Better Homes and Gardens®

Household Hints and Tips

Better Homes and Gardens®
Household Hints and Tips

A DORLING KINDERSLEY BOOK

BETTER HOMES AND GARDENS® BOOKS

Editor: Gerald M. Knox
Art Director: Ernest Shelton
Managing Editor: David A. Kirchner
Editor, Food and Family Life: Sharyl Heiken

President, Book Group: Jeramy Lanigan
Vice President, Retail Marketing: Jamie L. Martin
Vice President, Administrative Services: Rick Rundall

HOUSEHOLD HINTS AND TIPS
Editor: Rosemary Hutchinson
Project Manager: Angela K. Renkoski
Associate Art Director: Randall Yontz

CONTRIBUTING SPECIALISTS
James A. Hufnagel
Douglas A. Jimerson
Paul Krantz
Heather J. Paper
Rae Reilly
Mary Kay Shanley
Janis Stone, Ph.D.
Lois Warme
Dr. Loren A. Will

Original Title: Household Hints and Tips
© Copyright 1989, 1990 Dorling Kindersley Ltd., London.
© Copyright 1989, Meredith Corporation, Des Moines, Iowa, for
Maximum Food Storage Times for Pies, Bread, and Cakes, Soups,
and Casseroles, page 24; Cutting and Cooking Techniques, page
36; Using a Meat Thermometer, page 37; Grilling Frozen
Vegetables, page 38; Beverage Party Guide, page 40; Nutrition
information (except Tips for Vegetarians and Where to Find
Fiber), pages 44–45; Keeping the Children Occupied list, page
306; Calorie Tally, pages 366–369; Meat and Poultry Cooking
Times, pages 370–373; text for Choking illustrations, page 357;
Weights and Measures table, 374; Basic Food Groups chart, 375;
1988—Foods That May Cause Problems, page 301; 1986—
Vitamins and Minerals chart, pages 46–48; 1985—Clothes for a
New Baby, page 293; 1981—Faucet parts illustrations, page 227;
1980—screen illustration, page 223; Condensation, page 226;
Wiring Plugs (text and illustrations) and Wiring Self-Connecting
Plugs (illustrations), page 235; 1977—bamboo steamer lid
illustration, page 38.

Contents

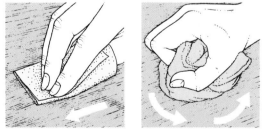

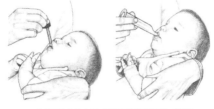

Use this book as a tool. Its carefully researched tips will simplify your life and encourage you to try things you may have thought were beyond you. It will save you time, trouble, and money, and turn housekeeping into a manageable task.

Finding the information you need

First, find the heading for the subject you're interested in. Below it are a number of tips set off by solid diamonds ◆. If you're looking for tools or materials to carry out a specific job, you'll find them indicated by an open diamond ◇. The open diamonds also help break down larger topics into quick-to-read categories.

Where special attention is needed, because the job may involve something potentially dangerous, the information will be preceded by this symbol: ‼ If some technique or product is particularly beneficial to the environment or if it is an alternative to using a commercial chemical, this will be noted by a leaf symbol 🍃 and the words "Green Tip."

Illustrations with captions show a variety of tips and methods, which whenever appropriate, are detailed in step-by-step order.

Tinted boxes or panels contain useful information in an easily identifiable form.

At the back of the book, an appendix contains a variety of charts filled with general information, a glossary of cooking terms, and a list of useful addresses. This list also gives descriptions of a number of consumer-service groups.

The comprehensive index at the back of the book will direct you right to the page that contains the advice you're looking for.

Organization

EVERYONE dreams of a cozy, neat, smooth-running household. But this dream does not come true on its own; it takes organization. Here are some hints to help you get things done and still have time to enjoy your home.

PRIORITIES

First decide what is important and what is not. Here is a list of top-priority items.

◆ Keep your home safe; fix bad lighting, faulty appliances, and trailing wires.

◆ Keep your home in good condition so trouble and large repair bills don't crop up later.

◆ Organize your home so it is comfortable. It should not be cluttered with too much furniture, nor so formal that you can't relax after a hard day.

◆ It should be neat and clean but not excessively so.

◆ Carefully make a budget plan so you can live comfortably within your income.

Set realistic goals

◆ If housework makes you irritable and bored, you may be overdoing it. Balance housework with personal time.

◆ Get your family to pitch in, but don't expect children to do everything perfectly.

◆ If you are out at work all day, look into the possibility of getting some cleaning help once or twice a week.

◆ Do the minimum to keep things under control rather than the maximum: Vacuum the main living areas once every two weeks rather than once a week if you can get away with it—some rooms don't even need that. Don't attempt too many tasks at once; better to do one or two jobs well than leave several half done.

◆ Keep a good supply of groceries on hand so you don't have to run to the supermarket too often. Purchase some items for quick and easy meals that family members can fix for themselves. This will free you from always having to prepare elaborate meals. If time and help are short, entertain informally.

EFFICIENT HOME MANAGEMENT

Here are some ways to get and stay organized.

Storage

Everything should have its place and should be easily accessible.
◆ Store kitchen utensils in compartments in drawers or hang them on hooks near the countertop, and keep plates near the sink or in the dining area.
◆ Store things off the floor if possible: Brooms can be hung on hooks, shoes can be placed on racks, etc. Keep all tools and equipment in a tool box or on hooks on the wall where they can be recognized and reached quickly.
◆ Store toys according to size or type (otherwise the large things may damage the small ones). Keep a toy box or bucket in each room where children can toss the toys in them for a quick cleanup.
◆ If you live in an older home that has a fuse box, it's a good idea to keep spare fuses, a fuse puller, a flashlight, and a small electrical screwdriver on the shelf right next to the fuse box. Keep spare light bulbs and plugs on hand, too.

Don't be a pack rat

Throw out what you don't need. A house full of old belongings means a house difficult to clean, and things going unused because you can't find them.
◆ Discard anything you haven't used for the last 12 months, especially clothing you don't wear or items your children have grown out of.
◆ Throw away broken-down, worn-out items, but be careful not to discard toys without asking the children first.
◆ Dispose of all expired medications by pouring them down the toilet.
◆ Get rid of all old magazines (newspapers can be useful for lighting fires or covering things while painting or cleaning). Offer them to a local charity or hospital.
◆ Remember that charity stores would like your belongings as long as they are clean and in fairly good condition.

Making lists

Making lists is an excellent way of organizing.
◆ Reminder lists on a blackboard or tackboard are useful if you want other family members to notice and remember dates, duties, and other items.
◆ A running shopping list is helpful; this way anyone in the house can write on it if they notice things have run out.
◆ Some people have a "To Do" list with notations of things to be done and phone calls to be made. These lists can be ongoing and dated. When a page becomes full, transfer the uncompleted jobs to another page and add others as they come up. Check off items as you finish them.

Yearly planners

◆ Offices have annual planners—a large wall sheet showing the entire year—so why not homes? Once they are filled in, there is no excuse for not knowing who has to be where and when.
◆ Fill in any important dates pertaining to the family such as:
Vacation dates, birthdays, and wedding anniversaries
School open houses, graduations, PTA meetings, and other school events
Planned visits to or from relatives or friends
Medical and dental appointments and service calls for cars or appliances.

THE HOME OFFICE

◆ Set aside some time every week to deal with phone calls, bills, and letters. You may not always need to use the time, but it's better to allow for it just in case.

◆ Make an ongoing list of people you need to get in touch with and keep it by the telephone.

◆ Keep current letters and bills in a box or folder that you go through regularly—once a week or month. File paperwork that has been dealt with in an indexed file so you can find it for future reference. Keep filing categories to a minimum so you won't forget what you have filed where.

USEFUL FILING CATEGORIES

Pending. Unpaid bills and letters that need to be answered.

Medical. To include paid bills, prescriptions, medical insurance invoices.

Other correspondence. A miscellaneous category.

Financial. Bank statements, mortgage papers, insurance papers, pension information, credit card statements, relevant correspondence.

Car. Car insurance papers, car loans, paid repair bills, details on your automobile club or association, relevant correspondence.

Home. Details of maintenance, repair, and decorating work; materials used and where you bought them; any other relevant information and correspondence.

Utilities. Receipts and relevant correspondence for gas, electric, telephone, water, and garbage removal services.

Warranties and instruction leaflets. For large and small appliances.

Hobbies and/or travel. This could include catalogs, suppliers of materials and tools, magazine clippings, relevant correspondence, information on clubs to which you belong.

FILING SYSTEMS

◆**Box files.** Large cardboard boxes, separately labeled, keep different categories of papers separate. Variations of those are "cut away" box files that leave the top half of the papers revealed. You can use a shoe box instead.

◆ **Accordion files.** These are indexed and particularly useful for filing receipts and paid bills.

◆ **Folders.** These are useful for papers you want to carry around with you.

◆ **Filing cabinets.** Double-drawer office filing cabinets are available in several colors. One should hold enough papers for even the most complicated household; two make excellent bases for a desk top.

◆ **Card index files.** Useful for addresses, business details from service people, or indexed information on particular interests.

◆ If you have a lot of paperwork—financial, medical, information on hobbies, or some aspect of running the home—use a specially designed indexed accordion file, or separate box files on a shelf out of the way of children. If you have a great deal of paperwork, you may find a small filing cabinet useful.

◆ Keep all documents relating to purchases—bills, receipts, and correspondence—at least until the purchase has been finalized and goods received, and, even better, until the warranty runs out in case there are problems.

◆ You may wish to keep receipts to add to a household inventory to be used for insurance purposes in case of a fire or theft.

◆ Always keep financial papers (bank statements and correspondence about mortgages and loans; credit card statements; bills and receipts; tax papers, etc.) and legal papers for seven years after you are finished with them. After that, you can throw them away.

MANAGING MONEY

◆Review and adjust your budget at least once a year. If you haven't made a budget, begin by totaling your household's yearly income, making sure to include any bonuses and dividends in addition to salary. Then list your fixed and variable expenses. Your mortgage payments and loan repayments would fall under the former; gifts, vacation costs, and clothing would fall into the latter. Add your expenses and deduct this from your income. If you have more money going out than coming in, pare down some of your luxury items, such as entertainment and gifts.

◆Always budget a contingency amount for unexpected expenses. You might consider putting the money in a higher-interest account since you won't be withdrawing it on a regular basis.

◆Check all bills carefully for their payment due dates to avoid paying extra charges. If you are paying a monthly bill, such as for a credit card, check your individual receipts against the statement.

◆As soon as you can, reconcile your bank statement and your checkbook. If you have trouble doing this, study the information found on most bank statements or ask your bank for help.

◆Take account of seasonal sales for saving substantial amounts on merchandise. Clearance sales, normally held after peak demand periods, also are good times for making savings.

◆Mail-order catalogs are not only useful for doing research on available products but also may help you make the best choice of an item away from the inducements of stores.

Credit, savings, and insurance

◆If you take out a loan, you will normally save money in the long run by making the largest down payment and paying it off in the shortest time you can manage.

◆Once you've finished paying off the loan, it is a good idea to continue putting the same amount into your savings account, since you probably won't miss the money.

◆A married woman should continue to keep some bills or credit cards in her own name in order to maintain her credit rating. This is especially important should circumstances change due to divorce or her husband's death.

◆Make two photocopies of all your credit cards. Carry one with you when traveling, and keep the other set at home.

◆Report all lost or stolen cards to the issuers immediately after you discover their loss. Or, sign up with a credit card protection service. For only a small fee, it will notify all the parties concerned should you lose a card and you only have to make one telephone call.

◆Treat your cash card from your bank's automatic teller in the same way as your credit cards: You must notify the bank immediately after you are aware it is lost or be subject to financial liability.

◆Put aside a fixed amount of money each month for savings. Protect your investments by spreading them among several different kinds, such as certificates of deposit, Treasury bonds, mutual funds, etc.

◆Make certain your family is protected by an adequate amount of life insurance.

WHAT TO STORE IN A SAFE-DEPOSIT BOX

◆**Property records.** Such as mortgages, deeds, titles.

◆**Personal documents.** Such as birth certificates, marriage licenses, divorce papers, military discharge papers, passports.

◆**Your home inventory.** A list of all valuables such as jewelry, furs, and electronic equipment, along with their photographs and serial numbers.

◆**Personal items.** Special-occasion jewelry, gold coins, medals, and silver.

◆**Stock or bond certificates; bank certificates of deposit.**

▼▼ Do not store your will, passbooks, or ◆ ◆ life insurance policies. Bank safe-deposit boxes usually are sealed in the event of death.

Food and Drink

SHOPPING GUIDE

THE QUALITY AND VARIETY of foods that you put into the shopping cart can make all the difference to your family's health. Include on your shopping list a balanced assortment of all the food groups, especially fruits and vegetables. Make a habit of check-ing the expiration dates on perishable products, and for optimal nutrition and quality, use them as far in advance of that date as possible.

PLANNING

◆Plan your meals ahead of time and make your shopping list at the same time. Be sure to include how much food you need, plus can and package sizes.
◆Post a running shopping list on the bulletin board and ask family members to add to it as they use things up.
◆Buy everything you need for a week's meals in one trip so you don't have to rush out to the store every other day.
◆Keep a good supply of staples so you don't run short of the basics.
◆Stock the freezer with meals you've pre-pared in advance for last-minute dinners.

Canned and packaged foods

◆It's always handy to have a certain number of canned and packaged food items on the kitchen shelves. Some of these are healthier than others. For instance, fruits canned in natural juices are much better for you than fruits packed in heavy syrup.
◆Read labels routinely (see *Understanding Food Labels*, page 18). If a product has sugar, fat, or salt listed at the beginning of the ingredients list, choose a different brand that lists these ingredients farther down or not at all. Ingredients are listed in order by weight, from the largest amounts listed first to the smallest amounts listed last.
◆Avoid dented cans, especially bulging ones. They may contain toxins that cause food poisoning.
◆Don't buy frozen food covered with frost; it probably has defrosted and then refrozen.

SHOPPING CHECKLIST

Staples

◇ Breakfast cereals
◇ Flour, baking powder, baking soda, cornstarch, sugar, and brown sugar
◇ Shortening and cooking oil
◇ Salt, pepper, spices, herbs, seasonings
◇ Mayonnaise or salad dressing
◇ Prepared mustard, vinegar, catsup, Worcestershire sauce, and hot pepper sauce
◇ Bouillon granules and soups
◇ Dried beans and peas, rice, and pasta
◇ Honey, jams, and preserves
◇ Coffee, tea, and cocoa
◇ Canned vegetables and fruit
◇ Canned fish, seafood, and meats
◇ Canned juices

Fresh or frozen foods

◇ Milk, eggs, cheese, butter or margarine
◇ Bread and rolls
◇ Vegetables and fruit
◇ Juices
◇ Poultry, fish, seafood, and meat

Vegetables and fruit

◆ Choose produce that you can hold in your hand and take a good look at. Steer clear of vegetables and fruit that are tightly sealed in plastic; they bruise and deteriorate rapidly.

◆ Choose fruits and vegetables that are in season, for the best value, and in a form that best fits your needs and storage capacity. Choose fresh items if you plan to use them in a day or two, frozen or canned if you want to keep them on hand.

Eggs

◆ Purchase clean, fresh eggs from refrigerated display cases. Most recipes are based on large eggs.

◆ Choose either white eggs or brown eggs. Their nutrition content is the same.

▼▼ Always discard any eggs with broken or
◆ ◆ cracked shells. They may have become contaminated with the harmful bacteria salmonella.

◆ U.S. Department of Agriculture classifications of eggs refer only to size and appearance, not the quality of the eggs. This must be marked on the cartons as:

◇ **Grade AA.** These have firm high yolks and thick whites. These are the best choice for fried or cooked-in-the-shell egg dishes.

◇ **Grade A.** These have slightly thinner whites; they are all-purpose eggs, equally good cooked whole or in recipes.

◇ **Grade B.** The whites are less thick and the yolks may be somewhat flattened and enlarged. They are good for use in recipes.

Shopping tips

◆ Check newspaper food ads. You may be able to plan several meals around the weekly specials.

◆ Divide your shopping list into categories, arranging the categories in the order they appear in your store.

◆ Shop only at stores you are familiar with so you don't waste time searching for items. Save trips to new stores for days when you have some time to browse.

◆ Besides foods and amounts needed, list advertised specials.

◆ Mark any items for which you have coupons, and have your coupons ready before you go to the store. Make sure, however, that you check to see if the special or the coupon brand is really the best buy.

◆ Once you are in the store, stick to your shopping list and avoid impulse purchases. Keep your eyes open, however, for unadvertised specials. Plan to buy fruits and vegetables in season and other needed items on sale at lower-than-usual prices.

◆ Shop for refrigerated or frozen items last, so they will stay cold longer.

CHECKING FOR FRESHNESS

Fresh food not only tastes better than food that's been lying around in containers and on supermarket shelves, it also retains the vital nutrients that less-than-fresh foods have lost. You can quickly learn to recognize fresh food because it looks bright and colorful, smells fragrant, and is usually firm to the touch.

Fish and meat

◆Fresh fish have clear, shining, slippery skins, bright bulging eyes, and distinct color and markings.
◆Fresh red meat should look silky and red rather than brown; the fat should be white, not yellow.
◆Choose poultry and game with pliable meat that is not dry-looking; the breast should be plump and lightly colored.

Vegetables

◇**Salad greens.** These should be bright green and free of brown edges and rotting leaves.
◇**Tomatoes and radishes.** Both should be bright red and firm without wrinkles or spots.
◇**Avocados.** Let them ripen outside the refrigerator. When still firm but with a slight give when gently squeezed, they are ripe. Brown streaks within are perfectly OK. The skins of some varieties blacken as they ripen.
◇**Root vegetables and tubers.** These should always be firm to the touch.
◇**Eggplant.** Ripe eggplant should be nice and firm, very shiny, and a rich purple color.
◇**Mushrooms and other fungi.** All types should be firm and dry, never slimy.
◇**Dried beans and seeds.** They should be brightly colored and plump.

Fruits and nuts

The fresh fruit you pick should be entirely free of moldy patches.
◇**Grapes.** Choose a bunch that is shiny, brightly colored, and firm.
◇**Cherries, plums, peaches, nectarines.** When ripe, these are firm and plump, just soft to the touch, and brightly colored, with smooth, unbroken skin.
◇**Berries** (strawberries, raspberries, blueberries). These should be firm and colorful. Because they spoil rapidly, eat them as soon as possible after purchase.
◇**Figs.** Ripe fresh figs always have a blush and should be plump and soft.
◇**Mangoes.** These should have a fragrant smell and a brightly colored reddish skin; if it is green all over, the mango will not ripen.
◇**Kiwi fruit.** The fruit should be firm and plump with an unbroken, fuzzy skin.
◇**Bananas.** These are ripe when the skin is bright yellow. They are underripe when green, and overripe when brown and mushy.
◇**Melons.** Choose plump, firm, and fragrant fruit without scars, bruises, or soft spots.
◇**Dried fruits.** They should be plump and juicy, not hard and leathery.
◇**Nuts.** Fresh nuts have glossy shells and should not rattle when shaken. They are easily shelled and free of the bitter taste common to stale nuts.

UNDERSTANDING FOOD LABELS

When shopping for food, get into the habit of reading labels. Once you understand their language, you will find that they reveal a great deal about the food inside. This is essential reading for people who care about good nutrition and of crucial importance for those with restricted diets. If you have cardio-vascular disease, diabetes, or food allergies, scrutinize the labels carefully every time you shop.

◆ By law, all prepackaged food must have the following information clearly stated on the label:

◇ Name of the food

◇ Description of the food if the name is not self-explanatory

◇ List of ingredients in descending order of weight, including any food additives, stabilizers, artificial colorings, and sweeteners

◇ Name and address of the manufacturer

◇ Net weight of the entire contents

◇ Country of origin, if imported

◆ Many products also carry nutrition information on their labels. These list serving size, number of servings, and calories per serving, along with the amount of protein, fat, and carbohydrates per serving. The percentage of the U.S. Recommended Daily Allowances for protein and seven other vitamins and minerals met by each serving also must be shown. Quantities of sodium, potassium, cholesterol, and saturated and polyunsaturated fats may be listed, too.

Expiration dates

◆ All prepackaged foods must be clearly stamped with an expiration date. The numbers are in large print and may be accompanied by the words "sell by," "use before," or "use by." In general terms, the expiration date indicates the maximum length of time that a product will retain its freshness and nutrient value. After that date, the product begins to deteriorate and spoil. The best advice is to buy and consume food as far in advance of the expiration date as possible.

FOOD ADDITIVES

Food additives are ingredients not normally present in the foods to which they are added. They are sometimes added for purposes other than nutrition, such as to preserve food or to make it more attractive.

◆ It is a good idea to become familiar with additives. Many supermarkets offer free leaflets detailing additives and their functions. When you pick up a product that is labeled "natural," "light," or "salt-free," you may not be getting exactly what you think. Check below to clarify some of these ambiguous terms.

◇ **Salt-free.** If you must restrict your sodium or salt intake, be aware that "unsalted," "no salt added," and "salt-free" all mean that no salt was added to the food during processing. But the food could still have significant levels of sodium in the form of preservatives or flavorings such as "sodium bicarbonate," "sodium saccharin," or "monosodium glutamate." In addition, check the sodium content per serving.

◇ **Natural.** This term should indicate a food that does not contain additives, preservatives, or artificial flavors and colors. The word is often used loosely, so check the label closely; the more additives listed, the less "natural" the food.

◇ **Whole wheat.** Don't assume that "wheat," "stone-ground wheat," or bread with "natural whole-grain goodness" means whole wheat. If whole wheat is not the first word on the ingredients list, the bread is not whole wheat.

◇ **Low fat.** Low-fat dairy products such as milk, yogurt, and cottage cheese must contain between 0.5 and 2 percent fat. Low-fat or lean meat can have no more than 10 percent fat.

◇ **Select, Prime, and Choice meat cuts.** The healthiest meat cuts—lean and low in saturated fat—are now labeled "Select." Those labeled "Prime" and "Choice" may be more tender and juicy, but they are higher in fat and generally higher in price.

FOOD STORAGE

Store foods in a well-ventilated cupboard or pantry—not over the range. Staples last longest in dark, airtight containers or in their original packaging. Fresh foods stored beyond the recommended time will spoil quickly; packaged foods steadily lose their flavor and nutrients over time.

STORING FOOD

Many foods can be kept a long time if stored correctly in a dry, well-ventilated cupboard, refrigerator, or freezer. Keep packaged and dried food in a cool cupboard and perishables in the refrigerator. (See also *Making the Most of Your Refrigerator*, page 21, and *Making the Most of Your Freezer*, pages 22 and 23).

Canned foods

◆ Canned foods (except rhubarb and prunes, which should be eaten within six months) will retain their quality for at least a year. Once a can is opened, transfer the contents to a covered dish in the refrigerator and consume the food within a day or two; otherwise the metal will affect the food.
◆ Foods in cans with deeply dented seams or swollen ends should not be eaten. They may be loaded with bacterial toxins that can cause severe illness.

Dried and packaged foods

◆ Store foods in their original package or in a tightly sealed container in a dry place. Unless indicated otherwise, foods kept in this manner will retain their nutritional value for as long as six months. After that period of time, they gradually deteriorate in quality.
◆ Coffee beans can be kept in airtight jars for up to three months; vacuum-packed coffee lasts up to a year. Once the vacuum seal is broken, coffee should be refrigerated.
◆ Keep dried beans, rice, flour, and dried fruits in a cool, dry place and out of direct sunlight. Once you've opened a package of

DRYING HERBS

Pick fresh herbs in the summer and dry them for winter use.

1 Gather herbs. Rinse and pat dry with paper towels.
2 Spread on a rack, or tie in small bunches, and hang them in a dry, airy, dark place such as an attic or not-too-hot airing cupboard.
3 Crush the dried herbs and store them in airtight jars in a cool place.

dried fruit, store it in the refrigerator.
◆ Store herbs and spices in dark, airtight containers, or in jars in a cool, dry cupboard, to keep them fresh. Ground spices stored in small quantities will keep for approximately six months. Whole herbs and spices that are stored correctly will keep their flavor for up to a year.
◆ You can freeze herbs either in small parcels wrapped in foil or chopped up in an ice-cube tray filled with water.

Meat and fish

◆Chill meat and poultry in the store's packaging. For longer storage, remove the packaging; wrap tightly in moisture- and vaporproof material—such as heavy foil, freezer paper, freezer bags, freezer plastic wrap, or freezer containers—and freeze.

◆Tightly wrap fresh fish in moisture- and vaporproof material before refrigerating or freezing.

Vegetables and fruit

◆Keep fresh fruits and vegetables in the crisper or in a loosely closed moisture-resistant bag or wrapping. Never wrap them tightly; they will spoil faster. Except for salad greens, do not wash produce before storing because the water can destroy some of the vitamins.

◆Allow fruits, especially grapes, plums, and pears, to ripen at room temperature before refrigerating to improve the flavor.

◆Before refrigerating fresh vegetables, remove any leafy tops because they deteriorate faster, and rinse and drain all leafy greens. If necessary, let tomatoes ripen before refrigerating; leave corn in the husks and beans and peas in their shells.

◆Onions, potatoes, and other tubers and root vegetables can be stored in baskets or wire racks that allow air to circulate. Place them in a dry, cool, well-ventilated, and dark place.

◆To keep a supply of fresh garlic on hand, peel the buds, then drop them in a jar with cooking or olive oil or vinegar over them to cover. Put on the lid and they will stay fresh in the refrigerator for weeks.

Dairy products and eggs

◆Store cheese, milk, cream, sour cream, yogurt, margarine, and butter tightly covered in the refrigerator.

◆Whole or skim milk and cream will stay fresh in the refrigerator for up to a week.

◆Margarine is good for six months to a year, butter only two weeks. Buttermilk, sour cream, and yogurt will stay fresh for two weeks.

◆Chill strong-flavored cheese in a tightly covered glass container.

◆Soft cheeses should be consumed within two weeks; hard cheeses will retain flavor and freshness for three to four months.

◆Keep eggs in the covered egg carton in the refrigerator and eat within a month for maximum freshness.

◆Chill leftover separated eggs in tightly covered containers (cover yolks with cold water).

◆To freeze eggs, break into a bowl and stir to combine. Add $1\frac{1}{2}$ teaspoons sugar or corn syrup, or $\frac{1}{8}$ teaspoon salt, per $\frac{1}{4}$ cup whole eggs (two whole) or $\frac{1}{4}$ cup yolks (four yolks). Egg whites require no additions. Place eggs in freezer containers or bags and freeze. Thaw in the refrigerator; use within 24 hours.

Bread, cakes, and cookies

◆Keep bread in a bread box or cabinet that allows some air to circulate; otherwise mold will develop and spread quickly.

◆Cover cakes, and refrigerate cream or custard cakes or pies.

◆Put cookies and crackers in airtight containers to prevent staleness.

Cooked foods

◆Cover and chill or freeze cooked foods and leftovers promptly. For freezing, use moisture- and vaporproof materials, such as heavy foil, freezer paper, freezer bags, freezer plastic wrap, or freezer containers. Keep cooked meat or poultry away from any equipment used with raw meat or poultry.

FOOD SAFETY

Keeping food safe to eat is as simple as keeping hot foods hot, cold foods cold, and all foods clean. The following pointers, and the food-storage timings on pages 24 and 25, tell you how.

Keeping foods safe

◆To prevent the buildup of illness-causing bacteria, cook foods thoroughly, especially meat, poultry, and dishes containing eggs. *Do not partially cook food, stop, then finish the cooking later.* Bacteria may grow between the cooking steps.

◆Since bacteria grow at room temperature, discard any cooked or chilled food that has been left out longer than two hours.

Cover leftovers to retain moisture while reheating. Be sure, too, to reheat the food completely.

Keep your refrigerator at about 40° and your freezer at 0° or below. Check them both periodically with an appliance thermometer.

◆Thaw meat and poultry in the refrigerator overnight. For faster thawing, place frozen packages in a watertight plastic bag in cold water. Change the water often. Or, defrost food in your microwave oven. *Do not thaw meat on the kitchen counter.*

◆Store leftovers in the refrigerator as soon as possible. *Do not let food cool on the counter.*

◆When shopping, pick up perishables last. Be sure frozen foods are solid and refrigerated foods are cold. If you live more than 30 minutes from the store, you may want to put frozen, refrigerated, and perishable foods in an ice chest for the trip home.

Since bacteria live all around us, always wash your hands with soap and dry them with clean cloths before you begin to cook.

When working with raw meat and poultry, wash hands, counters, and utensils in hot soapy water between *each* recipe step. Bacteria on raw meat and poultry can contaminate other foods. Never put cooked meat or poultry on the same plate that held any of the raw food.

MAKING THE MOST OF YOUR REFRIGERATOR

◆Store all perishable foods in the refrigerator at a temperature between 36° and 40°. To check a refrigerator's setting, leave a refrigerator-freezer thermometer in the refrigerator overnight.

◆For the most efficient operation, keep your refrigerator fully loaded, but with enough space between items for air to circulate.

▼▼Take care not to cover any vents in the ◆◆freezer compartment that send cold air to the refrigerator compartment.

◆Keep all packaged and prepared foods, leftovers, and dairy products tightly wrapped in moisture- and vaporproof material. Foods in general should be well wrapped, or placed in plastic containers, to keep odors from transferring and foods from drying out. Exceptions are fresh fruits and vegetables that spoil.

◆Put liquid to be refrigerated in tightly sealed containers; moisture that evaporates inside a refrigerator makes the unit work harder.

Defrosting refrigerators

◆If you do not have a frost-free unit, defrost your refrigerator regularly—when the ice is about $\frac{1}{4}$ to $\frac{1}{2}$ inch thick. Turn off the appliance and let the ice melt on its own, or help it along by placing pans of hot water in the freezer compartment. If you want to scrape out the ice, use a dull, plastic scraper. Put old towels in the bottom of the refrigerator and along the floor to soak up the water. When the ice is gone, wipe out the freezer compartment with a clean cloth rinsed in a mild detergent.

◆If you wipe the sides with glycerin (available in drugstores) after defrosting, the ice will come off easier next time.

◆To free a stuck ice-cube tray, soak a towel in hot water and apply it to the edges of the tray for a few seconds.

MAKING THE MOST OF YOUR FREEZER

◆ Use your free time every once in a while to cook up double batches of favorite dishes that freeze well. You also can freeze a supply of special ingredients that take time to prepare, like beef stock or pastry, so you can create more time-consuming dishes in a flash.

◆ Label foods to be frozen with masking tape indicating the contents, quantity, and date. Include other pertinent information such as "needs seasoning," "thin before using," etc. Be sure to put the tape on the container before freezing or it will not adhere.

◆ When assembling casseroles for freezing, line the dish with foil (use freezer wrap for tomato-based dishes), then freeze food in the dish. When frozen, remove from the dish, then wrap for storage. Food can then be returned to the same dish for heating.

Meat, poultry, and fish

◆ Freeze meat and chicken in the quantities in which you plan to use them—enough individual hamburger patties for the family, or a package of beef stew just large enough to feed the family.

◆ Raw or cooked meatballs can be frozen on a cookie sheet then transferred to a container, sealed, and put back in the freezer. This way they stay separate, and you can use as many as you want at any one time.

◆ Cooked meat will keep better if frozen unsliced, but if you freeze it in serving portions, pack it with a little gravy to help preserve flavor.

◆ Wrap fish and shellfish in heavy-duty foil or freezer wrap. Fatty fish and shellfish will freeze well for four months and lean fish up to eight months.

TIPS FOR HOME FREEZING

◆ Fresh foods to be frozen should be in perfect condition; otherwise they won't be at their best later.

◆ Food should be frozen quickly at 0° or below; place new packages against the freezer walls or shelves for quick freezing.

◆ Introduce fresh food gradually, adding only as much food as will freeze in 24 hours, about 3 pounds for each cubic foot of interior freezer space.

◆ Stack foods in groups and keep an inventory noting the dates stored to enable you to use foods within the correct time.

◆ Seal all foods in moisture- and vapor-proof freezer wrappings; exposure to air can give them an off-color and off-flavor and tough, dry surface known as "freezer burn."

◆ Cellophane tape is not recommended for sealing frozen foods, because it will not hold. Use ordinary masking tape; it is just as effective as special freezer tape and much cheaper.

◆ When freezing liquids, leave a ½-inch headspace at the top of the container to allow for expansion.

◆ Small amounts of stock and concentrated sauces or gravies may first be frozen in ice-cube trays and then transferred into plastic freezer bags for easy thawing later.

◆ It is best not to refreeze foods that have been frozen already and thawed, as this increases the risk of contamination by harmful bacteria and of spoiling the quality of the food. Never refreeze a food with an off-color or odor.

Fruits and vegetables

For best results, choose produce that is fresh, ripe, and unbruised; wash it well before preparation for freezing.

◆ Many seasonal fruits and vegetables can be frozen uncooked or partially cooked. Exceptions to the rule are salad greens, radishes, cucumbers, celery, uncooked tomatoes, scallions, and bananas, and potatoes, which all become mushy in the freezer. However, you can freeze mashed potatoes.

◆ Cook seasonal fruits and vegetables as you would tomatoes, squash, and berries, and put them into sauces, relishes, pies, soups, and casserole dishes before freezing them for future use.

◆ To freeze berries, place them on a cookie sheet and freeze. Then remove them from the sheet and put them back in the freezer in an airtight container; this way they won't turn to mush.

◆ Freeze leftover vegetables like chopped onions and green peppers in individual plastic bags for use in soups, sauces, and casseroles.

◆ Vegetables should be blanched before freezing to kill enzymes that cause loss of

WHAT NOT TO FREEZE

◆ Cream cheese and cottage cheese; they separate and break down when frozen.

◆ Hard cheese crumbles when thawed.

◆ Hard-cooked eggs become very leathery if frozen.

◆ Yogurt, sour cream, and mayonnaise all separate when frozen.

◆ Cream and custard pie fillings may separate, and meringue topping will shrink.

◆ Never store carbonated drinks in the freezer or they may explode.

◆ Be wary of freezing fish and shellfish; it may have been frozen already on its way to the store.

EMERGENCY ACTION FOR FREEZER BREAKDOWN

◆ Food will remain in good condition for at least 48 hours in the event of a power failure or breakdown, if the freezer is full and packed tightly—24 hours if it is partly filled.

▼▼ During the downtime, don't open
◆ ◆ the freezer to see how the food is holding up.

flavor and color. After blanching, rinse in very cold water, drain well, and pack at once.

◆ To prevent fruit from darkening, cover it with an ascorbic acid (vitamin C) solution. Dissolve $\frac{1}{2}$ teaspoon ascorbic acid crystals in $\frac{1}{4}$ cup cold water for each quart of prepared fruit. Lemon juice is often substituted but may affect the flavor.

Bread, cakes, and pastries

◆ Freeze balls of uncooked pastry, freezer-wrapped, up to two months; or roll pastry into circles 3 inches larger than your pie plates, stack with two sheets of waxed paper between layers, wrap, and freeze.

◆ Freeze baked or unbaked piecrusts in their pie plates, then wrap and stack with crumpled waxed paper between crusts. To freeze unbaked fruit pies, prepare as usual but do not cut slits in the top crust. Use a metal or freezer-to-oven pie plate. Cover with an inverted paper plate to protect the crust. Place in a freezer bag. Label and freeze.

◆ To freeze a baked pie, cook it in a metal freezer-to-oven pie plate and let it cool to room temperature. Cover with an inverted paper plate to protect crust. Place in freezer bag. Label and freeze. Do not freeze cream or custard pies.

◆ To freeze a frosted cake, put it in the freezer without any wrapping. Once it has frozen, wrap it and replace. This way the frosting won't stick to the wrapping. Remove the wrapping before thawing.

◆ Pack unbaked cookie dough in freezer containers, or shape into rolls or bars, and wrap tightly in foil or plastic wrap.

MAXIMUM FOOD STORAGE TIMES

PIES

◇ **Unbaked.** Store in freezer 2 to 4 months.
◇ Unwrap; cut slits in top. Cover edge with foil. Bake frozen pie in a 450° oven for 15 minutes, then in a 375° oven for 15 minutes. Uncover; bake about 30 minutes more or till done.
◇ **Baked.** Store in the freezer 6 to 8 months.
◇ Thaw in package at room temperature.

BREAD AND CAKES

◇ **Fresh breads, rolls, and biscuits.** Store in freezer up to 3 months.
◇ Thaw in package 1 hour or reheat in foil in a 300° oven about 20 minutes.
◇ **Cakes.** Store in the freezer up to 6 months.
◇ Unwrap; thaw at room temperature 1 to 2 hours.

SOUPS AND CASSEROLES

SOUPS AND STEWS
◇ Store in freezer 1 to 3 months.
◇ Place frozen food in a heavy saucepan. Cook over low heat, separating often with a fork until hot.

CASSEROLES
(Fish, poultry, or meat with vegetables or pasta)
◇ Store in freezer 2 to 4 weeks.
◇ Bake in a 400° oven for 1¾ hours per quart. Cover for the first half of baking time.

FISH AND SHELLFISH

RAW FISH
◇ **Fat fish.** Store in freezer 4 months; store in refrigerator 1 to 2 days.
◇ **Lean fish.** Store in freezer 8 months; store in refrigerator 1 to 2 days.
◇ Thaw in wrapping in refrigerator for 6 to 24 hours.

RAW SHELLFISH
◇ Store in freezer 3 months; store in refrigerator 1 day.
◇ Thaw in wrapping in refrigerator for 6 hours per pound.

POULTRY

FRESH POULTRY
◇ **Whole chicken and turkey.** Store in freezer 12 months; store in refrigerator 1 to 2 days.
◇ **Whole duck and goose.** Store in freezer 6 months; store in refrigerator 1 to 2 days.
◇ **Chicken pieces.** Store in freezer 9 months; store in refrigerator 1 to 2 days.
◇ **Turkey pieces.** Store in freezer 6 months; store in refrigerator 1 to 2 days.

COOKED POULTRY
◇ **Covered with broth, gravy.** Store in freezer 6 months; store in refrigerator 1 to 2 days.
◇ **Pieces not in broth, gravy.** Store in freezer 1 month; store in refrigerator 3 to 4 days.
◇ **Cooked poultry dishes.** Store in freezer 4 to 6 months; store in refrigerator 3 to 4 days.

MEAT

FRESH MEATS
◇ **Beef roasts.** Store in freezer 6 to 12 months; store in refrigerator 3 to 5 days.
◇ **Lamb roasts.** Store in freezer 6 to 9 months; store in refrigerator 3 to 5 days.
◇ **Pork and veal roasts.** Store in freezer 4 to 8 months; store in refrigerator 3 to 5 days.
◇ **Beef steaks.** Store in freezer 6 to 12 months; store in refrigerator 3 to 5 days.
◇ **Lamb chops.** Store in freezer 6 to 9 months; store in refrigerator 3 to 5 days.
◇ **Pork chops.** Store in freezer 3 to 4 months; store in refrigerator 3 to 5 days.
◇ **Ground and stew meats.** Store in freezer 3 to 4 months; store in refrigerator 1 to 2 days.
◇ **Pork sausage.** Store in freezer 1 to 2 months; store in refrigerator 1 to 2 days.
◇ Thaw roasts, steaks, and chops in wrapping in refrigerator, allowing 5 hours per pound.

COOKED MEATS AND MEAT DISHES
◇ Store in freezer 2 to 3 months; store in refrigerator 3 to 4 days.

PROCESSED MEATS

◇ **Bacon.** Store in freezer 1 month; store in refrigerator 7 days.

◇ **Frankfurters.** Store in freezer 1 to 2 months; store in refrigerator 2 weeks if vacuum-sealed package is unopened, 7 days if opened.

◇ **Whole ham.** Store in freezer 1 to 2 months; store in refrigerator 7 days.

◇ **Luncheon meats.** Store in freezer 1 to 2 months; store in refrigerator 2 weeks if vacuum-sealed package is unopened, 3 to 5 days if opened.

◇ **Smoked sausage.** Store in freezer 1 to 2 months; store in refrigerator 7 days.

◇ Thaw in wrapping in the refrigerator.

EGGS

◇ **Whites.** Store in freezer 9 to 12 months; store in refrigerator 2 to 4 days.

◇ **Whole eggs.** Store in freezer 9 to 12 months; store in refrigerator 4 weeks.

◇ **Yolks.** Store in freezer 9 to 12 months; store in refrigerator 2 to 3 days.

CHEESE, ICE CREAM, BUTTER AND MARGARINE

◇ **Cottage cheese.** Store in refrigerator 5 days.

◇ **Hard cheese.** Store in freezer 6 months; store in refrigerator 3 to 4 months.

◇ **Soft cheese.** Store in freezer 4 months; store in refrigerator 2 weeks.

◇ **Ice cream.** Store in freezer 1 to 3 months.

◇ **Butter.** Store in freezer 6 to 9 months; store in refrigerator 2 weeks.

◇ **Margarine.** Store in refrigerator 6 to 12 months.

STORING WINE

All wines, even the cheapest, should rest before being drunk, so buy wine at least two days, preferably longer, before you expect to drink it.

◆ Store wine in the dark because light causes deterioration. The storage area should be dry, airy, and draft- and vibration-free. Try to keep a constant temperature around 54° to 59°F.

◆ Never store wine in the refrigerator for more than an hour or so, particularly sparkling wines; they will get too cold and lose their flavor.

◆ Table wines that are to be stored for any length of time should be stacked horizontally on special racks or shelves so that the corks are kept moist and expanded. Store fortified wines (port, sherry, and so on) upright.

Serving temperatures

◆ Serve most red wines at room temperature, at about 65°F. Burgundy and Beaujolais and some light Italian red wines are at their best when served at about 61°F.

◆ Bring red wine up to room temperature slowly; it is better to serve it cold than to overheat it. Open the bottle a few hours before you want to drink it to let it breathe, and keep it in a warm part of the room.

◆ Serve dry white and rosé wines cold—at "cellar temperature," about 50°. Chill them in the refrigerator for about an hour before you serve them. Serve sweet white wines at a lower temperature than dry ones; chill for about an hour and a half before serving. Exceptions are the high-quality sauternes and German wines of the "Auslese" grade, which are better at a temperature of 57°, so chill for half an hour.

◆ Fortified wines, such as sherry, to be served as an aperitif can be slightly chilled. Put them in the refrigerator for half an hour before serving, although you can simply serve them with ice.

CHOOSING KITCHEN EQUIPMENT

WHEN IT COMES to choosing major appliances and time-saving equipment, one rule should apply: Shop around. With such state-of-the-art refinements as automatic sensors, computer monitoring systems, and no-fingerprint and stain- and scratch-resistant surfaces to choose from, you need to determine your priorities before you buy. You should buy the best—it will last longer—and add items gradually.

COOKING APPLIANCES

You can choose among freestanding kitchen ranges that fit between cabinets, built-in combination units, or separate cooktops and ovens.

◆ Microwave ovens, as separate appliances or as part of built-in units with conventional ovens below, are a great convenience.

◆ A separate oven and cooktop can be more expensive to install but are a good idea if you want to design a kitchen with individual work spaces and cooking areas. For example, if your kitchen is arranged around a "work island," the cooktop can be housed on its own in the center. The advantage of a separate oven is that it can be installed at a convenient height or incorporated into a space-saving design. Separating the cooking units also will enable you to use different fuels in your cooking; for instance, gas burners for easy regulation of the heat under the saucepan, and electrical monitoring in the oven.

Electricity

Electricity probably offers the greatest sophistication in cooking.

◆ An electric fan-assisted oven will cook faster than an ordinary oven because the heat is distributed more evenly.

◆ If you are short of space, you may want to install a built-in oven with two ovens in one—a microwave on top, and a self-cleaning conventional oven below, with one compact control panel for both.

POINTS TO LOOK FOR WHEN CHOOSING A STOVE

◇ Height of unit; it is more convenient if it is the same height as the kitchen counters.

◇ Good-quality finish; it lasts longer and is easier to clean.

◇ Automatic ignition on gas ranges.

◇ Size, shape, and number of ovens; some units have a main oven and a small economy one.

◇ A bottom-hinged oven can be more convenient for sliding pans into.

◇ An insulated oven door will help prevent accidental burns.

◇ Control panel on the top, rather than the front, is safer if you have young children.

◇ An interior glass door on the oven or glass panel in the door, and preferably an interior light will enable you to see the food without opening the door.

◇ Baking racks that slide out are easier to use.

◇ Economy element that heats up only at the center is good for small pans.

Useful features
◇ Continuous-cleaning oven.
◇ Digital timing device.
◇ Automatic temperature monitoring.
◇ Spit-roasting device.
◇ Stain- and scratch-resistant surface.

Gas

◆ Gas burners are easy to control; there is no residual heat when they are turned down.

Microwave ovens

◆ Ideal if you are out at work all day and want meals ready quickly in the evening.

◆ A microwave oven is cheaper to run than a conventional electric oven because the cooking time is so short.

◆ Microwave ovens can cook many foods but don't brown foods well. You can get browning dishes (see page 32) or buy a microwave with a broiler in the top.

◆ Microwave ovens are available with varying amounts of cooking power. Most larger models have 600 to 700 watts of cooking power; most compact models yield only 400 to 500 watts. The lower the wattage, the slower the rate of cooking.

◆ To find your oven's power levels if your owner's manual doesn't mention the percentage of power assigned to each power level, use this simple test. Fill two identical cups each with 1 cup water. Make sure the water is the same temperature in both cups. Cook 1 cup water on 100% power and record the time it takes to boil. Cook the other cup of water on the power level you want to test. If the water takes twice as long to boil as on 100%, you have 50% power. If it takes ten times as long, you have 10% power.

◆ The simplest microwave oven has two power levels: "defrost" and "cook." The most sophisticated microwave oven has an autosensor that automatically sets time and temperature for many different types of food.

◆ Control panels differ from oven to oven. Solid-state touch panels with digital readouts are the most accurate, because you can set your oven to the exact second of cooking time. Dials and slide controls are a little less accurate but adequately serve most purposes. They also are easier for some people to use.

◆ An oven shelf in your microwave makes cooking several dishes at the same time easier, especially with small amounts of food.

◆ Some have a turntable that helps cut down on the amount of stirring and turning necessary.

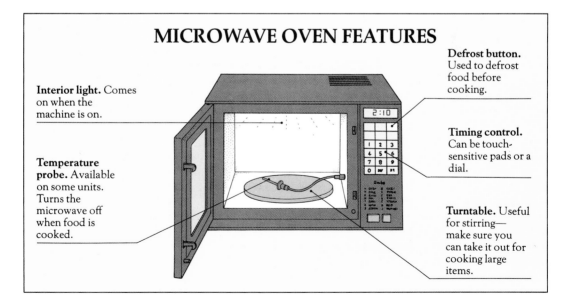

MICROWAVE OVEN FEATURES

Interior light. Comes on when the machine is on.

Temperature probe. Available on some units. Turns the microwave off when food is cooked.

Defrost button. Used to defrost food before cooking.

Timing control. Can be touch-sensitive pads or a dial.

Turntable. Useful for stirring— make sure you can take it out for cooking large items.

REFRIGERATOR AND FREEZER

◆ Make a note of the measurements of the unit and the space in the kitchen before you buy anything. Sizes vary enormously, from small worktop refrigerators to huge free-standing ones. You often can specify the size you want with the freezer either on the top or bottom, as suits your specific needs. Or you can choose a refrigerator with double doors, which has the refrigerator and freezer compartments side by side.

◆ Choose a refrigerator or freezer with a door that opens in the right direction for your kitchen. Some models have the door hinged on the right or the left; some are reversible.

◆ Choose a refrigerator with suitable fittings (sometimes simple shelves are more convenient than egg racks and cheese compartments). Adjustable shelves can be useful.

◆ State-of-the-art refrigerators have electronic monitoring systems that warn you with a beep if the door is open, or if the temperature is too high or low in any of its sections, which are individually programmed for temperature control. The monitor shows you the temperature in both sections and can be set for maximum cooling over a 24-hour period. Some of the newer model refrigerators feature textured no-fingerprint doors and porcelain-enameled interiors that make cleanup easy, as well as through-the-door ice and water dispensers.

◆ Frost-free refrigerators will save you time but can be less energy efficient. If you want automatic defrosting, choose a model that incorporates energy-saving controls.

◆ There are two types of freezers: chest freezers, which open from the top, and upright freezers, which open in front. Chest freezers hold more, but upright freezers are easier to use because you can see most items without unpacking other items.

◆ If you keep your freezer in the garage, invest in a freezer alarm to warn you if the temperature becomes warmer than it should.

STORAGE TIMES

Many freezers indicate storage times for different foods in words and symbols within. Some models have food charts inside the door with specific foods along with the particular length of time (usually indicated in months) that they can be safely stored.

KITCHEN TOOLS

Every cook has his or her own particular needs and will eventually discover which equipment is most useful. However, the list of basic equipment on page 29 should get you started.

◆ There is one overriding rule: Always buy the best. Badly made tools of cheap materials will be frustrating to use, may cause recipe failures, and will probably not last very long. It is better to buy durable equipment with a serviceable look rather than stylish utensils that are difficult to use.

Knives and utensils

◆ A good basic collection of cutting tools and utensils is essential in any well-equipped kitchen. Choose knives and utensils that are labeled "dishwasher safe" if you plan to soak them in water or wash them in the dishwasher. The best knives are those with blades made of carbon steel or stainless steel that can be easily sharpened. Knife handles should be shaped to provide a firm grip without slipping.

◆ Always use the knife that is specific to the particular cutting job at hand; all sharp-edged knives should be stored in a slotted rack or block to keep the edges sharp.

◆ Large chopping boards made of plastic or acrylic plastic sheets are the best surfaces for cutting on, and they can be put in the dishwasher. Wooden boards are not recommended because they can harbor harmful bacteria from raw meats or poultry.

Saucepans and bakeware

◆Select a range of pots and pans that are of suitable size and shape, will spread heat evenly, and are durable and easy to clean. Skillets should have comfortable handles and flat, thick bases that won't warp.

◆Nonstick finishes on cooking pans and bakeware protect the base metal and are easy to clean. Aluminum is lightweight and spreads heat evenly, but minerals stain it easily. Stainless steel is exceptionally durable and easy to clean. Cast-iron is heavy to handle but great for slow cooking. Copper utensils should be heavy-gauge and lined with another metal. Glass ceramic can go from freezer to top of range or oven to table.

◆Do not use cast-iron and copper pans to cook anything that contains vegetables because both metals destroy vitamin C.

◆For best results with cakes, breads, and other products that rise during baking, use bakeware with satin-finish bottoms and shiny sides.

BASIC KITCHEN EQUIPMENT

Preparation and Cooking Utensils
◇ Set of mixing bowls
◇ Set of dry measuring cups
◇ Clear glass liquid measuring cup
◇ Set of measuring spoons
◇ Wooden spoons
◇ Rubber spatulas
◇ Flexible metal spatulas
◇ Serrated knife
◇ Paring knife
◇ Utility knife
◇ Chef's knife
◇ Sharpening steel
◇ Vegetable peeler
◇ Meat mallet
◇ Long-handled fork
◇ Long-handled spoon
◇ Ladle
◇ Slotted spoon
◇ Pancake turner
◇ Tongs
◇ Kitchen scissors
◇ Bottle opener
◇ Can opener
◇ Corkscrew
◇ Rotary beater

◇ Grater and/or shredder
◇ Small and large strainers
◇ Colanders
◇ Kitchen timer
◇ Cutting board
◇ Rolling pin
◇ Meat thermometer
◇ Oven thermometer
◇ Wire cooling rack

Range-Top Cooking
◇ 1-quart covered saucepan
◇ 2-quart covered saucepan
◇ 3-quart covered saucepan
◇ 4- or 6-quart covered Dutch oven or kettle
◇ 6- or 8-inch skillet
◇ 10-inch skillet with cover
◇ 12-inch skillet

Bakeware
◇ Baking sheet
◇ 6-ounce custard cups
◇ Muffin pan

◇ 9-inch pie plate
◇ 8 × 4 × 2-inch loaf pan or dish
◇ 9 × 5 × 3-inch loaf pan or dish
◇ 12 × 7½ × 2-inch baking dish
◇ 13 × 9 × 2-inch baking dish or pan
◇ 8 × 8 × 2-inch baking dish or pan
◇ 9 × 9 × 2-inch baking pan
◇ 8 × 1½-inch round baking pans or dishes
◇ 9 × 1½-inch round baking pans
◇ 15 × 10 × 1-inch baking (jelly roll) pan
◇ 10-inch tube pan
◇ Various sizes of casserole dishes
◇ Roasting pan with rack
◇ Pizza pan

Food Storage Products
◇ Assorted refrigerator dishes
◇ Vapor- and moistureproof containers for freezing foods

◇ Foil
◇ Clear plastic wrap
◇ Waxed paper
◇ Large and small plastic bags
◇ Paper towels
◇ Assorted canisters for storing foods
◇ Juice pitcher

GADGETS

As you set up your kitchen, you will want to add several work- and timesaving appliances. The vast selection, with every convenience feature imaginable, makes it necessary to shop shrewdly. Choose gadgets that suit your cooking style, are durable, and are easy to clean.

Blender

This kitchen helper trims minutes from your cooking time by blending, chopping, and pureeing foods. To make the best use of your blender, follow these guidelines.

◆Cut fresh fruits and vegetables, cooked meats, fish, and seafood into ½- to 1-inch pieces before chopping them in your blender.

◆ Stop your blender often and check the size of the food pieces. Blenders work quickly and can easily overblend or overchop food.

◆Cube and soften cream cheese before blending it with liquid ingredients.

◆When blending thick mixtures, stop your blender often and use a rubber spatula to scrape the sides of the container.

◆For better control of the size of the pieces and to avoid overworking the motor, blend large quantities of foods in several small batches.

Food processor

A food processor not only blends, chops, and purees as a blender does, but it also slices and shreds. In addition, some food processors mix batters and doughs and knead bread doughs. Refer to your owner's manual to see if your model can perform these more difficult tasks.

Keep the following points in mind when using your food processor.

◆For even slices, fit the food into the feed tube as tightly as possible. If the food pieces lean to one side, you'll get diagonal slices.

◆When slicing foods with peels, place the food pieces in the feed tube so that the peel faces the center of the work bowl. That way, the blade of the slicing disk will hit the peel side first and cut through it, rather than scraping it.

◆Store the sharp food-processor blades and disks away from other utensils and out of the reach of young children.

Crockery cooker

This cooks food very slowly. All you do is prepare the dish, set the temperature, and forget about it until the food is done. The food is cooked in a ceramic pot that sits inside an insulated metal casing. Choose a slow cooker with a continuous slow-cooking cycle, indicated by fixed settings on the heat control since they are more versatile. Capacity varies from 6 to 20 cups, so choose one to suit your needs.

◆Do some of the chopping and measuring of ingredients ahead, if possible. Assemble the ingredients in a bowl, cover, and refrigerate till it's time to begin cooking. (If your cooker has a *removable liner*, assemble and refrigerate the food in the liner rather than in a bowl.)

◆Keep the lid securely on the crockery cooker during cooking, and be sure the food doesn't push against the lid. Because crockery cooking depends on the heat that builds up in the cooker itself, resist the temptation to peek or stir frequently.

◆To protect the crockery liner, avoid subjecting it to sudden temperature changes. For instance, do not preheat the cooker and then add cold food.

Toaster

◆If you have a large family that makes a lot of toast in the morning, get a toaster that can make four or six slices at once.

◆If you prefer thick pieces of toast, toasted English muffins, or bagels, choose a toaster with self-adjusting toasting slots and controls that monitor browning levels. Some toasters have a thermostat that allows you to toast frozen breads.

◆To avoid a buildup of crumbs that can catch fire in the toaster, choose a model with a removable bottom plate so you can empty out all the loose bread and clean the bottom easily.

Wok

The wok is a Chinese high-sided frying pan in which vegetables and small pieces of meat are very quickly stir-fried to retain their flavor and nutrients. It also can be used for deep-frying and steaming.

◆ All woks are suitable for gas stoves; traditionally woks are used over a fire.

◆ Woks are available for use on electric or wood-burning stoves; you also can buy electric woks.

◆ A two-handled wok is easiest to carry.

◆ Single-handed flat-bottomed woks that resemble a saucepan also are available.

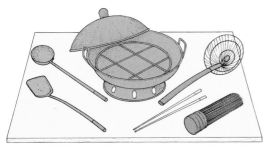

Wok equipment. *Spatulas, straining spoons, and chopsticks are used for cooking. A lid and inside rack are useful for steaming, and a bamboo brush is useful for cleaning the wok afterward.*

Electric coffee maker

There are three types of electric coffee makers: percolator, drip filter, and vacuum (cappuccino/espresso) machines. Each has a different method of forcing boiling water through a container of ground coffee.

◆ Check on the number of cups a coffee maker holds. Some can make up to 12 cups of coffee at a time; others, such as cappuccino and espresso machines, can make only one or, at most, two cups.

◆ Filter and vacuum machines use finely ground coffee and are economical. Percolators are simplest and keep coffee hotter. Check the capacity before buying one; some can't make fewer than two cups of coffee. Some machines have their own stainless steel filters; others need paper filters.

◆ If you prefer to grind your own beans, buy a unit with a built-in grinder.

◆ Check how long a coffee maker can keep coffee warm without spoiling the taste. Filter machines have an element in the base to keep coffee warm.

Kitchen thermometers

◆ **Meat thermometers.** These thermometers tell you when a large piece of meat reaches just the right doneness. The most common type is a needle-shaped instrument with a tube of mercury in the center. For an accurate temperature reading, make sure the tip of the thermometer is touching meat and is not resting on bone, fat, gristle, or the pan bottom.

◆ **Candy and deep-fat-frying thermometers.** These thermometers have different temperature ranges than meat thermometers. Some may be used for both deep-fat frying and candy making; others are calibrated specifically for candy making.

Before making candy, always test the thermometer's accuracy in boiling water. If the thermometer registers above or below 212°, add or subtract the same difference in degrees from the temperature given in the recipe. Remember to read the thermometer at eye level. If you live more than 1,000 feet above sea level, decrease the temperature given in the recipe 2 degrees for each 1,000 feet of elevation.

◆ **Appliance thermometers.** Use an oven thermometer to check the temperature of your oven. If your oven cooks too hot or too cool, you'll need to adjust the settings you use for recipes. Use a freezer thermometer to make sure your freezer registers below 0°.

MICROWAVES AND FREEZERS

Microwave ovens and freezers are natural partners. Both serve to retain the flavor, texture, and vitamin content of foods, and both save you time and money. The great convenience of using a microwave in conjunction with your freezer is that it can defrost food in minutes, eliminating the need to take food out of the freezer hours ahead of time. Some foods can even be defrosted and reheated in one step.

◆ Defrost food in the same-size container it was frozen in; otherwise, if the food has too much room, it will spread as it heats and the edges will cook too quickly. Loosen covers of containers, but leave the food covered as it defrosts. Transfer foods frozen in metal containers or foil to microwave-safe containers, because metal reflects the microwaves, causing sparks that can damage the oven.

◆ When defrosting food in a bag, pierce or slit the bag to prevent it from bursting, and always be sure to remove any metal ties.

◆ Stir foods from the edge to the center as they start to thaw; if they cannot be stirred, break them up to ensure even thawing.

◆ Place breads, cakes, and pastry on a double layer of paper towels. The paper will soak up any excess moisture and prevent the food from getting soggy.

Microwave tools and equipment

The vast selection of specialized equipment and gadgetry on the market makes microwave cooking all the more convenient, but in most cases you should be able to use the utensils and cookware you already have.

◆ The main thing to remember when deciding which container to use is that it must be made of a material that allows microwaves to pass through to the food without being absorbed or reflected by the utensil. It's very likely that most of your regular dishes and bakeware can go safely into the microwave — even your best china is probably fine as long as it isn't metal trimmed. If in doubt, you can test for micro-safety. Place the dish in the oven with a measuring cup filled with cold water next to it. Heat on High for 1 minute. If the dish stays cool and the water is warm, the dish is microwave-safe.

◆ Browning dishes will seal and brown fish and meats so they come out crisp.

◆ Use plastic roasting bags and boiling bags, but pierce them first to prevent bursting, and use only plastic ties. Use microwave-safe plastic wrap, waxed paper, or ceramic or glass covers to cover food while cooking. In many microwave ovens, small pieces of foil can be used to protect the edges of food from overcooking.

◆ Freezer-to-microwave dishes also can be used to serve foods directly from oven to table.

SUITABLE DISHES FOR A MICROWAVE

◆ You can use ovenproof ceramic, glass, and china dishes. Wood or straw baskets can be used for short periods.

◆ White paper towels and plates can be used for simple cooking and reheating, but avoid those with colored patterns, as the dyes may transfer to the food.

◆ Use round dishes, whenever possible, so food cooks evenly and doesn't burn in the corners.

◆ Choose deep dishes for casseroles that need to be stirred during cooking.

◆ Food cooks faster in shallow, open dishes because a larger surface area is exposed to the microwaves.

◆ Cookware made from microwave plastic works well; don't use lightweight plastic containers like margarine tubs since they may melt.

▼▼ Never use metal or metal-trimmed ◆ ◆ containers because they reflect microwaves and create sparks that damage oven walls and cause pitting.

DISHES, GLASSWARE, AND CUTLERY

You don't need elaborate sets of plates and glassware. Here is a list of basic pieces you can add to later.

Dishes

◆Choose a design that is not likely to be discontinued by the manufacturer for a while so you will be able to replace broken pieces and add to your set.
◆Every piece should be dishwasher-safe.
◆You will need:
◇Dinner plates
◇Salad plates
◇Dessert plates
◇Soup bowls (choose a shape that can be used for cereal, too)
◇Cups and saucers

Serving dishes

◆You also will need serving dishes; these do not need to be the same pattern as the china. Ideally you should have:
◇Vegetable dishes
◇Casserole dish
◇Large platter for meat or fish
◇Gravy boat
◇Salad bowl
◆Ovenproof dishes also can be used for serving.

Flatware

◆Silver flatware adds a touch of real elegance, but is expensive and needs regular polishing.
◆Stainless steel, although less formal, is available in a variety of different designs, often with wooden or plastic handles.
◆Buy flatware that has dishwasher-safe handles to save on hand washing.
◆Before you buy, hold the flatware as though you were using it. Check on its weight, balance, and sharpness, size, and shape; badly balanced flatware is difficult to manipulate.
◆Ideally you should have:
◇Dinner knives (if they are not very sharp, you may need steak knives, too)
◇Dinner forks
◇Dessert (or salad) forks
◇Teaspoons
◇Soup spoons
◇Serving spoons and large serving forks
◇Soup ladle
◇Salad servers
◇Carving knife and fork

Glassware

◆Plain, long-stemmed glasses are elegant and will do for any occasion, though they may be difficult to fit into the dishwasher. A shorter, sturdier stem can still look nice and is less likely to get broken. Choose glasses with heavy bases so they can't be knocked over easily.
◆Don't be misled by price: Some of the cheapest glasses are among the best looking.
◆Ideally you should have:
◇Tumblers for water, juice, or iced tea (A)
◇All-purpose wineglasses (B and C)
◇Small juice glasses
◇Old-fashioned glasses (optional)
◇Brandy snifters (optional) (D)
◇Liqueur glasses (optional) (E)

COOKING AND SERVING

Taking a few minutes each week to plan meals can save you time, work, and money.

◆Start by planning balanced meals. First, select main dishes. Then add breads or cereals, hot or cold vegetables, and fruits or salads to complement the main dishes. Next add beverages and desserts, if you like.

◆Choose dishes whose colors go together. Try not to choose foods that are all the same color.

◆Vary the sizes, shapes, seasoning levels, textures, and temperatures of foods.

◆Make sure you have all the necessary ingredients, and check the length of time a dish takes to cook before you start.

◆Don't plan elaborate meals if you are busy with hundreds of other things, and don't plan two complicated dishes at the same meal unless you have the time and enjoy cooking.

◆If you are a reluctant or new cook, work out a schedule for cooking before you start work. For example:

5:00 peel or chop vegetables
5:15 prepare ingredients for main dish and start cooking
5:30 prepare dessert
5:45 prepare salad and dressing
6:00 eat!

QUICK PREPARATION AND COOKING

◆For super-quick cooking, cut up ½ pound of potatoes, winter squash, or almost any dense vegetable into ¼-inch-wide sticks, cover and cook in the microwave, with 2 tablespoons water on High for 5 to 7 minutes; stir once. Drain, season, and serve.

◆Put peeled apples in water with lemon juice or ascorbic acid color keeper to stop them from turning brown.

◆For baked potatoes in a hurry, parboil the potatoes for 5 minutes before putting them in the oven, or put an aluminum skewer through them. Either speeds up the baking time by 15 to 20 minutes. Potatoes baked in the microwave taste great and are finished in a mere 4 to 7 minutes. Put a paper towel under the potato while it's cooking to absorb moisture.

◆Make a quick stock flavoring for stews by combining onion, garlic, and carrots in a blender with a small amount of water.

◆For cooking dried legumes in a hurry, instead of soaking overnight, bring water and legumes to boiling; reduce heat and simmer for 20 minutes. Let stand 1 hour. Prepare and

cook as normal with fresh water. Drain and rinse.

◆Get a head start on main-dish salads by storing cans of fruits, vegetables, and meats in your refrigerator. That way, they're already chilled when you're ready to use them. Or, if refrigerator space is at a premium, place the cans in the freezer for 30 minutes. But don't forget them. They'll burst if you leave them in too long.

◆Cut 10 to 15 minutes of meal preparation by buying chicken breast halves that are already boned and skinned. For recipes that call for bite-size chicken pieces, save even more time by buying the precut boned and skinless chicken breast pieces. All of the cutting and trimming will already be done.

◆Use your freezer and microwave oven to keep rice and pasta readily available. Place ½-cup portions in 6-ounce custard cups. Cover with clear plastic wrap and freeze for several hours. When firm, remove the portions from the custard cups and transfer them to a freezer bag or freezer container. Seal, label, and freeze for up to 6 months. To reheat, return the frozen rice or pasta to the custard cups. *Do not* add water. Cover with waxed paper. Micro-cook on 100% power (high) 1½ to 2 minutes for 1 custard cup till heated through.

ENERGY-SAVING COOKING

Energy saved during cooking also means that foods are cooked in less time and retain their fresh flavor, or very slowly using less power, thereby developing their full flavor.

Stir-frying

This cooking technique using a wok cooks food very quickly in a minimum amount of very hot oil, so that it retains its flavor, crispness, and nutrients.
◆ Add liquid to give food a burst of steam.

Using a wok. *Cut all the ingredients into even-sized pieces; cook items requiring the longest cooking time first.*

Microwave cooking

◆ Microwave ovens cook very quickly without the need for preheating and are much more economical than conventional ovens. Because food that has been cooked in a microwave continues to cook after it is removed from the oven, many recipes call for a "standing time" that allows the food to finish cooking outside of the oven—using no power at all.
◆ Cooking time is directly related to the amount of food in the oven. The more food cooking at one time, the longer it takes because the microwaves have to be "shared." For example, one baked potato takes 4 to 5 minutes, but two potatoes take about 8 to 10 minutes.

◆ Cooked foods reheat well in a microwave with close to their original flavor, color, and texture. When reheating, always stir foods from the outer edges (where foods cook faster) toward the center of the dish, pushing cooler food at the center back toward the edges. For foods that cannot be stirred, turn or rearrange the foods often.

Crockery cooking

◆ Use electric crockery cooking as a convenient and economical way to cook casseroles, soups, roasts, or stews ahead of time. Meals can be prepared in advance and slow-cooked overnight or while you are working.

Grilling techniques

Although gas and electric grills are easy to use, directions differ by brand. Refer to your owner's manual for operating instructions. To cook with a charcoal grill, read the tips that follow.
◆ After lighting the fire, leave the briquettes in a mound until they look ash gray during the daytime or glow red after dark. This usually takes about 20 to 30 minutes for standard briquettes and 5 to 10 minutes for self-lighting briquettes.
◆ Once the coals are ready, spread them out as follows.
For direct-heat grilling. Use long-handled tongs to spread the hot coals into a single layer. For more even heat, arrange the coals about $\frac{1}{2}$ inch apart. Place the food directly over the coals and cook uncovered. Cook burgers, sausages, kabobs, steaks, and chicken pieces this way.
For indirect-heat grilling. Use either a disposable foil drip pan or make your own. Place the drip pan in the center of the firebox. Then, using long-handled tongs, arrange the hot coals in a circle around the pan. Place the food over the drip pan but not over the coals, and cover the grill. Use this method when cooking roasts, whole chickens or turkeys, and other large pieces of meat.

SOUPS

◆The best soups have a homemade broth, but the following are convenient substitutes: Instant beef, chicken, or vegetable bouillon cubes or granules; ready-to-use canned beef or chicken broth; and canned condensed beef or chicken broth. Add fresh vegetables to instant bouillon and use the cooking water for the broth.

◆Use beef, lamb, pork, poultry, game, or fish bones to make a broth.

◆Use cooking water from vegetables or beans to make a vegetarian broth or to add to soups and stews.

Soup garnishes

◆Croutons, pastry cutouts, yogurt, or sour cream liven up any soup. Use crumbled bacon in vegetable soups.

◆Chopped herbs: Use sage for fish and cream soups; tarragon for consommé or mushroom, chicken, and tomato soups; thyme for fish, meat, and beet soups; watercress for fish soup; rosemary for cauliflower, chicken, pea, and spinach soups.

◆Sprinkle shredded cheddar, Swiss, or Parmesan cheeses onto small bread rounds. Brown quickly in the oven or under the broiler and float on top of each serving of soup.

CUTTING AND COOKING TECHNIQUES

CUTTING

◆**Cubing.** Cut the food into strips $\frac{1}{2}$ inch wide or more. Line up strips; cut crosswise to form cubes.

◆**Dicing.** Cut the food into strips $\frac{1}{8}$ to $\frac{1}{4}$ inch wide. Line up and stack strips; cut crosswise to form pieces.

◆**Chopping.** Cut the food into irregular pea-size pieces.

◆**Finely chopping.** Cut the food into irregular-size pieces, smaller than peas.

◆**Slicing and bias-slicing.** To slice, cut food crosswise, making cuts perpendicular to cutting surface. To bias-slice, hold knife at a 45-degree angle to cutting surface.

◆**Cutting into julienne strips.** Cut the food into slices about 2 inches long and $\frac{1}{4}$ to $\frac{1}{2}$ inch thick. Stack the slices, then cut lengthwise again to make thin, matchlike sticks.

◆**Shredding.** Push the food across a shredding surface to make long, narrow strips. (Or, use a food processor.)

◆**Finely shredding.** Push the food across a fine-shredding surface to make very thin strips.

◆**Mincing.** To cut into tiny, irregularly shaped pieces. For garlic, a garlic press can be used.

◆**Grating.** Rub the food across a grating surface to make very fine pieces.

COOKING

◆**Simmering.** Heat liquids over low heat till bubbles form slowly and burst below the surface.

◆**Boiling.** Heat liquids till bubbles form and rise in a steady pattern, breaking on the surface.

◆**Poaching.** Cook food partially or completely submerged in simmering liquid.

◆**Steaming.** Cook food in the steam given off by boiling water. Place the food in a perforated metal basket, a bamboo steamer, or on a wire rack set just above, but not touching, boiling water. Cover the pan and steam till the food is done.

◆**Stir-frying.** Cook food quickly over high heat in a lightly oiled wok or skillet, lifting and turning the food constantly.

◆**Deep-fat frying.** Cook food in enough melted shortening or cooking oil to cover. The fat should be hot enough (365° to 375°) so that the food cooks without absorbing excess grease, but not so hot that the fat smokes or food burns.

◆**Baking.** Cook food in the indirect, dry heat of an oven. The food may be covered or uncovered.

◆**Broiling.** Cook food a measured distance from the direct, dry heat of the heat source. A broiler also is used to brown or toast foods or melt cheese.

COOKING FISH AND MEAT

◆ Fresh fish and meat spoil quickly so eat them as soon as possible. Freeze fish and meat you don't plan to use in one or two days in freezer wrap or bags.

◆ Thaw meat or fish in the refrigerator, not at room temperature.

◆ Never leave raw or cooked fish or meat at room temperature for more than two hours.

USING A MEAT THERMOMETER

◆ Insert the thermometer into the center of the thickest portion of the meat. The thermometer should not touch any fat or bone or the bottom of the pan.

When the meat reaches the desired doneness, push the thermometer into the meat a little farther. If the temperature drops, continue cooking. If it stays the same, remove the roast, cover and let stand about 15 minutes.

Fish and shellfish

▼▼ Never overcook fish; it'll disintegrate or
◆ ◆ toughen.

◆ To bake, place a single layer of fish in a greased shallow baking pan. For fillets, tuck under any thin edges. Brush with melted butter or margarine. Bake fresh fillets or steaks in a 450° oven for 4 to 6 minutes per $\frac{1}{2}$-inch thickness. If fillets or steaks are frozen, increase baking time to 9 to 11 minutes per $\frac{1}{2}$-inch thickness. Bake dressed whole fish in a 350° oven for 6 to 9 minutes per half-pound.

◆ To poach, add $1\frac{1}{2}$ cups water, broth, or wine to a large skillet. Bring to boiling. Add fish; return to boiling. Reduce heat and simmer fresh fillets or steaks for 4 to 6 minutes per $\frac{1}{2}$-inch thickness. For frozen fillets or steaks, increase poaching time to 6 to 9 minutes per $\frac{1}{2}$-inch thickness. Poach dressed whole fish for 6 to 9 minutes per half-pound.

Poultry

◆ A bird will be easier to carve if it is taken out of the oven and allowed to rest—about 15 to 20 minutes for a turkey, less for smaller birds.

◆ Roasted poultry is done when a meat thermometer registers 180° to 185°. The drumsticks should move easily in their sockets, and the thickest parts of the drumsticks should feel soft when pressed.

◆ If you need cooked chicken for a recipe but don't have time to stew a whole bird, poach some chicken breasts.

◆ Only a small quantity of liquid is used for braising, so it is a good idea to check the liquid occasionally during cooking, adding a few tablespoons more liquid if needed.

◆ Roast duck or goose on a rack in a roasting pan to drain the fat.

Beef and pork

◆ Meat cuts vary widely in their tenderness, so choose a method of cooking to suit the cut. Tender cuts are best when roasted, broiled, or pan-fried. Less tender cuts should be cooked slowly in moist heat: pot roasted or braised.

◆ When grinding meat, put any other ingredients, such as herbs, onions, garlic, and bread crumbs, through the grinder or food processor with the meat; it saves time and improves flavor.

◆ Marinating is a cinch if you use a plastic bag. The meat stays in the marinade, and it's easy to turn and rearrange. Cleanup is easy, too. Just toss the bag.

◆ All meat loaves and patties should be cooked to 170° or till no pink remains.

◆ Pork is always cooked until well done and should be a uniform light gray color throughout. Use a meat thermometer; it should register between 160° and 170°.

◆ Pork cooked with bacon, spinach, tomatoes, or onion sometimes remains pink even when well-done. The same is true of grilled or smoked pork. So, when cooking pork mixtures with the ingredients above, or grilling or smoking pork, use a meat thermometer.

COOKING VEGETABLES

◆ Steaming takes a little longer than boiling but it is a healthier way to cook.

◆ To cook vegetables add them to boiling water to preserve the nutrients.

◆ Flavor with lemon juice and herbs instead of salt for a healthier, tasty seasoning.

◆ Cook root vegetables until they are tender; the older the vegetables, the longer this will take.

◆ Don't simmer old potatoes too vigorously or they will fall apart. Put them unpeeled in cold water and cook them gently with the cover on.

◆ Beets peel easily if you dip them in cold water immediately after cooking.

◆ Before frying onions, pour boiling water over them then pat dry; they fry faster this way.

◆ To dress up buttered, cooked vegetables, sprinkle them with toasted sesame seed; toasted chopped nuts; crumbled, cooked bacon; canned french-fried onions; slightly crushed seasoned croutons; snipped fresh herb; chopped hard-cooked egg; or sieved hard-cooked egg yolk.

Grilling frozen vegetables

◆ Fold an 18 × 36-inch piece of heavy foil in half to make an 18-inch square. Bring up the sides to make a pouch, using your fist to form corners. Place the contents of one 10-ounce package frozen vegetables in the pouch. Season to taste with margarine or butter and salt and pepper. Bring two opposite sides of foil together. Leaving space for steam to build, fold edges to seal securely. Seal ends. Grill directly over *medium-hot* coals about 25 minutes for peas or other small vegetables (about 30 minutes for larger vegetables) or till vegetables are tender, turning often.

STEAMING VEGETABLES

◆ Steaming is better than boiling; the vegetables don't touch the water, so they retain their flavor and vitamins.

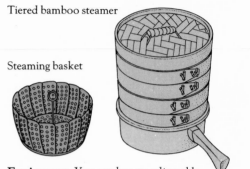

Tiered bamboo steamer

Steaming basket

Equipment. *You can buy an adjustable steaming basket that fits into most saucepans. Otherwise buy a tiered pan that allows you to steam one or more different vegetables together. The water sits in the bottom, and each layer has holes in the base for steam to pass through.*

COOKING EGGS AND DAIRY PRODUCTS

If you add eggs, milk, cream, or yogurt to soups or stews, always do so near the end of cooking time. They are less likely to curdle if you pour a small amount of the hot liquid from the soup or stew into the beaten eggs or dairy products, mix well, then return the mixture to the main dish.

Eggs

◆ If you plan to beat egg whites, separate the whites from the yolks about a half hour before you plan to use them. Bringing the whites to room temperature will help them whip up to a greater volume.

◆ To peel shells off hard-boiled eggs, salt the cooking water. When the eggs are cooked, rinse them quickly in cold water, and crack the shell at the ends.

◆ If you are not sure if an egg is hard-cooked, spin it on its side on a flat, hard surface. A fresh egg will spin unevenly; a hard-boiled egg will spin evenly.

◆Scrambled eggs will become watery and hard if you overcook them.

◆Cook omelets over moderate to low heat and check that the egg mixture is not more than $\frac{1}{4}$ inch deep in the pan. You don't have to turn the omelet over if you raise the edge with a spatula and shake the pan to keep the uncooked mixture moving freely.

◆If making a soufflé, don't open the oven before the time stated in the recipe, or it will sink.

Fresh and bad eggs. *A fresh egg should sink at once in a bowl of salted water and lie on the bottom (above left); a bad egg will float (above right).*

Cheese

◆When cooking with cheese, the main thing to remember is that excessive heat and overcooking turn it stringy and leathery. High heat also may cause a mixture of cheese, eggs, and milk to curdle.

◆When making a sauce, stir in the cheese toward the end and continue stirring just long enough to melt the cheese and blend it smoothly with other ingredients. Cheese melts quickly and evenly and blends readily with other ingredients if it is grated or shredded first. This is easier when the cheese is chilled.

◆Allow 4 ounces for every cup of shredded or cubed cheese called for in a recipe, 2 to 3 ounces per cup if it is hard-grating cheese such as Parmesan.

Dairy products

◆For safety and the best volume, whip cream straight from the refrigerator.

◆Use yogurt and ricotta cheese as low-fat alternatives to sour cream and regular cottage cheese.

YEAST BREADS AND MUFFINS

◆When the recipe gives a range for the amount of flour, use the minimum amount and knead in as much of the remaining flour as you can.

◆Knead the dough to the stiffness called for in the recipe. Kneading develops the gluten of the flour, which determines the final structure of the bread loaf. To knead, fold the dough over and push down with the heel of your hand, curving your fingers over the dough. Give the dough a quarter-turn, then fold over and push down again. Continue this fold-push-turn procedure until the dough is smooth and elastic.

◆Don't raise dough in a hot area because excessive heat will kill the yeast. Too much cold, on the other hand, will stunt the yeast's growth. The optimum temperature for raising dough is 80° to 85°. For best results, place the bowl of dough in an unheated oven, then set a large pan of hot water under the bowl on the oven's lower rack.

◆Let dough rise till it is nearly doubled in size. Don't let loaves rise to the top of the pan, because the dough needs room to rise.

◆For a soft and shiny crust, brush loaves with margarine or butter after baking. For a glossy, crispy crust, brush before baking with milk, water, or beaten egg.

◆Test for doneness by tapping the top of the loaf with your finger. A hollow sound means the loaf is properly baked.

◆If you live more than 3,000 feet above sea level, expect your dough to rise faster.

◆When baking several long, individual, or round loaves of bread at the same time, you'll need an extra large (17 × 14-inch) baking sheet. If you don't have this size baking sheet, go ahead and shape the loaves on two smaller baking sheets and let them rise as directed. Then, while you're baking one sheet, place the other one in the refrigerator. Don't bake the two sheets at the same time.

◆For evenly rounded tops on nut breads and muffins, grease baking pans or muffin cups on the bottom and only $\frac{1}{2}$ inch up the sides. Do this and your batter will cling to the sides of the pan instead of sliding back down.

PIES AND CAKES

◆ For a pie or crust that will be baked, select a glass pie plate or dull metal pie pan. Use shiny metal pans, which keep crusts from browning properly, only for crumb crusts that are not baked.

◆ Measure accurately. Too much flour makes pastry tough, too much shortening makes pastry greasy and crumbly, and too much water makes pastry tough and soggy.

◆ To roll the dough with little sticking, use a pastry cloth and a rolling-pin sleeve.

◆ If the pastry is baked without filling, prick it well with a fork. This prevents it from puffing up. (Do not prick pastry if the filling is baked in the crust.)

◆ After baking, cool pie on a wire rack. Allowing air to circulate under the pie keeps the crust from becoming soggy.

Making custard pies

For delicious, velvety, fuss-free fillings, follow these tips when making custard pies.

◆ To avoid spills, place the pie shell on the oven rack before adding the filling.

◆ To check for doneness, gently shake the pie. If the liquid area in the center is smaller than a quarter, the pie is done. The filling will continue to set after you remove the pie from the oven. Or, insert a knife near the pie's center. If the knife comes out clean, the pie is done. Note that the knife test may cause the filling to crack.

◆ After the pie cools, cover and refrigerate it till serving time. Cover and chill leftovers, too.

Making fruit pies

Follow these simple tips for delicious, picture-perfect fruit pies.

◆ To avoid messy spills in your oven, set the pie plate on a baking sheet or pizza pan.

◆ For a prettier double-crust pie, brush the unbaked top with milk, water, or melted margarine or butter, then sprinkle lightly with sugar. Or, brush the unbaked top lightly with a beaten egg or milk and skip the sugar.

◆ Store fruit pies at room temperature up to one day. Refrigerate for longer storage. Cover and refrigerate any pies that contain eggs or dairy products.

Serving cream pies

Cool cream pies for four to six hours before serving. For longer storage, cover and refrigerate. To cover meringue-topped pies, insert toothpicks halfway between the centers and edges of the pies. Loosely cover with clear plastic wrap. When cutting cream pies, occasionally dip your knife into water to keep it from sticking.

Cakes and cookies

◆ To grease cake pans, use a paper towel to evenly spread the shortening. If the cake will be removed from the pan, grease the bottom and sides; if it will be left in the pan, grease only the bottom.

◆ To keep drop cookie dough from spreading too much, drop it onto cool cookie sheets.

◆ For perfectly rolled cookies, keep any unused dough chilled until you need it. To avoid sticking, roll half of the dough at a time on a lightly floured surface with a floured rolling pin. For tender cookies, reroll the dough as few times as possible.

◆ If you use 100-percent-corn-oil margarine in your cookies, keep in mind that your dough will be softer than doughs made with regular margarine or butter. (Do not use spread, diet, or soft-style margarine products in cookie doughs. Your cookies will not turn out satisfactorily.) When using corn-oil margarine, make the following adjustments so your dough will be easier to handle:

◆ For sliced cookies, chill the rolls of dough in the freezer instead of the refrigerator.

◆ For rolled cookies, chill the dough before rolling it, or freeze it just until it's firm enough to roll.

VEGETABLE GARNISHES

◆**Tomato roses.** Cut a base from the stem end of each tomato (do not sever). Cut a continuous narrow strip in spiral fashion, tapering end to remove. Curl strip onto its base in a rose shape. Use with salads and dips.

◆**Scored cucumber.** Make a V-shaped cut lengthwise down each cucumber (or run the tines of a fork lengthwise down each cucumber, pressing to break the skin). Repeat at regular intervals around cucumber. Slice or bias-slice. Use with salads and dips.

◆**Onion brushes.** Slice roots from ends of green onions; remove most of green portion. Make slashes at both ends of the onion pieces to make fringes. Place in ice water to curl the ends. Use with steaks or roasts.

◆**Carrot curls/zigzags.** Using a vegetable peeler, cut thin lengthwise strips from carrots. For curls, roll up; secure with toothpicks. For zigzags, thread on toothpicks accordion-style. Put curls and zigzags in ice water; remove toothpicks before using. Use with salads, sauces, and thickened soups.

FOOD PRESENTATION

◆Keep a bunch of fresh herbs in the refrigerator so you can snip some for garnishing dishes.

◆Fresh peppers are available in red, green, yellow, purple, and even black. Use them to add a touch of color to salads and rice dishes.

◆Decorate fish or pieces of chicken with slices or twists of lemon.

◆A topping of grated cheese or bread crumbs, browned for a few seconds, can make all the difference to a basic casserole. Try a swirl of cream or yogurt to lift a dish.

◆Cold meats can be turned into works of art by carefully arranging different kinds together with sliced vegetables.

◆Plan your menu so everything is not the same color. Use dishes of one color to set off the food: white bowls for tomato soup or borscht and salad in glass bowls, etc.

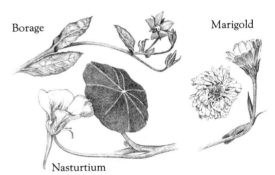

Borage   Marigold
Nasturtium

Flowers in food. *Scatter edible flowers over salads; nasturtium, marigolds, and the blue flowers of borage are all spectacular.*

Keeping food hot

◆Put hot food into heated dishes.

◆Keep casseroles in a low-temperature oven. Don't turn the oven off; the residual heat can encourage bacteria.

◆Trays with built-in heating units are highly effective for keeping dishes hot at the table.

Making lemon twists. *Cut lemon slices. Make a cut from the center of each slice to the edge, then twist.*

41

BEVERAGE PARTY GUIDE

If you're planning a party, beverages are a must. Here are a few tips you should consider before the festivities begin.

◆ Generally expect to use $1\frac{1}{2}$ ounces of liquor for each bar drink. This means you'll get about 16 drinks from a 750-milliliter bottle (fifth) of liquor.

◆ Chill beer to about 45° to 50°. For quick chilling, place the beer bottles or cans in a deep tub of ice cubes.

◆ Generally expect to use 3 ounces of wine for each drink, getting about eight drinks from one 750-milliliter bottle. For bigger parties, consider buying wines available in larger 1.5-liter bottles.

◆ Remember to make a variety of nonalcoholic beverages available to your guests.

◆ Keep punches cold by floating easy-to-make ice rings in the serving bowls. To make an ice ring, fill a ring mold with water and freeze till firm. Or, for a fruit-filled ice ring, line the bottom of the ring mold with citrus slices, berries, or melon balls. Add enough water to just cover the fruit. Freeze till firm. Then fill the mold with water and freeze till firm.

◆ Don't buy unnecessary types of bar glasses. Ten- or 12-ounce all-purpose glasses and 9- or 10-ounce stemmed wineglasses are suitable for nearly every drink and occasion. Disposable plastic glasses, available in various sizes, are convenient to use, especially at large parties.

Serving wine

◆ Uncork or decant red wine an hour or two before serving to allow it to breathe. It should be served at room temperature.

◆ If you want to check white wine for quality, open it an hour or so before serving. Replace the cork lightly before chilling the wine in the refrigerator.

◆ Don't open champagne or sparkling wines until just before serving or they will go flat.

◆ If the cork breaks, take a sharp pointed knife or a skewer and stab it into the cork against the side of the bottle and try levering the cork out. If the cork breaks up into the wine, decant it through a tea strainer (see below).

◆ Smell the cork after you remove it to make sure that it smells only of wine and isn't tainted by mold. There usually is a slight smell of cork in newly opened wine, which should disappear after a short time.

◆ Before serving, wipe the mouth of the bottle with a clean cloth.

DECANTING WINE

◆ For vintage wines, decant them to filter out any sediment. The decanter should be at room temperature. Pour wine slowly and steadily through a tea strainer and into the decanter, until the sediment begins to flow.

◆ Decant young red wine, such as Beaujolais nouveau, three or four hours before serving; for other wines an hour or two is sufficient. It is not necessary to decant champagne or sparkling wines.

Decanting wine. *You can filter wine that is full of cork bits through a tea strainer, set on a funnel, into a decanter.*

RESCUING DISASTERS

◆If a dish lacks flavor, try adding a little mustard, hot pepper sauce, or Worcestershire sauce. An herb or spice such as curry powder can help, too.

◆Bread crumbs, yogurt, cream, and parsley can help disguise saltiness.

◆If a somewhat flavorless dish won't take more salt or pepper, try onion or garlic powder, or lemon juice.

Soups, sauces, and dressings

◆Soup can be livened up with a dollop of sour cream, yogurt, or cottage cheese.

◆Grease on soups or sauces can be soaked up with a paper towel laid on the top or can be carefully spooned off. If you have time, chill the soup, then remove the congealed fat.

◆For crystal-clear soups, use broth that's been clarified. First, separate an egg. Save the yolk for another use. In a Dutch oven or kettle combine strained broth, $\frac{1}{4}$ cup cold water, and the egg white. Bring to boiling. Remove from the heat and let stand five minutes. Strain the broth through a large sieve or colander lined with several layers of damp cheesecloth for cooking.

◆Prevent lumps in cornstarch- or flour-thickened sauces by stirring constantly. If lumps do form, beat the sauce briskly with a wire whisk or a rotary beater.

◆To rescue hollandaise sauce, place a teaspoon of lemon juice and a tablespoon of curdled sauce in a bowl. With a wire whisk, beat vigorously until the mixture is creamy and thickened, then gradually beat in the remaining sauce, a tablespoon at a time, making sure that each addition has thickened before adding the next.

◆Improve an overly sweet sauce by adding a squeeze of lemon juice.

Meat, poultry, or vegetables

◆Crumbling pâtés can be served as a soft pâté from the bowl. If there's time, put them back into a food processor with a little bit of added butter, then remold.

◆Don't stir a burned stew: instead, pour the unburned part into another pot.

◆If poultry is overcooked, cut it up and use it for soups or with mayonnaise or salad dressing as a sandwich filling. Or, mix it with a white sauce and use it to fill crêpes.

◆Rice that has formed heavy wet lumps can be put in a ring mold, then baked in the oven for about 10 minutes. Turn it out and serve with sauce or stir-fried vegetables in the middle of the ring.

◆To make celery crisper, put it in a bowl of water and add ice. Leave it in the refrigerator for a few hours.

◆To make lettuce crisper, run it under cold running water and drain thoroughly.

Miscellaneous

◆Sticky pastry will never quite recover because the proportions are wrong. However, if you put it in the refrigerator for half an hour, then roll it out between two pieces of lightly floured waxed paper, it will at least cover a pie.

◆If a creamy frosting hardens in the refrigerator, let it sit at room temperature until it softens.

Moistening dry cakes. *If a cake is slightly dry, pierce it all over and pour brandy or fruit juice into it.*

◆If your coffee tastes bitter, put two or three cardamom pods into the pot while it is brewing.

◆To unstick dried dates, figs, or raisins, place them in a low-temperature oven for a few minutes.

HEALTHY EATING

FOOD NOURISHES US by supplying our bodies with protein, carbohydrates, fats, vitamins, and minerals. Protein helps build, maintain, and repair our bodies. Carbohydrates and fats provide the body with fuel. Various vitamins are needed as catalysts for chemical reactions in our bodies, and minerals are vital to good health.

NUTRITION KNOW-HOW

The easiest path to good nutrition is to eat a variety of foods. When planning meals, use the Basic Food Groups as a guide. The chart on page 375 tells which foods are in each group and how much of each you should eat.

Food nourishes us by supplying our bodies with protein, carbohydrates, fats, vitamins, and minerals. Most foods contain several of these nutrients, but no single food contains them all. That's why a healthy diet includes a variety of foods.

Protein

◆ Protein helps build, maintain, and repair our bodies. It also helps produce antibodies that ward off disease, and it contributes to the production of enzymes and hormones that regulate many of our bodies' processes.
◆ Protein is found in foods of both animal and plant origin. The proteins found in meat, poultry, fish, eggs, cheese, and milk are complete proteins. They can supply the body's need for protein all on their own.
◆ Plant forms of protein include legumes, rice, wheat, corn, and nuts. They're called incomplete proteins because, on their own, they can't meet our protein needs. But when two or more plant proteins are combined in one dish or are eaten together in a meal, they add up to a complete protein.

Carbohydrates

◆ Carbohydrates provide the body with fuel and are an important part of our diets, especially in starch form. Starches exist in potatoes, breads, cereals, and pasta.
◆ Besides existing in starch form, carbohydrates also are available as sugars. Sugars are found in fresh fruits, vegetables, some dairy products, honey, corn syrup, brown sugar, molasses, and table sugar.

Fats

◆ Fats provide a highly concentrated form of energy, and, despite all the bad publicity they receive, some fat is essential to our diets. Fats carry certain vitamins through our bodies and help cushion body organs. They give a staying power to our meals that keeps us from getting hungry too soon after we eat.

Vitamins

◆ Various vitamins are needed to spur chemical reactions in our bodies. This list and the chart on pages 46–48 describe some of the vitamins essential for good health.
◇ **Vitamin A.** This promotes the growth of normal skin. It also contributes to bone and tooth development, aids our night vision, and helps prevent eye disease.
◇ **Vitamin C (ascorbic acid).** This aids the formation of healthy bones, teeth, gums, and blood vessels. It also plays a part in the creation of collagen, which binds our bodies' cells together.

◇**Thiamine.** This helps regulate our appetite and digestion, helps us maintain a healthy nervous system, and helps our bodies use carbohydrates.

◇**Riboflavin.** This helps us use food efficiently, promotes healthy skin, helps cells use oxygen, and aids vision in bright light.

◇**Niacin.** This helps convert sugars to energy and keeps our skin, digestive tract, and nervous system healthy.

Minerals

◆Minerals are found in very small amounts in foods, but they're vital to good health.

◇**Calcium.** Gives strength and structure to our bones and rigidity and permanence to our teeth. It helps make sure, too, that our blood clots and our muscles contract.

◇**Iron.** This is an important part of every red blood cell. It plays a role in carrying oxygen through the body and also helps the body resist infections.

◇**Sodium.** Helps regulate the passage of

WHERE TO FIND FIBER

HIGH-FIBER FOODS
◇Bananas
◇Bran
◇Brown rice
◇Muesli
◇Dried beans and peas
◇Whole wheat bread or pasta
◇Baked potatoes
◇Leafy vegetables—broccoli, brussels sprouts, cauliflower
◇Corn

◇Rhubarb
◇Dried fruit

MEDIUM-FIBER FOODS
◇Apples
◇Oranges
◇Green vegetables
◇Nuts

LOW-FIBER FOODS
◇Peeled potatoes
◇Grapefruit
◇Lettuce
◇White rice or pasta

---

water and nutrients in and out of our cells. It also helps us maintain the proper balance of body fluids.

◇**Potassium.** Helps steady our body-fluid balance, too. It also regulates muscular contractions.

For a more detailed list of minerals, see the chart on pages 46–48.

Other dietary concerns

In addition to nutrients, food supplies our bodies with water, fiber, and cholesterol.

◇**Water.** Bathes our tissues, lubricates our joints, carries nutrients, takes waste away from our cells, and is built into the structure of many chemical compounds in our bodies. Water is part of all the foods we eat, but our bodies also need several additional glasses per day.

◇**Fiber.** This is the portion of food that can't be broken down (digested) in the body. Fiber passes through our intestines and carries waste products with it. To add fiber to your diet, eat plenty of fresh fruits and vegetables, grains, and whole-grain foods.

◇**Cholesterol.** Is essential to life, but most of us consume more than we need. Cholesterol makes up cell membranes, builds nerve sheaths, and provides raw materials for hormones. In adults, the liver and other organs manufacture enough cholesterol to meet most needs. Cholesterol usually is most concentrated in foods with saturated fats, such as meats, butters, and egg yolks.

TIPS FOR VEGETARIANS

◆Tofu (otherwise known as soybean curd) is a good source of protein.

◆Nuts and peanut butter are good protein sources.

◆Eat dried fruits for vitamin E and iron content.

◆Eat a wider variety of vegetables, especially dark green, leafy ones.

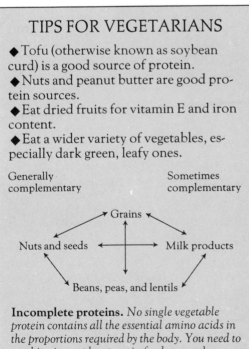

Generally complementary

Sometimes complementary

Incomplete proteins. *No single vegetable protein contains all the essential amino acids in the proportions required by the body. You need to combine incomplete protein foods to get them in the right proportions in your diet.*

HOW TO EAT LESS FAT

◆ Use lean cuts of meat and trim off all the fat. Eat more poultry and seafood.

Skim milk has 60 calories less per 8-ounce glass than whole milk.

Eat fewer white flour products and more whole wheat foods.

◆ Eat more raw vegetables; season cooked vegetables with herbs rather than salt and butter.

Substitute polyunsaturated oil for butter when cooking or use nonstick pans without added oil.

Use only a quarter of the margarine or butter you use now; use reduced-calorie cheeses in sandwiches or for spreading.

Cottage cheese made smooth in a blender can be substituted for sour cream in some recipes.

Use fresh fruit to satisfy your sweet tooth; canned fruit packed in natural rather than heavy syrup saves you 30 to 60 calories a serving.

Canadian bacon has one-third fewer calories than regular crisp bacon.

Calories and dieting

◆ Just as your car needs gas to run, your body needs calories to function. A calorie is the measurement of the energy supplied by food. A certain number of calories is necessary for body functions and activity. This number depends on your body size, sex, and stage of life. When more calories are consumed than the body needs, the excess is stored as body fat. Each pound of excess body fat is produced from 3,500 extra calories.

◆ Ideally the number of calories we consume should match the number we burn. But that's rarely the case. If you're among the many who carry a few extra pounds, try to lose weight through a combination of exercise and dieting. Once you reach your ideal weight, continued exercise will help you maintain it.

VITAMINS AND MINERALS

VITAMIN	Functions	Sources
A	Maintains mucous membranes and inner organs, helps build bones and teeth, promotes vision.	Carrots, broccoli, squash, spinach, liver, egg yolk, milk and dairy products.
D	Promotes absorption of calcium for strong bones and teeth.	Fish, milk, eggs. Made in skin by direct exposure to sunlight.
E	Prevents oxidation of essential vitamins, fatty acids. Needed for red blood cells, muscles, and tissues.	Green leafy vegetables, vegetable oil, whole-grain cereals and breads, liver.
K	Essential for blood clotting.	Cabbage, brussels sprouts, kale; other green leafy vegetables; milk.
Thiamine	Assists in release of energy from carbohydrates; helps synthesize nerve-regulating substances; promotes appetite.	Pork, liver, oysters, cereals, nuts, legumes.

VITAMIN	Functions	Sources
Riboflavin	Maintains skin and eye tissue; needed for energy release from macronutrients.	Dark green vegetables, whole grains, pasta, mushrooms, milk, eggs, meat, fish.
Niacin	Works with thiamine and riboflavin to produce energy reactions in cells.	Poultry, meat, fish, tuna, peanut butter, dried beans and peas.
Pyridoxine (B$_6$)	Participates in absorption and metabolism of fats and proteins; helps in formation of red blood cells.	Avocados, spinach, green beans, bananas, whole-grain cereals.
Cobalamin (B$_{12}$)	Needed for building of genetic material and functioning of nervous system.	Kidneys, meat, fish, eggs, milk, oysters.
Folic acid (Folacin)	Helps to form body proteins and genetic material; promotes growth; needed for formation of hemoglobin in blood.	Dark green leafy vegetables, fruits, soybeans.
Pantothenic acid	Needed for metabolism of macronutrients, formation of hormones and nerve-regulating substances.	Nuts, eggs, liver, kidneys, whole-grain bread and cereal, dark green vegetables, yeast.
Biotin	Needed for formation of fatty acids, release of energy from carbohydrates.	Egg yolk, liver, kidneys, green beans.
C	Helps maintain bones, teeth, and blood vessels; helps form structural collagen.	Citrus fruits, strawberries, tomatoes, melons, green pepper, potatoes.

MINERAL	Functions	Sources
Calcium	Needed for strong bones and teeth, muscle contraction, and normal heart rhythm, blood clotting, transmission of nerve impulses.	Milk, cheese, small fish eaten with bones, dried beans and peas, dark green vegetables.
Phosphorus	Works with calcium to promote strong bones and teeth; also needed for metabolism of fats and carbohydrates.	Liver and kidneys, meat, fish, eggs, milk and dairy products, nuts and legumes.
Sulfur	Helps build proteins, especially hair, nails, cartilage.	Eggs, meat, milk and cheese, nuts, legumes.
Chlorine	Part of fluid outside cells. Helps in formation of gastric juice and in digestive process.	Table salt (sodium chloride).

MINERAL	Functions	Sources
Magnesium	Helps regulate body temperature, nerve and muscle contractions, protein synthesis. Activates enzymes in carbohydrate metabolism.	Green leafy vegetables, whole grains, nuts, beans. (Magnesium may be lost in processing of packaged or canned foods.)
Sodium	Regulates water balance, muscle contraction, nerve irritability. Major component of fluid outside cells.	Salt, salted foods, soy sauce, monosodium glutamate, baking powder, cheese, fish, shellfish, poultry, eggs.
Potassium	Works with sodium to promote fluid balance, regulate muscle contraction and heart rhythm. Major part of fluid within cells.	Fresh fruits (especially oranges, cantaloupe, bananas), dark green vegetables, liver, meat, fish, poultry, milk.
Iron	Part of hemoglobin in blood. Transports and transfers oxygen in blood and tissues.	Liver, eggs, lean meat, legumes, whole grains, green leafy vegetables.
Iodine	Main part of thyroid hormones, which regulate basal metabolism and influence growth and development.	Iodized salt, seafood, vegetables grown near the sea, butter, milk, cheese, eggs.
Copper	Acts with iron to synthesize hemoglobin in red blood cells; helps form nerve walls and body's connective tissue.	Found in most foods *except* dairy products. Good sources: organ meat, shellfish, cocoa.
Zinc	Component of insulin and digestive enzymes; needed for protein metabolism.	Wheat germ and bran, whole grains, legumes, nuts, lean meat, fish
Fluorine	Component of strong teeth; prevents decay. May also be necessary for strong bones and to prevent bone loss in adults.	Water, either naturally or artificially added.
Chromium	Metabolism of glucose and protein, synthesis of fatty acids and cholesterol, insulin metabolism.	Corn oil, brewer's yeast, meat, whole grains.
Selenium	Works with vitamin E to protect cells against oxidative damage.	Seafoods, kidney, liver, some grains, depending on soil in which grown.
Molybdenum	Essential for function of certain enzymes, especially those needed in production of uric acid.	Meat, grains, and legumes.

ENTERTAINING

THE SECRET OF success is in planning. If you have everything organized beforehand, you will be able to enjoy your guests. Don't be over-ambitious: If you are new to cooking, don't try to produce the kind of meal you might eat in a restaurant. If you have young children and no help, make the meal informal; you'll enjoy it a great deal more. Plan the menu so you don't have lots of things to do at the last moment. If you are out at work all day, prepare as much as possible the evening before so it is less of a rush on the day of the dinner or party.

PREPARATION

◆Several days before, write down a menu that is seasonal, using the best fresh ingredients you can find. Try to plan a menu in which one or two courses can be made ahead and frozen, made the night before, or in the morning. Check your shelves and make a list of everything you need to buy.

◆Don't attempt anything you haven't done before or aren't sure about. Better to have one main dish with salads and a good cheese board than to attempt four or five complicated courses that need your constant attention and might go wrong.

◆Make sure there's a relaxed atmosphere. Don't feel that everything must be put away; things are what make your home interesting to others. It's also better to have guests chatting in a relaxed way in the kitchen with you than sitting formally in another room on their own.

◆Always provide nonalcoholic beverages for those who are driving and don't want to drink.

Menus

◆Combine dishes that are varied in taste, color, and texture as well as appearance and calorie value in each course. Try not to follow one course with another that has the same ingredients or one that is the same color; they won't be as appetizing.

◆Balance a rich, heavy dish with something light, such as a salad or fruit.

WHEN GUESTS ARRIVE

◆Plan a main dish that can cook with little attention. This way you'll be free to mingle with guests.

◆For vegetables, prepare pans of simmering water; add vegetables to pans when guests arrive. Or, you can place vegetables in a serving dish, and cook them in the microwave at the last minute.

◆Salads should be prepared and ready for the dressing, and the dressing made.

◆Hot desserts should be ready to go into the oven; cold desserts should be in the refrigerator.

◆If you have the oven space, warm plates in the oven if the meal is hot.

◆Red wine should be open and breathing at room temperature; white wine or champagne should be cooling in the refrigerator.

◆The table should be set.

◆Coffee should be measured out, ready to make; don't forget the cups, spoons, sugar, and cream.

◆Drinks, glasses, ice cubes, and snacks should be set out.

Setting the table

◆Don't have any extras on the table. All you need are condiments, beverages, serving spoons and forks, place settings, and a centerpiece. Keep everything else ready but on a separate table or in the refrigerator.

◆Lay out flatware so that the items you use first are on the outside of the arrangement and, as the courses proceed, follow from the outside in.

◆Tablecloths in neutral colors and made from fine cloth or lace work well for formal occasions, and tablecloths or place mats in bright colors and rough or nubby textures create a more casual atmosphere.

◆Have classic white or neutral napkins for formal occasions and colored and patterned ones for informal occasions.

◆Mix-and-match table settings include combining old with new, florals with geometrics, and plain with fancy to get a one-of-a-kind look.

Lighting

◆For evening meals, candles are important for lending atmosphere and are definitely the most flattering light you can have.

◆Candle flames must be above or below eye level, or those trying to talk across the table will be unable to see each other.

◆If candles are not enough, have dimmed background lighting that is not too brash.

Centerpieces

◆Make your centerpiece large enough that it doesn't look lost in the middle of the table, but small enough that it doesn't get in the way of glasses and other dinnerware.

◆Make sure the centerpiece is low enough that diners can see each other across the table.

◆Check that your centerpiece looks good on all sides; study it from all angles.

FOLDING NAPKINS

◆Napkins neatly folded into triangles or rectangles are all a dinner table actually needs, but if you have the time and inclination, you can fold napkins into all sorts of intricate shapes.

◆Most folding methods require a square napkin. Complicated folds need a large, well-starched napkin.

◆Make sure cloth napkins are ironed, and your hands and the working surface are clean.

The fan. *Lay the napkin out flat. Working away from you, make a series of narrow pleats (1).*
Fold the pleated napkin in half. Set the bottom of the fold into a wineglass and open out the pleats (2).

French fold. *Fold the napkin in thirds lengthwise, then make staggered folds to form steps or pockets.*

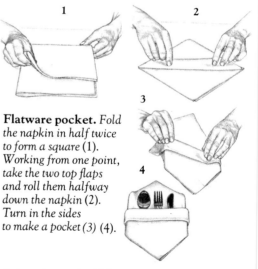

Flatware pocket. *Fold the napkin in half twice to form a square (1). Working from one point, take the two top flaps and roll them halfway down the napkin (2). Turn in the sides to make a pocket (3) (4).*

SERVING TIPS

◆ For formal meals without help, fill each guest's plate in the kitchen and carry it to the table.

◆ Put plates down in front of a guest from the left and take them away, when empty, from the right.

◆ Offer food in dishes from the left for guests to help themselves, and serve wine and water from a person's left.

◆ Serve soups—from a tureen—and dessert at the table on plates stacked in front of you; pass them to the right from person to person.

Seating arrangements

You may not want to be very formal at most dinner parties, but the rules are useful to know.

◆ The host sits at one end of the table and the hostess at the other.

◆ The male guest of honor sits on the right of the hostess and the female guest of honor on the right of the host. Couples do not sit together.

◆ Nowadays, there may be only one person giving a dinner party and there may not be an equal number of men and women, in which case put people you think will have something in common next to each other.

BUFFET PARTIES

These are practical ways of entertaining a lot of people at home, or a few people where seating is limited.

◆ One prominent flower arrangement should be enough, or you can make the food decorative in its own right.

◆ To ease congestion at the food table, put drinks and glasses on a separate table.

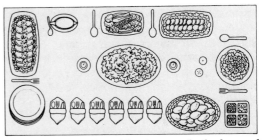

Arranging a buffet table. *Arrange the food around the table in menu order to prevent traffic jams.*

Renting dishes and glassware

◆ For very large parties, you can rent china, glassware, flatware, or serving pieces.

◆ Always shop around because there may be a large variation in price as well as quality.

ESTIMATING QUANTITIES

◆ Allow for the fact that people often have second helpings.

◆ The following are approximate quantities per person:

◇ $\frac{3}{4}$ to 1 cup soup for a side dish; 1 to $1\frac{1}{2}$ cups for a main dish

◇ 4 to 6 ounces fish

◇ 6 to 8 ounces meat on the bone

◇ 4 to 6 ounces meat off the bone

◇ 2 ounces rice, weight uncooked

◇ 2 ounces pasta, weight uncooked, for a main dish; 1 ounce for a side dish

◇ $\frac{1}{2}$ to $\frac{3}{4}$ cup vegetables

◇ 2 rolls

◇ 1 to 2 tablespoons sauce for main dishes or desserts

◇ $\frac{1}{2}$ cup fruit salad

◇ $\frac{1}{2}$ to $\frac{3}{4}$ cup ice cream

◇ 2 to 3 6-ounce cups coffee or tea per person

◆ The following are approximate quantities for multiple servings:

◇ 1 large head of lettuce will make a base for a salad for 6

◇ 1 large fruit pie for 8

◇ 1 loaf of bread will serve 16

◇ A two-layer cake will serve 10 to 12

◇ A large cheesecake will serve 10 to 12

CHILDREN'S PARTIES

◆Parties for kids can either be chaotic or delightful depending upon how well they are organized. It's best to invite a reasonable number of children so that things don't get completely out of hand.

◆Invite very young children to come with a parent or sitter. It's advisable not to invite children to come by themselves until they are at least 4 years old.

◆Give every child a name tag so that you and any visiting adults can more easily supervise the children by calling them by their names.

◆Clearly state the time the party will end on the invitation. One and a half hours is plenty for toddlers; two hours is ideal for 7- to 10-year-olds.

◆Young children prefer assorted bites of food such as popcorn and mini-pizzas, pita bread sliced to form a pocket and stuffed with imaginative fillings, brownies, and individual ice-cream cups. You can make delicious and healthy party snacks by mixing raisins, nuts, honey, and peanut butter together into little balls sprinkled with coconut and cinnamon for a sugar-free treat.

◆Fresh fruit salad, strawberry shortcake, or fruit dipped in chocolate is nice for children and adults. Remember to have food and drink for parents, too.

◆Make the cake in the shape of a teddy bear or fire engine and bake or buy two, one to have sliced and ready to eat so that children don't become restless waiting for a piece of the main birthday cake.

◆A low table with cushions or little chairs makes it easier for kids to get up and down without help. Cover the table with a plastic tablecloth taped to the underside so that it can't be pulled off accidentally.

◆Use gaily patterned paper products and disposable flatware that can be swept into a big plastic bag when the party is over. Save your linen tablecloths and napkins for grown-up parties.

Music and games

◆Invite a friend who plays a musical instrument to come over for a sing-along of some of the children's favorite tunes. "Ring Around the Rosey," "The Hokey Pokey," "Old MacDonald Had a Farm," and "Shoo Fly" are favorites that kids can act out along with the singing.

◆Active participation is much more fun for children. Movement games like "Hide-and-Seek," "Pin-the-Tail-on-the-Donkey," and "Musical Chairs" are great favorites of the under-fives, while older children enjoy team games like scavenger hunts or charades.

◆Dressing up is a winner at any age. Give them a box loaded with hats, scarves, old jewelry, and shoes, and let imaginations run wild.

Presents

◆If you want to avoid tears and tantrums, don't expect the birthday child to wait until the end of the party to open presents. Older children might wait until later, but toddlers should be allowed to tear happily into the gifts; that way frustration is minimized and all the children can share in the fun.

◆As each present is unwrapped, make a note of who gave what, and later on, after wearing or playing with each gift, let your child draw or write his or her appreciation on each thank-you note.

◆Call an end to the party by handing out party bags and coats; don't wait until the children are too tired.

◆Children love the inexpensive party favors—yo-yos, bubbles, marbles, jacks, jump ropes—sold in drugstores and toy-stores. Handcrafted favors will be treasured and can be great fun for the children themselves to make right at the party.

◆If the room is filled with balloons, offer one to each child as the children leave; the foil ones cost a little more but don't pop as readily as ordinary balloons.

Cleaning

ORGANIZING YOUR CLEANING

GOOD HOUSEKEEPING should be a matter of upkeep based on individual preference. It is up to you to decide what "clean" is, and then for you to maintain your home at that standard. It makes no sense to clean things according to a routine when, in fact, they are not dirty. Home is the place where the family gathers together, and while it should be generally clean and in order, it need not be spotless.

While thorough and routine cleaning is necessary in areas such as the kitchen and bathroom, where hygiene is all-important, cleanliness can best be achieved by straightening up as you go along. Have everyone in the family pitch in with the everyday housework and with a periodic sweep of all the closets. Even a child can help with housework. Just remember, a house with a reasonably clean and comfortable atmosphere is the place everyone loves to come home to.

TIPS TO MINIMIZE CLEANING

◆ Straighten up as you go along. Immediately wipe up anything that is spilled, including crumbs; by doing so, you will prevent stains, which are difficult to remove.

◆ Use a hard-wearing door mat to keep dirt out of the house. One that fits as a carpet does over the width of the entryway is best.

◆ You may want to encourage people to take their shoes off, or at least change their shoes, when they come in from outside; the carpet will stay clean longer.

◆ Wipe surfaces often so they never get so dirty that you have to use heavy, toxic household chemicals to get rid of the built-up grime.

◆ Make your life easier by dividing up the chores into things you must do every day or week, and things that can be left for a few months or that only need to be done once a year.

◆ You may want to make it a practice to eat in the kitchen or dining room, never in the living room or bedrooms. That way any mess will be concentrated in one part of the house.

◆ Eliminate clutter, as this creates more surfaces to keep clean.

◆ See that everybody in the house takes his fair share of the cleaning burden; encourage children to take responsibility for their own rooms.

CLEANING TACTICS

◆Try getting into the habit of returning items to their proper places once you have finished using them. Not only will you prevent a much larger cleanup job later on but you won't waste precious time looking for things.

◆Do small chores as they arise rather than putting them off.

◆Use laborsaving gadgets and appliances as much as possible, as long as they don't involve extra work. For example, for lots of chopping, a food processor makes sense, but for a single onion, a knife and cutting board are quicker and easier because you won't have to wash and dry the processor bowl, top, and blade.

◆When you are straightening up, carry a basket around to collect everything that's in the wrong room, then put it away when you arrive at its correct place.

◆Always follow the manufacturers' directions on cleaning supplies to avoid extra work. Do not use more than the recommended amounts; it is not only more costly but also is sure to involve extra effort in rinsing items off.

◆Always use a clean solution, mixing new cleaner and water as soon as the mixture becomes moderately dirty, or you will be redepositing dirt on the surface.

◆If you are going to make your own cleaning products, make certain they will be cheaper and be as safe and effective as commercial versions.

◆When dusting a room, it is more efficient to work around the room in one direction, starting from the door.

◆Always dust or polish furniture from the top down.

◆Do as many tasks as you can in one place before you move on to the next area; this will make cleaning faster.

◆The kitchen and bathroom are the two rooms in the house where strict cleaning and hygiene are paramount. Toilets and bathroom sinks should be disinfected and deodorized regularly. Kitchen countertops should be routinely wiped clean after food preparation to prevent bacteria, and the sink and drain area should be rinsed out with clear hot water after each use. Sweep the kitchen floor or damp-mop it as often as you can.

Parents with young kids

Let your standards slide a little without feeling guilty. It's better to spend time with your children than to be constantly chasing after their crumbs and scattered toys.

◆At their bedtime gather up all toys in a basket and carry them to the toy boxes. Then vacuum if it really needs it. In the morning you start off with a clean base. Don't worry about sweeping too much during the day. Just sweep up breakfast and lunch crumbs, wipe the mess from under the baby's chin, wipe sticky fingers immediately after a meal, and keep the floor or place where children play relatively clean.

◆Keep larger jobs, such as cleaning windows or the refrigerator, for weekends when your partner can take the children off your hands (or you can take them off hers). Don't worry about cleaning the drapes and upholstery; fit it in when you can.

◆Wash baby bottles immediately after use to prevent bacteria developing; don't leave children's cups and plates lying around too long before they are washed, especially if there are animals in the house.

At home all day

Cultivate your own interests and use your time creatively. Organize your day so that you only do housework in, say, the morning. Keep the afternoon free for your own activities or for spending time with your children.

◆Plan so that every day you: Clean the kitchen and bathroom; vacuum the main living areas; make your bed (any children should have made their own); straighten up the house.

◆Slot in extra tasks each day, for example:
Monday: Thoroughly clean bedrooms
Tuesday: Do the laundry
Wednesday: Iron the clothes
Thursday: Wash the windows or clean out the closets
Friday: Do the weekend shopping.

FREQUENT, REGULAR, AND OCCASIONAL JOBS

FREQUENT (daily or weekly)
◇ Straighten up the house
◇ Empty the garbage; clean garbage pail, if necessary
◇ Make beds
◇ Wash dishes or load or unload dishwasher
◇ Clean toilet and bathroom
◇ Clean kitchen counters and sink
◇ Clean pet dishes and the floor around them
◇ Clean out cat litter box, if you have one
◇ Vacuum living areas
◇ Dust
◇ Water the plants
◇ Do the laundry
◇ Sweep or scrub the floors
◇ Change the sheets

REGULAR (monthly)
◇ Give individual rooms, including hall, stairs, and landings, a thorough cleaning
◇ Alternate rooms from month to month
◇ Clean mirrors and tele-

phone, stereo, and other electric or electronic equipment
◇ Clean the oven, if necessary
◇ Wash the windows thoroughly in rotation

OCCASIONAL (two or three times a year)
◇ Defrost refrigerator
◇ Clean mineral deposits out of coffee maker and steam iron
◇ Clean out drains and gutters, particularly in the autumn
◇ Wash summer and winter blankets
◇ Wax floors
◇ Polish furniture
◇ Clean out closets

RARELY (once a year)
◇ Move heavy furniture and clean behind and under it
◇ Wash walls
◇ Shampoo carpets, upholstered furniture, and drapes, or get them cleaned

◇ Get chimney cleaned, if you have one
◇ Take out books and dust them and the shelves
◇ Get gas appliances serviced
◇ Clean filter in stove exhaust fan
◇ Get scissors, knives, shears, etc., sharpened
◇ Oil sliding door tracks
◇ Remove and clean light fixtures
◇ Clean screens and storm windows

Out at work all day

◆ Do a little cleaning at a time, whenever you can, and don't strain for perfection. Few people are able to do everything well, so save your energies for your family.

◆ Decide on the tasks that need to be done right away and those that you can put on hold for a while; relegate time-consuming tasks to the weekends, and work out a schedule for those jobs that can be done on a less regular basis.

◆ Vacuum the floors only when they need it or use a minivacuum for a quick spruce up of small areas until you can do the whole room.

◆ Clean the bathroom sink after using it, and wash out the tub or shower when you finish bathing; encourage everyone in the house to do likewise.

◆ To make coming home more pleasant, make up the beds and tidy the kitchen before leaving in the morning.

◆ When you clean the kitchen after dinner, set the table for breakfast. You'll have that much less to do in the morning.

◆ Set up a routine of simple chores to do in the evenings. Pick small jobs that you can easily finish with time enough left to unwind before sleep. Your evening routine could look something like this:

Monday: Put in a load of wash before going to bed and put it in the dryer when you wake up in the morning.

Tuesday: Dust and vacuum high-traffic areas.

Wednesday: Do your ironing while listening to music or watching television.

Thursday: Do the grocery shopping for the week.

Friday: Cook an extra casserole that you can freeze now and eat later.

HOW TO THOROUGHLY CLEAN A ROOM

1 *Open all of the windows to air out the room.*

2 *Remove scraps of paper, newspaper, and dead leaves of plants or old flowers; empty ashtrays and wastepaper baskets; put away any out-of-place items like papers or books.*

3 *Pick up any rugs. If cleaning a living room or bedroom, move all the small pieces of furniture out of the room. If cleaning the hall or entry, move out boots, coats, umbrella stands, and strollers.*

4 *Remove cobwebs and brush out closets.*

5 *Dust everywhere, including bric-a-brac. Wipe down the woodwork and clean all windows.*

6 *Vacuum the drapes and the upholstery.*

7 *Mop and polish the floor, or vacuum.*

8 *Shake rugs outside before putting them back in the room.*

9 *Replace all furniture, accessories, and ornaments, and polish them, if necessary.*

When cleaning a bedroom

In addition to the above items, you also should:

◆ Strip and air the bed.

◆ Put away clothing, towels, shoes, jewelry, toys, etc.

◆ Straighten the closets.

◆ Put clean sheets on the bed.

SPRING CLEANING

The first rays of spring sunshine show up all the splatters, smears, and dust that have accumulated on windows, walls, and furniture during the winter. Even rooms that have been regularly cleaned can benefit from some serious deep cleaning.

◆ It's a good practice every spring to thoroughly reorganize the house and get rid of accumulated junk, outgrown clothes, expired medication, and old canned goods.

◆ Tackle those areas that don't generally get the full treatment: The basement, the attic, behind the furniture, and under the stairs.

◆ Take it room by room, or choose a specific task and finish that before starting another, so that you don't wind up with several half-finished areas.

◆ Schedule an appointment with yourself for a specific task, and block out the time in which to work.

◆ Enlist the aid of family members; encourage them to clean out their closets and pile up belongings they never use that could go to someone in need.

◆ Small children are usually very happy to be "little helpers" with the dusting or sweeping, and even if they do very little actual cleaning they are learning how it's done.

THINGS TO REMEMBER WHEN SPRING CLEANING

◆ Take down pictures and clean the glass, the frames, and the wall behind them.

◆ Take down all accessories and clean them (and the shelf or wall behind them).

◆ Clean areas behind doors, above door frames, under tables, and behind and under chests of drawers and other large pieces of furniture that have been forgotten or skimmed over throughout the rest of the year.

◆ Remove cobwebs. Wash down moldings thoroughly.

◆ Polish all the furniture to clean and recondition it.

◆ Clean lamps and shades. Don't forget light fixtures; take them down to clean them, if necessary.

◆ Shampoo the carpets and upholstery, and get drapes washed or dry-cleaned.

◆ Vacuum thoroughly, then replace everything.

◆ Clean out all the kitchen cabinets.

◆ Take the opportunity to sort, give away, toss, or sell things you never use; you'll have less to put away.

CLEANING EQUIPMENT

◆When choosing your cleaning rags, remember that cotton fabrics, such as diapers, old towels, or undershirts, are more absorbent than synthetics, such as nightgowns.

◆Use lintless cloths when dry-dusting lightly soiled surfaces. Absorbent terry or other cotton cloths should be dampened with water or a little furniture polish to clean dust, smears, fingerprints, or soot. Always follow ___

___ e used on all wash-
___ nge can be used on
___ ceilings, wallpaper,
___ reas where liquids

___ are ideal for clean-
___ vily soiled, uncar-

CLEANING TIPS

◆Add a little water softener to the final rinse water when using sponges or mops to eliminate soap residue.
◆Baking soda sprinkled on a damp cloth or sponge makes a good nonabrasive cleaner for porcelain-topped appliances.
◆Use $\frac{1}{2}$ cup vinegar mixed with 1 tablespoon salt as a substitute for metal cleaner for copper and brass.

peted floors; and outdoor porches. Nylon brushes won't rot or become moldy.
◇**Brooms.** These should be used for quick, routine cleaning of hard floors.
◇**Dust mops.** For dusting bare floors between vacuuming. Keep mop pressed firmly on the floor, and follow the grain of the wood.

CLEANING KIT

___ ore than one level,
___ ing equipment up-
___ airs to save you

___ two
___ ed,

___
___ hard

___ de on

___ windows)
◆Bucket (better still, two)
◆Scrub brush
◆Cloths: For floors, wiping

kitchen and bathroom surfaces, dusting, window cleaning, and polishing
◆Dish towels
◆Toilet brush (one for each toilet)
◆Sponge for cleaning the bath
◆Dishwashing brushes. These can be used for general dishwashing, pets' plates and bowls, and for getting into corners when cleaning the sink.
◆Scouring pads

from running up and down the stairs.
◆If your hardware store doesn't stock what you need, try a janitorial supplier.

◆Cleaning agents: Furniture polish, silver polish, baking soda, white vinegar

ADDITIONAL EQUIPMENT
◆Bottle brush for cleaning vases
◆Floor polisher
◆Plastic toolbox or basket for carrying cloths and cleaning agents around the house
◆Carpet sweepers or mini-vacuums, either hand-held or floor models. These are great for small apartments, or if you don't want a large vacuum.

ECONOMY TIPS
◆A polishing mitt can be made from an old woolen sock.
◆Keep old toothbrushes—they are ideal for cleaning corners and metalware.
◆Large machinery, such as floor polishers and large wet/dry vacuums (useful if you have a flood), can be rented. It is almost never worthwhile to buy your own. They are expensive and bulky and need a lot of maintenance.

◇**Wet mops.** Use these for cleaning dirt and grime from large, rough-surfaced washable floors; mops should be wet but not sopping when used.

◇**Sponge mops.** These are best for cleaning smooth, moderate-sized washable floors. Use just damp; a squeegee end can be used to scrape off hardened dirt.

Vacuum cleaner

There are five basic types: Upright, tank/canister, wet/dry, hand-held, and central (built-in) system.

◇**Upright vacuum.** This takes less work than other types since you don't have to bend, but it can be clumsy for cleaning the stairs. Most uprights suck and brush; some even beat gently to raise the dust for sucking up. Beating can be rough on valuable carpets.

◇**Tank/canister vacuum.** This is light and portable, though cumbersome to carry upstairs. Cylinder vacuums are the best for smooth floors but not as good on carpet as the upright kind are.

◇**Wet/dry vacuum.** More efficient and flexible than an ordinary vacuum cleaner. For wet cleaning, it sucks up water or other liquid until the tank is full. Then a float will shut off the suction, and it is time to empty the tank and start again. For dry vacuuming you simply attach a cloth filter.

◇**Hand-held vacuum.** Convenient to use and store, some models are cordless. Good for cleaning small, lightly soiled surfaces and hard-to-reach areas quickly.

◇**Central (built-in) system.** Is quiet with no heavy equipment to carry. Good for cleaning carpets and above-floor cleaning.

WHAT TO LOOK FOR WHEN CHOOSING A VACUUM

◆Check how noisy it is; a noisy vacuum can be very irritating.

◆A long cord saves you from having to change outlets all the time while vacuuming. Automatic cord rewinding makes storage easier. Some models also store accessories inside the body.

◆Check the weight; a heavy machine is difficult to move around.

◆Check how near the wall it will go and how low under furniture.

◆Make sure the bags are easy to replace. Buy one with a large bag; small bags need to be emptied all the time.

◆For wet/dry cleaners, a 5-gallon capacity stainless or plastic tank is recommended, but you can get smaller ones.

◆Some tank/canister vacuums blow as well as suck; this can be handy for unblocking the hose or cleaning in tight places.

◆Variable speed can be useful if you have valuable carpets that need to be treated gently, as well as carpets that get a lot of use and need stronger suction.

◆Upright vacuums should have attachments such as expandable tubes and upholstery brushes for stairs and corners.

MAINTAINING EQUIPMENT

All valuable tools will work better and last longer if kept in good condition.

Vacuum cleaner

◆Remove lint, hair, or thread from the brushes and rollers frequently to prevent them from blocking the mechanism.

◆Check the cords where they enter the machine and the plug, and repair, if frayed. Check the hose and make sure it has no holes in it; a damaged hose won't suck properly.

◆Empty the bag before it gets too full to prevent dust from getting into the motor. Clean permanent vacuum cleaner bags by brushing them lightly. Do not wash them as this may loosen the weave of the fabric.

◆Replace the filter on tank/canister vacuums regularly—about every six months.

◆Replace worn vacuum brushes, because they don't pick up all of the dust.

Mops and brushes

◆ Wash wet mops in hot sudsy water after each use, and rinse thoroughly so soap residue does not build up and leave a dirty film on the floor with successive use. Rinse several times in clear, hot water. Shake to separate strings, and hang or turn upside down to dry (in the sun if possible). Store in a cool, dry place. Never keep a damp mop on the floor or in a bucket.

◆ You can tie a soiled mop head in a net bag and put it in the washing machine.

◆ Wash and rinse sponge mops after each use, then stand upside down to dry.

◆ Wash brooms and short-handled brushes in hot, sudsy water occasionally; they'll last longer. Beat the head up and down in the water so it reaches into the bristle tufts. Rinse well. Shake and dry in a warm place, with a rubber band around bristles to straighten them.

Carpet sweeper

◆ Frequently empty the dust compartment, and run your hands along the brushes to remove threads and lint.

◆ Unclip the brush occasionally, wash it in soapy water, and wipe out the inside; it will then sweep more efficiently.

Floor polisher

◆ Clean the polishing heads from time to time and attach new ones when they get too dirty. To clean them, stand the bristles in a shallow bowl of paint thinner until the polish has softened. Then rub the brushes clean with an old rag and air-dry.

Cloths

◆ Always rinse and wring washing cloths well after use so you don't spread the dirt from last time you cleaned. Wash all cloths and dustcloths when you have a machine load; wash chamois leather with pure soap (see page 90).

STORAGE

◆ Follow these suggestions for storing cleaning equipment, for practicality and safety. First, make sure everything has a place and is kept in its place. A tangled mass of equipment cannot be used to best advantage. Second, get everything off the floor.

◆ Store mops and brooms with their heads up so they keep their shapes.

◆ Hang carpet sweepers by their handles. The working part twists up, flush with the wall.

◆ Keep all household cleaners and other chemicals out of reach of children—preferably in a lockable closet.

◆ Put up hooks or shelves for vacuum cleaners, brooms, and mops, plus all attachments and accessories for cleaners, such as floor polish pads, vacuum cleaner bags, and dusting attachments.

◆ If you have a closet for cleaning supplies, clean it occasionally with a solution of mild detergent. Leave the door open until the closet is dry again. Then put the equipment back inside.

Organizing the cleaning closet. *Hang brooms and mops with their heads up between wooden dowel rods. If you stagger rows of hooks or rods, you will get more inside. Keep spare cloths and vacuum bags in boxes or in organized piles on a shelf.*

CLEANING THE KITCHEN

THE KITCHEN IS the room that gets most obviously dirty because of the grease and condensation caused by cooking. Daily cleaning is important to prevent a buildup of germs and the risk of food poisoning.

PREVENTING CONDENSATION IN THE KITCHEN

Condensation can be a problem in the kitchen because so much moisture is created in cooking. Ventilation, heating, and insulating are all necessary to combat it.

◆ Make sure there is sufficient ventilation in the kitchen, and, if necessary, have an exhaust fan installed. There are two types: One that extracts steam directly to the outside air, and another that filters and recirculates the air into the room. Both disperse steam and cooking odors very efficiently.

◆ Make sure the kitchen is adequately and constantly heated.

◆ Insulating cold walls and ceilings with sheets of expanded polystyrene and drywall before wallpapering will eliminate condensation. Thermal lined drywall, cork tiles, or tongue-and-groove-edged boards will have the same effect. Special vapor-barrier paint is also effective.

◆ Don't use a dryer in the room, or if you do, have it vented to the outside.

◆ Use a microwave oven when you can.

SINKS

◆ Clean the sink and drain area with a non-abrasive cleaner.

◆ Clean stainless steel occasionally with a commercial stainless steel cleaner if it is tarnished, looks cloudy, or is badly marked by water spots.

You also can use undiluted white vinegar, or a damp cloth dipped in baking soda to remove stains.

◆ Don't leave acidic foods such as vinegar, salad dressing, and fruit juices in a porcelain sink because they will stain it.

◆ To whiten a porcelain sink, fill it with lukewarm water and a little chlorine bleach, and let it soak for an hour or so.

▼▼ Bleach makes things white but not necessarily clean. Use it very sparingly; it can damage a variety of kitchen surfaces, as well as skin, eyes, and your water system.

◆ An occasional handful of baking soda down a drain, with boiling water poured over it, will keep the drain clear and fresh. Or use a commercial drain cleaner.

Remove rust stains. *Rub the surface of the sink with a cut lemon. If the stain is stubborn, keep working at it until it fades.*

◆Clean sink overflow openings and drains with a small toothbrush or a bottle brush.

Preventing blockages. *Keep a sink strainer over the drain all the time to prevent solid waste from accidentally blocking it.*

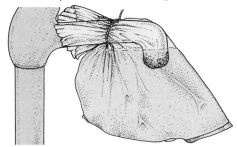

Faucets

Clean faucets with warm sudsy water or nonabrasive cleaner. Keep a dry washcloth handy to use as a chrome buff to rub away water spots and eliminate scrubbing.

◆Tackle mineral deposits on a faucet with a little nonabrasive cleaner on a toothbrush. You can also push the cut surface of a lemon onto the spout and press it around. Or, soak a paper towel with undiluted white vinegar and leave it on the stain for a while. The acidity of the lemon or vinegar neutralizes the alkalinity of the mineral deposit.

Removing mineral deposits. *Break down heavy deposits around the faucet by filling a small plastic bag with dissolved water softener and tying it onto the spout. Leave for about two hours. Repeat if necessary.*

KITCHEN UNITS

It is always a good idea to clean off the countertops just after preparing food to minimize germs and stains. Wiping up spills as soon as they occur is the best way to prevent permanent staining.

▼▼ Abrasive cleaners should never be used
♦♦ on plastic laminates because they will scratch the surface. Use mild liquid detergents or spray-on bathroom cleaners.

◆The greasy buildup from cooking can leave countertops covered with a sticky film. You can cut through the grease with rubbing alcohol, or, if the stains are persistent, dampen the area and sprinkle on a little baking soda; let it sit a while, then rub gently and rinse with clean water.

◆To remove tea stains or dye from a package or label from a plastic laminated countertop, use baking soda (see above), or use a very weak solution of bleach and water, 1 tablespoon to a quart. Wash and rinse thoroughly once the stain is removed.

◆Rub heat marks or stubborn stains on wooden countertops with equal parts of linseed oil and cleaning fluid, and rinse well with mild detergent. Or, try lemon juice or a commercial wood bleach, following the instructions.

◆Wipe slate and marble countertops regularly with a cloth wrung out in water and a mild detergent; both are porous so don't soak the surface (see also *Marble Furniture,* page 98).

◆Stains on marble can be removed with lemon juice or vinegar, but with great caution, making sure the acid does not affect the marble. Leave the lemon on for no more than 1 or 2 minutes; repeat if necessary.

◆If you find bugs, get rid of all contaminated food and wash out the cabinets with warm, sudsy water and bleach solution; don't use ammonia or insecticides in food cupboards.

KITCHEN EQUIPMENT

Clean any equipment used to prepare food as soon as possible after use to prevent bacteria growth. For the same reason, wipe all of the outer surfaces regularly with a damp cloth.

Range and oven

◆The easiest way to keep the range clean is to wipe up spatters when surfaces are still warm—and before they have a chance to burn on. Keep a damp sponge or cloth handy while you work so you can wipe up as you go along.

◆Once a month, or after a major cooking session, wash all the removable parts of the cooktop, such as burners and metal liner trays, in hot sudsy water. Give the whole surface of the range a good wipe down with a nonabrasive cleaner; use a nylon scouring pad for stubborn spots rather than scraping with something sharp that could damage the surface.

◆Clean burned-on marks on nondetachable electric elements with a stiff wire brush.

◆Clean enamel surfaces with liquid detergent and hot water. You can occasionally use a very fine steel wool, but rub gently so the enamel doesn't scratch.

◆Some electric ranges have heating elements that are flush with the surface of the cooktop. These must be kept very clean—even a tiny crumb on the element will slow down cooking time—since it is the contact of the entire surface with the base of the pan that heats the food.

◆For easy cleaning of burned-on grease in an electric oven, leave a bowl of full-strength ammonia in the cool oven overnight. The fumes will penetrate and soften the grease so all you have to do the next day is spray on more ammonia and wipe clean. Alternatively, you can sprinkle baking soda on the walls and floor of a warm oven, and leave it for an hour before wiping clean. Gas ovens with baked-on grease may have to be scrubbed with an abrasive cleaner.

◆For complete cleaning, new commercial oven cleaners are simple to use and nontoxic; they spray on with no fumes.

TIPS TO MINIMIZE CLEANING

◆Line the tray beneath an electric element with foil so if something boils over, all you do is change the foil.

◆To prevent food splattering in the oven, cover the dish with foil, or cook in a casserole with a lid or in a roasting bag.

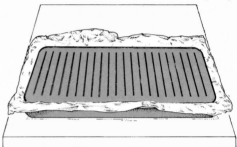

Keeping the broiler pan clean. *Line the bottom of the pan with aluminum foil, so if you broil greasy foods, the foil collects the drips while the pan stays clean.*

◆Traditional oven cleaners work well on heavily soiled gas or electric ovens but are very caustic. If you use them, wear rubber gloves, protect the floor with newspapers, and cover thermostats, heating elements, and light bulbs with aluminum foil.

◆**Self-cleaning ovens.** Refer to the owner's manual and follow instructions exactly. With most models, when the cleaning cycle is over, a light gray ash remains on the oven floor. Wipe it away with a sponge.

◆**Continuous-cleaning ovens.** These contain special linings that convert grease deposits into water and carbon dioxide whenever the oven is used, although heavier spills need to be scrubbed away. Protect the oven floor with foil and clean up spills when they occur.

◆Clean doors with a damp cloth dipped in dry baking soda; if necessary, rub stubborn marks with fine steel wool.

Exhaust fan

◆Clean the outside regularly to prevent a buildup of grease.

◆The fan filters that collect the grease must be cleaned or replaced regularly (some models indicate by a light when this is necessary), because they may catch fire. Check every six months or more often if you do a lot of frying. Change filters about once a year or as recommended.

◆To clean the exhaust fan, remove the outer cover and wash in warm water and detergent. Wipe fan blades with a damp cloth, but don't get them wet. Dry and replace the cover.

Refrigerator

◆Wipe the refrigerator out frequently. Use a cloth that has been wrung out in baking soda and warm water. Wipe bottles, jars, and containers before replacing them.

◆If you spill something in the refrigerator, clean it up right away; if left, it will probably start to smell or get moldy.

◆Defrost when ice in the freezer is about $\frac{1}{4}$ inch thick. Clean automatic-defrosting refrigerators about three times a year.

◆Once or twice a year, clean the condenser coils under, behind, or on the top of the refrigerator. Pry off the grille and vacuum with a crevice tool. Remove the drain pan at the bottom, and wash in soapy water.

Freezer

◆All freezers, even frostless ones, should be emptied and thoroughly cleaned every year. Standard freezers will need to be defrosted when the ice is about $\frac{3}{4}$ inch thick.

Cleaning a freezer.

1 Turn off the power. Remove all of the food, and wrap it up in newspapers and blankets or put it in a cooler to slow thawing.

2 To speed defrosting, place pans of hot water inside the freezer. Wipe out the inside with a solution of $\frac{1}{4}$ cup baking soda to a quart of warm water.

3 Turn the freezer back on at its lowest setting for an hour before replacing food. You can put an opened box of baking soda in the freezer to absorb unwanted odors.

Dishwasher

◆Clean regularly, particularly around the door seal where food particles get caught. Clean the filter after each wash, or the particles will be recirculated in the next wash.

◆Every so often, shake out the spray arms and use a pipe cleaner to clear the ports; scrub the filter screen (strainer) or basket with a stiff brush, and wipe down the detergent dispenser and the inside surfaces.

◆Dissolve mineral deposits by pouring a cup of vinegar into the empty tub and running the machine through the wash cycle.

MICROWAVE OVEN

◆Wipe out the inside with a damp cloth after use.

Cleaning a dirty microwave. *Put a dish of hot water in the oven. Add a slice of lemon and boil the water until plenty of steam is produced. Then wipe over the interior with a damp cloth.*

SMALL APPLIANCES

▼▼ Unplug electrical appliances from the
♦♦ wall before cleaning. Do not immerse
them in water.

Blender/food processor

♦ When you've finished using the appliance,
rinse the container in warm sudsy water.
Detachable blades and disks should be
cleaned one at a time under warm running
water. Use a small brush to avoid cutting
your fingers.
♦ Clean the bowl in a dishwasher or with
sudsy water; use a toothbrush to remove oily
deposits on the base.

Toaster

♦ Open up the removable plate at the bottom of the toaster, and gently shake out the
crumbs; wipe clean.
♦ Wipe the exterior with a damp cloth from
time to time.

Coffee maker

♦ Wipe off an electric coffee machine but
don't immerse it in water.
♦ If it is plastic, be careful not to scratch it.
Don't use scouring pads or abrasive cleaners.
♦ Clean stainless steel or chrome coffee
makers with a nonabrasive cleaner, then buff
up with a clean dry cloth.
♦ Dissolve mineral deposits in drip coffee
makers frequently by running a carafe of half
white vinegar, half water solution through a
brewing cycle, followed by a carafe of plain
water. Use a toothpick to clean residue from
the drip tube or dribble notch.
♦ To reduce mineral buildup, put a marble
or piece of loofah sponge inside a drip coffee
maker; mineral deposits will accumulate
there rather than on the element.
♦ If you use a commercial substance to take
out mineral stains, be sure to rinse the pot
thoroughly afterward, because these products can be highly toxic.

♦ **Teakettles or teapots.** Wipe enameled or
painted finishes with a damp cloth. Clean
stainless steel or chrome kettles with a nonabrasive cleaner, then buff with a clean dry
cloth. To remove discoloration in an aluminum teapot, fill it up with water, add 2
tablespoons cream of tartar per quart, and
boil for 20 minutes. When the water is cold,
scrub out the stains with a scouring pad.

Carving knife

♦ Unplug the knife, remove the blades, and
wash the parts separately. Wipe any greasy
parts with a damp (not wet) cloth.

Crockery cooker

♦ Some models allow you to take the
ceramic liner out and wash it, but the outer
casing must never be immersed in water,
unless it separates from the heating element.
♦ To clean the ceramic liner, empty out
contents, fill it with warm sudsy water, and
clean with a soft sponge, brush, or cloth.
Rinse well and wipe dry. If food is burned
on, let it soak.
♦ Don't use abrasive pads to clean the
ceramic liner.
♦ In hard-water areas, a whitish deposit may
appear on the inside of the liner. Remove this
with a mild liquid abrasive cleaner. Wipe
with a little vegetable oil to restore a sparkling look.
♦ Don't subject the liner to sudden temperature changes, or it may crack.

WASHING DISHES

♦ Get into the habit of rinsing dishes right
after eating so food doesn't have to be
scrubbed off the plate and the glaze is protected. Use cold water to rinse off egg or
milk, hot water for other foods. Hot water
sets egg and milk hard.
♦ Wash dishes in a plastic dishpan to prevent
chipping; fill the pan with hot sudsy water,
then wash the least greasy items first: Glassware and cups, then silverware, and plates,
ending with the pots and pans.
♦ A tablespoon of vinegar instead of liquid

PHOTOS FROM ANNABEL WRIGLEY

In designing her trailer studio, sewing teacher Annabel Wrigley asked for extra-large windows so kids could see outside while they work. Her husband, Darren, added a table,

Remove stains

BY JEANNE HUBER

Q I have a GE microwave oven. The white interior has yellowed in several areas. I have tried numerous products, scouring pads (Brillo & SOS), Comet and even bleach, with no success. Can you suggest something that might remove this discoloration?

Rockville

A Julie Wood, who manages public relations for GE Appliances, consulted with a home economist on the company's cooking team and wrote back.

Severely burned food, such as popcorn, can cause a yellow stain, Wood said. GE recommends placing a glass bowl with a cup of water and a tablespoon of lemon juice in the microwave and heating it until it is steaming. This should help loosen whatever is on the oven's interior. Then scrub the interior with a damp cloth and baking soda. Wipe off the residue, then wipe again with a clean damp cloth to make sure you've removed all of it.

"We do not recommend any additional cleaners beyond what is in our use and care manual and what we've listed above," Wood said.

Without knowing the model number of your oven, it's not possible to find the precise use and care manual that applies. However, one posted online that applies to numerous GE models says that you should unplug the oven before scrubbing the interior, and it lists only baking soda as suitable for the main interior. For the door and the surface of the oven that come together when the door closes, it recommends "only mild, nonabrasive soaps or detergents."

The world-famous store typically relies on a professional ultrasonic cleaning machine, says Vice Chairman Peter Schneirla. Instead, you can try this homemade solution that the store also uses: In a bowl, mix two parts hot tap water to one part ammonia, then soak your diamonds for several minutes. (Schneirla warns that, for some other stones, this solution might be damaging.) While the diamond is submerged, scrub it with a soft makeup brush or a baby's toothbrush. Rinse with warm water and pat dry. Repeat monthly or as needed.

GETTING CRYSTAL TO GLITTER
at Gump's

At this high-end San Francisco store, employees fill a spray bottle with a solution of one part rubbing alcohol to three parts water. (This formula, they swear, leaves no streaks or residue.) Then they spritz the crystal and wipe it dry with a clean white cotton cloth. They advise using a cotton swab to get at crevices.

REMOVING TARNISH ON SILVER
at Asprey

This posh big-city retailer uses the same stuff your mom did: Hagerty Silversmiths' Polish ($10 for a 12-ounce bottle). Using a soft cloth, spread a generous amount on your silver, wait a minute, then, using plenty

DUSTING COLLECTIBLES
at Hummel

For intricate porcelain figurines, a standard feather duster won't do. The M. I. Hummel team uses a paintbrush (with bristles that are at least three inches long) to sweep grit from surface details. Before reusing the brush, wash it with hand soap and warm water, then air-dry.

POLISHING WOOD
at Ethan Allen

Pieces in the showroom at this giant furniture retailer are kept gleaming with the company's own brand of polish (Ethan Allen Furniture Cleaner, $9.99 for ten ounces). Paula Mandeville, director of retail services, says you can use other polish too. Just be sure to use a clean foam pad to apply the product, then buff with a lint-free material like a cotton baby diaper or T-shirt.

CLEANING BLINDS
at Hunter Douglas

The company's trick: Clean vinyl shades with dryer sheets, which remove surface grit and reduce static cling. For wooden blinds, the company suggests that you vacuum with the soft-brush attachment to dust, then use Murphy's Oil Soap to spot-clean.   —*Patricia Greco*

Clean like a pro

Ever wonder how fancy retailers keep their goods gleaming? We've got the dirt on easy-to-do tricks.

MAKING DIAMONDS SHINE
at Harry Winston

of elbow grease, rub the item until the luster reappears. Use a clean cloth to wipe off any excess polish. Rinse silver if necessary—but never soak it in water for a long time, as it will tarnish.

detergent in the dishwater helps to remove grease.

◆Always rinse all the soapsuds off dishes with hot water, the hotter the better, so any bacteria are eliminated; hot water evaporates quickly, and dishes dry faster. Cold rinse water can leave visible film or spots on glasses and silverware. Skip towel-drying and use a dish rack instead.

◆To clean up burned pots quickly, fill them with sudsy water and bring to a simmer. For aluminum pots that are scorched, mix a quart of water with 2 tablespoons cream of tartar, boil for 10 minutes, and scour lightly, if needed.

◆When you are finished with the dishes, rinse out the sink and drain with clear hot water, wipe the faucets, spout, and drainboard, then wipe with a dry cloth to discourage water deposits. Wash sink mats in sudsy water, and rinse after each use. If they are very grimy, use a commercial tire cleaner (sold at automobile supply stores) to remove built-up scum. Rinse well.

◆Store steel wool pads in the freezer after each use so they won't get rusty.

◆Turn rubber gloves inside out, wash thoroughly in warm sudsy water; rinse well, and let them dry completely. Sprinkle with baking soda before turning right side out.

DISHWASHER

Most modern dinnerware, ranging from glazed enamel to the finest china, can be safely and efficiently cleaned in a dishwasher. Exceptions are hand-painted pieces with gold, silver, platinum, or cobalt-blue decoration, where the action of the dishwasher can remove the decoration.

◆A dishwasher can be cheaper to run than washing dishes by hand, and you can save energy by opening the machine after the rinse cycle is completed so the pieces can air-dry.

◆Dishwashers require very alkaline detergents; others create too many suds, so use only designated detergents. Always follow the manufacturer's instructions.

▼▼Avoid using too much detergent; it ◆◆makes too many suds and prevents the machine from cleaning properly. Sometimes it builds up an ugly chalky deposit that is difficult to remove from china and glass. In soft-water areas, fill your soap dispenser half full; in moderately hard-water areas, fill it three-quarters full; fill it up only in hard-water areas.

◆Check the water softener level, and refill regularly. If you don't, a film will start to appear on the dishes and glassware.

◆If there is a film on your dishes, check that the water is hot, try using more detergent, or try a new one. To remove the film, open the dishwasher after the rinse phase, remove all metal items, and on the bottom rack place a bowl containing 2 cups white vinegar. Wash and rinse again. Or, use citric acid in powder form as carried in most drugstores. Put a tablespoon of it into the dispenser instead of detergent and run the complete cycle through once or twice to get rid of the stains completely.

◆Get a dishwasher serviced regularly to prevent breakdowns.

TIPS FOR WASHING DISHES BY HAND

◆Wood, bone, and ivory handles that are glued on should be kept dry.

◆Lift stemmed glasses by the stem.

◆Use a plastic dishpan in the sink to prevent breaking china and glasses against the side of the sink.

◆Don't pile glasses on top of each other; dip each piece carefully.

◆To remove burned-on food, let the pan soak in cold water containing a little salt, overnight, or until food is soft. Boil water in the pan if food won't break up.

◆You can buy wooden wall-mounted dish drainers that can double as a plate storage area.

CHOOSING A DISHWASHER

◆ Measure the dishwasher and the space in the kitchen before you buy one.

◆ Do plenty of market research, since prices and quality vary.

◆ Some dishwashers are designed to take more plates than cups or glasses; others have interchangeable or removable baskets, which can be more useful. A removable lower basket allows you to get at the filters more easily to clean them.

◆ A machine with no central column is the most spacious.

◆ A filter with a grinder that automatically disposes of any food particles means you don't have to scrape the food off the plates before loading.

◆ An overflow pan is essential if your kitchen is not on a ground floor.

◆ Many dishwashers have a built-in water softener, which keeps mineral deposits from building up on glasses.

◆ Dishwashers may have numerous different cycles. A rapid cycle may be useful for some households constantly using cups or mugs; an energy-efficient cycle is good for not very dirty items. A prerinse cycle eliminates stale food smells if dirty dishes are kept in the machine for any length of time.

◆ Some machines have three spray levels, which means that hot spray will get to all the items.

◆ If you haven't got any under-the-counter space, you can buy a small portable machine that rolls to the sink or sits on the countertop and connects to the faucets.

Loading and unloading a dishwasher

◆ Remove large scraps from plates and pans before putting them in a dishwasher so they don't block the filters.

◆ Place dishes so soiled surfaces face toward the water spray.

◆ Avoid nesting dishes one inside the other so water can reach all surfaces. Never block small items with larger ones.

◆ Stack glasses, cups, bowls, saucepans, and oven dishes with rims downward so that they don't fill up with water.

◆ Put stainless steel, silver, or silver-plated flatware in separate baskets; if washed together, stainless steel can pit or stain the silver.

◆ Anchor lightweight items firmly between other items to keep them from falling into the bottom or overturning.

◆ Don't overload your dishwasher if you want perfect results.

◆ Always unload the bottom basket first; otherwise, drips from the top may land on the items at the bottom.

TIPS FOR USING A DISHWASHER

◆ Don't put anything in the dishwasher that isn't dishwasher safe.

◆ Don't put crystal in a dishwasher without a rinse aid as it may become "etched"—cloudy and scratched.

◆ Everyday glassware and flatware with wood or plastic handles should be washed in the low temperature cycle or in the top rack.

◆ The following items and materials are not suitable for dishwashers:

◇ Thin or heat-sensitive plastics

◇ Woodenware

◇ Valuable glassware

◇ Glassware with metal trim

◇ Fine or delicate china

◇ Hand-painted antique china

◇ Ironware

◇ Lacquered metals

◇ High-gloss aluminum

SPECIAL PROBLEMS

◆If you use a chopping board for onions or garlic, wash it thoroughly with a hard-bristled brush and wipe dry. Wash it right away, then wipe with a little mineral oil.

◆Wash insulated vacuum bottles with hot water and detergent or baking soda. Always store with cap off to prevent mold. Use a bottle brush to get the neck of the bottle clean. Don't immerse the bottle in water.

◆Don't immerse wooden salad bowls in water for more than a few seconds; the wood will dry and split. Wipe them immediately. Reapply mineral oil as a finish when needed.

China and porcelain

◆Rinse china used for egg or milk dishes promptly with cold water, then wash.

◆Rub tea and coffee stains on cups or mugs with a wet cloth dipped in dry baking soda or a salt-and-water paste.

◆Wash old china by hand in warm, not hot, water. If you wash or rinse china or glazed finishes in very hot water, very small cracks (crazing) can appear all over the dish. Don't soak pieces with gold glazes or trim; the water may lift the glaze off.

◆Always stack china carefully because the underside is often unglazed and may scratch the piece underneath it.

◆Wash glazed pottery by hand in warm water with a mild detergent to keep from damaging the glaze.

Plastic

◆A mild chlorine-bleach-and-water solution usually will remove food stains.

◆Soaking plastic ice-cube trays in full-strength vinegar for several hours will remove stains from hard-water buildup.

Glassware

◆Avoid extreme changes in temperature with all glassware; e.g., don't put cold glasses into very hot water—they will break.

NARROW-NECKED CONTAINERS

◆When cleaning, pour in some uncooked rice, a handful of dried beans, or some crushed ice. These will help scrub out the inside of a dirty vase or decanter. Add a small amount of liquid dishwasher detergent, fill with water, shake, and rinse.

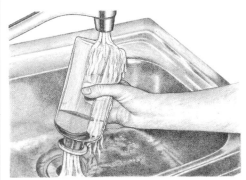

Drying a decanter. *After rinsing out, fill the decanter to the brim with cold water. Then turn it quickly upside down and allow it to empty while cold water, from the faucet, runs over the base. This seems to get rid of nearly all the water, and the rest will evaporate.*

◆Wash valuable glassware with mild detergent. Rinse in clear, hot water and allow to drain dry on a soft cloth, or polish with a linen cloth. Try not to wash very old glass, as it is easily broken; wipe it with a damp cloth.

◆Clean the crevices in cut glass with a soft bristled brush to keep it from scratching, then rinse carefully with warm water.

◆Clean baking dishes that have a sticky brown buildup by spraying them with oven cleaner and then, after the cleaner has soaked in for a few minutes, washing them in warm sudsy water.

◆To get rid of stains, cloudiness, or mineral deposits in glass vases, carafes, cruets, or decanters, fill them with water containing one or two teaspoons of household ammonia. Let them soak for a few hours, and then wash well and rinse with clear water.

GREEN TIP: If you don't want to use ammonia, shake some tea leaves and vinegar around in a glass to remove stains.

Knives and flatware

◆Carbon steel knives should be washed as soon as you are finished with them. Then dry them or hang in a warm place to prevent the blades from rusting.

◆Remove any corrosion on carbon steel knives by rubbing with steel wool or salt and waxed paper. Rinse well, then polish with a cotton cloth.

◆Clean silver flatware from time to time with silver cleaner. Wash it afterward. If working on your stainless steel sink, cover it with newspaper first because silver cleaner will mark stainless steel.

◆Remove egg stains from silver spoons by rubbing them gently with salt before washing them.

◆Don't leave stainless steel flatware in contact with salt in very hot water or with rhubarb, lemon juice, or vinegar; they all corrode it.

◆If stainless steel flatware comes out of the dishwasher spotted with mineral deposits, soak it in undiluted white vinegar. To prevent spots, use a rinsing agent.

Cast-iron and iron pans

◆Cast-iron cookware rusts easily, so it must be wiped after use with a damp cloth and dried right away. To remove caked-on food or rust, scour with coarse salt, and wash in sudsy water. Rinse and dry thoroughly, coat with vegetable oil, and store in a dry place. Place paper towels between stacked pots, and leave the lids off.

SHARPENING KNIVES

◆When sharpening knives on a steel or stone, be sure to hold the blade at a shallow angle (about 15 degrees); if held at the wrong angle, the blade may not sharpen.

◆If using a rotary grinder with little wheels, pull the blades through several times in the same direction so that you don't damage the blade. Knives with serrated edges do not need to be sharpened.

Using a mug. *You can sharpen knives on the unglazed base of a mug. Hold the blade at a slight angle and slide it in one direction.*

PREPARING IRON AND CAST-IRON

Buy preseasoned cast-iron pans if you can. Otherwise, you will have to "season" the pan with oil to keep food from sticking to the sides and to prevent it from rusting (see below). Before using a preseasoned pan, scour the pan to remove lacquer, rinse it, dry it, and grease the inside lightly with an unsalted fat. Grease it again before using it.

SEASONING CAST-IRON

1 *Remove the protective coat of lacquer by rubbing the pan with scouring powder and a stiff brush. Wash the pan in hot sudsy water, and dry thoroughly.*

2 *Coat the inside thinly and evenly with vegetable oil and set the pan in a 325° to 350° oven for two hours. Wipe off the excess oil when cool, rinse the pan, and dry it on a burner set at low heat. Grease it before and after use for the first few weeks.*

...ns

...water. Rinse ...st scrape, use ...soap.

...ng the pan or ...spoons cream ...oiling for 20

...oking acidic ...or lemon in it.

...ans

...but salt and acids in food can cause pit marks. Remove these marks with fine steel wool and scouring powder.

◆ To keep stainless steel sparkling, polish with a commercial stainless steel cleaner.

◆ Marks that result from stainless steel getting too hot can't be removed.

Tin bakeware

◆ Clean badly discolored bakeware by boiling it in white vinegar and water. Soften rust marks with cooking oil, then rub gently with a cloth. Don't use abrasives; they scratch.

◆ To make a pan rustproof, wipe all over with buttered paper, and place in a 350° oven for 15 minutes.

Nonstick pans

◆ Wash in warm sudsy water. If the black nonstick finish is wearing off, rub the inside surface with oil on a piece of paper towel.

Copper pans

◆ Remove protective lacquer on new pans before use (see right), or you will get lacquer all over the stove and in the food.

◆ Copper must be kept very clean to prevent a poisonous "green-rust" from developing. Always wash copper in hot soapy water after using acids, or it will tarnish.

◆ Copper pans are sometimes lined with a

CLEANING A PRESSURE COOKER

◆ Wash after each use but don't immerse the cover, or you may damage the gauge and clog the vents.

◆ Wipe the cover with a sudsy cloth, and rinse with a clean, damp one.

◆ Wash the gasket carefully; replace it if it gets worn out or stretched because it won't seal in the steam.

Cleaning the openings in the cover. *Draw a pipe cleaner through the holes several times; the dirt should collect on the fibers.*

tin or chromium plating that prevents copper from reacting with food. If the lining becomes worn, get the pan replated.

◆ Rub corrosion spots with a paste of equal parts white vinegar and salt, or lemon juice and salt. Rinse and dry. Corrosion also can be cleaned off with commercial copper cleaner. To remove the green patina, use a solution of half-and-half soapsuds and ammonia. Burned-on food can be removed by scrubbing lightly with scouring powder.

◆ You can make your own copper polish with equal parts salt, white vinegar, and flour. Rub the copper with this mixture until clean, then wash in hot water, rinse, and dry.

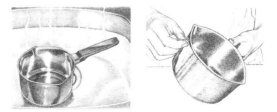

Removing lacquer. *Cover the pan with boiling water, let it sit until the water has cooled (above left). Then peel off the lacquer (above right).*

CLEANING BATHROOMS

BATHROOMS CAN BE a haven for germs and mildew, and they require thorough cleaning on a regular basis to remain sanitary and free of odors.

Knowing a bathroom's trouble spots can help you determine a cleaning routine that is simplified by doing a little every time you go into the bathroom. If you get into the habit of giving the toilet and sink a frequent wipe down with a squirt of cleaner, you will prevent them from becoming a regular breeding ground for bacteria. Keeping the room well ventilated will not only promote a fresh, pleasant smell but also will minimize condensation and dampness.

DEALING WITH MILDEW

Prevention is the best method for eliminating mildew, but if it is already present, try the following:

◆ Remove mildew and stains from tub and tiles by wetting the surfaces with water and then spraying them with a solution of 1 cup bleach and 1 quart water.

◆ Mildewed bath mats can be washed in the washer with detergent, bleach, and a few colorfast towels to help balance the load.

◆ If your shower or window curtains have mildew spots, try washing them in a mild bleach solution, using 1 tablespoon of bleach to every 2 cups of warm water. Rinse and wipe dry with a cloth.

BATHROOM FIXTURES

◆ Frequent wiping with a mild disinfectant cleaner prevents a buildup of dirt or mineral deposits and makes the use of strong cleaners unnecessary. Wipe all bathroom surfaces frequently, working from the cleanest (mirror) to the dirtiest (floor).

◆ Try to persuade members of your household to wash and rinse the bathtub or shower floor each time they use it. Keep the bathroom cleaning equipment in a known place so there can be no excuses for not using it.

Bathtubs and showers

◆ Scrub the tub and shower with a nonabrasive or a liquid disinfectant cleaner and a sponge. When stronger measures are necessary, use a brush or nylon scouring pad.

◆ To make quick work of bathtub rings, spray on foaming tile cleaner, let it work for a few seconds, and whisk away with a long-handled brush or sponge (it does the stretch-

ing for you), then rinse.

◆ If you live in a hard-water area, use water softener in the bath to minimize deposits. Rust marks can sometimes be removed with a commercial rust remover.

◆ If the bathtub has been damaged by rough treatment or stains from long neglect, you can have it professionally chemically cleaned or refinished. The finish won't be as durable as the original.

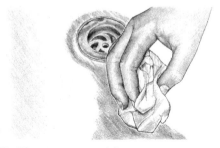

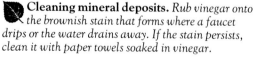

Cleaning mineral deposits. *Rub vinegar onto the brownish stain that forms where a faucet drips or the water drains away. If the stain persists, clean it with paper towels soaked in vinegar.*

SPECIAL PROBLEMS

◆If you use a chopping board for onions or garlic, wash it thoroughly with a hard-bristled brush and wipe dry. Wash it right away, then wipe with a little mineral oil.

◆Wash insulated vacuum bottles with hot water and detergent or baking soda. Always store with cap off to prevent mold. Use a bottle brush to get the neck of the bottle clean. Don't immerse the bottle in water.

◆Don't immerse wooden salad bowls in water for more than a few seconds; the wood will dry and split. Wipe them immediately. Reapply mineral oil as a finish when needed.

China and porcelain

◆Rinse china used for egg or milk dishes promptly with cold water, then wash.

◆Rub tea and coffee stains on cups or mugs with a wet cloth dipped in dry baking soda or a salt-and-water paste.

◆Wash old china by hand in warm, not hot, water. If you wash or rinse china or glazed finishes in very hot water, very small cracks (crazing) can appear all over the dish. Don't soak pieces with gold glazes or trim; the water may lift the glaze off.

◆Always stack china carefully because the underside is often unglazed and may scratch the piece underneath it.

◆Wash glazed pottery by hand in warm water with a mild detergent to keep from damaging the glaze.

Plastic

◆A mild chlorine-bleach-and-water solution usually will remove food stains.

◆Soaking plastic ice-cube trays in full-strength vinegar for several hours will remove stains from hard-water buildup.

Glassware

◆Avoid extreme changes in temperature with all glassware; e.g., don't put cold glasses into very hot water—they will break.

NARROW-NECKED CONTAINERS

◆When cleaning, pour in some un-cooked rice, a handful of dried beans, or some crushed ice. These will help scrub out the inside of a dirty vase or decanter. Add a small amount of liquid dishwasher detergent, fill with water, shake, and rinse.

Drying a decanter. *After rinsing out, fill the decanter to the brim with cold water. Then turn it quickly upside down and allow it to empty while cold water, from the faucet, runs over the base. This seems to get rid of nearly all the water, and the rest will evaporate.*

◆Wash valuable glassware with mild detergent. Rinse in clear, hot water and allow to drain dry on a soft cloth, or polish with a linen cloth. Try not to wash very old glass, as it is easily broken; wipe it with a damp cloth.

◆Clean the crevices in cut glass with a soft bristled brush to keep it from scratching, then rinse carefully with warm water.

◆Clean baking dishes that have a sticky brown buildup by spraying them with oven cleaner and then, after the cleaner has soaked in for a few minutes, washing them in warm sudsy water.

◆To get rid of stains, cloudiness, or mineral deposits in glass vases, carafes, cruets, or decanters, fill them with water containing one or two teaspoons of household ammonia. Let them soak for a few hours, and then wash well and rinse with clear water.

🍃GREEN TIP: If you don't want to use ammonia, shake some tea leaves and vinegar around in a glass to remove stains.

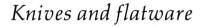
Knives and flatware

◆Carbon steel knives should be washed as soon as you are finished with them. Then dry them or hang in a warm place to prevent the blades from rusting.

◆Remove any corrosion on carbon steel knives by rubbing with steel wool or salt and waxed paper. Rinse well, then polish with a cotton cloth.

◆Clean silver flatware from time to time with silver cleaner. Wash it afterward. If working on your stainless steel sink, cover it with newspaper first because silver cleaner will mark stainless steel.

◆Remove egg stains from silver spoons by rubbing them gently with salt before washing them.

◆Don't leave stainless steel flatware in contact with salt in very hot water or with rhubarb, lemon juice, or vinegar; they all corrode it.

SHARPENING KNIVES

◆When sharpening knives on a steel or stone, be sure to hold the blade at a shallow angle (about 15 degrees); if held at the wrong angle, the blade may not sharpen.

◆If using a rotary grinder with little wheels, pull the blades through several times in the same direction so that you don't damage the blade. Knives with serrated edges do not need to be sharpened.

Using a mug. *You can sharpen knives on the unglazed base of a mug. Hold the blade at a slight angle and slide it in one direction.*

◆If stainless steel flatware comes out of the dishwasher spotted with mineral deposits, soak it in undiluted white vinegar. To prevent spots, use a rinsing agent.

Cast-iron and iron pans

◆Cast-iron cookware rusts easily, so it must be wiped after use with a damp cloth and dried right away. To remove caked-on food or rust, scour with coarse salt, and wash in sudsy water. Rinse and dry thoroughly, coat with vegetable oil, and store in a dry place. Place paper towels between stacked pots, and leave the lids off.

PREPARING IRON AND CAST-IRON

Buy preseasoned cast-iron pans if you can. Otherwise, you will have to "season" the pan with oil to keep food from sticking to the sides and to prevent it from rusting (see below). Before using a preseasoned pan, scour the pan to remove lacquer, rinse it, dry it, and grease the inside lightly with an unsalted fat. Grease it again before using it.

SEASONING CAST-IRON

1 *Remove the protective coat of lacquer by rubbing the pan with scouring powder and a stiff brush. Wash the pan in hot sudsy water, and dry thoroughly.*

2 *Coat the inside thinly and evenly with vegetable oil and set the pan in a 325° to 350° oven for two hours. Wipe off the excess oil when cool, rinse the pan, and dry it on a burner set at low heat. Grease it before and after use for the first few weeks.*

Aluminum pans

◆ Wash in mild detergent and water. Rinse with very hot water. If you must scrape, use steel wool pads saturated with soap.
◆ Remove dark stains by filling the pan or pot with water, adding 2 tablespoons cream of tartar per quart, and boiling for 20 minutes.
◆ Brighten aluminum by cooking acidic foods such as apples, rhubarb, or lemon in it.

Stainless steel pans

◆ Stainless steel is rustproof, but salt and acids in food can cause pit marks. Remove these marks with fine steel wool and scouring powder.
◆ To keep stainless steel sparkling, polish with a commercial stainless steel cleaner.
◆ Marks that result from stainless steel getting too hot can't be removed.

Tin bakeware

◆ Clean badly discolored bakeware by boiling it in white vinegar and water. Soften rust marks with cooking oil, then rub gently with a cloth. Don't use abrasives; they scratch.
◆ To make a pan rustproof, wipe all over with buttered paper, and place in a 350° oven for 15 minutes.

Nonstick pans

◆ Wash in warm sudsy water. If the black nonstick finish is wearing off, rub the inside surface with oil on a piece of paper towel.

Copper pans

◆ Remove protective lacquer on new pans before use (see right), or you will get lacquer all over the stove and in the food.
◆ Copper must be kept very clean to prevent a poisonous "green-rust" from developing. Always wash copper in hot soapy water after using acids, or it will tarnish.
◆ Copper pans are sometimes lined with a

CLEANING A PRESSURE COOKER

◆ Wash after each use but don't immerse the cover, or you may damage the gauge and clog the vents.
◆ Wipe the cover with a sudsy cloth, and rinse with a clean, damp one.
◆ Wash the gasket carefully; replace it if it gets worn out or stretched because it won't seal in the steam.

Cleaning the openings in the cover. *Draw a pipe cleaner through the holes several times; the dirt should collect on the fibers.*

tin or chromium plating that prevents copper from reacting with food. If the lining becomes worn, get the pan replated.
◆ Rub corrosion spots with a paste of equal parts white vinegar and salt, or lemon juice and salt. Rinse and dry. Corrosion also can be cleaned off with commercial copper cleaner. To remove the green patina, use a solution of half-and-half soapsuds and ammonia. Burned-on food can be removed by scrubbing lightly with scouring powder.
◆ You can make your own copper polish with equal parts salt, white vinegar, and flour. Rub the copper with this mixture until clean, then wash in hot water, rinse, and dry.

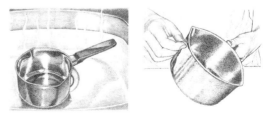

Removing lacquer. *Cover the pan with boiling water, let it sit until the water has cooled (above left). Then peel off the lacquer (above right).*

CLEANING BATHROOMS

Bathrooms can be a haven for germs and mildew, and they require thorough cleaning on a regular basis to remain sanitary and free of odors.

Knowing a bathroom's trouble spots can help you determine a cleaning routine that is simplified by doing a little every time you go into the bathroom. If you get into the habit of giving the toilet and sink a frequent wipe down with a squirt of cleaner, you will prevent them from becoming a regular breeding ground for bacteria. Keeping the room well ventilated will not only promote a fresh, pleasant smell but also will minimize condensation and dampness.

DEALING WITH MILDEW

Prevention is the best method for eliminating mildew, but if it is already present, try the following:

◆ Remove mildew and stains from tub and tiles by wetting the surfaces with water and then spraying them with a solution of 1 cup bleach and 1 quart water.

◆ Mildewed bath mats can be washed in the washer with detergent, bleach, and a few colorfast towels to help balance the load.

◆ If your shower or window curtains have mildew spots, try washing them in a mild bleach solution, using 1 tablespoon of bleach to every 2 cups of warm water. Rinse and wipe dry with a cloth.

BATHROOM FIXTURES

◆ Frequent wiping with a mild disinfectant cleaner prevents a buildup of dirt or mineral deposits and makes the use of strong cleaners unnecessary. Wipe all bathroom surfaces frequently, working from the cleanest (mirror) to the dirtiest (floor).

◆ Try to persuade members of your household to wash and rinse the bathtub or shower floor each time they use it. Keep the bathroom cleaning equipment in a known place so there can be no excuses for not using it.

Bathtubs and showers

◆ Scrub the tub and shower with a nonabrasive or a liquid disinfectant cleaner and a sponge. When stronger measures are necessary, use a brush or nylon scouring pad.

◆ To make quick work of bathtub rings, spray on foaming tile cleaner, let it work for a few seconds, and whisk away with a long-handled brush or sponge (it does the stretch-

ing for you), then rinse.

◆ If you live in a hard-water area, use water softener in the bath to minimize deposits. Rust marks can sometimes be removed with a commercial rust remover.

◆ If the bathtub has been damaged by rough treatment or stains from long neglect, you can have it professionally chemically cleaned or refinished. The finish won't be as durable as the original.

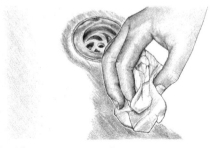

Cleaning mineral deposits. *Rub vinegar onto the brownish stain that forms where a faucet drips or the water drains away. If the stain persists, clean it with paper towels soaked in vinegar.*

◆Wipe acrylic bathtubs with dishwashing liquid, using a soft cloth. Rub resistant stains with half a lemon. Rub scratches with a little silver polish, then buff. Acrylic bathtubs are easy to take care of; they are not affected by bath salts and are nonporous.

◆Too much use of acid (i.e., very strong bathroom cleaner) and abrasive pads will damage bathtubs, sinks, and showers.

Faucets

◆Clean around the faucets with an old toothbrush dipped in nonabrasive cleaner.

◆Keep a dry washcloth handy to buff away water spots on fixtures and eliminate scrubbing later.

◆Gold-plated faucets scratch easily, so just use a soft cloth and warm water.

◆Mineral deposits can be cleaned with commercial cleaners that use acid to eat away the stain.

◆Use vinegar or half a lemon to remove mineral deposits. Leave it on the stain as long as needed. Repeat until the stain has dissolved.

◆If there is a heavy buildup of mineral deposits, hang a plastic bag full of dissolved water softener from the faucet (see page 61).

Shower heads

◆Shower heads clog up very quickly with mineral deposits in hard-water areas unless you have a strong jet. Take the shower head apart and clean it from the inside (see below). The harder your water, the more often you will have to do this.

◆Soak plastic parts in warm water and vinegar (1 tablespoon vinegar to 2 cups of water), or rub them with a slice of lemon to remove mineral deposits.

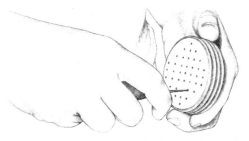

Cleaning the shower head. *Unscrew the head, and scrub with an old toothbrush or nail brush. Then poke a toothpick through the holes to clear them.*

Shower curtains and doors

◆Extend shower curtains after showering to allow air to circulate and thus prevent mildew spots from developing.

◆Wash canvas or cotton shower curtains in hot, sudsy water.

◆A prewash spray can help remove soap and scum buildup. Spray it along the bottom and let it soak till the buildup loosens. Then rinse thoroughly with hot water, and wipe down with a clean cloth.

◆Most shower curtains can be washed in the washing machine. To wash waterproof silk curtains, place them on a flat surface, and sponge them with a lukewarm solution of soap and water. Rinse with clear water, and hang up to dry.

◆When buying a shower curtain, look for one that is mildewproof and water resistant so it doesn't get marks.

◆Clean out shower door tracks with a toothbrush or cotton swab soaked in a mild solution of bleach and water.

◆ You can keep shower doors free of mineral deposits with frequent swipes of a squeegee and regular washings with a cloth soaked in sudsy water containing white vinegar.

Sinks

◆Wipe sinks frequently with a nonabrasive cleaner, rinse, and dry; never use abrasive cleaners, which may damage the surface.

◆Remove stains from marble-topped counters by soaking with a few white paper towels saturated with a hydrogen peroxide solution or full-strength ammonia, and leaving it covered with a piece of plastic. Polish the marble after cleaning.

Toilets

◆Scrub the inside of the toilet bowl frequently with a toilet brush, using the cleaner of your choice to remove deposits and waterlines and minimize germs.

◇ **Chemical toilet cleaners.** These will disinfect and deodorize at the same time.

◇ **White vinegar.** This is useful because it is safer to have around the home and can be poured into the bowl and left for an hour or so before flushing.

◆Remember to wipe the seat, handle, tank, under the rim, and the surrounding areas on a regular basis.

◆To remove old mineral buildup in the toilet, sprinkle $\frac{1}{2}$ cup of water softener around the bowl (above the waterline) immediately after flushing.

◆If you need to remove very bad buildups of lime, you may have to empty the toilet bowl first. Turn off the water valve to the tank, and flush until the bowl is empty. Place white paper towels over the discolored areas and saturate with a special cleaner or with white vinegar; let soak. This may have to be repeated several times. Finish by scrubbing with a plastic brush to remove any stubborn deposits.

◆Rinse your toilet brush in a fresh flush of water after cleaning, and occasionally wash it in hot water and disinfectant. Keep it free of mildew by letting it dry completely before putting it away.

THE DANGERS OF TOILET CLEANERS

▼▼Do not be tempted to double the
• • effectiveness of a toilet cleaner by using two different ones together. Different chemicals can combine to form explosive and toxic gases.

▼▼Bleach is not a cleaning agent; it just
• • makes things white. It will eventually damage chrome, laminates, and other plastic materials. Vinegar, lemon juice, and mild disinfectant are just as good, and they are safer.

▼▼Most toilet cleaners are poisonous.
• • Buy ones with childproof tops, and store out of reach of children.

BATHTUB AND SHOWER TILES

◆Wipe away soap spots or film from tile with a solution of water and water conditioner or a solution of 1 part vinegar to 4 parts water. Rinse, then dry with a soft cloth.

◆To take off soap scum and mildew, you can apply a coat of paste wax (the kind used for automobiles) onto bathtub and shower tiles, but be careful not to get any in the bottom of the tub or on the shower floor.

◆A coat of paste wax on chrome, plastic, fiberglass, marble, and other bath surfaces helps to repel dirt and hard-water deposits.

◆Wipe over bath surfaces with a nonabrasive cleaner on a damp cloth, then rinse, on a regular basis.

◆Bathtub tiles will stay shiny and free of soap scum with a quick wipe of a squeegee after the last shower.

FURNITURE AND ACCESSORIES

◆ Treat chrome towel racks as you would the faucets (see page 71).
◆ If you have a linen closet in the bathroom, take everything out from time to time, wipe the shelves, and let them dry before replacing the linens.

Wastebaskets and laundry baskets

◆ Avoid using metal wastebaskets in the bathroom; they will quickly become rusty.
◆ Line wastebaskets with a plastic liner, and if you are using disposable diapers, keep a pail especially for them; empty it daily.
◆ Scrub wicker occasionally. Do this outside with warm, sudsy water and salt. Let dry.

Medicine cabinet

◆ Regularly clear out the medicine cabinet and throw away used razor blades and other out-of-date items. Wipe the cupboard with a liquid disinfectant if it is very dirty, otherwise a damp cloth will do. Rinse and let dry.

Mirrors

◆ Wipe with a weak vinegar and water solution or a commercial glass spray.
◆ Remove hairspray with a little paint thinner on a cotton ball; the room should be well ventilated when you do this.
◆ Prevent condensation by rubbing with a little undiluted dishwashing liquid or an anti-fog product. Get plastic mirrors. They are less likely to fog.

Bath mats

◆ You can clean grimy bathtub mats with whitewall tire cleaner. Apply the cleaner outside, let it stand for a few minutes, then scrub a little and hose off. You also can clean the mat in the washing machine with a capful of bleach; let it air-dry.
◆ Machine-wash fabric mats with detergent and all-purpose bleach.

Sponges and washcloths

◆ Rinse thoroughly after use and wash occasionally in a weak solution of white vinegar and water. You also can put washcloths in the washing machine. Allow sponges to dry naturally, outside if possible.

Light fixtures

◆ Switch the power off before cleaning any bathroom light fixtures, and make sure your hands are dry, or you could get an electric shock. Wipe the bulb with a damp cloth. Replace the fixture when you're sure it's dry.

BATHROOM CHECKLIST

◇ Toothbrushes for the entire family
◇ Toothpaste, mouthwash, and dental floss
◇ Nail brush and nail scissors or clippers
◇ Washcloths or sponges
◇ Soap (bath oil and talcum powder are optional)

◇ Clean towels
◇ Toilet paper
◇ Toilet brush and cleaner
◇ Bathtub cleaning equipment
◇ Wastebasket and diaper bucket
◇ Laundry basket (optional)

CLEANING FLOORS

WHEN THE FLOORS in your home are clean, smooth, and shiny throughout, the rest of the house will not only look lovely and clean but also will be easier to maintain, because less dirt is being tracked through. Dry-mop often to pick up dust and grit, paying particular attention to the hall and entryways where most of the dirt is carried in. Wool or synthetic mop heads are best; their static cling attracts dust. Wipe across the entire area, pulling dust along as you go. Sponge mops that can be used damp or dry are great for sopping up spills and giving the floor a quick freshening up between washings.

TREATING HARD FLOORS

◆ Keep most nonwooden floors clean by sweeping and then wiping with a damp mop, using clear water. Others, such as slate and tile floors, benefit from heavy-duty washing now and then.
◆ A sealer and/or water- or wax-based polish will help to protect most hard floors.

Wooden floors

◆ For a quick cleanup, damp-mop a small area at a time using warm water, and wipe dry before continuing.

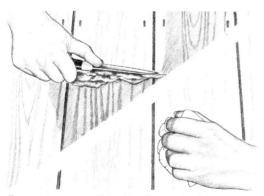

Removing ground-in dirt. *Scrape the dirty area gently with an old knife, working along the grain (above left). Then rub with paint thinner. Apply polish, give it time to soak in, then buff (above right).*

◆ For a more thorough cleanup, use a liquid cleaning wax containing turpentine or non-toxic dry cleaning fluid.

Cork floors

◆ If sealed, just mop from time to time. If polished, give a coating of wax polish sparingly no more than twice a year.
◆ Vinyl-coated tiles just need to be damp-mopped with detergent solution when dirty.
◆ Sealed cork that is in bad condition can be sanded and resealed.
▼▼ Cork floors that get too wet may crack;
◆◆ always dry the floor thoroughly after washing it.

Linoleum floors

◆ Too frequent washing of linoleum makes it brittle. Wash with warm sudsy water and dry each section promptly.
◆ Remove marks by rubbing gently with medium-grade steel wool dipped in turpentine or paint thinner; don't scrub. Then seal with an oil-based sealer to protect the floor.

Painted floors

◆ Painted floors can be wax-polished, and that makes them easier to clean.
◆ Damp-mop with mild detergent solution, using as little water as possible. Wash glossy enamel paint with hot water. Rub stubborn

spots gently with a nonabrasive scouring powder or fine steel wool.

Varnished floors

◆ Wash waterproof varnish with warm, soapy water. For nonwaterproof varnish, damp-mop with a mild detergent solution.

Vinyl and rubber floors

◆ Damp-mop with a mild detergent solution. Polish with water-base latex polish, and seal with a water-base sealant.
◆ Solvent-base cleaners or polishes will damage vinyl tiles and rubber flooring, and dirt can become ingrained in the cracks. Do not use wax polish, paraffin, or turpentine on rubber flooring for the same reason.
◆ Protect with water-base sealer.

Asphalt-tile floors

◆ Mop with a sponge mop squeezed out in mild detergent. Rinse and dry. Don't use abrasives or cleaning powders.
◆ If there are deep scratches, seal the areas with polyurethane sealer or seriously consider replacing the flooring, because asphalt tiles contain asbestos.
◆ Polish with a water-base latex polish. Don't use oil- or wax-base polishes, as they tend to soften the surface.

Brick and concrete floors

◆ Clean with a damp mop and mild detergent. Don't use soap on unsealed floors; it's difficult to rinse off.
◆ May be sealed with a penetrating masonry or cement sealer to make cleaning easier (this will also make it nonslip). Sealed floors can be wax-polished.

Marble floors

◆ Damp-mop weekly with clear water or a mild detergent. Wipe streaks and dirt with a damp sponge, then buff dry. For stubborn dirt, use dry borax and a damp cloth; rinse with warm water and buff dry. Marble is porous, so don't let it get too wet.

Quarry-tile floors

◆ Treat a newly laid tile floor with linseed oil and don't wash it for at least two weeks to let the oil soak into the tiles. Damp-mop with warm sudsy water and scrub if necessary.
◆ White patches on newly laid tiles can be wiped with a weak solution of vinegar and water. Rinse with clear water. (The patches are caused by the lime in the cement or grout.)

Slate and stone floors

◆ Wash with a mild detergent in warm water. Soap will form a scum that won't easily come off. Apply a little lemon oil to slate after it has been washed and dried to give it a lustrous finish. Remove all excess with a clean cloth.
◆ Protect stone floors with a cement sealer and wax polish.

Terrazzo floors

◆ Sweep and damp-mop as necessary. Use a mild detergent rather than alkaline cleaners such as ammonia or borax, because they will dull the surface. Similarly, avoid abrasive cleaners; they scratch the surface.

HEAVY-DUTY WASH FOR VERY DIRTY FLOORS

This method is suitable for terrazzo, ceramic, and quarry tiles and stone, marble, concrete, and vinyl floors. Do not treat wooden, linoleum, or cork floors in this way; they should be damp-mopped.

1 *Sweep and/or vacuum. Apply the cleaning solution recommended for your floor, with a wet mop (string or sponge).*

2 *Let it sit for 10 to 15 minutes. Don't allow the floor to dry out, but check that the water doesn't run under the baseboards. Scrub any very dirty places (usually by the walls and in the corners).*

3 *Wipe with a damp cloth rinsed frequently in clean water. Rinse thoroughly in order not to leave a film of detergent on the floor, which will prevent any polish from being absorbed and will make the floor slippery.*

WAXING FLOORS

All floors benefit from waxing; they are easier to clean, and a good shine will conceal all sorts of blemishes in any floor. Use the polish recommended for your flooring in the amounts suggested; too much will lead to a buildup of dirty polish, which will be difficult to buff.

Types of floor wax

◇**Solid paste.** Generally wax, this type of polish is suitable for unvarnished wooden floors, linoleum, and cork. It is hard work to apply and has to be done by hand. The shine lasts a long time.

◇**Liquid.** This type spreads easily and can be applied with an electric floor polisher. Can be wax or oil. The solvent evaporates, leaving the polish. Suitable for the same floors as solid paste. You will probably have to apply it slightly more often than solid paste.

◇**Water-base.** Generally silicone polishes, they are easy to apply and long-lasting. These can be used on all floors except unsealed wood, cork, or linoleum.

◆ You can thin some solid wax polishes with turpentine, but it is easier to use a liquid wax in the first place.

Applying wax polishes.

1 Apply the polish evenly and lightly with a soft cloth (paste) or a polisher (liquid solvent) and allow to soak in.

2 Buff with a floor polisher, or a broom head that has been covered and tied in a soft terry-cloth towel, or you can get down on your hands and knees and buff with a towel.

◆ Dampen the application pad or cloth with plain water before beginning to add wax. This makes applying and spreading wax easier, and prevents excessive absorption.

Applying water-base polishes.

1 Use a very clean mop. Wet the mop head and leave it damp.

2 Pour polish onto the mop head, and apply sparingly to the floor, spreading it until there are no bubbles left. Buff the floor as for wax polish above.

3 Build up the surface with two or three thin coats, buffing between coats. The first coat should cover the whole floor. The second and third coats should only cover the "traffic areas." Avoid splashing the walls and baseboards with wax; it is difficult to get off painted surfaces, and it can stain wall coverings.

TAKING OFF OLD WAX

When you have a big buildup of polish, it is best to remove all the old wax and start again.

1 *Mix a bucket of floor cleaner, preferably with a little ammonia in it, or use a commercial wax remover.*

2 *Apply plenty of this with a mop over a small area at a time and let it soak in (don't let it dry out).*

3 *As soon as the wax and dirt begin to dissolve, wipe them off with a sponge mop (above left). Scrub obstinate parts by hand or with a polisher, using bristle pads. Scrape the floor with your fingernail or a dull knife to see if you've removed all the old wax (above right).*

4 *Damp-mop with a clean mop. Then start on another section.*

5 *Do the whole floor again until you are sure it's completely wax-free. Let the floor dry thoroughly before you apply new wax.*

CARPET CARE

All carpets get dirty. No matter how careful you may be, dust from outside, soot from the street, or food crumbs will land on the best-maintained carpets.

◆ Routine maintenance will help to preserve and protect the life of a carpet. Vacuuming is the most efficient way of cleaning carpets; by vacuuming frequently, you can diminish wear and tear and reduce the necessity of frequent shampooing.

◆ For best results on rugs and carpets, use a vacuum with a beater brush—either an upright or a cylinder tank with a power nozzle. The brush agitates carpet fibers and loosens

dirt so it can be sucked away easily.

◆ Vacuum the main living areas, hall, and stairs as often as you can; don't wait until the carpet looks dirty.

Cleaning stairs

◆ Always start from the bottom of the stairs and work upward so you don't grind the dirt into the carpet.

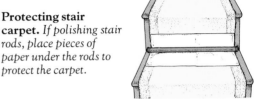

Protecting stair carpet. *If polishing stair rods, place pieces of paper under the rods to protect the carpet.*

Vacuuming techniques

Regular vacuuming can help protect floors, carpeting, and upholstery.

◆ Before you begin, pick up any debris, especially buttons and metal objects that could damage the hose or belt.

◆ For bare floors, indoor-outdoor carpets, and others with low pile, use a bare floor brush. For upholstery, draperies, and stairs, use the small upholstery attachment. For walls, use a dust brush. For cleaning around chair legs and furniture bases, at the edge of carpeting, in corners, and on radiators, use a crevice tool.

◆ Vacuum slowly and evenly with overlapping parallel strokes for the best results.

◆ Vacuums that have bumper plates can leave scuff marks on furniture legs. These can be covered up with shoe polish or felt-tip pen in a color close to that of the wood, or with a commercial scratch cover.

Unblocking a vacuum hose. *If the hose becomes blocked, unwind a metal coat hanger and use the "hook" to remove the blockage.*

CLEANING
A CARPET

◆To keep a carpet in good condition, deep-clean about once a year. You may want to dry-clean or shampoo the traffic areas more often, particularly if you have children or dogs.

◆Deep-clean before the carpet gets too dirty; left too long the dirt can be impossible to loosen. You have left it too long when there are obvious dark patches.

◆Call in a professional carpet cleaner if the carpet is old and/or valuable. Oriental carpets always should be cleaned professionally because they are sometimes touched up with hand-painting after they are made, and these colors often run.

◆Small throw rugs often can be cleaned in a washing machine.

◆Carpet tiles can be vacuumed, and individual tiles lifted and replaced or treated with carpet cleaner to remove stains.

Raising flattened carpet pile. *Rub up the pile with the edge of a small coin.*

◆If there are indentations in the carpet, raise them before wetting the surface. Try rubbing the areas with a coin (see left). Or, lay a wet terry-cloth towel, folded twice, over the flattened areas. Then steam them gently with a warm iron to lift the pile.

◆When selecting a cleaning product, check the label to make sure it is suitable for your carpet. Try to work on a clear, dry day so you can open the windows and doors wide to disperse chemical fumes and hasten drying. Pretreat heavily soiled areas.

Deep-cleaning a carpet

1 Take all the furniture out of the room. Put your drapes over a hanger, and hang it over the curtain rod.

2 Vacuum thoroughly (12 strokes over each section, overlapping each stroke). If carpet is not attached, vacuum underneath as well.

3 To make sure the colors won't run, do a test on an inconspicuous area of carpet using your chosen carpet cleaner (see opposite).

4 If the test is satisfactory, prepare the cleaner following the manufacturer's instructions. Apply the cleaner. If using the liquid cleaner, be careful not to let the backing get wet. If using foam cleaner, wait until the crystals have formed, then sweep or vacuum them up. If using a powdered cleaner, work the dry-cleaning solvent into the fibers then vacuum the residue.

TIPS FOR DEEP-CLEANING CARPETS

◆If carpet is only lightly soiled, try an aerosol spray foam, apply evenly, allow to dry, then vacuum. For a dirtier carpet, use a liquid cleaner that you scrub into the fiber with a brush or a home-type carpet shampooer.

◆Most effective for cleaning any carpet is a machine that sprays hot water and detergent into the fiber. Such equipment can be rented at hardware stores and supermarkets.

◆Be careful not to get the carpet too wet or it will soak through to the backing,

making the colors more likely to run and the carpet difficult to dry out.

◆Wool carpets are the easiest to clean because they absorb more moisture before becoming saturated and are more resistant to fungus if they get wet.

◆For carpets that might be damaged by water, use dry-cleaning granules. Sprinkle them on the surface, brush solvent in, then vacuum.

◆To slow dirt buildup, spray your clean carpet with a soil retardant or an anti-static chemical.

Protecting the wet carpet. *If you have to return furniture to the room before the carpet is completely dry, place a piece of waxed paper or foil, or coasters under the legs.*

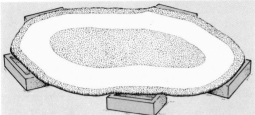

Drying a rug or unattached carpet. *You can help an unattached carpet to dry quicker by raising it on bricks or draping it over chairs to let the air circulate underneath.*

5 Test your cleaner for residue characteristics. This will help you determine what you need to remove from the carpet immediately after the deep cleaning (see below).

Testing cleaner residue

Carpets may attract dirt more quickly after deep cleaning because of the residue left during the cleaning process. To see what residue your cleaner will leave, follow these steps:

1 Prepare a small amount of cleaner according to the manufacturer's instructions.

2 Pour cleaner into a glass pie plate and place in a 200° oven until solution has evaporated.

3 Test residue by wiping glass surface with clean fingers.

4 If you get a dry powder on the glass, you'll also get one on your carpet and should be able to vacuum it up easily.

5 If you get a sticky or waxy residue, you'll have residue on your carpet that will attract and hold dirt. You won't be able to vacuum it up. Use hot water to remove all traces of residue.

Testing color-fastness

◆ Many carpet dyes run when they get wet, so test colors before cleaning.

1 Vacuum or beat the carpet. Dampen a piece of carpet with the cleaner.

2 Leave for an hour or so, then rub with a white cloth, or put several layers of white paper towel on the damp patch with a weight on top. The longer you leave it, the surer the test.

3 If there's no bleeding of color, go ahead and shampoo the whole carpet.

4 If there is slight bleeding, try the test again, but this time add acetic acid, white vinegar, or household ammonia to the mixture.

PRESERVING CARPETS AND RUGS

◆ Choose carpets that have been treated with soil-resistant chemicals; they are much easier to keep clean.

◆ Special chemical finishes to minimize static, or to keep the carpet from getting dirty and prevent spills from soaking into the fibers are available, but they may be difficult to apply and results may be unsatisfactory.

◆ Turn area rugs around periodically so that all areas wear evenly and are subject to the same amount of soiling.

◆ Before polishing furniture, cover carpet areas around and under legs and bases to prevent chemicals in polishes from discoloring the carpet.

◆ Carpet seams and edges can be prevented from fraying by being brushed with a liquid resin that locks the yarns in place as it dries.

Professional cleaning

◆ Always get an estimate, or preferably two or three estimates. Ask the company whether the price includes moving the furniture. Some cleaning companies offer a discount if they don't have to move the furniture out of the room. Most firms also offer soil-resistant treatments to prevent the carpet from quickly getting dirty again.

▼▼ If you have Oriental wool carpets, look
◆◆ for a carpet specialist who will clean them with a detergent using hand brushes. This applies also to old carpets.

PROBLEM CARPETS

Beater/brush upright vacuum cleaners, although adjustable, are too rough for delicate fibers such as silk. For these, use a canister/tank vacuum, or sweep by hand with a bristle brush.

◆ Get handmade carpets, particularly Oriental ones, professionally cleaned.

Coconut, sisal, rush matting

◆ Shake or beat matting outside once in a while, and vacuum dust trapped underneath. Scrub occasionally with sudsy water; dry flat.

◆ If the matting has been tacked down, vacuum regularly, because it gets very dusty.

◆ Entrance mats often have a rubber backing that traps dirt. Take the mat outside and beat the dust out. Occasionally scrub with sudsy water, rinse with a hose, and air-dry.

Fur and sheepskin rugs

◆ If the rug has a backing, it can be cleaned with powdered tailor's chalk or unscented talcum powder. Shake the powder over the fur, leave it for several hours, and then brush, and shake it out. You may need to do this several times.

◆ Wipe unbacked fur rugs with a cloth wrung out in lukewarm detergent water. Don't let the water go more than fur deep. It must not wet the skin.

◆ These rugs can be professionally cleaned by tanneries or some dry cleaners.

Braided rugs

◆ Some small braided rugs are machine-washable in warm water on a gentle cycle, particularly cotton and synthetic materials.

◆ You can protect a small rug by putting it in a pillowcase or laundry bag and securing it with a safety pin before washing.

◆ A powdered dry-cleaning solvent can be brushed into the rugs for deep cleaning. Then vacuum the solvent residue.

REMOVING STAINS

◆ Treat any spill as soon as it occurs. Marks that will disappear completely if treated at once are almost impossible to remove after they have dried out.

◆ Blot the spill quickly with paper towels or a clean, white towel. Scrape away solids.

◆ When using stain removers, always work from the outside edge to the center of the stain. Always blot, do not rub or brush, and don't let the carpet get too wet.

◆ Acid stain removers (lemon juice and vinegar) work better on wools and polyesters than alkalis. Alkali stain removers (borax, ammonia) work better on cellulose, cotton, jute, viscose, rayon, silk, and nylon than acids.

EMERGENCY ACTION FOR SPILLS

1 *Absorb or scrape up the spill right away, before it dries and marks the carpet.*

For liquids. *Pour on a generous amount of salt and leave for at least an hour, then vacuum, or blot up with paper towels. Change these as they become saturated.*

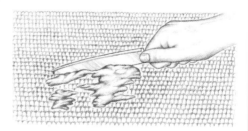

For solids. *Scrape them up carefully with the back of a knife; don't rub them into the carpet.*

2 *If the spill leaves a mark, apply the appropriate stain remover (see opposite and page 82).*

Stain removal kit

Keep everything in a small plastic toolbox or basket and out of reach of children. Label the box clearly so that others can find it easily.
◇Neutral detergent (one advertised as safe for fine fabrics) and foam carpet cleaner
◇Paint thinner, denatured alcohol, or turpentine
◇Household ammonia (always dilute with 10 parts water)
◇Dry-cleaning fluid containing perchloroethylene. Use straight from the bottle. *Do not* use lighter fluid, gasoline, paraffin, or carbon tetrachloride; the fumes are harmful.
◇Distilled white vinegar
◇Clean white terry-cloth towel
◇Soft bristled brush
◇White paper towels

TREATING SPECIFIC CARPET STAINS

◆When applying stain removers, work with small amounts to prevent the mark from spreading.
◆If you start removing a stain with one formula, let it dry completely before trying another. You can't tell whether the stain has gone until the carpet is dry.
◆If you are worried about the colors running, add a teaspoon of white vinegar, acetic acid, or household ammonia to the cleaner.

◆When you have finished the treatment, rinse with cold water, then blot dry with a clean paper towel.
◆For a common mixture that helps remove stains from carpeting, use this detergent-water-vinegar solution:

Mix together 1 teaspoon liquid dish or fine-fabric detergent, 1 quart warm water, and 1 teaspoon white vinegar.

DRINK STAINS

ALCOHOL AND SOFT DRINKS
Remove excess. Apply detergent-water-vinegar solution (see above). Rinse and blot dry.

COFFEE, BLACK
Remove excess. Apply detergent-water-vinegar solution (see above). Rinse and blot. Apply dry-cleaning solvent. Dry carpet and brush pile. Repeat if necessary.

COFFEE, WITH MILK
See COFFEE, BLACK

CREAM, ICE CREAM, MILK
See COFFEE, BLACK

FRUIT JUICE
See ALCOHOL AND SOFT DRINKS

TEA, BLACK
See COFFEE, BLACK

TEA, WITH MILK
See COFFEE, BLACK

WINE
See ALCOHOL AND SOFT DRINKS

BIOLOGICAL STAINS

BLOOD
Apply cold water, then blot. Repeat as many times as necessary. Rinse and blot. Follow directions for COFFEE, BLACK, if necessary.

FECES
See ALCOHOL AND SOFT DRINKS

URINE
Blot quickly. See ALCOHOL AND SOFT DRINKS

VOMIT
If dried, remove deposit with knife. Then clean with detergent-water-vinegar solution (see above). If wet, see COFFEE, BLACK.

Continued ▷

TREATING SPECIFIC CARPET STAINS (Continued)

HOUSEHOLD STAINS

BALLPOINT PEN
Rub stain with a clean cloth moistened with paint thinner or a dry-cleaning fluid (such as clothing spot remover). Keep turning the cloth so you are using a clean area all the time.

CANDLE WAX
Cover the wax with paper towels or brown paper. Iron with a warm iron so the wax melts and is absorbed. Continue with clean paper until all the wax is removed.
◆ Colored candle wax may leave a stain. Treat this with a little paint thinner on a white cotton ball. Don't soak. Vacuum when dry.

CHEWING GUM
Pick off what you can; treat the remainder with paint thinner or dry-cleaning fluid. You may have to repeat this several times.

FELT-TIP PEN
Try rubbing with paint thinner or dry-cleaning fluid, using a clean cloth. Repeat if necessary.

FOUNTAIN PEN INK
See BALLPOINT PEN

FURNITURE POLISH
See GREASE AND OIL

GREASE AND OIL
Dab with paint thinner on a cotton ball. Blot dry. Bad stains may have to be professionally cleaned.

MUD
Let it dry, then brush or vacuum. Treat residual stain with denatured alcohol, then with detergent-water-vinegar solution (see page 81). Rinse.

PAINT
Most paint stains cannot be removed once they are dry.

Acrylic paint. Wash out with diluted detergent, then dab with denatured alcohol.
Cellulose paints. Treat with cellulose thinners.
Latex paint. Wash it out with cold water while still wet.
Oil-base paint. Sponge with paint thinner if wet; if dry, try a commercial stain remover.

SHOE POLISH
Very carefully scrape off as much as you can. Dab with paint thinner.

SOOT
Cover with dry salt. Vacuum up. Blot with detergent-water-vinegar solution (see page 81). Rinse and dry.

TAR
Scrape off as much as you can. Dab with paint thinner on a cotton ball. Blot dry.

CLEANING WALLS AND CEILINGS

As with all cleaning, the more often you wipe or dust off the surface, the better. If you let a wall or ceiling become really dirty, you will have to work very hard to get it clean again; this could even mean you will need to redecorate.

Light colors require more maintenance than dark ones, since every finger mark or spot shows up. If you are bothered by marks that cannot be removed such as children's artistic attempts or permanent stains, cover the walls with one of the many washable wall coverings on the market.

General care

◆ If you have high ceilings, dust them with a clean, long-handled broom or an extended vacuum hose with a brush attachment. Don't use water until you are ready to wash the walls.
◆ A quick way of dusting is to use a clean dustcloth tied over a broom head, or a clean, soft broom.
◆ Keep a copy of the hanging instructions for wallpaper; they include care instructions.

WALL COVERING CARE SYMBOLS

These are the cleaning, or care, symbols. There are other symbols related to hanging coverings (see page 195).

Can be sponged	Easily washed
Can be washed	Can be scrubbed

Cobwebs

◆ Remove cobwebs when they are new. Once covered with grease and dust, they are much more difficult to remove.

◆ Spray a large piece of nylon net or cheese-cloth with a cleaning-and-dusting spray, wrap it around the end of a yardstick, secure with a rubber band, and remove cobwebs in high corners. Or, use the method shown below.

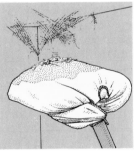

Clearing cobwebs.
Cobwebs cling to damp surfaces, so you can pick them off by using a damp mop or a broom covered with a damp towel.

WASHING WALLS AND CEILINGS

◆ To prepare walls for washing, dust them with a flannel cloth, or vacuum them; remove cobwebs, and spot-clean grimy areas with a heavy-strength household cleaner.

◆ Have one bucket for the cleaning solution and another for rinse water; two sponges or rags; a long-handled mop or squeegee for reaching into corners; rubber gloves; and a stepladder.

GREEN TIP: You can use all-purpose household cleaner, or mix a homemade solution of 2 tablespoons of ammonia or vinegar and 1 quart of warm water. For a heavy-duty solution, mix 1 cup ammonia, $\frac{1}{2}$ cup vinegar, and $\frac{1}{4}$ cup baking soda in 1 gallon warm water. First test the cleaning solution on an inconspicuous part of the wall.

◆ Work rapidly from the bottom, washing and rinsing a section no larger than 3 feet square at a time. If you start at the top, the cleaning solution may cause permanent stains as it drips down.

◆ Use white or colorfast rags or sponges because colored ones may leave stains; use rags rather than sponges on textured surfaces. Make sure you wring them out well.

◆ Rinse walls well with clear water and a clean sponge or rag; detergent left on the surface will attract more dust. On painted wood, dry each area before continuing. Change washing or rinsing water when it gets dirty.

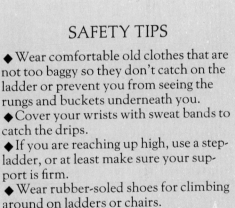

SAFETY TIPS

◆ Wear comfortable old clothes that are not too baggy so they don't catch on the ladder or prevent you from seeing the rungs and buckets underneath you.

◆ Cover your wrists with sweat bands to catch the drips.

◆ If you are reaching up high, use a stepladder, or at least make sure your support is firm.

◆ Wear rubber-soled shoes for climbing around on ladders or chairs.

◆ Don't use water near electrical wall sockets and lights; you could receive an electric shock. Likewise, make sure electrical appliances are disconnected before you begin, and do not pull out electrical cords with wet hands.

◆ Don't leave the bucket at the foot of the ladder where you could step into it on your way down, and always move the bucket before you move the ladder.

WALLS

◆Clean most walls with sponges soaked in all-purpose household cleaner or a home-made solution (see Green Tip on page 83). For painted walls, you can use a commercial paint cleaner, but follow directions carefully.

Latex paint

◆Remove surface dirt by brushing, washing, or vacuuming; clean small areas in corners and around light switches with a non-abrasive cleaner. Wipe down sills and other wooden surfaces with a lint-free rag moistened with denatured alcohol.
◆Most scuffs and marks can be wiped off with a homemade cleaning solution (see Green Tip on page 83), or by applying a paste of baking soda and water and rubbing lightly with fine steel wool.

Oil-base paint

◆Wash with warm water and soapless detergent, or with a homemade cleaning solution (see Green Tip on page 83).
◆When washing oil-base paints, use a drier cloth than for latex paints.
◆If cleaning textured paints, add a little borax to the water (1 ounce borax to each pint water). Rinse with clean water.
◆Remove stains with a commercial paste cleaner, mild scouring powder, or a paste of baking soda and water (see also page 87).

Mirrored walls

◆Use liquid glass cleaner to remove dirt.
◆For badly soiled areas, wipe with a solution of 2 tablespoons vinegar, 2 tablespoons ammonia or denatured alcohol, and 1 quart water.

Washable wall coverings

◆Textured vinyl wall covering can be cleaned with all-purpose cleaner or a home-made solution (see Green Tip on page 83) in lukewarm—never hot—water, applied with a thick absorbent cloth or a very soft nail brush. Wait a little, then rinse thoroughly with clean water.
◆Vinyl wallpaper must be dusted and/or damp-mopped frequently—dirt tends to make it brittle if left. Commercial dry-cleaning fluids can be used on vinyl. Don't use lacquer solvents; they melt the surface of the wall covering.
◆Embossed wall coverings get thickly encrusted dirt in the folds. Use a smaller brush, such as a soft toothbrush, to get the dirt out—make sure you get all the detergent out as well as all the dirt.

Nonwashable papers

◆Ordinary wallpaper, made of paper without a protective finish, is not washable. Brush it occasionally with a soft brush or broom head covered with a dust cloth, or a hand-held vacuum.
◆Rub marks gently with a damp cloth. Then gently pat the paper dry. Be careful not to rub the paper dry, or the surface will come off in tiny rolls.
◆Clean nonwashable papers with a commercial dough-type wallpaper cleaner, or you can use a gum eraser or crustless lumps of stale rye bread (see below). To make your own

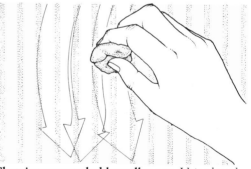

Cleaning nonwashable wallpaper. *Using bread rolled into balls, a soft eraser, or wallpaper cleaning dough, rub the wall with a series of wide sweeping downward movements, overlapping each stroke. Rub gently and don't rub upward or sideways. As the dough or eraser picks up dirt, turn it so that a clean area is always on the outside. Work patiently and carefully so you don't get streaky results.*

dough-type wallpaper cleaner, mix $2\frac{1}{2}$ tablespoons household ammonia and $1\frac{1}{4}$ cups water in the top of a double boiler. Add 2 cups flour and 4 teaspoons baking soda. Cook over a low heat about $1\frac{1}{2}$ hours. Cool. Store in a tightly sealed jar or a sealable bag.

None of these can work wonders on very dirty walls, so don't let the walls get too grimy before cleaning them.

◆Heavier nonvinyl papers can be sponged with mild white suds on a soft sponge and squeezed very dry. Use a light touch and very little liquid, and pat dry with a clean cloth.

Fabric and cork wall coverings

◆Dust the wall, then vacuum with the vacuum cleaner dusting attachment or a hand-held vacuum.

◆You can try a damp cloth wrung out in warm water if you're very careful. Check that any colors won't run on a small hidden piece of covering before tackling the whole wall.

◆If you are worried about cork becoming dirty, treat it with polyurethane sealer to make it like a washable wall covering.

Ceramic tiles

◆Treat as for oil-base paints (see opposite). Rub splattered tiles with a cut lemon. Leave for 15 minutes, then polish with a soft cloth.

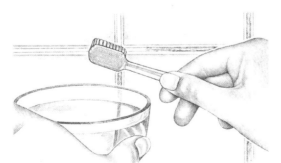

Cleaning discolored tile grouting. *Rub with a toothbrush using a commercial bathroom cleaner, or a half-and-half solution of chlorine bleach and water. If the stain won't clean up, it's better and easier to regrout.*

Wood paneling

Waxed or sealed wood panels require very little cleaning except dusting. If they do become dirty, wipe them with a sponge rinsed out in diluted detergent, or polish them with a liquid wax.

Unwaxed, varnished, or shellacked wood paneling can be cleaned with a mixture of $\frac{1}{4}$ cup gum turpentine and $\frac{3}{4}$ cup boiled linseed oil (not steam distilled). Apply and leave 15 minutes, then rub off.

◆Clean painted paneling with a detergent solution. Don't use abrasive cleaners.

◆Rub fine scratches on paneling with clear wax on a damp cloth, working in the direction of the grain.

Touching up discolored paneling. *Apply a small amount of shoe polish, dark wax polish, or commercial wood stain to the affected area.*

Brick walls

◆For unsealed brick walls, brush and vacuum the entire surface occasionally, about twice a year, pulling out all loose grit.

◆To clean stained brick, try spraying foam bathroom cleaner or a half-and-half solution of bleach and water directly onto the brick. Clean with a damp cloth or, where necessary, with a scrub brush; wash very gently if the bricks are soft and porous, taking care not to soak them. Other marks, such as crayon or paint, may come off with gum eraser.

◆Treat the bricks with a polyurethane sealer to protect them, then you can wash them with a detergent solution.

DECORATIVE MOLDINGS

◆ The quickest way to get at the dust that collects in the nooks and crannies of moldings is to fit the brush attachment or crevice tool to the end of the vacuum cleaner hose and apply suction to draw out the dirt. Where narrow crevices are thick with dust, use an old toothbrush.

◆ Protect delicate surfaces from scratches by attaching a piece of foam rubber or terry-cloth towel with a rubber band to the head of the vacuum attachment.

◆ To wash moldings that are grimy, mix 1 cup ammonia, $\frac{1}{2}$ cup white vinegar, and $\frac{1}{4}$ cup baking soda in 1 gallon of warm water. Fill a plastic spray bottle with the solution, and squirt it directly into dusty corners and crevices (see below left).

▼▼ Plaster moldings or those that are
◆◆ badly chipped and cracked can be damaged by water, so don't wash them.

Spray-cleaning moldings. *Using a plastic spray bottle, squirt cleaning solution directly into soiled places, then wipe off and spray with plain water. Dry with a terry-cloth towel.*

Cleaning in corners. *Use a paintbrush or an old toothbrush to get at the dirt in corners and crevices of the molding.*

CEILINGS

◆ It is far easier to keep a ceiling regularly dusted until it needs painting again than to try to wash it. Use the dusting attachment fitted to your vacuum hose, a long-handled feather duster, or a flexible broom head.

◆ If you must wash the ceiling, take it one section at a time, covering each area with a clean sponge soaked in a homemade solution (see Green Tip on page 83). By the time you've swabbed across a whole section, the dirt will be sufficiently loosened to go back and wipe it off with a clean cloth. Repeat the process across the entire ceiling. It's always a good idea to cover the floor and furnishings before you start.

◆ It is much easier to repaint a ceiling that is badly marred by soot and smoke, or blackened by burned-out fluorescent tubes, than it is to wash it.

◆ Ceilings with acoustic tiles don't usually show the dirt badly because their color and texture tend to camouflage most marks. They do, however, show the streaks and stains of water damage that can't be removed by washing. To conceal these, apply a primer or clear sealer to the tiles and paint them with latex paint when they are dry.

◆ Small stains that are hard to remove may be covered up with a dab of shoe polish in a shade that matches the ceiling color. White shoe polish on a white ceiling is easiest to cover and works best.

REMOVING STAINS

◆Scuff marks and fingerprints on painted walls can be washed off with diluted dishwashing liquid rubbed over the mark and rinsed off thoroughly. A mixture of 2 tablespoons ammonia or white vinegar in 1 quart warm water also will do the job.

◆To remove dirt and grease stains from washable wallpaper, sponge the soiled area thoroughly with a solution of mild liquid soap and cold water. Rinse with clear, cold water, and wipe dry with a clean absorbent cloth. Always do a patch test on the wallpaper before washing it, in case the color runs.

◆If bad spots on wallpaper have gotten worse from too much scrubbing, they may be covered with a patch of the same paper cut to fit (see page 202). That's a good reason why you should always keep the extra covering. You may need to expose the unused paper to sunlight before applying it to the wall so the new paper matches that on the wall.

◆Retouch spots that won't wash off a painted wall with some leftover paint. Put on a very thin coat, and try not to leave a hard edge. At first your touch-up job will look obvious, but it will blend in quickly.

Cleaning grease marks from wall coverings.
Make a thick paste from baking soda or talcum powder and dry-cleaning fluid. Spread the mixture evenly onto the wall, starting outside the stain and rubbing gently over and around it (above left), as you would on fabric. Let it dry out and then use a soft brush to wipe it off (above right). Two or three applications may be necessary.

REMOVING ADHESIVE TAPE AND GLUE

◆Masking tape that has been pressed down to protect the woodwork while painting should be removed before the final coat is dry. At this stage, if you peel off the tape in a slow even motion, it should come away easily.

◆When you need to remove tape that has been holding posters up for a long time, use oil-free nail polish remover to soften the glue base before you start. Peel the tape off carefully (see right).

◆If the tape leaves a mark on wallpaper where the dust has stuck to the glue, wipe this off with oil-free nail polish remover and absorb it with a warm iron over paper towels.

◆To remove glued-on pictures, spray them with a petroleum-base prewash spray, then after a few minutes rub with a piece of nylon net. If there is a residue of glue, sprinkle on some cornmeal or talcum powder, and rub with a dry cloth.

▼▼ Oil-free nail polish remover is safe to
◆ ◆ use on glass but may damage some paint and plastic surfaces. It gives off strong fumes and is highly flammable, so use it in a well-ventilated room.

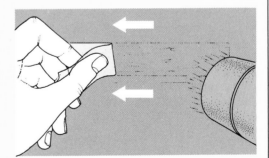

Peeling off adhesive tape. *Lift the top edge and then pull it back on itself, slowly and evenly, keeping it parallel with the wall. In this way, you lift the minimum amount of paper or paint with it. Try running a hair dryer along the tape as you pull it off; the warm air softens the glue.*

TREATING WALL STAINS

◆ When using water or other liquids, always test a hidden piece of wall covering first to make sure the colors won't run.

PAINT

UNIDENTIFIED STAIN
◇ **Water-base paints.** Dust then wash with weak detergent solution. Clean small areas at a time. Rinse and dry before doing the next part.
◇ **Oil-base paints.** Dust and wash with detergent solution. Rub residual stain with cut lemon or fine steel wool.

GRAFFITI
◆ Some felt-tip pens come out with detergent.
◆ Denatured alcohol or paint thinner may get rid of ballpoint ink.
◆ Wax crayon can sometimes be removed with an eraser.
◆ If you can't remove the graffiti, seal it and cover it with a new coat of paint.

GREASE
Rub with a strong detergent solution containing a little paint thinner, or use a kitchen cleaner.

WALL COVERINGS

UNIDENTIFIED STAINS
◇ **Washable and nonwashable wall coverings.** Rub over with stale bread, preferably rye. Don't use water.
◇ **Vinyl wall coverings.** See PAINT, water base.
◇ **Textured wall coverings.** Sponge with mild detergent solution.
◇ **Embossed wall coverings.** Rub with a bread ball or soft eraser (see page 84).

GRAFFITI
◆ For wax crayon, first absorb the wax with a warm iron over blotting paper or paper towels. If left with a color stain, it may come out with paint thinner, or rub gently with moistened baking soda on a damp cloth.
◆ Another method for crayon is to sponge with dry-cleaning fluid. Follow with a soap-and-water rinse on washable coverings or a damp cloth on nonwashable ones.
◆ There is no very satisfactory way to remove ink. If it's washable, try blotting it, then washing stain with detergent and hot water.
◆ Pencil marks can be removed with an eraser or a bread ball (see page 84).

◆ If dry-cleaning fluid leaves a ring mark, try the thick paste of baking soda or talcum powder and dry-cleaning fluid described for grease stains (see page 87).

GREASE
◆ **Washable and nonwashable wall coverings.** Draw out the grease with blotting paper or paper towels under a warm iron. Or, apply a paste of baking soda or talcum powder and dry-cleaning fluid, and brush it off when it has dried (see page 87). It may help to dab the residue with moistened borax.
◆ **Embossed wall coverings.** Dab with talcum powder, leave for a couple of hours, then brush off gently.
◆ **Vinyl wall coverings.** Dab with paint thinner or dry-cleaning fluid, then detergent and water.

CORK

UNIDENTIFIED STAINS
Sponge gently with warm water and detergent. *Do not* get cork very wet.

GRAFFITI
As for WALL COVERINGS (below left); anything more drastic will damage the cork. You may have to live with the marks.

GREASE
Rub gently with water containing borax or with a mild detergent solution containing a few drops of household ammonia.

GRASS CLOTH AND BURLAP WALL COVERING

UNIDENTIFIED STAINS
Rub gently with talcum powder. Leave for a couple of hours and then brush off gently. Don't use dry-cleaning fluids or upholstery cleaners.

GREASE
Use a dry-cleaning fluid or paint thinner, but test color first—this treatment will damage some of these coverings. If available, get professional advice.

GRAFFITI
Try dry-cleaning fluid.

SILK WALL COVERING

Call professional dry cleaners for all stains.

WOOD PANELING

◆ Any treatment will discolor the wood. Use wood stain to bring the wood back to its correct color.

UNIDENTIFIED STAINS
◆ If wax-finished, use furniture polish.
◆ If sealed, wash with mild detergent solution, rinse, and buff.

GRAFFITI
Try a mild detergent solution, followed by paint thinner, on a cotton ball.

BRICK AND NEW PLASTER

EFFLORESCENCE
(white crystals or powdery deposit)
Brushing with a dry paintbrush should get rid of it. If not, wipe with plain warm water. Repeat if necessary, allowing the wall to dry between washings.

UNIDENTIFIED STAINS
Wash with a solution of warm detergent with a handful of washing soda crystals dissolved in it. Rinse thoroughly.

GRAFFITI
Use paint remover and give it time to work on the marks before you scrape it off. Wash with detergent solution. If worse comes to worst, sandpaper off the marks.

GREASE
Sponge with paint thinner.

CLEANING WINDOWS

IT IS BETTER to clean your windows on a regular basis than to wait until a thick film has built up. Window glass that is washed frequently takes on a gleam and luster that adds to the warmth and beauty of your home. Dirty windows greatly reduce the amount and quality of light that comes into a room, and washing off the accumulated grime can be difficult.

WASHING THE GLASS

For best results, wash windows on an overcast day.
◆ When cleaning the inside, take down blinds, curtains, and bric-a-brac on the windowsill to avoid breakages and water damage.
◆ If the windows are not very dirty, cool clear water is fine for cleaning, or you can make your own cleaning solution by mixing 2 tablespoons household ammonia or white vinegar with 1 quart warm water. Have two buckets of clear lukewarm water or one of cleaning solution and one of clear water for rinsing. A chamois cloth is best for cleaning windows; but you also can use a lint-free linen dishcloth or strong paper towels. Squeegees on extendable handles make cleaning larger windows much easier.
◆ Spray the cleaner or water onto the glass, or use a sponge or rag that is completely wrung out to eliminate drips. Start at the top

of the window and work across in a horizontal direction. Use a toothbrush or cotton swab to get dirt out of the corners.

◆ If there are many panes in the window, work from the top in horizontal rows. While panes are still wet, wipe with a clean cloth squeezed out in rinse water.

◆ If you are using anything other than clear water to wash the windows, be sure to rinse them well to avoid a filmy residue.

◆ Dry with paper towels, crumpled newspapers, a chamois cloth, or lint-free rag. Remove any streaks with a soft, dry cloth.

Cleaning large areas of glass. *Use a rubber squeegee instead of a cloth. Work downward from the top of the pane (above left), wiping the blade on a cloth after each stroke (above right) so you are less likely to get streaky windows. Repeat for rinsing.*

CARE OF YOUR CHAMOIS CLOTH

Chamois may be more expensive than other cloths, but if well maintained, it should last for years.

◆ Don't use powdered cleaners or liquid detergents to clean the window if using chamois. The detergents react with the natural oils in the skin and destroy them. Use denatured alcohol, white vinegar, or clear lukewarm water.

◆ Wash the chamois cloth after use in warm water and soap flakes; rinse it out well in clean water. Do not wring out the water but squeeze the cloth gently and shake it out flat. Allow it to dry slowly, away from direct heat and never in sunlight, as heat and sunshine will destroy the natural oils in the skin.

◆ Crumple and rub the chamois when it is dry to bring back the softness.

TIPS FOR WASHING WINDOWS

◆ Clean the windows on a cloudy day or when the sun is not shining directly on the glass because sun causes streaks.

◆ Avoid scrubbing dirty windows with a dry cloth; it will scratch the glass.

◆ If temperatures are below freezing, you can add $\frac{1}{4}$ cup denatured alcohol or 1 tablespoon glycerine to keep the cleaner from freezing on the glass. Cleaning windows on a frosty day is risky because the glass will be brittle.

◆ Use all detergents and chemicals sparingly; to use too much causes streaks and leaves layers of residue. Never use soap because it is very difficult to rinse off. You can wash off hard specks and spots with warm tea on a sponge.

◆ Change the water frequently, especially water for rinsing.

◆ When cleaning windows inside and out, wipe one side of the glass with horizontal strokes, the other with vertical ones, so if you leave streaks and smears, you'll know which side they're on.

Using commercial window cleaners

◆ These are convenient to use and are available as aerosols, sprays, or liquid emulsions. Use liquid sprays because they evaporate quickly without leaving any buildup. The emulsions leave a white smear on the surface that is more difficult to wipe off.

◆ Wipe spray cleaner off with a soft, clean absorbent cloth (not paper towels, as they disintegrate too quickly when wet).

◆ If the window is very dirty, rinse off the worst of the dirt before applying a commercial window cleaner.

Cleaning the outside

◆ If you have screens on the outside of the windows, remove them and brush them with a vacuum cleaner brush, or with a stiff-bristled brush.

◆ For windows that are difficult to reach or higher than the first floor, hire a professional window cleaner.

◆ Don't sit on the window ledge and lean out to clean upstairs windows, and never use a ladder in a strong wind.

◆ Hang the wash bucket onto the ladder using an S-hook, available from any hardware store, or use a ladder with a platform. Don't carry the bucket or perch it on a narrow window ledge.

◆ You may be able to clean the outside from the inside by using a squeegee with an extendable and angled handle.

◆ Don't bother with magnetic window cleaners that go over the outside while you clean the inside. They sound great but are not easy to use effectively.

Keeping a ladder from slipping. *On soft ground, place the ladder on a piece of strong board. Nail a piece of wood to the board to wedge the ladder against so it won't slip.*

Removing paint, putty, and other marks

◆ You can get rid of fresh paint marks with turpentine, dry-cleaning fluid, or nail polish remover on a lint-free cloth. Dried paint can be softened with turpentine and scraped off. If you try slipping a very sharp knife under the paint and prying it off, make sure you don't scratch the window.

◆ Use a special tool (see above right) to scrape hardened paint off the window.

◆ Use ammonia to remove putty marks, or soften them with turpentine as for paint.

◆ Don't use nylon pads, steel wool, or abrasive cleaners on window glass, because they will scratch it.

◆ To remove labels from new windows, wet the surface of the glass and keep it wet. When the water has soaked in, the label usually slides or floats off.

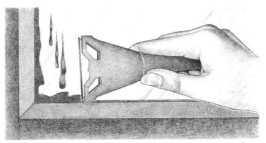

Scraping paint or dirt off the window. *Use only a flat razor-type paint scraper or a safety blade. Always work in one direction. Make one forward stroke, lift the tool off the glass, then make another forward stroke. Never scrape backward and forward; you risk scratching the glass.*

WASHING SCREENS

Dirty screens not only block out sunlight but also cause spots on windows when it rains. You can brush or vacuum screens periodically without removing them, but take them down to thoroughly wash them.

◆ Lay them flat on a smooth, cloth-covered surface, such as a picnic table topped with a plastic tablecloth. Scrub them gently with a brush and hot sudsy water, and then rinse with a hose. Shake off excess water.

SPECIAL PROBLEMS

◆ If the panes of glass on a piece of furniture, such as a bookcase with glass panels, are very dirty, dust them and then wipe the glass off with denatured alcohol on cotton balls. Squeeze the cotton balls so they are almost dry, and wipe with a circular motion to avoid leaving streaks. Change balls as soon as they are dirty.

Small-paned windows

These include windowpanes and louvered windows.

◆Don't use the squeegee method; unless you have your squeegee cut down to fit, it's impractical when dealing with lots of little panes. Wash them with a chamois or lint-free cloth.

◆You can leave these little windows for longer periods without cleaning them, because they do not show the dirt like large expanses of plate glass.

◆For little windows, it is probably worth using a commercial spray cleaner, because it saves time and effort. You can use the same cleaner to wipe the window ledges as you go along.

Stained-glass and leaded windows

◆Examine the window once a year for signs of weakness in the lead, which is shown by the window bowing out of its true vertical shape. If you notice bowing or cracks, get the window repaired by a professional.

◆ Most modern stained glass is pretty sturdy and can be cleaned as you would window-panes. Clean the corners with cotton swabs dipped in cleaning solution.

◆If you have glass you think is valuable or vulnerable, just be extra careful. Wipe occasionally with a damp cloth, but do it very gently. Don't use any commercial detergent or window cleaning product.

◆Never wash painted "stained" glass, because the paint is often loose on old glass, particularly heraldic glass, and this can be dislodged very easily and lost by washing. Dust with a very soft paintbrush or cloth instead.

ULTRAVIOLET FILTERS

It is possible to treat windows with an ultraviolet filter to protect valuable items and fabrics from being damaged by sunlight. There are many different types of filters available. Follow the manufacturer's instructions for cleaning because they vary. Here are a few general tips:

◆ Try not to touch the windows for at least a month after treatment with a UV-absorbent finish; you may damage it.

◆Detergents, cleaning agents, or denatured alcohol, if used on the windows, can all remove the special homeowner-applied finish. Similarly, don't use brushes, a chamois cloth, or paper towels.

◆Don't put adhesive tape on the homeowner-treated glass; it will destroy the coating.

Wooden window frames

◆ Use very little water when cleaning painted window frames, and change water often.

◆Remove fly specks from painted frames with cold tea, or use a soft cloth dipped in a mixture of equal parts skim milk and cold water. A rough cloth takes off fly specks better than a smooth one.

◆Rub sealed or varnished wood with cold tea or use a liquid nonabrasive cleaner.

◆Clean waxed wood with a mild detergent solution or fine steel wool dipped in liquid floor or furniture wax. Then polish.

Aluminum window frames

◆Wash with hot sudsy water, and use a scouring pad of finest steel wool to take off thick grime.

◆If window frames have oxidation deposits, use a light household abrasive cleaner, a mild detergent, or fine steel wool. After cleaning, apply car paste wax.

Painted, varnished, or sealed wood

◆ Sponge with warm water and detergent. Rinse and wipe dry.
◆ For bad marks, use a cleaning paste, but don't use abrasive powders or cleaners, because they damage the finish.

Lacquered finishes

◆ Wipe over with a damp cloth when needed.
◆ Remove fingermarks with a damp chamois cloth and rub with a soft dustcloth.
◆ Polish the surface with furniture cream or spray polish occasionally.

Gilded furniture

◆ Dust gently with a feather duster.
◆ Clean with a soft cloth lightly dipped in warm turpentine or paint thinner. (Warm these solvents by standing the bottle in hot water.)
◆ If any piece of gilt seems to be flaking, the object should not be cleaned. Get professional advice.
◆ Gilding should not be rubbed. If necessary, brush the dust off with a soft watercolor paintbrush. Never let water get onto a gilded surface; it will ruin the surface.
◆ Never retouch the gilding with any form of gold paint, because it gives a completely different effect and will discolor.

Stained gilding. *Remove stains by dabbing the surface gently with a raw onion.*

Veneer

◆ Treat according to the type of wood.
◆ Wipe up water spills right away to prevent them from marking the surface.
◆ Check veneered surfaces for bubbling when you clean them. Small blisters in veneer can be reglued (see page 251); get larger ones repaired professionally.
◆ **Marquetry.** Veneer surfaces inlaid with wood, shell, or ivory must be handled with care. Dust gently and try not to catch inlaid edges with your dustcloth. Lightly polish with a wax paste and buff occasionally, but never wash. (For candle wax and greasy stains, see page 96.)

Plastic laminates

◆ These are easily scratched, so don't use scouring powders or pads.
◆ **GREEN TIP:** You can remove light stains by rubbing with a damp cloth dipped in baking soda.
◆ Mop up spills, particularly berry juices, right away with hot sudsy water.
◆ For an ink stain, rub in undiluted dishwashing liquid. For stubborn stains, you can use toothpaste (see below), or apply a paste of baking soda and water and rub off after a couple of minutes.

Stubborn stains. *Rub a little toothpaste onto the stain with your finger to remove it.*

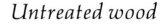

Untreated wood

◆ Unpolished or unsealed wooden tables, butcher block, and chopping boards should be scrubbed after use with sudsy water and a scrub brush, then rinsed and dried thoroughly.

▼▼ Wooden cutting boards are not recom-
♦♦ mended when cutting up raw poultry or
meat because bacteria from the poultry or
meat may get lodged in cracks and crevices of
the wood.

◆ Treat the wood occasionally with a thin
coat of mineral oil on a clean cloth or paper
towel (see below). Don't use vegetable oil; it
can turn rancid.

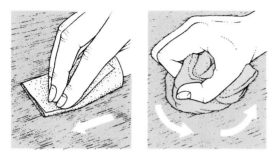

Reducing the shine. *If mineral oil has made the
wood too shiny, rub along the grain with fine sandpaper or steel wool (above left). Then rub with a soft
cloth, using a circular movement to buff the wood
(above right).*

Antique furniture

Regular dusting, so that every surface that
can be reached is free of dust, is the best way
to preserve antiques.

◆ Most antiques need only a light dusting.
Occasionally, buff the polished surface with
a clean, dry dustcloth or chamois cloth.

◆ Use a duster made of lamb's wool; feather
dusters break off and can scratch the surface.
Be particularly careful when dusting furniture that has pieces of molding or veneer
missing, because the pieces next to the gap
are usually loose.

🍃 **GREEN TIP:** You can remove greasy
marks with a chamois cloth wrung out in
vinegar and water (1 tablespoon vinegar to
1 cup water). Dry well.

◆ Polish only once or at most twice a year.
Apply polish sparingly and evenly, and rub
in well until a good shine has been built up. If
you put it on too thick, it will dry before you
have finished polishing, leaving the surface
smeared and making it difficult to buff.

◆ Try not to polish near pieces of wood that
are cracking or lifting. If wax gets under

them, it will be difficult to glue the loose
pieces back.

◆ If the dye in the polish is darker than the
wood, it will darken the appearance. If the
polish is lighter than the wood, make sure no
residue is left in the crevices, because it will
show up when the wax dries out.

◆ Use a paste wax or old-fashioned furniture
cream. Modern furniture cream is not recommended for antiques because, in order to
keep the wax and solvent in suspension, an
emulsifying agent has to be used. Although
many of these agents are harmless, it is
impossible to check all the polishes.

▼▼ Avoid aerosol furniture polishes and
♦♦ those with added silicones. These give an
instant shine, but the film does not fill
scratches and other surface blemishes as wax
does. With aerosol sprays, the solvent comes
out with such force that it can damage the
polished surface; where used a lot, the surface may acquire a milky look. There is no
remedy for this except stripping and resurfacing the object.

◆ Don't waste time trying to cure difficult
problems yourself; consult a professional.

◆ When cleaning a desk or chest of drawers,
check that the drawers run smoothly; if they
don't, loosen them with wax or talcum powder as described below. Always pull on both
drawer handles at the same time, and don't force
the drawer if it sticks.

Sticky drawer runners. *If drawers are not running
smoothly, take them out and rub a white candle along
the runners, or sprinkle talcum powder on them.*

Treating specific woods

◇ **Pickled or limed oak and pine.** Clean
with a chamois cloth wrung out in vinegar
and water. Dry and polish with furniture
cream.

TREATING STAINS OR MARKS ON WOOD FURNITURE

◆ Don't use oiled or treated dustcloths on waxed surfaces; they'll damage them.

◆ Wipe up spills immediately.

◆ Don't use excessive water on wood.

DRINK STAINS

ALCOHOL
Soak up immediately. Rub any mark with the palm of your hand to replace some of the grease the alcohol will have removed. Wipe with a little teak oil, furniture polish, or linseed oil, depending on the type of wood. Or, rub a paste of vegetable oil and salt onto the stain. Then remove the paste and give the piece a coat of wax polish.

COFFEE OR TEA
Wipe up immediately. See HEAT MARKS, WHITE

MILK
See ALCOHOL

SOFT DRINKS
See ALCOHOL

BIOLOGICAL STAINS

BLOOD
Wipe up right away. If natural wood, sandpaper the surface lightly and swab with hydrogen peroxide. Blood is unlikely to mark treated wood.

URINE
Wipe up quickly. Apply a little furniture polish or oil, then some scratch cover or shoe polish to restore the color.

HOUSEHOLD STAINS AND MARKS

ADHESIVES
Remove adhesive before it dries, then rub mark with cold cream, creamy peanut butter, or salad oil.

CANDLE WAX, GREASE, FATS, AND OILS
Veneered and inlaid wood. Cover mark thickly with talcum powder; cover that with a few layers of paper towel. Iron with a warm, dry iron. **Most furniture.** Remove mark with lighter fuel and a cotton ball.

◇**Waxed oak, mahogany, pine, walnut, beech, elm.** Dust and rub frequently. Polish occasionally with a light-colored wax polish. A cheap and easy method for cleaning oak and mahogany is to wipe with a cloth dipped in warm beer.

◇**Teak.** Once in a while, rub in teak oil or cream—never use wax polish.

◇**Cedar and hardwoods.** Remove marks with steel wool, rubbing along the grain. Treat with exterior-grade wood preservative.

◇**Composition board and plywood.** Wipe with a chamois cloth wrung out in warm water. Rinse with cold water and dry.

◆ Remove stains by rubbing gently with fine steel wool along the grain; don't scrub too vigorously or use harsh abrasives.

LEATHER FURNITURE

◆ Dust or vacuum leather upholstery, then clean with saddle soap when necessary. Use as little water as possible. When dry, buff with a soft cloth.

◆ Rub dark leather once or twice a year with castor oil to prevent cracking. On pale leather, use white petroleum jelly. Don't wax leather furniture; it won't absorb it.

◆ If leather furniture begins to look parched, sparingly apply a commercial leather conditioner with cotton swabs; leave for 24 hours so it will be absorbed, then polish with a soft, clean cloth. Or, sponge with a solution of 1 teaspoon household ammonia and 4 teaspoons vinegar and 2 cups water. Then apply castor oil on a soft cloth. When the leather is dry, apply a leather shoe cream.

HOUSEHOLD STAINS AND MARKS (Continued)

CIGARETTE BURNS
See HEAT MARKS, WHITE

COSMETICS
See ALCOHOL.

GRAFFITI
See WOOD PANELING
(page 89).

HEAT MARKS, BLACK
Rub with a cut lemon to
bleach the mark. When dry,
recolor wood with commer-
cial wood stain, scratch cover,
or shoe polish. Repolish
whole surface.

HEAT MARKS, WHITE
Remove stain with denatured
alcohol or paint thinner.
When dry, recolor wood with
commercial wood stain,
scratch cover, or shoe polish.
Repolish the whole surface.
**Plastic and lacquered fin-
ishes.** Rub with brass polish.
Wipe off polish before it
dries, then rub with a very hot
cloth (heat it in the oven or
under the iron). Repolish.

Oiled wood. Rub with teak
oil, furniture polish, or linseed oil.

INK
Absorb as much as you can
into a damp cloth, then rub
with a cut lemon.

PAINT
You won't be able to remove
old dry stains, so tackle the
mark as fast as you can.
Oil-base stains. Wipe with
liquid furniture polish or turpentine, then polish.
Water-base stains. Wipe with
soap solution.

SCRATCHES
Rub with a waxy substance of
a suitable color.
Ebony. Use black shoe polish,
wax crayon, or eyebrow
pencil.
Mahogany. Use dark brown
shoe polish, wax crayon, or
eyebrow pencil.
Maple. Use iodine diluted
with paint thinner. Dry and
rewax.

Oak. Use white or pale brown
shoe polish and rewax.
Pine. See OAK.
Red mahogany. Brush iodine
over surface with a fine brush.
Let dry and rewax.
Teak. Sandpaper gently
before rubbing with a half-
and-half solution of linseed oil
and turpentine. (These substances are flammable.)
Walnut. Rub with a piece of
nutmeat from a walnut.

WATER MARKS, BLACK
Rub surface gently with fine
steel wool until unfinished
wood is reached. Recolor or
stain wood. Repolish or oil
wood as necessary.

WATER MARKS, WHITE
Rub with very fine steel wool
and oil with the grain. Apply a
half-and-half solution of linseed oil and gum turpentine,
leave for 2 hours, and remove
with vinegar.

◆If the upholstery is badly damaged, do not
treat it yourself, but get advice from a professional restorer.

Seasoning leather upholstery. *Rub castor oil (for
dark leather) or petroleum jelly (for light leather) into
the surface of the leather with your fingertips (above
left). Then wipe it all off with a soft absorbent cloth
(above right).*

Vinyl or imitation leather

◆Wipe sticky marks with a cloth squeezed
out in a warm, detergent solution (not soap),
and polish with a soft cloth. Don't use wax or
cream polish; it tends to leave the surface
tacky.

Desk and tabletops

◆Wash with a damp cloth wrung out in
sudsy water. Occasionally rub with leather
conditioner. When using leather conditioner
avoid any embossed gilding and be careful
not to touch any surrounding wood, as it
may leave a mark.
◆Rub ink stains very gently with a cotton
ball dipped in paint thinner. Apply paint
thinner sparingly; it can remove the color.

OTHER MATERIALS

▼▼ If you are going to take a marble or glass
♦♦ top off a table to clean it, don't carry it
flat (both marble and glass can break under
their own weight). Instead, hold it vertically
to avoid breaking.

Metal furniture

◆ Most modern tubular metal furniture
needs only an occasional wipe with warm
sudsy water.

◆ Check about cleaning when you are buying
the furniture, because metal parts may have
been given a special nontarnish (lacquer)
finish. If you damage the lacquer, the metal
will tarnish.

◆ Generally, a thin film of silicone-wax polish will be enough to protect the surface.

◆ See *Cleaning Metalwork* (pages 102–105).

Cleaning wrought iron. *Remove loose dirt on
wrought iron with a bristle brush. Use a wire brush if
the metal is rusty.*

Glass tabletops

◆ Rub with lemon juice or vinegar, and dry
with paper towels. Buff with newspaper. You
can use ammonia or commercial glass or
window cleaner instead.

Marble furniture

◆ Marble is porous, so it stains and scars
easily. Don't let it get too wet; use coasters
under drinking glasses, and seal windowsills,
floors, and tabletops with a marble sealer.

◆ Wipe regularly with a damp sponge and
buff dry. For stubborn grime, use dry borax
and a damp cloth; rinse with warm water and
buff dry. To clean and polish, use a self-
polishing marble cleaner.

◆ To remove a stain, apply one of the mixtures given below, cover with plastic wrap,
and seal with masking tape. Let the peroxide
and acetone (available at chemical supply
stores) mixtures stand overnight; the rust
paste, a few hours. Sponge off the mixture
and buff the treated area. *For grease stains:*
Make a paste of powdered whiting or chalk
dust mixed with acetone. *For organic stains—
coffee, tea, fruit juices, tobacco:* Mix the whiting or chalk powder with hydrogen peroxide
instead of acetone and add a few drops of
ammonia just before applying it. *For rust
stains:* Use liquid rust remover as the solvent.

◆ You can sometimes remove white rings left
by drinking glasses or potted plants by rubbing with a high-quality marble-polishing
powder (tin oxide).

◆ If removing a major stain dulls the marble,
wet the area with water and sprinkle it with
the marble-polishing powder (tin oxide).
Rub with a thick cloth or use an electric
buffer.

◆ Consult a professional refinisher if stains
won't come off, or for treating antique or
valuable marble.

Wicker and bamboo

◆ Brush or vacuum regularly to prevent dust
from clinging, and wash with sudsy water
and borax, using a soft brush to get into the
crevices.

◆ If a piece is very dirty, it can be gently
scrubbed with soapsuds and an added capful
of ammonia, and rinsed well with water
containing a couple of tablespoons of salt.
Dry outside on a sunny day. The salt stiffens
the bamboo, and the sun will bleach it
slightly. If it becomes brittle, drenching with
clear water will help restore it.

◆ Rush, sea grass, or twisted fibers should
only be wiped when necessary with a damp
cloth.

CLEANING SOFT FURNISHINGS

THE SIMPLEST WAY to keep the upholstered furniture and drapes in your home in mint condition is to vacuum them regularly; this prevents surface dirt, dust, animal dander, food, etc., from settling into the fabric and creating lasting damage. Given this kind of regular attention, soft furnishings will retain their original colors and textures for many years.

TIPS FOR VACUUMING TEXTILES

◆ Use the general-purpose head for cleaning textiles, as brushes of any kind can roughen loose threads.

▼▼ A vacuum cleaner with extra-strong
◆ ◆ suction should not be used on textiles because it can pull out loose threads. Do not vacuum fringes or embroidered items that have beads or sequins on them; you could pull them off.

◆ A small, hand-held vacuum cleaner is ideal for most textiles. If you have many curtains and much upholstery, it would be worth investing in one of these, as they are light to carry around and far less cumbersome than any other type of vacuum.

UPHOLSTERED FURNITURE

◆ Vacuum the sofa, chairs, and any cushions regularly—whenever you do a thorough cleaning. Clean armrests, backs, and crevices with the upholstery attachment. Regular dusting and cleaning prolong the life of a sofa or chair.

◆ Before vacuuming, check under and around cushions for small toys or buttons, etc., that could block the vacuum.

◆ Deep-clean chairs and seats occasionally—before they look dirty. Remember that cleaned upholstery will rapidly get dirty again if you don't remove all the detergent or cleaner properly.

◆ Use silicone sprays on upholstered furniture to prevent dirt settling. Re-treat as recommended.

◆ Use commercial cleaning products that contain a soil-retardant.

Loose covers

◆ Removable covers can be cleaned, which makes them a good idea if you have young children.

◆ Stretch covers can be satisfactorily machine-washed at home. Larger cotton and linen loose covers may fit into a domestic washing machine, but it might be easier to wash them in the larger machines at a self-service laundry. They also may be taken to professionals for dry-cleaning and pressing.

◆ Iron loose covers on the wrong side so the fabric does not become shiny, unless it is glazed chintz, which should not be ironed. Many stretch fabrics are drip-dry and don't need ironing.

Ironing slipcovers.
Iron cotton and linen slipcovers on the wrong side while still damp. Put the cover on the sofa right away so it dries to the shape of the sofa.

Cushions

▼▼ Don't soak padding when cleaning, as
◆ ◆ this can cause foam and feathers to break
down or lump together. Some dry-cleaning
fluids can have the same effect.

◆ Dry-clean kapok paddings (a fiber from the
pods of the kapok tree) but not too often.
Kapok can get very lumpy if allowed to get
wet, making it uncomfortable to sit on.

◆ You may want to cover cushions with
removable covers.

Stains

◆ Quickly wipe up anything spilled, before it
sinks in far enough to damage the fabric.

◆ Blot liquids with salt or paper towels and
scrape off anything thick with a blunt knife.
If the spill leaves a mark, apply the appropriate stain remover; treat nonremovable
covers as for carpets (see pages 81 and 82) and
loose covers according to the specific fabric
(see pages 114–118 and 142–144).

CLEANING FURNISHING FABRICS

◆ Fitted covers can be cleaned in place
using a foam upholstery cleaner. The basic
rules are: Don't let the furniture get too
wet; brush all of the cleaner off the upholstery thoroughly; and don't let anyone sit
on it until it is completely dry.

◆ Test a hidden area before cleaning to
make sure the colors don't run.

ACRYLICS
◆ For nonremovable covers,
use foam upholstery cleaner;
don't rub vigorously.

◆ For removable acrylic
covers and curtains, wash in
warm water, with a cold rinse
and a short spin. The cold
water rinse will cool the fiber
so it won't crease. This also
applies to all other man-made
fibers.

◆ Pile fabrics may be brushed
lightly when dry.

◆ You can iron with a cool
iron, if necessary, after the
fabric is dry. Most of these
fabrics are drip-dry.

BROCADE
◆ Dry-clean all brocades,
because they are too heavy to
handle when wet.

CANVAS AND SAILCLOTH
◆ Scrub with warm sudsy
water; rinse in clear water. Dry
in the open air.

◆ Use a gum eraser for small
dirty marks.

COTTON AND LINEN
◆ Can be laundered, but remove stains beforehand. If
very dirty, soak in detergent
or soap suds in warm water.

Wash in hot water, and rinse
thoroughly.

◆ Iron on the wrong side with
a hot iron while still damp.

◆ Starch cottons before ironing them; they will look
better.

◆ Loose covers with piping
should be put back on while
they are still slightly damp;
otherwise the piping may
tighten, or even shrink.

GLAZED CHINTZ
◆ It should be dry-cleaned for
best results, but you can wash
it in the machine on a gentle
cycle and a cool rinse.

◆ Don't rub, twist, wring, or
bleach it, and, if the glaze is
permanent you should not
have to starch it.

OPEN-WEAVE CASEMENT
◆ Wash as for the weakest
fiber (see *A to Z of Fabrics*,
pages 114–118).

SILK
◆ Dry-clean silk taffetas and
brocades.

◆ Other silks and blends may
be very carefully washed (see
page 117).

◆ Iron while still damp with a
cool or a steam iron.

◆ Clean nonremovable covers
with foam upholstery cleaner.

TWEED
◆ Dry-clean woolen tweeds.

◆ Tweeds made with
polyester or acrylic can be
washed according to their
fiber (see *A to Z of Fabrics*,
pages 114–118).

◆ Clean nonremovable up-
holstery covers with foam upholstery cleaner. Don't rub
wool fabric while it is wet.

VELVET
◆ Can be cotton, acrylic,
rayon, or olefin. If in doubt as
to which fiber your velvet is
made of, have it dry-cleaned.
Many velvets are uncrushable,
spotproof, and easily washed.

◆ To remove creases on loose
covers, hang the cover in the
steam of a hot shower.

VELVETEEN
◆ May be cotton or viscose
rayon, so wash as appropriate
for the fiber (see *A to Z of
Fabrics*, pages 114–118). Shake
occasionally while drying, and
smooth the pile with a soft
cloth.

◆ May be dry-cleaned.

DRAPES AND CURTAINS

Remove dust and dirt from drapes by vacuuming, but don't use the brush attachments, because you may damage the fabric; use the upholstery attachments instead.

◆Clean drapes and curtains, or get them cleaned occasionally so they'll last longer. Follow the manufacturer's care instructions. Always test colors before washing; some colors may run.

◆ Small drapes and curtains can be washed in the washing machine, provided the material and the lining (if any) are the same; if not, one or the other may shrink.

◆Large drapes become very heavy when wet. Either take them to a self-service laundry that has large machines or have them professionally cleaned. Wash delicate fabrics by hand.

◆Remove hooks, weights, etc., before washing.

◆If the drapes are lined, wash as for the weakest fiber.

◆Stretch cotton drapes gently before hanging to dry so linings and drapes will still hang correctly.

◆Have fiberglass drapes dry-cleaned; don't machine-wash, twist, or iron them, because the fibers can break. If you wash them, wear gloves so you don't get fiberglass splinters in your hands. Rinse the tub well when finished.

◆Do not soak drapes or curtains made of rayon or silk.

Lace curtains

Soak in plenty of warm sudsy water with enough room so they can be gently moved around. Do not rub, twist, or wring; just move the fabric gently around in the water.

◆For extra body, dip freshly washed cotton lace curtains in starch to stiffen them.

◆Rehang nylon and polyester lace curtains while they are still slightly damp to allow the creases to drop, then you won't have to iron them.

◆Whiten "gray" nylon curtains with a nylon whitener. Rinse and drain them well. Faded areas where the fabric has been bleached by the sun can't be washed out or covered over by dyeing.

BLINDS

◆Dust them occasionally with a clean dustcloth or the vacuum cleaner, or put on cotton gloves and wipe the slats by hand. To wash metal blinds at the window, have two pails of water on hand—one with household cleaner or ammonia in it, the other with clear rinse water. Extend the blinds fully, with the slats horizontal. Starting at the top, wipe each slat with a sudsy sponge; then rinse with clear water and a fresh sponge.

◆Blinds also can be washed in the bathtub and hung over the shower-curtain rod to dry, or hosed down outdoors then hung on a clothesline to dry.

◆Spray wooden blinds with furniture cleaner, and wipe with a soft cloth. Don't wash them, because the wood may splinter if allowed to get too wet.

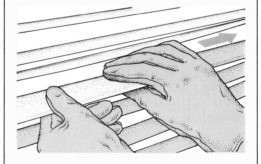

Quick way to clean blinds. *Put on a pair of old fabric gloves over rubber gloves, and dip your gloved fingers into a cold water and ammonia solution—1 teaspoon ammonia to 1 quart water. Now run your fingers and thumb along each slat.*

CLEANING METALWORK

METAL SURFACES don't last forever; they scratch easily and can wear away. Too much polishing is not good for metal and will eventually disfigure a metal object, so save yourself the work. If you think a piece is valuable, don't polish it yourself with commercial cleaners—take it to a jeweler.

Keep metal dry to prevent it from tarnishing (tarnish is caused by gases and moisture in the air acting on the surface of the metal). Rubber bands and plastic wrap can stain metals that tarnish, even through several layers of wrapping.

Silver

◆ If you use and wash your silver regularly, you won't have to polish it so often, which is easier for you and better for the silver. Wash after use in hot water and dishwashing liquid as soon as possible.

◆ Dust decorative pieces regularly, and wash them occasionally to keep them bright.

◆ You can remove small scratches by rubbing with jeweler's rouge, purchased in most jewelry stores.

◆ Wash and dry the silver before polishing it. Rub the polish in with a soft, dry cloth and a small, soft brush to get inside the crevices; rub lengthwise, not crosswise or in circles. Make sure no excess polish is left on the silver—it will cause it to tarnish again more quickly. Wash the silver, rinse it, and buff with a chamois or soft cloth.

◆ The best way to polish tarnished silver is by hand-rubbing it with commercial polish or a paste of baking soda and water.

◆ Always polish silver near an open window, because the tarnish gives off a sulfurous gas when it is cleaned.

◆ Coat a string with silver polish or a paste of baking soda and water, and rub it between tarnished fork tines.

▼▼ Abrasive cleaners will scratch silver, and
◆ ◆ bleach will permanently stain it, so these should never be used for cleaning.

▼▼ Be sure to use soft cloths; scratchy linen
◆ ◆ dish towels will damage silver.

TIPS FOR CLEANING METALS

◆ Wear cotton gloves when cleaning metal, otherwise the acid in your skin will tarnish the metal.

◆ Badly tarnished or dirty antique metals should be cleaned professionally.

◆ Never use silver cleaner on metals other than silver, gold, or platinum, unless specified.

◆ A drop of paint thinner on a cotton ball will quickly brighten silver pieces not intended for eating or containing food.

LACQUERED METAL

◆ Precious metal objects can be lacquered (coated with a special finish) to prevent them from tarnishing.

◆ Metalwork that has been lacquered does not need to be touched again for up to 10 years, except for an occasional light dusting.

◆ Lacquering should only be done by experts, because the preparation is complicated.

◆ Once metalwork has been lacquered, don't touch it with your bare hands because the acidity of your skin will still tarnish the metal.

◆ Handle lacquered metal carefully, because if the lacquer is damaged, moisture can creep in under the lacquer and tarnish the metal, making it impossible to clean. Lacquer is difficult to remove.

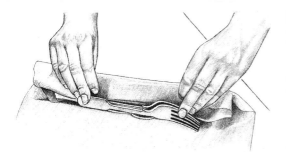

Protecting silver from tarnish. *Silver will tarnish more quickly in a damp or salty atmosphere. Wrap it in special bags or rolls of cloth saturated with a tarnish inhibitor, which you can get from jewelers or order as yardage through fabric shops. Or, you can use acid-free tissue paper.*

◆If using commercial silver dip, pour some cleaner into a jar and keep that for regular use. Never dip anything into your main supply, because it will become overcharged with silver that is then deposited back on the surface as mat silver.

🍃 **GREEN TIP:** Make your own silver-cleaning cloths by mixing a soaking solution of 10 parts cold water to 2 parts household ammonia and 1 part silver polish. Cut up several squares of cotton and saturate them in the mixture. Let them drip-dry.

◆To retard tarnishing, store silver in a chest or drawer lined with a special tarnish-inhibiting fabric, or wrap it in the fabric. Do not use plastic wrap or bags, because condensation can collect within and cause tarnishing or hard-to-remove spots.

CLEANING TOOLED SILVER

◆Use special silver cleaning brushes, and *only* use them for silver. Use a special plate brush, which you can get from a jeweler, or a child's soft toothbrush, to get into the grooves on large objects.

▼▼ Don't use a hard toothbrush or a
◆◆ paintbrush, because the bristles will scratch the surface.

Cleaning deep "valleys." *Use a cotton swab or cotton wrapped around the end of a wooden cuticle stick. Dip the stick in a liquid polish, and work it into the crevices to remove the tarnish. Rinse well.*

◆**Silver plate.** Treat as for silver but, since the silver is just a coating, clean items more gently.

◆**Gilt.** Never polish it or you will remove the gold completely, revealing the silver underneath, which will then tarnish. Dust occasionally.

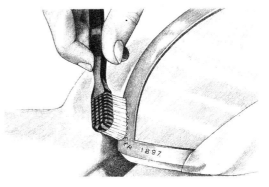

Cleaning engraved surfaces. *Use a soft toothbrush to rub each piece with straight strokes; don't rub in circles. Finish with a chamois or soft cloth.*

Gold and platinum

◆Platinum doesn't tarnish and is not affected by acids. Clean with detergent or a soap-and-water solution, and dab dry.

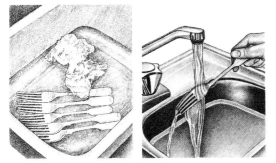

Cleaning household silverware. *Immerse the silver for 10 minutes in a bowl containing a handful of baking soda and some aluminum foil. Add enough water to cover the silver. (The tarnish collects on the foil—but it will also collect on any silver sticking out of the water.) Rinse in hot water and dry. Wipe with a soft cloth and air-dry. Then wrap in specially treated silver bags.*

◆ Dust precious gold lightly with a clean, dry cloth or a chamois cloth; ordinary cloths may harbor tiny particles of grit, which could damage the metal.

◆ Clean tarnished low-karat gold with silver polish. When not in use, wrap in a chamois cloth or acid-free tissue.

◆ Take a precious piece to a jeweler.

Chrome

◆ Wipe with a soft, damp cloth, and polish with a dry one. Very sticky chrome can be washed with a mild soap or detergent.

GREEN TIP: Polish the surface with a cloth dipped in apple cider vinegar.

▼▼ Don't clean chrome with harsh polishes; ◆ ◆ they will scratch it and damage the shine.

◆ A little paraffin on a damp cloth, or baking soda on a dry one, will clean greasy deposits. Rub burned-on grease with silver polish, powdered whiting, or baking soda.

◆ A thin film of silicone furniture polish protects chrome furniture.

Cleaning the inside of a teapot. *Chrome teapots can be cleaned inside with a cloth moistened with vinegar and dipped in salt.*

Stainless steel

◆ Wash in hot sudsy water occasionally, adding ammonia to the water (2 tablespoons per quart). Soak very dirty pieces in warm sudsy water. Wash sinks, countertops, or stove tops with borax. Avoid abrasives because they scratch the surface.

GREEN TIP: You can shine the inside and outside of a stainless steel pan by rubbing it with lemon juice or vinegar on a cloth.

Brass

◆ Lacquered brass does not need polishing, because polish can damage the lacquer. Wash occasionally in soapy water.

◆ If a brass object is very dirty, wash it in a solution of household ammonia.

GREEN TIP: You can clean very dirty brass with a lemon dipped in salt; a paste of equal quantities of vinegar, flour, and salt; or a paste of vinegar or lemon, and salt. Rinse off thoroughly; clean with brass polish.

◆ Polish with brass polish. Use a soft brush to get into engraved surfaces; a stiff brush could scratch the surface.

GREEN TIP: Instead of brass polish you can buff with mineral oil on a soft cloth.

◆ Ingrained dirt on brass objects such as fire tongs should be rubbed with steel wool or very fine emery cloth, unless they are antiques, in which case, get expert advice.

GREEN TIP: Clean the inside of brass serving containers with a household paste made of vinegar and salt.

▼▼ Wash and rinse brass pans thoroughly ◆ ◆ after cooking, and dry before storing to prevent any corrosion. Don't use metal polish on the inside of a brass pan you use for cooking; any residue could get into the food.

◆ Apply a thin coat of paste wax to outdoor brasses and lemon oil to indoor brasses to keep them staying bright.

Cleaning small brass ornaments. *Small objects can be boiled in water containing salt and vinegar. Rinse thoroughly and dry.*

Copper

Copper tarnishes by forming a greenish surface film (green rust), which can cause nausea and vomiting if eaten.

◆ Protective lacquer on new pans must be removed before the pan is used (see page 69).

◆ Clean the outside of a pan with a commercial copper polish, or make a homemade copper polish from equal parts salt, vinegar, and flour. Treat stubborn stains with a strong solution of household ammonia.

GREEN TIP: Buttermilk, vinegar or lemon juice, and salt will all remove corrosion on copper. Rinse and dry well.

Bronze

◆ Dust the surface lightly once or twice a year with a soft, clean dustcloth. Don't use a wire brush or harsh abrasives; they will damage the surface.

◆ Lacquered bronze only needs dusting and an occasional wiping with a damp cloth.

▼▼ Antique bronzes must be cleaned pro-
◆ ◆ fessionally. Don't attempt it yourself. Never wash antique or valuable bronze—it can cause rapid corrosion, which leads to "bronze disease," where the metal starts flaking away. Denatured alcohol should not be used on antique or valuable bronze.

◆ Remove any greenish blue deposits (verdigris) by scraping lightly with a knife or rubbing with a toothbrush. Heavy encrustations that won't scrape off should be washed with water containing 10 percent acetic acid. Rinse.

Cleaning bronze. *For not very valuable but very dirty pieces, wash with a soft brush in hot water and mild detergent. Rinse, dry, and buff.*

Pewter

◆ Keep it dry or it will develop a sort of gray film, and tarnish.

◆ Don't disturb the tarnish found on antique pieces; the piece may disintegrate.

◆ Polish with a suitable metal polish, or with powdered whiting and a little household ammonia or denatured alcohol for a bright finish. For a dull finish, rub with rottenstone and olive oil or a raw cabbage leaf (see below). Rub badly stained pewter with fine steel wool and olive oil.

Cleaning pewter. *Rub the surface with a raw cabbage leaf or the green part of a leek leaf. Rinse and dry.*

Lead

◆ Scrub with turpentine or paint thinner. Place a very dirty object in a solution of 1 part vinegar to 9 parts water with 1 teaspoon baking soda. Rinse in several changes of distilled water.

◆ Remove white deposits by boiling in several changes of clear water.

Wrought iron

◆ Remove rust by rubbing with steel wool dipped in kerosene. If the item is small enough, soak it in kerosene for a couple of hours, then rub with steel wool. Polish with liquid wax or paint it to keep it from becoming rusty again.

◆ Rub large objects (gates, table legs) with a bristle or wire brush. Wipe over the surface with paint thinner on cotton swabs; don't use water, the iron will rust again.

◆ Paint outdoor iron furniture, or it will be difficult to keep the rust under control. Remove all rust first. Then apply two or three coats of exterior-grade paint.

HEATER AND AIR-CONDITIONER CARE

M OST HEATING AND air-conditioning equipment needs only an occasional wiping down with a damp, sudsy cloth. Fireplaces and wood-burning stoves, however, involve a fair amount of time and attention, even though they provide a warm and cheerful focal point in a home.

FIREPLACES AND WOOD-BURNING STOVES

◆ Use blacking or a commercial cleaner containing graphite to clean metal parts and freestanding stoves. Brush the hearth while the damper is closed to prevent dust from flying around.
◆ If it is an old fireplace and you want it only for decoration, you can give it a thin coat of a mat black paint. (A thick coat would hide the decoration.) Thin the paint, if necessary, with paint thinner.
◆ Old steel and cast-iron fenders, grates, hearths, and irons can be burnished by a professional metal refinisher.
◆ Remove old paint with chemical paint stripper, then blacken or paint as soon as possible to prevent rust.

Grates

◆ Wood ashes may be left in the grate throughout the winter and will build up a good base for your fire; coal ashes should be cleared out more often, perhaps once a week.
◆ Before removing ashes, sprinkle damp coffee grounds over them to keep down the dust.
◆ Always put the ash into a metal container to take it to the trash can. Any hot embers will burn through paper and plastic.
◆ Use a plate dishwashing brush for cleaning a metal grate, and keep it just for the grate.
◆ If you have a slate hearth, wash and dry it,

and then coat it with lemon oil to keep it gleaming. Do this about every six weeks.

Brick fireplaces

◆ Clean with water or a commercial cleaner; never use soap, which leaves scum. For bad marks, apply undiluted vinegar, then rinse.
◆ For smoke stains, try using a half-and-half solution of bleach and water. Pour it into a spray bottle and spray directly upon the brick. Cover the entire surface, and scrub lightly. Rinse and dry thoroughly.

Stone fireplaces

◆ Clean with plain water only. If stained, use a bleach solution as for brick. Or, use a commercial stone cleaner.

Removing bad stains from stone. *Scrape these off the stone with a pumice stone.*

Tile fireplaces

◆ Wash ceramic tile hearths with hot water and detergent.

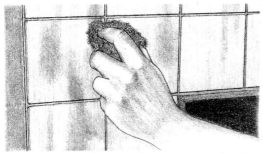

Cleaning stained tiles. *Rub stains very gently with steel wool or scouring powder.*

Marble fireplaces

◆ Wipe regularly with a cloth wrung out in water and mild detergent. Wipe dry and polish with a soft dustcloth.

◆ You can sometimes remove rings left by wineglasses or coffee cups by rubbing with a high-quality marble-polishing powder (tin oxide); otherwise, consult a professional.

◆ In a pinch, you can rub stained marble with steel wool, and then polish it with an electric buffer.

◆ If your marble fireplace has been painted, you will have to use paint stripper to remove the paint (see page 98).

Fire screens and andirons

◆ Dust the fire screen with a brush. If very dirty, wash it with hot water and detergent, or a cloth dipped in kerosene.

◆ Clean brass fire screens and andirons as for brass (see page 104). Use a toothbrush to clean between wires of the fire-screen mesh. Rub ends of andirons with a cloth moistened with kerosene to prevent rusting. Clean the handles with metal polish.

◆ Most metal polishes are flammable, so work away from the fire and wipe off all the polish before using the andirons again.

Chimneys

The drier the wood you burn, the more efficient the combustion and the fewer tar deposits you will get in your chimney.

◆ All chimneys in use should be cleaned at least once a year. If you burn wood, the chimney should be inspected four times a season for creosote deposits. If any deposits of creosote are detected, hire a chimney sweep to clean them out.

◆ Modern flues on wood-burning stoves are insulated with a double "skin" and also should be inspected four times a season, or once a month.

◆ If you have a box stove fitted into a closed fireplace by a short flue pipe, it is a good idea to cut a soot-cleaning hole with a well-fitted door above the fireplace to gain access for cleaning. You can hang a picture over this door when it is not being used.

INSPECTING A CHIMNEY

◆ Check whether a chimney is lined. It should be lined with either ceramic tile or metal. If it is not, lining the chimney will be a costly but very important improvement.

◆ The safest inspection is to look into the chimney from both the top and bottom openings.

RADIATORS AND HEATERS

Radiators require fairly frequent wiping when they are in use. Along with various types of heaters, they should be cleaned when cooled down.

Central heating radiators

Heat from radiators carries the dust up the wall and spreads it over the surface. Cleaning is difficult but worth the trouble.

◆ Clean radiators frequently during winter, less often when they are not in use.

◆ Use a vacuum cleaner to either suck or blow the dust out from behind the radiator. A good radiator brush or a feather duster will also work very well, or you can make your own tool (see below).

◆ Always cover the floor below the radiator with an old towel or piece of plastic when cleaning.

Making a radiator cleaner. *Find a stick, rake, or broom handle that fits down the back of the radiator. Tie a sponge on the end, and cover the sponge with an old sock. Change the sock when it gets dirty.*

AIR-CONDITIONER CARE

Keep your room air conditioners working efficiently by making sure they are as clean as possible.

◆ Wipe down the outside casing with a damp cloth on a regular basis.

◆ Once a month, remove the front panel and wash the filter in tepid water and mild detergent. Allow it to dry thoroughly before replacing it. Vacuum inside while the front panel is off, reaching all accessible surfaces.

◇ **Tubular heaters.** Keep the perforations clean by regular dusting. Don't cover with cloths or clothes, or the heater will overheat, which could cause a fire.

Electric heaters

◇ **Radiant heaters.** These need no particular maintenance other than the normal dusting and occasional wiping with a sudsy cloth.

◇ **Convector heaters and radiant convector heaters.** Dust regularly to keep the inlet and outlet grilles clean and free of dust and lint.

◇ **Oil-filled radiators.** Dust regularly, and occasionally wipe with a damp sudsy cloth.

◇ **Fan heaters.** These need occasional cleaning to remove dust and lint that may clog the grille.

Gas heaters

◆ Dust and wipe over bottled gas heaters occasionally with a damp cloth.

◆ Keep grilles free of lint.

◆ Don't block the inlet grilles of radiant convector heaters; you will prevent the air from flowing, and the elements will overheat. Some models have thermal cutout devices.

◆ Check the owner's manual for additional care.

Kerosene heaters

◆ Refer to the owner's manual for specific maintenance.

Cleaning an area heater. *Unplug the heater, and use your vacuum cleaner to blow through the grille, holding the nozzle about 4 inches away from the fan.*

CLEANING DECORATIVE OBJECTS

Decorative objects need frequent dusting and occasional washing. These tasks must be carried out carefully to prevent breakages. If the objects are very valuable, take them to a professional. Carry objects to be washed in a basket lined with plenty of tissue paper or towels.

CHINA AND GLASS

◆ Decorative china, ceramics, and glassware just need careful dusting every so often. If they get very grimy, wipe with a damp sudsy cloth, then with a clean dry one.

China and ceramics

◆ Wipe very fine china kept for display occasionally with a damp cloth, then dry with a linen towel.
▼▼ *Never* use detergents or bleaches on ceramics to try to remove stains.

CLEANING CRACKS IN PORCELAIN

◆ Cracks in fine porcelain often can be made less obvious by cleaning.

1 *Place a wad of cotton in warm water, squeeze it out, and then dip it in baking soda. Put the cotton over the crack, and leave it for several days, wetting the cotton occasionally.*

2 *Scrub gently with a fine bristle brush dipped in ammonia solution (1 teaspoon ammonia to 1 cup water). Rinse and dry.*

▼▼ Don't use cleaning powders or scouring powders on china or ceramics; they will damage both the glaze and the pattern.

Cleaning a raised pattern. *Brush with a soft brush to clean into the grooves.*

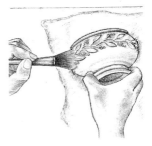

Glassware

▼▼ Don't touch glassware with painted or gilded decoration or antique glassware; the decoration may not be firmly fixed and could come off in your hand. Very delicately brush with a soft watercolor paintbrush or a photographer's lens brush.
◆ Glassware with metal mounts should only be dusted. If the glass is very dirty, clean it with slightly damp cotton swabs and dry right away. Don't let the metal get wet.

Handling a delicate glass. *Support the glass while cleaning or drying by cupping your hand under the bowl. Don't hold it by the stem, which can snap off very easily.*

TIPS FOR HANDLING CHINA AND GLASS OBJECTS

◆ Use both hands to pick up an object.
◆ Make sure you have plenty of elbow-room and are not likely to knock anything over.
◆ Never pick up a decorative object by its handle, or a delicate plate or bowl by its rim. They are often not strong enough to support the weight of the piece.
◆ Pick up objects with pieces sticking out by supporting the base with both hands.
◆ Don't grip figurines that have small

decorations such as flowers or leaves on them. The decoration is very vulnerable, and pieces can snap off.
◆ If washing china and glassware, use a plastic bowl so you don't chip the object. Don't put more than one item in the bowl at a time.
◆ Put glasses and cups down on a cloth or piece of paper towel to dry, never on a wet, smooth drainboard; they slide around too easily when wet.

Cleaning vases

◆Remove the whitish film that is left at the water line of glass vases with vinegar. Soak a cotton ball or paper towel with vinegar, and leave it on any ring for about five minutes to soften the deposit before you remove it.
◆ To get rid of plant and flower verdigris (the bluish-green deposits on copper, brass, or bronze), use a commercial cleaner that you soak in the vase, then rinse out.

GREEN TIP: Alternatives to commercial cleaners.
◆Fill the vase with dried beans or uncooked rice, and shake them around.
◆ Fill the vase with water, and put in 2 teaspoons household ammonia. Let it stand overnight, then wash and rinse.
◆ Put a little clean sand into the vase with a squeeze of dishwashing liquid and a little warm water. Shake well, let soak overnight, shake again, then rinse.
◆ Use toothpaste or baking soda—a heaping tablespoon to half a vase of warm water. Let it soak overnight, then rinse.

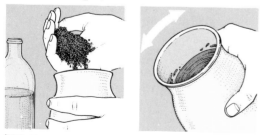

Removing plant stains from a vase. *Put a handful of tea leaves into the vase, cover with vinegar, and shake.*

LAMPS AND LIGHT FIXTURES

◆ When cleaning any lamp or light fixture, check that all cords are secure, unfrayed, and undamaged; replace if necessary.
◆Clean lamps and shades in the kitchen, bathroom, and workroom often; they are more likely to get dusty and greasy than those in other parts of the house.

Table lamps

◆ Take off the bulb and shade. Dust or vacuum the shade and wipe the bulb.
◆ Wash glass or plastic globes and reflectors in warm sudsy water. Rinse and dry carefully. Or, wipe with a chamois cloth dampened with denatured alcohol or paint thinner, then buff with a lint-free cloth.
◆Clean glass bases with a cloth wrung out in clear or sudsy water. You can use a toothbrush on cut glass to get into the crevices, but dry the glass well afterward with a paper towel or a lint-free cloth.
◆Porcelain bases, glazed stoneware, and china can be cleaned with a cloth wrung out in mild suds. Rinse and wipe dry with a paper towel or a lint-free cloth.
◆ Wipe marble and alabaster with a damp cloth. They shouldn't need any more attention, but if they do, follow the instructions for marble (see page 98).
◆ Metal lamp bases may be polished if they

have not been lacquered. But you shouldn't do this too often.

◆Lacquered surfaces only need dusting. Be careful—you can damage the lacquer by frequent cleaning (see page 102).

Ceiling or wall fixtures

◆Clean pendant fixtures regularly; bowl shades can become full of dead insects.

▼▼ Some fixtures, once put together, are not
♦ ♦ easy to remove, and once dismantled, are not so easy to put back together again. Be sure to read the manufacturer's care instructions, if you have them.

Dusting a ceiling light. *Dust with a feather duster; it's much easier on your arms than a cloth.*

Lampshades

For routine cleaning, vacuum lampshades lightly every so often to remove dust.

▼▼ Do not wash or wet a lampshade that has
♦ ♦ been put together with glue or staples; water will dissolve the glue and rust the staples, and damage glued-on trim.

Cleaning raffia and straw shades. *Vacuum often with the upholstery attachment. If they get really dirty, it is difficult to clean them. You can wipe with a damp cloth, but this is more likely to smear the marks than to get rid of them.*

For a more thorough cleaning, use the following directions.

◇**Fabric shades.** Brush off any dust, then swish the shade in a deep bath of lukewarm suds. Rinse in clear lukewarm water, then blot any excess water with a clean towel. Dry quickly out of direct sunlight.

◇**Glass and metal shades.** Dust with a dustcloth or a feather duster.

◇**Plastic and fiberglass shades.** Take down, dip in sudsy water, rinse, and hang to dry.

◇**Acrylic shades.** Wash in warm, sudsy water, and drain them on a terry-cloth towel.

◇**Paper shades.** Brush often with a feather duster. Do not attempt to wash. If they get very dirty, buy replacements.

◇**Parchment shades.** Wipe the surface gently with wallpaper cleaner, a damp cloth, or art gum eraser.

◇**Silk shades.** Get these cleaned professionally before they begin to look dirty.

SAFETY TIPS FOR CLEANING LIGHTS

◆Unplug lamps, and turn off the power before you begin cleaning light fixtures.
◆Never touch a light switch or light with wet hands.
◆If you are cleaning wall fixtures or ceiling lights, make sure you have a sturdy stool or ladder and somewhere to rest new light bulbs, a mop, cloth, or whatever you are cleaning with.

TIPS FOR CLEANING LAMPSHADES

◆Always remove removable lampshades for cleaning.
◆Some washable fabrics may be joined together with water-soluble glues, so don't plunge a lampshade into water unless you know it is safe.
◆Washable fabrics may not have washable linings so test them first.
◆Don't let metal lampshade frames get wet, or they might rust.

LIGHT BULBS

◆ Clean the light bulbs when you are cleaning the light fixtures. Take bulbs out of their sockets, and wipe them with a damp cloth. (This makes quite a difference as to how much light you will get from the lamp; you can lose 20 percent with a very dirty bulb.)

◆ Make sure a bulb is dry before you put it back to prevent electric shocks.

◆ Fluorescent tubes should be wiped with a damp cloth and changed when they start to flicker.

◆ Keep a supply of all the bulbs in use in your home so you can change burned-out bulbs when cleaning the light fixtures.

◇ **Metallic paper shades.** Rub with a solution of kerosene and paint thinner or turpentine—1 tablespoon turpentine or paint thinner to $\frac{1}{2}$ cup kerosene—and wipe off.

◇ **Nylon and rayon shades.** Detachable shades should be repeatedly dipped in warm sudsy water. Rinse in warm water. Dry quickly. Do not pull or stretch while wet.

◇ **Sunlamp reflectors.** These should be brightly polished to reflect as much heat as possible.

▼▼ Don't rub acrylic or any plastic shades, ◆ ◆ or you will increase the static, which attracts dust. Rub with an antistatic cloth if they seem to attract a lot of dust.

Chandeliers

◆ Dust them when you clean the room. More thorough cleaning depends on the material.

◆ Spray cleaners are available that allow the chandelier to be cleaned in place.

◆ Wipe over all parts of the chandelier with a cloth wrung out in sudsy water.

◆ Unscrew and clean all the light bulbs.

◆ While cleaning, take the opportunity to check the condition of the main chain and the ceiling fixture.

Kerosene lamps

◆ Clean kerosene lamps after each use. Wipe the chimney with a damp cloth or wash with sudsy water.

◆ Wash old brass lamps that have yellowed in mild detergent and water. Then buff with a soft cloth. Clean newer brass lamps as for brass (see page 104) and glass ones as for glass (see page 110). Lacquered brass will just need wiping over with a damp cloth.

◆ Wash the chimneys in mild detergent and warm water, and clean with a special chimney brush.

Trimming wicks. *Trim the wick with a pair of sharp scissors or a wick cutter. Keeping the wick trimmed prevents the lamp from smoking.*

CANDLESTICKS

▼▼ Tempting though it may be, do not ◆ ◆ use a knife to scrape off wax; you could scratch the candlestick.

◆ Wash china and crystal candlesticks in warm sudsy water; rinse and dry. Clean metal ones according to the metal they are made of. Wipe lacquered metal candlesticks with a damp cloth.

◆ Don't immerse weighted or hollow candlesticks in hot water.

Removing old wax. *Pour warm water into the candle holder to soften and remove old wax (above left). To soften wax from outer surfaces, cover your finger with a soft cloth, and push the wax off gently with your nail (above right).*

Home Laundry & Clothes Care

FABRICS GUIDE

ALL FABRICS require care if they are to stay in good condition. However, some fabrics need special care, so always check the care label when buying them.

CARE LABELS

In the United States, care labels are required by law on all wearing apparel except shoes, caps, hats, and gloves.

◆ Labels must:
◇ List washing or dry-cleaning instructions
◇ Be easily readable before purchase
◇ Be permanent for the life of the garment
◇ Alert consumers if any part of regular care could be harmful
◇ List if a garment cannot be cleaned by a certain method
◇ List water temperature and dryer settings if hot water and hot tumble drying will harm the item
◇ List an iron setting, if ironing is needed and hot ironing is harmful
◇ Mention if no bleach is safe or if only nonchlorine bleach is safe
◇ Warn if any dry-cleaning procedures are unsafe.

CLOTHING LABEL TERMS

Hot water: Water up to 150°
Warm water: Water between 90° and 110°
Cold water: Water up to 85°
Durable or permanent press cycle: Cool rinse before spinning to reduce wrinkling
With like colors: Wash with clothing of similar color and brightness
Dry flat: Lay out horizontally to dry
Block to dry: Reshape to original dimensions
Only nonchlorine bleach, when needed: Chlorine bleach may be harmful

CLEANING FURNITURE

FREQUENT DUSTING throughout the house is an essential task if you intend to keep accumulated dirt and grime from becoming permanent. Dust has a tendency to cling to surfaces and build up a filmy layer or sticky markings that can be difficult to remove. The best dustcloths to use are of soft cotton or flannel. These fabrics will not scratch furniture and will absorb dust naturally instead of just moving it around. It is especially important to dust regularly if you have animals in the house and/or family members with allergies or asthmatic problems.

WOODEN FURNITURE

Polish does not penetrate the surface and feed the wood, as people tend to think. All it does is fill some of the fine scratches and other blemishes, and it protects the surface, leaving a finish that is easier to dust. Polish, wax, and oil finishes need cleaning regularly to keep them in good condition.

◆ For cleaning and polishing the wood, mix equal parts of olive oil, denatured alcohol, gum turpentine, and strained lemon juice. Shake well and apply a small amount with a soft, lint-free rag (cheesecloth is ideal). Rub off excess polish with a soft, dry cloth, then buff to a shine with another cloth, preferably made of wool.

◆ Use a soft, old toothbrush to remove dirt stuck in corners. Polish carved furniture with a clean, soft shoe brush; dust with a feather duster.

Waxed furniture

◆Rub the surface with a clean, soft cloth, and polish occasionally with a small amount of furniture cream. To remove polish buildup, use a mixture of 1 part vinegar and 1 part water on a clean rag.

◆If the surface is scratched, try using a commercial scratch cover, always working along the grain and following the instructions provided.

◆Remove sticky marks with a cloth rinsed in warm sudsy water, then dry thoroughly and polish as above.

◆If in doubt about your treatment of the piece of furniture, get professional advice.

Alcohol spills on wood furniture. *Wipe up liquid immediately, and rub the area with your hand. The oil in your hand will help to restore some of that taken out of the wood by the alcohol.*

Dusting carved furniture. *Clean modern carved furniture with feather or lamb's-wool dusters, which are good at getting into the crevices. Do this fairly frequently or the dust will cling to corners and be very difficult to remove.*

A to Z OF FABRICS

ACETATE
Cellulose acetate fiber usually made from wood pulp.
◆ Dry-clean acetate unless the label specifically says a garment is machine-washable.
◆ If an acetate fabric is washable, use only warm water and a gentle cycle. Do not wring or twist. Hang on a hanger to dry.
◆ Iron on the wrong side with a cool iron.

ACRYLIC
Acrylic is used primarily in wool-like fabrics, sweaters, socks, upholstery fabric, blankets, and carpeting.
◆ Machine-washable: Warm wash, cold rinse.
◆ Lightweight acrylics can be drip-dried or dried in a cool tumble dryer.
◆ Heavy sweaters should be pulled into shape and dried flat on a towel.
◆ Brush pile fabrics with a soft brush when completely dry.
◆ Iron, if necessary, with a cool iron when completely dry, on the wrong side.

ALPACA See WOOL

ANGORA
Angora rabbit hair is often mixed with wool or nylon.
◆ Hand-wash and dry as for wool.

BONDED FIBERS
Two or more fabrics are fused together with adhesive.
◆ Machine-washable: Warm wash, cool rinse. Don't rub, spin, or wring; fabric will crease.
◆ Drip-dry; iron with a cool iron if necessary.

BROCADE
It has raised twill- or satin-weave designs on a plain, ribbed, twill, or satin background. It comes in a variety of fibers, such as acetate, cotton, silk, or a blend.
◆ All brocades should be dry-cleaned.

CALICO See COTTON

CAMBRIC See COTTON

CAMEL HAIR See WOOL

CANDLEWICK
A soft fabric made in a variety of fibers.
◆ Wash according to fiber (see care label).

CANVAS
A strong fabric often made from cotton or acrylic.
◆ Wash and iron as for the weakest fiber (see care label).

CASHMERE See WOOL

CHENILLE
May be made of a variety of fibers.
◆ Wash old chenille very carefully by hand in warm water.
◆ Don't iron. Stretch the fabric gently before hanging it to dry. Brush lightly to raise the pile.

CHIFFON
May be silk or a man-made fiber, such as nylon.
◆ Wash according to fiber (see care label). Do not wring; you can pull it out of shape.
◆ Use a cool iron when nearly dry, stretching gently in all directions and then into its correct shape.

CHINTZ See COTTON

CORDUROY
Can be cotton or cotton-polyester.
◆ Machine-washable: Turn inside out for washing, and wash as for most delicate fiber in the fabric (see care label).
◆ Smooth and shake the pile as it dries. Do not rub or the pile will be damaged.
◆ No ironing needed, but you may press gently while still damp, with several thicknesses of cloth between the corduroy and the iron.

COTTON

Natural fiber, sometimes used on its own, or combined with other fibers for strength.

◆ Machine-washable: White cottons are tough and can have a hot wash, hot rinse, and long spin, although you also can use a cold wash.

◆ Test colored cottons for colorfastness (see page 122), or follow care label. Wash similar shades together in case the color runs.

◆ Wash combined fibers as for weakest fiber (see care label).

◇ **Voile, organdy, and other delicate fabrics, and cottons with drip-dry or water-repellent finishes.** Treat according to the care label.

◇ **Muslin.** Can be starched.

◇ **Chintz.** Dry-clean or wash as for cotton, but don't rub, twist, or bleach. Don't iron chintz because this destroys the glaze. Can be starched.

◆ Iron cotton on the right side while damp, with a hot iron.

CREPE

Any fabric with a crinkled or pebbly finish; available in a variety of fibers.

◆ Wash according to fabric (see care label). Wool and silk crepes often require dry cleaning.

DAMASK

Made from a variety of fibers or blend of fibers.

◆ Treat as for weakest fiber (see care label).

DENIM

Can be pure cotton or cotton and man-made fiber blend.

◆ Wash new denim separately as it is usually not colorfast.

◇ **Cotton denim.** Machine-washable, but check care label and wash as for weakest fiber.

◆ Choose preshrunk denim, otherwise it will shrink.

◆ Iron as for cotton or as on care label.

DRILL See COTTON

ELASTOMERS

These are natural or synthetic fibers that can stretch to twice their normal size and yet return to their original shape; they include rubber and spandex. Also known as elastomeric fibers or elastofibers.

◆ Follow the care label, hand-wash in warm water, or give a gentle machine-wash.

◆ Rinse, short spin or roll in a towel; drip-dry.

◆ Don't iron.

FAILLE

Made of a variety of fibers.

◆ Treat as for weakest fiber (see care label).

FELT See WOOL

FIBERGLASS

Fine glass filaments.

◆ Hand-wash only: Wear rubber gloves and handle with care, moving the fabric around gently in warm suds. Don't wash with any other items and don't spin, wring, or iron.

◆ Hang over a rod or clothesline, then pull into shape. Don't hang with clothespins as this will break the fibers.

◆ Rinse the sink out well in case bits of fiberglass remain in it.

FLANNEL See WOOL

FLOCK FABRIC

Can be of various materials.

◆ Wash according to fiber (see care label).

◆ Roll in a towel to remove excess moisture. Then drip-dry. Don't spin or wring.

◆ Iron on the wrong side with a warm iron.

FOULARD

Used for silklike clothing, such as dresses, ties, and scarves.

◆ Treat according to fiber (see care label).

FURLIKE FABRIC

Man-made fur fibers.

◆ Treat according to fiber (see care label).

GABARDINE

Made from wool, wool blends, polyester, cotton-polyester blend, or other synthetic fibers. Fabric is woven to look like wool.

◆ Treat according to fiber (see care label).

A to Z OF FABRICS

GEORGETTE
Made from silk or man-made fibers.
◆ Treat according to the weakest fiber (see care label).
◆ Test for colorfastness (see page 122).

GROSGRAIN
Made from various fibers.
◆ Treat according to care label.

JERSEY
Made from a variety of fibers.
◆ Treat according to fiber (see care label).

LACE
Made from a variety of fibers.
◆ Hand-wash with powder or liquid specially formulated for delicate fabrics.
◆ Use enzyme-containing presoaks for short periods of time only. Take lace out as soon as it looks clean.
◆ Old or delicate lace can be washed and rinsed inside a pillowcase (or see page 124). Don't have it dry-cleaned, and never spin or tumble-dry, because the action will pull it out of shape.
◆ Squeeze, don't wring. Pull into shape while hanging to dry.
◇ **Cotton lace.** Starch, and iron with a hot iron on the wrong side.
◆ Man-made fibers shouldn't need ironing.

LAMÉ See METALLIC YARNS

LAWN
Fine fabric of cotton or cotton-polyester.
◆ Hand-wash in hand-hot water, or wash on a delicate machine cycle.
◆ Iron while damp, according to care label.

LINEN
Originally fabric made from flax; now the term is often applied to linenlike fabrics. Irish linen always means fabric made from flax.
◆ For linen made from flax, wash in machine using hot water. Starch, if desired. Hang to dry.
◆ For linen made from other fibers, treat according to fiber (see care label).
◆ Iron while still damp on the wrong side of the fabric, to prevent shiny patches.

LYCRA See ELASTOMERS

MERINO See WOOL

METALLIC YARNS
Aluminum threads coated with plastic and woven with other yarns.
◆ Dry-clean only.

MODACRYLIC
Similar to acrylic but weaker. Used to make furlike fabrics and fleecelike fabrics.
◆ Machine-washable in warm water; drip-dry.
◆ Iron with a cool iron, only if necessary.

MOHAIR See WOOL

MOIRÉ See SILK

MUSLIN See COTTON

NET
Refers to any open-weave fabric. Made from a variety of fibers.
◇ **Cotton net** may shrink when washed for the first time, so baste a deep hem, which you can let down after washing.
◆ Wash white net often; once it is gray, it is gray for good, although commercial whiteners can help to restore some of the whiteness.
◆ Rinse, drip-dry, and iron on the right side with a warm iron.

NYLON
A man-made fiber used on its own or mixed with natural fibers.
◆ Machine-washable: Wash often in warm water and rinse in cold water.
◆ White nylon may be rewhitened with a whitener. Don't use bleach; it will yellow.
◆ Wash delicate and pleated garments often to keep the pleats in. Dip them quickly up and down in the water. Don't twist or wring; short spin and drip-dry; hang on plastic hangers.
◆ If you take nylon to a dry cleaner, mark it clearly as nylon so the right chemicals are used.
◆ If exposed to direct heat or sunlight, the fabric will yellow permanently, so don't iron or line-dry.

ORGANDY
Usually made from cotton. Wrinkling is a problem (see care label).
◆ Hand-wash cotton organdy by squeezing gently in warm water and mild detergent.
◆ Treat organdy made from fibers other than cotton according to fiber (see care label).
◆ Iron on the right side while still damp, with a medium-hot iron.

ORGANZA
Can be made of various fibers.
◆ Treat as for fiber (see care label).

PIQUÉ
Made from a variety of fibers.
◆ Treat as for weakest fiber (see care label).

PLASTIC COATINGS
These coatings are added to fabrics for many reasons, including to give a leatherlike look, to minimize heat loss through the fabric, and to make items wind- or waterproof.
◆ Treat according to care label directions.

POLYESTER
Very strong and versatile man-made fiber. Won't shrink or stretch.
◆ Machine-washable: Hot wash, cold rinse. Tumble-dry.
◆ Wash pleated garments by hand; drip-dry.
◆ Use a cool iron, only if necessary.

POPLIN
Made from a variety of fibers.
◆ Treat according to fiber (see care label).

RAYON
Man-made fiber made of wood pulp. Weak when wet, strong when dry. Can look like silk, wool, linen, or cotton, but should be treated much more gently.
◆ Rayon fibers vary in their washability. Be sure to follow care label directions. If there are no directions, dry-clean.
◆ Iron with steam or while still damp.
◆ Shiny fabrics should be ironed on the right side, mat fabrics on the wrong side.
◆ Take care not to press over seams, as this will leave marks.

REP
Can be cotton or a mixture of cotton and man-made fibers.
◆ Treat as for weakest fiber (see care label).

SATEEN
Can be cotton or man-made fibers.
◆ Treat as for weakest fiber (see care label).

SATIN
Can be a variety of fibers.
◆ Lightweight satins may be washed as for the fiber (see care label).
◆ Heavy-furnishings satins should be dry-cleaned.
◆ Press satin on the wrong side while still slightly damp, using a warm iron.

SEERSUCKER
Can be cotton, polyester, or acetate.
◆ Wash according to fiber (see care label).
◆ Drip-dry. Do not iron.

SERGE
Can be cotton, wool, or either of these blended with man-made fibers.
◆ Treat according to fiber (see care label).

SHANTUNG
Made from a variety of fibers.
◆ Treat according to fiber (see care label).

SHARKSKIN
Made from a variety of fibers, often acetate.
◆ Treat according to fiber (see care label).

SHEEPSKIN
Wool from sheep, or may be acrylic.
◆ Machine-washable in the wool cycle.
◆ Can be shampooed in hand-hot water with a mild detergent. Rinse in warm water, squeeze, and dry away from direct heat.
◆ Can be dry-cleaned. Best taken to a specialist cleaner.

SILK
A natural fiber produced by the larva of a moth. Some silklike fabrics are made with man-made fibers.
◆ Check care label to see if washable; if so, hand-wash often in a mild soap or detergent to remove perspiration, which weakens the fibers. If in doubt, dry-clean.

A to Z OF FABRICS

◆ Dry silk away from direct sunlight, and don't soak in heavy-duty detergent, as both of these will weaken it. For best results, remove stains by dry cleaning. Tell the dry cleaner what the stain is.

◆ White silk may be bleached with hydrogen peroxide solution, but not chlorine bleaches.

◆ Treat wet silk gently; never rub it.

◆ **Brocade, taffeta, silk ties, and moiré:** Dry-clean only.

TAFFETA
Made from silk, wool, acetate, rayon, polyester, or nylon

TRIACETATE
Made from wood pulp and often blended with other fibers. Won't crease easily, stretch, or shrink, and dries quickly.

◆ Machine-washable: Short warm-wash/cold-rinse cycle.

◆ Use a cool iron, if necessary, on the wrong side.

TRICOT
Made of nylon or polyester.

◆ Treat as for weakest fiber (see care label).

TULLE
Fine net of cotton, nylon, or mixture of other fibers.

◆ Treat according to fiber (see care label).

◇ **Limp cotton tulle.** Dip in weak starch.

TUSSAH (or tussore) See SILK

TWEED
Made in a variety of fibers, especially wool and polyester.

◆ Treat man-made tweeds according to fiber (see care label).

◆ Dry-clean woolen tweeds.

VELOUR
Made in a variety of fibers.

◆ Treat according to fiber (see care label).

VELVET
Made in silk, cotton, or man-made fibers.

◆ Treat according to fiber (see care label).

VELVETEEN
Made in a variety of fibers, especially cotton or rayon.

◆ Treat according to fabric (see care label).

VISCOSE RAYON See RAYON

VOILE
Originally made in cotton or wool, but now made in a variety of fibers.

◆ Treat according to fiber (see care label).

WOOL
Natural fiber from sheep, lamb, or goat. Special wools from alpaca, camel, llama, and rabbit. Only soak it for short periods; wool shrinks easily when wet.

◆ Dry cleaning is the best treatment for wool.

◆ If you hand-wash wool, use a special cold-water wool detergent and squeeze water gently through; never rub.

◆ Machine-washable wools are available. Consult the care label.

◆ Avoid using a dryer. Either dry flat on a towel, or give a short spin and hang over a towel rack. Don't dry in the sun, because this will weaken the fibers.

◆ If the wool has shrunk after washing, stretch the garment while drying, first in one direction, then the other.

◆ Iron inside out with a cool iron and a damp cloth to avoid flattening the surface.

WORSTED See WOOL

LAUNDRY EQUIPMENT

Do A LITTLE research before you buy any piece of large equipment. Compare prices; features that save time, work, and energy; and warranties. Ask friends about their equipment and how pleased they've been with certain brands. Find out from the store or manufacturer how easy it is to get your machine serviced. Make sure the filters can be easily cleaned and that you can use any type of detergent. Buy units that stack if you don't have space for two machines next to each other.

WASHING MACHINES

◆ **Fully automatic washing machines.** These combine state-of-the art convenience with energy-efficiency and allow you to preselect the load size (small, medium, large, and extra large) along with the water temperature specified on the care label for washing and rinsing. This enables you to safely launder delicate fabrics, woolens, and lingerie at a suitable speed and temperature. Whatever the garment requires—a cold wash with cold rinse, a hot wash with warm rinse, and so on—can be preselected.

◆ **Semiautomatic washing machines.** These regulate temperature and washing times automatically, although the controls need to be adjusted from one cycle to the next.

◆ **Top-loading washing machines.** These usually are most efficient at removing ground-in dirt and can take larger capacity loads.

◆ **Front-loading washing machines.** These are space-savers; you can use the top as a work surface.

◆ Check the range of cycles on a washing machine—particularly useful cycles include one for an economy load and a separate spin cycle for hand-washed articles.

◆ Make sure your machine has sufficient room to vibrate. Allow a 1-inch space all around the washing machine.

◆ A washing machine should be installed in a heated room; if left in an unheated garage or utility room, for instance, water trapped inside can freeze and damage the machine.

▼▼ Completely drain a washing machine left
◆◆ in an unheated vacation home and have it professionally serviced.

▼▼ Don't use an extension cord to connect
◆◆ your washer; if water touches it, you could be electrocuted. Have the outlet moved or have a longer power cord installed.

Choosing automatic washing machines

◆ Additional features include capacities from 6 to 12 pounds of dry clothes, up to 20 different wash cycles, a memory that will run cycles in sequence, and a tumbling device built-in to boost the spin-drying operation.

◆ Some machines are portable and can be connected to the kitchen faucets by a length of hose.

Choosing clothes dryers

Dryers should be installed in places where the temperature is at least 45 degrees to cut drying time.

◆ The most versatile dryers automatically regulate timing and temperature and have a variety of cycles for different fabrics.

◆If you have condensation problems in your home, be sure your dryer is properly vented to the outside and that it collects all moisture within the unit.

TROUBLESHOOTING

Washing machines

◆If your washer won't start, check that the cord is plugged in, then for a blown fuse or tripped circuit breaker.

◆If your washer won't fill or fills slowly, there may be a kink in the drain hose or the hose may not be attached properly. If it is completely on the faucet but you can't straighten it out, replace the hose.

◆If oversudsing has blocked the drain or caused a leak, pour $\frac{1}{2}$ cup white vinegar mixed with some cold water into the washer; use a low-suds detergent to prevent the problem from recurring.

◆If the washer won't spin or begins to vibrate, the wash load may be off balance or too heavy. Remove some of the clothes or try to redistribute the load.

◆When the washing temperature is not right, check the faucets to make sure they are fully open and that the screens in the water inlet valve or hoses aren't clogged.

Dryers

◆If the dryer won't start, check the power supply and replace any blown fuses or reset any tripped circuit breakers.

◆If the dryer starts but the drum doesn't turn, the drum belt may need to be tightened or replaced.

◆If the dryer makes noise, look for a nail, screw, curtain hook, or other object caught in a drum hole.

◆If clothes won't dry, check to see if the lint trap or exhaust duct is clogged and needs cleaning. Also make sure the door is firmly shut and the seal is not worn.

MAINTAINING LAUNDRY EQUIPMENT

◆Don't overload a washer or dryer because the machines won't work as efficiently.

◆Wipe the equipment occasionally with a damp cloth.

◆Keep the machine door open to let the air circulate, except when children are around.

▼▼Don't use abrasive cleaners on the out-
◆ ◆ side of the machine; they will scratch it.

Washing machines

◆Use the right amount of the correct laundry detergent. Using more than specified will only make rinsing more difficult.

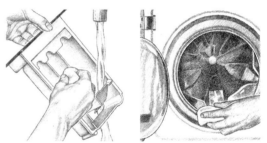

Keeping a washing machine clean. *Wipe out the soap, bleach, or fabric softener compartment regularly* (above left). *For front-loading machines, wipe the rubber door gasket where water often collects in the fold* (above right).

◆Check your hoses periodically by turning the water on and feeling for bulges. Replace hoses that have bulges.

Dryers

◆Remove lint from the filter after each use.

◆Check your dryer door for tightness by moving a piece of tissue paper around the door's edge while the dryer is on. Have the seal checked if the paper is drawn in.

LAUNDRY PRODUCTS

◆Always use the amount specified on the product; too little may be as bad as too much.

◆Most laundry products are toxic and should be stored away from children.

▼▼Don't mix chlorine bleach with am-
◆◆ monia, rust removers, vinegar, cleaning fluids, or acids. These chemicals can produce toxic gases when combined.

◆Use a low-suds detergent in front-loading machines. These also can be used for other machines.

🍃GREEN TIP: Cold water detergents are just as good as hot water detergents, and they save on energy. Use phosphate-free detergents to minimize water pollution.

◆If washing with granular detergents and cold water, make sure the powder has dissolved thoroughly before putting clothes into the water; undissolved detergent can cause white, powdery streaks on clothing.

◆Recommended amounts are based on average washing conditions of a 5- to 7-pound load, moderate water hardness, moderate soil, and average water volume. Adjust your quantity if conditions differ.

◆Add more detergent if you have a large amount of very dirty clothes to wash in very cold or hard water and you have extra water volume in a large-capacity washer.

◆Use less detergent when you are washing a small, lightly soiled load in very hot and very soft water with reduced water volume.

Enzyme presoaks

◆Often sold as enzyme-containing bleaches, these products work best on organic or protein stains, such as mud, egg, milk, or baby formula. They are not safe for silk, wool, cashmere, mohair, and angora.

◆Be sure to wear gloves when using these presoaks. They can irritate your hands.

Pretreatment sprays

◆The aerosol type contains petroleum-base solvents and is especially effective on shirt collars. Use it in a well-ventilated room because the fumes can be toxic.

◆The pump pretreatment spray is a detergent-base spray and may not work as well as the solvent-base type.

Fabric softeners

These are used for softening garments and towels. They also help reduce static cling. Some include whiteners to brighten the wash. There are three kinds of fabric softeners.

◆The first kind is added to the final rinse water in a machine or to hot or hand-hot water when hand-washing. They make ironing easier by reducing the friction between the fabric and iron and preventing static electricity from forming on man-made fibers.

◆The second type comes in sheets and is used in the dryer. This type does not soften as well as the rinse-cycle softeners and often does not evenly distribute the softener. With 100-percent polyester or nylon fabric, it may leave oily stains on medium and dark colors that will require rewashing.

◆The third type comes premixed with detergent. The softener is left on the clothes after washing and is activated by the heat from the dryer. These products do not soften as well as rinse-cycle softeners.

Bleaches

◆Most "all-fabric" bleaches are safe for colored fabrics and most fibers, with the exception of silk and wool. These may be purchased in powdered or liquid form.

◆Liquid chlorine bleaches must be diluted with water before they are used. These are the strongest and quickest of the bleaches. Properly diluted, they are safe for cotton, linen, rayon, and synthetics such as nylon and polyester. Colored clothing, particularly synthetics, may not be colorfast in liquid chlorine bleaches.

◆If you are unsure if a piece of clothing is silk or wool, test a hidden spot with fresh full-strength liquid chlorine bleach. Silk or wool fibers will dissolve.

◆You can speed bleaching action by using hot water.

WASHING AND DRYING

SORT THE LAUNDRY into dark and light piles, with reds and browns together, hot-wash items together, hand-wash items together, etc. Separate synthetics and lint producers such as towels. Never mix them. Before washing anything, make sure the pockets are empty; close zippers (open ones can damage other items as well as pull the clothes out of shape); fasten buttons; and mend any tears, however small.

HARD-WATER HINTS

Hard water is hard on your wash, because it doesn't always rinse well and leaves a detergent residue behind, so clothes and towels feel scratchy and stiff.

◆ Telltale signs of a hard-water area are bathtub rings; crusty deposits on faucets and shower heads; streaked or cloudy china and glassware; and extra soap or detergent needed to adequately clean.

◆ To help soften water, use nonprecipitating water softener. The amount you'll need depends on the hardness of the water and the amount of water and detergent used. If water feels slippery between your fingers, you're using enough softener.

◆ Your local water company or cooperative extension service agent can advise you on the hardness of your water, which ranges from soft through moderately hard, hard, and very hard.

◆ In hard-water areas, add a few tablespoons of baking soda to the load.

TESTING COLORFASTNESS

◆ Test on a hidden area, such as the hem. Some detergents and other additives may cause bleeding.

1 *Dampen a cotton pad and leave it on the fabric for 5 minutes.*

2 *If any dye comes off on the cotton pad, do not wash the fabric but get it cleaned professionally.*

MACHINE WASHING

◆ Use the amount of detergent manufacturers recommend.

◆ Don't wash more than you can dry easily at one time.

◆ If your wash turns pink or blue because you've added a garment of the wrong color by mistake, remove the colored article, then put all the affected garments back into the machine right away and put them through another complete wash cycle. Quick action may be enough to wash all the color out.

BLEACHING

▼▼ Always dilute chlorine bleaches,
♦♦ undiluted bleach will burn holes in
the fabric. Most garments that require
bleaching can be bleached in the automatic washer. Diluted bleach should not be
added until after the detergent wash cycle
has run about halfway through. Some
washers have an automatically timed
bleach dispenser.
♦ Check the care label to see if bleach is
safe on a fabric. If in doubt, follow
bleach bottle directions to test colorfastness on a hidden part of the fabric.
♦ Rinse fabric thoroughly after bleaching, and don't wash unbleached fabrics
with garments that have been soaking in
bleach; the bleach from the latter may

bleach the other in patches. Damaged or
discolored materials won't bleach evenly.
♦ Use a plastic container for bleaching
and test it first to make sure that it is
colorfast. Don't use metal containers;
they will rust.

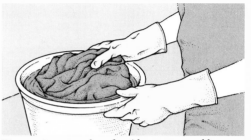

Protecting your hands. *Always wear rubber or
plastic gloves when bleaching fabrics.*

HAND-WASHING

Sort out hand wash according to the water
temperature recommended on the care label:
Cool feels cool to the hands; warm feels
comfortably warm; hand-hot is as hot as the
hand can bear.
♦ Pretreat spots and stains before hand-
washing.
♦ Wash delicate items such as silk lingerie by
shaking them in a jar filled with warm, mild,
sudsy water.
♦ Use soap flakes for hand-washing delicate
woolens or man-made fibers in hand-hot or
cold water.

SPECIAL PROBLEMS

♦ Wash frequently used garments and
fabrics often. This will prevent them from
graying and will make stains easier to remove
if spills occur.
♦ To brighten discolored or dull items, wash
in a permanent-press cycle using hot wash
water and a cool-down rinse. Use a cup of
water conditioner rather than detergent. If
condition persists, wash again with detergent
and all-fabric bleach.

Collars, cuffs, hems, and waistbands

♦ Dampen them and rub with heavy-duty
liquid detergent to coat any grimy marks.
Leave for 5 minutes then wash as usual.
Otherwise, use a commercial stain remover
(see page 140).

Elastic and elasticized garments

♦ To lengthen the life of clothing that contains elastic, wash frequently with detergent
and hottest water allowed by fabric. Laundering removes dirt and body oils, which
cause elastic to stretch and deteriorate.
♦ Dry elastic-containing items at lowest heat
setting and remove them when they're still
damp. Drying too much causes elastic to
shrink.

Knitted clothes

◆Knitted clothes should be cared for according to label directions for fiber content. Many knitted items can be machine-washed and tumble-dried. Hand-washing is needed for wool sweaters.

◆To wash wool knitted items, use lukewarm water, and a liquid detergent or special wool detergent, and gently squeeze the water through the garment. Never rub wool while wet; it will shrink.

◆Before washing a wool sweater, trace its outline on brown paper. Mix detergent and warm water. Allow sweater to soak for 3 minutes without stirring, swishing, or rubbing. If very dirty, repeat soaking. Then rinse with cold water. Squeeze and roll in a towel of similar color to remove excess water.

◆To dry a wool sweater, cover the paper outline with clear plastic (a cleaner's bag works well), then lay the sweater on the outline with rustproof pins and block it to its original shape. If you like, pin the edges to the outline with rustproof pins to prevent shrinking. Place in a warm place (not in direct sunlight) to dry.

◆Tailored wool clothes that have interfacings require dry cleaning.

Lace

◆Some laces, such as those found on nylon lingerie, are machine washable. Others, more delicate, need hand-care. Always consider the design and fiber of the lace when deciding

Washing old and delicate lace. *Pin it flat on a linen-covered board, using pins that won't rust. Sponge it clean with soapy water, rinse, and then leave it to dry on the board.*

whether to machine-wash.

◆Cotton laces frequently are starched. Washing removes starch or sizing, but lace can be starched again in a final rinse or with an aerosol starch during ironing to restore stiffness and body.

◆If lace is not washed when soiled, it will be difficult to clean and may become permanently stained.

Jeans

◆Turn them inside out before washing to prevent streaks.

◆New jeans should be washed several times to soften before wearing. However, frosted or prewashed jeans may have weakened fabric so that seams break if given unnecessary prewashing.

Baby clothes

These often get stained from formula and food, and the stains are sometimes hard to remove.

◆For best results, soak stains in cold water as soon as possible. Then rub them to remove at least some of the stain. Don't use hot water; it will make the stains permanent. If the stains are old, try an enzyme presoak.

Blankets

Have wool blankets dry-cleaned. Other fibers may be washed, but if they are bulky and heavy they may not fit into your machine. Take them to a self-service laundry or have them dry-cleaned, too.

◆If you machine-wash blankets, use the gentle cycle with least agitation and a very short spin.

◆Check the care label to see if a comforter can be washed; most synthetic comforters can be washed by hand or machine.

Pillows

Pillows take a very long time to dry, so always use a protective cover and pillowcase and wash the coverings frequently.

◆Feather pillows can be hand- or machine-washed. Inspect the ticking of your feather pillows before attempting to wash them by machine. If the weave is very tight with no apparent weak spots that will dissolve in washing, you may be able to machine-wash your pillows without losing feathers.

◆Feather pillows should be washed in covers on a gentle cycle and turned over halfway through the cycle (turn the machine off first).

◆Polyester or other fiberfill may shift during machine-washing, leaving the pillows quite lumpy.

Hand-washing pillows.

1 Immerse the pillow in a basin of luke-warm water with 1 ounce of baking soda or soap flakes, and squeeze the water through.

2 Rinse by lifting up and allowing them to drain and then immersing them again. Repeat the process, two or three times if necessary. If you use soapsuds, soften the first rinsing water with a tablespoon of ammonia to get rid of the soap.

3 Put the pillow through a short spin in a spin dryer if you have one; otherwise lay it out on a flat surface. Turn the pillow over several times until completely dry; this could take a few days.

Sheets

◆Sheets require frequent laundering (at least weekly). Dark sheets may show stains from body or hair oil after only one use. Frequent laundering reduces the likelihood of permanent staining.

◆Wash sheets in hot water with heavy-duty detergent and use bleach to sanitize. For dark colors, use all-fabric bleach and expect some fading.

◆Tumble-drying sheets at hot temperature and prompt unloading and folding will prevent sheets from wrinkling even if they are not permanent-press blends of polyester and cotton.

Towels

◆Wash frequently, using a hot cycle. If they

STARCHING

Cotton, rayon, and linen may be given stiffness and body with starch.

◆You can starch clothes in a basin in the sink after washing them in a machine. Then put them back in the machine and spin them to remove excess water. Rinse the machine afterward to get rid of starch deposits.

◆Spray starches are expensive but convenient and are good for collars and cuffs, and for freshening up garments between washes.

---

develop a sour odor, this may be due to incomplete soil removal and slow drying. Rewash in very hot water and all-fabric bleach.

Tablecloths

◆Inspect tablecloths before washing to identify food and wine stains. Pretreat stains according to type (see pages 142 and 143).

◆Store linens without starch to prevent attack by silverfish.

DRYING CLOTHES

Care labels usually indicate whether a fabric is suitable for tumble-drying, drip-drying, line-drying, or drying flat.

◆Most fabrics can be dried in a tumble dryer with variable heat, except for woolens, some knitted fabrics, delicate fabrics, and rubber.

◆If you wish to dry clothes outdoors, make sure the air is pollution-free. Don't dry wool or silk in direct sunlight, because it weakens the fabric and may turn it yellow.

◆Drip-dry lightweight acrylics, nylon, and pleated garments. Hang them on hangers, if possible.

◆Roll delicate fabrics, such as silks, chiffon, and crepe in a towel, or sandwich them between two towels to absorb excess moisture. Then hang them on a hanger indoors to dry.

IRONING

BUY DRIP-DRY or easy-to-care-for polyester cotton clothes and wash them correctly in order to minimize the amount of ironing you have to do.

Most fabrics are easier to iron if they are damp: Either tumble-dry them to the right dampness or spray them and roll them in a towel for an hour or two, or steam press them. Watch your iron temperature carefully. With too much heat, you can permanently damage synthetics and blends. If you don't have time to do all the ironing at one time, put the remaining damp clothes in a plastic bag and keep them in the freezer until you can finish them.

TYPES OF IRONS

The basic iron today is an iron with both steam and dry heat settings. Fancier models have a spray feature for spot dampening. All electric irons have heat settings marked either with the names of the fabrics they are suitable for, or with the dots corresponding to the care label code, or (as in older irons) numbered heat settings: 1 = cool, 2 = warm, 3 = hot, and 4 = very hot.

◆ **Dry heat settings.** These can be set to the heat required for the fabric you are ironing but cannot dampen it as you iron.

◆ **Steam settings.** Water in the chamber is turned to steam and automatically dampens the clothes as you iron.

◆ **Steam-spray settings.** These can shoot out a jet of steam when you operate a thumb control, which is good for quick dampening and for certain fabrics, such as linen, which crease heavily.

Choosing an iron

◆ Make sure the iron has a label with the Underwriters Laboratories seal verifying it meets U.S. safety standards.

◆ A closed handle gives a better grip and better balance, but an open handle (with a gap in the front) makes it easier to iron folds and pockets.

◆ Irons vary in weight. Choose an iron that feels right for you, but note that a very light iron may not be as effective at smoothing out creases as a heavier one.

◆ Self-cleaning irons allow for uniform flow of steam, because vents do not clog.

◆ Choose an iron where the cord will be least in the way; one with the cord on top is better for left-handed people. Cordless irons can be easier to use.

◆ Look for an iron with an indicator light that comes on when the iron is heating and turns off when it reaches the chosen temperature.

◆ Look for irons with a flat heel rest. They don't tip over as easily.

◆ An iron with an automatic shutoff feature lessens the chance of leaving an iron on accidentally.

◆ Steam irons are easier to fill if there's a water-level gauge or if the water container is made of clear plastic.

◆ Choose a steam iron that can be filled with tap water; it will save you from having to buy distilled water.

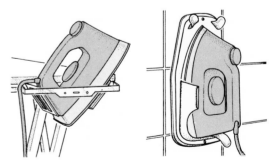

Storing the iron. *A heel rest stops the iron from tipping over when upright (above left). A wall bracket is invaluable for storing the iron when not in use (above right); you can put it inside a cabinet.*

IRONING BOARDS

Most ironing boards are adjustable in height. Find one you can set up and take down easily and one that does not weigh too much; some are cumbersome.

◆ They come in various widths: Choose one that suits the ironing you do.

◆ Make sure there is a secure heatproof plate to stand the iron on.

◆ Board covers that tie are available in cotton, or stain- and scorch-resistant material. They are often lined to retain the heat and make the ironing smoother.

◆ A cord holder is useful, attached to the board or to the iron, to keep the cord out of the way of the clothes.

◆ A sleeveboard, either loose or attachable, is handy for ironing sleeves and children's clothes.

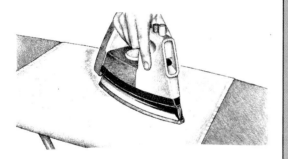

Cleaning the bottom plate. *While the iron is hot, rub it over a piece of coarse damp cloth held tight over the ironing board.*

MAINTAINING IRONS

◆ Rub scratches and stains gently with a piece of fine steel wool when the iron is cold.

◆ If your iron has a tendency to build up deposits, you can prevent this by using only distilled or filtered water in it.

◆ Clean irons with nonstick bottom plates with a cotton cloth or diaper dipped in warm water and detergent or baking soda. Never use an abrasive; it will scratch the bottom plate.

SAFETY TIPS

Wrapping the cord around the iron while it is hot may damage the cord.

◆ Always replace worn-out or frayed cords.

◆ Make sure you switch the iron off whenever you leave it unattended, even if it's just for a short time.

◆ Always switch off a steam iron to fill it; otherwise you could receive an electric shock.

◆ Always keep your iron out of the reach of children.

◆ If you're buying a new iron, look for one that automatically turns off when left unattended.

IRONING TECHNIQUES

◆Use a spray bottle and warm water to dampen clothes and make them easier to iron. After spraying, roll them up so the dampness becomes evenly distributed.

◆Let the iron stand for 5 minutes after you turn it on before you start ironing. The thermostat takes time to settle, and the initial temperature may be higher than you've set it at. Start with the items that require the lower iron setting first, then adjust the setting upward as you come to the sturdier fabrics, such as cotton and linen.

◆Always iron at the temperature given on the care label. When there is no label, iron clothes on the lowest setting.

2 Iron the sleeves, starting at the underarm seams. Run the point of the iron into the gathers at the cuff, and then work up toward the shoulder.

3 Iron the body, starting at the front panels and working around. Hang it up to air.

Ironing pants

This technique is for pants with a center crease down the legs. If you don't want creases, don't press right over the inner and outer edges of the legs.

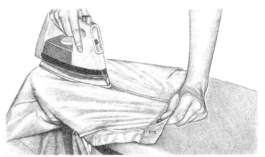

1 Iron the top of the pants first. Then lay the pants flat, legs on top of each other, with the side and inseams aligned.

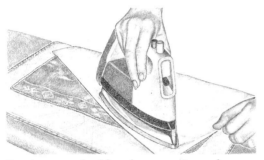

Ironing an embroidered pattern. *Lay a clean cloth on a folded blanket. Place the embroidery face-down on them. Put a thin dampened cloth on the back of the embroidery, and quickly apply a hot iron.*

Ironing a shirt

This technique also can be used for dresses. Always start at the top and work down.

1 Iron the collar wrong side up, and press from each point toward the center back. Then iron the cuffs.

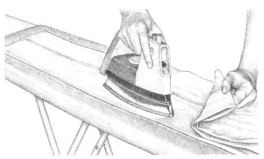

2 Fold back the top leg and iron the inside of the bottom leg. Turn the pants over and repeat on the other side. Then iron the outside of each leg, setting the creases with a damp cloth, if needed.

TIPS FOR IRONING

Use ironing when you want to remove wrinkles; use pressing when you're sewing.

◆ Pull flat articles (napkins, scarves) into shape before ironing to get them square.

◆ Steam the wrinkles from wool, or use a damp cloth and a light up-and-down motion instead of gliding.

◆ Iron dark fabrics, acetate, acrylic, crepe, flock fabric, cotton lace, linen, satin, silk, rayons, mat rayon, and wool garments inside out to prevent shiny patches from developing. Iron cotton (except for chintz), net, and silky rayon right side out while damp. Iron polyester and polyester-cotton mixtures either way.

PRESSING

Pressing involves an up-and-down motion with less pressure than ironing.

◆ For pressing, use a hot iron and a clean, damp, lint-free cloth.

◆ You can buy trouser presses, which press trousers overnight.

1 *Place the garment on the ironing board with the press cloth on top.*

2 *Press the iron down, then lift it, then press it again. Repeat all over the cloth.*

CARING FOR SPECIAL ITEMS

Take furs, velvet, suede, and other special fabrics in need of a thorough cleaning to a dry cleaner who is an expert at dealing with such garments. Unless leather clothes are stained, avoid dry cleaning because the beauty of leather is in the patina that develops over time; attempts to restore its original perfection can destroy the luster. Hang valuable coats and jackets on padded or wooden hangers to maintain their shape; cover them to keep the dust off but don't store them in sealed plastic bags.

DRY CLEANING

◆ Check the care label first, to make sure the garment can be dry-cleaned.

◆ Dry-clean any garments made of a fabric you are unsure about. Explain the cause of any stain on a garment and point out its location so that the cleaner will know how to deal with it.

◆ Dry-clean garments as soon as any grime shows around the collar and cuffs. The dirtier the garment, the more difficult it will be to get it really clean again.

◆ A professional dry cleaner may be able to remove stubborn spots and stains from washable garments.

◆ The best professional cleaners will repair damaged cuffs, collars, and pockets at the same time they clean.

◆ Always remove buckles and metal trimmings on clothes, because they can be discolored by the dry-cleaning chemicals. Some cleaners may do this for you.

LEATHER AND SUEDE

◆ Wear a scarf when possible with leather or suede garments to prevent perspiration and body oil stains.

◆ If a leather or suede piece gets wet, let it air-dry. Keep it away from heat.

◆ Store leather or suede garments in a cool, ventilated place. If a closet is too dry and hot, it will dry the leather or suede out; if it's hot and wet, mildew may form.

◆ If a leather garment is creased, hang it in the bathroom and turn the shower on hot so the room becomes steamy; otherwise press it with an iron at a low setting, placing heavy paper between the iron and the leather.

◆ Brush the surface of suede regularly with a terry-cloth towel or a suede brush to keep it clean and raise the nap.

◆ To treat rain or water spots, let the garment dry thoroughly, then rub it with a towel or brush. You can remove minor stains with a pencil eraser or very fine sandpaper.

◆ If your leather or suede piece has a major stain, take it to a professional who specializes in cleaning leather and suede. Don't try to clean it at home.

Brushing suede. *Suede should be brushed with a soft rubber or bristle brush, or a suede brush. Do not brush too hard, and do it in a gentle circular motion, eventually covering the entire surface.*

Reviving flattened suede. *Hold the article over a bowl of boiling water (above left), let the steam get into the nap, then brush it up with a soft bristle brush (above right).*

Leather gloves

If your gloves have label directions for cleaning, follow those. Otherwise, you can try this technique:

Washing leather gloves.

1 Squeeze water gently through the gloves, rinse with cool water, and press water out.

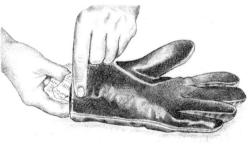

2 Dry at room temperature flat on a towel or stuffed with white paper towels.

3 When the gloves are almost dry, rub a bit of leather conditioner into their surfaces to restore pliability.

Boots, shoes, and bags

◆ Fill leather shoes, boots, and bags loosely with tissue or cotton socks when wet to keep their shape. Allow them to dry naturally, in a warm place but away from direct heat.

◆ To remove white stains and spotting, wipe off loose dirt and mud with a damp cloth; then dab the stained areas with a mixture of equal parts water and cider vinegar. When the items are dry, condition and polish them.

POLISHING BOOTS AND SHOES

Polish leather boots and shoes regularly with shoe cream or paste wax, matching the color carefully.

◆ First wipe the shoes, then apply cream or paste with a clean cloth or applicator, rubbing gently in a circular motion. Finish by buffing to a gloss, using a separate brush for different colors. With paste wax, buff with a towel or soft cloth.

◆ For a high-gloss shine, apply a second coat of paste wax on a piece of water-soaked cotton, let footwear dry, then buff again.

◆ Clean patent leather using a spray-on glass cleaner or a damp cloth and detergent. Buff with a soft cloth.

◆ Always use shoe trees in shoes, or rolled-up newspapers or magazines (covered in muslin or an athletic sock to prevent ink stains) in boots, to keep the shape of footwear while you are not wearing it.

◆ To cover scuff marks, use acrylic paint, indelible felt marker, or crayon in a matching color.

◆ Clean leather handles, which get dirtier quicker than the rest of the bag, with saddle soap, and then rub with leather conditioner. Buff the leather well.

◆ Dry-clean the lining of leather bags with cornstarch powder. Brush or vacuum it out well. Or, rub the lining with a damp cloth soaked in soapy water and then clean water. Allow to dry away from direct heat.

Washing imitation leather.

◆ Wipe with a damp cloth. Treat any marks with a paste of chalk and a few drops of water spread over the stain. Leave until dry, and then brush off.

CARING FOR SPECIFIC LEATHERS

◆ Most smooth leather can be spot-cleaned with mild soap and water.

◆ **Suede.** Brush suede with a rubber suede brush after each wearing.

◆ **Buckskin.** Remove dust by brushing with a bristle brush. Rub off difficult marks with fine sandpaper or use a commercial buckskin cleaner.

◆ **Alligator.** Buff frequently with a soft cloth after wearing. You will only occasionally need a shoe cream.

◆ **Pigskin.** Brush gently with a soft brush.

◆ Dry-clean leather clothing only when necessary. Be sure to take the clothing to a dry cleaner that specializes in leather.

Removing stubborn marks from buckskin. *Rub the skin gently in a circular motion with a piece of very fine sandpaper.*

FURS

◆ Get good furs professionally cleaned once every year to keep them in good condition.

◆ Shake a wet fur well and then hang it up to dry on a wooden hanger, in a well-ventilated place. Do not dry wet fur near direct heat, because it will become stiff.

◆ Some fake furs, such as are found in children's outerwear, are machine-washable and can be air- or tumble-dried.

◆ Many fake furs in adult garments must be dry-cleaned because of the leather or vinyl facings, linings, and inner construction.

◆ Some imitation leather and fur-trimmed garments lined with acetate cannot be successfully dry-cleaned or washed and must be thrown away if stained.

DYEING FABRICS

WASH ARTICLES BEFORE dyeing them to remove any starches or other treatments, and remove stains (see pages 142 and 143), so the fabric will take color evenly; you may even need to remove the color before you start if the article is blotchy. Bleach and fade marks cannot be taken out by dyeing, nor can scorch marks. Patterns will not be obliterated by dyeing, though they may be less obvious. A two-tone effect will be produced as colors are combined (see page 134).

A word or two of warning: Don't dye wool in a washing machine unless the garment is machine-washable—it will shrink; and polyester fabrics are difficult to dye. Polyester/cotton mixtures, however, can be dyed—the more cotton there is, the stronger the effect you will get.

DYES AND HOW TO USE THEM

Certain dyes work better on certain fibers; check the manufacturer's instructions carefully. Animal and vegetable fibers—cotton, wool, linen, silk, and rayon—absorb dye better than synthetics such as polyester, nylon, or permanent-press blended fabrics.
◆ Before dyeing any fabric, test a swatch to see if the dye will absorb well and produce the desired color.
◆ For the best penetration and colorfastness, most dyes are applied with hot water. Special cold-water dyes for use in batik and for dyeing wool without shrinking will take only on animal or vegetable fibers (see left).
◆ You can dye light colors with dark dyes, but you cannot dye light colors over dark fabric.

REMOVING COLOR

If the base color on a garment is blotchy, remove it before dyeing or it will not take the color evenly.
◆ Garments can be washed in color remover by hand or machine.
◆ Follow label directions of commercial color removers. They may not be effective on synthetic fibers that were solution-dyed.
▼▼ Ventilate the room when using color
◆ ◆ removers because the fumes are not pleasant.

TESTING FABRIC BEFORE DYEING

◆ Pull out a few threads, hold them with tweezers over a sink, and singe the ends with a lighted candle or match:
◇ If the threads burn only in contact with the flame and smell like burning hair, the fiber is wool or silk.
◇ If they burn then glow, the fiber is cotton, linen, or rayon.
◇ If they do not burn but melt and drip or form a ball, the fiber is synthetic.

Hot-water powder dyes

Hot-water dyeing can be done in the sink, on the stove, or in a washing machine.

◆Although directions will vary with the brand of dye, a general rule of thumb is use 1 package of powdered dye for each dry pound of fabric (about 3 yards) in 3 gallons of water.

Preparing hot-water powder dye. *Dissolve the dye in a bowl of hot water (1 package per pint), and stir well.*

For hand-dyeing in the sink or on the stove.

1 Prepare the dye mixture according to package directions.

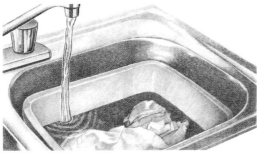

2 Wear rubber gloves to prevent dye from staining your hands. Immerse the wet, washed fabric unfolded into the dyebath and continue according to package directions.

3 Keep the dyebath hot while the color is developing (about 20 to 30 minutes) by adding extra hot water or simmering. Stir the fabric continuously with a wooden or stainless steel spoon until it is a shade darker than desired. (Keep in mind that a dyed article will always look darker when wet.) If dyeing in a pan on the stove, heat to simmering and stir constantly back and forth, up and down (not around and around) for 30 to 60 minutes. This is the best method for obtaining dark colors and deeper shades of other colors. (If the shade obtained is not dark enough, remove the article, add more dye, reimmerse the article, and repeat the dyeing process.)

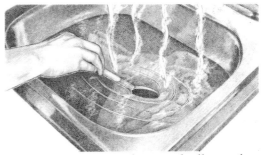

4 Rinse in warm, then gradually cooler, water until clear. Squeeze to remove excess water (never wring or twist), then place in the dryer or line-dry away from direct sunlight.

5 Always clean the sink or pan immediately after dyeing, with chlorine bleach or cleanser to prevent permanent stains from forming. If necessary, fill the sink with cold water, adding a capful of chlorine bleach.

Dyeing in the washing machine.

1 Fill washer with hottest water and add dissolved dye solution. Agitate briefly to mix. Place wet, unfolded fabric in the dye bath; set washer for longest wash cycle. Rinse and dry as above. For darker colors, reset to repeat wash cycle before washer empties.

2 Clean washer immediately with hot water, detergent, and $\frac{1}{2}$ to 1 cup chlorine bleach, using complete wash cycle. Clean lint trap and wipe spilled dye with a solution of bleach and nonabrasive cleanser. Plastic or rubber machine parts may be tinted, but the color will not come off on other washloads.

Liquid hot-water dyes

The procedure is the same as for powder dyes (see above), except that the amounts used will be different. Be sure to follow manufacturer's directions.

COLOR COMBINATIONS

A dye of one color applied to a fabric of another color will produce a different and often unexpected shade. For cotton:

◇ *Red and yellow will make orange or red.*

◇ *Blue and yellow will make green.*

◇ *Yellow and pink will make coral.*

◇ *Green and yellow will make lime.*

◇ *Light brown and red will make rust.*

◇ *Red and blue will make purple.*

◇ *Pale blue and pink will make lilac.*

◇ *Dark brown and light red will make a dark red-brown color.*

◆ Other fibers may produce different hues and shades, so be sure to test them.

SPECIAL PROBLEMS

If you plan to dye two matching pieces the same color, be sure you do it in one batch. It is very difficult to match colors from batch to batch because the amount of dye, weight of fabric, and the water temperature will vary.

Woolens

◆ To minimize shrinkage and prevent matting of wool in hot water dyes, use the stove method. Put the wool in lukewarm water first, slowly heat to a simmer, then transfer to the simmering dyebath. Move the wool gently in the liquid, pushing it up and down rather than stirring it. Finish by rinsing in very hot water; gradually make subsequent rinse water cooler until the water runs clear.

Lace

◆ If you want to dye lace to an ecru color, use cold tea instead of dye. In varying amounts, this will give a permanent color ranging from beige to old ivory, depending on how long you leave the lace in.

Feathers

Feathers are fragile and have to be treated very carefully if they are to last.

Dyeing feathers.

1 Hand-wash feathers gently in warm water, and then rinse in cold water.

2 Immerse the feathers in the dyebath while still soaking wet.

3 Raise the temperature of the dye by adding boiling water and maintain a constant temperature for 10 minutes exactly, moving the feathers gently but constantly.

4 Rinse the feathers until the water runs clear, and then leave to dry.

Leather and shoes

◆ Leather coats, suede, and so on should always be dyed by professionals.

◆ Satin shoes should be dyed with multi-purpose dye.

Dyeing canvas shoes. *Wash the shoes in hot water and detergent. Stuff them with newspaper and allow them to dry in a warm place out of direct heat. Then dye with an appropriate dye.*

GUIDE TO DYEING FABRICS

◆ Always test the dye on a hidden part of the fabric to see if it will take the dye and to check that the color is what you were expecting it to be.

SUITABLE FABRICS FOR DYEING

ACETATE
Good results with hot-water dyes only.

COTTON
Good results on all untreated cotton fabrics with all dyes.

LEATHER
Good results with a brush-on leather dye.

LINEN
Good results with all dyes.

NYLON/POLYESTER
Very good results with hot-water dyes.

POLYESTER/COTTON MIXTURE
Pale shades only with all dyes.

RAYON
Good results with all dyes.

SILK
Good results with hot-water dyes.

SUEDE
Good results with a brush-on suede dye.

TRIACETATE
Reduced shades with hot-water dyes. (Special instructions may be included.)

WOOL
Good results with all dyes. Don't rub wool.

UNSUITABLE FABRICS FOR DYEING

◇ **ACRYLIC**
◇ **FIBERGLASS**
◇ **"FINISHED" fabrics** (e.g. drip-dry and rain-repellent finishes) and permanent press

◇ **MODACRYLIC**
◇ **NATURAL SPECIALTY WOOLS** (e.g. angora, camel hair, cashmere, and mohair)

◇ **NYLON**
◇ **POLYESTER** (100 percent)
◇ **POLYESTER-WOOL MIXTURES**

STORING CLOTHES AND LINEN

FABRIC NEEDS room to "breathe," so it should never be so tightly packed that it becomes creased. Always clean clothing and linen before storing.

Cover hanging garments that are to be put away for any length of time or that are seldom used with a muslin or ventilated plastic bag to keep dust from collecting on the fabric. Keep linen in a cool place on slatted shelves so that air can circulate around it. Put hats in boxes, stuffed with tissue if necessary; never leave them lying on a flat surface—it may damage the brim.

CLOTHING

◆ Hang clothes in groups in the closet so that often-used and outdoor clothes do not rub against your seldom-used or more delicate dresses and suits.

◆ To make the best of space, create two tiers by putting up a closet rod above or below the main one. Hang shirts and blouses on the upper one, pants or skirts on the lower one.
◆ Cover long-sleeved garments with short plastic covers so the sleeves are not pulled in and creased.

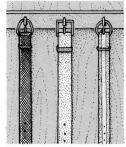

Hanging ties. *Hang them over an expanded curtain rod attached to the inside of the closet door.*

Hanging belts. *Hang them by their buckles from hooks on the inside of the closet door or in the closet itself.*

◆ Hang only knitted clothes or sweaters that are stable, such as double knits, to avoid stretching them out of shape. Fold knits carefully and store them in a drawer or on a shelf where they won't be too crushed.

Coat hangers

◆ Keep a good supply of sturdy coat hangers. Thin wire hangers are not good for clothes as a permanent arrangement. Ideally, hangers should be padded so they don't pull the clothes out of shape.

Ideal hangers. *Make sure the hanger fits the garment exactly. It should span the width of the shoulders, and the back should support the neck of the garment.*

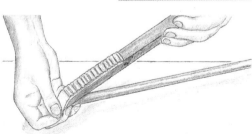

Keeping garments on hangers. *Stick strips of rubber at each end of a hanger to help prevent a garment from slipping off.*

DRAWERS AND SHELVES

◆ Divide shelves up into areas for sweaters, scarves, socks, underwear, or table and bed linen. This will keep them neatly arranged and make it easier to find things when you need them.

▼▼ Don't keep anything in plastic bags if
• • you have young children; the bags can cause suffocation.

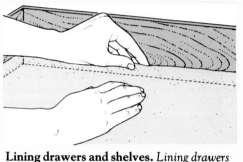

Lining drawers and shelves. *Lining drawers and shelves can help keep them clean. There are several types of lining products available. To line drawers, cut the lining 2 inches larger than the drawer on all sides and turn it up.*

◆ Use wooden hangers to hold weighty clothes such as suits, coats, and furs; they provide more support.
◆ Avoid hanging clothes from a loop at the back of the neck. The shoulders and the neck of the garment should be well supported.
◆ Make sure you hang garments centered on the hangers. If you don't, your clothes will look lopsided the next time you wear them.

Knitwear and shirts

◆ Store light-colored sweaters in plastic bags to prevent them from gathering dust.
◆ Don't squash sweaters into a drawer because you will damage the fibers, which may result in permanent creases.
◆ Store shirts on hangers, if possible; otherwise fold them and store them in drawers or on shelves.

FOLDING CLOTHES

FOLDING KNITWEAR

1 Lay the sweater facedown. Fold one side and arm to the middle. Fold the arm back down on itself. Do the same with the other side.

2 Fold the sweater in two, taking the bottom up to the top with the sleeves inside the fold.

FOLDING A SHIRT

1 Button the shirt to the top to prevent it from creasing and to stop the collar from becoming distorted.

2 Lay the shirt facedown. Turn both sides into the middle, with the sleeves lying flat down the back in line with the collar band.

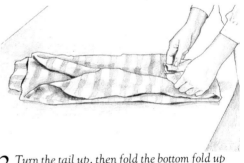

3 Turn the tail up, then fold the bottom fold up to the collar.

Pants and suits

◆ Fold pants along the crease and store on hangers. Tape a piece of folded cardboard or foam rubber to the hanger to prevent a crease mark from developing across the middle of the legs.

Dresses and skirts

◆ To hang long dresses, use skirt hangers with spring clips to hold skirts at the waistband.

Keeping pleats in. *Cut the foot off a stocking or half a pair of tights and draw pleated skirts and dresses through it. Store flat.*

Boots and shoes

◆ Build or buy a rack where shoes and boots can be stored neatly and where they will not rub together and mark each other. A shoe rack can be attached to the inside of the closet door or on a rail at the back of the closet, but make sure the shoes don't rub against the clothes.

◆ Buy a pair of shoe trees for each set of shoes, and put rolled-up magazines covered with clean cotton socks in boots, to make them last longer.

Hanging all-weather boots. *Punch a hole in the top of the rubber of each boot and put a piece of string through. Hang from a nail or hook.*

LONG-TERM STORAGE FOR CLOTHES

Always wash or dry-clean clothes before you put them away for the summer or winter.

◆ Fasten all buttons and hooks.
◆ Put tissue paper between the layers.
◆ Don't starch summer dresses before putting them away because creases will set.
◆ Don't pack clothes too tightly.

PRECIOUS LACE

◆ Completely cover garments, veils, and tablecloths made of valuable lace.
◆ Wrap antique laces in fully rinsed bleached muslin or acid-free tissue (available from museum supply stores).
‼ Don't store nylon lace in sunlight.

BED AND TABLE LINENS

◆ Place clean linen at the bottom of the pile so you use it in rotation. This will make everything last longer.
◆ Store comforters in large plastic bags on the top shelves of the closet or in drawers under the bed so that they don't become squashed.
◆ Don't starch the linens before storing. Starch attracts silverfish.

Leather and suede

◆ Shake the leather well before putting it away so creases don't set and so it maintains its shape.
◆ Rub leather shoes, boots, and bags with leather conditioner before storing them.
◆ Hang leather and suede garments in a hanging "wardrobe" made from heavy plastic to keep them clean.

Fur

◆ Shake fur gently outdoors before you put it away.
◆ Store in a well-ventilated place (the coldest you can find), or keep it in a sealed container. If stored clean, and storage space is not already infested, there is little likelihood of moths.
◆ Better still, have the fur professionally cleaned at the end of the winter and store it with a furrier.

MOTHPROOFING

All man-made fibers are mothproof, but when blended with natural fiber, the fabric is still susceptible to damage by moths and needs to be protected when it is put into storage.

◆ Pack clothes in airtight chests, or boxes or hampers with plastic linings, or hang them in mothproof bags.

◆ Sprinkle moth repellent between the layers of material.

◆ To repair damaged items, wash or dry-clean them. Then hang them on a clothes-line in bright sunlight and spray them with an insecticide labeled for fabric insect problems. Finally, place them in tight garment bags or in chests. Add naphthalene or paradichlorobenzene flakes to bags or chests. Use 2 ounces for every cubic foot of space.

PACKING CLOTHES

◆ When packing clothes to travel, make a list of the clothes and accessories so you don't leave something essential behind.

◆ If you are packing for children as well as yourself, make separate lists for them.

◆ Get together everything you want to pack and lay it out on a bed so you can see what you've got; you may find that you need only half of it.

◆ Fasten all the hooks and buttons before folding and pack everything facedown; it is less likely to crease. Put tissue paper between the folds to prevent knife-edge creases.

◆ Use a sturdy suitcase and never squeeze too much in; otherwise clothes are likely to be flattened.

Packing a suitcase.

1 First pack heavy things, such as shoes and books. Pad out the spaces with rolled-up socks, gloves, underwear, etc.

2 Heavy garments and suits go in next. Fold each garment to the size of the case and keep each layer as flat as possible.

3 Pack underwear and woolens. Lay breakable items on this layer.

4 Pack dresses or slacks next.

5 The top layer should be shirts or blouses. Make sure everything is packed tightly so it will not move around.

◆ Clothes for overnight or a weekend don't need this elaborate packing, but the same principles apply: Place heavy things at the bottom, pad out the shapes, and lay light things on the top.

STAIN REMOVAL

REMOVE SPILLS on fabric immediately, because once anything has soaked into the fabric, it is much harder to get out. Absorb or scrape up as much as possible—be very careful not to work more of it into the fabric.

Apply a stain remover as a secondary treatment only if the spill leaves a mark. If the stain is not greasy and the garment is washable, put the item immediately into cold water. Don't use hot water because it fixes the stain.

A stain will come out more easily if you work from the back, instead of pushing the mark further into the fabric by working from the front. Work in a circle around the mark, then in toward the middle to prevent a permanent "ring" from developing around it.

EMERGENCY ACTION FOR SPILLS

◆ **For solid matter.** Scrape off the substance as soon as you can, using the back of a blunt knife or spatula.

◆ **For grease marks.** Apply liquid detergent to the stain and rub it in, then wash at a high temperature. For unwashable fabrics, apply dry-cleaning solvent.

Removing liquids.
Working from the back of the fabric, dab liquids with paper towels or a clean cloth. Then soak the fabric in cold water, if possible. Do not soak dyed silk, moiré fabrics, or wool.

◆ **For liquids on unwashable fabrics.** Use talcum powder to absorb liquid. Treat residual stain.

STAIN REMOVAL KIT

Have a stain removal kit ready on hand for emergencies and keep it next to your carpet stain removal kit (see page 81). You will need the following things:

◇ *A clothes brush.*

◇ *Fine sandpaper for cleaning suede.*

◇ *Baking soda and other stain removal products.*

◇ *A collection of small sponges.*

◇ *Some white absorbent cotton material and paper towels to place behind a stain while removing it and to absorb any surface liquid.*

◇ *Some cotton balls for applying solvents, detergent, etc.*

◇ *A medicine dropper or syringe for controlled application of powerful solvents. Don't store solvents in them. Rinse thoroughly after use.*

◇ *A plastic spray bottle to squirt water onto a stain.*

▼▼ Keep all household chemicals in
◆ ◆ their original labeled containers. Post a poison control center number near your household chemical storage area. Do not store chemicals where children can reach them.

BLEACHES

Bleaches remove stains and heavy dirt from clothing and help sanitize clothes. Keep in mind, though, that the more you bleach, the faster your clothes will wear out.

Testing for colorfastness

◆ Before you bleach, be sure your colored clothing can be safely washed with bleach. Here's a simple test. Mix 1 tablespoon of liquid chlorine bleach with $\frac{1}{4}$ cup water. Place a drop of this mixture on a hidden seam edge. Let stand for 1 or 2 minutes, then blot dry. If the color of the fabric stays the same, it is probably safe for chlorine and oxygen bleaches.

Liquid chlorine bleaches

◆ Do not use for silk, wool, spandex, polyurethane foam, or rubber items.
◆ Too strong a solution may harm cotton, linen, and rayon. Be sure to follow manufacturer's directions.
◆ Colored items that are nylon, polyester or acrylic may fade. Check label directions.
◆ For best results, add diluted bleach 4 to 6 minutes before the end of the wash cycle. Don't pour full-strength bleach directly onto clothes. Or, use your machine's automatic dispenser, if it has one.
▼▼ Do not mix liquid chlorine bleach with
◆◆ ammonia, toilet-bowl cleaners, or rust removers. If mixed, these chemicals will release toxic fumes.

Other bleaches

◆ Liquid oxygen bleaches are milder and safer to use than liquid chlorine bleaches and work best in warm water. These are commonly sold as all-fabric bleaches.
◆ Dry-powder oxygen bleaches are the dry form of all-fabric bleach. Like their liquid counterparts, they are milder and safer than liquid chlorine bleach. Some brands contain stain-removing enzymes.

USING SOLVENTS

This is a secondary treatment for residual grease or oil stains. Solvents are used by professional dry cleaners. They can be bought as spot removers under various brand names, in liquid, aerosol, or paste form.
◆ You can use paint thinner, acetone, household ammonia (use with caution), or borax. Useful and safer substitutes for commercial products are: undiluted white vinegar, lemon juice, and petroleum jelly.

Removing the stain.

1 Place a clean paper towel under the stain to absorb extra moisture and the solvent.

2 Soak a clean cloth in the solvent and dab the stain, working in a circle outside the stain and moving into the center.
3 Rinse thoroughly and wash, if the fabric is washable. If you can't wash the garment, allow to air-dry in a well-ventilated area.

TREATING SPECIFIC STAINS

◆ Always work with small quantities of solvents, bleaches, or commercial stain removers.

◆ Always work near an open window and far from an open flame.

◆ Always test fabrics for colorfastness and strength before applying stain remover, and never use acetone on acetate fibers; it will dissolve the fabric.

◆ Let the fabric dry after applying one solvent, and rinse the fabric before applying another. Never mix solvents.

COSMETIC STAINS

DEODORANTS
Apply heavy-duty liquid detergent directly on stain; wash in detergent and warm water. A buildup of aluminum or zinc salts may be permanent.

HAIR SPRAY
Rub stain with heavy-duty liquid detergent. Then wash, using detergent and all-fabric bleach. If fabric is colorfast, wash tough stains in chlorine bleach.

LIPSTICK
Treat with dry-cleaning solvent then wash in heavy-duty liquid detergent. Rewash using detergent and all-fabric bleach. If fabric is colorfast, wash tough stains in chlorine bleach.

MAKE-UP
Rub stain with heavy-duty liquid detergent. Then wash, using detergent and all-fabric bleach. If fabric is colorfast, wash tough stains in chlorine bleach.

NAIL POLISH
Do not use nail polish remover because it dissolves some fabrics. Have item professionally dry-cleaned.

PERFUME
Do not use soap. Wash in detergent.

BIOLOGICAL STAINS

BLOOD
Wash right away in cold water. Don't use warm water.
◆ Hardened blood should be brushed off and the fabric soaked in cold water with heavy-duty detergent.

FECES
Absorb matter or scrape it off. Soak item in cold water. Then wash as usual.

URINE
Soak stain in cold water. Wash as usual. For stains on mattresses, sponge area with a mixture of water and detergent. Rinse with a mixture of vinegar and water. Let air-dry. If odor remains, sprinkle with baking soda. Let stand 24 hours. Vacuum residue.

VOMIT
Absorb or scrape off. Soak stain in cold water. Wash as usual.

FOOD AND DRINK STAINS

ALCOHOLIC BEVERAGES
Do not use soap. Wash with detergent.

BEER
Do not use soap. Wash in detergent in water as hot as is safe for fabric.

BUTTER
Pretreat stain with heavy-duty liquid detergent. Then wash fabric in water as hot as is safe for fabric.

CATSUP
Rub stain with heavy-duty liquid detergent before washing. Wash, using detergent and all-fabric bleach. If fabric is colorfast, wash tough stains in chlorine bleach.

CHEWING GUM

Put the article in the freezer, or dab the gum with ice cubes to freeze it, and then break it off. Spray stain with pretreatment product. Rub with liquid detergent. Rinse with hot water. Repeat if necessary. Wash with detergent.

CHOCOLATE

Scrape it off, rinse stain with cold water, and rub with heavy-duty liquid detergent. Wash with detergent and all-fabric bleach. If fabric is colorfast, wash tough stains with chlorine bleach.

COFFEE

Do not use soap. Wash with detergent.

COOKING FATS AND OILS

Wash in heavy-duty detergent and hot water. For difficult stains, use a pretreatment product on the stain before washing.

CREAM

Rinse in cold water and wash with detergent.

EGG

Soak stain in cold water and then wash with detergent.

FRUIT AND FRUIT JUICES

Do not use soap. Wash with detergent.

GRAVY

Rub stain with heavy-duty liquid detergent. Wash with detergent and all-fabric bleach. If fabric is colorfast, wash tough stains with chlorine bleach.

ICE CREAM

Soak in cold water. Wash with detergent.

JAM

Soak in cold water. Wash with detergent.

MAYONNAISE OR SALAD DRESSING

Scrape off excess with a dull knife. Wash in heavy-duty detergent using water as hot as is safe for fabric.

MEAT JUICE

Soak in cold water. Wash with detergent.

MILK

Soak in cold water. Wash with heavy-duty detergent.

MUSTARD

Wash with detergent and bleach as safe for fabric.

SOFT DRINKS

Wash with detergent; do not use soap.

TEA

Do not use soap. Wash with detergent.

VEGETABLE OIL

Treat stain with a petroleum-base solvent pretreatment spray. Wash with heavy-duty detergent in hot water.

WINE

Soak in cold water. Wash with detergent. Do not use soap.

"STAIN REMOVERS" TO AVOID

DISHWASHER DETERGENT

These products are designed for use in very hot water. They can irritate skin if used on clothing.

HAIR SPRAY

Although some sprays work on ballpoint ink stains, they often leave a gummy residue and perfume, which must be removed. It also can affect the color of some fabrics.

MILK

This is sometimes suggested to remove ink stains, but it doesn't remove the stain and may leave a protein stain.

WHITE VINEGAR

This may weaken cotton, rayon, acetate, triacetate, or silk fabrics. It also may cause color changes.

TREATING SPECIFIC STAINS

BALLPOINT PEN
Spray or dab with dry-cleaning solvent. Then rub with heavy-duty liquid detergent. Wash with detergent and all-fabric bleach.
◆ On suede, rub marks with fine sandpaper.

CANDLE WAX
Freeze the wax by applying ice cubes or by putting the item in the freezer; then break off the frozen pieces. Treat the residual stain with dry-cleaning solvent, then rub with heavy-duty liquid detergent. Wash with detergent and all-fabric bleach.

CRAYON
Spray or dab with dry-cleaning solvent. Then rub with heavy-duty liquid detergent. Wash with detergent and all-fabric bleach.

CRUDE OIL OR TAR
Treat with a petroleum-base solvent pretreatment spray. Then wash with heavy-duty detergent and hot water.

DYES
Cleaning marks caused by dyes is difficult. Rinse with cold water and treat with liquid detergent. If the stain persists, soak in a diluted solution of powdered all-fabric bleach. Then wash in detergent and bleach as safe for fabric.

ENGINE OIL
Treat with a petroleum-base solvent pretreatment spray. Then wash in heavy-duty detergent and hot water.

FELT-TIP PEN
Pretreat with heavy-duty liquid detergent then rinse well. If stain persists, soak in a diluted solution of all-fabric bleach. Then wash in detergent and bleach as safe for fabric.

FURNITURE POLISH
Treat with dry-cleaning solvent, then rub with heavy-duty liquid detergent. Wash as usual.

GRASS STAINS
Pretreat with heavy-duty liquid detergent, then rinse well. If stain persists, soak in a diluted solution of powdered all-fabric bleach. Wash with detergent and bleach as safe for fabric.

GREASE
Treat with a petroleum-base solvent pretreatment spray. Then wash with heavy-duty detergent in hot water.

INK (PERMANENT)
Pretreat with heavy-duty liquid detergent, then rinse well. If stain persists, soak in a diluted solution of powdered all-fabric bleach. Wash in detergent and bleach as safe for fabric.

INK (WASHABLE)
Wash stain with detergent; do not use bleach.

IODINE
Treat with sodium thiosulfate (available in photo supply stores as "acid fixer"). If solution contains other chemicals in addition to sodium thiosulfate, do not use. Some commercial stain removers also remove iodine.

MILDEW
Brush item outdoors so mildew will not spread in the house. Pretreat with heavy-duty liquid detergent. Wash in hot water with heavy-duty detergent and bleach as safe for fabric.

MUD
Soak in cold water with detergent or enzyme presoak. Wash with detergent in warm water.

PAINT (LATEX)
For best results, treat while stain is still wet. Soak in cold water. Then wash in cool water with heavy-duty detergent. Dried paint is very difficult to remove. Treat as for permanent ink.

PAINT (OIL-BASE)
Treat while stain is wet for best results. Spot-treat stain with thinner recommended for paint. Treat until stain is softened. Wash in heavy-duty detergent. Turpentine and rubbing alcohol are common paint thinners.

RUST
Do not use chlorine bleach; it sets the stain. Treat with a commercial rust remover.

SCORCH MARKS
If a fabric is thick and fuzzy, brush to remove charring. Pretreat with heavy-duty liquid detergent. Wash with detergent. If stain persists, rewash with detergent and all-fabric bleach.

SHOE POLISH
Spray or dab with dry-cleaning solvent, then rub with heavy-duty liquid detergent. Wash with detergent.

Household Contents

STORAGE

EVERYTHING NEEDS TO be stored somewhere, whether you use it every day or only once a year, so never underestimate the amount of storage you need. Putting things away, however, does not have to mean hiding them; you can make a display of some of the more decorative items.

ASSESSING YOUR REQUIREMENTS

◆When planning your storage, try to imagine how your needs will change over the coming years, and plan accordingly. For instance, if you are expecting a baby, allow space for everything from diapers to bathing equipment and strollers.

◆Make a list of all your possessions, and arrange them in such categories as: books; records; audio and video tapes; "collections;" kitchen equipment; clothes; shoes; paintings; bed linen; papers; toys; jewelry; electronic equipment; and so on. Then, working logically room by room, assess the potential in your home for storage space. Now decide what sort of storage/display would suit each category of possessions; for example, a glass-fronted cabinet for china, open shelves or specially designed cabinets for books, bureau or desk for papers, and built-in or freestanding closets and chests of drawers for clothes.

◆Have closets or shelves built into a small space, or look for a freestanding closet or shelf unit to fit the space.

◆Make sure that storage is in a convenient place—books near where you will want to read or refer to them, any kitchen equipment where it can be taken out and used with ease, and clothes where you can reach them.

Storage for small rooms

◆Use open storage in a small room; closed storage can make a room look smaller.

◆Make a display of your belongings rather than cramming them into the closets.

◆Don't take shelves right up to the ceiling because this makes a room seem small.

FINDING EXTRA SPACE FOR STORAGE

Most homes contain wasted spaces that have a lot of potential; for example, the space under the stairs or in corners, and alcoves in hallways, basements, or attics can be used to store many items.

UNDER THE STAIRS

◆ If the space is tall enough, use it to house a wall-hung telephone with a message board and a small table or shelf unit for telephone books, pads, and pencils.

◆ Store the cleaning equipment under the stairs, but organize the space so everything hangs neatly on the wall, as it does in a well-ordered workshop.

◆ Put a small cabinet, plus a stool, in the space and use it for storing shoes and shoe-polishing equipment. You could arrange boot trees or hooks for boot storage.

◆ Box in the space and use it as a cleaning closet or as extra storage for basic tools, etc.

◆ If the space is large, install a shower and sink. Make sure you can provide adequate ventilation to prevent condensation.

LANDING

◆ Build shelves for books or records, for example. A large draftproof landing with shelves and an armchair can even make a good corner for reading or listening to music.

◆ Use the space to make a hobby corner with a bench and shelves for all the equipment or papers.

◆ Put a hanging closet in the space for storing out-of-season clothes or seldom-worn evening wear.

BASEMENTS AND ATTICS

◆ Use these spaces as playrooms, provided they are not damp. They're ideal places to keep a model railroad, as the carefully designed construction won't have to be dismantled at bedtime.

TYPES OF STORAGE UNITS

There are three basic types of storage systems to choose from: Built-in, modular, and freestanding.

Built-in cabinets can be made to the full height of the room, taking advantage of all the available space. Freestanding systems can be easily reinstalled in a different room or house. Modular units may be freestanding or fixed. Those attached to the wall are more solid and can support heavier weights than freestanding units.

Built-in units

◆ A built-in unit provides good insulation against cold and sound and maximizes wall, floor, and ceiling space.

◆ Built-in closets may be designed to take in the full height of the room, fit into fireplace alcoves, turn a corner, or span gaps between furniture and kitchen fixtures.

◆ Closets with sliding or folding doors help to increase the working or living space of a small area.

◆ Choose units with interiors that can pull or swivel out on a hinge, or pivot to maximize use of space. Trays, drawers, or bins come in handy and can be set behind a hinged or flap door.

◆ Always measure precisely before buying; a fraction of an inch too large or small can make a crucial difference.

Modular units

These are composed of cubes, shelves, drawers, and cabinets that can be adapted or enlarged to suit your needs.

◆ Arrange them alongside each other to

cover a whole wall, or stack them on top of each other to form a pyramid or staggered storage. You can conceal inner storage areas with sliding or louvered doors, fold-out desk tops, and so on.

◆Shelves and desk tops can be placed over separated modules.

◆Shelves and drawers can be specifically arranged to provide interior storage for stereo equipment, cassettes, games, and other items you want off the floor.

Freestanding units

◆Choose this type of storage if you move often or if you periodically rearrange the furniture and the layout of rooms.

◆Prefabricated units can be easily taken apart and reassembled or incorporated into a piece of furniture or kitchen storage unit.

◆Freestanding units are often used as room dividers, although tall units should be weighed down at the bottom to keep them from toppling over.

◆Drawer kits come with side and corner pieces, and in some cases molded inserts can be added to create extra compartments.

ORGANIZING THE INSIDE OF A CLOSET

To maximize space in a built-in closet, plan it to accommodate adjustable shelves or drawers, closet rods, pullout wire baskets, and shoe racks.

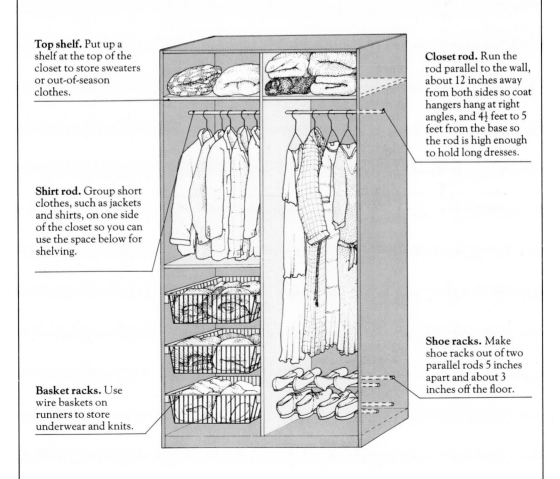

Top shelf. Put up a shelf at the top of the closet to store sweaters or out-of-season clothes.

Shirt rod. Group short clothes, such as jackets and shirts, on one side of the closet so you can use the space below for shelving.

Basket racks. Use wire baskets on runners to store underwear and knits.

Closet rod. Run the rod parallel to the wall, about 12 inches away from both sides so coat hangers hang at right angles, and $4\frac{1}{2}$ feet to 5 feet from the base so the rod is high enough to hold long dresses.

Shoe racks. Make shoe racks out of two parallel rods 5 inches apart and about 3 inches off the floor.

SHELVING

Well-placed shelving helps maximize the space in a home; it can be built into alcoves and corners or in the space created by the slope of an attic roof. Shelves can enhance the architectural features of a room while housing a multitude of books and assorted objects. Ideally, all shelving systems should be versatile so they can be moved to another room, extended, enlarged, or adjusted to hold different contents.

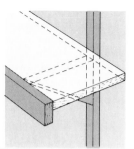

Making a shelf sturdier. *Attach a strip of hardwood along the front of a shelf to form a "lip" to make a thin shelf stronger. If the end of the shelf is visible, continue the strip around the end so the shelf looks neat.*

Shelving materials

There are three main types of shelving: permanent fixed shelving, adjustable shelving systems, and prefabricated shelving kits that can be assembled at home. The strongest and most expensive shelving is made from hardwood with the grain running in the direction of the shelf length. Softwood, particleboard, and plywood are not as solid as hardwood, but are the most commonly used materials for indoor shelving.

◇ **Particleboard.** Is readily available, reasonably priced, and supplied in standard widths, to be cut to the required length. Plastic-laminate-faced particle board wipes clean easily.

◇ **Softwood.** Is inexpensive, but prone to warping.

◇ **Plywood.** Can vary a lot in strength and cost, but can be stronger than solid wood, although it may not be as good-looking.

◇ **Glass shelves.** Can be used for ornamental, lightweight display; when built into a window they allow light to filter through,

providing a perfect spot for small plants and glass objects.

◇ **Metal office shelving.** Is the cheapest way to go; it can be spray-painted and provides the best support for heavy loads.

Shelving supports

A shelf collapses because it is unable to hold its load or because the supports are not securely mounted to the wall. Supports must be strong, spaced at reasonable intervals, and attached to a wall with screws long and thick enough to anchor them firmly. A variety of shelf supports is available for homemade shelving; some kinds are suitable for a flush wall, and others fit into an alcove.

◆ For strong, built-in shelving, use brackets, or wooden or metal supports that run along underneath the shelf to support its back edges and are secured to the wall.

◆ For adjustable shelving, use metal or wooden uprights with slots at intervals for shelf brackets so you can vary the distance between shelves.

◆ For lightweight, adjustable shelving, use pegs, dowels, plastic studs, clips, or wires that are inserted into holes in wooden uprights.

◆ Fixed supports also can be used to make a built-in shelf system, and adjustable supports are useful for a freestanding unit.

Plate supports. *If you want to display plates on a shelf, nail a thin strip of wood along the shelf near the back edge to prevent the plates from slipping.*

MAXIMUM DISTANCES BETWEEN SHELF SUPPORTS

The heavier the load, or the thinner the shelving material, the closer the brackets.

Material	Thickness of shelving	Distance between uprights
Hardwood	¾-inch	36 inches
	1-inch	42 inches
Softwood	¾-inch	24 inches
	1½-inch	48 inches
Plywood	¾-inch	30 inches
	1-inch	39 inches
Medium particle-board	¾-inch	27 inches
Laminated particle-board	⅝-inch	16 inches
	¾-inch	27 inches
	1-inch	36 inches
Glass	⅜-inch	27 inches

TYPES OF SHELVING

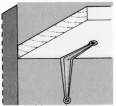

Metal brackets.
Angled metal brackets are the cheapest strong shelf brackets.

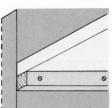

Wooden supports.
Use these as side supports for a permanent shelf and along the back of a long shelf.

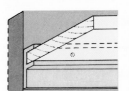

Metal clip shelf.
Use this angled metal strip to support the back edge of a shelf.

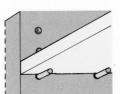

Wooden adjustable shelving. *Use for display shelving; you can't see the supports.*

MOUNTING SHELVES

◆ Draw a plan to scale on paper before you start putting up any shelves. Then mark the positions on the wall with a pencil. Make a note of light switches and electrical outlets, and be careful not to hammer or screw into any concealed wiring.

◆ Attach shelf supports to a load-bearing wall or studs in the wall, if the shelves are to support heavy items such as books.

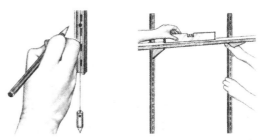

Putting up adjustable shelving. *Attach the top of the first upright loosely to the wall. Hang a plumb line (or use a weight on the end of a piece of string) from the top to align it vertically (above left) and mark the point for the bottom screw. Get someone to hold the second upright in position while you lay a shelf between the two and place a level on it (above right). Mark the screw positions.*

Partition, or hollow, walls

The load-bearing points of partition walls are the wooden uprights (called studs). They are usually 16 or 24 inches apart and are covered with drywall.

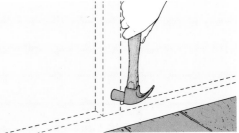

Finding the wall studs. *Tap along the wall lightly with a hammer and listen for a change in sound between the hollow board and the solid stud. Make your drill holes at the spot where you hear a dull sound.*

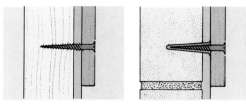

Securing the brackets or uprights. *Attach them with screws that are long enough to go through the wall into the stud to a depth of at least $\frac{5}{8}$ inch (above left), or into brick and plaster to the same depth (above right).*

◆ Partition, or hollow, walls are too thin to allow a screw to grip sufficiently. A variety of wall anchors (see below) are needed to hold the screw in place. These are inserted like a closed umbrella into a predrilled hole in the wall. Once inside the wall cavity, the anchors spread out to hold the fixture in position.

◆ Always attach the fixture securely to a stud (see above), so the shelves can carry a reasonable weight without pulling loose from the wall. For extra support, span two studs with a batten and add brackets between them.

◆ **For solid walls.** Make sure the wall isn't damp or crumbling before you start to mount shelves. To check, bore a hole with a bradawl or small masonry drill in an inconspicuous spot at the base of the wall. Screws will not grip on their own in solid brick or plaster walls, so in most cases you will have to use a wall anchor that matches the screw size (see below).

WALL ANCHORS

◆ Use anchors for board thicknesses of up to $\frac{3}{4}$ inch and toggles for board thicknesses of up to about $1\frac{1}{2}$ inches.

◇ **Solid-wall anchors.** These expand to grip the inside of brick or plaster walls when the screw reaches the end. Use lead anchors in masonry; use plastic ones in plaster or drywall.

◇ **Hollow-wall anchors.** These have metal shoulders that expand as you turn the bolt. They also are called Molly bolts.

◇ **Spring toggle.** This type has twin arms that spring apart inside the wall cavity.

IDEAS FOR STORAGE AROUND THE HOUSE

◆ Use baskets to store toys. Choose baskets that are big and roomy with strong handles. They also can be used to carry toys when visiting.

◆ Store large items, such as skis or surfboards, under beds if you haven't got a spare closet, an attic, or a basement.

◆ Use insulating cork to make a bulletinboard for the kitchen, workroom, or children's bedroom; it is thicker than other types of cork.

◆ Make a wall panel with lots of differentsized pockets—out of striped deck-chair canvas, for example—and hang it in the kitchen or on the back of a child's bedroom door. Sew large paper clips and/or hooks into the bottom for gloves or notes.

◆ If you have a hallway with a high ceiling, build a pulley system and hang bicycles near the ceiling.

Kitchens

◆ Run a narrow shelf around the kitchen walls or along one wall for herb and spice jars, sauce bottles, salt and pepper mills, and all the little things that so often get misplaced.

◆ Fix wire baskets to the insides of cabinet doors to hold miscellaneous cleaning items, shoe-polishing equipment, etc.

◆ Use glass jars and metal boxes for dry food. They can look very decorative in a row on a shelf. The glass also is a good idea, because you can see how much you have left. Use colored glass; otherwise the food will deteriorate too quickly.

◆ Hang stemmed glasses upside down from slots in wood or shelves.

◆ Hang cups and mugs from cup hooks under upper kitchen cabinets or shelves, where they will be decorative and out of the way at the same time.

◆ Use wicker baskets as vegetable racks; they let the air in and look attractive.

◆ If drawer and closet space is limited, buy wire mesh panels or make your own ladder

MAKING LADDER WALL STORAGE

1 Measure the height and width of the space. Cut (or have cut for you) two battens of ½-inch lath in the length you require for the uprights. For the crossbars, cut more lengths of lath—enough to leave gaps of ½ inch between the bars.

3 Make hooks from wire coat hangers, using a pair of pliers, or buy some butcher's hooks from a kitchen supply store.

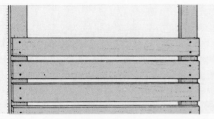

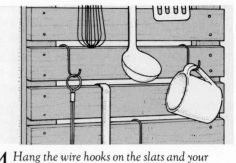

2 Screw the uprights to the wall, then nail the crossbars to them at right angles, leaving a ½-inch gap between each bar.

4 Hang the wire hooks on the slats and your utensils on the hooks. Hang implements with hooked handles on the slats, too.

rack storage panels (see above), or screw hooks into perforated hardboard and hang utensils from them.

◆ Run a metal bar across the room and hang baskets and pans from it.

◆ Pottery mugs or jugs are handy for storing wooden spoons on the counter.

◆ Use a filing cabinet to hold large kitchen equipment, such as saucepans or large, rarely used items.

◆ Store plates in a wall-mounted wooden plate rack.

◆ Keep a shelf for cookbooks, a notepad, and correspondence so they are within easy reach when you need them.

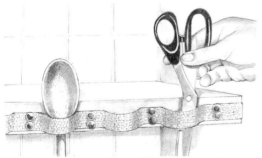

Making storage pockets. *Edge shelves with strong carpet binding, tacked firmly at intervals, leaving gaps wide enough for scissors, spoons, and other utensils.*

Children's rooms

◆ Plastic milk crates make good stacking storage for toys, puzzles, and small games. The crates also make good shelf units for shoes, books, and clothes.

◆ For toy boxes that are easy to move from room to room, use colored plastic stacking boxes.

◆ A rattan mirror with a shelf or a set of shelves (or several all over the wall) can hold tiny books, dollhouse furniture, or toy models in an older child's room.

Bedrooms

◆ When buying a bed, buy one with large drawers underneath to increase storage space.

◆ Make built-in closets by installing floor-to-ceiling sliding doors, or a curtain across an alcove, or sliding doors and an end panel against a wall.

◆ Use an old-fashioned wicker laundry hamper to store out-of-season clothes.

Bathrooms

◆If you don't have space for a separate cabinet in the bathroom, build one around the sink. If you use it to store cleaning equipment, and there are young children in the house, it must be lockable.

◆Put the children's bath toys in a string bag and hang it from the wall over the tub, or over the faucet, so they are out of the way when you take a bath or shower.

Workshops

◆Hang work tools on perforated hardboard. Paint the profile of each item on the board so you can see where everything should go (and if anything is not where it should be).

◆See-through storage drawers are easy to install under any surface.

◆Look at office-supply catalogs for colorful and useful storage ideas.

◆Use two filing cabinets to make a base for a desk and to provide extra storage.

Hall

◆Large wicker baskets or large ceramic crocks make good umbrella stands. Put a plant saucer in the bottom to catch any drips.

◆Place a wooden hat stand in a small hall for coats and hats. Or, you can put up a Victorian mirror that has narrow shelves and hooks on it. These are useful because they provide a place for gloves and hats, or for letters and messages.

Wall baskets. *Hang wicker baskets on the wall— one for each member of the household—and put letters, telephone messages, and gloves in them.*

KITCHEN DESIGN

◆When designing a kitchen, make sure the main work centers—dish-washing, storage, food preparation, and cooking— are conveniently laid out, with sufficient counter room between them.

◆To avoid having people crossing your paths too often, locate work centers away from traffic paths to and from doors.

◆Many kitchens feature a cooking island that centers the preparation of meals in one area and sitting, eating, and family functions in another so they can comfortably overlap.

◆Kitchen/family room plans make it easy for a busy parent to keep an eye on the kids while preparing meals.

◆Kitchen doors should be glassed in, so a child or person carrying food can be seen approaching.

◆Good lighting is essential in a well-designed kitchen and will depend on the location of your range and work surfaces. Adjustable spotlights offer good directional lighting over the stove or sink.

KITCHEN UNITS

◆Set wall cabinets back far enough so that you have plenty of room to work at the counter without bumping your head on cabinet doors or corners. A wall cabinet should be no less than 18 inches above the counter space; a smaller gap than this does not allow room for most of the common kitchen appliances.

◆Work surfaces should·be at a comfortable height to avoid unnecessary strain and

Worktop height. *Ideally the work surface should be 2 to 3 inches lower than your elbow when you stand at it. Mount units on plinths if they are too low.*

accidents. Most ready-made units come with countertops about 2 feet deep and about 3 feet from the floor.

◆ Choose kitchen units that are fitted with a built-in bottom recess about 6 inches high and 3 inches deep to allow room for your toes, so you can stand close to the work surface in comfort.

◆ Do not put your gas range near a door or window where the draft may regularly blow out the pilot light and make it tricky to relight.

◆ To minimize risks, make sure all controls on electrical appliances are well out of the reach of children.

LARGE KITCHEN
By having cabinets along two walls there is plenty of room for storage as well as an eating area in this 14-foot-square kitchen.

Range hood Get one with a fan ducted to the outside to minimize cooking odors.

Dishwasher Install it near the sink because it needs to be near the water supply.

Shelf Mount a narrow shelf near the stove to hold herbs and spices during use.

Built-in oven and cooktop These can look neater and be easier to clean than freestanding appliances.

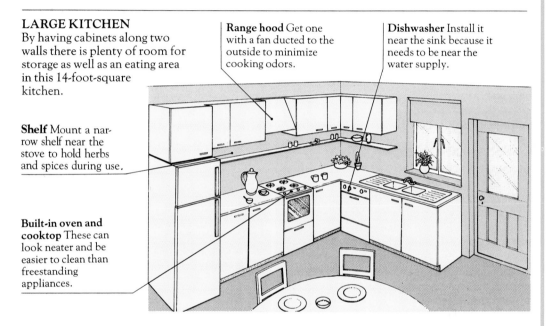

GALLEY KITCHEN
With careful planning you can pack a great deal into a very small space. This kitchen is approximately 6 × 7 feet.

Refrigerator/freezer A combined unit is better if space is limited.

Pot rack Pots and pans make a good wall display and are instantly accessible.

Wall plate rack Useful for plate storage. Make sure the wall can support the weight.

Wall-mounted oven This is useful if you want more low-level cabinets.

Garbage Keep a can under the sink so you don't trip over it; you can mount it inside the sink cabinet door.

Shelf A shelf running the length of the wall is best; things can fall more easily off short shelves.

LIGHTING

Plan your lighting and install fixtures and switches before decorating a room, because plaster or wallboard may need to be removed to run wires up inside the wall. Plan all the lighting for a room before buying.

TYPES OF LIGHTING

There are four different types of lighting: General overhead lighting, task lighting, directional or accent lighting, and lighting that is primarily decorative.

◆**General overhead lighting.** Use this for background or ambient lighting in a room. The most familiar type is the fixture that hangs from the ceiling. You can almost double the amount of light by reflecting it off a white wall or ceiling.

◆**Task lighting.** Use it to light an area where someone is reading or working. To prevent glare, conceal the light source from the person working, and position it so that his or her shadow doesn't fall across the work.

◆**Directional or accent lighting.** Use this to highlight features in the room, such as plant leaf patterns, architectural arches, or alcoves, or to light displays and paintings.

◆**Decorative lighting.** To add to the room decoration, use lamps that are decorative in their own right, such as tiffany lamps with their stained-glass shades, or lamps in the form of sculptures.

Downlights and uplights

Downlights are cylindrical or square lighting fixtures that can be positioned high up on a wall or in the ceiling so they direct a shaft of light downward. They can be recessed or semirecessed into the ceiling, or they can be mounted on the surface. Narrow beams create highlights and shadows, and broad beams provide more diffused lighting.

Uplights send their beams upward, creating a lighting effect mainly by reflecting light off the ceiling.

◆Use both kinds to complement general lighting when all the lights are on or to give soft, reflected light at times such as in the evening, for example, when you don't want the main lights on.

◆You can use wall lights, freestanding tall spotlights, standard lamps, or discreet floor spotlights as uplights.

BULB SHAPES

◆Globe bulbs are good for lanterns or lamps with shades that let you see the bulb; normally clear, frosted, or white.

◆Use three-way bulbs when variable light supply is desired.

◆Use candle-shaped bulbs in some wall lights or chandelier fittings; can be clear, white, or twisted.

◆Choose a long-lasting bulb for hard-to-reach areas like a high-ceilinged foyer, kitchen, or outdoors. These bulbs can last for years.

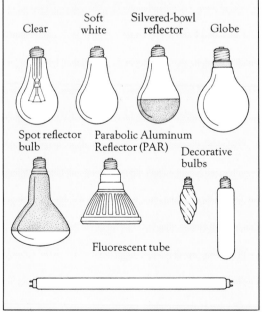

Standard incandescent bulbs

Clear Soft white Silvered-bowl reflector Globe

Spot reflector bulb Parabolic Aluminum Reflector (PAR) Decorative bulbs

Fluorescent tube

GLOSSARY OF COMMON LIGHTING TERMS

A-bulb. Standard light bulb.

Baffle. Panel that conceals bulbs for indirect lighting.

Ballast. A device fitted to fluorescent tubes and high-intensity discharge lamps to prevent them from consuming as much electricity.

C-bulb. Cone-shaped bulb.

Ceiling light. Hanging ceiling fixture.

Cold beam bulb light. A spotlight bulb with a special reflector that reduces the heat of the beam.

Diffused light. Light filtered evenly through a translucent material.

Direct light. Light coming directly from a fixture to a surface.

F-bulb. Flame-shaped bulb.

Fluorescent light. Glass tube coated with phosphor powders and containing an inert gas and mercury vapor at low pressure (available in different whites as well as colors). Can be found in circular and also U-shapes.

Incandescent bulb. Light bulb that contains a small filament wire, which when heated by electricity, emits light. Comes in various shapes, wattages, and colors, and gives off a golden light.

Indirect light. Light bounced off another surface before it reaches its destination.

Lumen. A standard international unit used to measure the amount of light falling on a particular surface.

Metal-halide bulb. Produces white light (commonly used for outdoor floodlighting).

Neon bulb. Colored bulb used for decoration only.

PAR lamps. Parabolic aluminum reflectors have enclosures of heavy glass and built-in reflecting surfaces.

Reflector bulb. Bulb that has a built-in reflector.

R-lamps. Lamps that have reflector bulbs.

Silvered-bowl bulb. There are two kinds. One has a silver coating, the amount of which determines the width of beam spread. The other has an internally silvered bulb that gives a sharply defined beam.

Spotlight. A single light source producing a direct beam.

Strip lights. A series of small incandescent bulbs on a chrome, brass, or wood base.

Track lighting. One or more fixtures mounted on a pre-wired metal track connected to a single electrical outlet.

Tungsten-halogen bulb. Incandescent light with halogen gas that gives a brighter light and lasts longer.

Volt. Unit expressing the potential of an electric circuit.

Wall washers. Fixtures that direct beams of light at the wall.

Watt. Unit of power describing the electrical output of a bulb. Ordinary bulbs range from 25 to 200 watts.

LIGHT FIXTURES

Most light fixtures come under one of two headings: Directional, such as spotlights, which beam concentrated shafts of light into a specific area; and diffused, such as ceiling-mounted fixtures, which provide overall illumination in a room. Some fixtures can provide both kinds of lighting; for example, spotlights can provide ambient background lighting if bounced off a light-reflecting surface, and ceiling lights fitted with an upward- or downward-pointing opaque shade can produce directional lighting.

Before choosing light fixtures.

◆Decide what kind of atmosphere you want in the room and take note of the position of windows and the amount of natural light.

◆If you want to create small pools of atmospheric light in strategic areas of a room, consider buying several decorative lamps.

◆Determine how much light a fixture will give out and how much will be taken up by the shade; also consider the shape of the beam and whether it should shine upward or downward.

◆A single ceiling-mounted fixture is usually not adequate for anywhere other than a small kitchen or bathroom; the best plan is a combination of fixtures that will provide a pleasing blend of general and specific light.

◆Be careful not to aim high-voltage spotlights directly at valuable furniture, paintings, or plants; they can produce a damaging amount of heat.

Ceiling-mounted lighting

These are traditionally positioned in the center of the ceiling for overall lighting.

◆ For maximum versatility, use them with a dimmer switch and a mechanism that lets you lower it over a dining or coffee table and pull it up again for general lighting.

◆ Ceiling-mounted lights should be used with more modern directional lighting and lamps; otherwise the light they distribute will be insufficient and bland.

Built-in lights

◆ These can be recessed or semirecessed to provide discreet lighting; you can't see the light source.

◆ If you want to be able to direct the light at an angle, install "eyeball" downlights, which can be swiveled in their sockets.

◆ Use one recessed ceiling light to light a

LIGHTING TIPS

◆ Fluorescent lights consume less than half the electricity that incandescent lights use, but they cost more to install.

◆ Position outlets to allow flexibility, and install light switches within easy reach as you enter a room.

◆ Three-way switches are very practical at the top and bottom of a staircase or by the bedside; install dimmer switches so you can vary the lighting level in a room.

◆ You need about 20 watts of lighting per square yard of space.

◆ Use wall lights to make a room look smaller and ceiling-mounted lights to make a room look lower.

◆ Several table or floor lamps scattered about the room will give a softer effect than one central one. They won't be any more expensive to run if you use low-wattage bulbs.

◆ Make a room look broader by directing ceiling lights toward a wall to flood it with an even amount of light; this is especially effective against pale walls.

---

space above a coffee table, for instance; use several for general lighting for a whole room. If you use several downlights, arrange the switches so you don't have to have all the lights on at the same time.

◆ Place a ceiling downlight close to a wall to effectively light the wall space; the reflection will provide unobtrusive general lighting.

Wall lights

◆ Use wall-mounted fixtures to provide general diffused light instead of, or in addition to, a central ceiling fixture.

◆ Use them to illuminate dark hallways, stairs, and landings when the ceiling fixture is too high up to provide adequate lighting.

◆ For background light, try a pair of wall fixtures with uplighting shades. The light reflected from the ceiling can be made discreet or very bright, depending on how pale the ceiling is and how bright the bulb.

◆ Wall lights can be used to highlight special decorative features in the home, such as plants or pictures.

◆ For an unusual effect, use a ship's bulkhead light vertically instead of horizontally.

Spotlights

◆ The great flexibility of spotlights makes them a practical choice for multipurpose lighting. Available in many shapes and sizes, they throw out a shaft of light in wide or narrow beams that can be directed wherever you choose.

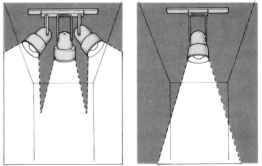

Using spotlights. *Use a cluster of spotlights on one light fixture for good general lighting (above left) and a single spotlight to light a particular part of a room (above right).*

◆Spotlights can be surface mounted or recessed into a wall or ceiling and also can be clamped onto headboards, desks, or bookshelves.

◆To maximize the light from one electrical source, install lighting track that can hold and power several spotlights at once. More sophisticated systems allow you to operate different sets of lights independently.

◆Single spotlights can be used for accent lighting of plants or paintings, or to direct concentrated light onto a reading or work surface.

◆Ordinary tungsten bulbs, when used in spotlights, give a harsher light than internally silvered varieties.

Positioning a desk lamp for writing. *Place a desk lamp on the left of a right-handed person and vice versa for a left-handed person, so there is no glare, and no shadow falls across the paper.*

Portable lamps

◆If you like to be able to change your lighting arrangement now and then, movable lamps are a good choice since they can be easily switched from one spot to another.

◆Traditional table lamps and standard lamps with translucent shades give a diffused light; spotlights and desk lamps provide directional light for close work.

◆Direct a freestanding lamp upward at a low, white ceiling to give good reflected light for reading along with overall background light.

◆Use a traditional table lamp to produce enough light for easy reading and writing and also to lend a relaxed feeling to a room.

Desk lamps

These come in an assortment of shapes with a stand or clamp-on attachment. The latter type is practical if space is limited.

◆Traditional and modern desk lamps emit directional light for close work. Choose an adjustable model for the added advantage of pointing the light exactly where you need it.

◆Desk lights also can double as spotlights and, if directed at a wall, will bounce off and spread into a diffused light.

◆Look for high-tech desk lamps with miniature halogen bulbs; they give efficient, longer-lasting, and cheaper light.

Fluorescent lighting

Although widely used in kitchens and work areas where bright, even light is needed, this lighting also can be used decoratively.

◆Use small fluorescent lights and filament tubes to light the space under kitchen cabinets above the countertops, at the top of alcoves with shelves, or under glass display shelves or cabinets.

◆Fluorescent fixtures consume very little power and stay cool, so they can be used in tight spaces.

◆You can have boxed fluorescent tubes built into closets, with a spring switch on the door so the light goes on and off when you open and close the door.

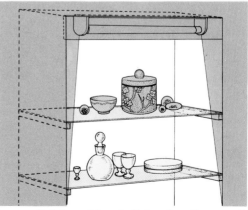

Accent lighting with strip lights. *Install a strip of lights above shelving to create effective accent lighting on displayed objects.*

LIGHTING FOR SPECIFIC PURPOSES

Because each living area in your home has a different function and atmosphere, lighting requirements will vary from room to room. Lighting should neither dazzle nor obscure. Living and dining rooms should have a complementary blend of diffused, decorative, and direct lighting, and kitchens and bathrooms need even, bright light. In bathrooms and kitchens, check that all outlets are enclosed. Don't overload outlets, and make sure that electrical cords do not trail across counters and near sinks.

HALLWAY AND STAIRS
◆ Make sure that these are always well lit to prevent accidents, as well as to look warm and welcoming. Install a porch light.
◆ Use spotlights on a track or in a cluster for good general lighting.
◆ Use a bright bulb if there is only one ceiling-mounted fixture, so there is enough light.
◆ Use wall-mounted lights on the stairs.
◆ Install two-way switches on the stair-case, particularly if you have more than one flight of stairs, to make switching on and off easier.
◆ Decorate dark halls with pale colors so light is reflected off the walls.

LIVING ROOM
◆ Use accent or directional lighting to highlight pictures and sculptures, arches, alcoves, or plants.
◆ Use table lamps or spotlights to illuminate activity areas; lighting that can be lowered and raised is practical for dining areas or over a low coffee table.
◆ An indirect light near the television set will reduce eye strain while watching.

KITCHEN
◆ Good general lighting and directional lighting are essential in the kitchen if you are to have your workspace well lit.
◆ Install separate switches for all the different lights so that you don't have to have them all on at the same time.

BEDROOM

◆ In a bedroom install good general lighting to dress by, bedside lights to read by, and a light inside the closet.

◆ Reading lights by the bed should be high enough to shine onto the book without casting a shadow but not so high that they shine directly into your eyes.

◆ If your bedside table is usually cluttered with alarm clocks, books, radio, etc., mount your bedside lamp on the wall.

◆ If yours is a double bed, make sure the light doesn't shine into your partner's eyes or is so bright as to keep him or her awake if he or she doesn't want to read.

BATHROOM

◆ Line the sides of the mirror with bare bulbs or spotlights in stage-dressing-room style. Light then falls above, below, and to each side of your face, providing good overall illumination for shaving or applying makeup.

◆ Plastic- or glass-enclosed ceiling fixtures are the best choice for bathrooms because, unlike metal, they are resistant to steam and condensation.

◆ Fluorescent fixtures are practical if installed behind a suspended ceiling or valance.

◆ Remember that all lights near a bath or shower should be out of reach of the water spray to prevent electric shocks.

CHILD'S ROOM

◆ Use wall-mounted lights in a child's room instead of freestanding fixtures or adjustable or fragile lamps that can be broken. Use sturdy fixtures with an authorized safety symbol that can be positioned on the wall or ceiling, away from small fingers.

◆ Install a dimmer switch if your child is frightened of the dark, or leave a glowing nightlight in a baby's room.

HOUSEPLANTS

Plants will enhance almost any interior by bringing the colors and forms of nature into your home. A simple arrangement of fresh flowers or a seasonal display of dried flowers that captures the colors of summer or fall will instantly transform a stark room into a warm and welcoming one. Always select plants whose needs match the conditions of light, heat, and humidity you can provide.

KEEPING PLANTS HEALTHY

Good common sense and awareness to the basic needs of plants go a long way toward keeping them healthy. You can get great pleasure and fulfillment from watching plants thrive under your care.

◆ Rainwater is ideal for plants; otherwise lukewarm tap water is fine.
◆ Before watering more delicate plants, let the water stand overnight in a bucket so it reaches room temperature and some of the chlorine evaporates.
◆ Water cacti once a month and succulents about twice a month.

The best way to water. *Either water with a long-spouted watering can directly under the leaves into the soil (above left) or immerse the pot in water to just below the soil level and let it soak until the soil glistens (above right). Let it drain.*

Encouraging bushy growth. *Some plants, such as Swedish ivy and philodendron, have a tendency to grow long stems with few leaves. If one of your plants gets leggy, pinch out the growing tips to encourage more growth from the base of the stem or plant.*

Watering

Each plant has its own watering needs according to size, natural habitat, and time of year; actively growing plants need a lot of water, but during the winter resting phase, these plants will need far less.
◆ As a rule, water potted plants only when they need it; let them almost dry out between waterings. Drooping leaves and limp stems are signals that they need more water, but don't wait until that stage.

TIPS FOR WATERING

◆ Water according to a plant's needs rather than by routine or you may overwater. Too much water floods the roots leaving them cold and deprived of air.
◆ The larger the leaf surface of a plant, the more water it will need.
◆ Be particularly careful not to overwater in winter.
◆ Never leave a plant standing in a tray of water; it may rot.

Feeding

Healthy plant growth depends on an adequate supply of plant nutrients—nitrogen for leaf growth and phosphates for root development—together with small amounts of trace elements. The amount of each nutrient contained in a fertilizer should be on the label.

◆ A hungry plant has a washed-out, listless look. Hunger signs are: A lack of growth; weak stems; small, pale, or yellowing leaves; lower leaf loss; and few or no flowers.

◆ Use a weak mixture of liquid houseplant fertilizer every time you water. During the winter months, skip the fertilizer solution.

◆ If you don't have houseplant fertilizer, dissolve an envelope of unflavored gelatin in hot water, let it cool to room temperature, and water with the mixture.

◆ Mix liquid fertilizer in water as directed and feed only at the strength given (or less) in the instructions; don't apply undiluted fertilizer; it can burn leaves and roots.

◆ Overfeeding will damage the plant and discourage growth. Underfeeding will encourage disease or pests.

◆ New or recently repotted plants will not need feeding for about three months, depending on the plant and type of soil. Plants potted in a soilless mixture (peat-moss-based, etc.) need feeding after about six weeks.

Light

◆ The majority of plants like to be kept in semishade or filtered sunlight but out of direct sun that can burn the leaves.

◆ Plants with variegated leaves need more sun than other plants, because the sunlight brings out their color.

◆ Flowering plants will need some sunlight to get them to flower. Cacti and succulents need more light than other plants and can stand direct sunlight.

Temperature

◆ The two temperature ranges that suit most plants are "warm," from 60° to 70° and "cool," from 50° to 60°. Most popular houseplants are from the tropics and do best in the warm temperature range; other types—mainly evergreens and flowering species—prefer cool conditions. In general, avoid fluctuations of more than 15° to 18° between daytime and nighttime temperatures in rooms where plants are growing.

◆ Many houseplants need to be kept at a slightly cooler temperature during the winter rest phase, a period when root growth is encouraged and top growth discouraged.

Humidity

◆ Grouping plants together increases humidity because of the moisture given off from the damp soil and foliage of surrounding plants.

◆ Mist-spraying regularly will provide plants with sufficient humidity, but be careful not to spray leaves while they are exposed to direct sun; the combination can burn them.

◆ A plant is suffering from a lack of humidity if: Leaves begin to shrivel or scorch; the tips of plants with long narrow leaves, such as palms or ferns, begin to dry out; and buds fall off or flowers wither.

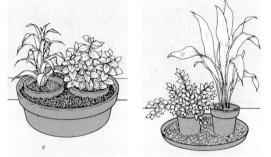

Increasing moisture levels. *If the weather is very dry, "double-pot" by burying plants and their pots in a waterproof container filled with moist peat moss (above left). Or stand pots in a dish of pebbles and keep the pebbles wet almost to the top (above right).*

Plant pests and diseases

◆ Check your plants often, and act at once if you spot trouble. You might save an expensive plant if you catch problems early.

◆ Keep affected plants away from other plants while you treat the problem to prevent it from spreading.

REMEDIES FOR COMMON PESTS AND DISEASES

APHIDS (plant lice)
(Greenfly, blackfly, grayfly, or orangefly)
◆ Remove these because they suck sap in shoot tips and flower buds, distorting growth. They also secrete a sticky substance that attracts mold, and they carry virus.
◆ Wipe them off with your fingers and thumb if there are not too many of them; otherwise spray with soapy water.

RED SPIDER MITES
Look out for these in the winter when your house's atmosphere is warm and dry. The spiders are almost invisible to the naked eye. You'll notice their webs on the underside of leaves.
◆ Spray an infested plant with a biologically safe houseplant insecticide. Mist plants daily in dry weather to prevent a recurrence.

MEALY BUGS
These are about ¼ inch long and look like blobs of cotton. On the leaves, they protect themselves with a white water- and insecticide-proof "wool."

◆ Wipe small infestations off with a damp cloth or cotton swab.
◆ Spray more severe infestations weekly with a biologically safe houseplant insecticide.

SCALE INSECTS
Seen as small, brown, waxy disks that attach themselves to veins on the underside of leaves. They suck sap and secrete a sticky honeydew substance that attracts mold.
◆ Wipe off with a damp cloth or cotton swab.
◆ If badly infested, the leaves will turn sticky and yellow; throw the plant and pot away to prevent the insects from spreading.

BOTRYTIS (gray mold)
◆ Cut away and destroy all affected parts and take out moldy potting mixture. Destroy a badly affected plant.
◆ Spray with a biologically safe fungicide.
◆ Improve ventilation and reduce watering and mist-spraying to prevent a recurrence.

CROWN AND STEM ROT
The crown and stem may become soft and rotten as a result of overwatering or of keeping the plant too cool.
◆ If you catch it early enough, you could try cutting away the rotten areas, dusting the rest of the plant with sulphur, and rerooting it. If the plant does not respond quickly, throw the plant and pot away.

VIRUS
Normally shows as yellow or pale green patches or white streaks on leaves, and causes distortion or stunting of the plant.
◆ Throw the plant and pot away. There is no cure, and it can spread to other plants.
◆ Treat any aphid infestation; aphids carry virus.

Repotting

◆ Repot plants into a larger pot when the roots show through the drainage holes and when the potting mixture dries out very quickly. Do this in spring just before the plant starts its main growth period. If you do it in winter when the plant is dormant, the roots won't spread into the new soil.
◆ Repot into a pot that is only slightly larger than the old one; otherwise you encourage too much root growth instead of leaf growth.
◆ If your plant is well-established in a large pot and you don't want the plant to grow much taller, "top-dress." Gently scrape away the top soil and replace it with new potting mixture.

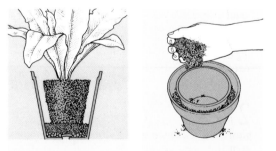

Repotting a plant. *Line the base of the new pot with drainage material so the plant will sit at the same level (above left). Place the old pot inside the new one and fill the gap with potting mixture (above right). Remove the pot and insert the plant, fill gaps with potting mixture, and pack soil down well.*

PLANT CARE WHILE YOU GO ON VACATION

◆ If there's no one available to water your plants, use one of the automatic watering methods. The length of time you can leave plants depends on the weather and the thirst of the plants. Test your chosen watering method for a time while you are at home to give yourself an idea of how long the water will last.

◆ "Double-pot" your plants in a container of moist peat moss (see page 161). This way they will have water for a couple of weeks.

◆ Buy self-watering containers that will keep a supply of water for a limited period. These are available from garden centers. Some self-watering containers store enough water for up to a month.

THE PLASTIC BAG METHOD

◆ You can "bag" your plants for periods of up to a week—no longer because the plant may begin to rot. Don't leave "bagged" plants in direct sunlight; they will produce too much condensation and are more likely to rot.

1 *Water the plant well. Push four bamboo stakes taller than the plant into the soil at equal intervals around the rim of the pot and angled outward so the bag does not touch the leaves.*

2 *Put the plant and pot into a clear, airtight plastic bag, big enough to enclose the plant completely. Seal the top of the bag with adhesive tape. This way the water is recycled into the soil after evaporating from the leaves.*

Capillary matting

Although sometimes difficult to find, capillary matting works well for plants in plastic pots with drainage holes. Clay pots tend to absorb the water rather than pass it to the plant.

◆ Use capillary matting if you have quantities of plants to leave. Some plants can be left for two to three weeks, and the matting can be reused several times.

◆ If you have no time to buy capillary matting or can't find it, try using water-soaked newspapers instead.

Using a capillary mat. *Place one end of the mat in a sink or bathtub filled with water and the other end on the drainboard or a shelf behind the bathtub; the end that is in the water should be lower than the level of the plants. The mat absorbs the water and the plants take up the water as they need it.*

Making a watering wick. *For individual plants or plants in clay pots, make a wick using any water-absorbent material, such as cotton shoelaces or oil-lamp wicks. Push one end firmly into the root ball and trail the other end into a container of water.*

GUIDE TO EASY-CARE VARIETIES

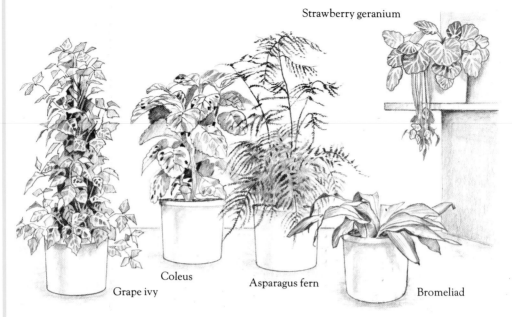

Strawberry geranium

Coleus

Grape ivy

Asparagus fern

Bromeliad

GRAPE IVY
Cissus sp.
◆ Perfect plants for beginners. *C. antarctica* (kangaroo vine) has light green leaves and the *C. rhombifolia* (grape ivy) has darker leaves. Use as a room divider or to cover a wall.
Position Needs warm filtered sun. Likes good ventilation in very hot weather. *C. antarctica* can stand drafts.
Size Can grow to a height of 6 feet with a spread of 2 feet in two years.
Watering Needs plenty of water in summer, less in winter. Spray if the foliage becomes dry.

COLEUS
Coleus blumei
◆ Coleus plants have a great variety of brilliantly colored leaves. Group several plants together to get the full effect of their colors.
Position Plenty of sunlight to bring out the color. Keep them somewhere that is continuously warm.

Size Grows to a spread of up to 18 inches in one year.
Watering Keep the soil moist. Spray occasionally.

ASPARAGUS FERN
Asparagus setaceus
◆ A vigorous fern related to the vegetable asparagus.
Position Stand it on a windowsill where it will get plenty of light, in a warm temperature.
Size Produces stems up to $3\frac{1}{2}$ feet long.
Watering Water enough to keep the potting mixture slightly moist, but no more.

BROMELIADS
◆ Some of the easiest plants to grow, bromeliads have prominent, colored leaves.
Position Keep in a warm temperature, with filtered sun.
Size Grows to about 1 foot.
Watering Water when the potting mixture looks dry, pouring the water into the center "cup" of the plant with a narrow-spouted watering can.

STRAWBERRY GERANIUM
Saxifraga stolonifera
◆ Compact plant with veined leaves and little plantlets hanging from red, threadlike stems. Ideal for a hanging basket or high on a shelf.
Position Needs plenty of light and an hour or two of morning sun to help keep its leaf coloring.
Size The main plant reaches about 8 inches.
Watering Keep the root ball moist but not too wet.

SWISS-CHEESE PLANT
Monstera deliciosa
◆ Ideal for "decorating" an empty corner because of its stylish, sculptural shape.
Position Likes a warm, shady position.
Watering Water thoroughly, but allow the potting mixture to become almost dry before watering again.
Other care Use a moss stick to provide a support for the plant and to supply moisture

Swiss-cheese plant

Rubber plant   Kentia palm

Cast-iron plant

Silk oak

through the aerial roots to the upper leaves. Clean old leaves regularly.

SILK OAK
Grevillea robusta
◆ A good indoor treelike shrub with evergreen, fern-like leaves.
Position Keep in a cool, sunny place.
Size Can grow to 5 feet in two years.
Watering Water liberally from spring to autumn, sparingly in winter.
Other care Encourage bushy growth by pinching out the main shoot when it is young.

RUBBER PLANT
Ficus elastica
◆ Use it in a group of plants or on its own as a decorative feature.
Position Likes a warm, shady spot.
Size Can grow to 6 feet tall.
Watering Water when not quite dry. Stand in a bucket of water to let it soak up as much

as it wants.
Other care Clean the old leaves occasionally, not the new ones.

KENTIA PALM
Howea belmoreana
PARLOR PALM
Chamaedorea elegans
◆ The Kentia palm is a tall, elegant plant. Ideal for the corner of a room. Buy young parlor palms, as the leaves become coarse with age.
Position Warm filtered sun.
Size A Kentia palm reaches heights of up to 8 feet; parlor palms take several years to reach 3 feet.
Watering Water regularly, but keep well drained so the roots don't stay wet.
Other care Avoid sudden temperature changes.

CAST-IRON PLANT
Aspidistra elatior
Position Use it in a shaded corner where other plants won't grow. Likes cool filtered sun.

Size Grows to a height/spread of 3 feet.
Watering Water it well, especially in summer, every time it dries out. Don't keep it waterlogged. Feed every two weeks in the growing season.
Other care Polish the old leaves from time to time with a commercial product.

SUCCULENTS AND CACTI
◆ Good plants for beginners as they can stand a great deal of neglect and bad treatment.
◆ Succulents and cacti need sunshine and good ventilation. They all like warmth in the summer growing period and a cooler, dry, winter rest period. For best results, keep them on a very sunny windowsill and, if possible, give them a period outdoors in the summer.
◆ Give less water in the autumn and winter.

CUT FLOWERS

◆Cut garden flowers early in the morning, before the sun reaches full strength (or in the evening), because the heat of the sun draws moisture from the petals. Flowers that are cut on a hot day won't last as long.

◆When choosing flowers, make sure the petals are firm and a vivid color, the foliage is green and not beginning to wilt, and the stems are not dark or slimy.

◆Avoid buying flowers that have been left outside in the sun; ask the florist to wrap them so the heads are protected from wind and heat.

◆Choose buds that are just opening; very tightly closed buds may never open. Daffodils are the exception; they are nearly always sold in bud and will open well and last a long time.

Making flowers last longer

◆Cut flowers will last much longer if their stems are treated so they can take up water quickly (see below).

◆Add fresh water to the vase and mist-spray the flowers daily. A teaspoon of sugar added to the water will renew the flowers.

◆Keep fresh, cut flowers out of direct sun, heat, and drafts.

◆Remove any dying heads right away, as they emit ethylene gas that can cause wilting of the other, healthy flowers.

PREPARING STEMS

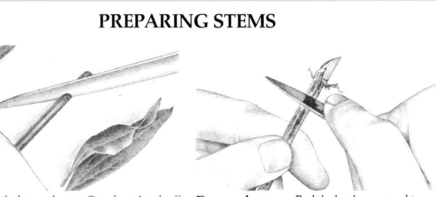

1 *Remove the bottom leaves. Cut about ½ inch off the end of the stem in case it was sealed while out of water. Cut on the slant.*

For woody stems. *Peel the leathery outer skin off the bottom about ¾ inch, or crush it with a mallet.*

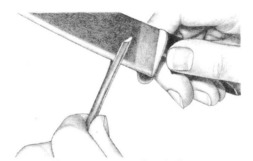

2 *Split all stems except woody or hollow ones to about ½ inch from the bottom.*
For large, hollow stems. *Turn the flower upside down, fill the stem with water, then plug it with cotton.*

Hellebores and tulips. *Pierce through the stem at intervals, or score from the head to the stem end with a needle to prevent an airlock in the stem that could keep water from the flower.*
3 *Place the stems in deep water and leave them there a few hours or overnight.*

DRYING FLOWERS

Gather flowers only when the weather is dry, and choose those that are not fully developed; they will keep their color better.

◆ Begin the drying process as soon as possible after picking; avoid putting flowers in direct sunlight as this causes colors to fade.

Air-drying flowers

Most flowers, grasses, and seed heads can be dried in this way. Always remove the lower leaves on the stems, because they shrivel up and slow down the dehydration process.

◆ Wire the heads of flowers on weak stems for extra support before you dry them (see below right).

◆ **Hanging flowers to dry.** Arrange them in small bunches and tie the stems with a rubber band so the bunch stays together as the stems contract. The bunches should not be too large or the flowers in the middle won't dry and will become moldy. Hang the bunches upside down in a warm, dry, well-ventilated space such as an attic or cellar (near the hot-water heater). They are ready when they feel completely crisp and dry to the touch.

◆ **Drying upright.** Use this method for flowers or grasses with very delicate heads. Leave the flowers standing in a little vase until they become crisp and dry.

◆ **Drying flat.** You can dry most grasses, seed heads, and pods in open boxes or laid out flat on newspaper or brown paper.

Using a drying agent

This is the technique to use if you want dried flower heads that look like the fresh plant. It is the best method for preserving roses and delicate flowers that lose some of their color when air-dried.

◆ Use equal parts of borax and alum for the more delicate flowers, and silver sand or silica gel crystals for hardier varieties. Silica gel dries flowers in two or three days; the other agents can take up to three weeks, depending on the density of the flowers.

Drying flower heads.

1 Remove stems from flowers and wire the heads (see below).

2 Cover the bottom of an airtight container with a 1-inch layer of drying agent. Place the flower heads in the container, making sure they do not touch.

3 Gently sprinkle more of the agent over the petals through a sieve. When the flowers are covered by at least 1 inch of powder, seal the container and leave in a warm, dry place.

4 Look into the container every two or three days to see if the petals have become papery and dry.

WIRING FLOWER HEADS

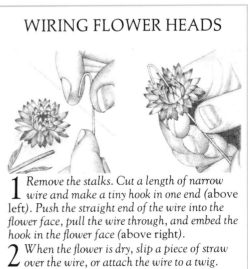

1 *Remove the stalks. Cut a length of narrow wire and make a tiny hook in one end (above left). Push the straight end of the wire into the flower face, pull the wire through, and embed the hook in the flower face (above right).*

2 *When the flower is dry, slip a piece of straw over the wire, or attach the wire to a twig.*

ANTIQUES AND VALUABLES

Treat your antique furniture with respect, but don't be afraid to use it. You'll get many years of enjoyment from your antiques and valuables, and they will achieve a nice patina with use. Get valuable pieces that are damaged repaired as soon as possible.

IDEAL CONDITIONS

Ideally, it is best to protect antique furnishings from all extremes of heat and cold, dryness or dampness. Sudden changes in temperature and humidity should be avoided, if at all possible, in the rooms where valuable pieces are housed. Even a sudden move from an unsuitable environment to a suitable one can be as bad for furniture (especially a piano) as leaving it where it was. Try to improve the conditions of the space where your antiques are kept until you can transfer them to more ideal surroundings.

Light

Any light can affect the color of wood to a surprising degree; it makes light wood darker and dark wood lighter.

◆ Use adjustable shutters or blinds to regulate sunlight coming into a room so antique pieces are shielded from direct sun.

◆ Place antique furniture out of direct sunlight, particularly if the surface is inlaid with dark and light wood, because bright light can destroy the effect completely. This type of damage can't be reversed without removing some of the finished surface.

Heat

◆ Extreme or constant heat can dry wood out and cause it to split. It also dries out fabric and paper, making them very fragile. Don't take the risk of putting antique objects, books, or furniture too close to radiators, portable heaters, or a fireplace.

◆ If you use accent lighting to highlight antiques, be sure to use only low-voltage lights because ordinary spotlights can produce a heat that is damaging to wood and paintings.

◆ If you have a weekend home filled with some valuable pieces, leave your heating on (even on low) all winter if possible, so you don't subject the furniture to sudden changes of temperature. Check your thermostat to ensure that it is well regulated.

Dampness

Dampness in the form of condensation or wet basements or walls can cause mold to develop, warp furniture, damage polished surfaces, and rot fabric.

◆ Put antique furniture against insulated walls and on carpeted or wooden floors. Bare stone or bricks and outside walls can be cold and often very slightly damp. Avoid hanging paintings against a damp wall or in the bathroom.

Humidity

◆ Ideally, keep valuables at a humidity level of 50 to 60 percent. It is safer for a room to be too humid than too dry. With humidity above 70 percent, molds might form. Below 40 percent, paper and water-absorbent materials become brittle; wood shrinks and may then warp and crack. Buy a hydrometer to keep a check on humidity levels.

◆ If your house is very dry, install a humidifier that fans vaporized water into the air to raise the humidity level.

MAINTAINING FURNITURE

◆ Make sure the legs of any antique furniture share an even weight. If a piece of furniture sits off-balance for some time, it may warp slightly, and this can be difficult, or even impossible, to mend. If the floor is uneven, put shims under the legs to compensate.

◆ Try not to overload old furniture because this weakens the joints. Drawers, particularly, can fall apart if they are stuffed too full.

◆ Keep any pieces that fall off the furniture. Simple repairs can sometimes be done at home; difficult repairs, or repairs to very valuable pieces, should be done by a professional restorer.

▼▼ Do not put a new seat cover over an old
◆ ◆ one. This will make the seat too big, and you can break the seat rail joints trying to force the seat into the frame.

◆ Inspect your antiques for any signs of damage or deterioration at least once a year, whether they are actually in use or being stored in a separate room.

◆ If a drawer is sticking, ease it out and rub a candle along the runners, or sprinkle talcum powder on them (see page 95).

◆ On bookcases and armoires, make sure that any interior catches are locked before you close the second door; otherwise the doors might fly open and split the wood around the lock.

◆ Polish brass hardware on wooden antiques at the same time you polish the wood. Use lemon oil or a homemade paste of equal parts salt, vinegar, and flour. Commercial brass cleaners are not recommended for brass fittings on wood; they not only make the brass unnaturally bright, but they also often leave smears and white marks on the wood around it. Such smears can be removed only by a professional restorer.

◆ Remember to use a writing pad or desk blotter when writing at an antique polished table to avoid scratching the surface.

MOVING ANTIQUE FURNITURE

◆ Move and handle items as little as possible to avoid damaging them. Don't move a heavy piece of furniture on your own, even if it's small; get someone to help you carry it by the lowest load-bearing part.

◆ Before you move furniture, remove any drawers and other loose parts so they don't fall out during the move. Shut all doors firmly and lock them if possible to prevent them from swinging open. If they won't lock, secure them with adhesive putty (see below). Never tip a piece of furniture back on its legs or turn it without lifting it because you will weaken the legs. Lift it, then move or turn it. Carry stools and chairs by the legs to avoid weakening the seat joints.

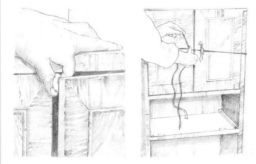

Securing cabinet doors. *If the doors won't stay shut, place a bit of reusable adhesive putty in the corners (above left). Then tie a length of string around the piece to secure it (above right)*

Carrying marble or glass tabletops. *Lift and carry them in a vertical position. Carried horizontally, they can break under their own weight.*

Care of various surfaces

◆ Clean inlaid surfaces of boulle (marquetry that uses thin sheets of brass or pewter, tortoiseshell, mother-of-pearl, and ivory) with a soft brush or a hair dryer set on cool. Never use a dustcloth or chamois because the surface may be loose and the cloth or leather could catch in the metal and pull pieces out.

◆ Leave flaking lacquer alone because treatment is difficult. Likewise, don't rub gilded furniture and never let water get onto gilt; it will damage it permanently.

◆ Most attempts to repair or touch up gilded furniture with any form of gold paint will be unsatisfactory because the paint produces a completely different effect and will soon discolor, leaving the gilding in worse condition.

Storing antique furniture

◆ Keep the storeroom clean, well ventilated, and dry, because wood and upholstery are very susceptible to attack by moths and mold.

◆ Store valuable pieces in a dry place, because the wood may warp or become moldy if allowed to get damp.

◆ Cover furniture with a clean dustcover to protect it from light and dirt while it is in storage. Wash dustcovers at least once a year and never put dirty dustcovers onto clean furniture.

◆ Dustcovers must be made from a light, closely woven cotton. Make fitted covers with double-stitched seams (see page 269) because loose threads can stick to upholstery or catch and pull off pieces of veneer and metal decorations.

▼▼ Be very careful when you put on and ◆ ◆ take off dustcovers or you may damage the furniture.

CARING FOR VALUABLES

Follow the guidelines below for preventing damage to valuables, but if repairs become necessary, get the advice of a professional before attempting anything yourself.

Books

◆ The temperature of a room in which books are kept ideally should not be higher than 60°. Never put them above a radiator; the heat can seriously damage them.

◆ Make sure the room is not too dry. If books get too dry, the paper and the binding will become brittle and the adhesives will deteriorate.

◆ Put similar-sized books together for support, and lay very large books on their sides, as they may be too thick or heavy to support their own weight. Be sure not to stack books too tightly because you can damage the bindings.

◆ When moving valuable books, wrap each one in clean paper and pack it on its side in tough cardboard boxes padded with blankets so the books can't slide around.

◆ Dust all your books about once a year. Work on one shelf at a time and start with the top shelf. Have a sturdy table next to you to put the books on.

◆ If dust has gotten inside a book, open up the book, blow the dust very gently, page by page, or brush it out with a soft watercolor paintbrush. Knocking books together to get rid of the dust will damage the bindings.

Taking a book down from the shelf. *Push the books on either side forward so you can get a firm grip. Never pull a book out of a bookcase by the top of its spine or by gripping it with your fingernails; this can damage the binding.*

Dusting a book. *Hold the book by its front edge to keep it closed so you don't transfer the dust to the inside. Gently brush along the top edge with a clean, dry, soft brush. A shaving brush is ideal.*

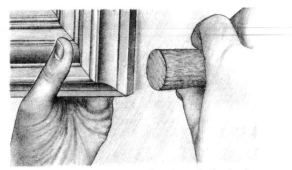

Protecting paintings. *Attach corks to the back of a painting on an outside wall to allow air to flow between the back of the painting and the wall to prevent condensation damage.*

Papers

Handle paper valuables as little as possible. Modern papers are made from poor-quality materials and are apt to yellow and disintegrate. Older paper made from linen fiber is much stronger and stays white.

◆ Keep paper flat to prevent it from warping. Store it in an airtight box interleaved with acid-free tissue. Pick it up by the margins and support it with the palm of your hand, or use the acid-free tissue.

◆ Dust very gently with a soft brush. Don't brush very brittle paper.

Paintings

◆ Hang paintings out of direct sunlight, drafts, and dampness, and keep artificial light on the paintings low. Do not hang pictures on freshly plastered walls, above radiators, or on sections of walls that have hot pipes or internal flues.

◆ Use low-voltage spotlights or hang pictures away from a direct source of electric light. Valuable paintings or paintings on wood, metal, paper, or vellum can be damaged by the heat of the lights.

◆ Support large, heavy frames underneath to prevent the miters from opening under the strain. Either hang the picture so the base is resting on a piece of furniture, or attach small blocks of wood to the wall for the frame to rest on.

◆ Choose varnished or sealed wood frames because they are easier to clean.

◆ When taking down a painting with a carved or fragile plaster frame, lower it onto a pillow or other padded surface to avoid damaging the frame.

◆ Keep works of art on paper (watercolors, drawings, and prints) framed under glass to prevent the surface from collecting grime.

◆ If a drawing or print gets damp, dry it between layers of blotting paper to keep it from buckling as it dries (see below).

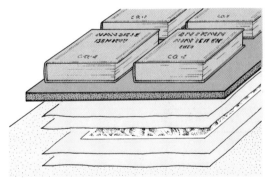

Drying a damp drawing or print. *Take it out of its frame and place it between several pieces of thick blotting paper. Put it under a gentle, even weight (a piece of veneer-covered board and a few books are ideal). Change the blotting paper nearest to the surface of the drawing after an hour, again after another hour, then after two hours. Change the paper every 12 hours for a couple of days.*

CLEANING PICTURES

OIL PAINTINGS

▼▼ Cleaning a valuable painting demands
◆ ◆ expert attention. Take it to a restorer instead of trying to do it yourself.

◆Dust pictures with a very clean dustcloth or
brush. If you use anything that is even slightly
greasy, it will grind the dust in. Even a speck of
dust can act as a focus for condensation.

◆Brush mold off the surface of a painting
with a soft brush. Move the painting to a warm,
dry place for several weeks to dry it out.

◆Apply a very thin film of cream furniture polish after dusting to brighten the surface. Generally don't do any more to a painting. However, if
the painting has been in a very smoky place, and
you are adamant about cleaning it, there are commercial cleaners on the market that are effective.

As an alternative, moisten a cotton ball in an
ammonia solution ($\frac{1}{2}$ teaspoon household ammonia to 1 cup cold water) and wipe the painting. Then apply a thin layer of wax polish and
rub gently.

WATERCOLORS, PRINTS, AND DRAWINGS

▼▼ Watercolors are very difficult to clean, es-
◆ ◆ pecially by an amateur. Consult a
professional.

◆Remove surface dust by rubbing very gently with a ball of bread. This will absorb a little
dust without damaging the paper or the paint.
Real erasers are too rough. Never use water, as
even old watercolors will run.

Cleaning an oil painting. *Dust the painting lightly with a cotton rag or a clean, soft brush. Don't use soap, water, bread, or an eraser because the smallest speck left on the painting will attract moisture.*

Cleaning works of art on paper. *Very gently stroke the surface of the paper with a ball of bread. Don't drag the bread across it. Brush any crumbs away gently with a watercolor paintbrush.*

PICTURE FRAMES

◆Wipe wooden frames with a cloth squeezed
out in warm sudsy water, then polish with a
little cream furniture polish.

◆Gilt frames that are not valuable can be
cleaned with a dry-cleaning solvent, or use a
cloth dipped in a little warm turpentine or paint
thinner. Warm by standing the bottle in a bowl
of hot water. Don't touch valuable frames.

▼▼ Try not to touch the picture while you are
◆ ◆ cleaning or touching up the frame; you
may damage it.

◆Dust ornate frames lightly. The beading
comes off very easily if it gets wet or if it gets
knocked in any way.

Touching up scratches. *Touch up modern gilt frames with gilt paint; you can buy small pots from art suppliers. These paints are poisonous, so don't lick your fingers while working with them.*

Cleaning the glass. *Wipe the glass with a cotton ball dipped in a solution of white vinegar and water, or just warm water.*

Enamel

◆ Handle enamel very carefully; it is actually multilayered glass fired onto a metal base, and it is easily chipped. Enamel can't be repaired without being reheated and that can do more damage.

◆ Dust rarely with a watercolor paintbrush. Never use water; it can seep between the layers and lead to corrosion.

Ivory, bone, and horn

◆ To sustain the warm white color of ivory, horn, and bone, expose them to light. Keeping them in the dark accelerates the yellowing associated with aging. If you always store ivory-handled flatware in a chest or keep ivory piano keys covered, they will eventually darken and yellow.

▼▼ Keep these materials out of intense sunlight and away from any form of heat such as radiators and spotlights. Heat and direct sunlight dry them out and cause cracking.

◆ Dust frequently with a soft, clean cloth; dust carved ivory with a watercolor paintbrush. Ivory should not be washed because it absorbs liquid, and this can cause it to swell.

◆ To clean ivory piano keys, apply a small amount of baking soda with a damp cloth and gently rub one key at a time. Wipe the keys clean with a damp cloth and buff dry.

◆ To whiten slightly yellowed ivory, try rubbing it with a half-and-half solution of lemon juice and water. To remove yellow stains, rub with a cotton ball dipped in peroxide; leave in the sun to dry. There is no need to bleach old ivory—the yellow patina is valued.

◆ You can polish ivory, bone, and horn with a cotton ball dipped in almond oil.

Tortoiseshell

◆ Keep it out of sunlight or strong artificial light. Even a small amount of light can cause tortoiseshell to lose its luster and eventually turn it white and milky-looking.

◆ Rub dried tortoiseshell with repeated coats of linseed oil or wax polish. If this doesn't work and the piece is valuable, take it

Polishing whitened tortoiseshell. *Remove the top layer with very fine sandpaper, working as gently and evenly as possible. When the white layer is removed, polish the surface with jeweler's rouge or wax polish on a soft cloth.*

to an expert. If the piece isn't valuable, remove the dead layer and repolish the layer beneath (see above).

◆ Clean tortoiseshell that is in poor condition with a paste made by moistening jeweler's rouge with a couple drops of olive oil. Rub in gently with a soft cloth, leave for a few minutes, then polish with a clean dustcloth. Tortoiseshell in good condition can be cleaned with furniture cream. Wash imitation tortoiseshell in warm soapy water.

◆ You can repair broken pieces with an epoxy resin adhesive, using another piece of tortoiseshell to patch the first piece. Boil the new piece to soften it enough for cutting, cut it to shape, then flatten it by putting a heavy weight on top. Glue it into place.

Lacquer

◆ Keep lacquer in a place that doesn't vary much in temperature. It's particularly prone to damage from moisture.

◆ You can repair mass-produced 19th-century lacquer with model aircraft paints or nail polish. For a good deep red, mix nail polishes together and test on an inconspicuous spot.

▼▼ Don't attempt to retouch valuable old lacquer or flaking lacquer; the results will be unsatisfactory.

Wooden boxes and ornaments

Water and wood don't mix well. Wood absorbs water and will crack, warp, or soften if it stays wet for any length of time.

◆If a box has a missing hinge, look for a similar more battered box that has hinges you could use as replacements; otherwise, find a jeweler who can make a hinge.

◆Use household glue to repair or replace worn baize or leather.

◆Keep old cylinder music boxes out of direct sunlight and away from any form of heat, because the shellac cement used to secure the mechanism slowly melts and sinks to the bottom of the cylinder. Don't clean, oil, or touch the mechanism of a music box yourself; take it to a professional repairer.

◆Run the mainspring of a music box down before moving it, to reduce the risk of an accident. In midtune, the teeth of the comb are leaning on the cylinder and could break if you then jolt the box.

Clocks and watches

◆Have your clocks and watches repaired, cleaned, and oiled professionally.

◆Take wind-up watches and pendulum clocks to a professional restorer about once a year to be cleaned and oiled; modern clocks and watches probably will need to be sent back to the manufacturer. Tiny wristwatches—worn like pieces of jewelry—work harder than others and should be cleaned and oiled every eight months. If a watch gets wet, take it to a jeweler immediately before it gets rusty and stops working.

◆You don't need to clean electric clocks because the mechanism is sealed, and therefore protected from dust.

◆Get cracks in wooden clocks sealed by a jeweler to keep the dust out of the works, particularly if the clock is valuable or old.

◆If the weights in a pendulum clock are suspended from ropes, try to get them replaced with chains because ropes create lint, which can get into the mechanism.

WINDING CLOCKS AND WATCHES

◆Always turn the hands clockwise, never counterclockwise, or you will damage the works.

◆Wind a clock with its own key. Memorize the number of turns needed.

◆Wind pocket watches once a day, preferably at the same time each day, to keep them running smoothly. Wind small wristwatches twice a day.

◆To wind an old watch without damaging the spring, place your thumbnail and middle fingernail just below the winder and press them together. This forces the winder out just far enough for you to be able to set the hands. Pull it a little further to wind it up; never pull it right out. Wind backward and forward between your finger and thumb. If you keep winding forward, you are more likely to overwind the mechanism.

Setting the time on a striking clock. *Turn the hands clockwise and wait for the clock to finish striking before moving them farther. For example, if the clock strikes at every quarter, wait at each quarter-hour marking until it has completed striking. If you don't do this, the clock will strike at the wrong time.*

◆If you drop your watch in seawater, put it in ordinary water in an airtight container, so that the salt doesn't oxidize and start to rust the mechanism. Take it to a jeweler as soon as possible.

Dolls

Most collector's dolls have unglazed porcelain (bisque) heads and limbs, and wooden or fabric bodies. Some have wax heads and limbs and fabric bodies.

◆ If the head is badly damaged, don't try to salvage the doll—it will be almost impossible to repair.

◆ Repair damage around the leg sockets with the hardest kind of plastic padding, such as the kind used to repair car upholstery. Repair damage to the main part of the body with plastic padding or tiling cement.

◆ Repair fingers and toes of porcelain dolls with barbola paste (from a modeling shop) or cold-set modeling clay.

◆ Look in doll antiques shops for replacement eyes.

◆ If the hair is matted, comb it from the bottom up. Wash the hair with a very weak solution of shampoo or dishwashing liquid and water. Gently squeeze the hair in the solution; don't get it too wet and don't rub it or the tangles will get worse. Avoid washing a doll's hair if it is on a gauze mount. The water can damage the gauze and the glue.

◆ Clean wax dolls with a cotton ball dipped in cold cream. Clean bisque dolls with a cotton ball dipped in a weak liquid detergent solution.

◆ Don't throw away a doll's clothes, no matter how dirty or raggedy they may be. They may indicate its age.

Combing out a doll's hair. *Separate small locks of hair at the bottom (around the neck), and gently tease the tangles out; work through the wig this way.*

Mending small cracks in wax dolls. *Wipe a cotton ball dipped in turpentine or paint thinner over the crack. Apply the liquid sparingly because these substances soften the wax and remove paint.*

Home entertainment equipment

▼▼ Unplug your TV, stereo, compact-disc
◆ ◆ player, or computer before cleaning it.

◆ Apply spray cleaners to your dustcloth rather than directly to the appliance, otherwise you may damage the wiring or clog the ventilation or sound-projecting holes. You can spray directly onto a TV screen.

◆ Clean TV, stereo, and speaker cabinets made of plastic with a cloth dipped into mild soap and warm water and wrung nearly dry. Clean metal cabinets and chrome with a soft cloth moistened with a little white vinegar, rubbing alcohol, or window cleaner.

◆ Keep your sound system and VCR covered when not in use to prevent dust buildup. Vacuum the ventilation louvers and speaker grilles periodically.

◆ Clean VCR heads only when the picture becomes fuzzy or streaked. Try playing a tape on the "fast scan" or "high-speed search" settings for 30 seconds or so. If this doesn't work, use a head-cleaning cassette.

◆ Store videocassettes in the original cardboard or plastic sleeves, upright, with full reels on top, and away from direct sunlight, excessive heat or cold, and moisture. Keep away from electronic equipment, especially stereo speakers, which have magnetic fields that can erase your tapes.

▼▼ Handle CDs by their edges only and
◆ ◆ always store in their cases. Scratches, fingerprints, and dust can affect their quality.

◆ To clean CDs, first rinse the unlabeled side under lukewarm water. If necessary, wipe with a nonabrasive, lint-free cloth after the rinse, working from the center outward with radial strokes, not in a circular motion.

JEWELRY

YOU CAN PRESERVE the beauty and radiance of almost any piece of jewelry by cleaning or polishing it on a regular basis. Examine your jewelry closely before each wearing so if any piece is loosening, you can get it repaired before a vital stone is lost. If a valuable pearl or beaded necklace shows any signs of weakening, it should not be worn until you can have it restrung. When hand-washing, remember to remove your rings; do the same during energetic activity, as even very slight knocks can affect their shape.

CARING FOR YOUR JEWELRY

◆ Keep all pieces of jewelry in separate boxes or compartments of your jewelry case, or hang them up. Plastic ice-cube trays are ideal for small pieces such as rings and earrings.
◆ If there is the slightest chance of anything becoming scratched, wrap each piece individually in tissue or cotton padding.
◆ Prevent tarnish on cheap costume jewelry by covering it with clear cellulose lacquer (from art stores) or clear nail polish. Cover the whole surface carefully so air will not get in. Let it dry completely before you wear it. Remove old lacquer with nail polish remover or lacquer thinner and re-lacquer the object.
▼▼ Don't lacquer a valuable piece yourself;
◆ ◆ take it to a jeweler.

Gold and platinum

◆ Rub gently with a piece of chamois; don't use an old cloth or rag, because it may contain grit that can damage the metal.
◆ Treat gold-plated items with great care—the gold will rub off eventually.
◆ Keep gold and platinum jewelry in separate boxes or wrapped in tissue because they scratch easily.

CLEANING TIPS

◆ Wash jewelry without stones with mild detergent and hot water using a soft-bristled toothbrush. To loosen very stubborn dirt, add a little household ammonia to the washing water. Rinse in hot water and dry with a soft cloth. If you have an oral-hygiene appliance, use the jet spray for the final rinse.
◆ Use a commercial jewelry cleaning fluid for cleaning jewelry with stones. Read the manufacturer's instructions carefully first. Don't use hot water because it may expand the settings (especially prong settings) and clasps, and the stones may fall out.
▼▼ Don't use ammonia or commercial
◆ ◆ cleaner for jewelry with pearls or coral; acids dissolve them. Never use silver cleaner on anything except silver, gold, or platinum; it may cause damage.
◆ Clean stones and beads on a necklace with a brush dipped into dry baking soda; don't use water, because it may rot the string.

Silver

◆ Wrap sterling silver in jeweler's bags and cloths, which are treated with a tarnish inhibitor.
◆ Clean with a commercial silver polish specially formulated for jewelry. Do not leave polish on the silver, as it will tarnish again more quickly and could leave marks on your clothes.

◆ Don't let silver jewelry come into contact with egg, fruit juices, olives, perfumes, salad dressing, salt, vinegar, and so on; they all tarnish silver.

◆ Make your own silver dip with 1 part washing soda to 20 parts water in an aluminum pan. Dip the silver into the mixture, rinse in hot water, and dry with a soft cloth. Don't use this dip for pieces with stones; the setting could loosen.

Cleaning pearl necklaces *Rub gently with a clean, soft chamois cloth. Work carefully between the beads to remove the film of dirt that pearls pick up from their wearers and from the atmosphere.*

Diamonds

◆ Rub them occasionally with a clean, soft cloth to maintain their sparkle. Use a soft toothbrush or a soft eyebrow brush to loosen dirt in the back of the setting.

◆ Boil diamonds (but no other stones) very briefly in a household solution (see below).

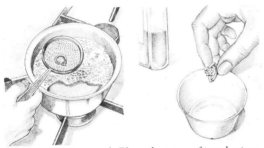

Cleaning a diamond. *Place the piece of jewelry in a small strainer or a piece of cheesecloth (above left). Prepare a weak solution of soapsuds and water, containing 1 or 2 drops of household ammonia, in a saucepan and bring it to a boil. Dip the diamond into the boiling liquid just for a moment, let it cool, then dip it into $\frac{1}{4}$ cup of rubbing alcohol (above right). Then lay the diamond on paper towels and let it dry.*

Crystalline stones

◆ For amethysts, aquamarines, emeralds, garnets, sapphires, rubies, topaz, and tourmaline, add 1 tablespoon ammonia to $\frac{1}{2}$ cup warm water; immerse jewelry. Scrub with a soft toothbrush and rinse in clear water. Dry on a lint-free cloth.

Lapis, malachite, and turquoise

◆ Clean pieces with a solution of detergent and cool water and a soft brush.

Jet

◆ Clean with a soft brush dipped in warm, sudsy water. Rinse in cold water and dry. Washing decorated jet can damage the decoration.

◆ You can remove greasy marks with fresh bread rolled into a ball.

◆ Dust carved jet with a soft paintbrush.

Pearls

◆ Wash pearl rings, bracelets, and earrings with a cloth dipped in warm water and mild detergent. Rinse and buff with a flannel cloth.

◆ Pearl necklaces should not be washed because the water can rot the thread. Clean each pearl individually.

◆ Wear pearls as much as possible; contact with skin keeps them white and lustrous. For the same effect, rub a little olive oil over the pearls and dry with a chamois cloth. Pearls lose their luster and discolor if left in a box.

Amber

◆ Rub amber with 2 drops of linseed oil on a cotton ball. Remove any oily residue, then buff with a chamois cloth.

◆ You can clean greasy marks on amber with a ball of bread or by wiping it with almond oil.

◆ Don't touch amber with alcohol or any solvent; it will leave it with a mat surface. Be careful with perfume and hair spray because they contain alcohol and solvents that damage amber.

Opals

◆ Dry-wash them in powdered magnesia. Put them in a jar of powder, shake gently, then leave overnight. Brush the powder away with a soft brush.

▼▼ Try not to subject opals to extreme
◆ ◆ changes of temperature and handle them carefully, because they are very brittle.

Removing stubborn stains from ivory. *Smear a stiff paste of whiting and a few drops of peroxide onto the mark. The paste must not be too runny, because the ivory will absorb the liquid. Leave the piece out in the sun until the paste is dry. Then wash it off with denatured alcohol and dry thoroughly with a soft cloth.*

Jade

◆ Wash in warm, soapy water. Use a soft toothbrush to get at the dirt in crevices or at the back of the setting. Dry with a soft cloth.
◆ Clean grease marks with cotton dipped in denatured alcohol. Don't let a glued setting soak in water; the glue will loosen.

Ivory

◆ Expose ivory to the light if you don't want it to yellow too quickly. Ivory will turn yellow with age, but this process is accelerated by keeping it in the dark.
◆ To store ivory, wrap it in acid-free tissue instead of cotton padding. Cotton padding absorbs moisture, which can damage the ivory.
◆ You can rub ivory with a soft cloth dipped in almond oil to give it a good protective coating. Don't use water to clean ivory—it absorbs liquid and swells up, and may crack.
◆ Take old or valuable ivory to a professional to clean. Don't try to do it yourself because you may damage its patina.
◆ To lighten slightly yellowed ivory, try rubbing it with a half-and-half solution of lemon juice and water. To give it a good cleaning, rub with a cotton ball dipped in peroxide, and place it in the sun to dry.

Wood

◆ Wipe wooden bangles, necklaces, pendants, and brooches with a damp cloth. Do not wash them with water because this may stain or warp the wood.
◆ Polish sparingly with a wax polish, or rub in a little olive oil.

Glass

◆ Wash in warm water and detergent. Use a soft brush to get at crevices or patterns. Glass should not be washed with very hot water as it may crack. Only leave it in the water briefly, otherwise the stones may become loose.
◆ Polish glass objects, such as a bracelet, with a silver cloth or stainless steel cleaner. Rub scratches with a chamois cloth and jeweler's rouge, pressing lightly. Polish a glass stone with white vinegar and water.

Plaster and acrylic paste

◆ Don't wash plaster or paste jewelry, because water dissolves it. Wipe off dirty marks with a clean cloth dipped in denatured alcohol or diluted ammonia.

Acrylic

◆ Sponge acrylic jewelry with lukewarm sudsy water. Then wipe dry with a damp, clean cloth.
◆ Polish out scratches with a silver polish. Wash the polish off thoroughly or it could come off on your clothes.

REPAIRING JEWELRY

◆ For the most part, do home repair work on costume jewelry only. Let a professional repair your fine jewelry.

◆ Tighten loose prongs of very soft metal, by pressing them down with your thumb. You also can press very gently with a knife handle or use a pair of jeweler's pliers.

◆ When replacing an old stone, pick off the old glue. Clean both the stone and the setting, then roughen the surfaces with a pin or a piece of emery board. Replace the stone using an epoxy resin adhesive, and leave for the full drying time given in the instructions before wearing the piece again.

◆ To make unknotting chains easier, first dust them with a little talcum powder. If knots are stubborn, place a drop of baby oil on a sheet of waxed paper, lay the knot in the oil, and work it out with two pins. Clean the chain in ammonia or warm sudsy water.

RESTRINGING BEADS

◆ Use nylon stringing thread; it doesn't fray as quickly as cotton.

◆ Tie a knot between each bead or group of beads, particularly if they are valuable. Then if the thread breaks, only a couple of beads will drop off, and there will be less chance of losing them. Also, the knots make stringing more flexible and beads will not rub against each other.

◆ Check the clasp before restringing. If it's losing its flexibility, get a new one. If it is valuable, get it repaired.

1 Gather the beads together in a fold of newspaper or around the edge of a box top. If they are graded in size or color, lay them out in the right order.

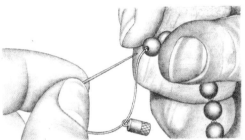

3 When you have made the final knot, pass the thread through the clasp, then back through the last bead.

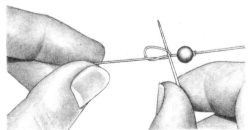

2 Tie a knot 3 inches from the end of the thread and feed the first bead onto it. Make a second loop, stick a needle into it, and use the needle to pull the loop as close to the bead as you can.

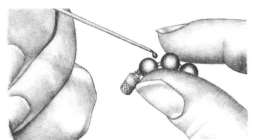

4 Tie a knot between the last two beads. Put a tiny drop of adhesive to keep it there. Put a little glue on the ends of the thread to keep it from fraying.

5 Tie the other side of the clasp onto the other end, and put a drop of adhesive onto the knot.

ASSESSMENT AND INSURANCE

For assessment purposes, jewelry is divided into ornaments, which are made of precious metal and stones, and costume jewelry, which is made of nonprecious metal and stones.

◆Check to see if jewelry is hallmarked. The hallmark is a row of small letters and pictures stamped into the article. Together they will tell you how old the object is, where it was made, and who made it. Jewelry made of silver, gold, or platinum will be hallmarked. A "lion passant" (a lion walking to the left and holding up one paw) on a piece of silver means that it was made in England and that it is sterling silver—sterling silver must be at least 92.5 percent pure silver. If you see the letters EPNS on the back or base, the item is silver-plated.

◆Check the karat value of gold, which

TYPES OF PEARLS

◆To check whether pearls are natural or artificial, draw them through your teeth. Natural and cultured pearls feel rough when drawn across the teeth, artificial ones will feel absolutely smooth.

NATURAL PEARLS
Pearls consist of layers of calcium carbonate, which is produced by oysters and clams as protection against pieces of grit or a particular parasitic worm in their shells. These are the most expensive type of pearl.

CULTURED PEARLS
Cultivated by placing a tiny bit of mother-of-pearl (lining of a shell) in the oyster shell. The oyster immediately starts to cover it with calcium carbonate. These are normally slightly cheaper than natural pearls.

ARTIFICIAL PEARLS
Made from hollow glass lined with fish scales in order to achieve a pearl-like effect.

---

should be stamped on it. Pure gold is 24 karat. The purer the gold, the softer it is, so hardly anything is made of pure gold; most fine jewelry is made of 14- and 18-karat gold.

◆Buy precious jewelry from reputable and well-established stores or jewelers. Jewelry by designer craftsmen may have a high value if the craftsman has a good reputation for his or her work.

◆Antique jewelry, found in antiques shops and junk shops, may have a high value because of age, but beware of high-priced, old costume jewelry, which might be worth very little.

Insurance

◆Take out an "all risks" policy if you have valuable jewelry. This can be taken out either as an extension to the policy. for home contents or as a separate policy to provide more coverage. "All risks" policies are designed to cover your more valuable possessions against loss or damage by any cause; this includes fire, theft, and accident, inside or outside the home.

◆Read the small print carefully. In spite of the title "all risks," there are always exclusion clauses, such as limits to the amount you can take out of the country or no coverage for radioactive contamination or riots. You often can overcome limits or exclusions in a policy by paying an additional premium. This is not likely to be very large and is usually worth the extra expense.

◆Keep receipts for all expensive pieces of jewelry. If an item is old, get a written assessment from an expert, or a shop that specializes in the field, every year when renewing your insurance.

◆If possible, take photographs of all your jewelry and keep these with your policies.

Painting and Decorating

ORGANIZATION

MEASURE AND MARK accurately all of the surfaces to be decorated so that you can estimate how much paper or paint you need.

Make sure you have all the tools you need before you start; don't just make do with what you have in the house—you could lose hours of work. You will need: A sturdy ladder (aluminum ladders are lighter and cheaper than other types); dropcloths, newspaper, and plastic sheets covering floors and furniture; stripping and sanding tools; putty knife and filler; a bucket for mixing wallpaper paste, etc.; a paint tray; and a selection of brushes, rollers, and cloths.

An easy way to remember how you had things previously is to photograph the room before you begin.

THE WORK SEQUENCE

◆ Work on one room at a time so you get each job finished and can use the rooms that are not being decorated. Clear the room first. If possible, take out all the furniture and store it somewhere for the entire time. If that's not possible, take anything you may need from drawers and closets. Move the furniture into the middle of the room and cover it with dustcovers. Remove loose rugs, curtains, and pictures.

◆ Remove door and window fixtures (handles, door plates, hooks, locks, bolts, and catches) and light fixtures to prevent them from being splashed with paint or stripper.

◆ Tape plastic wrap around switchplates and outlets to keep water from getting into them.

Covering wall fixtures. *Cut a piece of plastic wrap to fit, and tape it over the fixture using masking tape. Make sure no water can get under it.*

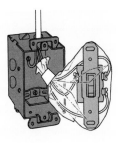

ORDER OF WORK

◆ Prepare for decorating: Fill any cracks, patch the plaster, scrape and sand damaged areas, and clean dirt from all surfaces to be painted or papered. Then decorate in the following order:

◇ *Ceiling*
◇ *Walls and alcoves* (if painting)
◇ *Doors*
◇ *Windows*
◇ *Baseboards*
◇ *Radiators*
◇ *Walls and alcoves* (if wallpapering)

◆ Bare patches of wood or plaster need a preparatory coat of primer to seal them before you paint or paper.

◆ Always repaint or repaper in the same order.

Protecting floor coverings. *Attach plastic firmly to the baseboard and corners, using double-sided tape.*

◆ Assemble all the equipment you will need so you have everything right at hand.

◆ Roll up rugs and place them out of your way; cover the rolls with old sheets or plastic drop cloths. Spread drop cloths out flat on the floor, and secure the corners so there is no risk of tripping over them.

◆ Wait until the paint or wallpaper paste is completely dry before putting furniture back in place.

MEASURING A ROOM

◆ You need a good, retractable measuring tape, a calculator (unless your mental arithmetic is very good), a piece of paper, and a pencil.

Walls. Measure the floor-to-ceiling height of each wall, leaving out any baseboard or frieze. Then measure the width of each wall, without deducting window and door areas, and multiply the width by the height for the total wall area. For example, a wall measuring 10 feet high by 11½ feet wide has a total area of 115 square feet.

Ceilings. Multiply the widths of two adjacent walls. Calculate the ceiling area of the alcoves in the same way and add this to the ceiling measurement.

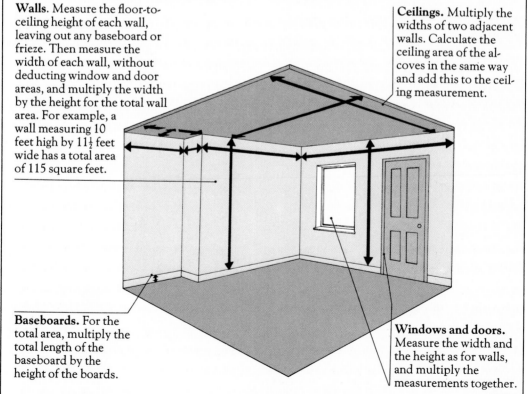

Baseboards. For the total area, multiply the total length of the baseboard by the height of the boards.

Windows and doors. Measure the width and the height as for walls, and multiply the measurements together.

PREPARATION

How HAPPY YOU are with the results of your new decorating depends on how well you prepare. If you ignore flaws and cracks, they may rapidly reappear and may even be exaggerated against a new finish, leaving you with no choice but to start over again.

How much preparation is necessary depends largely upon the age and condition of your house. But, whatever its age, make sure every surface in it that is to be painted or decorated is smooth, clean, and dry before you start decorating. This means removing all dirt, filling any cracks or holes, and replacing deteriorated wallboards. Old woodwork that is badly chipped or flaking should be stripped to the bare wood and primed.

WALLS AND CEILINGS

◆ Check the condition of the existing paint or plasterwork. If it is sound, wash the surface with a diluted ammonia solution and rinse thoroughly with clean water. If it is uneven, or has hairline cracks, try covering it with lining paper or wallpaper that can be painted over. Bigger cracks should be filled.

◆ A newly plastered wall should be left to dry for several weeks before sealing with a primer or a thin coat of latex prior to decorating. New wallboard (drywall) should be given a coat of primer sealer beforehand.

◆ Dried water stains should be coated with an oil-base sealer, otherwise they will show through any water-base paint.

Stripping wallpaper by hand

It is always better to strip off old wallpaper than to try to paper over it; otherwise, any peeling and blistering, or even a bold pattern in the old paper, may show through the new.

◆ **Stripping standard wallpapers.** Most are removed by soaking with warm water, using a large brush or a sponge, and then by scraping. A little laundry soap or liquid detergent added to the water will loosen the old paste and speed up the soaking process. Scrape as evenly as possible so you don't gouge new holes in the wall.

◆ **Stripping vinyl wallpapers.** These are easily peeled off by lifting the bottom edge of the paper with your fingernail or a stripping knife, then peeling each length straight up and off the wall. Vinyl wall coverings have a thin layer of backing paper that will remain on the wall as you pull the top layer off. If it is not torn, this can be left on as a liner for the new wallpaper. If it is torn, remove it.

◆ **Stripping difficult papers.** Washable and overpainted papers are made to withstand water, so soaking the surface does not always do the trick. First, score the surface with a steel brush or a serrated scraper, then soak the paper and scrape it off. If you can't get all the paper to come off, rent a steam stripper. These are simple to use and eliminate the mess of soaking and scraping. Steam passes through a plate held close to the wall, loosening the paper sufficiently so you can easily scrape it off as you go along.

Filling cracks and holes

Even the smallest hairline crack will show through a new paint job, if it is not carefully filled and sanded first.

◆ You can use standard, interior-grade cellulose putty for most inside plaster or wooden surfaces. It comes in tubs or tubes of ready-to-use paste, or in a powder form that you mix up with water to a creamy consistency.

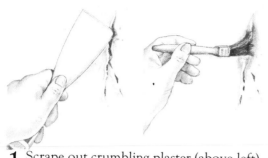

2 Pack and smooth in the filler a little at a time with a putty knife; if the crack is deep, let the filler dry before applying another layer.

3 Leave the final layer of filler slightly raised above the surface, and let it harden for a few hours.

4 When the filler is dry, rub smooth to a flush finish.

5 Seal the filler and the area around it with the recommended primer or latex paint before decorating.

1 Scrape out crumbling plaster (above left) and dampen each crack (above right).

SANDING AND SANDING EQUIPMENT

Sanding, whether by hand or machine, is the best method for smoothing wood or plaster surfaces, or making surfaces slightly rough to provide a gripping surface for paint or varnish.

◆ Power sanders are quicker for large areas but are not effective in corners or difficult spaces. They will need to be sanded by hand instead. Sanders can generally be rented.

◆ To achieve a smooth finish, start with coarse sandpaper and work through the grades to finish with fine paper.

◆ When sanding wood, always work along the grain to get the smoothest finish.

◆ To prevent wet-and-dry paper from clogging, dip it often in water and rub it on a piece of soap to lubricate it. (This applies only if you are sanding by hand.) Don't dampen any other type of sandpaper or you won't be able to use it. To clear clogged sandpaper, slap the back of the paper hard against the edge of a table, or run the back of the sheet up and down over the edge of a table or workbench.

◆ When using a disk sander, make sure that only the outer edge of the disk is in contact with the wall surface.

SANDPAPERS

◆ These can be used by hand or machine. Several types are available, in grades ranging from very fine to very coarse. They are marked on the back of the papers.

POWER SANDERS

◇ **Orbital sanders** (finishing sanders). These are the most widely used of the power sanders; they move at high speed in a series of tiny orbits to give a fine finish on wood and painted surfaces.

◇ **Belt sanders.** These are used for heavier sanding jobs and to sand or strip wood and metal quickly.

◇ **Sanding attachments.** These can be fitted to an electric drill. Disk sanders are used to sand wood, metal, and plastic. Wire wheel brushes have a gentler action. Foam drum sanders are used on curved surfaces.

Sanding by hand. *Wrap a sheet of sandpaper around a sanding block or a block of cork, wood or rubber. This makes sanding by hand easier and also helps you to apply pressure evenly.*

WOODWORK

◆Before priming, rub down bare woods with sandpaper to make them smooth. For bare softwoods, apply shellac over knots and areas of resin (see *Filling Knots in Wood*, page 186) to keep the resin from oozing out.

◆ Wipe bare hardwoods that are oily with a rag soaked in paint thinner, so the paint can stick to the wood's surface.

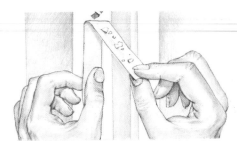

Testing for unsound paint. *Apply a strip of masking tape to the paint. If, when you lift it off, it pulls paint away, the paint is unsound. Strip the affected area and then prime it before painting.*

◆Sound paint can be left; just rub it lightly with a fine sandpaper to provide a grip for the new paint.

◆If the paint is blistered, cut the blisters with a knife and rub them smooth. Then apply shellac, fill any holes, and prime.

◆When stripping a door, strip all of the moldings before working on the rest of the door. The paint on the panels will protect the wood if your scraper slips.

STRIPPING EQUIPMENT

SCRAPERS
◆ Use scrapers to lift paint off woodwork and walls.

Flat scrapers. *These are good for stripping paint off large surfaces.*

Flat scraper

Shave hook. *This is particularly useful for moldings around doors and windows.*

Shave hook

HEAT STRIPPERS
◇**Gas blowtorch.** Use this to remove oil-base paint that is covering a large surface area. It is simple to operate, easy to light, and can be used with a pressure regulator.

◇**Hot-air gun.** This blasts out a powerful stream of heat that will melt the paint in its path. Special nozzle attachments can be used for stripping paint in difficult places and for shielding the glass when stripping a window frame. Some hot-air guns are noisy and heavy to use.

◇**Chemical strippers.** The alternative to heat stripping, these are practical for removing paint from intricate moldings or corners that could be scorched by a blowtorch or hot-air gun. They can be used on water-base and most oil-base paints.

◇**Peel-off strippers.** Quick and easy types of chemical stripper are applied in paste form and left to dissolve layers of paint that are simply peeled off later.

Heat stripping

◆Use a blowtorch or a hot-air gun for stripping brick, stone, and hardwoods.

◆ When using a hot-air gun, point the stream of heat directly on the area until the paint begins to soften after a few seconds.

▼▼ Do not use heat strippers on plaster-
◆ ◆ board (drywall), particleboard, hardboard, or softwoods such as pine, redwood, or cedar, because these materials could catch fire. Don't use heat for wood that is to be left unpainted because it could scorch it.

Using a heat stripper.

1 Hold the blowtorch about 6 to 8 inches from the surface to be stripped. Start at the top and run the flame over the paint until it starts to melt.

2 As the paint starts to melt and shrivel up, use a sharp scraper to quickly peel it off into a metal tray. Try to catch the melting paint in the tray before it hits the floor.

3 Remove all the softened paint before it hardens again, and then run the heat stripper over any remaining paint until it slides off. Use a shave hook for peeling the paint off moldings.

4 Smooth the surface with medium-grade sandpaper and rub away any scorch marks or paint will not adhere to it.

Dry scraping

This is the cheapest and safest way of stripping paint, but it is hard work and better left to areas where the paint peels off readily.

Using a two-edged scraper.
1 Score the surface lightly using the serrated edge of the blade.
2 Remove the paint with the plain edge, being careful not to scrape the wood.

Chemical paint strippers

These are ideal for stripping surfaces that could be easily scorched with a heat stripper. Use them to remove old paint from window frames, moldings, and other intricate surfaces, as well as natural woods that are to be left unpainted.

Using chemical strippers.
1 Apply a thick layer of the stripper with an old brush; after a few minutes the paint will shrivel and can be scraped off.

2 Remove any remnants with the scraper and steel wool soaked in alcohol, then rub with sandpaper until smooth.
♦ **Peel-off strippers.** Apply a thick layer of paste with a putty knife and let it eat through the layers of paint. After several hours, the layer can be easily peeled off with gloved fingers, leaving a clean subsurface.

Filling knots in wood

♦ Knots in bare wood must be sealed before painting to prevent resins from oozing out and staining the paintwork.
1 After filling cracks with wood putty and sanding them smooth, soak wood knots and any resinous patches with shellac on a clean paintbrush, making sure you cover the edges.
2 Let the wood dry for a couple of days, then apply primer before painting.

PAINTING

Top-quality paint will serve you well not only as decoration but also as protection for the internal and external surfaces of your home. High-grade paints are simple to apply, cover beautifully, and last far longer, saving you lots of money in the long run. An unknown, cheap brand will, more often than not, look or feel inferior and not last as long.

When choosing paint, keep in mind that cost is not always the best guide to quality. The best advice is to buy a well-known brand from a reputable home center. With routine care, newly painted surfaces can sustain color and coverage for up to 10 years.

CHOOSING PAINTS

◆ First determine what kind of paint is suitable for the various surfaces that are to be redecorated. Water-base (latex) paints are ideal for walls and ceilings. Oil-base paints (alkyds) provide the best coverage for woodwork and metal surfaces.

◆ Buy enough paint in one batch to do the whole job; this is particularly important if you are having the color custom-mixed, since pigments can vary from batch to batch. If you are mixing the paint yourself, make a note of the quantity and names of pigments used.

◆ When selecting the color of paint, bear in mind that the combined effect of the color on the walls and ceiling may intensify the shade you choose by as much as 50 percent above the manufacturer's color chart.

◆ Be sure to test the color (the bigger the swatch, the better) on an inconspicuous part of the wall before you make your final decision.

Preparatory paints

Whether brand-new or stripped, all bare surfaces that are to be painted will need a coating of primer and a base coat to provide an even surface for the final covering paint. This is especially relevant when dealing with new or stripped wood, or if a dark color is to be covered with a lighter shade.

◆ You do not need to prime previously painted surfaces.

◆ Primers and base coats, whether oil- or water-base should be compatible with follow-up layers of paint.

◆ **Primers.** These are designed to seal the pores of bare surfaces, reduce absorbency, and provide a uniform finish. Make sure you use the primer that is recommended for the particular surface you are redoing. Most woods will take a standard white or pink wood primer. Latex primer may be used but wood primer will give a better result. Multi-purpose primers are available but most primers are designed for a specific surface.

◆ **Base coats.** These are used as a follow-up to the primer to further prepare the surface prior to using a topcoat. They contain strong pigments that serve to hide underlying colors and thereby reduce the amount of final covering paint that is needed.

Topcoats

◆ These are divided into water-base (latex) paints for painting plaster, wallpaper, and masonry and brick surfaces; and oil-base (alkyd) paints that are mainly used on wood and metal. Both are available in exterior and interior grades.

◆ **Latex paints.** These are widely used on walls and ceilings, because they spread well and dry rapidly to a smooth, even finish.

◆ On new surfaces, it is common to use a thinned latex and water coating as a primer. On previously painted or papered surfaces, latex should be built up coat by coat, allowing each layer to dry in between.

◆ Water-base paints are unsuitable for metal, because they can rust the surface, and for wood, since the water content raises the grain, producing a rough finish.

◆ **Alkyds.** These are mainly used as a protective finishing coat for wood and metal, because they are tough and hard-wearing. They are usually preceded by a primer and base coat, especially on bare woods and new surfaces.

◆ Alkyds need to be more thoroughly brushed out than latex and should be applied in thin coats to avoid runs. There also are nondrip alkyds that go on in a thicker layer without much brushing.

◆ Make sure the room is well ventilated when using alkyds, because they dry slowly and have a very strong smell.

◆ To make oil-base paints go farther, dilute them with paint thinners.

◆ **Alkyd enamel paints.** These oil-base paints need no primer and give a very high-gloss finish, but they are expensive.

Specialty paints

◇ **Anticondensation paint.** This provides an insulating film between a cold surface and a humid atmosphere, and thereby reduces condensation.

◇ **Textured paint.** Used to hide cracks and irregularities in walls and ceilings. Some brands are self-texturing and automatically leave a patterned surface; others are textured after application with sponges, combs, or brushes.

◇ **Masonry paint.** A durable exterior latex that contains bulking materials for filling gaps, hiding cracks, and preventing erosion.

◇ **Floor paints.** These are strengthened with epoxy resins and rubber to withstand heavy foot traffic.

◇ **Polyurethane paints.** Use these tough, hard-wearing paints for radiators, pipes, and metal windows—they withstand moisture and hard knocks.

PAINT FINISHES AND QUANTITIES

Selecting a paint finish.

◆ Flat, semigloss and high-gloss finishes are available in the two main paint types. Each has its own advantages.

◇ **Flat paint.** With its suedelike softness, it is good on most walls except those subject to frequent soiling. Although some flat paints are scrubbable, the cleaning results are less satisfactory than with other finishes. Dark, flat paint shows stains more than lighter varieties.

◇ **Semigloss paint.** Combines the softness of a satiny surface with the durability and washability needed in heavy-use areas, such as the kitchen, bathrooms, and children's rooms.

◇ **High-gloss.** The most washable finish, stains penetrate it least, and soil comes off most easily. Glossy paint also has a decorative effect, giving a lacquer or enamel look.

Estimating paint quantities.

◆ Generally, a gallon of paint will cover about 400 square feet. Provide the dealer with the size of your room (the total length of all walls multiplied by the room's height) and the number of openings (see page 182).

▼▼ Make sure you tell the dealer if you
◆◆ plan to use a different type of paint on woodwork and doors.

◆ Remember to allow for any extra space taken up by alcoves and chimneys.

◆ Include windows and doors as part of the surface unless they are very large.

◆ When estimating for windows, in general allow $2\frac{1}{2}$ square yards for a small window, $4\frac{3}{4}$ square yards for a medium-size window, and 6 square yards for a large window.

◆ If the surface is very porous, you will need two or even three base coats, even after sealing.

◆ On a textured surface you will need to use more paint, or add water to the first coat.

◆ You will need fewer coats for nondrip paints, because they are thicker.

◆ You will need extra coats if painting a light color on top of a dark color.

◆ Semigloss latex may need more coats than a flat latex.

PAINTING TOOLS

◆ Use high-quality tools; they last longer and provide a better finish.

Brushes

◆ Buy brushes with natural bristles for alkyds. Even though they are more expensive, they have a longer life, and the bristles don't fall out as easily.

▼▼ Latex paint will make natural bristles
◆ ◆ stick together and become moplike. Use synthetic ones.

◆ Foam brushes are inexpensive, disposable, and adequate for many projects.

◆ You will need:

◇ A 4-inch brush for applying paint to walls and ceilings

◇ A 2-inch brush for painting baseboards and doors

◇ A 1-inch brush for painting window frames and other narrow areas

◇ A cutting-in brush with angled bristles for painting around windows

◇ A radiator brush with a long handle and angled head for painting behind radiators.

Rollers

◆ Use rollers if you want to cover large areas quickly and easily. They spread latex paints better than alkyd paints.

◆ Rollers are the best tools for painting textured walls and ceilings; for a smooth finish, use a roller with a short pile; for a lightly textured look, a medium pile; and for a deeply textured finish, a long pile.

◆ Use mohair covers for glossy finishes, and lamb's-wool covers for solvent-base paints. Synthetic foam covers are all-purpose but don't provide the best finish.

◆ Use a different cover for each color.

◆ Buy a paint tray if you are using a roller; this allows you to distribute the paint evenly.

◆ Attach an extension handle to the roller for painting high walls and ceilings. (Make sure your roller has a hole in the handle to take the extension.) You can buy one or make your own from a broom, mop, or long, window squeegee handle.

◆ Choose sturdy rollers without raised seams on the cover; less sturdy ones will deteriorate quickly.

◆ Use 3-inch-wide trim rollers for painting baseboards and door panels. You may find a brush handier for corners and around electrical outlets.

Foam pads

Pads are light, faster to use than brushes, and are more or less splash-free, but they are expensive and often leave a disappointing finish. As with rollers, you can use them for large areas but not for corners.

◆ Buy a paint tray for flat pads that have a handle on the back. For pads shaped like a paintbrush, use an ordinary paint bucket.

◇ **Edging pads.** These have small wheels for cutting in between a wall and a ceiling (they won't get into corners). Keep the wheels paint-free, and be careful not to get too much paint on the pad.

◇ **Sash and crevice pads.** These are useful for reaching difficult places.

◇ **Long-handled pads.** These are good for radiators and other places that are hard to reach.

Cutting-in brush   Paintbrushes   Foam brush   Paint pads   Roller and tray

CLEANING AND STORING PAINTING EQUIPMENT

BRUSHES

◆ If you've been using latex paint, wash the brushes in water and detergent as soon as you have finished painting to keep the bristles supple and ready to use again.

◆ Clean brushes used for lacquers and oil-base and polyurethane paints with paint thinners, turpentine, or a commercial paintbrush cleaner. Then wash out the brushes.

◆ Dry brushes with the bristles held together in the right shape with a rubber band to keep them in good condition.

Storing brushes in water or solvent. *Drill a hole through the handle of the brush and thread a piece of wire or a thin stick through it. Place this over the rim of a jar. This ensures that the bristles do not touch the bottom and lose their shape.*

◆ During short breaks, wrap brushes tightly in plastic wrap or foil, or leave them with their bristles immersed in clean water or solvent (see below left).

◆ To store brushes overnight, wrap them in newspaper or plastic with a few drops of turpentine on their bristles.

◆ Oil-base paints that are very sticky can be removed by rubbing bristles with linseed oil after the initial cleaning.

◆ To soften old, hard brushes, agitate them in paint thinner.

ROLLERS

◆ Before washing rollers, roll them out on newspaper to remove the excess paint.

◆ If used with latex paints, wash rollers in warm detergent, then rinse; use turpentine if oil-base paints have been used.

◆ Rinse, squeeze, and shake out before hanging up to dry. Cover with plastic wrap when dry.

◆ Clean pads in the same way as rollers; store them flat and unwrapped.

PAINTING A ROOM

◆ As a general rule, paint a room from top to bottom, so that dust does not fall onto wet paint, and any drips can be retouched later. Keep a damp cloth handy to remove dust, drips, and blobs.

◆ When applying latex, close the windows so the paint does not dry too quickly; it is important to have time to blend the edges of each section while they are still wet.

◆ If paint does not cover well, don't try to thicken it, but let it dry and apply an extra coat. For a perfectly smooth finish, two or three coats may be needed.

Ceilings and walls

◆ Try to complete ceilings and individual walls in uninterrupted sessions so you are working in the same light. If you stop midway, the dried paint line will show through the final finish.

◆ If you plan to use a roller, first coat the corners of the room and where the ceiling meets the walls with a narrow brush; a roller will not reach these areas.

◆ Paint around windows and door frames with an angled cutting-in brush, in order to better control where you put the paint.

◆ Small bubbles may show up if you are painting with water-base paint over wallpaper. They should disappear as the paint dries. If not, remove them (see below).

Removing bubbles on wallpaper. *Slit bubbles with a utility knife or razor blade (above left), dab the slit with wallpaper paste and flatten to the wall (above right). Let it dry out and then repaint.*

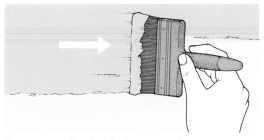

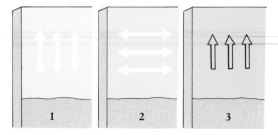

Painting walls. *Apply the paint in horizontal bands; it is less tiring and you are less likely to drip paint. To make overlaps less noticeable, keep the bottom edge (or top if you are starting on the ground) of each band fairly ragged and blend while wet.*

WOODWORK

◆ Use an oil-base or enamel paint to protect wood from wear and tear.

◆ You must use a base coat for alkyd paint even if the existing paintwork is sound; sand between coats to give the paint a surface it can stick to.

▼▼ Try not to overload the brush with ◆ ◆ paint, or you will get drips down the surface. Don't allow the paint to build up in ridges at the edges; these will spoil the smoothness of the surface. Applying too much paint to the top and not enough at the sides is a common mistake and causes drips.

◆ You need not paint the top edge of a door unless it can be seen from the stairs or landing, although it will be more difficult to clean if left unpainted.

Flush doors

◆ To paint flush doors, use a 3-inch brush for the door and a 2-inch brush for the edges; these give the best finish. Start at the top corner on the hinge side and work in

Painting door edges. *Hold the door open by tapping a wedge under it to expose its hinge and latch edges for painting. Don't close the door until the paint has dried thoroughly.*

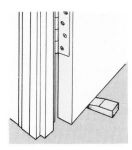

Painting flush doors. *Paint small sections at a time. Begin with vertical strokes (1), brush across them with horizontal strokes (2), and end with light upward strokes (3).*

10-inch-square sections until you reach the bottom corner on the knob side.

Paneled doors

◆ Use a 1-inch brush for the framework and a 2-inch or 3-inch brush for the panels.

◆ If painting panels and framework in contrasting colors, paint one color first, let it dry for three days, and edge it with masking tape before applying the second color; this way you prevent one color from bleeding into the other.

▼▼ Don't put masking tape on until the ◆ ◆ paint is very dry, and don't leave it in place for more than a day in case it pulls the paint off with it. Pull it off very slowly and carefully (see page 87).

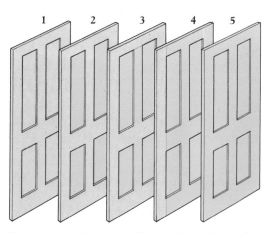

Painting paneled doors. *Paint in this order: Moldings (1), panels (2), central verticals (3), horizontals (4), and outer verticals and edges (5).*

PAINTING WINDOWS

DOUBLE-HUNG WINDOWS

1 *Push the bottom sash up and the top sash down until there is an 8-inch overlap. Paint the meeting rail of the top sash and then the verticals.*

2 *Almost close both windows, and insert matchsticks between the frame and the window to prevent them from sticking. Then paint the rest of the top sash.*

3 *Paint the bottom sash, catching any drips from the vertical sections.*

4 *Paint the frame. Close the windows and paint the runners (but not the cords).*

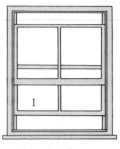
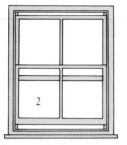

CASEMENT WINDOWS

◆ If one window is fixed, start with the one that opens, because it will dry fastest.

1 *If your windows have crossbars, paint the rabbets of these bars first and then the crossbars themselves (see below). Use a cutting-in brush.*

2 *Paint the crossrails. If your windows don't have crossbars, paint the crossrails first.*

3 *Paint the side verticals and edges.*

4 *Paint the frame and then the sill. Paint the stay last so you can open or close the window while you are painting it. If paint gets onto the hinges, wipe it off before it dries or it will be hard to remove.*

Painting around glass. *To guarantee a neat edge around windowpanes, protect glass with a paint shield or strips of masking tape before painting the woodwork. Remove masking tape before the final coat of paint is dry.*

Cutting in. *Place the brush on the bar about $\frac{1}{8}$ inch from the edge of the glass and carefully push it toward the edge. Press down lightly and draw the brush along quickly to make a long, clean line.*

Baseboards

◆ Use a 2-inch brush; this is the best size for the average width of baseboards.

◆ Dab a cutting-in brush into the corners and crevices to draw away excess paint.

◆ Prevent paint from smudging onto the walls and carpets by using masking tape, cardboard, or a carpet shield (see below).

Using a carpet shield. *Place the shield against the baseboard so the edge tucks under it and covers the edge of the carpet. Leave it in place until the paint is completely dry.*

Stairs and staircases

◆ It is most important to set up a safe working platform so you can reach even the least accessible parts without danger.

◆ The best sequence of work is as follows: The landing ceiling, the walls of the staircase from the top down, the stairs, banisters, and handrail.

◆ Try to keep people off the stairs and avoid moving the doors until the paint has dried,

---

PERFECTING PAINTED WOODWORK

Teardrops, wrinkles, specks, pimples, and brushmarks in the paint, flaking, loss of gloss, and having the previous coat show under the new one are caused by not cleaning and sanding the surfaces properly, overloading the brush, or overthinning the paint.

◆ Allow the paint to harden for a week, then rub it down with sandpaper, clean the surface, and apply a fresh coat of paint more carefully.

SETTING UP A SAFE WORKSTATION

◆ Wrap cloth around the top of the straight ladder to prevent it from slipping or damaging the wall.

1 *Put up a sturdy step-ladder on the top landing. Lean a long ladder against the wall opposite the landing, with its foot lodged against a stair riser.*

2 *Link the ladders with boards. For spans longer than 5 feet, use two planks, one on top of the other, secured with nails and strong tape.*

---

because this spreads dust, which sticks to wet paint.

Pipes and radiators

◆ For difficult areas, such as a radiator, use a 1-inch brush and a crevice or radiator roller or brush.

◆ Paint when pipes are cold and allow to dry thoroughly before you turn the heat on again. Otherwise the paint may blister or not stick to the metal.

◆ Check old pipes and radiators for rust; they may need to be treated and primed before you paint them. Copper pipes don't need primer; just give them a coat of base coat and alkyd.

◆ Never paint connections or fitting nuts on radiators or pipes; you may not be able to undo them.

◆ When painting pipes, start at the top and work down so you can catch any paint drips.

◆ When pipes are close to the wall, hold a piece of cardboard behind them to shield the wall from paint.

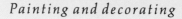
WALLPAPERING

M ODERN WALLPAPERS come in a wide variety of designs, colors, and textures to suit the purpose and ambience of any room. Some papers such as silks and woven fabrics are purely decorative; vinyls and washable papers are easy to clean; textured papers help to conceal an imperfect surface; others have insulating and water-resistant properties.

Select high-quality wall coverings, because they are easier to put up and will last longer. If you can't cover an entire room in an expensive paper, incorporate a few panels of it against a harmonizing but less costly backdrop.

CHOOSING WALL COVERINGS

◆Before buying wallpaper, check the symbols on the packaging to see how easy the paper will be to care for. Washable papers are cheap and easily maintained. Prepasted wall coverings are much easier to hang than those you have to paste yourself.

◆Choose easy-strip wall coverings if you think you will want to change the covering at a later date. With these, you peel off the front part and leave the backing as a lining for the next covering.

◆Check lot numbers on rolls before unwrapping them; they should be the same on all rolls from the same batch.

Estimating wallpaper quantities

Standard wallpapers come in rolls of about 33 feet × 21 inches. Lining-paper rolls are usually slightly wider and come in both standard and economical large rolls.

◆Measure the distance around the room and the floor-to-ceiling height (not counting baseboards and moldings, but adding 4 inches to the totals to allow for trimming after hanging). Multiply one by the other to find the square footage. The amount of usable paper in a single roll will cover about 30 square feet.

◆Find out the distance between the repeats in the pattern; this will affect the quantity you need. Add 10 percent for waste when choosing a large pattern.

WALL COVERINGS QUANTITY CHART

Check this chart to estimate the number of 30-square-foot rolls you will need.

HEIGHT OF ROOM	CIRCUMFERENCE OF ROOM								
	30 feet	38 feet	46 feet	54 feet	62 feet	70 feet	78 feet	86 feet	94 feet
7 feet	4	5	6	7	8	9	10	12	13
8 feet	5	6	7	9	10	11	12	14	15
9 feet	6	7	8	9	10	12	13	14	15
10 feet	6	8	9	10	12	13	15	16	18

TYPES OF WALL COVERING

◆**Machine-printed papers.** These are moderately priced. The selection is wide, and most are well designed and durable. One reason these papers are moderately priced is because they're printed on high-speed presses, which reduces the manufacturing cost.

◆**Hand-printed wallpapers.** These are more costly than most other kinds, with prices varying a great deal depending on the background material used. Though this type of covering is called "paper," the selection also includes designs printed on linen, foil, vinyl— even silk.

Ordering hand-printed wallpapers may mean a wait of several weeks. These papers are usually not pretrimmed, and fragile coverings should be hung by a professional. Some may even need lining papers.

◆**Washable wall coverings.** These include several types of materials that range from "wipeable" to downright scrubbable.

Plastic-coated wallpaper allows you to wipe off spots with a damp cloth. Vinyl-coated, fabric-backed papers, and polyvinyl-chloride wall coverings are labeled "scrub-

bable," meaning they can withstand frequent brisk scrubbings over a long time. Grease and smoke stains will come off with no damage to the surface.

◆**Prepasted papers.** These already have an adhesive coating when you purchase them, so they save time and effort. Just dip them into water or wet the back with a sponge. Prepasted papers can go over old wallpaper (except vinyl), as long as the paper is smooth and tight to the wall.

Prepasted papers also come in 12-inch squares for even easier application than rolls.

◆**Strippable wall coverings.** These can be pulled off the wall in full strips without steaming or scraping. The main advantage of this type of wall covering is the ease of removal when it is time to repaper or paint. It's a particularly good advantage with vinyl, as you should never try to hang new wall covering on top of old vinyl. Most fabric-backed vinyls are strippable, but some vinyls are not.

Any wall covering can be made strippable if a quick-release adhesive is used. However, only fabric-backed, fairly heavy grades of wall coverings

are actually durable enough to be used again.

◆**Grass cloth and fabrics.** These are laminated to paper, and sold in rolls in wallpaper stores. Some of these specialty coverings are cork, felt, burlap, and synthetic or natural-fiber grass cloth. Cork is glued to a paper in feather-thin slices. Felt, which has insulating and sound-deadening qualities, is now moth- and flame-proof. Burlap is available in many colors and is often vinyl-coated for soil resistance. Grass cloth comes in a range of colors and textures from smooth to nubby. These coverings are hung in the same way as regular wallpaper, but should be used with lining papers for best results.

◆**Cushion-backed wallpaper.** This is a washable vinyl covering designed to mask cracked plaster or imperfect wall surfaces. It also can be used on rough concrete- or cinder-block walls. The embossed cushion and woven glass fiber backing prevent this wall covering from conforming to the irregular surface of the wall.

WALLPAPER CARE SYMBOLS

Wallpaper manufacturers are now using these international symbols to indicate the type of wallpaper and how it should be used.

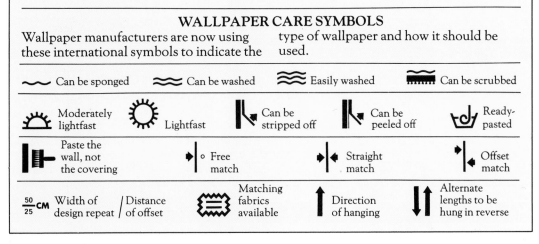

EQUIPMENT

◆A platform stepladder is essential so you can reach the ceiling level safely.

◆If the wallpaper is not prepasted, you need a long table to lay it on while you paste it. Folding paste tables are cheap; otherwise, use a flat door or board on two supports.

◆For prepasted wall coverings, you don't need a long table, just a soaking tray or pan of water to immerse the paper in. A table will come in handy for laying out and marking up the lengths of wall covering.

Wallpapering tools

You will need:

◇**Measuring tools.** A steel tape measure or a yardstick, and a pencil.

◇**Cutting tools.** A pair of sharp scissors with long blades and a utility knife or pair of small scissors for trimming around light switches, outlets, etc.

◇**Straightedge or steel ruler.** For cutting textured wall coverings.

◇**Seam roller.** To make sure seams are well pasted down and for patching wall coverings. Don't use it on embossed wall coverings, because it will flatten them.

◇**Plastic buckets.** One for paste, one for water.

◇**Pasting brush.** Use a 4-inch paintbrush or a paint roller with a foam cover.

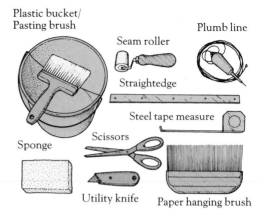

Plastic bucket/ Pasting brush — Seam roller — Plumb line — Straightedge — Steel tape measure — Scissors — Sponge — Utility knife — Paper hanging brush

◇**Cloth or sponge.** To wipe the table clean for the next piece of wallpaper.

◇**Glue size.** For sealing bare plaster; you also can use diluted wallpaper paste.

◇**Wallpaper paste.** See below.

◇**Plumb bob.** To enable you to hang the paper vertically. You can improvise a plumb line by using a small flat weight and a length of fine cord.

◇**Paper hanging brush.** For smoothing the wall covering into place, fitting it into angles, and getting rid of bubbles. Choose one with soft flexible bristles. You can smooth down vinyls with a sponge instead of a brush, because it doesn't matter if you get paste or water on the surface, provided you wipe it off fairly quickly.

Wallpaper pastes

◆Allow 1 to $1\frac{1}{4}$ pints of paste for each roll (more if it is heavily embossed, because paste collects in the hollows of the surface).

◆Choose the correct paste for the wall covering you are about to hang, so it adheres properly. There are several types:

◇**Universal paste.** Can be mixed up to suit different types of wall covering.

◇**Cellulose paste.** Suitable for all types of wallpaper except vinyl.

◇**Premixed paste.** Only economical for heavy textiles and high-relief and embossed papers.

◇**Cold-water paste.** Best used on heavier papers.

◇**Fungicidal paste.** For standard wallpapers to be used in areas of condensation, and for washable and vinyl wall coverings.

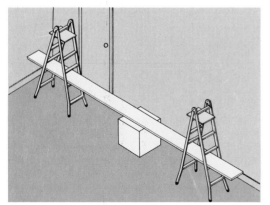

Constructing a platform. *When papering ceilings, you need a scaffold board and two stepladders to create a platform on which you can walk the length of the room. Support the planks in the middle.*

HANGING WALLPAPER

◆Paper the ceiling before the walls so paste can't drip onto a newly papered wall.

◆Start papering on the wall adjacent to the wall with the main window so cut strips end up on the darkest wall in the room.

◆Hang lining paper on previously painted surfaces or on new plasterwork. This will prevent the top layer of wallpaper from creasing and stretching. The paste also dries faster on lining paper.

◆Leave lining paper for 48 hours before hanging the top covering, so it can dry.

◆Apply a coat of glue size or diluted wallpaper paste to the wall or lining paper to create a slippery surface that will make it easier to position the wallpaper.

Hanging lining paper

◆Each length should be the full length of the wall or ceiling; don't join pieces—it's difficult to get a perfect seam.

◆Butt the pieces against each other; don't overlap them or the seam will be visible.

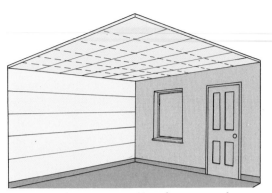

Putting up lining paper. *Hang lining paper horizontally for walls, and at right angles to the final covering for ceilings (indicated by the dotted lines). This ensures that the seams of both layers do not meet, which would make them bulky.*

CUTTING OUT WALLPAPER

1 *Measure the height of the wall at the point where the first length will be hung.*

2 *Cut the first length about 4 inches longer than this measurement to allow for trimming. If the pattern is bold, decide where you want the first motif to go and cut the paper accordingly. Mark the top of the length on the back of the paper, and number the piece.*

3 *Measure and cut further lengths as required until you get to the end of the roll. (A roll should give four lengths unless the repeat is very large or your ceilings are especially high.) If the paper is patterned, watch the match carefully. Use leftovers to paper above doors, and above and below window openings.*

4 *When cutting stepped patterns, mark the back of the first length "cut 1" and the back of the second length "2." The third length will be an exact match for 1 and the fourth a match for 2 and so on.*

Pasting and folding wall coverings

◆Keep the brush well coated with paste, and brush it along the center of each length, then out to the edges. This will prevent the paper from coming away from the wall in patches or along the edges.

◆Put each length aside after you have pasted it, to absorb moisture and become supple, while you paste the next length or hang the previous one. Leave medium-weight papers for about five minutes and heavy-weight papers for about 10 or 12 minutes. If there are no instructions, leave the paper until it is supple. Keep the soaking time constant between lengths.

▼▼ Try not to prepare so many lengths that
◆ ◆ you no longer have any room to move around in.

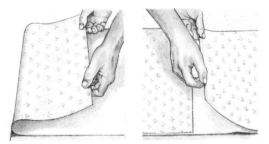

Folding wallpaper. *Fold one end to the middle, pasted sides together (above left). Fold the other end over to meet the first in the middle (above right). Don't crease the fold.*

HANGING PAPER IN TRICKY AREAS

RADIATORS

◆ If you can't remove the radiator, tuck enough paper down behind it to give the impression that the wall is completely papered. Use a long-handled roller or pad to smooth the paper onto the wall.

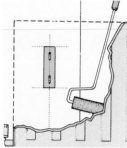

Papering behind a radiator. *Cut slits in the paper before pushing it down behind the radiator so it will go around the brackets that hold the radiator in place. Use a long-handled roller or paint pad to smooth the paper.*

CORNERS

◆ Hang full lengths until you are less than a full width away from a corner. When you reach the corner, measure between the edge of the covering and the corner of the room in several places. (The distances may differ—very few homes have perfectly straight walls.)

Papering a corner. *Cut a length of paper about ½ inch wider than the widest measured distance between the corner and the wall covering; paste it, and hang it. Turn the overlap neatly onto the other wall and brush it down. Paste the edge of the next length over it.*

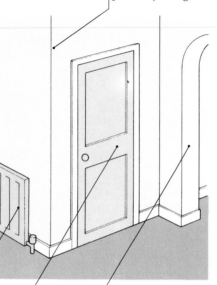

DOORS

◆ When you reach the door, measure the distance between the edge of the covering and the door frame in several places. Cut an L-shape out of a full-length piece, about 2 inches less than the height of the door and 2 inches wider than the distance between the paper and door to allow for trimming. Hang the paper from the ceiling to the top of the door frame. Make a diagonal cut in the paper in the corner of the door frame (see below). Crease the paper along the top of the frame and cut it. Crease the paper along the vertical, and trim. Smooth the paper into place.

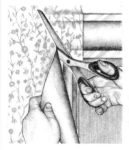

Trimming paper around a door frame. *Make a diagonal cut in the extra trimming, about 1 inch long, for the angle between the top of the door frame and the vertical.*

ARCHES

1 *Paper the outer walls first. Trim to leave a 1-inch margin of wallpaper to be folded under the edge of the arch.*

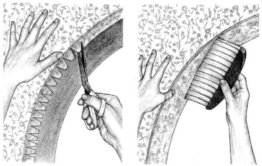

2 *Make small V-shaped cuts in the edge of the paper to allow for the curve of the arch (above left). Fold the flaps around the edge and smooth them down. Paper the inside of the arch in two pieces cut to the exact width of the arch, and butt the joint neatly at the top. Smooth the paper down (above right).*

WINDOWS
Papering dormer windows. *Leave a 1-inch margin of extra paper on the paper from the outer wall into the dormer. Cut accurate triangular pieces to cover the dormer walls, and overlap the margin.*

Papering window recesses. *Paper the inside walls first, cutting the paper to align exactly with the edge of the outer wall. Then hang a length on the outer wall, with a small margin overlapping the papered recess. Match the pattern (if there is one) carefully.*

ELECTRICAL OUTLETS
◆ Turn off the power before touching any switch, receptacle, or light fixture.
◆ To paper around a fixture, remove the fixture and paper over its box, just as you would treat a switch or receptacle—or leave the fixture in place and paper around it.

Papering around switches and receptacles. *Remove the cover plate and hang paper as if there were no box underneath. Then make diagonal slits from opposite corners, trim away triangular flaps, and replace the cover plate.*

Papering around fixtures. *Paper up to the fixture, cut a slit across paper, and smooth paper around fixture. Make a series of radial cuts from the center to the edges of the fixture. Trim off triangles by running a knife around fixture's perimeter.*

STAIRCASES
◆ Set up a safe workstation (see page 193).
◆ It is easiest to hang the longest length first and work away from it in both directions. Make sure each piece is long enough to allow for the slope of the stairs.

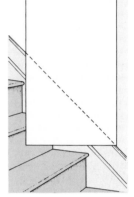

Papering a staircase. *Hang the paper in standard way, then crease it along the baseboard, and trim off the excess.*

FIREPLACES
◆ With very wide mantelpieces, treat the wall above and below the shelf as two separate areas. Hang the top half first and then the bottom. Match the pattern carefully and make a neat butt joint where the two pieces meet. Chimney breasts look best if the seams and overlaps are on the recessed walls.
◆ If the mantelpiece spans only part of a wall, hang the length of wallpaper as one piece.

Papering around a fireplace. *Brush on the top half of the paper, and cut it along the rear edge of the mantelpiece. Brush on the bottom half of the paper and mark out the contours of the fireplace with the back of a pair of scissors. Cut out the shapes and smooth the paper into place with a brush.*

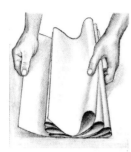

Folding ceiling paper. *Fold this alternately back on itself then forward, accordion fashion.*

Covering walls

1 Use a plumb bob to mark a true vertical on the wall in pencil before hanging the first length (or use a chalk-covered string as for ceilings).

2 Hold the length exactly against this line, and brush it with firm strokes from the middle outward.

3 Push the paper into the angles of the wall with the bristles on your brush.

Papering ceilings

◆ Get someone to help you if you can. Papering ceilings is very tiring.

1 Keep the paper parallel to the main window in the room; otherwise the seams will be visible.

2 Make a guideline on the ceiling for the first length of paper (see below).

3 Position the top flap of the folded paper in the corner in the angle between the wall and ceiling. Brush it into position.

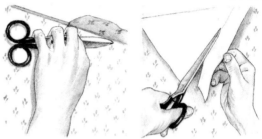

4 Use the back of the scissors blade to mark the angles on the wall covering (*above left*). Pull the paper away from the wall and trim it along the marked lines (*above right*).

MAKING A GUIDELINE

1 *At the ceiling of each of the walls adjacent to the main window wall, measure out the width of the paper and make a mark. On one of these marks, pin or nail one end of a string coated with colored chalk.*

2 *At the mark opposite, hold the other end of the string taut with one hand, then reach up with the other hand and snap the string gently against the ceiling so that it leaves a line parallel with the window wall. This will be your guide for starting the first length of paper.*

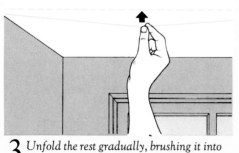

3 *Unfold the rest gradually, brushing it into place against the guideline, walking along the platform as you go. Crease and trim the ends.*

HANGING WALLPAPER BORDERS

◆ Use borders and friezes to make a room look taller, lower, or simply more finished. Borders and friezes also can be used to coordinate colors in a room or add a bit of accent color.

◆ Put them up at the level of picture rails, use them as a vertical wall border, as the trim to a sloping ceiling, to finish off an area of wall tiles in the bathroom, or to outline a door.

◆ Don't apply a border or frieze until at least 48 hours after hanging the wallpaper, to allow the paper to dry. Hang them using an ordinary adhesive.

OTHER WALL COVERINGS

◆ Textured wall coverings can give a room a warm feeling and also can ward off condensation. Many act as heat or sound insulators.

◆ For thin or shiny materials, put up lining paper first, otherwise every small flaw will show. Lining paper helps heavy and textured coverings to adhere better. If the covering is semitransparent, paint the lining paper with a coat of a neutral-colored latex.

◆ Paste coverings that have a paper backing as you would an ordinary wallpaper; they are easier to hang than unbacked fabrics.

◆ Be very careful not to stretch or stain fabric coverings. Modern wall coverings usually can be spot-cleaned, but silks have to be cleaned professionally, and even then may be impossible to get clean again.

Silk

◆ Check your measurements carefully before you cut; silk is very expensive.

◆ Cut and trim the fabric with a utility knife against a straightedge to prevent fraying.

◆ Paste the wall, not the fabric, and make sure there are no lumps in the paste, because they will show through. Smooth the fabric to the wall with a clean seam roller.

Grass cloth

◆ Paste this as you would any other wallpaper, but cover the face of the paste table with a strip of lining paper to protect the face of the fabric.

◆ Don't fold the cloth—this will leave permanent, hard crease lines on it.

◆ Apply the lengths directly to the wall and smooth them down with a paint roller. Make a crease line for trimming at the corner of the wall and ceiling and at the baseboard. Wait until the adhesive is completely dry before trimming each length with a sharp knife against a steel ruler.

Burlap (hessian)

◆ Treat paper-backed burlap like any other wallpaper. For unbacked burlap, paste the wall and not the burlap. Flatten each strip in place with a roller.

◆ Get someone to help you—burlap is easily stretched. Try to line it up right the first time.

◆ Overlap strips, and finish all the walls before you trim.

Trimming burlap. *Cut through each overlap with a very sharp utility knife held against a steel ruler. Remove the excess, and press the seam. Trim the top and bottom with a utility knife against a wide-bladed scraper.*

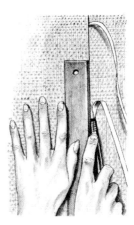

Fabric

◆ Paste the wall, and then smooth the fabric into place with a paint roller, overlapping the edges. When dry, trim the edges with a utility knife against a steel ruler.

◆ You also can staple fabric to thin strips of wood or a wooden framework around the wall. Fold the fabric under at its edges first, to stop it from fraying. This is a good method for pleated or gathered wall coverings.

Foil

◆ Paste foil with a foam roller. Immerse prepasted foil in a trough of water to activate the paste. Hang each length of foil from the top down and smooth onto the wall with a clean sponge. Make sure you match the pattern carefully because foil attracts the eye. Trim the top and bottom edges, butt the lengths, and flatten the seams with a roller.

PATCHING WALL COVERINGS

If a piece of wall covering gets torn, you may be able to stick it back on again using a dab of latex adhesive. Rub off surplus adhesive with your fingers. A badly torn or marked piece of wall covering will need a patch.

WALLPAPER

1 *Tear a ragged piece of paper to fit entirely over the damaged area. (Torn edges are less noticeable than cut ones.)*

2 *Paste the patch and stick it over the area, taking care to match the pattern accurately.*

3 *Leave it to dry for a few minutes and then roll with a seam roller (or a rolling pin).*

VINYL, BURLAP, OR GRASS CLOTH

1 *Cut a piece of the wall covering to match the pattern, and make sure it is slightly larger than the damaged part.*

2 *Hold the piece against the wall and cut a square through both layers with a very sharp utility knife. Take out the old patch. Paste the new one and fit it into the gap.*

3 *Roll it lightly with a seam roller to get rid of any creases.*

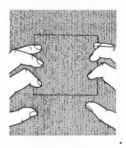

TILING

T ILES ARE A DECORATIVE and practical way to cover large surface areas with a range of materials that offer great scope for individual style and design. Hard-wearing and resistant to heat and moisture, tiles require little maintenance and can be laid by anyone, with a little practice and patience.

PREPARING THE SURFACE

◆ Always take the time to plan out the best starting point and sequence for laying tiles; the placing of the first tile determines the end result. (See *Marking a Floor or Ceiling for Tiling*, page 206.) Remember to allow for grouting joints when mapping out the tiling area.

◆ All surfaces must be sound, level, and dry before tiling begins; any unevenness will show through soft tiles and eventually crack or damage hard tiles; it is nearly impossible to align tiles accurately unless the wall or floor is perfectly flat. Hold a long, flat piece of wood against the surface vertically, horizon-

tally, and diagonally to test for "see-sawing." If the surface is not sound or level, it may be necessary to realign it.

◆ Resurface walls with drywall, and floors with particleboard or plywood. Old, uneven floorboards can be coated with a latex compound to fill the gaps and cover nailheads. Use exterior-grade hardboard (shiny side up), particleboard, or plywood for resurfacing; it does not need to be sealed. Make sure there is enough under-floor ventilation to prevent moisture from collecting and rotting the floor.

◆ Floorboards that are sound should be scrubbed with warm sudsy water before laying new tiles. And all boards should be firmly nailed, or the adhesive might not stick.

◆ If you plan to lay ceramic or quarry tiles on floorboards, get an expert to verify that the floor will be able to support the weight.

◆ When tiling over painted surfaces, make sure they are sound (see page 185). If they are, rough up the paint with sandpaper to take off the shine and provide a grip for the adhesive.

◆ Old wallpaper and flaking or chipped paint will have to be stripped off before tiling.

◆ Leave old ceramic tiles on the wall if they are flat and firmly attached. It is much easier to apply new tiles on top or to replace a few damaged tiles than to remove them all.

◆ To remove old ceramic tiles, use a brick chisel and a small sledgehammer. To remove old vinyl, cork, or polystyrene tiles, use a garden spade. After all the tiles are off, use a hot-air gun to strip off the old adhesive. If the tiles seem stuck for good, you will have to tile over them. Brush on a coat of special primer and then a coat of latex-based self-leveling compound. Make sure that the adhesive for the new tiles you use is compatible with the compound. (Ask at your tile shop.)

◆ Brush very powdery cement floors with a stabilizing agent and fill any cracks with mortar. If necessary, prime the floor with diluted PVA adhesive and then apply a self-leveling compound according to the manufacturers' instructions. Work in small sections because it sets quickly. Allow the compound to dry out for two weeks before laying the tiles.

TILING WALLS AND CEILINGS

◆ Make a plan of the wall on graph paper to work out where to put the tiles, especially if they are patterned or you want to insert a patterned tile randomly among plain ones.

◆ When you have finished tiling a bathroom or kitchen wall, spread a silicone sealant

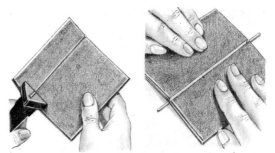

Cutting tiles. *Score along the surface with a tile cutter, then hold the tile in pincers and squeeze the handle to break the tile in two (above left). If you do not have pincers, score the surface of the tile, then place the tile faceup on top of two matchsticks lined up under the scored line (above right). Press your fingers lightly on the edges of the tile on either side of the line, and it should break along the line.*

TILING EQUIPMENT

◇ **Tile cutter.** There are many types, but the most commonly used ones have a cutting wheel and a pair of snappers to break the tile along the scored line.

◇ **Sharp utility knife and a straightedge.** For cutting soft tiles.

◇ **Clippers, pincers, tile saw.** For cutting ceramic tiles.

◇ **Vise.** For holding tiles while you saw-cut curved edges.

◇ **Tenon saw.** For cutting wood tiles.

◇ **Tile file.** For smoothing rough edges.

◇ **Cardboard.** For making templates for difficult spaces.

◇ **Furring strips, string, and a T-square.** For positioning wall and ceiling tiles.

◇ **Hammer, nails, screws, screwdriver, and level.** For attaching furring strips.

◇ **Staple gun.** For attaching soft tiles to furring strips.

◇ **Adhesive.** Use a thin-bed adhesive for smooth surfaces, and a thick-bed adhesive for uneven floors. Choose a waterproof adhesive for bathrooms and other places likely to get damp or wet.

◇ **Trowel or spatula.** For applying adhesive; for polystyrene tiles you need an old paintbrush.

◇ **Notched plastic spreader.** To distribute the adhesive evenly.

◇ **Grout.** Premixed grout is the easiest to use, and it is available in many colors. If you can't get the right color, buy powdered grout and add pigment.

◇ **Rubber grouter, squeegee or spatula, or a sponge.** For filling the joints.

◇ **Tile spacers or a box of matches.** For spacing tiles. Choose the type of spacers that are shallower than the tiles; they don't need removing— you just grout over them.

◇ **Thin stick with a rounded end, or a stick for frozen treats.** To run along the grouting between the tiles.

◇ **Large sponge.** For wiping the tiles clean.

along the line where the tiles meet the bath or kitchen surface, to keep water from seeping down behind it. A more expensive but better-looking alternative is to fit curved edging tiles or a curved plastic strip along the adjoining edges. In a kitchen, you also can fit wooden molding where the tiles meet the work surface.

Ceramic tiles

1 Nail a horizontal furring strip lightly to the wall where you want the base of the bottom row of tiles to begin. This will support the tiles until the adhesive has dried.

2 Start in the bottom left-hand corner, or in the middle of the wall if the pattern is a large one, so the cut tiles will be at the edges. Smooth a layer of adhesive over about a square yard of wall with a trowel.

3 Draw a notched spreader horizontally over the area so that its teeth touch the wall surface.

4 Place the first tile on the furring strip, and press it into the adhesive with a slight twist, so it is in full contact with the adhesive.

5 Lay the tiles in horizontal strips. If using straight-edged tiles, place spacers or matchsticks between each tile and each row of tiles to make an even gap for grouting. Butt universal tiles (ones with angled edges) against each other.

6 Leave the tiles to dry for at least 12 hours before grouting them. Remove the furring strips and spacers (unless they are the type that remain), and then grout.

CUTTING CERAMIC TILES

◆ For angles, score the surface and then chip away at the excess tile with pincers or pliers.

◆ File rough edges with a tile file, working away from the glaze so you do not damage it.

◆ Some tile breakers are a bit flimsy. If you have many tiles to cut, or if they are difficult, rent a sturdy floor tile cutter; it is much quicker.

Cutting curves. *Make a template of the curve on cardboard and trace the outline onto the upper surface of the tile. Fix the tile in a vise, and use a tile saw to cut the shape out of the tile.*

GROUTING

◆ Use a grouting cement to keep dirt and water from getting under the tiles.

◆ Use a waterproof grout to prevent dampness in areas where there is heavy condensation or running water, and on surfaces you wash regularly; otherwise, the adhesive may not stick.

1 *Spread the grout onto the surface of the tiles around the gaps.*

2 *Use a rubber squeegee blade or a piece of damp sponge to work it well into the gaps between the tiles. Sponge the tiles clean.*

3 *When you have covered the whole area, draw a thin stick with a rounded end, such as a stick for frozen treats, along each joint to press the grouting firmly down. Wipe clean again.*

Mirror tiles

◆ If the walls are cold, heat the room first, so the self-stick tabs on the tiles adhere.

◆ Mount a sheet of particleboard to the wall if it is not absolutely even. If you stick mirror tiles to an uneven surface, they will produce distorted images.

◆ Mirror tiles do not need grouting; you can butt them up against each other.

Cork tiles

◆ Leave cork tiles unwrapped in the room 24 hours before laying them, so the cork can adjust to the atmosphere.

◆ Use a straightedge and a very sharp utility knife to cut cork, or it may crumble. Always cut cork tiles with the smooth side up.

◆ Apply these tiles in the same way as ceramic tiles, but use a special cork wall tile adhesive, and butt them closely together.

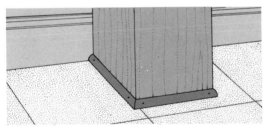

Finishing cork tiling. *Where cork tiling is taken up to exposed edges, protect the edge with quarter-round shoe molding.*

Acoustic ceiling tiles

◆ Make sure the surface is clean and dry. Mark the ceiling with chalk lines as you did for the floor (see page 206). Spread acoustic tile adhesive across the tile, from edge to edge. Working from the middle outward, position the first tile so that it lines up with your crossing chalk lines in the middle. Butt the tiles up to each other.

▼▼ Acoustic tiles should not be placed di-
♦ ♦ rectly above a stove where they may be a fire hazard.

CUTTING AN ACOUSTIC EDGE TILE

1 *Place the tile to be cut exactly over the last full tile in the row. Put another tile on top and butt it against the wall.*

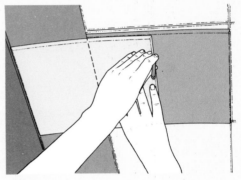

2 *Trace the edge of the top tile (the edge away from the wall) onto the tile beneath it, which is the tile to be cut.*

3 *Score along the line with a sharp utility knife. The cut tile will fit into the gap.*

TILING FLOORS

◆ When laying down any type of tiled floor covering, start in the center of the room and work outward to the baseboards.

◆ Since few rooms are exactly square, make sure that you mark the center point (see page 206), adjusting it to leave at least half-tile widths at each baseboard, then work outward.

◆ Most floor tiles raise the surface at least a $\frac{1}{2}$ inch, which will cause the door to bind against them. Trim the lower edge of the door or attach rising butt hinges to allow it to rise as it opens.

Vinyl and cork floor tiles

◆ **For vinyl tiles.** Peel off the backing paper for self-adhesive vinyl tiles or spread vinyl adhesive (for nonstick types) just before laying the tiles. Make sure the pattern is going in the right direction, then press each tile down firmly, butting up the edges closely.

◆ **For cork tiles.** Lay them in the same way

as vinyl, but use a cork-flooring adhesive for nonstick tiles.

◆ Cork tiles without a protective, washable

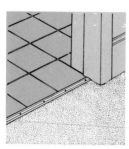

Fitting a threshold bar. *If the tiles start at a doorway, fit a wooden or metal threshold bar over the edge of the tiles to prevent them from becoming scuffed.*

finish will need to be sealed with wax or polyurethane before the room is used.

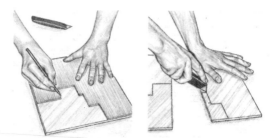

Fitting tiles around intricate spaces. *Make a cardboard template of the shape, and trace the outline onto the tile (above left). Cut the tile into several pieces, then cut out the shapes with a sharp utility knife. Fit them around the space (above right).*

MARKING A FLOOR OR CEILING FOR TILING

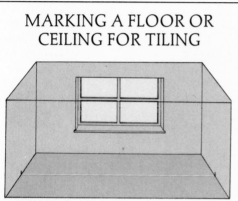

1 Chalk a length of string, stretch it between the centers of the two shortest sides of the room, and attach it to the base of the walls.

2 Pluck the string with your fingers so that it snaps back onto the floor and leaves a chalk line. Measure the line to find the center. Using a T-square, mark a short line, at right angles to the line. Stretch the chalk string along the short line and attach it to the base of the walls. Snap it to mark a line that runs between the walls.

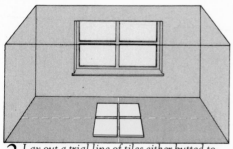

3 Lay out a trial line of tiles either butted together or with a grouting space between them, from the center to all four walls. Adjust them so the border tiles will be more or less equal in size; this will make them look better.

Wood tiles (parquet panels)

◆ Wood tiles are usually grouped together to make up a larger "parquet panel" in a basket-weave pattern; they also can be separated and arranged in different patterns.

◆ Unpack the tiles and leave them in the room for a few days before fitting so they can adjust to the temperature and humidity level in the room.

◆ Start by spreading enough adhesive for one panel of tiles, and lay the first panel straight down without sliding it around; if adhesive oozes onto the wood, wipe it off right away with a damp cloth.

◆ Once you have laid the first row of panels, spread the adhesive in blocks of about 5 feet square, lay the next row, and so on.

Fitting wood tiles. *Allow for a ½-inch gap between the cut tile and the baseboard, because the wood may expand a little after you have laid it. Cut shapes as you would for vinyl or cork, in pieces, but use a backsaw or power saber saw.*

◆ Leave an expansion gap of $\frac{1}{2}$ inch around the edge of the floor, using a cork strip to help maintain the gap as you go. Lay all the complete panels before you cut and fit for edges and intricate spaces.

◆ Untreated tiles should be sanded smooth and sealed with wax or polyurethane sealant.

Ceramic, clay, and quarry tiles

1 Make sure the floor is sound and level; if it is wooden, seal the floor with a primer beforehand.

2 Spread a thin layer of ceramic floor-tile adhesive over 1 square yard at a time.

3 Press and twist each tile into position so it is firmly bedded down.

4 Wipe away any surplus adhesive, and clean out the joints in preparation for grouting.

5 Grout the joints when the tiles have been in place 24 hours. Since tiles should not be walked on for at least 48 hours, wait another day before using the room.

◆ Seal unglazed ceramic and quarry tiles with wax or polyurethane sealant.

REPAIRING TILES

◆ **For vinyl tiles.** Pry off the old tile and clean the area thoroughly. Be careful not to damage the surrounding tiles. Apply adhesive to the floor. A new tile will soon fade to match the rest.

◆ **For acoustic tiles.** Scrape off the old tile. Trim off the bottoms of grooved edges and spread adhesive across the back of the new tile, to about $\frac{1}{2}$ inch from each edge; stick the tile in place.

◆ **For ceramic or quarry tiles.** If a tile has a small crack or chip, it's better to leave it alone; you may do more damage to the wall or surrounding tiles. If you do replace one, make sure the replacement is the same size, color, and thickness as the old one.

Replacing a ceramic tile. *Work from the middle outward, cracking the damaged tile into small pieces with a hammer and chisel and chipping out loose bits. Clean out the area, apply adhesive, and position the new tile.*

Replacing a wooden floor tile. *Chisel out the central block and lift out the surrounding pieces. Scrape the floor surface clean, and vacuum thoroughly. Stick the new blocks in place with flooring adhesive. If the new blocks are slightly raised above the others, plane them down when the adhesive has dried.*

CUTTING CLAY AND QUARRY TILES

1 *Mark the desired shape and size on the tile with a pencil. Hold it on top of a brick, and tap a row of chips along the pencil marks with a hammer and masonry chisel.*

2 *Hold the tile in both hands, and hit the chipped line smartly against the corner of the brick; the tile should break along the line.*

For corners and narrow pieces. *Chip away at the marks with a pair of pincers until you reach the chiseled marks.*

FLOOR COVERINGS

TOP-QUALITY floor coverings keep their appearance and last longer than cheaper versions. Different types have different characteristics: Wall-to-wall carpeting is warm, comfortable, and reduces sound; area rugs provide warmth and color over wooden or tile flooring; and sheet vinyl makes an excellent waterproof barrier for kitchens and bathrooms.

ESTIMATING QUANTITIES

Many retailers have a free estimating service; but to do it yourself, use these guidelines.

Measuring the floor.

1 Sketch an outline of the room including doors and windows. Measure the room's length and width from the bottom of the baseboard to the deepest part of the door threshold, allowing for alcoves, doorways, and other protrusions, and mark the maximum measurements on the plan. Include the interiors of closets in your plan.

EQUIPMENT

◆ Foam-backed carpet needs cutting and fitting equipment; carpet tiles need trimming equipment only.

◇ *Trimming knife with curved and straight heavy-duty blades and large, sharp scissors*

◇ *3-foot steel ruler*

◇ *Knee kicker*

◇ *Double-sided carpet tape*

◇ *Adhesive spreader*

◇ *Metal edging for edge of floor covering and for joining floor coverings*

◇ *Putty knife*

◇ *$\frac{3}{4}$-inch and 1-inch carpet tacks*

◇ *Heavy-duty stapler (with rustproof staples)*

◇ *Angled and standard tackless strips (grippers)*

---

2 Add 3 inches for trimming in each direction, and allow for any waste that will be caused by pattern matching.

3 Choose a width of flooring that will waste the least amount of floor covering. Ask the retailer whether or not you can buy a length plus a narrow strip, or if you have to buy a wider roll and waste a strip at the edge.

Estimating for stairs.

1 Working from the top tread down, measure each tread and riser, and add the height of a riser to the overall length. This allows for the carpet to be tucked under at the bottom and for moving it up and down every so often to even out the wear.

2 Add $1\frac{3}{4}$ inches to the length of each tread to allow for the bulk of the underlay and for tucking into the tackless strips.

3 Measure the width of the treads. If they have open sides, allow $\frac{1}{2}$ inch for turning under at each edge. On winding staircases, measure along the outer edge for the longest length. Allow for tucking in and moving the carpet up and down, as for straight stairs.

◆ Add enough to the measurement of the landing carpet for it to overlap the top stair riser and be tacked down.

CHOOSING FLOOR COVERINGS

◆ Choose a carpet grade that is suitable for the traffic through the room. Many carpets are classified into "wear factor" categories, (see right). Jute-backed carpet is hard-wearing but expensive. Foam-backed carpet is cheaper and easier to lay, but it is not as hard-wearing, and is not suitable for areas such as stairs. Hair, wool, and twisted yarn carpets are hard-wearing.

◆ If you are buying sheet flooring for a kitchen or bathroom, make sure it is not slippery when wet.

◆ Don't use carpet in a bathroom. It is very difficult to dry, and wet carpets fade, smell musty, attract mildew and germs, and are hard to clean.

◆ For stairs, choose a carpet that won't show the backing at its edges, such as a carpet with bound edges.

◆ Use carpet remnants and squares that have unbound edges for small rooms; butt against the wall to prevent fraying.

CARPET QUALITY

Grade	Use
1	Rooms with very light traffic, e.g. study, bedroom
2	Secondary rooms
3	Lightly used living rooms
L	High-quality carpets with a long pile, but not for heavy traffic
4	Rooms in heavy use
5	Very heavily used areas

PADDING

◆ All carpets need a separate padding. Good-quality padding will improve a carpet's heat- and sound-insulating properties and make it last longer.

◆ Jute- or paper-backed rubber padding is best for most carpets.

◆ If you have under-floor heating, use a heavy felt padding.

◆ Foam-rubber padding can be used in bedrooms and other rooms that don't get much heavy traffic, but it flattens easily and needs felt paper underneath it to prevent the backing from sticking to the floorboards.

◆ Use felt paper padding under foam-backed carpet and foam-rubber padding. Use felt paper padding also when there are gaps between the floorboards not wide enough to warrant a complete resurfacing with hardboard.

◆ You can use individual stair pads under stairs—they are much easier to put down than a length of padding.

CARPETS

◆ Broadloom is the easiest to lay in square or rectangular rooms, because it is made in generous widths, which means there is much less cutting and tacking to do.

◆ Body carpet is practical for oddly shaped rooms and for stairs, because its narrow width is easier to cut; it is also cheaper, because you are less likely to waste carpet. It can be professionally joined to make wider widths if necessary.

◆ Carpet tiles are easy to lay and trim, and can be lifted and washed, or replaced, individually. They are a reasonably cheap form of carpeting.

MATTING

◆ Rush and split-cane matting usually are sold in 1-foot squares, which can be sewn together to cover larger areas. They are very hard-wearing, need no padding, and can be loose-laid onto wood or concrete.

◆ Coconut, coir, and sisal matting need no padding;

some may have a nonslip backing. Good as door matting or for a hallway.

◆ Plastic matting is cheap, available in bright colors, and easily washable; it is suitable for kitchens and bathrooms.

SHEET FLOORING

◆ Sheet vinyl comes in roll widths of up to 13 feet and in unlimited lengths. Most rooms can be covered with one sheet. "Lay-flat" vinyls are easiest to lay, don't tear, and need no adhesive. Also, unlike other vinyls, they don't shrink. Use cushioned vinyl to hide slight irregularities in the floor; it is also more comfortable and quieter to walk on than other vinyl floor coverings.

◆ Sheet rubber is slightly more difficult to lay than vinyl but is hard-wearing, quiet, and waterproof. It is available with various raised designs, which make it nonslip.

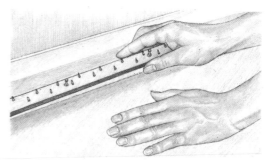

LAYING FLOOR COVERINGS

◆Leave floors that are treated with wood preservative for several months before covering them; otherwise, the treatment may damage the covering.

◆For large areas of carpet and stairs, it is best to hire a professional carpet layer.

◆If possible, mark up the new flooring outside or in a larger room than the one you are covering to make the task easier.

◆Put vinyl and linoleum in the room 24 hours before laying to acclimatize.

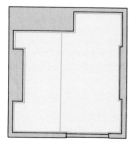

Making a template for the floor covering. *Cut a template of the floor using lengths of carpet padding, which can be taped together to form the room shape. If replacing vinyl, use the old floor covering as a template for the new one.*

Preparation

◆The floor must be smooth, dry, clean, and firm. If you are covering floorboards, secure loose boards first and hammer in any protruding nails.

◆Remove old vinyl sheeting, and scrape away sections that are stuck to the floor.

◆If a cement floor has indentations, or is slightly uneven, coat it with a latex floor-leveling agent before filling with cement mortar.

◆If the floor is very uneven, lay plywood or particleboard to give a smooth base for the floor covering (see also page 202).

◆Vacuum thoroughly to remove dust and grit before putting down any floor covering.

Laying padding

1 Lay the carpet roughly in position before fitting the padding, or you may damage it by dragging the carpet over it. Roll half the carpet back; lay half the padding at a time.

2 Secure tackless strips (grippers) in a continuous line around the edges of the room, $\frac{1}{4}$ inch away from the wall, angling the pins toward the wall. Nail tackless strips onto wood floors, or use hardened pins or an adhesive recommended by the manufacturer for solid floors. If you are not using tackless strips, stick double-sided tape to the edge of the floor to secure the carpet.

3 Anchor the padding 2 inches from the baseboard. Secure padding to a wooden floor with rustproof staples; use dabs of adhesive on a solid floor.

▼▼ Don't put extra thicknesses of padding
◆ ◆ on well-worn areas of flooring.

Laying felt paper padding. *Join the strips of padding before you secure it. Lay strips of double-sided adhesive tape along the edges of the room 2 inches from the baseboard, and secure the padding to the tape.*

Laying jute-backed carpet

1 Position the carpet so about $\frac{1}{2}$ inch of material turns up against two adjoining walls.

2 Hook the carpet to tackless strips or tack it down on one side.

3 Stretch the carpet across the room (see opposite), and hook it onto the rest of the tackless strips or tack it.

4 Trim the edges and tuck them under the baseboard using a putty knife.

STRETCHING JUTE-BACKED CARPET

◆ Use a knee kicker—it makes the job of stretching the carpet much easier (you can rent one). Use the muscle just above your knee to operate the tool.

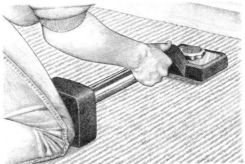

1 Hook the carpet onto tackless strips in one corner so it is secured for 1 foot along the wall on each side of the corner.

2 Attach the carpet to the tackless strips at an adjacent corner. Then attach it firmly along the wall between the first and second corners.

3 Smooth the carpet over to the corner diagonally opposite the second corner. Secure it onto the tackless strips along the wall connecting it and the first corner.

4 Kneel on the carpet with your back to one of the completed sides, press the teeth on the knee kicker into the carpet, and knock the padded end forward with your knee. Continue until you reach the wall facing you. Hook the carpet onto the tackless strip. Repeat this along one edge and then do the same for the last unattached edge. Trim the excess carpeting to about ½ inch, and push it under the baseboard.

Laying foam-backed carpet

◆ You can get tackless strips with extra large pins for foam-backed carpet, but it may be easier to use double-sided carpet tape.

◆ Lay the carpet on the floor, and make sure there is ½ inch extra all around to allow for trimming.

◆ Roll the carpet back, and stick down the tape. Roll the carpet back down, and press it onto the tape. Roll back the other half, and repeat.

◆ Foam-backed carpet needs no stretching.

Fitting floor coverings into difficult spaces. *Trim the covering so 2 inches rests against the wall. Make a series of release cuts in the covering until it lies flat. Then trim the pieces and slip them under the baseboard or onto the tackless strips.*

Trimming foam-backed carpet. *Hold a sharp trimming knife at an angle with the handle pointing away from the wall so you don't cut away too much.*

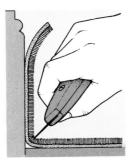

Laying carpet tiles

◆ Follow the same planning and laying sequence as for floor tiles (see pages 205 and 206).

◆ Secure the first tile with double-sided carpet tape and loose-lay the rest.

◆ Secure tiles in doorways with a metal edging strip to prevent the edges from getting scuffed and frayed.

PATCHING FLOOR COVERINGS

CARPET

1 *Buy a piece of carpet exactly like the one being patched, or take a piece of carpet from somewhere where it won't be missed. Lay the new piece on top of the damaged area and cut through both layers with a sharp knife.*

2 *Cut a piece of jute slightly larger than the patch. Lay double-sided carpet tape on the floor under the hole, and stick the jute down.*

3 *Apply latex adhesive along the edges of the hole and the patch to about halfway up the pile. Let it dry (until the adhesive is semi-transparent).*

4 *Fit the patch into the hole, and tap lightly around the edges to make a good bond.*

VINYL

◆ Use a scrap to patch large tears.

1 *Lay the scrap over the tear, and match up the pattern with the rest of the covering.*

2 *Using a utility knife, cut through both pieces of floor covering to make a patch larger than the tear.*

3 *Remove the damaged piece, coat the new piece with adhesive, and press it into place.*

Laying sheet vinyl

◆ Put sheet vinyl into the room 24 hours before you want to lay it to get it to room temperature. This makes it easier to lay. Turn the heat on if you are laying vinyl in winter.

◆ Loose-lay it, leaving it overlapping up the wall all around by about 4 inches, because it will probably shrink.

◆ Don't bother to glue down the very cheap vinyls, nor those that are intended to be loose-laid.

◆ If you are gluing the covering down, use the recommended adhesive. Glue cushioned vinyls around the edges, but glue other types under the entire surface.

◆ Roll back half the sheet and apply the adhesive to the floor. Roll the sheet back down and press it down onto the floor. Sweep it with a broom to get it absolutely flat. Repeat with the other half.

◆ If you have to lay two sheets, overlap the edges, and cut through both thicknesses as they overlap, using a utility knife against a steel ruler. Peel away the excess. The cut edges should fit together perfectly.

Cutting around corners and intricate shapes.
Trace around the shapes on cardboard with a pencil held against a 1-inch-wide strip of wood. Retrace the shape 1 inch inside the template outline onto the covering.

Repairs and Maintenance

BASIC TOOL KIT

Having an all-purpose tool kit on hand makes home repairs less of a hassle and prepares you for almost any household emergency. For one-time repairs you can rent power or specialty hand tools from specialist suppliers.

ESSENTIAL TOOL KIT

◆ Keep a basic tool kit handy for emergency household repairs.

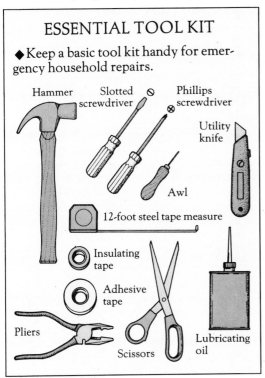

Hammer   Slotted screwdriver   Phillips screwdriver

Utility knife

Awl

12-foot steel tape measure

Insulating tape

Adhesive tape

Pliers

Scissors   Lubricating oil

Hammers

◇**Claw hammer.** A 16-ounce curved claw hammer with an unbreakable handle of tubular or solid steel or fiberglass is the most useful for driving a wide variety of fasteners as well as for pulling them out. You might also want a 13-ounce version that is easier to swing and more accurate to use. Choose a hammer with a cushion grip to deter shock.

◇**Ripping claw hammer.** A 20-ounce hammer is useful for rough work such as removing studs.

◇**Specialty hammers.** These include *tack hammers* with magnetic heads to hold and drive tacks; *ball peen hammers* with round and flat heads for metalwork—the ball end is used to shape the metal, and the flat end drives chisels and punches; *mallets*, which have large, wooden, hard rubber or plastic heads and are used to drive chisels and assemble wood joints; and *mason's hammers* and *sledgehammers* with their more substantial heads, which are used for working with brick, block, and concrete.

Screwdrivers

◇ **Basic slotted screwdrivers.** These include a heavy-duty square blade, medium square blade, small square blade, stubby, and offset.

◇ **Cabinet screwdrivers.** These have special straight-sided tips to drive or remove countersunk screws without marring the surrounding material.

◇ **Phillips screwdrivers.** These have multiple edges on their tips for more turning power. For general-purpose work, you will need three sizes.

◇ **Specialty screwdrivers.** Include those for particular jobs, such as electrical and jeweler's screwdrivers. Others make jobs faster, such as spiral ratchets that spin screws in and out, and screwdriver bits that are used in hand braces.

◆ Choose a screwdriver to fit the screw's slot; if the tip is too narrow, it will ride up out of the slot and damage the screw. If the tip is too wide, it will damage the material around the screw head when the screw is driven flush with the material.

◆ A variable-speed power drill that is also reversible is tops for driving and removing lots of screws.

Pliers

◆ Pliers perform three major tasks: holding, turning, and cutting. Holders have smooth jaws or fine serrations; turners have coarse teeth designed to turn nuts and bolts; cutters feature smooth jaws with cutting edges to snip wires, nails, and small bolts and screws.

◆ Your toolbox should include at least two of the following types: *slip-joint pliers, lock-joint pliers,* and *diagonal pliers.*

◆ An almost limitless range of specialty pliers exists including *rib-joint, long-nose, four-position adjustable, lineman's, nippers,* and those that pull staples, form wire loops, and retrieve small parts.

◆ Wrap the jaws of pliers with adhesive bandages or tape to prevent them from marring delicate soft woods and plastics.

◆ Wrap rubber bands around the handles to transform your pliers into a vise for small projects, or use lock-joint pliers.

◆ To insulate handles for electrical work, wrap them with electrical tape. Tape also adds padding for a comfortable grip.

Wrenches

◇ **Adjustable-end wrenches.** Available in sets; 6-, 8-, and 10-inch ones will be able to tackle almost any job requiring a wrench.

◇ **Allen wrenches.** Also known as hex-key wrenches, they are generally packaged in sets of assorted sizes. These are used to tighten setscrews and those with allen-type heads.

◇ **Specialty wrenches.** These include *pipe wrenches,* which are ideal for plumbing jobs; *open-end, box-end, combination,* and *socket wrenches,* which are fixed-jaw relatives of adjustable wrenches; *socket wrenches with ratchet handles,* which are built for speed; *nut drivers* to fix hex nuts and screws; and an *offset box wrench.*

Saws

◆ For most basic home repair and minor improvement projects, you can get by with three handsaws: an 8-point crosscut saw, a keyhole saw, and a hacksaw.

◇ **Crosscut saw.** Works best across the grain of wood; a *ripsaw* cuts best with the grain.

◇ **Keyhole saw.** Makes tight-radius cuts on large, thick material; a *coping saw* is better for sharper curves.

◇ **Hacksaw.** Will cut practically anything, but its specialty is metals.

◇ **Backsaw.** Actually a small fine-tooth crosscut saw, it is used for cutting miters and other exacting work.

◆ Portable power saws are cheaper, more flexible, and easier to store; stationary power saws are more accurate and versatile. Choose portable ones for repairs and improvement projects, stationary ones for cabinet- and furniture-making.

◇ **Jigsaw or saber saw.** One with variable speed should be your first purchase. It can crosscut, rip, miter, bevel, and cut holes in almost any material.

◇ **Circular saw.** One with enough blade capacity (usually $7\frac{1}{4}$ inches) to handle a 45-degree cut in 2-inch-thick materials will rip long boards and paneling quickly.

NAILS, SCREWS, AND SCREW ANCHORS

◇ **Common and box nails.** For general use, these have flat broad heads that won't pull through. Coated ones have more holding power than uncoated ones.

◇ **Casing and finishing nails.** Small-headed and suitable for finishing work on cabinets and trim. Casing nails hold better, but finishing nails leave a smaller hole.

◇ **Brads.** Tiny finishing nails for thin moldings and paneling.

◇ **Masonry nails.** For hanging pictures and nailing into brick and block walls.

◇ **Wood screws.** With either straight-slot or Phillips (cross-slot) heads, these come in three kinds: flathead screws that can be driven flush with the surface or concealed; roundhead screws that sit atop the surface; ovalhead screws for decorative applications.

◇ **Lag screws.** Give extra holding power in wood.

◇ **Plastic or nylon screw anchors.** For securing screws in solid walls. Anchors and toggles are used in cavity walls.

Files, rasps, and planes

◆ Files and rasps perform the same job. Files remove and smooth metal and plastic; rasps finish only wood.

◇ **Double-cut file.** Removes lots of material.

◇ **Single-cut file.** Is used for smoothing.

◇ **Serrated rasp.** Cuts quickly for a usable smooth surface.

◆ For most home projects, you need only smoothing and block planes.

◇ **Smoothing plane.** For all-around work that encompasses jointing and smoothing.

◇ **Block plane.** Used for end-grain work.

◇ **Specialty planes.** Include *jointer planes* for squaring the edges of the materials so they can be joined with adhesive or fasteners; *rabbet planes* for cutting rabbets for joints; *spokeshave planes* for irregular surfaces and curves; and *model-maker's planes* for small jobs on wood and metal.

Knives and scissors

◇ **Utility knife.** Buy one with replaceable blades because this type is cheaper; for safety, buy one with retractable blades. Ideal for laying flooring; cutting paper, fabrics, and leather; and stripping wire.

◇ **General-purpose scissors.** A range of straight, curved, and keyhole shaped blades are available for cutting fabric, paper, and other pliable materials.

◇ **Tin snips.** These have straight or curved blades for cutting sheet metal or screens.

Chisels

◆ Wood chisels are needed for shaping mortises, and cutting and smoothing wood joints.

◇ **Butt chisels.** Remove lots of wood and are useful for tight spots.

◇ **Pocket chisels.** For use by hand or with a hammer.

◇ **Paring chisels.** Thin-bladed chisels for very fine work.

◇ **Gouges.** These are rounded for outside and inside cutting.

◆ Cold chisels cut rusted bolts, rods, thin bar steel, bricks, blocks, and stone.

◇ **Cape chisel.** Used normally to gouge metal.

◇ **Flat chisel.** Will shear metal and can cut bolts and screws.

◇ **Diamond-point chisel.** Makes V-shaped cuts and grooves in metal.

◇ **Bricklayer's chisel.** Cuts and forms masonry and stone materials.

Drills

◇ **Electric drill.** Use a one-speed drill for simple jobs only, such as drilling holes in wood or soft walls; use a variable-speed drill for drilling through brick or stonework. A drill with hammer action can be rented for tough jobs. For greater versatility, choose a drill/driver, which has a clutch that facilitates driving screws.

◇ **Push drill.** This is excellent for drilling small holes in wood, plastic, and metal. For larger holes use a *brace*.

◇ **Breast drill.** This handles lots of pressure; your body supplies the push while your hands hold and crank.

Measuring tools

◇ **Retractable steel tape measure.** For measuring long lengths and round measures.
◇ **Steel ruler or straightedge.** For measuring and for cutting against with a utility knife.
◇ **Carpenter's level.** For determining a straight horizontal line.
◇ **Plumb bob and line.** For determining a straight vertical line. You can use a weight tied onto a piece of string instead.
◇ **Combination square.** For establishing right angles.

Adhesives

◆ A wide range is available that will join almost any materials and make bonds that are often stronger than the original materials.
◇ **Contact adhesives.** Used to apply plastic laminate and wood veneer, and to repair veneer. Good holding power and excellent water resistance.
◇ **Epoxy adhesives.** Will bond almost any material to any other material and have excellent holding power and water resistance.
◇ **Latex-based adhesives.** Will bond fabric, carpeting, canvas, and paper. Fair holding power and water resistance.
◇ **Mastics.** Include latex- and resin-based. The former bonds ceiling tile, floor tile, and paneling. The latter is used for ceramic, plastic, wood, and cork. Good holding power and water resistance.
◇ **Paste adhesives.** Used for applying wallpaper and other thin paper bonds. Good holding power but poor water resistance.
◇ **Plastic adhesives.** Used for wood, glass, plastics, pottery, china, and model work. Fair holding power and good water resistance.
◇ **Polyvinyl resin** ("white glue"). Bonds wood, plywood, hardboard, and paper. Good holding power, but poor water resistance.
◇ **Resorcinol and formaldehyde.** Bond wood, plywood, hardboard, and reclaimed wood products (chipboard). Excellent holding power and water resistance with resorcinol; poor water resistance with formaldehyde.
◇ **Rubber-based adhesives.** Bond wood, wood to concrete, paper products, plastic, and cork. Fair-to-good holding power and good water resistance.
◇ **Cyanoacrylates** (so-called instant-bonding adhesives). Bond rubber, plastics, metals, hardwoods, ceramics, and glass. Excellent holding power and fair water resistance.

Tapes

◆ For most jobs, a selection of electrical, duct, and masking tape will do the trick. For specialty tasks, choose a tape designed for the job.
◇ **Electrical tape.** Insulates electrical wires but also can be used to temporarily stop leaks in plumbing pipes, garden hoses, and auto hoses. It can be used to tape handles of hammers and ball bats for extra grip.
◇ **Duct tape** (plastic-coated cloth tape). Can repair most plastic articles, fabric, and metals. Also use it for sealing joints in heating, cooling, and clothes dryer ducts.
◇ **Masking tape.** Protects woodwork during painting, but it is also good for sealing packages, clamping together light materials for gluing, and protecting wood and metal furniture surfaces from damage during moving.
◇ **Aluminum foil tape.** Patches most metals. Also use it as a backup material for auto body repairs and for sealing ducts, gutters, and downspouts.
◇ **Double-face tape.** Holds light materials together while they are being sawed, drilled, nailed, or screwed. Also can be used to apply carpet and wall tiles.
◇ **Pipe-joint tape.** Wrapped around pipe threads, it stops leaks. Can make nut-and-bolt assembly easier and deters rust.
◇ **Transparent weather-strip tape.** Seals windows, doors, storm windows, and air conditioners.
◇ **Plastic decorative tape.** Comes in many colors and is used for minor repair jobs and decorative accents.
◇ **Strapping tape.** A heavy-duty product, it comes in handy for making temporary repairs and for reinforcing packages.

Caulks and sealants

◇**Acrylic latex.** A good general-purpose sealant that is fast-drying. It is ideal for filling small cracks and joints, patching plaster walls, and sealing around baseboards and window trim. It can be painted.

◇**Vinyl latex.** Highly adhesive as well as water- and weatherproof, this type is excellent for use around wet areas such as tubs and showers.

◇**Butyl.** It is exceptionally good for sealing seams in gutters and around roof flashings, storm windows, and air conditioners. Great, too, for joints between metal and masonry and for filling cracks or joints. Remains flexible after setting; can be painted.

◇**Silicone.** A very expensive product that is best saved for small jobs where exceptional adhesion and long-lasting elasticity are necessary. It is ideal for sealing around tubs, showers, and outdoor outlets and fixtures. Paint does not adhere well to most kinds.

Abrasives

◆A general tool kit should contain some very fine to very coarse aluminum oxide abrasives plus some very fine to medium steel wool.

◇**Aluminum oxide.** Comes in a wide range of grades ranging from extra-coarse 36 to extra-fine 220. Used to sand wood, metal, plastic, and fiberglass.

◇**Emery.** Comes in three grades—fine, medium-coarse, and extra-coarse—and is used to polish metals.

◇**Flint.** Fine, medium, and coarse grades are useful for light-duty sanding and sanding tacky surfaces.

◇**Garnet.** Comes in the same wide range of grades as aluminum oxide (above) and is used for woodworking projects.

◇**Silicon carbide.** Comes in the most popular grades as well as an extensive range of fine grades from very-fine 180 to ultra-fine 600. Used to sand floors and smooth glass, fiberglass, hard plastics, soft metals, and finishes between coats.

◇**Tungsten carbide.** In coarse, medium, and fine grades, it is used to remove stubborn finishes.

◇**Steel wool.** Ranges from No. 3 coarse to No. 0000 extremely fine. It is used to remove rust or corrosion from metal and to smooth the surface between finish coats.

◇**Pumice.** Comes in coarse to fine powder versions and is used to smooth finish coats.

◇**Rottenstone.** Comes in coarse to fine powder and is used to smooth finish coats.

◆Use open-coat papers on materials that are gummy and tend to clog the abrasive particles. For materials that won't clog the particles, use closed-coat papers.

Lubricants

◇**Penetrating oil.** Used to loosen rusted and balky screws, nuts, and plumbing connections.

◇**Light machine oil.** Used to lubricate and protect tools, and silence squeaky hinges; use it with steel wool to remove rust.

◇**Powdered graphite** (without oil). Ideal for lubricating locks since it doesn't attract dirt and dust.

◇**Silicone spray.** All-purpose lubricant that doesn't congeal during cold weather.

◇**Paraffin wax.** Helps windows and doors glide more easily, and makes screws easier to drive in.

Patching materials

◆These are indispensable for indoor and outdoor repairs.

◇**Wood putty.** Comes in stick or paste form and fills gouges, cracks, and nail holes in wood; can be sanded and painted.

◇**Patching plaster.** For filling large or deep holes and cracks in plaster and drywall.

◇**Spackling compound.** For filling narrow cracks, small indentations, and nail holes in walls.

◇**Joint compound.** Comes premixed to a gooey consistency for filling joints between drywall panels. Also good for large and small patching jobs.

◆Specialized materials for patching, such as *roofing cement; vinyl, epoxy,* or *latex concrete patch; stucco patching compound; gutter seal; mortar* for brick joints; and *plastic metal fillers,* can be purchased at a good lumberyard or home improvement center.

STORING MATERIALS

◆ Do not throw tools together in a heap; it makes it harder to find what you need later.

◆ Make sure that the storage system you choose will not damage blades or any other working part of the tool. If tools are pressed together, they can easily be damaged or blunted.

◆ Make sure that tools are always put back in the right place so that you can find them the next time.

◆ For ready access to tools, construct a storage system from wooden racks, or use plastic or wire tool-hanging clips mounted to the wall or to perforated hardboard, and hang tools from them.

Perforated hardboard Paint the outline of the tool for each space so you can see where it should go.

Paintbrushes Hang them on hooks to make sure their bristles stay in shape.

Shelves These are useful for storing containers with harmless or non-flammable liquids, or reference books.

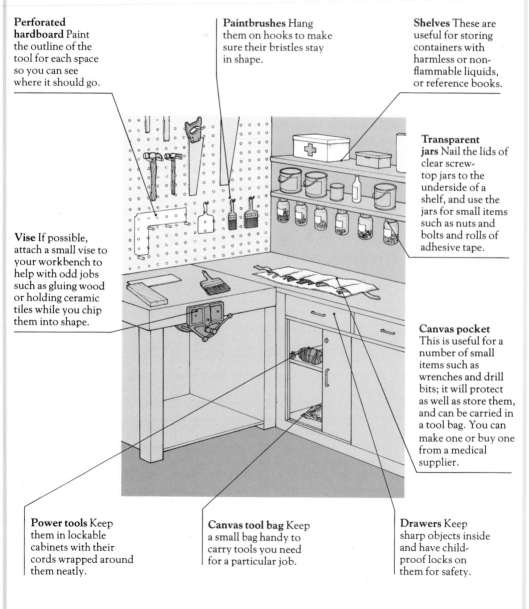

Transparent jars Nail the lids of clear screw-top jars to the underside of a shelf, and use the jars for small items such as nuts and bolts and rolls of adhesive tape.

Vise If possible, attach a small vise to your workbench to help with odd jobs such as gluing wood or holding ceramic tiles while you chip them into shape.

Canvas pocket This is useful for a number of small items such as wrenches and drill bits; it will protect as well as store them, and can be carried in a tool bag. You can make one or buy one from a medical supplier.

Power tools Keep them in lockable cabinets with their cords wrapped around them neatly.

Canvas tool bag Keep a small bag handy to carry tools you need for a particular job.

Drawers Keep sharp objects inside and have child-proof locks on them for safety.

HOUSEHOLD REPAIRS

THROUGHOUT the year, the typical homeowner will tackle a wide variety of tasks. Some jobs are regular occurrences like cleaning out gutters and replacing storm windows with screens, but the majority are unexpected and can involve any area of the home inside and out.

The following pages cover a variety of jobs that you should be able to manage, but if you are in any doubt, call a professional, especially if you have problems with your roof.

When doing your own home repairs, be alert to the risks of each job. Most accidents occur because people are careless with tools and equipment. A little common sense and a knowledge of correct repair techniques can help you steer clear of accidents.

SAFETY GUIDELINES

Avoid most accidents by keeping the following guidelines in mind.

Safety equipment

◇ **Safety goggles.** Those with plastic lenses always should be worn when operating power tools, grinding or chipping, working above your head, or striking metal against metal.

◇ **Dust mask.** Keeps you from inhaling dangerous particles into your lungs when sanding or working with insulation.

◇ **Cartridge respirator.** Guards against toxic paint and solvent fumes.

◇ **Gloves.** Protect your hands from chemicals, insulation, and abrasive or sharp objects.

◇ **Earplugs.** Good to wear when you are working with noisy power tools.

Ladders

◆ Set a ladder base on firm, level ground, at a distance from the wall equal to one-quarter the ladder's length; on soft ground, set the ladder on a board so it won't sink in; use rubber safety shoes on the ladder feet.

◆ Make sure the ladder reaches at least 3 feet above the highest level at which you are likely to stand.

◆ Be sure the rung hooks of an extension ladder are locked in place; no section should be extended more than three-quarters of its length.

▼▼ Don't stand on the top two rungs.

Glass and fiberglass

◆ When dealing with broken glass or fiberglass, always wear thick gardening gloves to protect your hands, sturdy shoes to protect your feet, and goggles or sunglasses to protect your eyes from flying fragments or from strands of fiberglass.

◆ Wrap pieces of glass in newspaper, then seal the package with masking tape before you throw it away so that no one can get cut by fragments of glass.

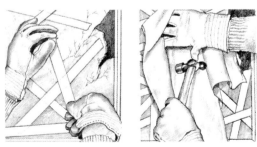

Removing glass from a frame. *Put strips of adhesive tape over the glass to hold the fragments together* (above left), *and cover the glass with a cloth as you break it* (above right).

Flammable materials

Many adhesives, paints, varnishes, and solvents are flammable and/or toxic.

◆Don't work near an open flame. Turn off pilot lights.

◆Work with a window open or make sure there is plenty of ventilation to clear the fumes away quickly.

◆Keep fire extinguishers in the house and in your workshop—one type for electrical fires, another for all other fires (see page 320).

Sharp instruments

◆Never leave sharp instruments lying around unattended, even for a second, particularly if you have children.

◆Follow instructions to the letter when using all cutting tools, and don't allow young or inexperienced people to use them without supervision.

Electricity

◆Be very careful when hammering into walls and floors that you are nowhere near wiring (or water lines).

◆Always turn the main power supply off if you are working on or anywhere near wiring. Double-check that the circuit is dead by plugging in an electrical appliance (one that you know is working) and trying to turn it on. Or, use a continuity tester.

◆Always unplug power tools before leaving them unattended.

◆Check the cords of all power tools for cracks or breaks before using them; don't try to patch a damaged cord—get it replaced.

◆Keep extension cords away from your work; you could cut through them.

◆Never touch any electrical item or the main service panel when your hands are wet.

◆Turn off an overheated tool immediately and let it cool down before using it again.

Gas

◆The main shutoff valve is located on the inlet pipe next to the gas meter. Some shutoffs have handles that can be manually operated; others have a key that can be turned only with a wrench. Both types are open when the handle or key is parallel to the pipe, closed when perpendicular to it.

◆If you smell gas, check that no gas burners have been left on accidentally, or that no pilot lights have blown out. Never try to find a gas leak in the dark by using a match, and never turn on an electric light; either could ignite the gas. Always use a flashlight.

◆If you can't find the source of a leak, turn off the main shutoff valve, open all doors and windows, and call your gas company.

▼▼ Never attempt to repair a gas leak your-
◆◆ self; there is always danger of an explosion.

Testing a gas pipe for a leak. *Smear a fairly strong solution of concentrated dishwashing liquid over the connections; it will bubble where the gas is leaking.*

FLOORS AND FLOOR COVERINGS

◆Cover gaps between the floor and the baseboard with quarter-round, also known as shoe molding (see below). A cheaper, temporary way is to squeeze some caulk along the gap.

◆Fill wide gaps between floorboards with wooden strips. Glue the strips at the sides

Covering floor cracks with shoe molding. *Press the strip flat on the floor, and nail it to the baseboard only. As the gap expands and contracts with varying temperatures, the strip can move.*

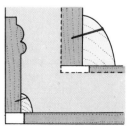

MAKING PAPIER-MÂCHÉ

1 *Tear up newspapers into small pieces. Mix a solution of wallpaper paste to a slightly stronger consistency than the manufacturer suggests for use when papering.*

2 *Work the paste and paper together, keeping the mixture fairly dry.*

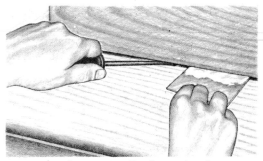

Fixing creaking stairs. *Pry the tread and riser slightly apart, then push wooden or cardboard wedges thickly coated with glue into the space. Trim off any protruding edges and cover with molding.*

driving block to tap polyvinyl-resin-glue-coated wooden or cardboard wedges into the space between the tread and riser. After driving in the wedges, cut them flush with the riser, using a utility knife, and replace the molding to conceal them (see above).

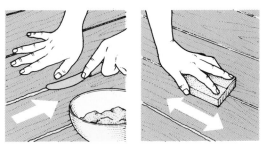

Filling gaps with papier-mâché. *Squeeze the papier-mâché or filler into the cracks with an old knife or putty knife (above left). Let it set completely and then sand it flush with the boards (above right).*

with polyvinyl resin adhesive and then tap them gently into the gap with a hammer. Let the glue dry for 24 hours and then plane the strips so that they are level with the floorboards.

◆ Fill small gaps between boards with plastic wood or, for a less-expensive solution, use papier-mâché (see above).

◆ For loose boards, locate the floor joists by finding the existing nailheads. Hammer 1-inch-long floor nails, or brads, through the boards and into the joists.

◆ Stop floorboards from squeaking either by securing loose boards or by blowing powdered graphite between the noisy boards to act as a lubricant.

Stairs

◆ Stair squeaks usually are caused by a loose tread that rubs against a riser when someone steps on the stair.

◆ First try lubricating the stairs by forcefully blowing powdered graphite or talcum powder into the joints, where the backs of the treads meet the risers.

◆ If lubrication doesn't help, remove the shoe molding and use a hammer and a

Floor coverings

◆ Bind carpeting and rugs, and sisal, coir, and coconut matting to prevent fraying.

1 Make sure that the floor covering and tape are clean. Trim the edges of the floor covering with a pair of large, sharp scissors.

2 Cut a piece of 3-inch binding tape to the right length and apply a latex-based adhesive to half the width of the tape. Apply adhesive to the same width on one edge of the matting. When both are nearly dry, stick the two coated sides together, which should make an immediate bond.

3 Turn the matting over and do the same with the other half of the tape and the matting.

4 Tap along both sides with a hammer to make sure the tape bonds well.

WINDOWS AND DOORS

◆Seal gaps around window frames with a butyl or acrylic latex sealant that has some elasticity to allow for movement. A general-purpose filler should be satisfactory for gaps in wood joints indoors. Clean all surfaces thoroughly before applying filler or it will not adhere.

◆Repair cracked windowpanes temporarily by sticking clear waterproofing tape over the crack on both sides. You can even use the tape to cover a hole in the glass temporarily. Use polyethylene sheeting as a temporary pane for a broken window.

◆If handles and locks begin to work loose, tighten the screws.

◆To repair rattling windows, fit an insulating strip between the frame and the window; this also will stop drafts (see page 238).

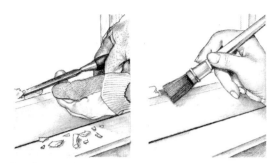

Replacing damaged glazing compound. *If compound has fallen off a window, scrape away the old compound (above left), and brush a little linseed oil where the new compound is going to go (above right). This will prevent water from getting in and rotting the inside of the window frame. Apply new compound with a putty knife.*

Screens

◆Check caulking on the frames of combination units, vacuum dirt from the screen, and clean oxidized aluminum with car polish.

REPLACING A WINDOWPANE

1 *Put on a pair of tough gloves. Remove the broken pane of glass (see page 219). Scrape out the compound with an old chisel or putty knife and tap out any remaining fragments of glass with the handle of a hammer.*

2 *Measure the size of the opening at several points and get a piece of glass cut ⅛ inch smaller than the opening on all four sides.*

3 *Pull out the glazier's points with a pair of pliers and clean and roughen the window recess where the glass fits with a scraper so the new compound will adhere. Prime the groove with linseed oil or turpentine.*

4 *Apply a ⅛-inch-thick bead of glazing compound, and press it into the recess with your fingers. Then set the new glass firmly into place but don't apply pressure at the center of the pane.*

5 *Using a putty knife, gently push glazier's points into the sash (using two points on each side for small panes and a point every 4 to 6 inches for large ones).*

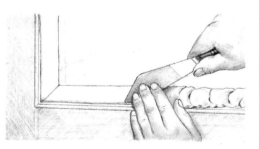

6 *Roll more glazing compound into a rope about ¼ inch thick and spread it around the outside edges. With a putty knife, smooth and bevel the compound to form a neat seal between the glass and wood. If compound sticks to the knife, wet the knife with turpentine.*

7 *Scrape off excess compound from inside the window and clean off fingerprints with cotton balls dipped in denatured alcohol.*

8 *Wait for seven days before painting. Paint should overlap the glass about 1/16 inch for a tight weatherproof seal.*

◆ Clean screens by blasting them with water from a hose, then scrub with a stiff brush.

◆ Paint steel screens with a pad. To unclog holes, turn screen over and scrub with a dry pad. Let dry; paint other side.

◆ Paint wood frames whenever they need it. Shrinkage and warping greatly undercut their weather-stripping value.

◆ Reinforce loose corner joints with mending plates. Corrugated fasteners work especially well for mitered joints.

Patching metal screens. *Cut a section larger than the opening; unravel a few strands. Fit over hole; bend strands back.*

WALLS

◆ Many modern homes have interior walls of drywall, also known as gypsum board and plasterboard, which is relatively quick and easy to apply compared to plaster. It is composed of a fire-resistant gypsum core sandwiched between two layers of paper, and it improves the insulation and soundproofing of a room. Drywall also can cover a solid wall or a previously plastered wall, and it provides a good base for many wall treatments, such as paint, wallpaper, tiles, and paneling.

◆ Plastered walls are found mostly in older homes applied over a base of wood lath, metal mesh, or masonry. (In newer homes plaster is often applied over a special gypsum wallboard.) Plastering walls requires a great deal of skill, time, and expense.

Repairing drywall

Drywall repairs range from fixing minor dents and holes to replacing entire panels. You can repair most minor problems yourself, but adding new walls should be left to a professional.

◆ To fill small dents and holes, sand the depression to roughen the surface, then pack with premixed joint or patching compound.

If the patch shrinks as it dries, apply more coats. When it is dry, sand it flush with the surface or smooth it with a damp sponge.

To patch a hole in drywall

1 Use a utility knife to trim the edges of the hole so they are clean.

2 Cut a piece of drywall that is slightly larger all around than the hole.

3 Make a hole in the center of the piece and thread a string through it. Attach a nail to the string on the white side of the board and tie a knot in the string on the gray side.

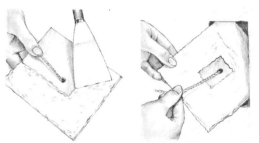

4 Spread some compound on the gray side (*above left*). Holding the string, put the new patch of drywall into the hole, and guide it forward with the string (*above right*) until you are holding it flush against the back of the hole. Keep it firm against the wall.

5 Fill the hole with compound, leaving enough room for a finishing coat. When the compound is almost dry, cut off the string and apply a finishing coat.

Repairing plaster walls

Small cracks and holes in plaster are within the scope of an amateur, but large areas of damage should be handled by a professional.

Patching a hole with a wood lath base

1 Using a cold chisel and hammer, dig back several inches from the damage. Undercut at the edges for a stronger repair.

2 If there is wood lath behind the hole, staple wire mesh to it to give the patching material a better grip. Thoroughly dampen the hole's edges and backing.

3 First fill the hole's edges with patching plaster for medium-size holes or ready-mix for large holes. Then work toward the center. Apply two or three thin coats. Allow time to dry between coats.

4 For a slick finish, run a wet brush across the patch, followed by the trowel's edge.

SOLVING COMMON DOOR PROBLEMS

STICKING DOOR

◆ If the door is tight on the hinge side, there is probably too much paint on this edge of the door. Strip it off and re-paint the area.

◆ If the door is tight on the jamb side, pare off some wood from the hinge recesses in the frame with a chisel. Coat door edges and jambs with paraffin.

◆ If a door scrapes the floor when it is opened and shut, place a sheet of coarse sand-paper on the floor under the door and pull the door over it backward and forward several times until it moves easily.

◆ If the door sticks on the floor, remove it and plane only as much as necessary from the bottom.

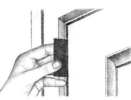

Finding out where a door sticks *Close the door onto a strip of carbon paper. The carbon will rub off onto the door at the point of contact.*

HINGES

◆ For loose door hinges, tighten the screws.

◆ To fix a squeaking door, oil all hinges or coat them with silicone spray. Lubricate exterior hinges with grease rather than oil.

RATTLING DOOR

◆ Stop a door from rattling either by installing weather stripping inside the frame (if the door has shrunk), or by moving the strike plate closer to the lock on the door.

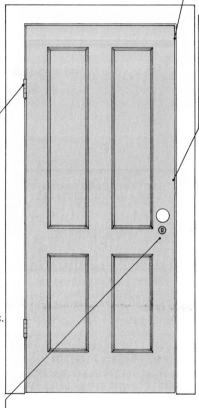

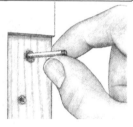

Packing screw holes. *If the holes are too big for the screws, remove the hinges and plug the holes with matchsticks. Replace the hinges.*

1 *Close the door and mea-sure the gap between the doorstop and the door.*

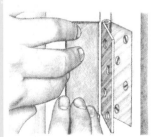

Fixing a loose door. *If the door is loose on the hinge side, first support the bottom of the door with wedges, and unscrew and remove one hinge at a time. Pack each recess with card-board and replace the hinge.*

STICKING LOCK

◆ To loosen a sticking lock, try ap-plying a light lubricating oil and operate the lock vigorously a few times, or put a little powdered graphite onto the key by rubbing a pencil lead along the key, working it into the lock that way.

2 *Unscrew the strike plate and move it toward the doorstop by the same amount as the gap you have just measured. Extend the recess with a chisel. Fill the old screw holes with wood plugs, drill new holes, and replace the strike plate.*

WATERPROOFING

Moisture is a particular problem in basements, but other rooms also may be vulnerable to the effects of poorly maintained gutters and roofs, or condensation.

◆ If your basement floor or walls chronically sweat, or if puddles of water collect on the floor, it will be necessary to track down and correct the source of the problem to prevent your home's foundation from being undermined.

◆ If damp patches appear on the walls of top-floor rooms, have the roof inspected. Slipped, cracked, or missing roof tiles or shingles may be allowing water to come through.

◆ Check gutters late in the fall after most leaves are down and in the spring before any heavy rains begin. Mud and leaves not only clog up gutters and downspouts, they also hold moisture that causes rust, rot, and corrosion.

◆ After you have fixed the cause of any moisture damage on walls, wait until the wall dries out and then paint the outside with a silicone water repellent before redecorating. Remove any peeling paint or paper inside, and paint the wall with a sealer. Redecorate over the sealer.

Roofs, gutters, and downspouts

◆ At least once a year, look at the roof through the attic and scan it through binoculars from the backyard to check for damaged shingles and a faulty chimney or flashing. If you have a flat roof, go up and have a look at it, if possible.

◆ Vinyl-clad screens keep leaves out of gutters. Just slip them under the first course of shingles and fasten with roofing nails.

◆ To extend your reach when cleaning out gutters, fasten a hook to the end of a long pole or board, then use it to rake debris toward you.

◆ Hose your gutters clean. Begin at the high end of each run or in the middle of runs with spouts at both ends. Sometimes you can blast out a spout blockage with hose pressure. If not, break up the jam with a plumber's snake.

◆ If the insides of your gutters are beginning to rust, scrape and wire-brush them, then apply a thin coat of roofing cement.

◆ Patch a rusted-out gutter with lightweight metal or heavy roofing paper. Cement the patch in place, then coat with more cement.

◆ To renew wooden gutters, sand them down to bare wood and apply linseed oil. Let them dry, then apply two coats of roofing cement.

◆ Make certain that all gutters slope toward their outlets, because standing water causes most gutter problems. Check the slope by pouring some water into the gutter and watching what happens. Eliminate sags by lifting the gutter section slightly and bending the hanger with a pair of pliers.

◆ Special wire strainers eliminate downspout clogging. You must still clear the debris around the strainers.

◆ In joining two pieces of spout, crimp the end of one so it will slip into the other. The upper section always goes inside.

TIPS ON USING ROOFING CONTRACTORS

◆ Get a contractor to look at the roof first to establish what has to be done.

◆ Before choosing one, make sure the contractor is a member of a reputable professional organization, in case of problems arising from the workmanship.

◆ Get opinions and estimates from two or three roofers. Look for items that may have been left out.

◆ An estimate should specify:
All materials needed;
Whether cleaning up and clearing away debris, rubble, and old materials are included (as they should be);
Whether the job is simply to replace shingles or to make the roof waterproof;
Statement that the work will conform to a satisfactory standard building code of practice;
Guarantee of work.

CONDENSATION

Damp walls, dripping pipes, rusty hardware, and mildew are all indicative of condensation. This is caused by excess humidity in the air, usually from an internal source such as a basement shower, washing machine, or unvented dryer. It also can be caused by a significant temperature difference between the wall and the inside air. To keep condensation in check:

◆ Install a dehumidifier or window exhaust fan.

◆ Improve ventilation; you may have to fit adjustable vents into window glass.

◆ Make sure walls and windows are well insulated. Use warm wall coverings and storm windows.

◆ Maintain an even temperature throughout the house and avoid oil or gas heaters that produce moisture.

Checking for condensation. *Tape a piece of aluminum foil or a mirror to the dampest spot and wait 24 hours. If it is foggy or beaded with water, suspect condensation.*

Belowground moisture

In addition to condensation, moisture can penetrate basement walls and floors as:

◆**Seepage.** Suspect this when there is general dampness on the floor or a particular wall, especially down near floor level. It can be checked as for condensation (see above). Seepage results when surface water forces its way through pores in the foundation or an expansion joint. There may also be poor roof drainage or a leaky window well. The remedy is to improve surface drainage. An interior sealer may work on a relatively minor problem area, otherwise waterproof the foundation from outside.

◆**Leaks.** Apparent localized wetness that seems to be oozing or even trickling from a foundation wall or floor is usually due to cracks resulting from normal settling, faulty roof drainage, or a grade that slopes toward the wall. A single hole may be plugged from inside, or, you may have to dig down and work from the outside. If leaking is widespread, waterproof the entire foundation wall and install drainage tiles.

◆**Subterranean water.** This may first appear as a thin, barely noticeable film of water on the basement floor. Test by laying down vinyl sheet goods or plastic for two or three days. If moisture is penetrating, it will dampen the concrete underneath. This condition may happen only in rainy periods because a spring or high water table is forcing water up from below under high pressure. A sump pump may be required if drainage tiles around the perimeter of the foundation or floor are not able to direct water to a lower spot or a storm sewer.

RECOGNIZING ROT

◆ Dry rot is a fungus that can penetrate brickwork and plaster and cause serious decay if not checked. Signs include:

◇ Wood that crumbles when you probe it with a sharp knife.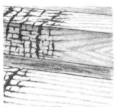

◇ Wood that breaks up into rectangular cubes and has a gray, feltlike fungus on its surface.

◇ White rootlike strands or fluffy growths like wool, which soon change color and resemble bright, rusty red dust.

◇ Bulging, warped, or cracked plaster.

◆ Wet rot spreads only as far as the moisture has penetrated and will not grow into brickwork. Signs are:

◇ Darkened wood, cracks along the grain of the wood, flaking paint.

◇ Dark brown, narrow strands of fungus.

PLUMBING

Y OU CAN handle many plumbing repair jobs yourself by following our guidelines below. Doing the repairs yourself will avoid the expense of hiring a plumber. Some useful tools to keep on hand include a "plumber's helper," also called a plunger or force cup; a "plumber's snake"; chemical drain cleaner; and assorted washers, screws, and O rings.

LEAKS

Water can escape from faucets and pipes, though the former is usually more annoying than serious, as is the latter. A leaking faucet, however, does waste water and, if it is a hot water faucet, it wastes energy and should be repaired as soon as possible.

Leaking faucets

◆Though faucets vary in style, they all fall into one of two broad categories:

◇**Compression or stem faucets.** These always have separate hot and cold controls. Turning a handle to its off position rotates a threaded stem. A washer at the bottom of the stem then compresses into a seat to block the flow of water.

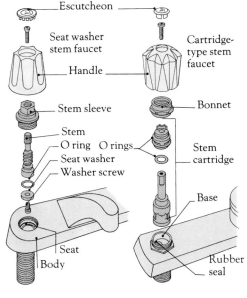

Escutcheon

Seat washer stem faucet

Handle

Stem sleeve

Stem
O ring O rings
Seat washer
Washer screw

Seat
Body

Cartridge-type stem faucet

Bonnet

Stem cartridge

Base

Rubber seal

◇**Noncompression faucets.** These have a single lever that controls the flow of hot and cold water. There are four types named for their different operating mechanisms: a tipping valve faucet, a disk faucet, a rotating-ball faucet, and a sleeve-cartridge faucet.

◆Stem faucets are the most leak-prone of all types. Repairs are needed generally because of a worn washer, a pitted or corroded valve seat, or deteriorated packing.

To change a washer

1 Turn off the water at the main entry or at the shutoffs below the sink or lavatory.

2 Pry out the decorative escutcheon on the faucet handle. Back out the screw and remove the handle. Lift it straight up.

3 Remove the packing nut. Use an adjustable wrench or a pair of slip-joint pliers. Then simply turn out the stem.

4 The seat washer, held in place by a screw, is at the bottom of the stem. You may have to replace the stem's O rings as well.

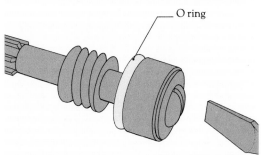

O ring

5 A worn washer will be grooved, pitted, and/or frayed. When you replace it, clean the entire valve stem with fine steel wool.

6 Before you reassemble an older faucet, be sure to wind packing around the stem, then install the packing nut.

Leaking pipes

◆ When you notice a leak, turn off the water at the main supply valve or at a shutoff valve. This takes pressure off the line.

◆ If the leak is behind a wall, in a ceiling, or under a floor where you can't get at it, you will have to call a plumber immediately.

◆ If, however, the leak is visible and not of great magnitude, you can probably get away with making a temporary patch and can replace the pipe or call a plumber at your leisure.

◆ A patch can be any material that will stop the flow of water, such as a piece of rubber and a C-clamp, several layers of plastic tape, or a length of garden hose split and tied around the pipe. Even better is an emergency patch kit. However, in a pinch, you can do the following:

◇ For tiny leaks, wrap the pipe with several layers of plastic electrician's tape. Wind the tape 6 inches each way from the hole.

◇ If the leak is at a connection, spread epoxy putty around the leak with a putty knife. It will dry quickly.

◇ Special metal clamps with rubberlike inner lining inserts are available. You can tighten these clamps with a screwdriver.

Making a temporary repair to a cracked pipe. *Cover the crack with a piece of solid rubber blanket. Fasten with an adjustable hose clamp size 16 or 12.*

Noisy pipes

Water moves through pipes under considerable pressure and can produce a wide variety of noises. Depending on the cause, there are a number of things you can do to decrease the sound.

◆ **Water hammer.** This is the loud bang you hear when you open a faucet, run the water, and quickly close the faucet. The same noise is often produced by automatic washing machines when a solenoid valve snaps shut. Most house fixtures have an air chamber, which eventually fills with water and causes "hammer." To fix, first drain the system. Then refill the pipes (the air chamber will fill with air again and there shouldn't be further noise for several years). If your system doesn't have chambers, install a chamber at the faucet fixture. This provides a cushion of air on which the bang can bounce. To install a copper-coil air chamber, break the supply line and add a T fitting.

◆ **Machine-gun rattle.** This signals a faucet problem. Try replacing the washer.

◆ **Whistle.** Somewhere in the system a water valve is partly closed. The water, under pressure, narrows at the valve and causes the whistle. Simply open the valve as far as you can. If a toilet whistles, adjust the inlet valve.

◆ **Running water.** Check for leaks at toilets, sill cocks, your furnace humidifier, and your water softener.

◆ **Soft ticking or cracking.** This is usually caused by a hot water pipe heating up with water after being cool. Try muffling it with insulation.

◆ **Bangs.** These may result from water pressure in the pipes causing them to knock against their metal hangers. Have someone quickly open then close the faucet to cause a bang; often you can see the pipes move. Nail pipe hangers so that they hang just below the pipes. Soundproof any pipes that touch the hangers with short lengths of rubber hose. Split the hose lengthwise and slip it around the pipes.

CLOGGED DRAINS

◆Hair, bits of soap, and other debris can gum up a sink stopper. To remove some types of stopper, just turn and lift.

◆Try clearing a drain with a plunger before using a commercial drain cleaner. Drain cleaners are caustic and poisonous; it is important to follow instructions exactly.

◆If you can't unclog the drain with a plunger or snake (see right) you will have to get into the trap beneath the sink. Place a bucket underneath; remove the trap by unscrewing the coupling nuts holding the trap, beginning with the higher one.

Clearing a stopped-up sink with a plunger. *Block the sink overflow by covering it with a cloth. Fit the rubber cup tightly over the sink drain and pump it up and down to create a vacuum, which will release the blockage.*

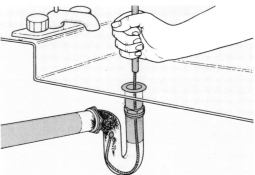

Clearing a blockage with a "snake." *If a plunger won't work, try a plumber's snake. Thread it down and through the trap. If this doesn't do the job, remove the trap and flush it. Now you can get the snake into the main drain.*

TIPS FOR PREVENTING DRAIN CLOGS

◆About once a week, throw a handful of baking soda followed by hot water into the sink. Or, pour in 1 cup of vinegar and after 30 minutes, run very hot water through the drain.

◆Pour cooking grease into an empty jar or can; never pour it down the sink.

◆Squirt greasy pans with dishwashing liquid, fill them with hot water, and allow them to soak for a little while so the fat breaks up into smaller particles before you wash the pans.

◆To retrieve metal items such as flatware or pins that have fallen into the drain, attach a magnet to a piece of stiff twine and use this to "fish" for the item.

◆Use a metal or plastic trap over the drain to catch sizable debris.

▼▼Don't put the following substances
◆◆down your drain, kitchen sink, or toilet—not only will they block up the drains but they also will make them smell very unpleasant:
◇Coffee grounds
◇Tea leaves
◇Hair
◇Disposable diapers
◇Sanitary napkins

Cleaning a garbage disposer

GREEN TIP: Put a slice of lemon into the disposer to make it smell sweeter.

▼▼Don't use drain-cleaning chemicals
◆◆because they are caustic and may damage the unit.

◆To clear the unit of greasy food, try throwing ice cubes in and running the disposer. The ice should congeal the fat, allowing the unit to grind it into disposable pieces.

HOW TO AVOID BLOCKING A GARBAGE DISPOSER

Don't deposit the following:
◇Metal   ◇Cardboard
◇Plastic   ◇China, glass, or flatware
◇Rags   ◇Large bones
◇String   ◇Hot or cold fat
◇Cotton balls ◇Bottle caps

Clearing a garbage disposer jam

1 If the garbage disposer jams, shut off power to it. Then remove the splash guard and survey the situation. Once you locate the obstruction, insert the end of a broom or mop handle into the grinding chamber and pry against the turntable until it rotates freely.

2 If the garbage disposer shuts off while in operation, wait about five minutes for the motor to cool, then push the reset button on the bottom of the disposer. If it won't start, make sure the unit is plugged in and that the fuse or circuit breaker is functioning.

Blocked toilet

▼▼ Don't keep flushing a blocked toilet—it
◆ ◆ will overflow.

◆ Unclog a blocked toilet with a plunger, or if the blockage is deep, use a special snake to break it up. Push and turn the handle simultaneously to maneuver the auger and remove

the blockage.

◆ If you don't have a plunger, use an old towel tied around the toilet brush. If you can't solve the problem easily, call in a plumber.

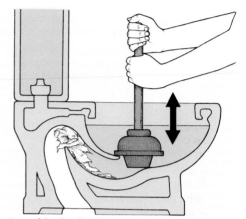

Clearing a blocked toilet. *Use a plumber's friend over the hole in the bottom. Work the plunger hard and vigorously, and don't give up too soon. Spread petroleum jelly on the plunger's rim to aid suction.*

STEAM AND WATER HEATING SYSTEMS

◆ Have your central heating system flushed out once a year by a heating engineer or plumber to get rid of any rust or sludge that could damage the pump or cause "cold spots" in the radiators.

◆ Bleed your radiators if they have not been used for a while. If a radiator is warm at the bottom but cold at the top, or if it makes a constant gurgling sound, there is probably an air lock in the system, which bleeding the radiator will solve.

◆ If air locks occur frequently, get a plumber to replace the vent valve with a special air eliminator, which has a valve in it to allow air to escape.

BLEEDING A RADIATOR

1 *Turn off the radiator. When the water is warm, not hot, turn the vent valve at the top counter-clockwise with a radiator key. When air starts to escape, stop turning.*

2 *As soon as air stops escaping and water starts to flow, tighten the valve again.*

EMERGENCY PLUMBING

◆ Turn off the electricity if the water is near any wiring, because water conducts electricity. Mop up as much water as possible and get the leak repaired as quickly as you can.

▼▼ Don't turn the electricity back on until
◆ ◆ you are sure that the wiring is dry, or you could get a shock when you touch the switch.

Constantly running tank

◆ Stop any water flow by pulling up the flush valve (see opposite, top). This will give you time to investigate the problem.

◆ Check the float ball. If it is damaged, buy a new one. Unscrew the old ball and fit the new one onto the arm. Make sure you get one the right size for your tank; if you use the wrong size, it may not stop the flow. A pitted or corroded ball seat needs scouring with a steel wool pad.

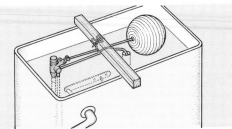

Stopping the overflow. *Pull up the flush valve (ball cock) and tie it to a clothes hanger or a strip of wood that has been laid across the top of the tank.*

◆ If the ball is not damaged, the float arm that supports the ball may be incorrectly angled so that the ball sits too high and won't shut off the flush valve. If the float arm is plastic, loosen the nut on the arm and lower the ball; if the arm is metal, bend the ball end down with pliers so that the ball sits lower and the water pushes it up sooner.

◆ Check the washer in the flush valve; if it is worn, the valve will drip. To replace it, switch off the water supply to the tank, remove the pin that attaches the arm to the valve, then remove the washer and replace it with a new one.

Overflowing washing machine/dishwasher

◆ If your machine empties into a sink, you may simply have left the plug in. Unplug it to drain the water, and then deal with the overflow.

◆ If an automatic machine starts to overflow, turn the dial until the machine begins to empty. Then spread as many towels as you can all over the floor, to sop up the excess water, especially if the floor is carpeted or if there are electrical outlets at floor level.

◆ If the overflow is caused by the wrong detergent, put the wash (or the dishes, if the machine is a dishwasher) through several rinse cycles to clean the soap off. Make sure that you always put the right amount of detergent in the machine and that you always use the detergent specified for your type of machine.

◆ Check that the filter and the detergent compartment have been put back properly in the washing machine.

◆ If the overflow is due to a problem with the machine, drain it as above, turn it off, unplug it, and call in a professional before using it again.

Thawing a frozen pipe

Frozen pipes must be thawed immediately upon discovery, or they may burst.

◆ If a pipe freezes, first shut off the water supply at the main shutoff valve, then open the faucet nearest the frozen pipe so that it can drain as it thaws.

◆ If the frozen pipe is concealed in a ceiling, wall, or floor, shine a heat lamp 8 to 12 inches from the surface.

◆ If the pipes are in tight quarters, wrap them with hot towels and pour hot water over the frozen section, or wrap a heating pad around the pipe. You also can run a propane torch, hot air gun, or hair dryer along the pipes little by little until the water runs again.

▼▼ Don't use an open flame to thaw frozen
◆ ◆ pipes behind walls, ceilings, or floors, or near gas lines.

◆ Always thaw frozen pipes gradually in case there are already cracks that could cause a flood.

Burst pipe

1 Turn the water off at the nearest shutoff valve or main shutoff on your meter and turn on all the faucets to drain the system.

2 If the damaged pipe is fed from the water heater, close the gate valves connecting the tank and pipe.

3 Place a bucket under the leak and keep emptying and replacing it as it fills.

◆ If the pipe has burst but the ice has not yet melted, you may be able to detect the damaged area—the ice may glisten through the crack; this often occurs at a joint. Wrap a rag tightly around the crack and put a bucket under it to catch the drips, or wind plastic electrical tape tightly around the split to about 3 inches on each side, and call the plumber.

ELECTRICITY

A S LONG AS you keep safety in mind, tackling many electrical repairs is easy. But if the job is more complicated, it is a good idea to get hold of a detailed electrical how-to manual and follow the procedures to the letter. Make sure, too, to check your local building code.

GLOSSARY OF ELECTRICAL TERMS

Amp Unit measuring the amount of current in a circuit.
Circuit Complete path around which an electric current flows.
Conductor Substance such as a metal wire that carries an electric current.
Ground The pathway along which a current flows to the ground safely, if a short occurs.
Fuse A protective device that cuts off the current when the circuit overloads or if a short develops in the system. Instead of fuses, newer homes have resettable, switchlike circuit breakers.
Live (also hot) The wire of a cord carrying the current to where it is needed, or any

terminal to which the live wire is connected.
Neutral The core of a wire cable that carries the current back to its source or the terminal to which the neutral wire is connected.
Service panel Also called the fuse box or circuit breaker box, this unit is the central point of origin for all the circuits that carry electricity to every part of the home.
Short circuit A circuit that deviates from its normal pathway, passing through wires or objects that may not be grounded and cannot handle the great amount of heat generated, and that may melt or catch fire.

Volt Unit measuring the electrical pressure that drives the current around a circuit.
Watt Unit measuring the amount of power consumed by any electrical device. Utility bills are based on the number of watts, in thousands consumed each hour. The common term is kilowatt-hour.
Wiring Under the color-coded system, "hot" wires may be red or black, neutral is white, and the ground is usually green or bare copper.

SAFETY WITH ELECTRICITY

▼▼ Before working on any circuit, make
◆ ◆ sure you shut off all the electricity at the service panel, either by pulling out the relevant fuse or switching off the main circuit breaker. At the same time, shut off power to the specific circuit you are working on; then plug in an appliance you know to be working, or use a testing device to double-check that the circuit is dead. Leave a note on the service panel explaining to others what you are doing, so they do not unknowingly switch the circuit back on.

▼▼ Don't use a fuse with a higher amperage
◆ ◆ than you need; the circuit may overload, overheat, and start a fire.
◆ Make sure all appliances with metal bodies are grounded to prevent shocks. Make sure that all appliances have double-insulated wire, particularly those without a ground wire.

▼▼ Don't ignore an unusual smell; check
◆ ◆ the plug of any electrical equipment that's switched on. If there's a short, the plug may be overheating and melting the plastic.
◆ If a plug feels warm to the touch, switch off the power, take the plug out of the outlet, switch off the circuit breaker or remove the appropriate fuse, and check the wiring in the plug and outlet. They may be overheating

because of a short and could eventually catch fire if not fixed.

▼▼ Don't touch electrical equipment with
◆ ◆ wet hands, feet, or cloths; water is a conductor of electricity, and you will get a shock if it touches a live surface.

▼▼ Don't use electrical equipment in the
◆ ◆ bathroom unless it has an outlet that is protected by a ground fault circuit interrupter (GFCI). If water should come in contact with a GFCI, the circuit instantly shuts down. GFCI outlets have two buttons between the receptacles that you use to test and reset the device; alternatively, some bath receptacles are protected by a special GFCI circuit breaker in the service panel.

◆ Check plugs and cords regularly for wear or damage and fix loose connections immediately or they may become dangerous. Never allow a cord to become frayed or worn. If it does, repair˙ it with insulating tape as a temporary measure only—it is not as safe as a permanent repair; replace it with new cord as soon as possible.

◆ Don't run cords under carpets; they may become worn, which will expose the wires. If the bare wires touch each other, they will short the circuit. Also, you may forget to check whether cords are worn if they are hidden under carpets.

▼▼ Don't hammer nails into walls near
◆ ◆ switches or sockets or through floors where there may be electric lines (and water or gas pipes); you may electrocute yourself, flood the house, or cause a gas leak.

▼▼ Don't use water to put out a fire in an
◆ ◆ electrical appliance unless the power is off, because it will cause a short circuit and make everything the water touches live. Use a fire extinguisher designed specifically for electrical fires or a multipurpose extinguisher.

▼▼ Don't improvise when replacing a fuse.
◆ ◆ The fuse is there to protect you and cut off power to an area with a short, preventing a fire or electric shock.

◆ When using power tools such as saws and hedge trimmers, be especially careful that you don't cut through the cord and possibly electrocute yourself.

BASIC TOOL KIT

◆ Keep a selection of basic tools together for everyday electrical repairs or emergencies. The best place for them is in a box of their own near the service panel where you can reach them easily in case the electricity suddenly is cut off. The essential items are:

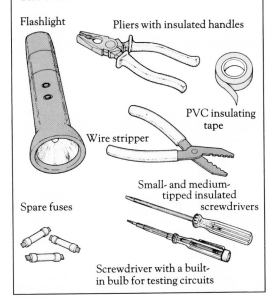

Flashlight

Pliers with insulated handles

PVC insulating tape

Wire stripper

Spare fuses

Small- and medium-tipped insulated screwdrivers

Screwdriver with a built-in bulb for testing circuits

BASIC TROUBLESHOOTING

◆ Electrical home repairs should be safe if you follow the correct procedures and use the right tools for the particular job at hand. For example, use only a plastic fuse puller for removing cartridge fuses; always use a continuity tester to check connections, and so on.

◆ Label the circuit breakers in the main service panel (or fuses in the main fuse box) according to the circuits they monitor. This will make it easier to identify a faulty circuit quickly.

◆ Whether you are joining wires to switches, receptacles, or in midcircuit, for safety's sake, make all the connections inside a box.

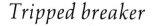

Tripped breaker

The circuit breaker is a heat-sensing, spring-loaded switch that instantly shuts off the circuit if even the slightest imbalance occurs. It is more effective than the older fuse box system because it provides extra protection against any dangerous current leakage.

◆ Most circuit breakers have three switch positions: on, off, and tripped, a midway position showing that the circuit has been overloaded and is off. Sometimes a red flag shows in a tripped breaker.

◆ An overload is usually a result of using too many appliances at the same time. You must correct the problem before resetting the breaker.

Resetting a breaker

1 If the switch is tripped, you generally only need to turn off extra appliances or one of the circuit's bigger electricity users; then switch the breaker to off before flipping it back on.

2 If the breaker trips again, suspect a short. To locate one, systematically unplug electrical items until the breaker holds. A defective plug, loose wires in an outlet box, or a frayed cord may be the problem you are looking for.

▼▼ Don't use high-wattage bulbs unless
♦ ♦ specified; they can melt insulation and cause a short.

◆ If a major appliance trips the line repeatedly and you're sure the circuit is not overloaded, call an electrician.

◆ If cracked insulation has exposed a wire and caused a short, wrap the wire with several layers of electrical tape.

Blown fuses

If you have an older home that hasn't been rewired, chances are you have a fuse box rather than a modern circuit breaker box. The two serve the same purpose, but instead of tripping as a breaker does, a fuse "blows" when too much current is in the circuit. The most common fuses still in use are the plug and the cartridge fuse. Always wear rubber-soled shoes and stand on dry ground when working at a fuse box.

▼▼ Don't install a "bigger" fuse to remedy a
♦ ♦ chronically overloaded circuit. Wiring that gets more current than it was designed to handle heats up and can catch fire.

Pulling a fuse

1 Check the metal strip through the window of the plug fuse. A melted strip and discolored fuse window indicate there is a short circuit; a clear window and a broken strip indicate an overload. Locate and correct the problem (see left) before replacing the fuse.

2 Turn off the main switch or pull out the main fuse block before you begin. Leaving one hand free, grasp the blown fuse by its glass rim, and unscrew it.

3 Make sure that you replace the fuse with one of the same amp rating. Restore the power.

4 To determine if a cartridge fuse has blown, pull out its fuse block and remove the fuse with a plastic fuse puller (see below). Touch the probes of a continuity tester to the ends of the fuse. If the tester doesn't light, the fuse is blown. Insert a new fuse into the spring clips by hand.

▼▼ Don't touch the ends of a cartridge fuse
♦ ♦ right after removal; the ends may still be very hot.

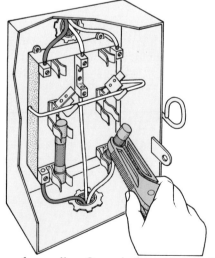

Using a fuse puller. *Grasp the fuse with the puller. Do not touch the fuse with your hands even after it has been pulled—the ends get hot.*

Wiring plugs

Faulty plugs, cords, or light sockets pose the most common shock and fire hazards; they also are very easy to repair. Any plug that is cracked, broken, or charred should be re-placed immediately.

Wiring flat-cord plugs

Some of these have a core that you attach the wires to, then snap into a shell. Others attach much like the quick-connect plugs do (see below).

1 First slip the shell onto the cord, peel apart the wires, and strip away about ½ inch of plastic insulation from each wire.

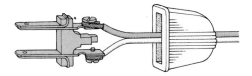

2 Twist the exposed strands together and curl each wire clockwise to form hooks big enough to wrap around each screw terminal.

3 Tighten down the screws, replace the insulator disk, and snap the cord into the shell.

Wiring round-cord plugs

These usually have either two or three wires and must be fitted to plugs with terminal screws. If these screws are coded, remember to connect the black wire to the brass-colored screw, the white to the silver screw, and the ground wire to the green screw.

1 Begin by cutting off the old plug, slipping a new one onto the cord, and stripping away insulation.

2 Tie a knot large enough so that tugging at the cord can't loosen the electrical connections.

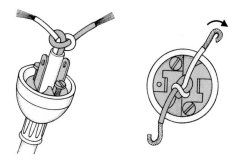

3 Twist the wire strands tightly together and with a pair of long-nose pliers, shape clockwise hooks.

4 As you tighten the screws down over the wires, tuck in any stray strands. Make sure all wires are neatly inside the plug cover, and slip on the cardboard cover.

WIRING SELF-CONNECTING PLUGS

Installing this type of plug takes about the same time as changing a light bulb. The only tool you need is a sharp knife or a pair of scissors.

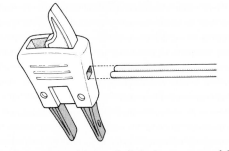

1 *Snip off the old plug. Lift the lever on top of the new plug and insert the zip cord at the side.*

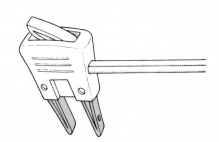

2 *Closing the lever pierces and holds the wire, and you're done.*

Fluorescent lighting

◆ Fluorescent tubes rarely burn out abruptly. When a tube won't light, try wiggling its ends to be sure they are properly seated. If this doesn't help, and yours is a rapid-start tube, you may have to remove the cover of the fixture and look for bare wires or loose connections. Make sure you turn off the power to the circuit first.

◆ Replace a tube that glows red at each end, any old tubes that flicker, and ones that start to go black near the end. Select a new tube of the same wattage as the old.

◆ Older, delayed-start fluorescent lights flicker as they light up. If a new tube continues to flicker as it comes on, make sure the starter is correctly seated by pushing it in and turning clockwise. If it still flickers, replace the starter.

◆ If the fixture makes a humming sound, has an acrid odor, or drips a tarlike substance,

DIAGNOSING PROBLEMS

Some electrical problems can't be dealt with by yourself. Call an electrician when:
◇ You are unable to find a short after fuses have blown
◇ You are not sure how to tackle a particular electrical job
◇ There are problems with the wiring of the house
◇ The wiring system is old and looks as though it could be dangerous.

chances are the ballast at the heart of the fixture is wearing out. If this is the case, it is usually cheaper to replace the entire unit.

ELECTRICAL FAULTS IN APPLIANCES

SYMPTOMS	PROBLEM	SOLUTION
◇ The cord is hot and the appliance stops working. ◇ A fuse blows the main fuse box, or the circuit breaker trips. ◇ There is a peculiar rubbery or hot smell and the plug or socket becomes a yellowish singed color.	Poorly insulated live and neutral wires, which cause a short circuit. Or, the cause may be an overload, a result of too many appliances in use at one time.	Check the wiring in the plug and then check the cord. If either is old or damaged, replace it. Make sure that extra appliances are turned off.
◇ The appliance gives a shock to anyone who touches it, the fuse blows, or the circuit breaker trips.	A poorly insulated live part of the plug or cord is touching a metal part.	Check the wiring to the appliance, especially where the cord is connected, and repair or replace any damaged sections.
◇ The appliance or plug starts a fire. ◇ The fuse blows, or the circuit breaker trips as soon as the appliance is switched on.	A live wire is poorly insulated, causing the current to flow to ground.	Check the cord and the plug, and repair any damaged wires.
◇ The appliance stops working. ◇ The plug is hot enough to catch fire.	Broken wires or loose connection within an appliance.	Check the wiring and the connections in the plug and in the appliance, and repair any damaged or loose wires or connections.

INSULATION AND ENERGY SAVING

INSULATION helps you make the most of precious energy. In a house that is badly insulated, as soon as heat is generated, it disappears through the roof, walls, and floors, up chimneys, out doors and windows, along with much of the money you are spending each year to heat your home. If you keep your home well insulated, your fuel bills will be lower, the rooms will heat up more quickly and cool down more slowly, and you will be warmer.

HEAT LOSS FROM YOUR HOME

Windows From 10 to 30 percent of heat in your home is lost through window glass. There are temporary forms of double glazing you can put up yourself, but have storm windows installed professionally.

Floors Around 16 percent of the heat lost goes through ground floors. Floor insulation is best done by a professional.

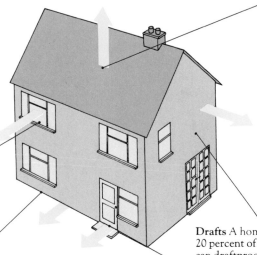

Roof and attic The roof accounts for about 25 percent of the heat lost in an average home. This can be cut to 8 percent by insulating the attic, one of the easiest and most cost-effective improvements you can make on your heating expenses.

Walls About a third of heat lost from a home goes through the walls. Cavity walls are easily insulated by an expert; solid walls, less easily.

Drafts A home can lose between 10 and 20 percent of its heat through drafts. You can draftproof your home quite easily.

WEATHER STRIPPING

◆ By using a variety of inexpensive materials, you can seal outside walls, keep outside air out, and inside air in. A tight seal at doors, windows, and anything else you can open will prevent heat leaks. In addition to the materials below, caulks and sealants (see page 217) will fill gaps between immovable materials where air could penetrate.

◇ **Spring metal or vinyl strips.** These are fairly easy to install. Cut with snips, then tack in place. These are invisible on installation.

◇ **Rolled vinyl and felt.** Also fairly easy to install. Cut with scissors or snips, then tack in place. These are visible.

◇ **Self-adhesive foam.** Very easy to apply. Snip it with scissors, peel off the backing, and press it in place. Not very durable, however.

◇ **Interlocking metal strips.** These are the most expensive materials and come in several different configurations. They need to align exactly, so they are fairly difficult to install. Use them on doors and casement windows.

◇ **Door shoes, sweeps, and thresholds.** Some mount on the bottom of the door; others replace an existing threshold. Installation can be tricky for some types, but relatively easy for others.

◆ Before working on windows, inspect each one carefully for loose or missing chunks of glazing compound, dried-out caulk around the window frame, and deterioration of the sill. All these problems must be rectified before attaching the stripping.

◆ Doors should not be warped, out-of-square, or deteriorating around the edges, or the weather stripping will not be efficient. A poorly weather-stripped exterior door can leak up to twice as much air as a window in the same condition.

WEATHER-STRIPPING DOORS AND WINDOWS

DOORS

◆ Choose weather stripping that is designed for doors because it is more durable.

◆ Pet flaps are also a source of drafts—choose one that closes on a magnet or is radio-controlled by the pet's collar. If you have a cat, try to persuade it to use a litter box during the winter, and tape up the flap.

◆ You will need a bottom-of-the-door device that withstands lots of traffic but clears any carpeting.

◆ Hang a heavy, lined curtain on a rail fixed to the back of the front door as an additional form of draftproofing. Don't attach the rail to the door frame or the curtain will get caught continually and become a nuisance.

◆ Stop drafts coming through a mail slot by fitting a flap to the back of it (see below right).

◆ Use durable brush or tubular strips around the door to deal with drafts between the door and the frame. Position these so the brush or soft tube touches the face of the door. For under-door drafts, treatments range from self-adhesive plastic strips to waterproof thresholds and door sweeps. Door sweeps are easiest to install, with one part fitted to the threshold and the other to the door. The sweep needs to be adjusted so it is flush with the floor.

FILLING GAPS

◆ For narrow gaps, fit self-adhesive foam-filled vinyl stripping to the sides of the frame of hinged doors and windows; this is the cheapest and easiest to use but will not last more than about two years.

◆ For wide gaps and for greater durability, fit rolled vinyl or felt strips in the form of a flexible tube to the door or window frame; when the door or window is shut, the tube is squashed flat and the gap is sealed.

◆ You also can use vinyl or spring metal V-shaped strips, which fit to the frames and compress upon closure to form a seal. For irregularly shaped gaps, caulking guns with silicone or acrylic latex sealants can be used. These expand and contract with changing conditions.

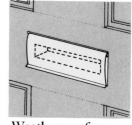

Weatherproofing a mail slot. *Fit a close fitting flap to the inner side of the mail slot so that the flap swings inward only when something is pushed through slot.*

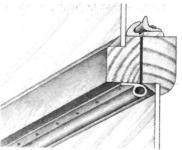

Weather-stripping double-hung windows. *From the outside, tack strip insulation along the under side of the upper sash so it presses against the top of the lower sash.*

Securing plastic weather stripping. *This strip is often sold in rolls so it can be difficult to get it to stay in position, even though it has double-sided tape on one side. Position each length on the frame, then secure each length top and bottom with brads.*

INSULATION FOR YOUR HOME

◆Insulating materials function like giant sponges, with millions of tiny air pockets that trap heat. The more pockets per inch of thickness a material has, the higher its R-value and the warmer it will make your home.

◆Insulation is rated by inches of thickness; to compute a material's total R-value, multiply the thickness by its R-value per inch.

Insulating with loose fill. *Use loose fill for insulating areas difficult to reach, such as the odd shapes around chimneys or between unevenly spaced joists. It must have a vapor barrier laid down before being spread, and must also be treated with a fire retardant.*

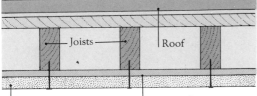

Joists — Roof

Insulation board | Plaster ceiling

◇**Batts.** Generally fluffy fiberglass or rock wool sections, they are moisture- and fire-resistant and come with or without an attached vapor barrier. They are used in unfinished attic floors, rafters, crawl spaces, walls, and ceilings.

◇**Blankets.** Also of fiberglass or rock wool, they come in continuous rolls and are used in the same areas as batts.

◇**Loose-fill insulation.** This can be either poured or blown into cavities. The most common are fire-retardant cellulose fiber, vermiculite, perlite, fiberglass, and rock wool. Used for unfinished attic floors, especially with irregular joist spacing, and for finished wall and floor cavities.

◇**Foam** (urethane). Also can be used to insulate finished walls, floors, and ceilings from the outside.

◇**Rigid insulation.** Consists of polystyrene, polyurethane, or polyisocyanurate that is molded and extruded into boards. It is used for roofs, ceilings, walls, foundations, and basement walls.

Insulating attics

◆If your attic will never be anything but dead storage space, insulate only the floor. If,

Laying blanket or batt insulation. *Wearing thick gloves, goggles, and a face mask, unroll the insulation in the attic, and cut it so it fits the spaces between the joists (above left). Press the strips down so that they fit snugly (above right).*

however, it is finished or will be finished later, also insulate the ceiling and walls.

◆If you need a separate vapor barrier, staple 2-mil polyethylene between the joists. Seal all seams with tape.

◆Be careful not to jam batts or blankets against the roof; leave space at the eaves for air flow.

◆When you encounter diagonal-bridging or other obstacles, cut for a snug fit. Otherwise, heat will slip away through the gap.

▼▼Don't cover recessesd light fixtures, or
◆ ◆ exhaust fans; this could cause a fire.

◆For loose-fill, nail in baffles at the eaves. Insulation should cover the top plate but not obstruct air flow needed for ventilation. Pour the insulation between joists, then level it off with a board. Don't leave any low spots.

◆Add collar beams overhead if your attic has none. Plan the height, cut the beams to fit, then nail to the existing rafters. Staple batts or blankets to the collar beams, vapor-barrier side down. Continue on down the knee walls to the floor.

◆If you are adding to old insulation, cut it and push it to the back of the cavity. Slash any vapor barrier with a sharp knife. Then place the new material directly over the old. Staple the flanges to the rafters, vapor-barrier side down, lapping as you go.

◆If your attic is finished, you must make openings to get at spaces above collar beams and behind knee and end walls.

◆Lay loose-fill, blanket, or batt material between joists in the knee-wall space. Use a broom to poke into hard-to-reach spots.

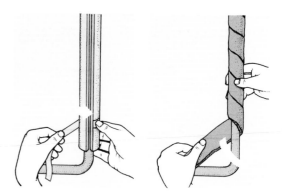

Insulating pipes. *The easiest and cheapest method of insulating pipes is to buy lengths of polyurethane foam tubing, which are available in sizes that fit standard pipes (above left); otherwise use strips of left-over batts or blankets and wind the strips around the pipes in a spiral (above right).*

Pipes and ducts

◆Sleeves to insulate pipes come in various lengths. A slit lets you fit the sleeve on the pipe, then you glue down the flap.

◆At ends or corners, cut short lengths to fit pipes as closely as possible. Use a fine-blade hacksaw or sharp utility knife.

◆At pipe junctions, wrap all the uncovered areas with spongy insulation tape. Peel off the backing and wrap like a bandage.

◆Wrap ducts with 2-inch duct insulation and seal all joints with duct tape.

◆Where ducts run between joists, cut blankets of insulation to surround ducts and staple them to the joists. Seal joints between the blankets with duct tape.

◆For other ductwork, wrap insulation carefully around all four sides. The vapor barrier should always be on the outside.

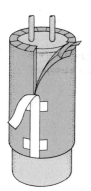

Insulating water heaters. *Water heater blankets are available in kit form in different sizes to fit most tanks. You also can make your own from fiberglass wrap that has a vapor barrier, securing it with wide tape. They are especially useful if your unit is located in an unheated space.*

INSULATING WALLS AND FLOORS

The amount of heat lost through the walls depends on the type of house. In general, the more outside walls you have, and the larger the roof area, the more insulation required. The amount of heat lost through floors also varies with the type of floor. For example, solid concrete is usually warmer than a wood frame floor, but it can be damper.

Walls

It is best to leave exterior wall insulation to professionals because the existing siding, plaster, or drywall has to be penetrated or removed and the walls have to be injected (if they are cavity walls) or covered with some insulating material.

◆Have cavity walls insulated by high-pressure injection. This is the best form of insulation, but it is expensive.

◆To insulate solid walls, have them clad in siding or stucco. This is the only form of insulation that really works on these walls.

◆Walls can be insulated from the inside by erecting a wood frame in front of them and insulating it, but again this is best done by a professional.

Unfinished walls are a snap to insulate. You just friction-fit batts or staple up blankets. Be sure not to compress the insulation.

Floors

◆Insulate floor surfaces by covering them with carpeting (particularly foam-backed carpeting) and padding, cork or wood floor tiles, or vinyl floor coverings. However, these coverings will not provide effective insulation if there are gaps in the floorboards, so make sure you seal the gaps before you cover the floor (see page 220).

◆Get a professional to insulate below the floor. Floor insulation is worth doing but is messy because it involves pulling up floorboards, if it is a wood floor, or digging around concrete if it is a concrete floor. The costs vary greatly but the insulation should pay for itself within about six years.

WEATHERPROOFING WINDOWS

Heat loss through windows can be reduced by various means.

◆**Double glazing.** A way of fitting two panes of glass into a window with a gap between them to prevent the substantial heat loss common through a single pane of glass.

◆**Storm windows.** Another method of fitting a second layer of glass onto windows that reduces drafts, makes heating and cooling systems work more efficiently, and cuts fuel bills.

◆**Pop-in shutters.** Made of foam insulation board, these can be made to fit tightly inside a window frame and can be attractive if covered with fabric.

◆**Insulated roll-up shades.** Available ready-made or in kits that you can assemble yourself. Running along tracks mounted on the window frame, shades are nearly as effective as foam shutters, but more expensive.

◆**Transparent vinyl sheeting.** Sealed to the inside of a window frame with clear polyethylene tape, this is an effective temporary measure, which provides good insulation and plenty of light at a low cost (see below).

FITTING TRANSPARENT VINYL SHEETING

1 Make sure the window frames are clean and dry, then cut a piece of vinyl sheeting $\frac{1}{4}$ to $\frac{1}{2}$ inch larger on all sides than the whole window area.

2 Attach the vinyl sheeting to the top edge of the frame with a thin piece of wood (furring strip), pulling the sheet down by the bottom

corners. Tack it to the bottom edge of the frame with another furring strip. (You also can use clear polyethylene tape to attach the sheeting, but furring strips are more secure.)

3 Then do likewise on each of the remaining two sides of the window. Trim the excess edges with a utility knife.

EFFICIENT HEATING

Central heating systems are efficient and economical. They can use gas, oil, electricity, or solid fuels, such as wood or coal. Gas is the cheapest and most versatile fuel; it can power a variety of furnaces, does not have to be stored, and is easy to control. Most homes today are heated by forced air or hot water. Electric heat is generally expensive, but makes sense in some areas where it costs less than either gas or oil. Steam heat, found in older homes, is rarely installed now.

Central heating

◇ **Fluid central heating systems.** These use hot water or steam that moves through pipes to radiators or convectors in living areas. (In a hot water radiant heating system, the water moves through tubing concealed in the ceiling, walls, or floor.)

◇ **Forced-air systems.** These use air as a heating medium and distribute it via ducts to vents in floors, ceilings, or walls.

◆ If possible, get the system serviced once a year to keep it running efficiently.

◆ If you have a fluid central heating system, get the repairman to flush it out when servicing it, and to add a special rust inhibitor to the water. This will remove any rust that may have accumulated and allow the water to move easily.

◆ If some radiators or registers do not get warm, while others get very hot, your system is not well balanced. Get your heating installer to have a look at the whole system.

◆ Fit a sheet of aluminum foil behind your radiators, particularly if they are on outside walls, or fit radiator wall panels to the back of the radiators. These will reflect the heat back into the room instead of allowing it to escape immediately through the wall.

◆ Don't draw drapes over a radiator, because they prevent the heat from coming into the room. Instead, mount a small shelf above the radiators to deflect the heat into the room, and hang drapes so that their bottom edges brush the shelf.

Controls

By controlling both the temperature and the timing of central heating, you can save a lot of money on fuel bills.

◆ Install a clock thermostat that allows you to easily control the temperature and the time period during which the central heating system is operating. These combine tempera-

---

SOLAR POWER

GREEN TIP: Unlike almost every other energy source we use, solar energy is clean, safe, and renewable, and there is no waste. However, installing an active solar heating system is liable to be expensive and will take about 10 years to pay for itself. In many regions it can only contribute to the hot water system, rather than provide all your hot water.

◆ Get a guarantee for at least 10 years (the average time it will take to pay for itself) if you have solar heating installed.

Passive solar heating. You need large expanses of glass facing the hottest sun. Replace skylights with special glass panels or build a solar greenhouse. The temperature inside rises higher than outside as the glass lets in the rays of the sun, which become trapped inside as heat. The glass does not let the heat out again.

Active solar heating. Install a flat plate collector that absorbs the heat and heats water circulating inside the plate. Once the water is heated, it can be stored in a tank for "on-tap" hot water, or you can use it to supplement an existing hot water supply.

◆ To get the highest efficiency, plan on 1 square yard of collector per person. Any more will reduce the amount you save.

◆ Make sure the collectors are tough enough to withstand all weather conditions since they will be placed on the most exposed part of the house.

---

ture control with time control, so you can set different temperatures for different times of the day or night.

◆Control the temperature of the whole house by a thermostat mounted on the wall of an easily accessible room such as the living room. Make sure that each radiator has its own valve so you can turn it off completely and don't have to heat rooms that aren't in use. Individual radiator thermostat valves that can be set to maintain a particular temperature are a good idea because they enable you to keep each room at a constant temperature.

◆Get the main thermostat checked once a year—when the system is serviced, for example—to make sure it is regulating temperature accurately.

Furnaces

◆Have an old, inefficient furnace replaced, particularly after insulating your home; it will consume much more energy than is necessary. Remember that if your house is well insulated, it will require a smaller furnace, which will consume less energy.

◆Choose a furnace with sufficient capacity for your needs—one that is too big for your needs is expensive to run. Make sure that it is big enough to run the radiator or vent system. Modern furnaces are compact and can be fitted on a wall or inside a cupboard.

◆Place oil and gas furnaces with balanced flues on an outside wall.

◆Have the furnace serviced once a year to make sure it is running efficiently.

BUILDING A FIRE

1 Remove the soot and ashes from the old fire (you can leave wood ash as it makes good kindling for fires through the winter). Keep large cinders and half-burned logs.

2 Place a few cinders or coals at the bottom of the grate to create enough ventilation for the fire to draw well when you first light it.

3 Spread a few pieces of bunched-up newspaper over the coals or roll a sheet of newspaper diagonally until you have a long, thin log. Fold it into a "V" and continue folding each arm until you have a short accordion shape. This will burn slowly but surely so the fuel catches well.

4 Over the paper place some short dry kindling sticks, crisscrossed or laid side by side and not too tightly packed.

5 Place fire starters under the kindling to help you start a fire, if the fuel you are using is not quite dry or a bit "green" (unripe).

6 Place a few pieces of wood on top, using smaller rather than larger pieces, so the fire does not collapse before it has caught.

SAVING ENERGY

Gas and oil are the cheapest fuels you can use for heat and hot water. Electricity is the least efficient fuel to produce and is generally an expensive way to heat the whole house.

◆If your home has little or no insulation, you may be wasting three-fourths of the money you are spending to heat it. With proper insulation, you can cut down on this loss by almost half.

◆Caulking and weather-stripping all windows and doors (see page 238) will save you about $50 a year in heating bills, and the investment will pay for itself within four years. Storm window installation (see page 241) can save $200 a year in heating costs and recoup your investment after about $5\frac{1}{2}$ years.

◆If you have access to large supplies of cheap or free wood, a wood-burning stove could be an economical and comfortable option for heating some living spaces, such as a den or family room.

Heating and water

◆Set thermostatic valves on radiators at their lowest comfortable room temperature. Most heating systems are set at 70 degrees in the living room, 64 degrees in the hall and 60 degrees in the bedrooms. However, few of us need to be as warm as that and reducing the thermostat by 4 degrees can lower energy consumption by 10 percent.

◆Close radiator valves and warm air dampers when rooms are not in use, so you don't waste heat.

◆Keep the doors of warm rooms closed to contain their heat.

◆Repair dripping hot-water faucets (see page 227); they waste a surprising amount of fuel.

◆Take showers rather than baths because they use much less hot water, and the savings built up over a year can be considerable.

◆You can save at least 18 percent on the cost of operating your water heater by lowering its thermostat from the usual 140 degrees to 120 degrees. If you insulate a heater located in unheated space, you'll cut between $8 and $20 from yearly energy costs (see page 240).

◆Insulate hot water or steam pipes, or forced-air heating ducts to increase their efficiency and to lower the costs of the system (see page 240).

Windows and doors

◆Fit heavy, lined drapes in front of windows; make sure they have many folds to trap the warm air in and that they provide a seal down the sides and at the bottom. Put up a valance if necessary to create a seal at the top of the curtains. Similarly, when putting up blinds, make sure the base lies on the sill.

◆Don't open windows when a room becomes overheated; turn down the thermostat instead.

Lighting

◆Turn off the lights when you are not using a room.

◆Install dimmer switches, because they save energy. Consider using fluorescent bulbs because they consume less electricity than incandescent types.

Kitchen equipment

◆Make sure the seals on refrigerator and freezer doors are sound and no cold air is escaping from them. Replace or repair them if necessary.

◆If possible, place refrigerator and freezer in a cold place or against an outside wall; their fans will not have to work so hard to keep them cool and will use less energy.

◆When cooking, keep lids on saucepans to contain heat inside them; your food will cook faster and you'll use less energy.

◆Use a pressure cooker where possible; it cooks food faster than an ordinary pot, so it uses less energy. Or, use a crockery cooker because it consumes very little electricity (see page 35).

◆When cooking, cover the burner with the saucepan to maximize your use of the heat generated. With electric burners and radiant heat surfaces, use flat-bottomed saucepans and keep the cooking surface clean so that the pan is in full contact with the heat source.

◆Use a microwave oven; it uses much less electricity than a conventional oven because the cooking time is shorter.

◆Use a timer to keep track of cooking time rather than peeking in the oven. Each check can cost as much as 25 degrees.

◆If possible, start the self-cleaning cycle of an oven while it is still warm.

◆Put as many dishes in an oven at the same time as you can. Leave one or two inches of space around each dish and adjust cooking times as necessary.

◆Before you turn the oven on, arrange the racks to accommodate your dishes; it saves energy and is safer.

DISHES, GLASSWARE, AND FURNITURE

REPAIRING DISHES, glassware, and furniture can be extremely expensive and may take a long time, if you are lucky enough to find anybody to do it. With a bit of experience and confidence, you can do a great deal of your own restoring. Mend broken china and glass as soon as possible and make sure that the edges of the pieces are clean when you stick them together.

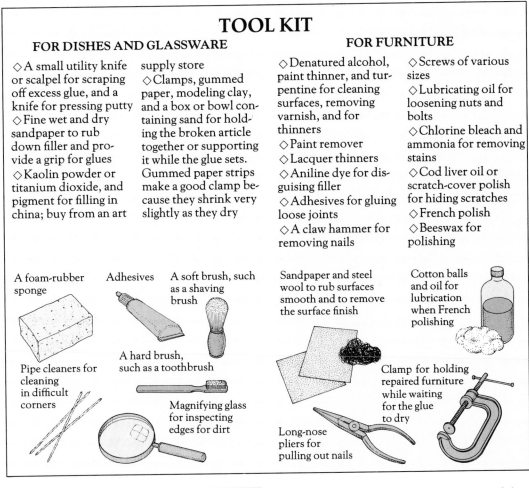

TOOL KIT

FOR DISHES AND GLASSWARE

◇ A small utility knife or scalpel for scraping off excess glue, and a knife for pressing putty
◇ Fine wet and dry sandpaper to rub down filler and provide a grip for glues
◇ Kaolin powder or titanium dioxide, and pigment for filling in china; buy from an art supply store
◇ Clamps, gummed paper, modeling clay, and a box or bowl containing sand for holding the broken article together or supporting it while the glue sets. Gummed paper strips make a good clamp because they shrink very slightly as they dry

FOR FURNITURE

◇ Denatured alcohol, paint thinner, and turpentine for cleaning surfaces, removing varnish, and for thinners
◇ Paint remover
◇ Lacquer thinners
◇ Aniline dye for disguising filler
◇ Adhesives for gluing loose joints
◇ A claw hammer for removing nails
◇ Screws of various sizes
◇ Lubricating oil for loosening nuts and bolts
◇ Chlorine bleach and ammonia for removing stains
◇ Cod liver oil or scratch-cover polish for hiding scratches
◇ French polish
◇ Beeswax for polishing

A foam-rubber sponge

Adhesives

A soft brush, such as a shaving brush

Pipe cleaners for cleaning in difficult corners

A hard brush, such as a toothbrush

Magnifying glass for inspecting edges for dirt

Sandpaper and steel wool to rub surfaces smooth and to remove the surface finish

Long-nose pliers for pulling out nails

Cotton balls and oil for lubrication when French polishing

Clamp for holding repaired furniture while waiting for the glue to dry

DISHES AND GLASS

◆ If you can't make the repair right away, carefully place the pieces in a plastic bag and seal it to keep out dust and grease.
◆ Before you start the repair process, clean the broken edges so the glue will stick. Wipe the edges with a piece of silk; don't use cotton, because it will leave bits of lint behind.
◆ If you think there is any dirt on the broken edges, and if the break is an old one, wash the pieces gently in mild detergent and water. Allow to dry thoroughly.
◆ Try not to touch the broken edges with your fingers; you could leave grease to which the glue won't adhere.

◆To remove old glue, boil it off slowly in soapy water, or try to rub it off with acetone and a clean cloth.

◆Don't boil cracked china; it will weaken the crack further.

Mending broken china

1 Clean the edges of the broken pieces, then lay them out in the order you want to put them back together. Use a box filled with fine silver sand to hold the largest piece to which other broken pieces will be attached.

2 Fit the pieces together dry to see how they fit.

3 Glue the edges of the first two pieces and stick them together. For extra support, place masking tape along the joint until the glue sets. Allow each piece to set slightly before adding further pieces. Remove surplus adhesive from the joints as you add each piece.

Repairing a rounded object. *Glue the object together and wrap rubber bands around it to hold it until the glue dries. This must be done carefully to prevent the bands from pulling the repair apart.*

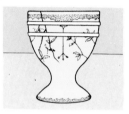

Repairing chips

◆Use epoxy adhesive to fill the gaps in chipped dishes; it has the same texture as china when dry and won't be visible.

ADHESIVES

Most adhesives set faster in a warm atmosphere. To speed the process, place repaired pieces by a warm stove or radiator or blow with a hair dryer.

◆Follow the instructions exactly for the type of glue you use (see page 216). Different types of glue have to be applied in different ways. With epoxy adhesives, for instance, you apply a very small amount to each surface and then join them at once. The less you use, the stronger the bond will be.

EPOXY ADHESIVES
◆Apply epoxy to any household china or pottery but bear in mind that—should you make a mistake—once the adhesive has dried you cannot dissolve it.

◆Remove surplus epoxy when the glue is beginning to set and you can get the point of a sharp knife underneath it to peel it off. If you try sooner, the glue will smear; if you leave it too long, you won't be able to remove it at all.

◆Be careful to get the seam right the first time; once an epoxy adhesive has set, it is permanent. Quick-setting epoxy gives you about five minutes to work with and sets to full strength within eight hours. The slower setting varieties give you more time to work on the joints but need to be held in place for several hours while the glue sets.

◆Leave repairs made with epoxy adhesive for at least 10 hours to ensure a proper set.

OTHER GLUES
◆Use water-soluble glues for valuable china and glass, because the glue can be dissolved and the piece taken apart and mended again, if necessary. Check the manufacturer's instructions to see that the glue is suitable for the material you are repairing.

▼▼ Don't use these glues for everyday
◆◆ dishes, because they won't stand up to a lot of washing, particularly in the dishwasher.

Filling cracks

1 Make your own mixture from epoxy glue and kaolin powder or titanium dioxide. Color the filler with the appropriate pigment before making the repair.

2 Press the filler down into the crack with a knife blade or the tip of your finger.

3 Make sure the gap is completely filled, and leave the filler slightly higher than the surrounding area.

4 When the filler has hardened, rub it down with the finest grade of abrasive paper so that it is flush with the surface. Paint over the repair if necessary and varnish.

Mending glass

◆ Take very old glass to a professional re-storer because a repair can easily go wrong; newer glass is easy to mend yourself.

◆ Before you attempt any mending, make sure the edges of the glass are thoroughly clean by washing them in warm water and dishwashing liquid. Rinse in clear water and polish them with a lint-free cloth that will not leave any fibers behind.

◆ To break down any grease on cut glass, soak the pieces for a few hours in soapy water with a few drops of ammonia added.

◆ Mend the glass as if it were china, but roughen the edges of the broken pieces with sandpaper so the adhesive can cling to the glass.

◆ Remove the surplus glue before it sets— but not too soon or it may smear.

▼▼ Don't use cyanoacrylate glues on glass
◆ ◆ because they are water soluble and the bond will not last long.

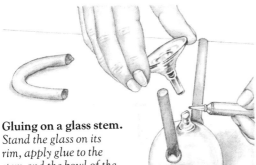

Gluing on a glass stem.
Stand the glass on its rim, apply glue to the stem and the bowl of the glass, and stick the stem on, supporting it with 2 pieces of modeling clay.

RESTORING FURNITURE

◆ Revive old and fading varnished wood with a fresh coat of varnish. First remove the old finish to get a smooth surface.

◆ Repair broken furniture as soon as possible to minimize damage.

Gluing wooden furniture

◆ Before regluing, remove all traces of the old glue and dust thoroughly.

◆ Glue well any furniture that gets rough treatment, or it will soon fall apart.

◆ Use a wood glue, which is unaffected by moisture. In the past, moisture was the downfall of glues because it dissolved them, making them useless.

◆ Work in a warm room; the glue will dry faster, speeding the repair process.

◆ Apply the glue to both surfaces and allow it to soak in for two or three minutes before sticking them together; this will help to form a stronger bond.

Clamping joints. *Cover or bind the wood with a cloth to protect it. Use clamps, brackets, or string to hold the joints under pressure while the glue is drying.*

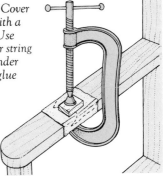

Metal trim

◆ Tighten loose screws or remove and re-place (see page 248); otherwise the joint will be weakened, and could split the wood.

Removing screws and nails

To remove a tight screw, put a few drops of oil or vinegar around the edge and let it sink in. An obstinate screw may loosen if you turn it clockwise a fraction while pressing down hard.

◆ Use the correct size screwdriver so you don't damage the slot in the head of a screw while trying to remove it.

◆ If a nut or bolt can't be loosened, apply a few drops of oil or vinegar to it and let the oil or vinegar sink in before applying your wrench once again.

◆ If nails are tightly embedded, you may be able to remove them by tapping them through from the other side.

◆ Remove protruding nails with a claw hammer. You also can use pliers, but first wrap a piece of cardboard around the nail to protect the wood from the pliers.

Tightening loose knobs
Take loose wooden knobs off doors and drawers, saturate strips of old sheets or handkerchiefs in wood adhesive, and stuff them tightly into the hole. Then work the screw of the knob into the hole until it holds firmly; leave until dry.

Working with small nails. *Hold very tiny nails in position with a piece of plastic putty while working on furniture. This will make them easier to handle.*

FILLING SCREW HOLES

Screws sometimes work loose and won't tighten because they have created too big a hole in the wood.

1 *Remove the screw and line the hole or coat the split with wood adhesive.*

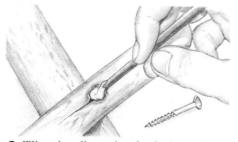

2 *When the adhesive has dried, plug the hole with plastic wood.*

3 *Replace the screw or use a new one of the same size.*

Legs

◆ If a wobbly leg has a wing nut holding it, the nut probably only needs tightening up. If the leg has old screws, you may have to remove them and replace them with slightly thicker (but not longer) ones.

◆ It is easier to add to uneven legs than make them shorter; if you add too much or too little, you can easily correct it. Only tiny differences are usually involved, so use very thin slivers of wood to build up the leg until you've got the balance right. Cut a piece as near in size to the diameter of the leg as you can and glue it on with a polyvinyl resin adhesive.

◆ To stop chair or table legs from scratching a polished floor, hammer a nail-on stud into the base of each leg. These are slightly adjustable, since you hammer them in only as far as you need; they also can be used for leveling uneven legs.

Reinforcing legs.
When gluing legs, wait until the glue is completely dry, and reinforce each leg by gluing a small block of wood inside the back corner.

Refinishing

◆ To find out what kind of finish is on a piece of wood, rub a drop of turpentine into it. If the wood comes out bare, the surface is coated in oil or wax, which can be removed with turpentine. If the sheen remains, it has been stained or varnished.

◆ If you can't work outdoors, work in a well-ventilated room and take frequent fresh air breaks. Read the label thoroughly before opening a can of remover; procedures and hazards vary from product to product.

◆ To remove varnish, use a paste, semipaste, or liquid remover. Use a non-flammable, nontoxic paste for indoor work. Apply generous amounts of remover to the furniture. When the old finish has softened, lift off as much as possible with a putty knife.

Don't scrape the varnish off with a sharp object, because it may mar the wood. Clean off the residue with steel wool, lifting the pad often as you work and dipping it in solvent or water to remove sludge.

◆Use a lacquer thinner to remove lacquer; apply it with a cloth. The thinner liquefies the lacquer and evaporates, leaving a hard, smooth finish.

VARNISHING, STAINING, AND POLISHING

APPLYING VARNISH

1 *Thin the first coat with 10 percent paint thinner and apply. Allow to dry for 6 to 12 hours.*

2 *Apply another three coats with a good-quality, clean paintbrush, using a flowing motion and letting each coat dry for 6 to 12 hours before applying the next.*

3 *When the last coat is dry, sand the surface lightly with fine-grade sandpaper. Remove any dust with a clean rag moistened with paint thinner.*

APPLYING STAINS, OILS, AND WAXES

1 *Use a clean, soft, lint-free rag to spread a first coat sparingly, working along the grain to get the most even finish.*

2 *If a stain is too light, add extra coats, but only when the previous coats are dry. If it is too dark, sand it down lightly. With wax stains, apply two coats for a good finish. If you are applying teak oil, make the second coat thinner with a few drops of turpentine, and let it dry for 24 hours. For a good finish, rub it down with fine steel wool and then polish.*

FRENCH POLISHING

1 *Remove any wax from the surface with fine steel wool, paint thinner, and fine garnet sandpaper,* or remove dirty polish with a commercial brass polish that is mildly abrasive and will not harm the surface underneath. Do this with care.

2 *Pour French polish onto a wad of cotton until it is soaked (right) and then wrap it in a clean lint-free cloth to form a smooth pad. Press it gently onto a spare piece of wood to get rid of excess polish.*

3 *Pour a few drops of linseed oil onto the wood surface for lubrication (above left) and then sweep the pad over the surface in figure eights, making sure you cover all the edges (above right). Increase the pressure as the polish fades, and when the polish is dry, refill the pad and apply another coat. Apply several coats, allowing each one to dry before applying the next.*

◆*Keep the pad in an airtight jar while waiting for each coat to dry to keep it moist and clean.*

4 *Six hours after the last coat, make a new pad with a double thickness of lint-free cloth, and wet it with denatured alcohol. Work it gently along the grain to achieve a good finish.*

SCRATCHES AND STAINS

▼▼ Don't treat a piece of furniture your-
♦♦ self if you think it may be valuable;
you may ruin it. For safety's sake, have it
repaired professionally instead.

REPAIRING SCRATCHES

A scratched surface can be dis-
guised with varnish, cod liver oil
and polish, or beeswax.

Using varnish

1 *Thin the varnish with a little*
denatured alcohol. Then apply
several coats of the thinned
varnish to the scratched surface with
a small paintbrush. Allow each coat
to dry before applying the next one so
you get a smooth finish.

2 *When the repair stands*
slightly above the surface,
allow it to dry before rubbing it
flush with fine sandpaper.

3 *To restore the shine, apply a*
thin coat of polish with a soft
cloth.

Hiding scratches. *Pour cod*
liver oil into the scratch and
let it soak in. Then polish as
usual. You also can rub the
scratch with a commercial
scratch-cover polish.

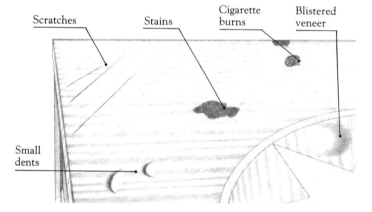

Scratches Stains Cigarette burns Blistered veneer

Small dents

REMOVING SMALL DENTS IN WOOD

1 *Remove the finish with paint*
thinner and a soft cloth.
Then place a clean, damp cloth
over the dent in the surface.

3 *Repeat this process as often*
as necessary until the wood
has risen sufficiently (this may
take a few hours).

Filling in scratches. *Melt bees-*
wax, stain it with an aniline dye
so it is darker than the wood,
and press it into the scratch with
a spatula or knife.

2 *Move a hot iron back and*
forth over the cloth, until the
wood absorbs the water and
swells to fill the dent.

4 *Allow the wood to dry*
thoroughly. Sand it down
with fine garnet sandpaper, re-
stain it, and polish it well.

REMOVING CIGARETTE BURNS

◆Rub with very fine garnet sandpaper and color the wood with matching artist's paint. Polish it when dry.

REMOVING STAINS

1 *Take off the top coating of dust and wax with a paint stripper.*

2 *Use diluted chlorine bleach to loosen the varnish (this will also get rid of surplus paint stripper). Don't mix chlorine with any other cleaner or you may produce a chlorine gas, which is highly poisonous. For deep stains, use ammonia.*

3 *Rub with fine-grade steel wool. Revarnish (see page 248).*

RESTORING BLISTERED VENEER

Repair small areas yourself but leave larger ones to a professional.

1 *Cut the blister along the wood grain with a sharp knife.*

2 *Using the knife blade, ease some polyvinyl resin adhesive into the cut.*

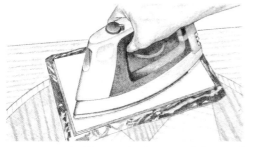

3 *Cover the blister with aluminum foil, several layers of blotting paper or brown paper, or a folded sheet; press with a hot, dry iron.*

4 *Turn the iron off after a minute or so, but leave the weight on the blister until the glue has set.*

REPAIRING CANE

◆Glue broken pieces of cane in place with a contact adhesive.
◆If the damage to cane baskets and chairs is extensive, turn the job over to a professional.

Reviving sagging cane. *Apply two cloths soaked in a solution of hot water and baking soda (or half vinegar and half water), one on each side of the cane; press the cane upward from below. Go over the whole surface. Rub with a dry cloth and let it dry, preferably in the sun.*

LEATHER FURNITURE

◆Treat leather on desks regularly with warm petroleum jelly or castor oil rubbed in with a soft cloth. Wipe treated leather furniture with a soft cloth only.
◆Patching leather upholstery is tricky. Get a professional to do it.

Renewing leather desk tops

1 Cut the sheet of new leather about $\frac{1}{2}$ inch bigger all around than you need.

2 Get the base for the new leather absolutely smooth and clean; otherwise every grain of grit will show through it.

3 Coat the wood and the new leather with wallpaper paste, position the leather on the wood, and press it into place.

4 Smooth the leather with a soft cloth to get rid of any bubbles and creases. Let it dry for an hour and then use a metal ruler and utility knife to cut off the excess leather around the edges. Be careful not to scratch the wood.

HOUSEHOLD PESTS

To KEEP pests from invading your home, make sure you don't provide them with food, water, and shelter. Food should not be left out in the open but stored in metal or glass containers, and all surfaces should be kept free of crumbs. Sink areas must be kept dry, and there should be no stagnant water near the house. Garbage cans should be kept tightly closed. All cracks and crevices must be filled, and all torn screens repaired.

If, in spite of all you do, you suffer from an infestation of any pest, contact the public health department or a professional pest exterminator.

ANIMAL PESTS

◆ Make sure that pets and children can't get hold of poisoned bait. Lock cabinet doors if poisoned bait is inside.

◆ Remove dead mice and rats immediately, particularly if you have used a poisoned bait, so that pets don't eat them and get poisoned.

Mice

◆ Keep all food packed in metal or glass containers so mice cannot get at it.

◆ Keep all garbage tightly covered to deter scavenging mice.

◆ Block all possible entry holes, especially in the pantry, in food cabinets, and under the sink.

◆ Keep a cat. Cat scent alone is enough to discourage mice and keep them away.

Discouraging mice.
Hang sprigs of mint in your kitchen cabinets, or place them on the shelves. Rub the plants often to release their scent.

◆ Set traps and bait them carefully. Peanut butter, bacon, and cake are good baits. Put the traps at right angles to the walls in places where you know the mice will go. Check the traps regularly, throw away dead mice, rebait and reset the traps.

◆ To prevent mice from becoming shy of your traps, bait unset traps for two or three days as above, and secure them with thread or wire. When you do set the traps, to avoid catching your fingers, use a pencil to move the traps near the wall.

◆ If you use poisoned bait, follow the directions carefully. You may have to persevere for several weeks. Other mouse poisons are very dangerous and should be used only by professionals.

Rats

◆ If you see a rat near your home, call the public health department immediately. They will deal with the problem quickly. It is important that you do this because rats carry a variety of diseases.

◆ Don't leave anything lying around that rats could use as a nest. This includes old rags or cushions in a shed, household waste in a trash can without a cover, or uncovered garden compost.

◆ Buy commercial poison baits for rats. However, some rats have developed an immunity to poisons, and it may be wise to use two different kinds. Check with your local public health department if necessary. Some poisons are ready to use; others have to be mixed with bait.

INSECT PESTS

◆For a bad infestation that you find difficult to get rid of, call your local public health department.

◆To keep many insect pests away, vacuum the house thoroughly and regularly, and keep all surfaces clean.

◆Apply insecticides around window frames, baseboards, and cracks.

◆Electric bug zappers will deter flying insects from pool, patio, and picnic areas at night but are ineffective against bees, wasps, and mosquitoes.

▼▼ Do not place a chemically treated pest
◆ ◆ strip in a sickroom, an infant's or elderly person's room, or where an animal could reach it. Avoid placing it near where food is prepared.

◆Choose your pesticide according to the insect rather than using an all-purpose pesticide.

◆In a pinch, if you have no bug spray on hand, hair spray can be used to immobilize a flying insect, making it easier to swat.

Ants

◆Follow the ants' path as they carry away crumbs to find where they leave the house and to locate the nest. Destroy the nest with a

---

SAFETY WITH INSECTICIDES

◆Read and follow package directions and warnings carefully.

◆Remove food, utensils, pets, and their dishes before spraying indoors; wear rubber gloves when spraying.

▼▼ Don't use pesticides near children or
◆ ◆ older people, and once you have sprayed a room, don't reenter it for at least 30 minutes.

◆Store pesticides in their original containers, tightly closed, in a locked, well-ventilated area away from heat and direct sunlight.

◆Wrap empty containers in thick layers of newspaper and dispose of them properly.

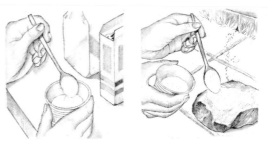

Making an ant killer. *Mix one part of borax with one part of powdered sugar (above left). Scatter it over a piece of stone or wood near the entrance to the nest (above right). The ants are attracted by the sugar and poisoned by the borax, which is not harmful to humans or animals.*

suitable insecticide, following the instructions on the packet carefully.

GREEN TIP: Sprinkle a few crumbled bay leaves on windowsills to prevent ants from invading your home. To keep them from your sugar and flour canisters, once a month place a couple of bay leaves inside.

Bedbugs

Bedbugs may be found in old and new homes, in mattresses, crevices in furniture, in window and door frames, baseboards, loose wallpaper, and cracks in plasterwork.

◆Spray bed and upholstery springs, webbing, slats, and frames liberally with an insecticide containing malathion, or pyrethrum, wetting them thoroughly with the insecticide. Pay particular attention to the seams and tufts of mattresses. Spray baseboards as well as cracks in walls and floorboards.

◆Don't sleep in the room or on the bed while the insecticide is still wet, and air the room thoroughly before sleeping in it; the insecticide is harmful to humans.

Cockroaches

Cockroaches are large brown beetles that feed on food, glue, starch, and garbage. They like moist, warm, dark areas.

GREEN TIP: Try sprinkling boric acid powder in kitchen and bathroom cabinets away from children and pets.

◆ Treat cracks and crevices with a household formulation of chlorpyrifos, diazinon, malathion, or propoxur; set feeding traps with amidinohydrazone.

◆ If you have a bad infestation, call the exterminator.

Fleas

◆ Treat pets regularly with flea powder. Although animal fleas can't live on humans, they can and will bite them.

▼▼ Never use a flea powder intended for one
♦♦ sort of animal on another. Also, dogs and cats may be made ill by preparations that are applied incorrectly. Don't let flea powder come into contact with an animal's eyes or mouth because it will cause irritation.

◆ Take your pet to a veterinarian if it won't take the treatment, or if you are unsure about how to treat the animal correctly. Tell the vet what you've been using; some insecticides react badly when combined with others.

◆ While treating your pet, make sure you clean the whole house out. Vacuum carpets, under rugs, crevices, baseboards, cushions, upholstery, and anything soft and warm. Burn the contents of the vacuum bag. Flea eggs can hatch in two to 12 days in warm conditions, but in cool temperatures they may remain dormant for months.

◆ Wash, burn, or throw away the animal's bedding and replace it with cotton sheeting or paper, or use a disposable bed and bedding (a cardboard box will do very well) until you are sure the fleas have gone. Burn and replace the box every few days to make sure that you get rid of the fleas completely.

Natural treatment for a pet with fleas. *Soak walnut leaves overnight with water (above left), and wash your pet's fur with the mixture (above right). Let the mixture dry and then brush and comb the fur vigorously.*

Mites

These are minuscule spiderlike insects that live where dust and general debris collect. They attack the warm, soft folds of the body and bite, causing itching, swelling, and sometimes fever.

◆ Dust and vacuum thoroughly, and spray insecticide in all areas where dust can gather.

◆ Clean any bird cages in your home, and spray with a suitable insecticide.

Flies

Flies can spread at least 30 different diseases to people and animals. They lay their eggs in rotting meat and other garbage, and they multiply quickly in hot weather.

◆ Keep all food and garbage tightly covered and clean the trash can with disinfectant regularly, particularly in summer.

◆ Don't keep piles of compost or manure near the house, because they attract flies.

◆ Use a fly swatter.

◆ If you want to use an insecticide, use contact poisons, which can be sprays or sticky strips, and are absorbed, or use internal system poisons (systemic poisons), which the flies eat.

◆ Make sure all windows and doors have screens. Be sure to repair any tears or holes.

◆ You can use herbs to get rid of flies. Put sprigs of elder, lavender, mint, pennyroyal, rue, or southern-wood in vases, or hang them up; rub the leaves frequently so that the scent is released.

Protecting pets against fleas. *Antiflea grooming brushes, collars and disks are available in pet shops, and an antiflea insecticide is available in powder, aerosol, and tablet form.*

Wasps and hornets

◆If there's a nest in the backyard or on the wall of the house, contact an exterminator who will destroy the nest for you.

◆If you destroy the nest yourself, use a suitable insecticide, and follow the manufacturer's instructions carefully. Store the insecticide out of the reach of children. Don't smoke while spraying, wear rubber gloves, and remember that the insecticide is probably poisonous to you, too.

Mosquitoes

◆Cover all rain gutters, and try to eliminate all puddles and any other standing water near the house. Mosquitoes breed in water and multiply quickly.

◆Spray with pyrethrum (a pesticide derived from the pyrethrum plant), but don't use it near fish ponds and pools, because it harms fish and pond plants.

◆To get rid of mosquitoes in the bedroom at night, give the room a sharp squirt of insecticide before you go to bed.

◆To keep mosquitoes away, use an electrical device that plugs into the wall and dissolves a special tablet. This device can be used with the window open.

GREEN TIP: Use screens at all windows and doors to keep mosquitoes out. Air-conditioning also can help.

Keeping mosquitoes away. *Use mosquito "rings" (often made of pyrethrum), which burn down slowly. The rings must be used with the windows closed.*

Moths and ticks

Before they die in early autumn, the little silvery moths that fly around the house lay their eggs in cotton and woolen materials, and furs, which provide food for the larvae when they hatch (see mothproofing, page 139).

◆Clean all clothes, bedding, and furnishing fabrics before you store them, because moths breed in dust and dirt.

◆Clean out drawers, closets, and chests periodically, and check the clothes for signs of moths; clothes that are in use fairly often are not likely to be at risk.

◆Clean storage chests, scrape out all the dusty debris lying at the bottom, and then vacuum the chest.

Keeping moths away. *Place sachets or balls of moth deterrent (see page 139) between fabrics in drawers, chests, or wardrobes. Renew them every six months or so.*

◆If you use mothproofing aerosols, air out fabrics after spraying before you fold them or hang them away, because aerosols smell (although the smell does eventually wear off). Don't use aerosol moth-repellents on furs because they damage them.

◆Ticks can easily fall off and hide in the crevices and baseboards of your house. Spray suspected infested areas with a household formulation of malathion or diazinon.

Keeping materials moth-free. *Store blankets, eiderdowns, furs, curtains, and clothes in airtight containers. Wrap them in sealed polyethylene bags for extra protection.*

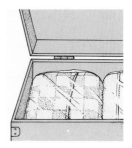

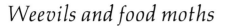

Weevils and food moths

◆Check the dried foods in your cabinets regularly for signs of little maggoty worms and beetles. Also, small moths that fly out when you open your kitchen cabinets are a sign of weevils (flour beetles) or food moths. Throw out all dried food in the cabinet—the moths may have laid eggs in any of the containers.

Keeping weevils out. *To deter weevils and food moths from laying eggs in flour, rice, dried beans, and grains, place a bay leaf in each of the containers.*

Silverfish

Silverfish live on starch and glue so they can damage fabrics and books.
◆Treat doors, windows, baseboards, cupboards, and pipes with a household formulation of diazinon, malathion, or propoxur.

Termites

Termites gain access to structural wood through beams that touch the soil, cracks in concrete slabs, and masonry or concrete-block footings.
◆A sure sign of termite infestation is a mud-shelter tunnel that leads across a concrete foundation to woodwork. Beams that have been badly eaten may sound hollow when rapped. A pointed tool will sink easily into the wood.
◆To prevent infestation, keep firewood piled away from your house on a metal platform; pretreat wooden structures, such as fences and play equipment, that come into contact with soil, and get rid of tree stumps near your house.
◆Controlling an infestation involves special equipment and the use of pesticides permitted to licensed applicators only. Contact a termite exterminator to check out the extent of the damage and to treat the foundations of the house, if necessary.

HOME SECURITY

M OST BURGLARIES are opportunistic rather than planned, so the best way to protect your home from intruders is to make it very difficult for them to break in. Ask a reputable security expert to recommend the best types of locks and alarm systems. Always lock all doors and windows, use timers to control lights, and leave a radio on when the house is empty, and cancel deliveries and mail when you go out of town.

VULNERABLE AREAS OF A HOME

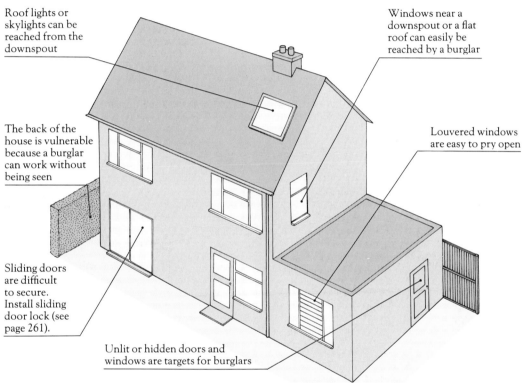

Roof lights or skylights can be reached from the downspout

Windows near a downspout or a flat roof can easily be reached by a burglar

The back of the house is vulnerable because a burglar can work without being seen

Louvered windows are easy to pry open

Sliding doors are difficult to secure. Install sliding door lock (see page 261).

Unlit or hidden doors and windows are targets for burglars

MAKING YOUR HOME SECURE

◆Windows are the most vulnerable points of any house. Make the act of locking windows as habitual as locking the front door.
◆Make sure windows near a flat roof on an extension or a garage are fitted with locks—they are particularly vulnerable.
◆Basement windows, often obscured by shrubbery, are a favorite entry point for burglars. Keep them locked.
◆Never leave windows that are near a downspout or a flat roof open, even if they are on the second floor, because they are still accessible to burglars.
◆Install iron bars over skylights that have external hardware; they are very easy to open and can be more vulnerable than ground-floor windows because a burglar may work on them without fear of being seen.

SECURITY DOS AND DON'TS

GENERAL TIPS

Change the cylinders in locks when you move into a new home—someone may have copied the real estate agent's key.

◆ Install a peephole with the widest possible view; 180-degree fish-eye lenses are the most effective.

Keep hedges in the front and along the side of your home trimmed low, and cut back trees and shrubs at the front.

Climbable shrubs are invitations to nimble burglars. If you must have a tall plant right next to the house, choose something prickly.

Keep ladders locked away safely in a garage; don't leave them lying around outside because they could be used by an opportunistic burglar.

◆ Don't put your stereo, TV, videocassette recorder, etc., where they can be seen easily from the street. The sight of them will encourage a passing burglar. If possible, engrave your social security number on valuables.

◆ Don't label keys, in case they find their way into the wrong hands.

◆ Don't reveal your name or whereabouts on your telephone answering machine.

◆ Don't leave your phone number on the telephone. A burglar may write down your number so the next time he can call to see if you are out.

◆ Don't leave a window open for a pet— install a pet flap instead.

◆ Don't lock internal doors. To a burglar, a locked door indicates that there are valuables in the room and he will kick or jimmy his way in.

◆ Get a small safe installed in your home, in a discreet place.

◆ Store bicycles and tools in a garage or shed and make sure the door is securely locked; never leave the toolshed door open because the tools could be useful for a burglar.

◆ Get a dog, if possible. Most burglars are wary of them, particularly if they bark.

SECURING YOUR HOME WHILE YOU ARE AWAY

◆ Lock all external doors and windows even when leaving the house for a short while.

Don't leave drapes drawn during the day; it is a sign that you are not at home and if burglars get in they can work without being seen.

Close drapes when you are going out at night so that would-be burglars cannot see that you are not home.

Close the garage door when going out in the car—an empty garage is a sign of an empty house.

Don't leave any signs that no one is at home, such as a lot of mail in the mailbox or newspapers on the doorstep.

◆ Don't leave door keys under a mat, on a string in the mailbox, in a plant pot, or anywhere near the door. If you can think of good places, so can a burglar, and

burglars know all the hiding places. Leave your keys with a neighbor or a friend who lives nearby.

◆ Don't leave notes on the front door for someone you expect to call or to cancel deliveries; this is a sure sign that you are out.

◆ If you are going to be away for a while, cancel all deliveries, unless a neighbor can take them for you regularly.

◆ Get a friend or neighbor to watch your home, turn the lights on, and draw the drapes at night, remove mail from your mailbox, and, if possible, to leave a car in the driveway while you're away. Depending on the season, ask them to mow the lawn or clear the snow.

◆ Put valuables in a bank if you are going to be away for some time.

◆ Make the back of your house as inaccessible as possible, particularly from adjoining houses; more than 60 percent of break-ins take place at the back of the house.

◆ Buy locks from a reputable locksmith, not from a chain of hardware stores or a door-to-door salesman; copies of the keys may have been made. Make sure the package is sealed. The best type are those with registered keys, which can be copied only on the authority of the owner or the person renting the property.

Lighting up your home. *Install efficient lighting at the back door and don't block out any streetlights. The more the door is hidden from view, the more vulnerable it is.*

Alarms

◆ Have an alarm system installed to deter intruders and make it easier to catch them. Experienced housebreakers know how most systems work so they may not be deterred, but casual burglars might be dissuaded.

◆ Have a warning device installed that dials an emergency service when the alarm is set off and reads out a prerecorded message to the operator, or alerts the headquarters of the alarm manufacturers who can inform your local police department in seconds. The prerecorded message should operate even when the telephone line is busy (burglars have been known to phone a victim's house from a phone booth then leave the receiver off the hook), and the system ought to be fitted with a delayed action audible alarm in case the police are slow to act.

◆ If you cannot afford an alarm system, try to find an alarm box that fits onto an outside wall. It may fool burglars and deter them from trying to break in.

Lighting

◆ If you don't want to leave lights on at night, install a light that contains an infrared detector: When someone walks past the detector, the light is activated and is switched on. These lights can be installed inside and outside your home.

◆ Leave lights on in the living room and kitchen when you are out in the evening to suggest that someone is in. Buy a timer switch that turns on lights at a preset time to simulate activity.

DOORS

Outside doors are a common entry point for burglars and should be protected with both locks and bolts. Don't rely on a simple night latch to protect an outside door; it is very easy to force open from the outside.

◆ When choosing any door lock, make sure to ask for a five-pin cylinder and always use wood screws of the right length.

◆ A mortise deadbolt is the strongest type of lock you can buy and should be fitted to each outside door. When locked, the bolt shoots into a slot in the door jamb, and locks into position so that it can't be jimmied open with a credit card, for example, or forced back out of the door jamb. The most secure types come with a beveled spring latch and a deadbolt.

◆ If you are an experienced do-it-yourselfer, you will find fitting locks easy; otherwise get a locksmith to install them for you.

Exterior doors

◆ There should always be at least two locks on the front door: An automatic deadbolt latch to hold the door firmly closed when you are in the house, and a mortise deadbolt to make it impregnable when you are out.

◆ A door chain adds to your security and can be slipped on when someone knocks (only do this then because they are a fire risk), giving you time to shut and lock the door and phone for help should someone try to force his or her way in. Make sure the links of a door chain are forged and the chain is heavy and attached to the chain plate with strong screws for maximum strength.

◆Burglars most often try to break in at the back door if there is less risk of being seen, so this too must be well protected. Fit a mortise deadbolt with a handle; for extra security, the back door also should be fitted with bolts— one near the top and another near the bottom of the door frame.

◆Outside doors should be at least 1 to 2 inches thick and solid, so they cannot be kicked in easily, and so the wood will not be weakened when a mortise deadbolt is installed.

◆Outward opening doors are a vulnerable point because the hinges are exposed making it easy to knock out the hinge pins and force the door open. You can solve this problem by fitting two hinge bolts on the hinge side of the door, one a third of the way from the top, the other a third of the way from the bottom (see opposite, top). Then the door cannot be lifted off its hinges.

◆If you live in an apartment building, arrange with other occupants to have an entryphone system installed and agree not to let in strangers or callers for other residents who live in the building.

◆When you are at home, leave a key in the inner cylinder so you can exit quickly in an emergency.

◆For an external door with glass panels, fit a rim lock that is key-operated only on both sides of the door; if a burglar smashes the

SECURING A DOOR

◆Make sure each external door has enough hinges to make it secure—three is best—and to keep the door from being pried off its hinges if one hinge is removed.

◆Fit appropriate locks on all external doors to make them secure. A mortise deadbolt and a rim lock and two locking bolts are ideal.

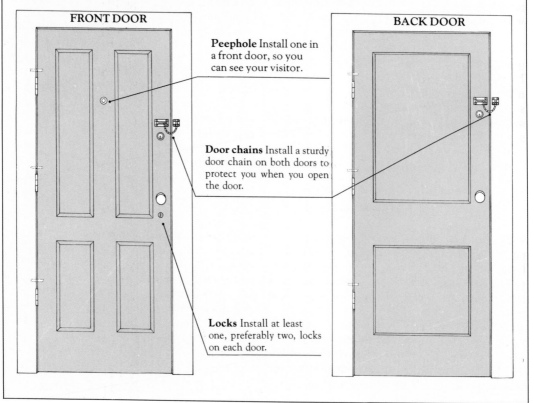

FRONT DOOR

BACK DOOR

Peephole Install one in a front door, so you can see your visitor.

Door chains Install a sturdy door chain on both doors to protect you when you open the door.

Locks Install at least one, preferably two, locks on each door.

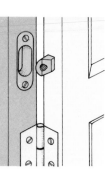

Fitting hinge bolts. *Fit these to doors with vulnerable hinges (doors that open outward for instance). They lock the door at the hinged side, which is often the weakest part of an old door.*

Fitting a strike plate. *Fit a steel strike plate to the door frame to hold the bolt of a mortise deadlock; this provides extra protection against crow bars. To give adequate protection for the door frame, the strike plate should be 7 to 10 inches long and should be secured by at least four staggered screws.*

glass he will not be able to undo the lock. **Note:** Rim locks with latches are totally inadequate on their own. A good kick will splinter the staple that holds the bolt, and a steel ruler or even a credit card can be used to slip the latch.

Patio doors, sliding doors, and French windows

◆If you have glazed doors leading to the patio or backyard, it is a good idea to put laminated safety glass in them or burglar-proof glass that can't be smashed. You can also fit key-operated locking bolts in addition to the main locks.

◆To make aluminum sliding doors less prone to break-ins, you can install a sliding door lock that screws to the top and bottom of the fixed frame. A key-operated bolt prevents the door from sliding or from being lifted off its track.

◆French doors can be made much more burglarproof by installing sliding bolts at the top and bottom on the door that closes first and a double cylinder deadbolt on the door that opens first.

Garage and shed doors

◆If there is access to the house through the garage, keep the garage door and access door securely locked.

◆Use a strong padlock on a toolshed door; it should have at least five levers or six pins so that it cannot be picked.

◆For overhead garage doors, if you plan to be gone for extended periods, drill a hole through the track and fit a padlock; repeat on the other side.

◆If you have a garage-door opener, purchase a lock especially made to go with it.

Securing a shed door. *In addition to a regular lock, it is worth fitting a long bolt that can be secured with a padlock. An ordinary bolt with a padlock can be pried off.*

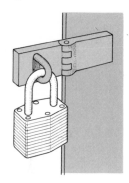

WINDOWS

Any windows that are accessible from the ground or via a tree or the roof should be safeguarded with appropriate locks.

◆Always measure the window frames first to make sure you buy locks that fit their width and thickness.

◆You can buy window locks that allow you to leave the window locked yet slightly open for air circulation.

◆Remember to remove the keys from window locks and keep them in a place where they can't be seen or reached by a burglar, but where they can be found quickly in the event of a fire.

◆Install locks with nonretractable, one-way screws.

◆Consider fitting bars across basement windows to protect them.

Double-hung windows

There are several devices for locking the two halves of a double-hung window together and for preventing either half from being moved.

◇**Wedge locks.** These have a dual strike plate system that allows the window to be locked while slightly open.

◇**Rod locks.** These are keyed devices that project a rod through both sashes, avoiding the glass.

◇**Horizontal and vertical sash locks.** These face away from the glass, providing greater security. The locking section is screwed to the top rail of the lower sash; the hook section is screwed to the bottom rail of the upper sash.

◇**Ventilating window bolts.** These are fitted in the same way as sash locks and will hold the window closed or in a ventilating position.

◆You also can make a double-hung window more secure with a simple metal screw, sold at a locksmith's, that slips into a hole in the sashes' meeting rails and is retracted with a special key that comes with the screws. A clipped-off steel nail can be used in a similar fashion and drawn out with a magnet.

Casement windows

◆For a casement window that opens with a crank handle, you can simply remove the handle so the window cannot be opened; otherwise install the same type of chain lock as used on doors. Fasten it down with the biggest screws the lock can take.

Sliding windows

These locks are quick and easy to install and require no tools.

◆The lock attaches onto the window track, and either a grip, key clamp, or thumbscrew keeps the window from sliding.

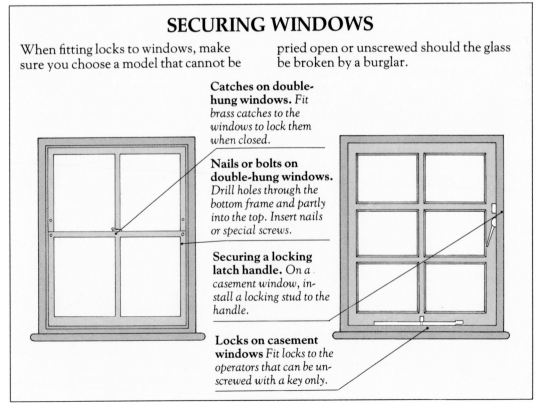

SECURING WINDOWS

When fitting locks to windows, make sure you choose a model that cannot be pried open or unscrewed should the glass be broken by a burglar.

Catches on double-hung windows. *Fit brass catches to the windows to lock them when closed.*

Nails or bolts on double-hung windows. *Drill holes through the bottom frame and partly into the top. Insert nails or special screws.*

Securing a locking latch handle. *On a casement window, install a locking stud to the handle.*

Locks on casement windows *Fit locks to the operators that can be unscrewed with a key only.*

Home Sewing

SEWING EQUIPMENT

IF POSSIBLE, keep your materials and sewing equipment in an area where they don't have to be constantly cleared away, so you can pick up a job at the point where you left off. If you have very young children, be careful not to leave needles, pins, and scissors lying around.

BASIC SEWING KIT

There are basic items that you will find useful for general sewing and repairs—these are listed below. When you buy a pattern, read the back to find out the equipment and materials you will need.

Cutting tools

◇ **Dressmaking shears.** For cutting fabric; the angle of the lower blade allows the fabric to lie flat while you cut it. You can get left-handed and special dressmaking shears for sheer fabrics and synthetics.

BASIC ESSENTIALS

◆ Keep the following selection of essential materials and equipment in one place, such as a sewing box or basket, for on-going repairs and emergencies.

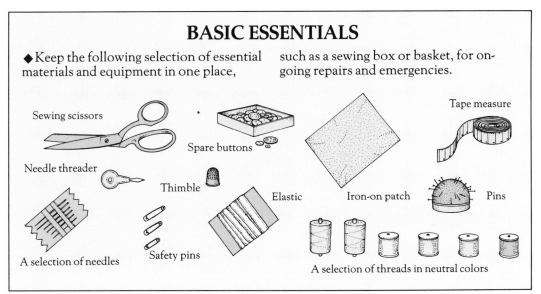

Sewing scissors

Spare buttons

Tape measure

Needle threader

Thimble

Elastic

Iron-on patch

Pins

A selection of needles

Safety pins

A selection of threads in neutral colors

◇**Pinking shears.** For cutting a zigzag, fray-resistant edge. Good for finishing seams and raw edges on fabrics that don't fray easily, but not for cutting out paper patterns because the paper will dull the blades.

◇**Small sharp-pointed sewing scissors.** For snipping the ends of thread. Protect ends when storing with rubber knitting needle tips or a cork. Store in unused eyeglass case.

◇**Seam ripper.** For cutting seams open, picking out threads, and slashing machine-made buttonholes.

◇**Rotary cutters.** For cutting leather, leatherlike material, multiple layers of fabric, and spongy knits and ribbing. Use with a cutting mat to protect the cutting surface.

Marking and measuring

◇**Tape measure.** The most useful are 60 inches long.

◇**Sewing gauge.** Get one with a marker that you can set at any point, for measuring hems and pleats, and spacing buttonholes.

◇**Yardstick.** For long straight measurements of curtains, checking the direction of the material's grain, and marking hems.

◇**Tailor's chalk.** For transferring pattern markings onto fabric.

◇**Marking pencil.** For accurately marking pleats, buttonholes, pocket positioning, etc. Available in chalk and leadlike versions.

◇**Tracing wheel.** Used with dressmaker's tracing paper to transfer pattern markings to the wrong side of fabric.

◇**Fabric marking pen.** Marks on right or wrong sides of fabric. Plain water or steam removes water-soluble inks. Other inks evaporate in two to three days.

Pins and needles

◇**Pins.** Should be of nonrust, stainless steel; use ones with ballpoint heads for knits; ones with large heads for loosely woven fabric.

◇**Needles.** Keep a supply of different ones. "Sharps" are medium length with round eyes and used for most fabric weights; "betweens" are smaller, thinner, and better suited to taking fine stitches; milliner's needles are longer for basting; crewels are medium length with long eyes for easier threading.

◆Pins and needles can be sharpened with an emery board.

◇**Needle threader.** Will make threading easier; you also can try holding the needle against a contrasting background to the thread.

◇**Thimbles.** Make sewing heavy, stiff, or multilayered fabrics easier. If too loose, cover the inside with pieces of adhesive tape.

◇**Pincushions.** The safest way to store pins. Ones that fit around the wrist are convenient. Magnetic pin holders should not be set on a computerized sewing machine.

Threads

◇**Thread.** The kind you need will depend on the kind of fabric to be sewn. Mercerized cotton is for cotton and linen; polyester and cotton-covered polyester are for general use plus knits and synthetics; silk is for silks and wools, and tailoring; buttonhole twist or topstitching thread is for decorative topstitching, buttonholes, and sewing on buttons; basting thread is for basting and tailor's tacks.

◆Always use a spool of a slightly darker color than the fabric.

◆Keep the thread end neat by catching it in the notch or groove of the spool.

◆Use clear monofilament thread for fabrics of hard-to-match colors.

◆Cut thread at an angle; the cut end should go through the needle and be knotted.

Notions

◇**Seam binding.** Useful for hemming and binding the edges of fabric. It comes in stretch lace for a decorative finish. Bias seam binding should be used on flared hems and facings. Tricot binding is sheer and lightweight.

◇**Fasteners.** Keep a selection of hooks and eyes, snaps, buttons, and safety pins.

◆Tie together same-size buttons with dental floss or keep on large safety pin.

◇**Elastic.** Use to repair underwear and other elasticized garments.

◇**Zippers.** These come in different types and sizes.

STORAGE

If you do a lot of sewing, the first essential is to choose an area in the house that can be turned into a well-organized work space, where everything is at hand.

◆ Use a closet, chest of drawers, or shelves for large items, lengths of fabrics, clothes in the process of being made, and for patterns and sewing books.

◆ Arrange separate storage for smaller items so they don't get mixed up. Tiny chests of drawers, glass jars, and small boxes are ideal.

Storing small items Use glass jars or small wooden boxes, or keep a selection of baskets of various shapes and sizes.

Work box Keep your basic kit for repairs in a toolbox so that you can take it into another room.

Plastic boxes Use these for storing scraps, lace, and other special bits and pieces such as ribbons and trimmings.

Storing spools of thread Divide up a desk drawer into compartments or fit a flatware tray into it to hold spools of thread and prevent them from unraveling.

Ironing equipment Mount wall brackets for the iron, the ironing board, and sleeveboard, if you have one, so they are nearby.

Locks Put childproof locks on low drawers or cabinets.

Spare fabric Use an old trunk for unused lengths of fabric.

THE SEWING AREA

In addition to your machine, a few other items are required in order to produce the highest quality work.

◇ **Work table.** Should be stable so it can be used to hold the machine and level to cut out patterns on the surface.

◇ **Work lamp.** This should be adjustable so it throws light on any part of your work area.

◇ **Full-length mirror.** This is essential for checking hems and fitting clothes.

◆ To help keep your work area clean, attach a small paper bag to the end of your machine table to catch scraps of fabric and thread.

Choosing a sewing machine

◆ If you do a lot of sewing, and especially if you use heavy fabrics or make large items, choose a sturdy machine that can tackle a range of heavyweight and lightweight fabrics and keep its tension constant.

◆ Check that the tension can be adjusted easily; most machines have a separate dial for this, which makes it easier.

◆ Buy a machine with a bobbin that is easy to take out and put back again.

◆ Some machines have storage space for bobbins, feet, and other sewing accessories. Others have a separate storage box.

◆ Check that you can lower the feed for sewing on buttons and doing free-motion embroidery.

◆ Make sure the machine has a seam gauge marked on the throat plate to keep the seam a specific distance from the edge.

◆ Machine accessories such as special-purpose feet greatly increase the versatility and efficiency of a sewing machine. The most useful include:

◇ **A zigzag or all-purpose foot.**

◇ **A straight stitch foot.**

◇ **A zipper foot.**

◇ **A buttonhole foot.**

◇ **An overedge foot.** For seam allowances that fray easily or are bulky

◇ **An embroidery thread foot.** For making decorative stitch patterns.

◆ The overlock machine, or serger, stitches the seam, trims off excess fabric, and finishes the edges in one operation. It also can create decorative effects. If you sew a lot, you may want to consider buying a serger to use along with your regular sewing machine.

Maintaining your machine

New machines will have a comprehensive manual giving full instructions for that particular machine. Handbooks for older models sometimes can be obtained from the manufacturer or dealer.

◆ Every time you use your machine, remove dust and lint from the bobbin and its holder, and from under the needle plate with a small firm-bristled brush. Do this regularly so the mechanism doesn't get clogged.

◆ Tighten sewing plates and other fittings regularly, using a small screwdriver. Most machines are provided with one. If your

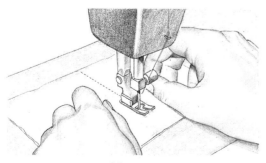

Removing excess oil from your sewing machine. *Stitch through a folded scrap of fabric after oiling to remove any excess oil and prevent it from getting onto your sewing.*

EASY MACHINE SEWING

◆ Guide the fabric evenly, without pulling or pushing it.

◆ To get a straight seam, watch the presser foot not the needle.

◆ If you are a beginner, practice stitching several rows and turning corners on a double piece of fabric. Experiment with different types and weights of fabric, changing the needle if necessary.

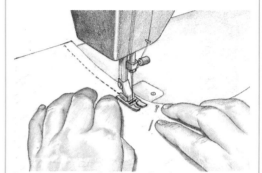

Stitching around shapes. *Stitch points, curves, and scallops before trimming or clipping, otherwise you might distort the shape during stitching. Move the fabric gently while stitching so you follow the curved line exactly.*

Securing the ends of seams. *Reverse the stitch back over the previous stitching for about ½ inch to secure the threads.*

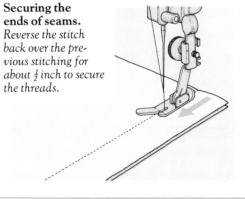

machine doesn't have one, get a replacement from a sewing machine shop or use the smallest standard screwdriver available.

◆ Service and oil your machine regularly according to the manufacturer's instructions, to keep it running smoothly.

◆ To reduce wear and tear on your foot pedal by keeping it from creeping across the floor as you sew, attach a rubber suction cup or a piece of foam rubber underneath.

SOLVING COMMON MACHINE PROBLEMS

Many minor machine problems can be fixed at home without having to take the machine in for repair. The manual provided with your machine will probably describe the most common problems and how to correct them.

GETTING THE TENSION RIGHT

◆ The tension is balanced when the top and bottom threads interlock in the center of the fabric and the stitches look the same on both sides of the fabric.

◆ Uneven stitches or "looping" and puckering of the fabric are caused by faulty tension. If the loops are on the top, the top tension is loose in relation to the bottom tension. If the loops are on the bottom, the bottom tension is loose in relation to the top.

◆ When making any tension adjustments, first use the top tension-adjusting dial or knob. Adjust the bottom tension only as a last resort because it is often difficult to do. To adjust the tension, follow instructions in the manual.

◆ If you still have problems with the tension, check that you have the right thread for the fabric, that the needle has been inserted correctly and is not blunt or damaged, and the machine is threaded correctly.

Positioning the needle correctly.
Fit the needle into the machine so the rounded side faces the direction from which you will thread the needle. The long groove helps guide the thread to the eye.

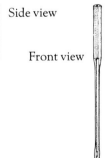
Side view

Front view

THE TOP THREAD BREAKS

◆ Check that you have inserted the needle correctly.

◆ Check that you have threaded the machine properly.

◆ Look carefully at all the parts the thread has to go through; if any part is rough or damaged, it may break the thread. Replace any damaged part if necessary.

◆ Make sure the needle is not blunt or broken.

◆ Check that the needle is not too fine for the thread.

◆ The thread may be brittle with age; use new thread.

◆ There may be a knot in the thread. Pull extra thread through the needle until you are sure the knot is clear.

THE BOTTOM THREAD BREAKS

◆ The bobbin case may be inserted incorrectly. Make sure it is in the proper position and not loose.

◆ The bobbin may be too full. Unwind and remove some of the thread.

◆ The hole in the throat plate may be damaged or rough. Replace the throat plate if necessary.

◆ The bobbin tension may be too tight; try adjusting it.

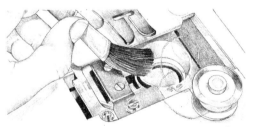

Cleaning the bobbin case. *If there is dirt or lint in the bobbin case, this may affect the tension of the bottom thread. Clean the case regularly with a small stiff-bristled brush.*

THE BOBBIN THREAD WON'T FEED

◆ The bobbin case may be threaded incorrectly; check the instruction book.

◆ You may not have allowed enough thread to come out of the bobbin. Always allow about 3 inches.

◆ Check that the needle is correctly threaded—consult the instruction book to make sure.

◆ Hold the needle thread to engage the bobbin thread as you turn the wheel.

SOLVING COMMON MACHINE PROBLEMS

SNARLS AND LONG LOOPS IN THE STITCHES

◆ Clean the bobbin area; there may be dust or lint blocking the thread path.

◆ Check that the bobbin has enough thread—it may need refilling.

◆ Make sure the tension is set correctly.

◆ The thread may have been inserted incorrectly in the bobbin case, which will affect the tension. Check the instruction book.

◆ The needle may be the wrong size for the fabric, so check the pattern or instruction book. Use fine needles, or the lower numbers, for sheer fabric, and thicker needles, or the higher numbers, for heavier fabrics.

◆ You may be using the wrong throat plate, so check your instruction book to make sure.

◆ The timing between the needle and take-up lever may need adjusting. Consult your instruction book.

◆ The needle may be damaged or blunt.

THE NEEDLE BREAKS

◆ You may be pulling the fabric with your hand so that it is bending the needle, causing it to hit the needle plate and break.

◆ The fabric may be too thick for the needle; try using a thicker needle.

◆ Check the needle; it may not be inserted correctly or it may be bent or blunt.

SKIPPED STITCHES

◆ The wrong type or size of needle may have been inserted.

◆ Check that the needle is not blunt or bent, or has not picked up lint from synthetic materials. Clean it or change it.

◆ The needle may be inserted incorrectly or not pushed up far enough into the clamp.

◆ Use the throat plate with the small round hole if you are not zigzagging.

◆ Increase the pressure on the presser foot.

THE THREAD BREAKS ON KNITS OR OTHER STRETCH FABRICS

◆ You may be using the wrong thread. Stretch fabrics require stretchable threads. Use polyester or cotton-covered polyester thread.

◆ Try stretching the fabric slightly as you stitch it.

◆ The stitch length and/or tension may be wrong. Adjust it following the instructions in your instruction book.

THE FABRIC PUCKERS WHEN STITCHED

◆ If the fabric is lightweight or sheer, the stitches may be too large; keep them small.

◆ Reduce pressure on the presser foot.

◆ If the fabric is tightly woven, the stitch may be too short; lengthen it.

◆ The needle size may be too thick for the fabric; change to a needle of a lower number.

◆ Make sure the bobbin is evenly wound. Rewind it if necessary.

◆ Check the stitch tension to make sure it is balanced.

◆ Keep fabric taut as you stitch by holding fabric with one hand behind the needle and one in front.

THE MATERIAL DOES NOT FEED IN A STRAIGHT LINE

◆ The presser foot may be loose or bent.

◆ The needle may be bent.

◆ You may be pulling or pushing the fabric without realizing it.

◆ Increase pressure on the presser foot.

THE MACHINE TURNS HEAVILY

◆ The machine may be dirty, not lubricated, or oiled with unsuitable oil. Check manual for correct procedure.

SEWING TECHNIQUES

Most basic sewing involves only a few standard seams and stitches. Once you have mastered these, you can make or alter almost any garment and tackle almost any other sewing job. If you are a beginner and intend to sew clothes for yourself and your family, or to create upholstery and drapes, you may find it worthwhile taking classes that teach basic techniques.

BASIC SEAMS

For general-purpose sewing, there are just three basic seams you need to know how to put together.

Plain seam

This is the most basic seam and the simplest one to sew.

◆ Sew two pieces of material together, $\frac{5}{8}$ inch away from the edge, with the right sides of the fabric together. Press the seam allowances open to flatten them.

◆ Machine-stitch them with a straight or zigzag stitch to prevent them from fraying.

Flat-fell seam

A strong seam that is used for jeans and sportswear.

1 Make a flat seam with the *wrong* sides together. Press to one side.

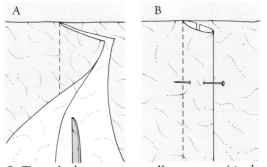

2 Trim the bottom seam allowance to $\frac{1}{8}$ inch from the stitching (A—*above*). Press

under the top seam allowance $\frac{1}{8}$ to $\frac{1}{4}$ inch and pin it flat to the garment (B—*below left*).

3 Machine-stitch along the folded edge, and press the seam flat.

Double-stitched seam

This narrow seam is good for sheers and knits.

1 Stitch a plain seam. Use a straight stitch for woven fabrics or a narrow zigzag for knits.

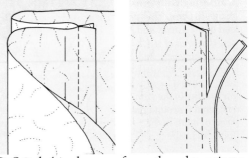

2 Stitch $\frac{1}{8}$ inch away from the edge using a straight stitch or zigzag stitch.

3 Trim close to the stitching. Press to one side.

MARKING AND MEASURING

WHETHER you are working from a purchased pattern or creating one of your own, it is most important that measurements are correct and the important points on the pattern are transferred accurately to your fabric. While you are making the garment, you should continually check its fit, always trying it on with the clothes you intend to wear it with.

MARKING

Marking is a very important part of sewing because it allows a greater degree of accuracy; your efforts will be well rewarded.

◆ Mark fabric after you cut the pattern pieces out and before you remove the paper patterns. Mark all the symbols that show you how and where the garment pieces are joined together and shaped, and mark the position of the darts, pockets, pleats, gathering lines, and center front and back.

◆ Mark all seam lines if you are inexperienced, and intricate seam lines whether you are experienced or not.

Tailor's chalk

Tailor's chalk or a marking pen or pencil is one of the quickest marking methods. However, it may not show up on sheer fabrics.

1 Push a pin through each symbol on the pattern and both fabric layers.

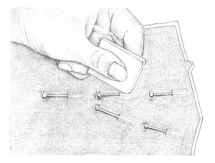

2 Take the paper pattern off and make marks at each pin on the wrong side of each fabric layer. You can substitute white soap on washable fabrics.

Tailor's tacks

These must be used on fabrics where other marks would not show up.

1 Use a long length of doubled, unknotted thread, and make a small stitch on the pattern line through both pattern and fabric.

2 Pull the needle through, leaving at least 1 inch of thread behind.

3 Make three or four stitches at the same point, leaving the thread very slack.

4 Cut the threads at their center point (*above left*), and lift the pattern off the fabric, taking care not to pull out the thread markings (*above right*). If you are working on two layers of material, gently open the material up, and cut the threads between the layers.

Tracing wheel

The wheel is used with dressmaker's carbon paper or tracing paper. It is not very clear on patterned or transparent fabrics.

◆ Place the colored side of the paper down on the wrong side of the fabric, and trace the markings with the wheel with short firm strokes.

MEASURING FOR DRESSMAKING

Measuring back waist length. Measure from the base of the neck (bend the head forward and feel most prominent bone) to the waist.

Taking your high bust measurement. Measure across the widest part of the back, under the arms, then above the full bustline. If the difference between this and the full bust is more than 2 inches, use the high bust measurement to select a pattern size.

Taking the shoulder-to-neck measurement. Measure from the base of the neck to the shoulder edge. (Shrug your shoulders to find where the base of your neck is.)

Taking your bust measurement. Measure across the widest part of the back, under the arms, then across the full bustline.

Measuring your waist. First tie a string snugly around your waist—it will roll to your natural waistline. Then measure around your waist at this point.

Measuring sleeve length. Put your hand on your hip; take the tape measure along the outside of your arm from the shoulder joint around the elbow and down to the wrist.

Taking your hip measurement. Measure your hips around the fullest part below the waist.

Measuring dress or skirt length. Measure from the back of the neck down the center back or from the waist down.

Measuring pant length. Measure from the waist down the side of each leg to the ankle, and from the crotch down the inner side of each leg to the ankle.

Measuring crotch depth. *Sit on a firm, flat chair, feet flat on the floor, and measure from the side of your waist down to the chair seat.*

Measuring crotch length. *Measure from the back waist through the legs to the front waist.*

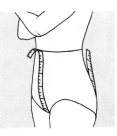

RIPPING OUT SEAMS

◆A seam ripper makes pulling out seams much quicker and is easier to control than a razor blade or scissors.

▼▼ If you do use a razor blade, use a
◆ ◆ safety blade.

◆If the thread is tight, you will find it easier to cut a stitch in the top thread every ½ inch or so along the seam. Then pull out the underneath thread.

◆If you use a pair of scissors for ripping seams, use sharp pointed ones because these will enable you to ease out the thread in a loop before you cut it.

Cutting stitches. *Cut a few stitches and then pull the seam apart gently so you can see the stitches clearly before cutting the next section.*

Ripping out with a pin. *Pull up very small stitches with the point of a pin. This method prevents you from accidentally snipping the material.*

RENEWING AND REPAIRING

If a garment wears through in one part, but the rest of the garment is perfectly all right, don't throw it away, because it may be possible to replace the worn part.

◆Collars and cuffs are often the first areas of a garment to wear through. If you can catch them before they've gone too far, just stitch a piece of cotton tape over the part that is about to fray. This is perfectly acceptable for old work shirts.

Making a new collar

1 Rip open the old collar and its "stand" (the upright base piece).

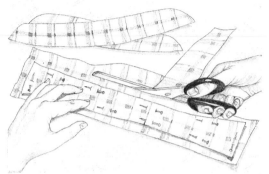

2 Using the old collar and stand as your pattern, cut two collar sections and two stand sections. Make these pieces ⅝ inch larger than the area of the original stitching, to allow for seams. Cut interfacing for the collar and its stand in the same way.

3 Pin or fuse the interfacing to the wrong side of the underpiece of the collar, and lay both collar sections right sides together. Pin and stitch the three outside edges.

4 Trim the seam allowance, turn the collar right side out, and press.

5 Attach the interfacing to the wrong side of one stand piece.

6 Sandwich the collar between the two stand pieces, right sides together, with the interfacing at the bottom.

7 Match the top edge of the stand with the bottom edge of the collar. Pin it in place on the collar, then stitch the entire stand seam, securing it to the collar.

8 Trim the seam and then cut notches in the curves. Turn the collar stand down so the right sides are showing, then press the seam allowance inward along the inside edge of the stand.

9 Pin the unpressed edge to the outside of the shirt neck, with right sides together, and stitch.

10 Fold over the pressed edge of the stand to the inside neck edge to enclose the neck edge with the stand. Pin and hand-stitch it onto the shirt.

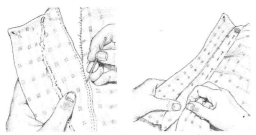

Turning a collar. *As an alternative to making a new collar, you can "turn" it. Rip open the collar from its "stand" (above left), turn it around so that it is back to front, and sew it on again with the frayed edge on the underside of the collar (above right).*

Cuffs

1 Rip open the cuffs and use them as a pattern for the new cuffs.

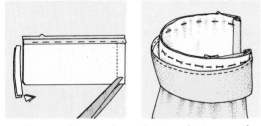

2 Pin or fuse and stitch interfacing to the wrong side of the new fabric. Trim the seam allowances (*above left*), then turn to the right side, and press. Press in the seam along one edge, and lay the unpressed edge on the main part of the sleeve, right sides together (*above right*). Adjust the sleeve fullness carefully, or press the tucks, and pin the cuff in place.

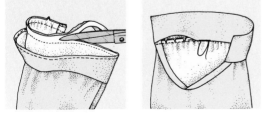

3 Stitch the seam, and trim the seam allowance (*above left*). Notch the edge of the sleeve fabric. Turn the pressed edge of the cuff over to the inside of the sleeve, and hand-stitch it to the seam line (*above right*).

4 Press seams flat, then make buttonholes, if necessary.

Replacing a coat lining

1 Use a seam ripper to take out the old lining, leaving some of the markings on the sleeves, collar, and body of the coat to tell you where the lining was attached. Notice whether the lining is attached at the bottom or is loose all the way along the hem.

2 Rip open each separate piece of lining, then iron it to get it absolutely flat. Cut the new pattern from it.

3 Sew the new pieces of lining together as for any garment.

4 Pin the lining into the coat—right side out, center back to center back, side seams to side seams—and stitch in place.

5 Hem the bottom of the lining as on the original lining so that it hangs in the same way. Turn the sleeve hems under, and slip-stitch them loosely to the coat.

Replacing pockets

◆ If you are going to give a coat new pockets as well as a lining, do this before lining it.

◆ Take out the old pockets, making note of which direction they go and exactly how they were attached. Then use the old pockets as a pattern for the new ones.

Hems

The easiest way to repair a torn hem is simply to raise the hem so the tear is hidden.

◆ Make a temporary repair with a strip of adhesive tape.

◆ Silver-colored duct tape is useful for temporarily holding up the hems of jeans; it can even last through several washings.

◆ Use iron-on tape for more permanent repairs. Stitch it into place if the garment is going to be washed a lot, and especially if you want to machine-wash it.

EMERGENCY REPAIRS

ZIPPERS

◆ If a zipper unexpectedly breaks and pulls apart, cut away one or two teeth, thread the tab back on, and sew the broken part together.

◆ For a zipper that is sticking but un-broken, you can rub both sides of the teeth with a lead pencil—the graphite in the lead is a lubricant—or with a bar of soap or candle, to get it gliding again.

◆ If a zipper tab is hard to grab, put a safety pin or piece of string through it.

Remedy for a broken zipper. *If a tooth at the bottom breaks, pull the tab up above the broken teeth. Use an overcasting stitch; sew the teeth together to form a base below which the zipper cannot slide.*

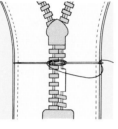

ELASTIC

A snapped or stretched elasticized waist-band can be repaired easily.

1 *Open up part of the seam and pull the old elas-tic out.*

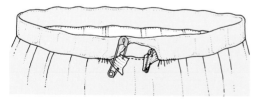

2 *Cut the new elastic to the right length, attach a safety pin to one end, and guide it through the casing. Pin the free end of the elastic to the casing to keep it from being drawn through by mistake.*

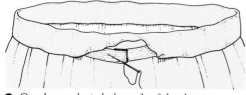

3 *Overlap and stitch the ends of the elastic to-gether. Pull the casing back over and stitch.*

BUTTONS

◆ Replace buttons on children's apparel and work clothes with sturdy topstitching or heavy-duty thread, and use elastic thread for a waistline button.

Strengthening buttons
To prevent buttons under strain from pulling out or tearing the surrounding fabric, stitch on a rein-forcing button or a square of interfacing fabric at the back.

PATCHING

◆ Use fabric patches for holes that are too big for darning, and cut the patch to match the grain of the fabric. For convenience and quick repairs, use ready-made adhe-sive patches. These can be ironed on and are strong enough for all patching jobs, especially for repairing jeans.

◆ Before ironing a patch on heavy cotton, put a piece of aluminum foil under the hole to intensify the heat and keep the patch from adhering to the ironing board or other layer of fabric.

1 *Trim the edges of the tear and cut the patch 1 inch larger all around than the hole.*

2 *It is a good idea to line the patch up around the hole before you iron it on, because once pressed down, it adheres instantly and can't be adjusted.*

◆ You can hand- or zigzag-stitch around the patch afterward for greater strength.

ALTERING CLOTHING

◆For best results, rip out the entire seam and restitch it rather than altering just the places that don't fit. Always try on the garment at the pinning stage.

◆For a neat finish, press all the creases flat after opening any seams or darts, and again after restitching them.

Shortening a hem

1 Rip out the hem and press the garment so that it lies flat.

2 Mark and measure the new length (see page 270). Cut off the excess material, but leave a hem allowance of at least $1\frac{1}{2}$ inches. If it is a flared skirt, leave a hem allowance of about $\frac{3}{4}$ inch.

Lengthening a hem

1 Rip out the hem and press to flatten the material.

2 Measure and mark the new hemline. Pin and stitch in place; press.

3 You can camouflage a permanent hem crease with decorative topstitching or trim.

◆To lengthen your child's too-short pants, sew on colorful calico, flannel, or other patterned cuffs. Cut two cuffs the circumference of the pant leg plus $\frac{1}{2}$ inch for seams and double the desired height plus $\frac{1}{2}$ inch for seams. With right sides of fabric together and using a $\frac{1}{4}$-inch seam, sew the short end of each cuff together to make two circles. Let the hems down. With raw edges matching, stitch right side of cuff to wrong side of pant leg. Turn remaining raw edge under $\frac{1}{4}$ inch. Turn cuff down. Place folded edge over cuff-pant seam; stitch close to fold. For maximum length, leave the cuff down. If length permits, turn cuff up; tack to pant leg.

◆If there is not enough hem allowance to lengthen a garment, you can make a false hem using ready-made hem binding. Lay the binding against the edge of the fabric, right sides together, and pin it. Machine-stitch about $\frac{1}{4}$ inch from the edge (above near). Trim the

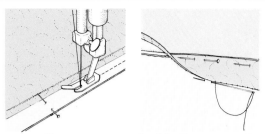

seam allowance, turn the binding up to the inside, and press along the seam. Slip-stitch the false hem to the wrong side of the fabric (above right).

Altering skirts

◆If the waist is too large, open the waist seam or the waistband at the sides. Open the existing side seams and take in an equal amount of excess material at both seams. Stitch new seams and press them open. Trim away excess material.

◆If the hipline is too snug, reduce the seam allowance an equal amount along each of the lengthwise seams.

◆If a child's skirt is too big, make a series of decorative tucks in the waistband.

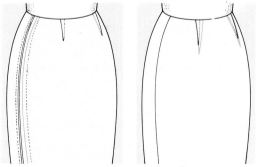

Letting out a tight skirt. Remove the waistband and open up the side seams. Mark a new seam (*above left*) and machine-stitch it. If moving the seam enlarges the waistband too much, take in darts (*above right*). Make a new waistband or extend the old one and stitch to skirt.

ADJUSTING PATTERNS

Compare your measurements with the pattern's to discover the places that need alteration. Few commercial patterns fit without some altering to individual needs.

◆ It is usually best to choose a pattern according to your full bust measurement and alter the other parts if necessary. But if you are very full-busted, you may find it better to buy according to your high bust measurement (see page 275).

◆ Keep grain lines and "place on fold" lines straight when altering a pattern, or the fabric will not hang properly.

◆ Very often when you alter something in one pattern piece, you will need to make a corresponding alteration to another piece. For example, if you add to the side seam of a bodice, be aware of the effect on the sleeve seam.

◆ If a pattern is being shortened a lot, alter skirts and pants at both the alteration line marked on the pattern and the lower edge.

◆ When altering the back waist length, alter the front length to match.

BUST

◆ To raise bust darts slightly, mark the position of the new dart point above the original. Draw new stitching lines to the new point, and taper them onto the original stitching lines.

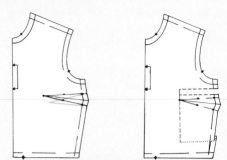

Lowering a bust dart. *Mark the position of the new dart point on the pattern below the original one. Draw new stitching lines to the new point, tapering them into the original stitching lines (above left). Or cut an "L" shape in the pattern above and beside the dart, and take a tuck below the dart deep enough to lower it to where you want it to be (above right).*

WAIST

◆ If you have to add or subtract a large amount at a skirt waist, distribute the changes among all darts and seams.

◆ When altering the waist of pants by a large amount, alter side seams, darts, and tucks.

Increasing the waist of a circular skirt. *Lower the cutting line at the waist by one-quarter of the needed increase. But be careful—it is easy to cut away too much. Lower the seam line by the same amount.*

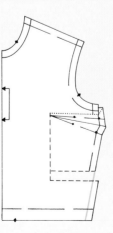

Raising a bust dart substantially. *Cut an "L" shape in the pattern, below and beside the dart. Take a tuck above the dart deep enough to raise it to where you want it to be.*

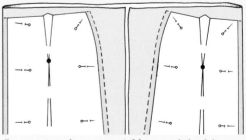

Increasing the waist. *Add one-eighth of the total amount to each side of both pattern pieces. If increasing the waist of a skirt with four pattern pieces, add one-sixteenth to the side of each piece.*

Shortening pants

1 Pin a tuck in the leg just above the old hem to mark the desired length.

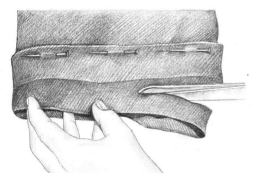

2 Measure the surplus fabric in the tuck, which will be twice the depth of the tuck. Measure the depth of the old hems or cuffs, then rip out their stitching. Cut the measured amount of tuck off the bottom.

3 Finish the raw edges, then pin and stitch the new hems or cuffs to the same depth as the original ones.

Straightening pant legs

1 Rip out the hem or cuff. Turn the pants inside out and lay them flat.

2 Mark a straight line from the knee to the hem on both sides of each leg, and stitch along the marked lines.

3 Trim the seam allowances and press open. Restitch the hems or cuffs.

Expanding a pant waist

1 Rip out the waistband at center back and also the center seam. Undo any darts or gathers.

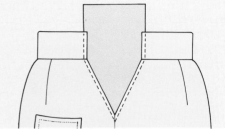

2 Cut a wedge-shaped insert from the same or similar weight fabric. Make the insert as wide as you need plus seam allowances, and taper it to a point.

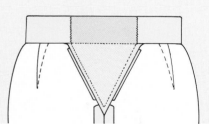

3 Turn the pants inside out, and machine-stitch the inset (point down) into the waistband and the seam.

4 Restitch any darts and gathers if necessary.

Taking in a pant waist

1 Rip out the waistband and center seam. Cut out the excess fabric.

2 Pin the tuck at the center back and taper the material from the waist down. Restitch the seam. Press the seam open and trim the excess seam allowance.

3 Restitch one of the bottom edges of the waistband to the pants, with right sides of the fabric together.

4 Turn under a hem on the other edge of the waistband and stitch it to the inside of the pant waist.

FUR AND LEATHER

◆Get valuable furs repaired by a professional furrier; cheaper furs or odd pieces can be mended at home.

◆Take care with your measuring and cutting, and make sure there is enough fabric for what you intend to do, because once the fur is cut, you can't alter it.

◆When cutting fur, cut only the skin itself and use a razor blade or crafts knife for cutting, never scissors or pinking shears. Scissors and shears will leave bald spots through which you will see the seams.

◆Use a glover's or leather needle, which is three-sided, to sew the fur, and use a very fine one so you don't damage the pelt.

▼▼ Don't draw the stitches too tightly or the
◆◆ fur will pucker. You may find it helpful to put a strip of cardboard between the seam to hold the work taut.

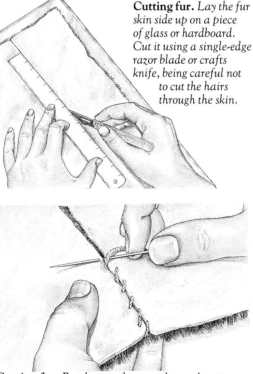

Cutting fur. *Lay the fur skin side up on a piece of glass or hardboard. Cut it using a single-edge razor blade or crafts knife, being careful not to cut the hairs through the skin.*

Sewing fur. *Put the cut edges together so they just meet, and make sure the hairs all run downward. Overcast the pieces, using heavy-duty topstitching or carpet thread, being careful to take up only the edge of the skin.*

◆Repair leather bags with patches of leather, using rubber cement. Other leather goods should be professionally repaired.

Shortening a fur coat

1 Rip out and turn back the lining of the hem. On the skin side of the fur, chalk a new length and cut it carefully with a single-edge razor blade.

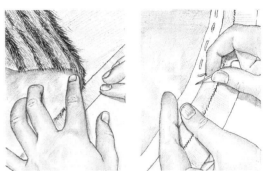

2 Place tape or a wide binding against the edge of the fur side (*above left*). Hand-stitch it to the edge of the skin side with very small overcasting stitches. Baste a narrow strip of soft fabric (flannel, for instance) around the skin side of the fur (*above right*).

3 Turn the tape to the inside and catch-stitch it to the flannel.

4 Cut the lining to length and slip-stitch it into place.

REPAIRING LEATHER GLOVES

◆ Mend skin gloves using a glover's needle made for leather work.

◆ Repair worn fingers by buttonhole-stitching with silk thread around the worn part. Then work in narrowing circles until you have filled the hole with closely worked stitches.

Repairing seam splits. *Repair splits between fingers with rows of buttonhole stitch, working lengthwise.*

PATCHING FUR

◆ To patch fur, use a piece taken from the inside of either the facings or the sleeves so that it matches.

◆ If the worn part is near the hem, you will probably have to shorten the garment slightly.

1 Check that the patch matches in color and that the pile runs downward.

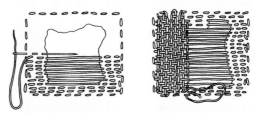

2 Cut away the worn part of the garment. Then cut out a patch exactly the same size as the worn part, and place it in the hole.

3 Sew the edges of the patch and the garment together with small overcasting stitches.

4 Use a fine brush to groom the hairs around the patch, working in the direction of the fur.

SWEATERS

Favorite sweaters are often in perfectly good shape except for a run or slightly worn cuffs. These can be repaired very easily.

◆ When mending sweaters try to match the color, fiber content, and weight. Then you can produce an almost invisible mend.

◆ Use a crochet hook to catch a dropped stitch. Hold it with a temporary stitch or safety pin until you have time to pick up the whole row.

Darning

Darning is appropriate for mending small holes or frayed areas. If skillfully done, it can be nearly invisible.

◆ Use a wooden darning egg for a sock or other knitted fabric or a sleeve; use an embroidery hoop for a flat piece of woven fabric.

◆ Darn under good light and with a fine needle. Darn like materials: cotton with cotton, wool with wool, etc., and use the same thickness of thread as in the rest of the garment. If possible, use a thread from an inside seam or fabric scrap; otherwise, choose a thread as nearly like the thread of the fabric as possible.

◆ Always keep the stitch tension even and not too tight when darning; pulling the stitches taut can cause puckering.

Darning a garment. *Working on the right side, take a tiny backstitch near the edge of the hole to anchor the thread, but don't knot it. Make small running stitches around the hole and fill it in with side-by-side stitches running parallel to the fabric yarn (above left). Then weave across these stitches at right angles (above right).*

Darning gloves. *Darn gloves while wearing them to keep the work taut. Wear the right glove on the left hand if you are right-handed and vice versa. "Weave" the repair as described above.*

HOME FURNISHINGS

Making your own curtains, furniture covers, bed and table linens, and other home furnishings is both economical and practical. Many household items are not difficult to make, and if you sew your own, you can choose your own style and fabric.

ESTIMATING THE FABRIC

◆ Be generous rather than exact in your measurements in case the fabric shrinks in cleaning.
◆ If the fabric has a large patterned design you will have to add one extra motif for each new length of fabric. For example, if the fabric has a pattern that repeats at 10-inch intervals, allow for an extra 10 inches on each new length of fabric.

Crisscross curtains

These can be made up in pairs so the two curtains overlap at the top with a single heading and the same rod.
◆ To measure the width, you need 2 to 2½ times the window's width for medium-weight fabrics and three times the width for sheers and lightweight fabrics.

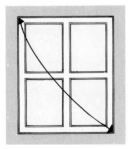

Measuring for crisscross curtains. *Measure from the top left-hand corner of the window in a loose curve to the bottom right-hand corner. Add the desired amount for the tail, plus 6 to 8 inches for the heading, hem, and shrinkage. Multiply the total by 2.*

◆ Measure each window. Even if all the windows look the same, they rarely are.

Shades

The amount of fabric you need depends on whether the shade will be set inside the window frame or above it.

Measuring for a shade mounted inside the window frame. *Measure the width of the glazed area and add 3 inches to determine the width of the fabric. Measure from the top to the bottom of the window frame and add 12 inches for the length.*

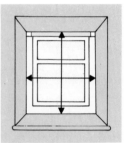

Measuring for a shade mounted above the window. *Measure the width of the window frame and add 3 inches to establish the width of the fabric. For the fabric length, measure the length from the roller to the bottom of the window and add 12 inches.*

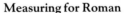

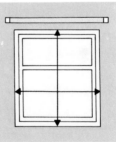

Measuring for Roman shades. *Measure the width of the recess and add 2 inches. Measure the depth of the recess and add 10 inches. You will need the same amount of material for the lining. These fit into a window recess and hang in pleats when drawn up.*

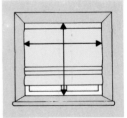

CURTAINS AND DRAPERIES

◆Curtains are usually made of sheer or lightweight fabric and have a casing or pocket for the rod, and sometimes a heading above the casing.

◆Draperies are generally of heavier fabric and need heading tape or stiffener sewn across the top.

◆**Estimating yardage.** Measure from the top of the rod to the desired length—less $\frac{1}{2}$ inch for clearance for floor-length draperies. Add hem allowances (2 to 4 inches for curtains, 4 to 8 inches for draperies), headings (2 to 4 inches for curtains, 4 to 8 inches for draperies), and casings (the diameter of the rod plus $\frac{1}{4}$ to $\frac{1}{2}$ inch for ease).

◆**To determine the finished width.** Measure the length of the rod and double it for fullness (triple it for sheer fabric). Allow for side hems: $1\frac{1}{2}$ inches for curtains; $2\frac{1}{2}$ inches for draperies; add 1 inch for seams if you are joining panels.

◆Divide the finished width by the fabric width to determine the number of panels needed. Multiply the finished length per panel by the number of panels and divide by 36 to find the yardage.

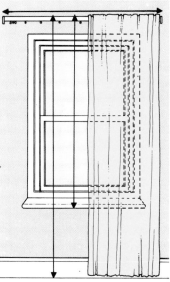

PLEATED HEADING TAPES

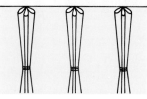

Pinch pleats. *Add an extra allowance of 4 inches per curtain length. Place the rod high enough so the curtains fall in long, graceful folds.*

Box pleats. *For a plain fabric, you'll need $2\frac{1}{2}$ times the length of the rod. For a patterned fabric, increase the width to allow for matching.*

CORNICE AND VALANCES

When measuring the fabric to cover a cornice or for a valance, allow for the "returns," the two sections of a valance or valance board that bend back at each end to meet the wall.

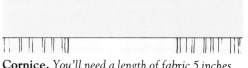

Cornice. *You'll need a length of fabric 5 inches longer than the rod including returns and about 2 inches deeper than the box itself.*

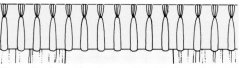

French-pleated valance. *Double the width of the rod to get the total width. Measure the length, and allow for hems.*

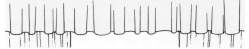

Shirred valance. *Measure the valance rods including the two returns. Double it for fullness (triple it for sheer fabric), measure the length, and allow for hems.*

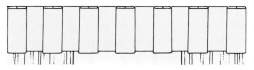

Box-pleated valance. *You'll need $2\frac{1}{4}$ times the rod length, plus 6 inches—20 inches for patterned fabric. Measure the length and allow for hems.*

Austrian shades

These shades fit just under the top lip of the window recess and should hang flush with the wall to look neat. Because they use a lot of fabric, you will need to join several lengths, preferably along the lines of the vertical tapes so you can't see the seams.

◆ To measure for an Austrian shade, measure the width of the window recess and double it, adding 1½ inches for side hems. For the length of each panel, measure the height of the window, and multiply it 2½ times, adding 8 inches for the hem.

Slipcovers

When making a slipcover, use the covers already on the piece of furniture as a guide for the new pattern. Adapt these basic instructions for your particular piece.

◆ To measure the length you need, follow these instructions.

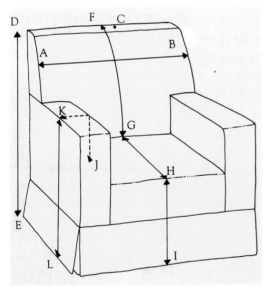

1 Measure from the left to right across the chair back (A–B) to give you the width of the fabric you will need. Find the center back at the highest point where the front covering fabric joins the back over the top of the chair (C). Mark it with a pin or tailor's chalk.

2 Measure the outside back down to floor level (D–E) and then the inside back

to the junction of the back and seat (F–G). Add 5 inches for tucking in.

3 Measure the seat from back to front (G–H), plus 5 inches for tucking in. Measure from the seat down to the floor (H–I).

4 Take the measurement of the inside arm from the outside seam over the curve to the seat (J–K), plus 5 inches for tucking in. Multiply by 2 to allow for both arms. Measure the outside arm from outside seam to the floor (K–L) and multiply by 2.

5 Measure the front facing of the arms or scroll, and multiply by 2.

6 For loose cushions, measure length, width, and depth. Add to the overall estimate an amount for self-piping, about 3 feet.

Bedspreads and dust ruffles

◆ Make the bed before you measure it, to allow for the thickness of the bedding.

◆ Use a flexible tape measure; where it is not long enough for the whole distance, pin at the place where the tape ends and continue measuring from the pin.

◆ Allow 2 inches for seam allowances, and add 5 inches to the length and width for hem allowances.

◆ Measure the length of the bed from head to foot, allowing 14 inches for pillow tucking in. Now measure the top width from edge to edge. Measure the drop.

◇ **For a full spread.** Measure from the edge of the top to ½ inch from the floor.

◇ **For a coverlet.** Measure from the top edge to 3 inches below the mattress.

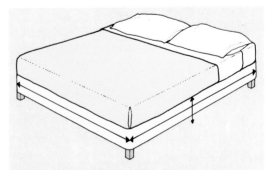

Measuring for a dust ruffle. *Measure the length and width of the box spring for the top. For the length, measure from the top edge of the box spring to ½ inch from the floor to allow for the drop.*

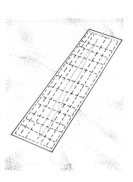

REPAIRING FURNISHINGS

Repairing a torn sheet. *Lay wide tape over the tear, turn the ragged edges under, and machine-stitch over the tape several times.*

A variety of home furnishings with minor tears and holes can be repaired so they look good and last longer.

Sheets

◆ Mend tears by stitching cotton or cotton-polyester tape or a scrap of fabric to the damaged area (see above right).

◆ Putting worn sheets "sides to middle" is a good old-fashioned way to get them to last almost twice as long. Although you end up with slightly narrower sheets with a seam down the middle, they are useful for beds or for making linings for sleeping bags, where the seam can be positioned to one side. Don't wait until the middle of the sheet is about to wear out completely, catch it when it begins to look a little bit worn. Otherwise you will have to cut away more of the sheet when you repair it.

1 Make a small cut in the middle of the sheet at the hem, and then tear it right down to the bottom. This will give you a straighter line than cutting.

2 Trim away any part that looks really worn, and turn the sides to the middle. Make a double-stitched seam up the middle (see page 269) and hem the outside edge.

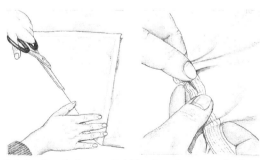

Make fitted sheets. *Fold back each corner of a flat sheet 12 inches, and cut off the triangular piece (above left). Turn up the hem and stitch a length of elastic onto the inside edge (above right). Stitch the elastic securely at each end.*

Blankets

◆ To mend a blanket, darn it as though it were a sock (see page 283), using yarn of the same thickness as the blanket yarn.

◆ When you've finished darning, brush the blanket gently around the hole to bring up the pile and hide the damaged area.

◆ Zigzag fraying edges.

Towels

◆ Reinforce a frayed edge with zigzag stitching or binding. Trim the edge first and then machine-stitch binding of a matching or contrasting color to the edge.

◆ Repair a hole with an appliquéd motif.

Re-covering a comforter or quilt

◆ Use sheeting material so you don't have to make seams in the fabric. Use 200-thread count to prevent feathers from poking through.

1 Measure the quilt, allowing extra for side, top, and bottom seams, and any seams you may have to make.

2 Measure around the outside of the quilt or comforter, and prepare any pleated trimmings and piping that you need.

3 Baste the sides of the fabric right sides together, with the trimming between them turned to the inside. Then machine-stitch all around, but leave an opening big enough to get the quilt into (will be most of one end).

4 If you are going to quilt the cover to the comforter, sew up the gap with neat stitches. If not, attach snaps or a strip of self-fastening tape to the open edges.

5 For the quilt stitching, lay the quilt flat on the floor or on a big table, arranging it inside the cover as evenly as you can; pin it at the corners, sides, and middle. Baste along the old stitching, which you should be able to feel with your fingertips through the fabric, starting at the center. Do the stitching by machine if you can get the material under the foot, otherwise do it by hand. Make sure the stitches go right through the fabric.

DECORATIVE PIPING

◆ Use piping to decorate the main seams of a slipcover and to strengthen the cover at its weakest points or to finish off the edges of a coverlet.

◆ If you are using covered piping, it is less time-consuming to make a continuous length and cut as required. One yard of narrow material will make about 73 feet of 1½-inch piping.

◆ Wash the piping cord before covering it if it is not preshrunk, and allow it to dry; otherwise it will shrink when you wash the slipcover.

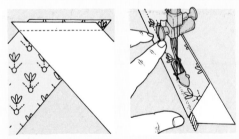

Making piping. *Cut the material into strips on the bias. Join the strips together with stitching on the lengthwise grain (above left), and press the seams open. Fold the material in half lengthwise, then lay the cord in the fold. Stitch close to the cord, using the piping foot or zipper foot on your sewing machine and stretching the bias material slightly as you work (above right). Roll the finished piping around a wide piece of cardboard to keep it from tangling.*

Refilling a quilt

Feather-filled quilts are expensive to refill with new down; you may be able to add some filling from an old pillow or cushion.

1 Put the new down into a pillowcase to contain it. It is best to use an old pillowcase because in the refilling process you are going to have to stitch up the pillowcase, which may damage the fabric.

2 Using a seam ripper, undo the quilting and the stitching in the middle of the seam at one end of the quilt.

3 Sew the top of the down-filled pillowcase to the opening you have made in the quilt, using fine neat stitches.

4 Gently shake the feathers from the pillowcase into the quilt. Unstitch the pillowcase from the quilt and close the opening in the quilt, using very close, even, small stitches. Shake the down evenly throughout the comforter, then lay it flat on the floor and quilt-stitch it as for the re-covered comforter above.

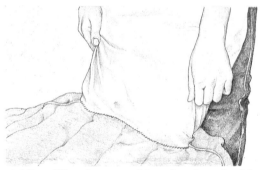

Adding filling from a cushion. *Sew the ends of the filled pillowcase to the quilt along the seam lines. Gently shake the feathers down into the quilt.*

Child Care

DAY-TO-DAY CARE

WHILE raising children can be one of the most rewarding activities of life, it also can be frustrating. Trying to keep up with the demands of child care can take up a lot of your time and energy. But with a little planning, some of the helpful shortcuts in this chapter, and a reminder to yourself to stay flexible, you can make the most of the time you have with your children.

USING A BABY-SITTER

◆ When you interview a person not recommended by a close personal friend, ask for the names and phone numbers of other clients and see whether they were pleased with the person.

◆ Try to find out whether you share the same ideas about child care.

◆ Show the baby-sitters where things they will need are kept and provide them with details about your house—how to regulate heat, how to lock and open the doors, and how to operate appliances.

◆ Tell the baby-sitters when and what to feed your child and advise them of your child's likes and dislikes.

◆ Make sure the sitters know when you will return and where you can be reached. Also, provide them with the name and telephone number of a responsible friend, relative, or neighbor who can be called if you can't be reached.

◆ Write down the telephone numbers of your physician, hospital and emergency room, fire department, and police and post them by the phone.

BATHING

Make bathtime fun and relaxing with plenty of playtime included—it can quickly become a highlight of a baby's week with the added bonus that your child will be less likely to develop a fear of the water.

◆ The most common baby bathtubs are made of molded plastic with a nonskid surface and are big enough for the baby to kick and splash in. If you are short of space, get an inflatable tub that can be deflated and stored between baths. It is fine to use the kitchen sink, too; just scrub it well before and after using for the baby.

◆ For sponge baths, place a fitted sponge liner or a folded towel in the bottom of the baby tub or kitchen sink to provide a soft, nonskid cushion.

◆ Make sure that the room and bath water are comfortably warm; test the water with either your wrist or elbow.

◆ Keep all the bath articles handy on a small tray or in a basket near the tub or sink.

◆ Use only mild, pure soap with no perfumes or deodorants so it won't dry out baby's skin.

GIVING A BATH

While baths are an important part of a baby's routine they are not necessary on a daily basis. Three baths a week is normally sufficient, although you may want to wash your baby more often in the summer.

You will need:
◇ One or two soft bath towels large enough to wrap the baby completely. Receiving blankets may be substituted for towels
◇ Cotton balls
◇ Soft, terry-cloth washcloths
◇ Soap and baby shampoo
◇ Clean diaper
◇ Clothes

1 *Fill the bath. The water temperature should be the same as your baby's body temperature and feel comfortably warm. Place the towel on a firm surface near the bathtub.*

2 *Place your baby on the towel with the undershirt and diaper on. Start from the face and head and work downward. Wash the baby's face with clear water. Clean only the outer areas of the ears using a soft cloth or moist cotton. Dry the face.*

3 *Pick the baby up in the "football carry" with your arm under the baby's head and back and your hand holding her head. Lean over the tub. Shampoo the head gently but thoroughly, using your fingertips but not your nails. Rinse thoroughly. Towel-dry the hair immediately.*

4 *Remove the baby's undershirt and unfasten the diaper but keep in place. Soap your baby's chest and stomach. With your hand under your baby's*

armpit, turn her over. Then pull down the diaper and soap the back and buttocks.

5 *Place your baby on her back. Remove the diaper and soap the abdomen and genital area. Carefully lift your baby up by her ankles so you can reach and clean all the creases in the diaper area. Wash the legs and feet and between the toes.*

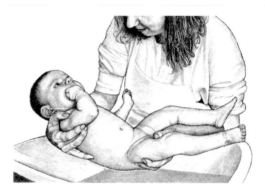

6 *With one hand supporting your baby's head and the other supporting the legs, place your baby in the tub. While you keep a firm grasp on the upper part of your baby, rinse her quickly, but thoroughly with a soft washcloth.*

7 *Then, carefully lift the baby out of the tub. Immediately wrap her in a large towel, and gently, but thoroughly, pat completely dry.*

8 *Baby powder, oils, or creams are not necessary after bathing. If you use any of these items, do so sparingly. Powder can get into the baby's lungs. Oils or creams can clog the baby's pores and promote rashes. Instead, just put a clean diaper on the baby and dress her quickly.*

Washing a very young baby

For the first three or four weeks, until the navel (or circumcision) is healed, it is better to give a baby a sponge bath than to wash the infant in a tub. First lay your baby on a firm padded surface undressed to the undershirt and diaper. Using moistened cotton balls or a soft washcloth, clean the face. Use a new piece of cotton for each eye to prevent infection passing from one eye to the other, and wipe around the outer ears only. Shampoo the scalp three times a week with mild

soap or no-tears shampoo and rinse holding baby in "football carry."

Sit down with your baby on your lap; remove the undershirt and unfasten the diaper but don't remove. Soap the baby's neck, chest, arms, and hands, including skin creases. Rinse the neck, chest, arms and hands with clean, warm water. Rinse soap from the folds of skin. Pat your baby dry; don't rub. Gently but firmly supporting her head, turn her on one side to soap and rinse her back and buttocks; pat dry. Remove your baby's diaper and soap and rinse the abdomen, genitals, legs, and feet. Wash gently around the navel until it heals. Dry her immediately and dress quickly.

Supporting an older baby. *Even if a baby can sit upright, put your arm around him and hold onto the thigh farthest from you. Put a nonskid mat in the bath for a baby to sit on.*

TIPS FOR SAFE BATHING

◆ Use a rubber safety mat. Don't let your baby slip down under the water or try to see if he can sit unsupported—he might tumble in. A bad fright could scare a baby and create a dislike of baths for a long time.

▼▼ Never leave a baby or young child
◆ ◆ alone in the bathtub; he could slip and hurt himself. A baby can drown in very shallow water.

◆ Put cold water into the bath first, then hot, so that the surface of the bath doesn't get too hot.

◆ Use the "football carry" (see page 290) to pick up a squirming, soapy infant.

Washing an older baby

◆ Introduce your baby to the family bathtub gradually. Place the old, small bathtub in the big one to bathe him. After a few baths, remove the little tub and fill the big one with a small amount of water. Each time you bathe your child, fill the bathtub a little higher.

◆ Make bath time a treat by having a special set of toys. Household items such as plastic colanders or funnels, measuring spoons, or ice-cube trays all make good toys.

◆ Let the water out of the bath after you take the baby out; the sound of the water going down the drain might be frightening.

Overcoming fear of water. *Fill the kitchen sink with a couple of inches of warm water. Put a towel on the drainboard and some of your baby's favorite toys in the sink. Sit him on the towel and, while keeping hold of him, let your baby paddle in the water.*

Shampooing the hair

Try to make hair washing as pleasant as possible; making a game out of the lathering and rinsing will help your child enjoy having his hair washed.

◆ Don't pour water directly over your child's head; lean your child back in the tub or over a sink and, while holding the shoulders, support the head. Direct the water away from the forehead and back toward his hair.

◆ Have a dry washcloth or towel handy to mop up any drips. To avoid stinging the baby's eyes, use a no-tears shampoo.

◆ If your child really hates having her hair washed, make the sessions fun by letting her participate: Get in the bath with her and let her wash your hair; let your child wet her own hair and apply the shampoo; or encourage your child to wash a doll's hair.

Fear of baths

Many babies enjoy their baths right away, while others howl in protest the minute they get wet. It may take eight or 10 baths before they get used to the water. Probably the easiest way of overcoming any fear is to make bath times as happy and relaxing as possible, with plenty of playtime included.

◆ If your child is afraid of the water, try to figure out the reason, then change the circumstances. Fear could be caused by a bathtub that is too large, too much water in the tub, having water splashed on the face, or the memory of slipping under the water.

◆Reintroduce your reluctant bather to the water gradually. Give a sponge bath on a towel outside the tub and immerse the baby in the water for rinsing only.

◆Put some favorite toys in a bowl of water on the bathroom floor next to the baby so that playing with the toys will get him used to being near water again. You can then reintroduce shallow baths—feet first, making it a game.

CHANGING DIAPERS

◆Change your baby's diaper after every bowel movement, and as necessary when wet. A fresh diaper also should go on after a bath and after a feeding.

◆It isn't necessary to wake a baby to change a wet diaper; babies wake up on their own if too wet or uncomfortable.

◆If you live in a large house, keep a set of diaper changing equipment downstairs to save you from running up and down stairs.

◆Assemble all the paraphernalia before you start. You need:
◇Changing mat
◇Disposable or clean cloth diaper
◇Diaper pins with plastic heads or masking tape
◇Cotton balls and baby wipes
◇Soft, terry-cloth washcloth
◇Clean clothes
◇Distracting toy

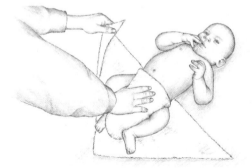

Changing a boy's diaper. *Lay a clean diaper over a boy's penis as soon as you take the old diaper off because boys often urinate into the air when changed.*

◆Change the diaper on a work surface at waist level or on the floor.

◆Make sure the new diaper is not too tight by running your fingers around the legs; if it is too tight, it will rub your baby's legs and cause a rash.

Using disposable diapers

◆Disposable diapers are convenient because they eliminate laundering. They also cut down on skin rash, odor, and irritations. Even if you use cloth diapers ordinarily, keep a supply of disposables for emergencies and for traveling.

◆Keep a diaper pin or a roll of masking tape handy in case you tear an adhesive tab, or if one won't stick.

◆Disposable diapers come in different shapes for boys and girls, and in different thicknesses according to weight.

CHANGING A DIAPER

1 *Take off the dirty diaper, using the front of it to wipe off any feces, then fold it and slide it under the baby's bottom.*

2 *Wipe the genital area with baby wipes and cleanse the skin with a damp washcloth or moistened cotton balls. Pat dry with a soft clean cloth, making sure to dry all the creases and folds in the baby's skin.*

3 **Using a disposable diaper.** *Open out the diaper with the adhesive tabs at the top. Lift the baby's legs and slide the diaper under so that the top aligns with the baby's waist. Bring the front up between the baby's legs and smooth the sides of the diaper around the baby's tummy so they tuck under neatly. Unpeel the adhesive tabs and pull them firmly over the front flap to secure the diaper.*

4 **Using a cloth diaper.** *Fold the diaper into the triple-absorbent fold (see page 293). Slide the diaper under so that the baby's waist aligns with the top edge. Bring the diaper up between the baby's legs. Hold it in place and first fold one back edge, then the other, over the front central panel. Secure the diaper with one pin in the middle for a small baby; use two side pins for bigger babies.*

Using cloth diapers

GREEN TIP: Cloth diapers are much less expensive to use in the long run than disposable brands, and are recommended by environmentalists because they can be reused.

◆ Keep your fingers between diaper and skin when putting diaper pins through the fabric, to avoid jabbing the baby.

◆ Whether you launder diapers or use a diaper service, keep a two-gallon covered pail for soiled diapers next to the changing area. Diaper services often provide a deodorized, lined container.

◆ After removing a dirty cloth diaper, scrape or shake any stools into the toilet and flush. Rinse the diaper thoroughly in clear water, wring it out, and drop it into the pail.

◆ **Triple-absorbent fold.** This is the neatest and most absorbent method of folding a diaper. Fold in fourths and place on a flat surface with the open edges to the top and right. Holding the bottom layers firmly with the right hand, with the left hand pull out the top corner to form an inverted triangle on top of the remaining layers of diaper. Turn the whole diaper carefully over, so the pointed edge is at the top right-hand corner. Fold the square of diaper now on the left into the center of the triangle in thirds, to form a thick, central panel.

Diaper rash. Most of these irritations will improve if diapers are changed as soon as they become wet or soiled, and if your baby goes without a diaper as often as practical until the rash has entirely healed.

◆ When you must diaper, use two or three thicknesses of cloth diapers and omit plastic waterproof pants; they retain heat and moisture and aggravate diaper rash.

◆ **To treat diaper rash.** Apply petroleum jelly or a mild protective ointment after cleaning and drying the skin. An ordinary lightbulb directed toward the exposed area from a few feet away can speed healing. Cool compresses, soaked in a solution of one teaspoon salt to a pint of water, may be applied intermittently.

◆ Zinc oxide should not be applied while the skin is still inflamed but may be used after the rash has healed to prevent new inflammation.

CLOTHES

◆ Keep a record of your child's measurements and update it regularly; then you are less likely to buy the wrong size.

◆ If you plan to have more than one child, buy unisex clothes, particularly when the children are young, so you can use them for the next child. Children usually grow out of clothes before they wear out.

◆ Choose machine-washable, permanent-press fabrics. Blankets should be acrylic; hypoallergenic materials are a wise choice when available.

◆ Pick clothes for convenience; they should be simple to put on and take off and easy to turn back or open for diaper changes.

◆ For everyday wear, one-piece jump suits that snap from neck to ankles in stretch fabrics that will expand as the baby grows work well.

◆ Buy T-shirts and undershirts with envelope necks, since they are easier to get over the baby's head.

CLOTHES FOR A NEW BABY

Buy the minimum amount beforehand. Once the baby is born, you will find out which clothes are the most useful and then you can get more.

◇ 6 undershirts, short-sleeved—opening at the front with side snaps, or pullover-type with adjustable neck
◇ 3 kimonos, long-sleeved, with snaps
◇ 3 sacques, short-sleeved, with snaps
◇ 6 one-piece jumpsuits, with snaps; choose lightweight ones for summer
◇ 1 sweater, synthetic and washable
◇ 6 receiving blankets
◇ 4 plastic pants
◇ 4 pairs of socks or booties
◇ 1 wool or acrylic blanket for an outer-wrap, or a quilted zipper bag with hood
◇ 1 hat: cotton for summer, woolen for winter

◆ Don't buy too many clothes for the baby. Babies will outgrow each size quickly. For maximum wear, start with six-month size. Buy winter clothes at least one size too big; they'll last longer.

Dressing and undressing

◆ If your child won't make a fist when you are putting on a sweater, give him a small toy to grasp at, making a fist, so you can dress him easily.

◆ Attach gloves or mittens to a long piece of string or yarn that you can thread through the arms of the coat.

◆ If the ends of shoelaces become frayed, coat them with clear nail polish or wrap some tape around them.

◆ Up until around 18 months, your child will be better able to remove clothes than put them on. Therefore, dress him in clothes that can't be removed easily, such as night-clothes that snap in the back or shirts that pull over the head.

◆ Keep your toddler's overall straps from slipping down by pinning them together with a large safety pin where they cross.

◆ For older children, buy pants with elasticized waists; children find them easier to put on or pull down when they go to the toilet. Don't buy zippered pants for a small boy; he could catch his penis in the zipper.

◆ Put a keyring on a zipper pull tab so that small hands can hold onto it more easily.

◆ Put a badge or clear marking on the front of a garment so your child can easily tell the front from the back.

Babies' and toddlers' shoes. *Washable fabric shoes with elastic around the ankles are ideal indoor shoes for babies and toddlers because they don't fall off (above left). For older toddlers look for shoes with self-grip fastenings so they can dress themselves (above right).*

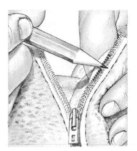

Fixing sticking zipper. *To ease a sticking zipper, rub pencil lead or soap over it so that it glides easily.*

CRYING

Hunger is the most common cause of crying in very young babies, but anything from bright lights, a hard surface, or a sudden loud noise to boredom or the need for physical comforting can make a baby cry.

◆ Comfort your baby promptly when she is crying; this will give your baby a sense of security knowing that her needs will be met.

◆ Babies often cry because they are too hot or cold. Feel the back of your baby's neck. If it is sweaty, remove a layer of clothing or a blanket. If the baby feels cool and/or the diaper is wet, add clothing and change the diaper.

◆ If your baby continues to cry, carry her around with you in a sling or shawl for a while, so that she can hear your heartbeat, which is very comforting.

◆ Try wrapping a very young baby firmly in a shawl before putting her down to sleep; this can make your baby feel more secure.

◆ Try rocking a crying baby to and fro in a rhythmic, tick-tock way. Holding babies in an upright or semisitting position seems to work better than cradling them in a horizontal posture. Some parents find that a car or bus ride can settle a persistently crying baby.

◆ Many small babies cry when they are bored. Put pictures or a baby safety mirror on the side of the crib beside the head so there is something to look at (see page 296).

◆ Crying seldom signals a real emergency. Despite parents' fears, an open diaper pin is rarely the cause. A medical explanation is usually indicated by other signs such as fever, decreased appetite, etc.

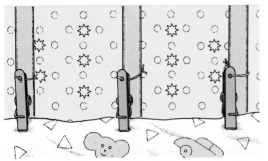

Keeping a baby warm. *Tie clothespins to the side of the crib and attach them to the blanket or quilt to hold it in place.*

SLEEP

A newborn baby should fall asleep the moment he is tired. To help your baby settle down:

See that the room is comfortably warm.

Darken the room at night.

◆Rock the baby gently or just place your hand on a cheek or shoulder. Babies find this soothing.

Make bedtime as happy and relaxing as possible; babies will be more likely to sleep through the night if they are relaxed and feel secure. With an older baby of about six months or so, develop a routine that helps him to unwind at the end of the day—bath, drink, into bed, and talk to the baby, read a story, and/or sing a song.

Don't play exciting or rough games near bedtime; your child will be wide awake and won't be able to go to sleep.

Be sure you don't give the baby a bottle to take to bed. The sugars in milk, formula, or juice contribute to the growth of bacteria that cause tooth decay. If a baby sucks on a bottle all night, he can develop "baby bottle tooth decay." If you want to offer a few extra ounces of milk, hold the child in your arms for the feeding.

Don't discourage your baby from taking up a security habit such as thumb sucking or holding a favorite blanket or stuffed toy; it will help your baby fall asleep more easily and he will grow out of the habit after a while.

Musical mobiles above the crib can lull babies to sleep.

If your baby resists bed night after night, say goodnight firmly and leave him to cry for

about 10 minutes; then, and only then, go back in. One such return is probably all right in order to check that your child is not ill.

Coping with night wakers

◆If your baby is very young, always respond to the cries to discourage insecurity later. Take turns with your partner so that you both get some sleep. Both of you should try to get to bed early at least twice a week.

◆Babies may wake during the night and cry or call out in a darkened room in a silent house because they need to be reassured that you are still nearby. The baby usually will calm down if you go to the cribside, lift him, and speak a few words in soft, reassuring, and loving tones.

◆Don't change a diaper routinely in the night unless it is really wet. This activity may wake your child up and make getting back to sleep difficult.

◆Make sure the child is the right temperature. If he feels sweaty or hot, remove a blanket if necessary. If the baby seems cold, or gets cold easily, put a safety heater with a thermostat in the bedroom to keep the temperature constant.

◆If your child wakes up because he is afraid of the dark, put a nightlight in the room or install a dimmer switch and leave a light on low all night.

◆If your child has a nightmare, distract him as quickly as possible. Hold and reassure your child with soothing words or songs until the crying stops. Then point out the familiar surroundings, and remind your child that you are always nearby. It is best not to make too much of the incident, or transfer the child to your bed, as this could encourage a habit of nightly awakening.

◆Don't keep checking on a sleeping baby; you may end up disturbing him. Keep such checking to a minimum (say, just before your own bedtime).

◆Check for diaper rash—a common cause of discomfort that can wake a baby up.

Early risers

◆Leave some soft toys or a busy box in the crib so your baby has something to play with after waking up. Make sure that the room is not too dark in the morning so that there is enough light to play by.

◆Don't leap out of bed at the first murmur or your baby will start to expect it; she can play for a while.

Storing small objects. *Plastic margarine or ice-cream containers are ideal for storing little dolls, marbles, and small blocks.*

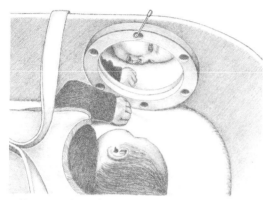

Alleviating boredom. *Tie a little plastic mirror to the side of the crib, so that the baby can gaze at it when she wakes up.*

PLAY

Toys are a baby's learning tools. They can be anything from improvised games made from common household objects to expensive items from a toy store. What is important is that the baby enjoys playing and learning.

◆**Up to six months.** Babies love watching anything that moves, such as mobiles; objects that make a noise, such as rattles; and plastic bottles filled with beans.

◆**Six to 10 months.** Offer brightly colored and noisy rattles or toys with bells; musical boxes provide endless fascination; a baby mirror will give pleasure; activity boxes are suitable for play in bed or bath.

◆**10 to 12 months.** Give push-and-pull toys like trains, cars, or walking dogs; toys on strings can be drawn by the child; chalks, crayons, and simple paintbrushes can be used for first attempts at drawing.

Reducing mess

◆You can make a tray for paint jars by cutting out holes in a block of plastic foam. This will prevent the paints from tipping over; otherwise, buy paint jars with non-spill lids. Store paintbrushes and jars in flatware trays.

◆Whenever your child is doing any gluing, painting, or other messy activity, cover the table and surrounding floor with newspaper.

SAFETY TIPS FOR TOYS

▼▼Never let your baby have anything
◆ ◆ small enough to swallow: no marbles, small shells, beads, or chess men. Babies love putting things in their mouths and all these items can choke them if swallowed accidentally.

◆Make sure painted toys are lead free, because lead is poisonous.

◆Don't give a child toys with sharp edges because they can cause injuries. Metal toys can be very dangerous.

◆Never leave a young baby alone while he is playing; he could swallow something or cut himself.

◆Buy soft toys displaying a safety label because they have to be made to a particular standard. Don't buy toys with loose pieces, eyes held in place with wire, or seams that look weak; your child could choke or get hurt on the eyes or particles of stuffing.

◆Always buy nontoxic paint for children—they often suck brushes or lick their fingers.

Protecting clothes.
If your child is painting, protect clothes with a plastic apron with elasticized sleeves. These also are useful if your child is "helping with the dishwashing."

◆Encourage children to put things away. Shoe boxes make great doll beds or barns for toy animals. They also are ideal for storing dolls' clothes or a child's favorite treasures.

◆Label boxes and jars with brightly colored labels or stickers so that you know where everything is.

◆Keep a basket in each room for collecting scattered toys for an easy cleanup—one per child if you have room, then you won't mix up prized possessions.

IMPROVISED TOYS

YOUNG BABIES

Everything is interesting at this age. Here is a list of safe and entertaining objects you can find around the house:

◇Things that roll: empty cardboard toilet-paper or paper-towel tubes

◇Round objects: oranges or grapefruit, balls of string or wool

◇Flat things and hard things: a table mat, a ruler, wooden spoons

◇Light things made of foam rubber: a shaped bath sponge. (Don't give your child a sponge once she has teeth because she could pull pieces off and swallow them.)

◇Things with holes big enough for a little hand or finger: napkin rings, rolls of tape and so on

◇Rattly things: a plastic jar with beans or beads inside (but only if the lid can be tightly screwed on and taped)

◇Large and fairly heavy (but safe) things: a football or a cushion

◇Things with interesting textures: strips of felt or other material

◇Kitchen utensils: a plastic sieve, or measuring spoons for playing in the bathtub

Suitable toys for young babies

OLDER BABIES AND TODDLERS

◆Start a dress-up box. Old shoes, shirts, skirts, dresses, hats, and scarves will provide endless entertainment. Real uniforms (you can sometimes get them from second-hand shops) are always fun.

◆Make your own finger paints by mixing 2 fluid ounces liquid starch with 4 drops of food coloring.

◆Make modeling dough by combining flour and salt (3 parts flour to 1 part salt) and add this to 1 part water. The dough can be colored with food coloring and will keep for a week or so in an airtight container.

◆Make nontoxic glue from 1 part flour and 2 parts water with a teaspoon of salt. Put the flour and salt into a saucepan and stir the water into the flour slowly until it is absorbed. Simmer the paste for five minutes and allow it to cool before use. This also is a good paste for making papier-mâché (see page 221).

◆Keep rolls of drawing paper, available from artist's supply stores, on a paper towel dispenser so that it is always close at hand when you need it.

Hand puppets. *Make puppets by drawing faces on brown paper bags, or sewing faces on old socks.*

FEEDING BABIES AND TODDLERS

How and what to feed babies and young children are important decisions parents need to make. Breast-feeding is healthiest for a baby and simplest for you, but bottle-feeding can be perfectly satisfactory. Once you have weaned your child onto solid food, it is important to vary the diet so that your child doesn't get bored with food, as well as to make sure that the amount and variety of nutrients are sufficient.

BREAST-FEEDING

Mothers who breast-feed their infants will find that it has many welcome advantages.
◆ Breast milk is the most convenient because it is always on hand and always at the right temperature.
◆ Mother's milk contains the exact nutrients, in the proper quantities, that a baby needs for optimal growth. (La Leche League International, the organization behind the return of breast-feeding in the United States, estimates that you could hire cleaning help for six months with the money you save on commercial formulas and baby food.)
◆ Natural immunities are conveyed through mother's milk, and research indicates that breast-fed babies enjoy prolonged protection against numerous viral infections, and have fewer allergies and eczemas.

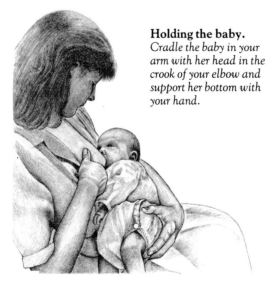

Holding the baby.
Cradle the baby in your arm with her head in the crook of your elbow and support her bottom with your hand.

◆ The benefits of nursing your newborn infant have as much to do with satisfying basic emotional needs of love, warmth, and security as with hunger. Ask that your baby be put to your breast as soon as possible after delivery, and bring her to your breast regularly in the first days after the birth (even if she dozes off and doesn't feed) to establish a bond between you.
◆ **Putting your baby to the breast.** Draw her toward you until her cheek brushes just near the nipple; your baby will then turn toward it instinctively to suck. See that your baby takes all of the nipple and the pigmented area around it (the areola) into her mouth so she can suck properly without causing you to develop sore nipples.
◆ Don't pull the baby off the breast. Insert your little finger into the corner of the mouth, or press gently on the chin to break the suction.
◆ Breast-fed babies usually want to nurse every two to three hours. Don't worry about your ability to produce milk: the more milk your baby takes the more you will make.
◆ **Expressing milk.** If you need to get back to a job, or would like your partner to share night feedings, you can express your milk into a bottle and this can be given to the child in your absence.
◆ Most women hand-express their milk or use a breast pump. To ease the process considerably, look for a battery-powered breast pump.
◆ Many women keep their milk production on schedule by expressing during working hours and putting the milk into a chilled vacuum-sealed bottle. Expressed milk will keep in the refrigerator for 48 hours and in the freezer for up to six months.

TIPS FOR ENSURING A GOOD MILK SUPPLY

◆ Get as much rest as possible, particularly when the baby is very young. Go to bed early whenever you can. Take small naps, while the baby is sleeping.

◆ Drink at least 12 cups of fluid a day to assist milk production. Remember that whatever you ingest will be carried in your milk to the baby; avoid alcohol and caffeine in anything other than small amounts while breast-feeding. Make sure you have a well-balanced diet of fresh and nutritious foods.

◆ Release tension regularly through gentle exercise, quiet reading, or a warm bath so that it doesn't interfere with your natural reflex to "let-down" the flow. Feelings of calmness and confidence enhance milk production.

◆ If you are seeing a physician about a medical problem, make certain he or she knows you are breast-feeding. Certain medications such as laxatives, diuretics, contraceptive pills, and antibiotics can reduce milk supply.

BOTTLE-FEEDING

The majority of babies are bottle-fed at sometime during the first year and thrive, so whether you use formula from the start or later decide to switch from breast milk to formula, it is unlikely to affect your child's growth and well-being.

◆ The great advantage of bottle feeding is that both you and your partner can provide nourishment. It also means getting back to work sooner if you need to; others can easily feed your child in your absence.

◆ Bottle-fed babies feed about six times a day, once every four hours, taking about two ounces at each feeding. The amount increases as the baby grows older so that the number of feedings is gradually reduced.

◆ The baby should be held in a semisitting position with the head propped in the crook of your elbow to keep the airway open and to ease swallowing. A baby that is fed while flat on his back may gag.

◆ A line of bubbles will rise through the milk to indicate that the baby is feeding successfully. If the flow shuts off, move the bottle in the baby's mouth from time to time to break the suction.

◆ Check the milk flow before feeding your baby by inverting the bottle; the milk should come out at several drops a second. A steady flow is too fast and means the hole in the nipple is too large. Milk that comes out too quickly can choke a baby. Remember, too, to test the temperature of the milk before you give it to baby (see right).

Using formula

Commercial formulas are developed to contain the essential ingredients of mother's milk.

◆ Most formulas use cow's milk as the principal source of protein; others use vegetable protein from soybeans to provide an alternative for babies with allergies to cow's milk.

◆ Most formulas are prepared in one of the following ways:

◇ Powdered formulas are mixed with warm water.

◇ Liquid concentrates also must be mixed, usually 1 part concentrate to 1 part water.

◇ Ready-to-feed formulas are poured directly into the bottle and require no mixing.

◆ Once the formula is warmed or at room temperature, give it to the baby right away; warmth encourages bacterial growth, which could make baby sick. For the same reason, always throw leftover milk away.

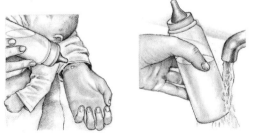

Getting a bottle to the right temperature. *Stand the bottle in a bowl of hot water to warm it. Test the temperature of the milk on your wrist before you give it to the baby* (above left). *If it is too hot, hold it under cold water* (above right).

How to hold the bottle. *Keep the bottle at an angle so that the nipple will always be full of milk; otherwise the baby will take in air with the milk, which will produce gas.*

Sterilizing bottles

◆ Disposable bottles eliminate the need for sterilizing bottles—just zip off a plastic sack from the roll, and place it in the holder.

◆ Ready-to-serve, single-serving bottles are the ultimate in bottle convenience and are great for short day trips.

◆ Be sure to always wash your hands with soap and hot water before sterilizing bottles; this will eliminate any bacteria that could upset your baby's stomach.

◆ If you're using traditional-style bottles, rinse out bottles and nipples after each use, and run them through the hot wash and rinse cycle in your dishwasher.

◆ If you don't have a dishwasher, or doubt the purity of your water supply, sterilize equipment in the following way:

1 Wash and rinse the used bottles, rings, and nipples, then fill each bottle with the amount of water directed, cover with the nipples and caps, and boil in a sterilizer for 25 minutes.

2 After the bottles have cooled, remove them from the sterilizer and store them at room temperature until needed.

TIPS FOR BOTTLE FEEDING

◆ Hold the baby in a slightly sloping position—head higher than feet; otherwise she may gag or be sick.

◆ Don't force the baby to finish a bottle; she will know when she has had enough.

▼▼ Never leave a baby alone with the
◆◆ bottle propped up on a cushion when feeding. The wrong angle may cause the baby to take in too much air, causing discomfort or choking.

STARTING SOLID FOOD

◆ The American Academy of Pediatrics' Committee on Nutrition recommends introducing solid food sometime between four and six months. Any earlier is taxing to the baby's intestinal tract, which is not yet developed enough to handle nutrients other than those in breast milk or formula.

◆ Start by serving a couple of spoonfuls of solids along with the normal milk supply, then gradually reduce the amount of milk. Try one type of food at a time.

◆ Cereals usually are the first solid food a baby should have. Start with rice since it is the mildest and most readily digested cereal.

◆ Fruit is usually the next food to be introduced. Bananas can be prepared easily by mashing up a teaspoon or so in formula or milk. Applesauce, strained pears, and strained peaches usually follow.

◆ Vegetables can be introduced after two to four weeks. At first, they should be served separately from other foods. Start by serving strained, mild-flavored vegetables such as squash or sweet potatoes.

◆ Strained meats come next, usually a month after you've started serving vegetables. Meats are important because, as babies drink less and less milk, they need a new source of protein, iron, and vitamins.

◆ If you want to feed your baby an entirely vegetarian diet, check with your pediatrician to ensure that the selection of foods you've chosen supplies all needed nutrients.

◆ A change in the color and consistency of bowel movements is a normal result of a change in the diet, but if you've just added a new food and your baby develops diarrhea, constipation, a skin rash, etc., wait for several days before trying it again.

◆ When buying baby food, check the age group and contents label carefully.

◆ Give your child plenty of fluid. Diluted fresh fruit juice is nutritious and won't decay the teeth as will sugary fruit drinks.

IDEAS FOR HEALTHY SNACKS

Plan snacks carefully and consider them as a complement to the whole day's nutrition. Serve different foods in snacks and at mealtimes so your child doesn't lose interest in meals.

◆ Try serving frozen yogurt or ice milk in place of ice cream; they have less fat.

◆ If your baby has some teeth, try finger foods; they make eating easy and fun. Start with crackers, an apple slice, or a crunchy bread rusk.

◆ Cubes of cheese make a healthy snack and help to prevent tooth decay by neutralizing acids in the mouth.

Making snacks inviting. *Cut pieces of cheese into unusual shapes, or lay pieces of fruit out in a pattern or to look like a train or an animal.*

FOODS THAT MAY CAUSE PROBLEMS

Frequently cause problems

Berries	Corn	Nuts, oils,
Buckwheat	Cow's milk	extracts
Caffeine	Dairy	Peanut
Chocolate	products	butter
Citrus fruits	(all)	Pork
and juices	Egg whites	Wheat
Coconut	Fish (all)	Yeast
Cola drinks		

Sometimes cause problems

Bananas	Cottonseed	Potatoes
Beef	oil	(white)
Celery	Garlic	Prunes
Cherries	Melons	Spices
Chicken	Mushrooms	Spinach
Coloring	Onions	Tomato
agents	Peaches	products
	Plums	Vitamins

Seldom cause problems

Apples	Ginger ale,	Lamb
Apricots and	noncola	Lettuce
juice	carbonated	Oats
Bacon	drinks	Pears and
Barley	Grapes and	juice
Beets	juice	Pineapple
Carrots	Honey (not	and
Cranberries	good for	juice
and juice	babies)	Raisins

Freezing puree. *If you prepare too much puree, freeze it in ice-cube trays. You can thaw the blocks in the microwave, if you have one.*

Homemade food

◆ When preparing homemade food for infants, cook the food until very tender and remember to remove all stringy material and chunks from the food to prevent choking.

◆ Use fresh fruits and vegetables whenever possible. Cook in a minimal amount of water to maintain the nutrient content.

◆ The quickest and easiest way to puree foods for a baby is with a blender or food processor. Hand-held blenders in particular are good for small quantities.

Children who won't eat

◆ Don't force a child to eat or meals will become a battleground. Take the food away calmly and try again later when she is hungry. Don't give the child any snacks between meals for a while, until her appetite returns.

◆ Try making a game out of eating. Put vegetables on a piece of bread to form a face, serve food on a doll's plate, or give your child some blunt plastic "grown up" silverware.

◆ Let your child help you prepare snacks or meals; it may create more interest in the food.

GOOD NUTRITION AT A DAY-CARE CENTER

◆To make sure your baby's nutritional needs are met while he is cared for in your absence, spend some time talking with the operators of the facility to determine their attitudes, expectations, and competence.

◆A good facility makes appropriate foods available to children of all ages, but does not use food to reward or punish them. Children should be encouraged but not forced to eat.

◆Many facilities have a dietitian on staff or on call to prepare a varied menu consisting of selections from all food groups. You should ask to see the facility's meal plan.

◆Children who remain in a day-care facility for nine or more hours each day should be served at least two meals and two snacks.

◆If your baby is under 18 months old, you should be allowed to provide formula or hand-expressed breast milk. You also should be able to supply the foods you want your child to eat, along with feeding schedules.

◆A well-run day-care facility will not prop bottles in babies' mouths and leave them unattended while feeding.

◆Areas should be specially designated for eating only and the facility should enforce strict hand-washing routines (for children and staff), especially after they've used the toilet, changed diapers, or blown their noses, before they've brushed their teeth, and before and after they've eaten.

Minimizing mess

◆Confine eating to the kitchen or dining area so that mess is concentrated in one part of the house.

◆Have the baby use a bib when he starts on solids to keep clothes clean and stain-free.

◆If your baby doesn't like the stiffness of a bib, try using a cloth diaper or a terry-cloth hand towel to protect clothes.

◆Put newspaper or plastic sheeting under the high chair or table to protect the floor.

◆Keep the baby well away from walls with expensive coverings when eating: it is great fun for kids to see how far food will fly.

◆Attach a paper-towel holder to the wall near the high chair or to the back of the high chair so you'll be prepared for spills.

◆When your baby decides it is time for him to feed himself, let him. Besides allowing your child to use a spoon, prepare some foods that can be eaten without one, which makes for less mess and less frustration for both of you. Cut fruits and vegetables into cubes or slices minus the skins and seeds; shape mashed potatoes or rice into little bite-size balls, or cut bread into cubes.

Choosing a bib. *Use a plastic molded bib with a crumb catcher (above left) for a baby who is learning to feed herself or for a toddler; it's easier to contain the mess. Use machine-washable terry-cloth bibs for babies, since the plastic ones can rub the neck. The best are those with sleeves and a plastic backing (above right).*

◆Buy bowls with rubber suction pads on the bottom, which help to keep the bowl from being hurled onto the floor. Look for training cups with a weighted base, which help reduce spills.

TRAVEL AND OUTINGS

THE BEST time to set out on any trip with babies is immediately after they have been fed and changed.

If possible, ahead of time, find out what facilities are available where you are going; some places have a special room for feeding and changing, which is a real boon if you are going to be out for some time. Avoid places that do not have elevators or don't allow strollers at all. Plan your trips and outings when the roads and stores will be least crowded; avoid rush hours if you are using public transportation.

TAKING CHILDREN ON OUTINGS

◆ Always carry spare diapers and baby wipes and other changing items. If your child is bottle fed or on solid food, make sure you have sufficient supplies and a bib.

◆ If you will be eating out, ask for a table away from the main centers of activity. Have your own snacks for your baby and a selection of toys. Most restaurants provide high chairs or booster seats.

◆ Use a carrier or backpack for your child that leaves your hands free.

◆ Shop in the morning when the supermarkets are least crowded. Use a belt to secure

---

BUYING A STROLLER OR BABY CARRIAGE

◆ Choose a stroller with a wide wheelbase to prevent it from tipping over. Strollers with turnable—instead of fixed —front wheels are easiest to maneuver.

◆ Make sure the seat belt is sturdy, snug, and easily operated.

◆ See that the brakes are secure, convenient, and cannot be child-operated.

◆ Make sure there is a safety lock to keep the stroller from collapsing.

◆ Get a stroller with an adjustable seat so your child can lie back to sleep.

◆ Any built-in shopping basket should be positioned low on the back, directly above or in front of the rear wheels for maximum stability.

◆ **NOTE:** Look for the JPMA "Certified" seal on strollers you're buying.

Stroller. *Choose a stroller that can be opened with one hand and folds compactly, for ease of carrying.*

Carriage/stroller. *If you want an old-fashioned baby carriage get a carriage/stroller that converts into a compact stroller unit when your baby grows out of the carriage.*

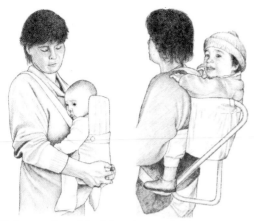

Baby carriers. *Use fabric slings to hold a young baby against your chest; make sure that the head is well supported (above left). Once a baby can support his head, he can be carried in a backpack (above right). Make sure the shoulder straps are well padded or they will dig into your shoulders, which is uncomfortable.*

your child in the cart, if necessary. Wheel the cart down the center of the aisles to keep your child from grabbing groceries as you pass by.

◆ Attach strings to your child's toys so you can fasten them to your cart or stroller.

◆ Dress your older child in bright colors so you can easily spot her when you go shopping. Toddlers and children like to wander in the aisles and can easily get lost.

Stroller safety

▼▼ Never leave your child unattended in a
◆ ◆ stroller. If you leave a stroller, park it so that it won't roll into the street, even if the brakes fail.

▼▼ Never put loaded shopping bags on the
◆ ◆ handles of a stroller—you might tip it backward. Choose a stroller with a basket underneath.

▼▼ Never push your stroller or carriage out
◆ ◆ into the street until you are certain there is nothing coming.

▼▼ Never tie a dog to a stroller; it may
◆ ◆ decide it likes something across the street and pull the stroller over.

▼▼ Never take a stroller with a baby in it on
◆ ◆ an escalator; always use an elevator or take the baby out and fold up the stroller before you step on the escalator.

CAR TRAVEL

◆ Secure babies and toddlers in special seats (choose the correct one for the child's weight to provide adequate protection). Put an older child in a child's safety seat. Don't put a child in the same safety belt as you: If there is an accident, your weight will crush the child.

◆ Always check that children's fingers will not be trapped when you close the door.

◆ Never turn around to talk to a child when you are driving. If the children are fighting, pull over at a safe place, stop the car, and iron it out. If you are on a highway, get off at the nearest exit.

◆ Always use child locks on rear doors, so you can open the door from the outside but the children can't open it accidentally. If your car doesn't have them, get some installed.

◆ Check that your child is correctly buckled into his car seat, that the seat is correctly buckled into the car, and that the shoulder straps fit snugly.

◆ Teach your child to always get out of the car on the sidewalk side—never into traffic.

◆ Make sure that your child knows not to lean out the car window or put a hand or arm outside, even when the car is stationary.

◆ It is never safe to leave your child unattended in a car, even for a short time.

▼▼ Don't leave hard or sharp things lying
◆ ◆ around inside the car. These will become missiles if the car stops suddenly.

◆ Encourage children to play quietly. Constant chatter, giggling, or yelling is distracting to the driver.

Long car trips

◆ Bring small cartons of fruit juice with straws for the children. Drinks can help to prevent travel sickness.

◆ Take some apples, dried fruit, or cubes of cheese for nibbling instead of cookies or candy. For young children, wrap apple slices in plastic wrap (to stop them from turning brown) and carry them along.

◆ Stop every hour or so for a few minutes and let the children stretch their legs; it'll relieve the boredom and release tension.

◆Keep a changing mat in the car for quick diaper changing, or a plastic potty if you are in the middle of potty training.

◆Keep a garbage bag in the car for litter and some paper towels and baby wipes for sticky fingers and faces.

◆A child's hanging shoe bag, placed over a side rear window, can be filled with toys and also serve to block out strong sunlight.

Train and plane trips

◆Bring enough entertainment with you so that your children won't spoil everyone else's journey by being bored. Take rattles or soft toys for young babies, books or games for toddlers and a pack of cards or a magnetic game, such as chess, for older children.

◆Choose a window seat if you are breast feeding; you'll have more privacy.

CAR SEATS

Under federal standards, all child seats must now be marked with the date of manufacture and the words "dynamically crash tested."

◆Infant car seats will provide protection until a child is about 9 to 12 months old (about 17–20 pounds). The safest model for an infant is a rear-facing seat (see below).

◆You can buy a convertible car seat designed to face rearward for infants and forward for children up to 4 years old or 40 pounds.

◆Use adjustable safety belts in combination with a car booster seat for children 3 and older, until they are tall enough to see out of the window (see below).

Toddler's car seat.
Buy one that has an adjustable back for greater comfort. Some seats fit into adult safety belts; others need a harness secured to the car frame.

Booster seat. *Use this in conjunction with a shoulder-lap seat belt for children who have grown out of the car seat (from 40 to 65 pounds) so that they can see out of the window.*

Rear-facing baby seat. *The safest model for infants, this can be used with an adult safety belt, on the front or back seat of the car.*

HOW TO AVOID TRAVEL SICKNESS

Travel sickness is perfectly real and very inconvenient and unpleasant for everyone, although it's not serious.

◆ If your child suffers from travel sickness regularly, check with your doctor and ask him or her to recommend some travel sickness medicine.

◆ Give your child a nutritious snack before setting out—nothing too rich or oily though.

◆ Take plenty of water and juice. Sucking mints or crystallized ginger can also help to prevent the feeling of nausea.

◆ Keep strong brown paper or plastic bags handy to be used as sick bags if worse comes to worst.

◆ Keep a window open—fresh air usually helps. Keep the heater as low as possible; a stuffy car can contribute to travel sickness.

◆ Take with you food, drink, bibs, etc. as you would in the car, because there may not be dining facilities.

◆ Take disposable diapers, baby wipes, lotions, etc., in your hand luggage. And carry several plastic bags with you for dirty diapers acquired on the way.

◆ When flying, call the airline before reserving your ticket to find out what facilities are available for children. Get a direct flight if possible, so that you won't have to change planes. Request a bulkhead seat, preferably near a window. These are the seats at the front of each compartment, and they have more room for changing and stowing bags and bits and pieces. If you are flying overnight, ask for a special "sky cot" so that the baby can sleep in it during the flight.

KEEPING THE CHILDREN OCCUPIED

When preparing for long journeys with children, leave battery-operated toys behind in favor of simpler objects. Wrap some of the small objects in boxes of their own, then put everything in one large shoe box or backpack. If you're traveling with more than one youngster, make sure each child has a personalized shoe box.

For Toddlers
◆ small, soft doll and bottle
◆ small cars, boats, and trucks and small cloth bag with drawstring to keep them in
◆ small reusable drawing slate
◆ small blocks that fit inside one another
◆ plastic animals with movable but not removable parts
◆ sunglasses
◆ small unbreakable mirror
◆ small, soft hairbrush
◆ plastic pinch clothespins

For Preschoolers
◆ small sewing cards (made from punching holes in picture postcards) and shoelaces
◆ small doll, clothes, and doll bottle
◆ play money
◆ small cars and boats
◆ reusable drawing slate
◆ cube puzzle with movable but not removable parts
◆ picture books
◆ cassette storybook and song tapes
◆ sunglasses
◆ old maid card game

For 5- to 7-Year-Olds
◆ card game
◆ colored pipe cleaners
◆ hourglass-shaped three-minute timer
◆ reusable drawing slate
◆ dot-to-dot book
◆ colored pencils (with pencil sharpener)
◆ pad of paper
◆ cube puzzle with movable but not removable parts
◆ storybooks
◆ sticker books
◆ unbreakable magnifying glass

Pet Care

CHOOSING A PET

WHEN CHOOSING a pet, start at the library; get to know about pets from books first. Then, think of the conditions and space you have available and the characteristics of the animal: Dogs can be boisterous and noisy and need to be walked at least once a day, whereas cats are more discreet and relatively self-sufficient; both will leave hair on the furniture. Of the smaller pets, hamsters usually come out and play at night but sleep during the day, so they are not much fun for children. Guinea pigs are friendly and make good starter pets.

A word of warning that applies to all pets—steer clear of any animal that shows signs of aggression.

DOGS AND CATS

◆ It is usually best to buy a dog or cat from a reputable breeder so you know the animal's parents and ancestry.

◆ Don't buy puppies or kittens over the telephone; go and see them before making your choice because you may not like them.

◆ If you take your children to see the puppy or kitten before buying it, don't let the sight of their eager faces make you forget your selection criteria and keep you from examining the animal carefully.

◆ Ask the owner to provide documentation for the puppy or kitten. This should include the vaccination certificate signed by a veterinarian, if the animal is of an age where it should have had any injections. If the animal has a pedigree, you should also be given a pedigree form and registration transfer form.

◆ If any vaccinations have yet to be given, find out when they are due.

◆ A puppy or kitten must be at least six weeks old before it is taken from its mother because it needs to be fed by her until then and can suffer psychological problems if separated any earlier.

Choosing a dog

Dogs are devoted and offer protection and companionship, but they also need regular care and attention. They are ideal where someone is at home most of the day and regular walking and feeding times can be kept.

◆ Take your time in choosing a dog that suits your own life-style, personality, and environment. Larger dogs are expensive to feed and need a lot of exercise; small dogs take up less space but may be yappy; medium-sized dogs are usually sociable and good with children. Remember that a dog will be with you for around eight to 15 years.

◆Ask yourself if you want a male or a female. Males are more outgoing but more likely to wander; females are somewhat more home-loving but will come into season, will attract males, and are very likely to become pregnant unless you take precautions, such as walking them on a leash whenever they are in season, fencing your yard, or getting them spayed.

◆A mixed-breed of dog will usually be healthy and stable; pedigree dogs may be inbred and more high strung.

◆If you want a pedigree dog, consider several breeds. Read books or dog magazines to find out how much a particular breed will eat, how much exercise it will need, and note any particular idiosyncrasies related to the breed. Talk to friends who have dogs about their dog's characteristics. Go to a dog show to get a view of different breeds and how well-behaved or temperamental they are.

Buying a dog

There is one golden rule: Always make a careful study of the animal's condition and state of health. Never buy a sick animal.

◆One of the main considerations is the dog's personality; avoid an animal that cowers or is excessively boisterous.

◆If you buy at a kennel or pet store, look at the other animals there to make sure they are happy and healthy.

◆Ask to see the animal's parents if possible. Their temperament will give you a clue as to how the puppy will turn out.

◆Have a veterinarian examine any dog you are thinking of buying. He or she will be able to confirm that the dog is old enough to be taken from its mother, and that it is free of worms and generally healthy.

◆Puppies must be vaccinated against canine distemper, canine parvovirus, canine lepto-spirosis, canine viral hepatitis, and rabies. Ask your veterinarian about other diseases that your puppy may need to be immunized against. A puppy must not be allowed out for two weeks after each vaccination, because it will not be protected against the disease. The first injection is usually given at 10 to 12 weeks, the second at 14 to 16 weeks (see page 315).

◆The best time to bring a pup home to its new family is between six and seven weeks of age. Have food, water, and a cozy bed of its own waiting for it. Don't handle it too much at first.

SPOTTING A HEALTHY PUPPY AND KITTEN

◆A healthy puppy should be plump without being bloated.

◆The eyes should be bright and alert without cataracts or discharges.

◆Inspect the skin and ears; they should be without irritations and smell clean.

◆Check that the feces in the pen are well-formed.

◆The body should be well-proportioned, not spindly.

◆If it is a male, make sure it has two testicles.

◆When buying a kitten, look for a healthy, good-natured one. It should be lively and inquisitive, with bright eyes, a smooth coat, clean and dry ears, a pink mouth with white teeth, and a damp nose. The abdomen should be slightly rounded but not hard; make sure there are no lumps (a sign of hernia).

Clean, pink mouth

Clean ears

Clean eyes

Clean nose

Smooth coat

Clean abdomen

Clean ears

Clean eyes

Cold, clean nose

Smooth coat

Plump abdomen

Buying a cat

A cat will develop an affectionate bond with its owner, but will remain far more independent than other pets. Cats are not expensive to feed, and will exercise and clean themselves. They can live indoors happily, so are ideal pets for city apartment dwellers.

◆Select a cat that is playful and friendly. With kittens, choose the bigger, first-to-come-forward animal, rather than the smallest, meekest member of the litter, which is apt to be sickly. A healthy cat should live for 12 to 14 years or longer.

◆ Wherever you obtain your cat, arrange for a checkup at the veterinarian's, and make sure that the kitten is given all the necessary vaccinations at about the time of purchase. An adult cat should have been vaccinated as a kitten and been given regular "boosters" thereafter.

◆Make a grown new cat feel at home by putting a little butter on its paws; the good taste will be linked with the new family so that it is less likely to run back to its previous home.

Providing for a new cat. *Make sure you have a litter box and bed waiting for your kitten or cat, and its own food and water bowls.*

SMALL ANIMALS

These are mostly trouble-free, provided you give them plenty of scope for exercise within their cages, enough food and water (very important), and clean out the cages regularly.

Rabbits, hamsters, gerbils, guinea pigs, mice, and rats

◆It is best to get all these from a pet shop or breeder, so you can be reasonably sure they are healthy. The breeder also will be able to give you advice on feeding habits and routine care.

◆If you are thinking of buying these animals

from a pet shop, ask the owner how long they have been there; the longer they have been cooped up with animals of the same species, the more likely that the females are going to be pregnant.

◆When buying one of these animals, look for shiny fur, bright eyes, healthy skin, and liveliness.

◆ Most of these animals need exercise equipment in their cages; this is available from most pet shops.

◆Don't get more than one hamster for a cage because hamsters are solitary and territorial, and will fight with each other. Rabbits, gerbils, guinea pigs, mice, and rats, however, like company—get two females unless you want them to reproduce.

◆Rabbits are suitable only for a home with a sizable yard because they need a large run to play in.

Birds

Caged birds make good pets, and a few birds can be kept at a fraction of what a large dog costs. Seed-eating birds, such as parakeets and canaries, are economical to feed because their food is nonperishable and can be bought in bulk.

◆Buy all birds from a breeder if possible; they are usually healthier than birds in a pet shop. The breeder also will be able to advise you about their needs and care.

◆If possible, pick out your birds personally from the breeder so you can inspect them. It is usually best to buy birds bred in the current year as they adapt to new surroundings quickest.

◆Parakeets are relatively cheap to buy and keep, are lively and colorful, and sometimes learn to mimic human speech. They will live for about seven or eight years and some for more than 10 years.

◆Canaries, like parakeets, are lively and attractive, and they have a pretty song. They are less excitable than parakeets.

◆If you want more than one parakeet or canary, but don't want eggs, get two cocks; hens tend to squabble. For other types of birds, check with the breeder.

FEEDING

THE STATEMENT "we are what we eat" applies to animals as well as people. Dogs and cats need protein, fat, carbohydrates, vitamins, minerals, and fiber, for optimum health. And like us, they enjoy an occasional change or a treat. It is also vital that they have a clean supply of drinking water daily.

DOGS AND CATS

▼▼ Keep cat and dog bowls separate from
♦ ♦ each other, and wash them carefully every day.

♦ Don't feed cats on dog food, because they need more vitamins and proteins than dogs and will not get sufficient nutrients from dog food alone.

Feeding dishes. *Shallow dishes are best for cats; higher, narrow-necked ones are suitable for long-eared dogs. Plastic dishes may discolor your pet's nose.*

Giving your dog the right bone. *Rawhide bones are the best choice, as animal bones can cause severe problems. However, the odd natural bone provides hours of pleasure and to some extent it also cleans the teeth and exercises the jaw. The only safe bones are large "knuckle" bones that won't splinter. If you can, keep an eye on your dog while it eats.*

to feel its ribs along its chest without them sticking out or being buried in fat. The coat should be smooth and shiny.

▼▼ Never give your dog pieces of backbone,
♦ ♦ fish, or poultry bones, or any well-cooked bones; they can be sharp or may splinter and lodge in the dog's throat.

Feeding a dog

♦ A dog needs certain nutritional components in the right proportions; variety is not necessary. It isn't a good idea to give your adult dog as much food as it will eat; a dog often goes on eating long after it is full. Follow label guidelines; the quantity that produces the best results in terms of growth is about 80 percent of what a dog would eat if unchecked. Most dogs over 12 months have one balanced meal a day.

♦ Quality canned, dried, or semimoist packaged dog foods provide a balanced diet. The quality of generic and private label dog food varies.

♦ If a dog is fed correctly, you should be able

Feeding a cat

♦ Variety is the key when it comes to a cat's menu. Accustom a kitten to a wide variety of food from the day it is weaned, so it doesn't become a fussy eater. Pet cats should have a diet that is 25 percent protein.

♦ High-quality cat foods are formulated to contain all of what a cat needs.

♦ Dry food may cause kidney and bladder problems. If you use it, you must provide plenty of fresh water at all times. Provide milk only if your cat will drink it; most cats prefer water.

▼▼ Don't feed a cat poultry bones as these
♦ ♦ can splinter and choke the cat.

SMALL ANIMALS

Most small animals need their diet supplemented with fresh fruit and vegetables to provide them with extra vitamins and nutrients.

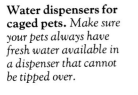

Water dispensers for caged pets. *Make sure your pets always have fresh water available in a dispenser that cannot be tipped over.*

Feeding birds

◆ Give birds seeds with husks as the basis of their diet. Millet and canary seed are good staples for parakeets and canaries; sunflower seeds are good for parrots. Talk to breeders about seed mixtures for other types of birds.
◆ Hard-billed birds, such as canaries and finches, and soft-billed birds, such as mynahs, have different requirements and must be fed appropriate diets accordingly.
◆ Avoid colored millet "treats" because the coloring can be harmful to birds in large quantities.
◆ Supplement seed with fruit, such as apples, bananas, and grapes, and green vegetables, such as spinach, to give birds extra vitamins.
◆ Provide grit (available from pet shops) to aid the bird's digestion.

Trimming your bird's beak. *Wedge a piece of cuttlebone into the side of the bird's cage every so often, so that your bird can keep its beak and claws in trim.*

Feeding rabbits

◆ Give rabbits commercial pellets and supplement them daily with carrots, grass, lettuce, and dandelion leaves.
◆ Make sure the rabbits have enough drinking water, because the pellets are dry and absorb water when they are swallowed.

Feeding hamsters and gerbils

◆ Give them about a tablespoon of hamster mix per day. You can buy this premixed from a pet shop or mix it up yourself.
◆ Hamsters need some green food every day: chickweed, clover, cow parsley, dandelion leaves, and grass are good. Avoid cabbage, because it makes their urine smell, and carrots, which stain their fur.

Feeding guinea pigs

◆ Feed them on pellets or a special mix, available from a pet shop. Be sure the mix contains vitamin C, a unique requirement for guinea pigs. You must provide adequate drinking water with these dry foods because guinea pigs get very thirsty.

Giving guinea pigs a treat. *Supplement the diet of your guinea pigs with vegetables, such as cabbage and cauliflower leaves, grass or fresh hay to help digestion.*

Feeding mice and rats

◆ Mice and rats should be fed pellets and given treats made from stale bread and dried oats soaked in milk. Fruit and tomatoes and hamster mix are also good for variety.

EVERYDAY HEALTH CARE

PREVENTION is better than cure, so if you make sure your pet has a well-balanced diet, provide it with clean surroundings, and inspect it regularly for infection, you can steer clear of most health problems.

GENERAL HEALTH AND HYGIENE TIPS

◆Choose a healthy, lively animal to begin with, and be aware of any conditions or diseases to which the breed is prone.

◆To keep your pet happy and satisfy its territorial instincts, provide it with an area of its own for eating and sleeping.

◆Keep all bedding, cages, and feeding utensils clean, warm, and dry—hygiene is a critical factor in maintaining health. Clean bird cages twice a week, rodent cages once a week, and cat litter boxes daily.

◆Make sure dogs and cats receive the necessary boosters against common diseases. Ask your vet about any local diseases your pet should be immunized against.

◆Check the eyes, ears, nose, mouth, feet, skin, and genital and anal areas regularly to ensure they are free of dirt, discharge, and abnormalities. De-flea and de-worm every six months or so, but never use preparations meant for dogs on cats; cats are more sensitive to toxins.

◆Always keep animal dishes separate from the family's.

GENERAL CARE

◆Groom all furry animals regularly to remove loose hair and clean the skin. Regular grooming also helps strengthen the bond between an animal and its owner.

◆While grooming, check for fleas or lice and take appropriate action.

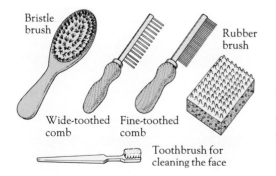

Bristle brush

Rubber brush

Wide-toothed comb   Fine-toothed comb

Toothbrush for cleaning the face

Grooming kits. *Use a wide-toothed comb first to break up long, matted fur, and then a fine-toothed comb. Brush with a bristle brush, following the direction of the hair growth. Brush the hairs around a cat's face with a toothbrush. To groom a short-haired cat, use a fine-toothed comb and a rubber brush.*

Dogs

Frequent grooming is a good practice; bathe your dog whenever it gets dirty, or if it seems to have a lot of dandruff. While a dog is molting, brush it daily.

◆Always groom the coat before bathing, to reduce tangling and matting. Never use household detergents or a harsh soap; they can cause skin reactions. Use a mild dog or baby shampoo and warm water. It is easiest to wash a dog with a hand-held shower spray.

◆Towel-dry or use a hair dryer if the dog will accept it. Dry shampoos are ideal for a quick cleaning if the dog is not very dirty.

◆Inspect the inside of a dog's mouth every month. Foul breath and eating difficulties may indicate that something is wrong.

Clipping a dog's claws. *Trim your dog's claws so they are just clear of, or just touching, the ground. Use dog nail clippers; don't overclip, or you will cut the nail bed.*

HANDLING AN INJURED ANIMAL

DOG

◆Approach an injured dog cautiously and talk to it reassuringly. Try to put an improvised muzzle, made from a tie or a bandage, around its snout to stop it from biting, unless it has a chest injury or has trouble breathing.

◆To move a dog, pull it onto a blanket or slide a blanket under it, if possible; with the help of two other people to support the head, back, and pelvis, lift it.

CAT

◆Cats in pain may bite or strike with their claws. Don't move an injured cat unless it is in danger; get the owner first. Don't raise or prop up its head because its airway may become blocked and it won't be able to breathe. If you do have to move it, slide a blanket or sheet under it and carry it to a quiet, warm place.

◆To restrain a frightened cat, hold it by the scruff of the neck and apply firm but gentle pressure with your other hand placed over its chest.

BIRD

◆Approach an injured bird slowly, to avoid frightening it.

Picking up an injured bird. *Gently scoop it up with both hands, with your index and middle fingers on either side of its head. Place it in a dark, warm, quiet place, preferably an enclosed box.*

Cats

Long-haired cats molt all year round and need daily grooming (15–30 minutes); short-haired cats require only two grooming sessions per week.

◆Stains should be removed from the face daily; use a warm, weak salt solution.

◆To prevent a buildup of tartar, once a week, clean a cat's teeth with a soft tooth-brush dipped in a salt solution.

◆To prevent a buildup of wax in the ear and subsequent irritation, clean out the ears using one or two cotton balls lightly moistened with oil or rubbing alcohol.

◆Untrimmed claws may grow into the pad of the paw; use sharp scissors or nail clippers to cut off the white tip, making sure not to cut the quick.

◆Use a seam ripper to tease apart badly matted hair prior to brushing.

◆Brush talcum powder or fuller's earth into a long-haired cat's fur to keep it from matting; brush it off immediately.

◆Polish a short-haired cat's coat with a piece of silk or velvet, or a chamois leather cloth to bring out its glossiness.

Making a scratching post. *Nail a piece of wood vertically to a base (you can cover it with carpet) to provide a scratching post for an older cat or one that is confined indoors. This will help keep your cat's nails trimmed naturally.*

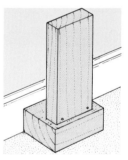

Birds

◆Get a parakeet's beak or claws trimmed by the veterinarian if they are getting too long. If the beak is not cut, it will curl around and eventually prevent the bird from feeding. If the claws are not cut, the bird may not be able to perch or walk properly.

Small animals

◆Most small animals such as hamsters and mice will groom themselves. If you want to groom them, use a soft baby's brush. Guinea pigs in particular may need brushing because they have longer fur.

COMMON DISEASES

ABSCESSES
Common in cats, especially unneutered males; also can occur in hamsters and gerbils.

Symptoms
Painful swelling or foul-smelling, creamlike or blood-colored discharge from wounds.

Treatment
Take a cat to the vet, who will probably prescribe antibiotics and may lance or surgically drain the abscess. For hamsters and gerbils, bathe the area with water and a mild antiseptic. When the abscess breaks, gently squeeze it to drain it.

ALLERGY
Common in dogs.

Symptoms
Itchy and inflamed paws, armpits, abdomen, and thighs, or large raised blotches on the animal's skin.

Treatment
Take the dog to the vet, to identify the cause.

ANEMIA
Occurs in all animals as a result of worms, infection, disease, or injury.

Symptoms
Poor appetite, weakness, high temperature, pale eye color.

Treatment
Take the animal to the vet, who may give it antibiotics and a blood transfusion.

ASTHMA
Affects dogs, cats, mice, and rats.

Symptoms
Harsh breathing and coughing.

Treatment
Take dogs and cats to the vet for advice and treatment. For mice and rats, place them in a dust-free environment for 10 days and reduce the amount of dry foods. Don't give them any milk.

CANCER
This can affect any animal.

Symptoms
Variable, depending on type and site; skin cancers usually are noted as growths, while cancer in other sites may produce listlessness and organ dysfunction, such as hepatitis, kidney failure, and anemia, or other signs.

Treatment
Go to the vet; never wait for swellings to grow large. Small cancers may be successfully treated.

COLDS AND CHILLS
Can affect most animals.

Symptoms
Lethargy, sneezing, and shivering, loss of appetite, and wet discharge from nose and eyes. Persistent coughing may be diagnosed as bronchitis. In addition, birds with colds puff out their feathers.

Treatment
Take a cat, dog, or bird to the vet, who will probably give it antibiotics. For a guinea pig, isolate the sick animal and keep it warm; feed it bread soaked in warm milk. If it doesn't improve within three days, take it to the vet. For mice, rats, hamsters, and gerbils, isolate the sick animal in a box smeared with a vapor inhalant and keep it warm. Feed it small pieces of food mixed with cod liver oil.

CONSTIPATION
Affects dogs, cats, and birds.

Symptoms
In dogs and cats, constant straining and squatting to no effect. In constipated birds, the droppings are white.

Treatment
Add bran (for fiber) to the food and give mineral oil by mouth.
If persistent, refer to a vet.

DERMATITIS (Eczema)
Common in dogs and cats.

Symptoms
Itching and scratching; licking or even biting the skin; and loss of hair.

Treatment
Take the animal to the vet to find the cause; it may be mites, an allergy, or germs lodged in the skin.

DIARRHEA
Can affect any animal.

Symptoms
Frequent liquid bowel movements and soiled fur or feathers.

Treatment
For dogs and cats, stop all food for 24 hours, but provide them with continual water in small amounts. If it persists, take the animal to the vet. Feed hamsters and gerbils, guinea pigs, mice and rats, and birds on dry food only until the problem clears up.

DISTEMPER (Hard pad)
Affects dogs only.

Symptoms
High temperature, nasal and eye discharge, prominent blood vessels in whites of eyes, severe diarrhea, and sometimes vomiting, frothing at the mouth, and epileptic fits.

Treatment
Immediate treatment by a vet. This is a serious disease, so prevention is better than cure. Get your dog vaccinated and don't forget the boosters.

EAR INFECTION

Inflammation of the ear in cats and dogs, although guinea pigs can get it from seed husks that get stuck in their ears.

Symptoms
Head shaking, scratching, and a foul-smelling discharge from the ear.

Treatment
Depends on the cause, so take the animal to the vet. With a guinea pig, you can sometimes dislodge a husk with a cotton swab.

FLEAS AND LICE

These affect most animals.

Symptoms
Scratching and excessive grooming; these parasites or their droppings are visible if you inspect the animal's fur.

Treatment
Apply antiparasitic aerosols or powders specifically marked for dogs and cats. Apply flea powder for cats to hamsters and gerbils, guinea pigs, mice, and rats.

HEATSTROKE

Usually affects animals locked in a car directly in the sun on a warm day or ones left outside without shade.

Symptoms
Distress, gasping, unconsciousness, convulsions.

Treatment
This is an emergency; use cold towels and, with large dogs, water hosing, to bring down the temperature. Call the vet.

INJURIES

Treat as soon as possible to prevent infection.

Treatment
Cuts or bites can be treated by washing in warm water and a mild antiseptic. More serious injuries must be treated by a vet who will advise on care after treatment.

SCALY FACE

Common in parakeets

Symptoms
Horny, yellow crusts on either side of the beak and sometimes on the legs.

Treatment
Liquids or lotions are available from pet shops to treat it; disinfect the cage.

WORMS

Affects dogs and cats.

Symptoms
Poor growth, anemia, and general unfitness are symptomatic of roundworm; small segments of worm found sticking to the fur under the animal's tail are symptomatic of tapeworm (this usually affects adult animals only).

Treatment
Use antiworm treatments approved by your vet. All puppies and kittens should be routinely dewormed.
▼▼ Tapeworms and round-
♦ ♦ worms found in cats are of different species from those in dogs. Do not give cats tablets or medicines prescribed for dogs (or vice versa).

VETERINARY CARE FOR DOGS AND CATS

DOGS		
VACCINATION	**WORMING**	**SPAYING/CASTRATING**
First vaccination 6–8 weeks in high-risk areas.	3 weeks old. Then every 2–3 weeks until the puppy is 16 weeks ($3\frac{1}{2}$ months) old.	Spay a bitch between 6 and 12 months of age.
10–12 weeks in normal areas.	6 months later.	Castrate a dog from 6 months to a year.
Second vaccination 14–16 weeks.	Every 12 months.	
Third vaccination (canine, parvovirus only) 4–5 months.		

CATS		
VACCINATION	**WORMING**	**SPAYING/CASTRATING**
First vaccination 8–10 weeks.	At 5–6 weeks old.	Spay a queen at 4 months or later.
Second vaccination 12–16 weeks.	Every 4 months for tapeworm.	Castrate a tom at 9 months or later.
Boosters every 12 months.	Every 6 months for roundworm.	

PET CARE WHILE YOU GO ON VACATION

◆ Get a good friend or neighbor to feed and exercise your cat or dog every day and clean out litter boxes; otherwise you will have to board your animals at a kennel.

◆ Leave small pets with a friend or neighbor; they are easier to take care of than dogs or cats so most people are less reluctant to take care of them.

◆ If you are leaving a cat alone over the weekend, buy double bowls with a lid and a timing device. Fill both bowls before you leave, then set the lid on the second bowl to open at the next day's feeding time.

TIPS FOR LONG CAR JOURNEYS

◆ Taking your pet regularly on short rides several weeks before a long car trip may help to prevent motion sickness and apprehension.

◆ Bring along plenty of paper towels.

◆ Take a dog for a long walk before a trip; bring a covered litter box along for a cat; it may run away if let out of the car.

◆ Give your pet a drink and about one-third of its normal feed before departure unless you know it can't tolerate any food.

◆ On very long trips, give your pet a small meal after 4 to 5 hours. A little food in the stomach can help it settle down.

◆ Stop every 2 to 3 hours along the road to give a dog a chance to stretch, relieve itself, and drink.

TRAVELING WITH PETS

◆ Make sure in advance you can take animals on public transportation; most trains and buses do not accept them.

◆ Before a long trip, have your pet examined by a veterinarian; ask for a certificate of good health and proof of vaccinations, and carry the papers with you.

◆ If you are traveling to a foreign country, make sure your dog's shots are current and comply with the regulations of the country. Find out if the country you are traveling to has quarantine restrictions.

◆ Prepare a travel kit containing a vacuum-sealed bottle for water, a water bowl and feeding dish, food, a leash, flea spray, a brush, a blanket, and a toy.

◆ Take along supplies of the pet's usual food. This helps prevent stress caused by unfamiliarity and diarrhea from changes in diet.

◆ Carry small dogs and all cats in a well-ventilated pet carrier; birds and other small pets should be in cages or gnawproof boxes.

▼▼ Weaned puppies younger than 8 weeks
◆ ◆ should not be shipped.

▼▼ Air travel is not recommended for
◆ ◆ females that are in heat or nursing.

◆ Most dogs and cats, if started young, travel well in autos, but as a rule, dogs are much happier car passengers than cats.

◆ Cats can behave in a distressed manner and interfere with your ability to drive if left loose in a car; they are better off in a carrier.

◆ Keep dogs in a carrier or in the back of the car behind a metal grille; remove their leashes.

▼▼ Don't ever leave animals in a hot car;
◆ ◆ they dehydrate quickly and can die from heatstroke. Always keep a car window slightly open to provide air.

Putting a cat in a basket. *Don't chase the cat around the house. Close the doors and windows and leave the carrier open. Wait for a quiet moment, then lift the cat up with one hand under its chest, using the other to stroke its back gently. Put it in bottom first and keep your hand on its back while you close the door.*

TRAINING CATS AND DOGS

THE AIM of training animals ranges from simple control within the home and acceptable behavior outside it, to strict obedience-style training. It is essential to toilet train your dogs and cats. If you also train them to obey certain commands, you will find that they are easier to get along with and better behaved. This is especially important with large, energetic dogs. Dogs and cats should wear collars with tags that bear your name and phone number.

OBEDIENCE AND HOUSE-TRAINING

◆ Give your dog or cat a name as soon as you get it and use the name frequently, so that it becomes used to it. A short name is best because it has more immediacy when it is called out and animals respond to it better.

◆ Begin toilet training puppies and kittens as soon as you get them. The younger they are, the quicker they learn.

◆ Start early to praise good behavior generously, with a stroke or pat and encouraging sounds, and give the animal a firm scolding when it behaves badly. Teach your dog or cat the meaning of "No" (i.e., stop what you're doing at once). Say it firmly but not aggressively. If necessary, restrain the animal physically from doing what it is not supposed to, until it understands.

▼▼ Don't hit your dog or cat. You may
◆ ◆ injure it, or it may grow to fear you and become difficult to approach.

◆ Don't feed a dog or cat from your table; it will start to expect it and beg. Also, this is not hygienic.

Toilet training a puppy. *To begin with, confine the puppy to one room and spread newspapers over the floor. The puppy will soon restrict itself to one area and you can remove the surrounding paper.*

floor. Gradually move the newspaper toward the door. Then move the paper outside, and finally remove it altogether. When there is no paper, the puppy will know that the only place it can relieve itself is outside.

◆ Take the puppy out when it wakes, after a meal, and after a period of activity. Watch it closely and try to catch it before it urinates. If it looks anxious or uncomfortable, walks in a circle, whines, or barks, act promptly; take it outside and stay with it until it relieves itself, and then praise it immediately.

◆ Never punish a puppy for accidents. Ignore it (this is punishment enough) when it goes where you don't want it to, and praise it when it gets it right.

◆ Once you start taking your dog for walks, encourage it to relieve itself in the gutter, not on the sidewalk or in parks. (In some places you must sweep up and dispose of the feces.)

House-training dogs

◆ Try keeping your puppy in an open-sided wire crate whenever it is not being supervised, played with, fed, watered, or exercised. If, in addition to a small bed, it has just enough room to turn around, it will try hard to keep its crate clean.

◆ Or, at night keep the puppy penned in a room or part of it with newspaper on the

Behavioral training for dogs

Dogs are pack animals. You are your dog's pack leader and you should develop a firm control so that it knows where it stands.

◆ Only one member of the household should train a dog; otherwise it will get

FOUR FUNDAMENTAL COMMANDS FOR A DOG

"HEEL": The dog must walk at the same pace as you on your left side. Repeat "Heel" regularly and point to your leg. Give a sharp jerk on the leash if it veers off, and leave the leash slack when the dog keeps close. Teaching this command will take patience and time.

"SIT": With your leash hand, lift the dog's chin upward and press gently but firmly on the dog's rump with the other, while giving the command to sit in a quiet but firm voice. When the dog sits, stroke it and praise it.

"COME": Command the dog to sit, then walk a few yards away. Turn and call the dog by name, stressing the command "come," while giving a little tug on the leash to show your dog what you mean.

"STAY": Make the dog sit. Holding the leash vertically and taut, command "stay" and walk around the dog in an ever-widening circle. Correct any attempt to move with a gentle but firm jerk of the leash. Repeat the command as you gradually move out of its sight. The dog should stay until you return.

confused. Once it has learned the commands, other members of the family can use them, but not all at once.

◆ Keep the lessons short and make them fun so that the dog doesn't get bored. Develop a bond of affection with the dog and make it feel pride in its achievements.

◆ Attend dog-training classes with your dog if you can—you may find them useful.

◆ Train the dog to accept a collar and leash early on. Use the leash while you train the dog to obey commands; in time, you will find that the leash won't be necessary.

◆ Discourage your dog from jumping up to greet you, however tempting it is to invite it to do so when it is a puppy. If it grows into a large dog, you will soon regret its jumping up. A firm "No" and a definite push down will help to stop the habit.

◆ Persistent bad habits can be cured eventually if you are consistent about diverting the dog's attention.

◆ Allow your dog to bark at strangers—a barking dog is a very effective burglar deterrent. But teach it to stop when you say "No."

◆ When teething, or if left alone too much, puppies and young dogs often chew up

shoes, clothes, books, and furniture. Keep all chewable temptations out of reach and give rawhide bones (see page 310) and other legitimate chewable things. Don't give a dog an old shoe because it will think that it is allowed to chew all shoes, old and new.

House-training cats

Cats are instinctively clean and prefer not only to relieve themselves in private but also to bury their waste.

◆ Provide a litter box for an indoor cat or new kitten. Keep the box in a quiet area. A kitten may have to be confined to the area around the box but will soon learn. Remove solid litter from the box at least once a day.

◆ To train a kitten to use the backyard, put the box outside and take the kitten to it after it has had a meal. Eventually remove the box and place the kitten on a suitable spot for scratching a hole.

🍂 **GREEN TIP:** Scatter orange peel over areas of the yard where you don't want cats to defecate. They don't like the smell and will stay away.

Protecting wooden furniture from puppies. *To stop a puppy from chewing on wooden furniture, dab oil of cloves on the wood.*

Using a cat flap. *If you have a backyard, allow a ready means of access to it, such as a cat flap. Some cat flaps are simply a swing door; others are more sophisticated and are activated by a device on the cat's collar.*

Health and Safety

SAFETY IN THE HOME

M OST ACCIDENTS occur at home and many of them are preventable, so it is important that your home be as safe as possible. This is especially true if you are living with elderly people, who are less quick to react to hazards and can be seriously injured, or young children.

ROOM-BY-ROOM SAFETY

To ensure that there are no accidents waiting to happen in your home, check the recommended safety features illustrated on the following pages. Take note of the layout and location of items from room to room and how alterations might be made to increase the level of safety throughout your home.

General Safety Tips
◆ Check all electrical cords. They are dangerous if frayed or cracked and should be replaced without delay.
◆ Furniture should be solid so that it can't be easily pulled or tipped over.
◆ Make all upper-story windows safe by installing safety stops, catches, or bars.
◆ Replace cracked vinyl or linoleum flooring or tiles. If you have smooth-tiled or hardwood floors, use a special polish to make the surface nonskid. Repair or replace rugs that are unraveling or lifting at the corners.
▼▼ Never keep a loaded gun in the house
◆ ◆ and keep guns and ammunition locked up separately.
◆ Keep all machinery and tools locked away.
◆ Avoid furniture (generally upholstered pieces and beds) that is made of polyurethane foam because the foam gives off lethal fumes if it catches fire.
◆ When visiting friends who have no children, check the house for possible hazards for your own youngsters. Breakable or sharp objects, accessible cleaning chemicals, furniture placed beneath open windows, and fireplaces without screens are all potentially dangerous.

Electricity

◆Cover empty outlets with outlet covers so children can't poke things into them.

◆Don't leave electrical cords where children can reach them or let the cords trail across a room, under a rug, or behind curtains.

▼▼Don't touch any electrical appliance,
◆ ◆ socket, or switch with wet hands; you could receive an electrical shock.

◆Buy only electrical equipment with an Underwriters Laboratories label on it, which shows that it has been checked and has passed certain safety regulations. Use only fuses and circuit breakers with the U.L. label on them.

◆To prevent an accident, turn off any electrical appliance and unplug it before checking or repairing any piece of equipment. Turn the main power off before checking a socket or light fixture, or changing a fuse in the fuse box.

◆Replace frayed cords; taping them up is not good enough.

◆Replace damaged plugs immediately; they are dangerous.

◆Check an appliance (or get it checked) if a plug feels unusually warm to the touch or has scorch marks (see chart on page 236).

Medications and household chemicals

◆Buy chemicals and medications with child-proof tops and always keep them in a locked cabinet (don't leave the key lying about where a child could find it).

▼▼Leave chemicals in their original bottles;
◆ ◆ never put a poisonous substance in a container that previously held a harmless substance; your child may confuse the two and try to drink it.

◆Keep medications and chemicals in clearly marked containers; discard out-of-date medications.

◆Don't leave aerosol cans where a child can reach them; the nozzle is easily depressed and the force of the spray could cause injury to the eyes.

Fire safety

◆Store paints, paint thinners, and other flammable materials in their original containers—away from fire sources.

◆Keep trash in covered containers and dispose of it regularly.

◆Develop a family escape plan by sketching the layout of each floor in your home, including windows, doors, and stairways. Mark out *two* escape routes from each room.

◆Hold frequent fire drills, including some at night, so everyone will know what to do.

◆Install at least one smoke detector in the hallway leading to the bedrooms; consider installing one on each level. If the detector is battery operated, check batteries annually.

◆Keep plenty of fire extinguishers; put one in the kitchen and at least one on each floor.

FIRE SAFETY FOR APARTMENT DWELLERS

◆Never block windows or doors with heavy furniture.

◆In case of fire, crawl to the door and feel the knob. If it is hot, the fire may be right outside your door. Do not open the door until you know it is safe.

◆If the hall is passable, use one of your predesignated escape routes. Do not use the elevator. It may stall due to heat or loss of power.

◆Check for smoke before entering an inside stairwell. If it is safe to enter, walk downward—do not run.

◆If you must return to or remain in your apartment because escape routes are blocked, open a window slightly to let smoke escape. Do not break the window; you may need to close it if there is smoke outside.

◆If you are stuck in the apartment, wet towels and sheets and stuff them around the doors; close all vents and air ducts.

▼▼Do not jump; you may not survive
◆ ◆ the fall.

Bathroom

Safety in the bathroom is focused on preventing falls, poisoning, and electrocution.

◆ Be sure that neither you nor anyone else touches any plugged-in electrical appliance while body or hands are wet.

◆ Avoid using electric space heaters, hair dryers, or radios near water.

◆ All bathroom outlets should be equipped with ground fault circuit interrupters to prevent the possibility of fatal shock.

◆ Never leave a child under age 4 alone in the bath, even for a minute. Children can slip under and drown in a small amount of water.

◆ Don't position electrical switches, outlets, or equipment where you can accidentally touch them from the bathtub.

◆ Use nonskid mats in the bath and shower; grab bars are practical for children, the elderly, and the disabled.

Grab bar. Place in the bath or shower, and near the toilet to help the elderly and disabled.

Shower door. This should be plastic or shatterproof glass that doesn't splinter if it breaks.

Bathroom door. Install a door with an outside lock release to prevent children from getting locked inside accidentally.

Cleaning equipment. Keep all toilet-cleaning chemicals in a cabinet with childproof locks.

Bath mats. Use nonskid ones, particularly if you have a tiled or polished bathroom floor.

Toilet. Clean it weekly to minimize germs, and keep the lid closed to discourage your child from putting his or her hands in it. Never mix toilet cleaners; they give off dangerous fumes.

Kitchen

More accidents occur in the kitchen than in any other room in the home. This is because the kitchen is a busy place that is full of potential hazards such as hot oil and appliances, sharp knives, jagged cans, and breakable objects. It is important, therefore, to take precautions in order to reduce the dangers.

◆ Have electrical outlets installed at countertop level. You should have at least four to six to avoid overloading the circuit. Don't let electric cords of appliances hang down from countertops. Head injuries may result from youngsters pulling appliances down upon themselves.

Electric appliances. Unplug appliances when they are not in use so your child can't turn them on by accident.

Cleaning equipment. Keep household cleaning materials, whether soap powder or bleach, out of the reach of children; most of them are dangerous if swallowed. Keep all original containers since you will need ingredient information quickly in an emergency.

Pets' bowls. Either feed the animals outside or keep the bowls out of a child's reach and where no one else can trip over them. Clean them out after each use.

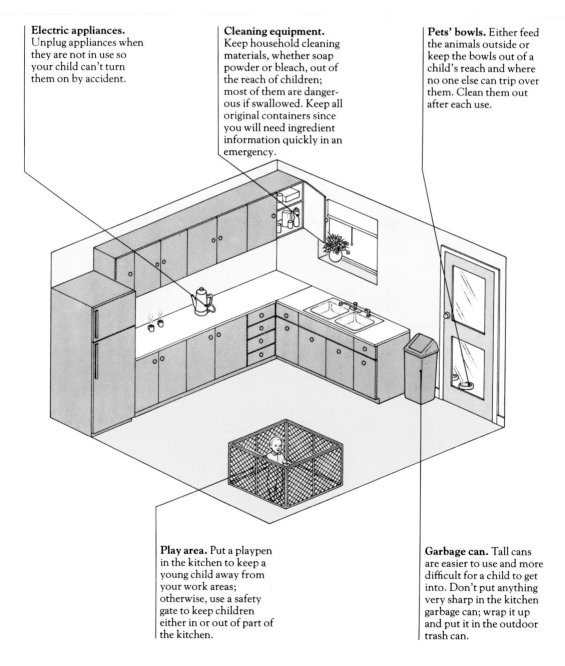

Play area. Put a playpen in the kitchen to keep a young child away from your work areas; otherwise, use a safety gate to keep children either in or out of part of the kitchen.

Garbage can. Tall cans are easier to use and more difficult for a child to get into. Don't put anything very sharp in the kitchen garbage can; wrap it up and put it in the outdoor trash can.

◆ To avoid spills, do not install microwave ovens above shoulder height.

▼▼ Never leave hot fat unattended for even
◆◆ a minute; it ignites spontaneously when it reaches 400 °F and is the cause of most kitchen fires. The danger sign is when fat starts to smoke.

◆ It is a good idea to have a nonskid surface for the kitchen floor; avoid overwaxing and use nonslippery floor polish.

◆ Keep dishcloths and paper towels away from the stove; they can easily catch fire.

◆ Keep hot food and drinks away from the edge of countertops or tables.

◆ Install a smoke detector, but position it away from cooking appliances.

Stove. Turn pot handles so your child can't reach them and you don't knock them over accidentally. Use the back burners when possible.

Fire precautions. Keep a fire extinguisher handy along with a box of baking soda by the stove. Position a smoke detector away from appliances.

Sharp knives. Keep knives out of the reach of children. The best place for them is on a knife rack, to help keep their edges longer. You could put a rack on the inside of one of the doors. Never leave knives lying on the countertop.

Storage. Try not to put everyday items above shoulder height; they'll be difficult to reach. Don't put heavy things too low; you could strain your back trying to get them out.

Child locks. Put child-proof latches onto all cabinets and drawers to prevent young children from getting into them.

Floor. Make sure it is a nonskid surface; wipe up greasy spills immediately, to prevent an accident.

Table. Be careful of using a cloth that may be pulled; even a crawling baby can reach up and grab it. If you leave anything on the table, make sure that it is in the middle, well out of reach.

High chair. Position it away from countertops, doors, and passageways. Always use a safety belt, and never leave your child unattended.

Living rooms

Because the living room or family room (or den) is a center for much day-to-day living, it should be hazard free.

◆ Keep all television, video, and stereo equipment out of reach and turned so the backs cannot be played with.

◆ Don't leave anything belonging to your child above the fireplace or on a windowsill where he or she may try to get at it. Place your treasured objects out of reach.

◆ Tape electrical cords along the floor, and run extension cords behind furnishings where they cannot be tripped over or played with.

◆ Always use a screen around a fireplace or woodburning stove; if possible, it should be firmly attached so that it can't be pulled over by a child.

Liquor cabinet. Always lock up alcohol when you are out of the room. Even a small amount of alcohol can seriously harm a child.

Television, video, and stereo. Unplug them during thunderstorms to prevent fires and harm to the equipment.

Houseplants and flowers. Some plants are poisonous to children if ingested. Place them out of reach.

Breakable objects. Move anything you value out of a toddler's reach; nothing is safe.

Outlet covers. Protect exposed and unused outlets by plugging with an outlet cover.

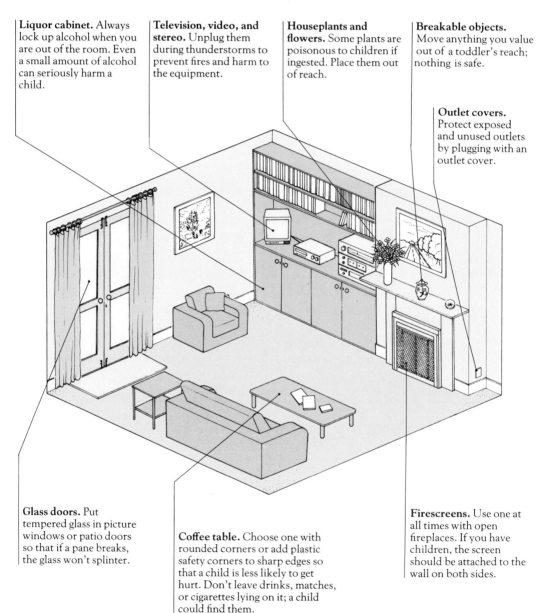

Glass doors. Put tempered glass in picture windows or patio doors so that if a pane breaks, the glass won't splinter.

Coffee table. Choose one with rounded corners or add plastic safety corners to sharp edges so that a child is less likely to get hurt. Don't leave drinks, matches, or cigarettes lying on it; a child could find them.

Firescreens. Use one at all times with open fireplaces. If you have children, the screen should be attached to the wall on both sides.

Bedroom

Keeping bedrooms safe is essential, as there will be times when you may be half-asleep when moving through them during the night and early morning hours. Safety awareness in a child's bedroom is especially important.

◆ Install a night-light with an electric eye that turns the lamp on automatically at dusk.

◆ An exposed radiator can be topped with a shelf to keep you from accidentally resting against it while it is hot.

◆ Always buy fire-resistant sleepwear for children. Do not use handmade sleepwear. Avoid the use of a pillow in an infant's crib; there is a risk of suffocation.

◆ Install childproof locks or tempered glass in a child's bedroom windows if they are above the ground floor.

◆ Leave a night-light on for those who get up to use the toilet.

◆ Don't smoke in bed.

◆ Never turn an electric blanket on if it is wet.

Windows. Put safety catches on the windows if the bedroom is on an upper floor. Don't put any furniture under a window; your child could climb out.

Lighting. Use wall-mounted or ceiling lights in a toddler's bedroom; never use freestanding table lamps, a child could burn herself.

Baby intercom. Get an intercom if your child's room is a long way from the living area, so you can hear any cries.

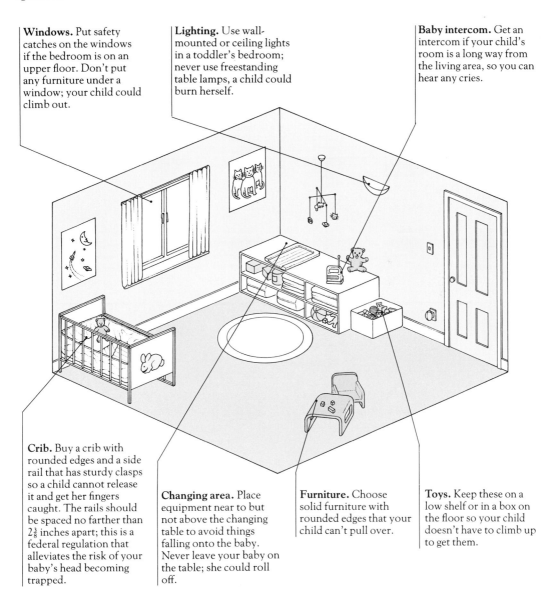

Crib. Buy a crib with rounded edges and a side rail that has sturdy clasps so a child cannot release it and get her fingers caught. The rails should be spaced no farther than $2\frac{3}{8}$ inches apart; this is a federal regulation that alleviates the risk of your baby's head becoming trapped.

Changing area. Place equipment near to but not above the changing table to avoid things falling onto the baby. Never leave your baby on the table; she could roll off.

Furniture. Choose solid furniture with rounded edges that your child can't pull over.

Toys. Keep these on a low shelf or in a box on the floor so your child doesn't have to climb up to get them.

Entrance hall

◆Check that your lighting is sufficient to illuminate the hall and any staircases and that it does not cast deceptive shadows. Install a light switch at the top and bottom of the stairs.

◆Keep stair carpeting well maintained to reduce the risk of anyone tripping on it and falling over.

Double rail. Get an extra handrail attached to the wall for someone who has difficulty climbing the stairs.

Banister supports. These should be close enough together so a child cannot get his head stuck in them.

Front door. Make sure the door closes properly and the lock is high enough so your child can't pull the door open and run into the street.

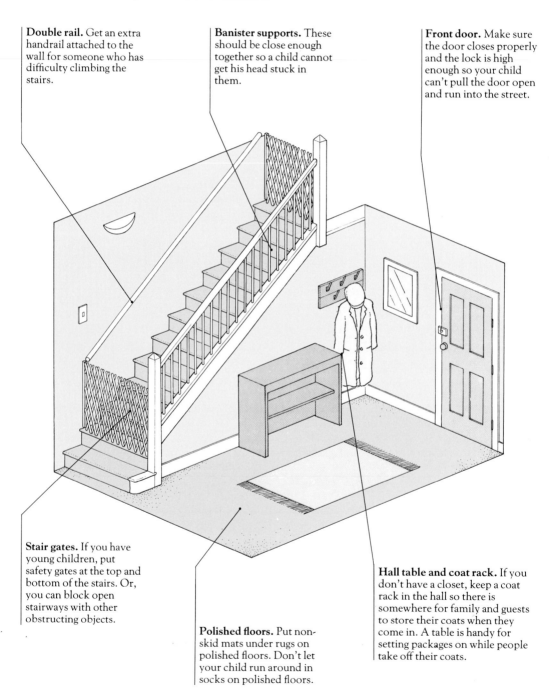

Stair gates. If you have young children, put safety gates at the top and bottom of the stairs. Or, you can block open stairways with other obstructing objects.

Polished floors. Put non-skid mats under rugs on polished floors. Don't let your child run around in socks on polished floors.

Hall table and coat rack. If you don't have a closet, keep a coat rack in the hall so there is somewhere for family and guests to store their coats when they come in. A table is handy for setting packages on while people take off their coats.

HOME NURSING

WHEN people are so ill that they are forced to stay in bed, a lot of comfort and reassurance is needed. Short, frequent visits are best. Use them to straighten the bed, bring a drink, sponge the patient's face and hands, chat for a while, and other such activities.

As the patient begins to recover, boredom is the main problem. Keep a supply of books, magazines, puzzles, or other items around the room.

SURROUNDINGS AND GENERAL COMFORT

If someone is likely to be ill for some time, try to position the bed so the patient has a pleasant view, either out the window or of something interesting in the room. Put a table by the bed for books, a radio, flowers, drinks, fruit, or a reading light.

◆ To keep the patient as comfortable as possible, plump up the pillows throughout the day and straighten out the sheets at least twice a day. Offer frequent opportunities for the patient to wipe his face and hands with a warm damp cloth, particularly if the patient has a fever.

◆ Use cotton sheets; they are more comfortable if a patient has a fever. Change the sheets if they get clammy or wet.

◆ To make bedmaking easier, use fitted sheets and a comforter. Shake the comforter every day to keep the filling even.

Sitting up in bed. *If a patient wants to sit up in bed, bank about five pillows: One at the base of the headboard, parallel to the bed; two leaning inward, one from each side; then two higher across the top.*

Temporary backrest. *Use an upturned chair and tie padding onto the legs to protect the wall or headboard. Fix a shoe bag to the bedside table or by the bed. The patient can store glasses, tissues, paperbacks, and other small items in it, and keep the area free of clutter.*

Children

◆ For most illnesses, it is not essential that your child stay in bed all day. If she feels well enough to get up and play in the house, it is usually safe to allow it. Check with your physician to see if your child can be outside for a little while if there is no fever and the weather is fine.

◆ If your child does not feel like getting out of bed or if your physician has advised plenty of rest, your child may be happier lying on a bed made up on the couch, or wherever you are working, so that she feels a part of things and is reassured by your presence. This will also make it easier for you to monitor your child.

◆ You can help alleviate boredom by providing a variety of amusing or creative things to do like drawing or pasting pictures in a scrapbook, but remember that sick children may not have the energy to concentrate on demanding games or projects.

Long-term patients

◆Leave a hand bell beside the bed if you are in another part of the house, or get a portable baby intercom.

◆If the patient is very confused, get a bed guard to prevent him from falling out.

◆Make your house accessible and comfortable for visitors so they will be encouraged to visit; bedridden people get bored and lonely.

◆If the patient will be in bed for some time, remove bedside clutter regularly and make room for fresh flowers, colorful pictures, and posters or wall hangings. Change the pictures every so often, so the patient doesn't become bored, but don't do this if the patient is easily disoriented.

◆If the patient is feeling strong enough, it can be a great relief to get out of bed and sit up in a chair for a little while, such as while you attend to the bed or at meal times.

◆Even if you are sometimes worried and harassed, try to be cheerful and optimistic. Get as much support as you can.

WHEN TO CALL A PHYSICIAN

◇Persistent coughing and hoarseness

◇Unexplained dizziness

◇Excessive indigestion or any mild but persistent indigestion after meals, especially if it prevents sleep at night

◇Persistent difficulty in swallowing

◇Chronic sleeplessness

◇Chronic or prolonged tiredness without an obvious cause

◇Persistent and recurrent pain anywhere in the body

◇Persistent loss of appetite or weight

◇A skin rash, a sore that does not heal, or an unexplained change in the color of skin or complexion

◇An unexplained swelling, especially in the abdomen, joints, or legs

◇Lumps or growths, even if they are painless or under the skin, especially if they keep growing

◇Unaccustomed breathlessness after exertion

◇Persistent and excessive thirst

◇Any problems with vision, such as seeing double

FOR CHILDREN

It is important that you call your pediatrician if you notice any of the following symptoms in your child:

◇A raised temperature over 102°F, or a temperature of 100.4°F accompanied by any obvious sign of illness that lasts more than three days

◇A raised temperature accompanied by convulsions

◇A low temperature that is accompanied by cold skin, drowsiness, quietness, and listlessness

◇If your baby has been vomiting or suffering from diarrhea for more than six hours

◇If vomiting or diarrhea is accompanied by severe abdominal pain

◇If a baby who is less than 6 months old suddenly stops eating for no apparent reason

◇If your child appears very listless for no apparent reason

◇Dizziness, particularly if your child has recently had a bump on the head

◇Severe right-sided abdominal pain

◇Headache accompanied by dizziness or blurred vision

EMERGENCIES

Get medical help immediately if you notice that an adult or child:

◇Stops breathing, or breathing is difficult and the person starts to turn blue or is unconscious

◇Has a deep wound and is bleeding badly, or has a serious ear or eye injury

◇Has a serious burn

◇Has a suspected broken bone

◇Has swallowed a poisonous substance or has been bitten by a poisonous insect, an animal, or a snake

Entertainment

◆Keep the patient supplied with plenty of books, newspapers, and writing materials, particularly during recovery. If the person likes books but is unable to read, get some books on audio tape. These are ideal for children as well.

◆A television can be a great companion for someone confined to bed; one with a remote control switch saves the patient from having to get out of bed to change channels. A radio/cassette player and a good selection of tapes are essential.

◆Let your child play with things not normally allowed in bed, such as crayons and paper jigsaw puzzles (on a tray). Dolls to dress or books of easy word puzzles are also good forms of amusement. Magazines and scissors for cutting out can provide hours of play.

CHANGING THE SHEETS FOR A PATIENT IN BED

1 *Remove the top bed covers. Turn the patient onto one side and move her as near to the edge of the bed as you safely can.*

2 *Roll the old sheet lengthwise until it is against the back. Roll the new sheet in half along its length and put it on the bed beside the old one. Tuck it in on one side.*

3 *Roll the patient over the two rolls and onto the new sheet. Remove the old one and tuck the new one in on the other side.*

NURSING

◆Always carry out the physician's instructions exactly. Keep a note of how much sleep the patient has had, how much has been eaten and drunk, and whether there has been much pain.

Temperature

In most people, body temperature varies between 97.8°F to 99°F but the average normal body temperature is 98.6°F. Readings outside the range of normal should be reported to a physician. Various factors influence a reading, so do not take a temperature immediately after a person has been very active, had a bath, eaten a full meal, taken a hot or cold drink, or smoked a cigarette.

◆Temperatures may be taken orally, rectally, or under the arm. Special thermometers are made for the different areas.

◆Battery-operated digital mercury thermometers are the easiest to read. Any type of mercury thermometer is more accurate than those using heat-sensitive chemicals.

◆A child's temperature should be taken rectally with a rectal thermometer until he is old enough to have it taken orally. You should wait until your child understands not to bite on the thermometer.

◆For babies and young children, thermometers with the quickest reading times are

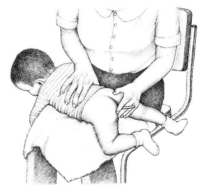

Using a rectal thermometer. *Lubricate the tip with a little petroleum jelly, and hold it between your first and second fingers with your palm resting on the baby's buttocks. Gently insert the tip no more than 1 inch into the rectum. Leave for two minutes.*

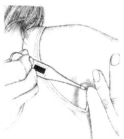

Taking a child's temperature under the arm. *Sit your child on your lap, put the thermometer into the armpit, and lower the arm over it; leave for five minutes.*

Taking the temperature by mouth. *Place the thermometer under the tongue and tell the patient to close the mouth; leave for two minutes.*

best; babies lose heat more rapidly than adults.

▼▼ Never leave a young child alone with a
♦♦ mercury thermometer. If the thermom-

eter breaks, both the glass and the mercury can be dangerous.

♦ To be sure of a correct reading with a mercury thermometer, shake it until the mercury falls below the 95°F mark.

♦ For confused patients or those who have difficulty breathing through their noses, take the temperature under the arm instead. This is normally 0.5°F lower. Be sure to keep the thermometer in place 10 minutes for adults and five minutes for children.

Pulse and breathing

The rate, regularity, and strength of the pulse and breathing are good indications of a person's health. A normal pulse is even and strong; a fast, weak, or a slow pulse may indicate illness. Normal breathing is even; rapid, slow or shallow breathing is abnormal.

♦ The average pulse rate varies with age; for a

COPING WITH FEVERS

You should consult your physician if an adult has a fever lasting longer than three days, or if he has accompanying symptoms such as severe headache with stiff neck, abdominal pain, or painful urination. Also call your physician if the sufferer is a child under 6 months, a child known to suffer febrile seizures, or an elderly person.

♦ Remove any excess clothing and/or bed covers and make certain there is a good supply of fresh air. Frequent changes of pajamas or nightgowns and bed linens are refreshing.

♦ Offer plenty of cold, tart, nonalcoholic drinks to replace fluid lost through sweating. If there is diarrhea or vomiting, increase the amount of fluids.

♦ Give adults the recommended dose of aspirin or aspirin substitute.

♦ Children should be given junior forms of aspirin substitute. They should not be given aspirin in any form; there is the danger of it leading to Reye's syndrome, a rare illness that causes inflammation of the brain.

♦ Try tepid sponging; children particularly benefit from being wiped down with water.

♦ Offer small, light meals and avoid milky foods that coat the tongue.

♦ Apply cold compresses if the patient has a headache; a few drops of cologne may be added to the water.

TEPID SPONGING

1 *If your child's temperature has been above 104°F for over half an hour, and undressing hasn't reduced it, sponge her all over with tepid water until temperature is below 100°F. Take temperature every five minutes until it drops.*

2 *Cover with a cotton sheet but don't let the child get too cold. Sponge again if the child starts to get hot again. Call your physician.*

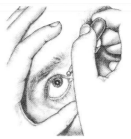

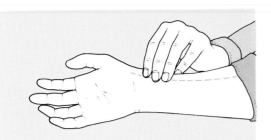

Taking the radial pulse. *Put three fingers on the patient's wrist, just below the palm of the hand on the thumb side. Do not take a pulse with your thumb or fingertips because they have a pulse of their own. Count the number of beats in 15 seconds and multiply by four to get the number of beats in a minute.*

healthy adult it should be about 72 beats a minute.

◆ A baby's pulse will be faster, about 100 to 120 times a minute; a child's pulse approaches the adult rate at age 8.

◆ A healthy adult breathes 16 to 20 times a minute, while a healthy newborn baby breathes 30 to 50 times a minute.

◆ The most convenient place for taking a pulse is at the wrist.

◆ If possible, count respirations while the patient is asleep.

Giving medicine

◆ Give the recommended dose—no more, no less—at the correct intervals throughout the day. Read the pharmacist's instructions on the label each time you give the medicine to make sure of the dose, especially if you are giving different medications throughout the day.

◆ **For babies.** If a baby won't take medicine on a spoon, get a medicine spoon tube or use a dropper; or try dipping a clean finger into the medicine and letting the baby suck it into his mouth.

◆ **For older children.** Suggest that your child hold his nose while taking the medicine—that way he won't taste it—or have his favorite drink ready to wash the taste of the medicine away. You can crush tablets between two spoons and mix the powder with jam.

◆ Children often hate being given ear or eye drops, especially if the drops are cold, so warm them slightly by standing the bottle in warm, not hot, water for a few minutes.

Giving eye drops. *Tilt the patient's head back and to one side, so that drops can't run from an infected eye into a clear one. Pull down the lower lid and let the drops fall between the eye and the eyelid.*

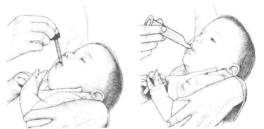

Giving medicine to a baby. *Fill a dropper with the required dose (above left) or pour it into a spoon tube (above right). Wrap your baby in a blanket to keep her from struggling.*

Dealing with vomiting

Vomiting should always be taken seriously because it can rapidly cause dehydration, particularly in a baby or young child. (A baby may spit up small quantities of curdled milk after a feeding, but this should not be confused with vomiting.) Vomiting has many causes, but in most cases it happens without warning and after a single bout the person is back to normal. Consult your physician if the vomiting continues over a 4- to 6-hour period, or if it is accompanied by diarrhea, or a fever, or an earache.

◆ Put the patient to bed and place a large bowl within easy reach.

◆ Give frequent, small amounts of liquid, preferably cold water, every 10 to 15 minutes to replace the lost fluids.

◆ You can give fruit juices, but they must first be diluted; do not give milk.

◆ Feed bland foods until nausea and vomiting have passed; reintroduce solid foods slowly.

◆ Wipe the patient's face with a cool damp cloth after she has vomited. Offer a toothbrush to brush away the taste. A hard candy, mint-flavored chewing gum, or peppermint tea also will help.

GIVING A BED BATH

If a person cannot get out of bed, give him a bed bath every day, particularly if he has a fever; the patient will feel more comfortable, and it will help prevent bedsores. You'll need:

◇ A bowl of warm water and some soap
◇ Two washcloths (one for the face and hands and one for the rest of the body)
◇ Two large towels
◇ Toothbrush, toothpaste, and a cup of rinsing water
◇ Clean pajamas or nightgown
◇ Cosmetics, talcum powder, or skin cream as required. (Ask the patient about any particular likes or dislikes.)

1 Help the patient take off his clothes, but leave him covered with a blanket.

2 Half-roll one of the towels up lengthwise. Roll the patient toward you onto one side and place the rolled towel against the back. Roll the patient gently back over the towel and unroll it across the bed (see page 329).

3 Then let the person wash his face and hands with a damp washcloth, or do it for him.

4 Remove the blanket and cover with another towel, then uncover each part in turn for washing. Start from the feet and work upward; change the water after washing the groin and genital area.

5 Help the patient brush his teeth. Remove the towels, then help him into clean clothes.

Feeding the ill

Anyone who is ill can survive without much food for a while, but a continuous intake of liquids is essential to prevent dehydration by replacing bodily fluids that are lost through sweating out a fever, diarrhea, or vomiting.

◆ Encourage a sick child to drink throughout the day by varying the drinks as much as possible. Offer diluted, fresh fruit juices mixed with soda water to make them fizz, or freeze fruit juice to make iced treats which are ideal for sore throats.

◆ Arrange a child's food into interesting shapes or faces, and offer some of her favorite foods. Try not to get impatient if your child has no appetite; she will eat more as she begins to get well.

◆ Offer a sick adult frequent small helpings of simple nutritious food rather than large, elaborate meals. Garnish the servings to make them attractive and colorful.

Giving fluids. *If a patient cannot sit up easily or finds it difficult to drink comfortably, use a beaker with a lid and a spout, or a flexible straw.*

Lifting and moving a patient

◆ Turn a bedridden patient regularly to prevent bedsores.

▼▼ Never try to lift an adult patient by
◆◆ yourself; you could strain your back.

Lifting a patient. *With a partner, stand facing each other, one on each side of the patient. Grasp each other's wrists under the patient's thighs and join hands around the back. Ask her to put her arms around your shoulders, then lift her up; she should sit in the well formed by your arms.*

MOVING A PATIENT UP IN THE BED

1 Sit the patient up. Sit on the bed, one person on each side of the patient, with one knee on the bed (your knee should be level with the patient's hip). Ask the patient to put his arms over your shoulders.

BEDSORES

Bedsores, or pressure sores, are ulcers that develop on the skin of bedridden patients. They commonly occur at the shoulders, elbows, lower back, hips, buttocks, knees, ankles, and heels—places where the weight of the body presses down and cuts off the blood supply to the area. Bedsores heal slowly and only if the pressure is minimized as much as possible.

◆ Adjust the position of the patient at least every two hours.

◆ Wash and dry pressure areas carefully, especially if the patient has some incontinence. Barrier creams can be used for added protection.

◆ A sheepskin under the buttocks and slippers under the heels relieve pressure.

◆ Use cushions and pillows between the knees and under the shoulders.

◆ You can buy a convoluted-foam mattress that has air moving through it, relieving pressure and stimulating blood circulation.

2 Grasp each other's wrists under the patient's legs, and put your other hands at the level you want to move the patient to. Lean in toward the patient to support the armpits and stand up, using your knees to push the patient forward.

NURSING THE ELDERLY

Caring for older patients can be a sensitive matter; you need to be aware of their special needs but also treat them as adults. Trying to balance this attention to needs with providing sufficient privacy will be difficult. The key is to be kind and sympathetic, and always to allow people to do what they are able to without any help. Elderly persons often need more time to consider questions and put forward their wishes. Be patient and listen to what they have to say. If the person is confused, you may have to go over things many times until he understands.

◆ When approaching a blind person, always introduce yourself clearly to allay anxiety and alarm.

◆ When you approach deaf people, you should be clearly in the line of vision. Articulate carefully so they can read your lips; offer to write things down if they have trouble following you.

◆ Unless your physician says otherwise, it is best for the person to be up and about rather than confined to bed.

◆ If the person is confined to bed, toilets are preferable to bedpans. There are sanitary chairs in which a frail person can be taken to the bathroom. A raised toilet seat also may prove more practical for certain patients.

◆ Protect the mattress with a waterproof sheet if the patient is incontinent. Don't deny the person fluids; however, do not give drinks just before bedtime.

◆ Install extra handrails near showers, bathtubs, and toilets.

◆ Nonslip mats should be placed in the shower; shower seats enable people to wash sitting down.

◆ Keep the room temperature at 68°F at least; the elderly can't regulate their own body temperatures efficiently.

◆ Persons without teeth need a soft diet; a mincer, food processor, or blender will come in handy. But don't forget the flavor. Many elderly people lose their appetites and become anorexic because food does not taste or smell as good to them as it used to.

IMPORTANT INFECTIOUS DISEASES

◆Consult your physician as soon as possible to get the diagnosis confirmed if you suspect any of the following conditions.
◆If a patient's condition starts to deteriorate or if a patient develops any new symptoms, call your physician immediately; there could be a complication.

DISEASE	SYMPTOMS	TREATMENT
CHICKEN POX Viral disease that is usually mild in children but can be more severe in rare adult cases. **Incubation period:** 7 to 21 days ◆ Your child will be infectious from 5 days before the rash appears until all the spots have scabs.	Headache; fever; and raised, red, itchy spots over the whole body, which develop into tiny blisters, mainly on face and trunk, leaving scabs. The fever dies down when the spots appear. Eventually the scabs will drop off.	◆Treat fever with aspirin substitute, soothe spots with calamine lotion, and give warm baths containing a handful of baking soda. ◆Keep fingernails short and clean; discourage scratching. If your child is still in diapers, change them frequently and leave them off when you can. ◆Your physician may prescribe anti-infective cream if spots are infected, and a sedative. ◆Consult your physician immediately if the patient has difficulty breathing and a high fever.
GERMAN MEASLES (RUBELLA) A highly contagious viral infection. The illness is mild, but if contracted by a woman during the first 3 months of pregnancy, it may affect her baby. One attack usually gives immunity for life. Girls should be immunized at puberty if they have not had the disease. **Incubation period:** 14 to 21 days	Slight fever, swollen glands in the neck, and pink rash on face, neck, and body. The rash disappears after 1 to 3 days. ◆Infectious from 7 days before the rash appears until 4 days after.	◆ Treat fever with an aspirin substitute. ◆Keep the patient away from anyone who might be pregnant, and from school and public places. ◆Bed rest if necessary.
INFLUENZA A viral infection of the respiratory tract usually occurring in small outbreaks in the winter months. Different viruses may be the cause. 　A specific form of influenza called hemophilus influenza type/B (HIB) can lead to meningitis (see opposite).	Chills, fever, headache, muscular aches, loss of appetite, and fatigue. Usually followed by a cough, sore throat, and a runny nose. Chest pain also may be present. 　HIB has the additional symptom of a stiff, aching neck.	◆Bed rest in a warm, well-ventilated room. ◆Painkillers should be taken to relieve aches and pains and to reduce fever. Don't give aspirin to children. ◆Warm fluids may soothe a sore throat, and steam inhalation will soothe the lungs. ◆If HIB is suspected, see a physician immediately.

DISEASE	SYMPTOMS	TREATMENT
MEASLES A contagious viral disease usually of childhood. One attack usually gives immunity for life. Infectious from onset of first symptoms until 4 days after the appearance of the rash. **Incubation period:** 10 to 14 days	Sore eyes, intolerance of bright light, sneezing, coughing, runny nose, and a high fever, and sometimes white spots inside the mouth. The fever begins to subside by the fourth day, when a rash appears behind the ears and on the forehead, and spreads over the entire body.	◆Give aspirin substitutes to control any fever. ◆Tepid sponging can control fever also. Give plenty of fluids to prevent dehydration. ◆Bathe sore eyes with water; your physician may prescribe drops. Darken the room. ◆Antibiotics may be necessary if there is secondary infection.
MENINGITIS Inflammation of the membranes that cover the brain and spinal cord can be caused either by a virus or a bacterium.	Fever, severe headache, nausea and vomiting, intolerance of light, and a stiff neck. In viral meningitis the symptoms are mild and resemble influenza. In bacterial meningitis the symptoms develop more rapidly and are sometimes followed by drowsiness and the loss of consciousness. There may also be a red, blotchy skin rash.	Viral meningitis requires no special treatment; bacterial meningitis is a medical emergency that needs to be treated with large doses of intravenous antibiotics.
MONONUCLEOSIS Also known as "the kissing disease," it is a viral infection that mainly affects teenagers and young adults. It is debilitating and can last for 6 months. The virus may reappear during the 2 years after the first attack, so watch for symptoms.	High temperature, runny nose, sore throat, aches, pains and tiredness, perhaps a rash behind the ears, that spreads to the forehead, and swollen neck glands.	◆Make sure the patient gets plenty of rest. Your physician may recommend an aspirin substitute to reduce the fever. Offer plenty of fluids. ◆In some cases, corticosteroid drugs are necessary to reduce severe inflammation. ◆Keep the patient occupied because depression is very common with this illness.
MUMPS An acute viral disease transmitted through the saliva of an infected person and usually affecting children. One attack usually brings immunity for life. Infectious from 3 days before the glands swell until 7 days after the swelling has subsided. **Incubation period:** 14 to 28 days	Swelling and tenderness of glands on the sides of face and neck (just below the ears and beneath the chin), usually beginning on one side and sometimes appearing on the other side in a day or two. It can cause swollen, painful testicles or lower abdominal pain in females. Other symptoms may include headache, dry throat, painful swallowing, fever, and vomiting.	◆Treat fever with an aspirin substitute and tepid sponging. ◆Liquidize food if eating is difficult. Give plenty to drink and encourage rinsing of the mouth to alleviate dryness. ◆Give the patient a hot water bottle wrapped in a towel to hold against the swollen area. ◆In moderate to severe cases the child may need to play in bed the first few days.

IMMUNIZATIONS

The incidence of certain infectious diseases has declined dramatically since routine immunization programs were introduced. It is necessary to continue such programs to ensure protection. Some types of immunization are aimed at the general population and are given primarily in childhood; others are intended for specific groups of people, such as those exposed to local outbreaks. Moreover, immunization may be necessary before going abroad (see below).

CHILDHOOD IMMUNIZATION

DISEASE	TIME	REACTION	PROTECTION
DIPHTHERIA, PERTUSSIS (WHOOPING COUGH), TETANUS	Injections at 2 months 4 months 6 months 18 months 4 to 6 years	Child may become feverish; the site of injection may become sore	Diphtheria and tetanus must be repeated
POLIO	Oral vaccine at 2 months 4 months 18 months 4 to 6 years	None	Must be repeated
MEASLES, MUMPS, RUBELLA (GERMAN MEASLES)	Injection at 15 months	Child may become feverish and have slight rash	Unknown
TETANUS, DIPHTHERIA	Injection at 14 to 16 years	Child may have localized swelling and soreness for 48 hours.	Must be repeated every 10 years
HEMOPHILUS INFLUENZA TYPE B	Injection after 18 months	Child may have slight fever and localized swelling, tenderness or redness	Provides immunity until natural immunity develops

TRAVEL IMMUNIZATION

IMMUNIZATION	REASON FOR IMMUNIZATION	EFFECTIVENESS
YELLOW FEVER	Compulsory for entry to some countries and advisable for visits to others within yellow fever zones in Africa and South America. May also be needed when traveling from yellow fever zones to neighboring states or to some Asian countries.	Injection at least 10 days before going abroad gives near 100 percent protection for at least 10 years. Certificate provided.
CHOLERA	Occasionally compulsory for entry to some countries in Asia and Africa. Also advisable when traveling to many other Asian, Middle Eastern and African countries.	Usually 2 injections give moderate protection for 6 months. Other precautions against cholera needed in epidemic areas.

TRAVELING ABROAD

When traveling outside the United States, it is a good idea to find out about the health risks in the country you are visiting and the precautions you can take. Some immunizations may be advisable for the traveler's protection, and a physician should be consulted about individual requirements.

◆Consult your physician at least two months before departure; some vaccinations take time to become effective; others cannot be given together.

◆Carry a sufficient supply of prescribed medications and any necessary over-the-counter drugs that may be subject to control in other countries.

◆If you are taking prescribed medicines, check with the embassies of the countries you plan to visit to see if there are any restrictions on bringing them with you.

◆Carry a letter from your physician giving details of any prescribed drugs, in case you need it to help you through customs.

◆Have a dental checkup if you will be away for more than a short time and you have any doubts about your teeth. It may be difficult and expensive to get treatment while you are away.

◆If you are visiting or even stopping over in a country that has malaria, ask your physician about antimalarial tablets. These need to be taken before, during, and after your visit.

IMMUNIZATION	REASON FOR IMMUNIZATION	EFFECTIVENESS
TYPHOID	Recommended when traveling anywhere outside of the U.S., Canada, Europe, Australia, and New Zealand for anyone who has not received immunization or a booster within the past five years.	2 injections, 4 to 6 weeks apart, give moderate protection for about 5 years, after which a booster is needed.
TETANUS	Advisable for anyone who has not received childhood immunization or a booster within the past 10 years.	Injection is highly effective, with booster needed every 10 years.
POLIO	Advisable for anyone who has not received childhood immunization or a booster within the past 10 years.	Oral doses are highly effective, with booster needed every 10 years.
IMMUNE SERUM GLOBULIN	Recommended when traveling to any country where hygiene and sanitary standards are low to protect against viral hepatitis, type A.	Injection gives moderate protection for up to 3 months.
MEASLES	Advisable for anyone who did not receive childhood immunization and who has not had measles.	Injection is highly effective and gives lifelong protection.
DIPHTHERIA	Advisable for anyone who did not receive childhood immunization and is shown by a test to be nonimmune.	Injection is highly effective.
HEPATITIS B, RABIES, MENINGITIS	Recommended only for individuals or groups at special risk through occupations, nature of visit abroad, and so on.	Injections—all highly effective.
SMALLPOX	No longer necessary, as the disease has been eradicated.	

MEDICAL SUPPLIES

KEEP A well-stocked medicine cabinet and first-aid kit in the home; you never know when a member of the household will become ill or have an accident. Although you often can improvise for first aid, it is much better to have correct supplies.

Check the contents of the first-aid box and medicine cabinet every so often; replace items before they run out.

MEDICINE CABINET

◆ Medicines should be stored outside the bathroom to protect them from dampness, light, and heat. If the label says to, keep them refrigerated. The medicine cabinet should be kept out of a child's reach and locked at all times.

◆ Check the expiration date of medicines frequently and safely dispose of those that have expired.

◆ Never give medicines to anyone other than the persons for whom they were prescribed.

WHAT TO KEEP IN THE MEDICINE CABINET

◇ Two mercury thermometers; one oral, one rectal

◇ Medicine dropper and medicine spoon

◇ Aspirin and aspirin substitute (acetaminophen) to help reduce fevers

◇ Calamine lotion for soothing sunburn, bites, stings, and rashes

◇ Mild antiseptic for minor wounds

◇ Bottle of ipecac syrup to induce vomiting in case of poisoning

◇ Petroleum jelly

◇ Currently prescribed medicines

▼▼ Do not keep any tablets that are
♦ ♦ chipped, cracked, or discolored, and capsules that have softened, cracked, or stuck together.

▼▼ Do not keep any ointments or
♦ ♦ creams that have changed odor or appearance or that have tubes that are cracked, leaky, or hard; discard liquids that have thickened or discolored.

FIRST-AID KIT

◆ Keep supplies in a clean, dry, airtight container so that they will remain sterile.

◆ Label kit clearly and put it somewhere easily accessible but not in the bathroom—the supplies can get damp and moldy.

◆ Check the package when buying bandages; the seals on sterile bandages must be intact.

WHAT TO KEEP IN A FIRST-AID KIT

Absorbent bandages—three medium-size, one large, and one extra large

Box of individually wrapped adhesive bandages

Open-weave bandages

Elastic bandages for strains and sprains

Skin closures for gaping wounds

Gauze dressings

A triangular bandage to make a sling

Roll of sterile cotton

Selection of safety pins

Round-ended tweezers

Small pair of scissors

Hydrogen peroxide

Mild antiseptic cream

USEFUL HOUSEHOLD ITEMS

◇ Packets of frozen peas make good ice bags because they mold to the injured part of the body.

◇ An elastic belt can be used to strap sprains; a leather belt can support a broken arm.

◇ Baking soda can be added to a bath to relieve itching or to warm water to soothe bee stings.

◇ Vinegar can be dabbed undiluted, or mixed half-and-half with water, onto wasp or jellyfish stings to soothe them.

◇ Rolled-up newspapers or a broom handle can make a temporary splint for a broken limb.

FIRST-AID TECHNIQUES

No HOME is completely safe from accidents; knowing the correct procedures can help you act quickly and prevent a situation from becoming any worse. There are a few points that are worth remembering. If possible, stay with the injured person and get someone else to call for the ambulance or physician. If that is not feasible, make the person comfortable, then call for help. If there is more than one victim, deal with the most seriously injured first; if a person has several injuries, first treat the most serious one.

LIFESAVING TECHNIQUES

In order to survive, everyone needs a constant supply of oxygen to every part of the body. To achieve this, you must be able to breathe in order to take air containing oxygen into the body, and the blood must be circulating to carry the oxygen around the body. An accident victim's vital needs are commonly abbreviated A B C:

A An open AIRWAY
B Adequate BREATHING
C Sufficient blood CIRCULATION

EMERGENCY ACTION FOR A SERIOUSLY INJURED VICTIM

This is a summary of the treatment; the techniques are described in more detail on the following pages.

1 *Send someone to telephone for an ambulance, while you stay with the victim.*

2 *Open the victim's airway and check to see if he is breathing (see page 340).*

3 *If he is not breathing, try clearing the airway (see page 340), then check breathing again.*

4 *If he is still not breathing after you have cleared the airway, give four breaths of mouth-to-mouth*

resuscitation (see page 341). Then check the heartbeat (see page 341).

5 *If the victim's heart has stopped beating, begin cardiopulmonary resuscitation (see page 342). Continue mouth-to-mouth and cardiopulmonary resuscitation until heartbeat is restored, then continue with mouth-to-mouth.*

6 *If the heart is beating, continue mouth-to-mouth until breathing is restored.*

◆It is always worth starting resuscitation; even if the person's breathing or heart doesn't start, you may keep his system going long enough for a physician to be able to take over. Brain cells will start to die after only three minutes without oxygen.

Opening the airway

◆Tilt the victim's head back to allow him to breathe; when a person is unconscious, particularly if lying on his back, the airway can be blocked by the tongue falling back across the top of the windpipe, by vomit collecting in the back of the throat, or by muscles in the throat relaxing and closing off the windpipe.

1 Put one hand under the back of the neck and the other on the forehead, and gently tilt the head backward. This will extend the neck to open the air passage.

2 Take your hand from the neck and push the chin upward to lift the tongue forward, away from the airway.

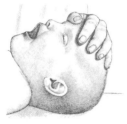

Opening a baby's airway. *Lay him on a firm surface and press very gently on the forehead to tilt the head slightly. Don't press it back too far or you'll block the airway.*

Checking breathing

◆To find out if the victim is breathing, kneel down beside him and put your ear as close as possible to the victim's mouth. Look along the chest and abdomen to see if you can detect any rise-and-fall movement; listen and feel for any breaths against your face.

Clearing the airway

◆If the victim isn't breathing, place him on his back and attempt to open the airway; quickly clear the mouth and airway of any foreign material.

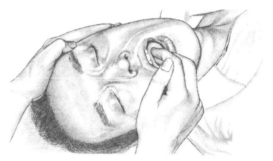

Lifting out debris. *Sweep around the victim's mouth with your index finger, removing any foreign bodies that can be seen or felt. Do not search for a hidden blockage; the victim could choke before you find it.*

Mouth-to-mouth resuscitation

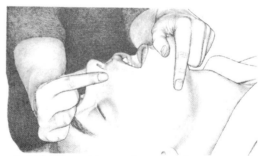

1 Lift the chin and press back on the forehead; the chin should point directly upward. Pinch the nostrils. Take a deep breath, seal your lips tightly around the victim's open mouth, and breathe at the rate of 12 breaths per minute, one every five seconds.

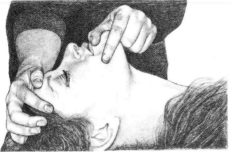

◆If the victim has swallowed a poisonous substance or is injured around her mouth, give mouth-to-nose resuscitation to prevent poisoning yourself. Put your thumb against the victim's lower lip and push it against her upper lip to seal the mouth, then put your mouth over her nose.

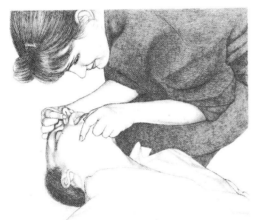

2 Give four quick breaths, taking a deep breath between each one. Remove your mouth and turn your head toward the victim's chest. Listen for air leaving the lungs and look to see if the chest is moving.

3 If air does not easily move in and out of the victim's chest pull or push the victim's jaw from behind into a jutting-out position, to prevent the tongue from falling back into the victim's throat. If breathing still does not occur, use the Heimlich maneuver (see page 349) to open the airway.

4 If the heart is beating, continue mouth-to-mouth resuscitation at the rate of one breath every five seconds, until you see the victim beginning to breathe on his own.

5 Watch carefully in case breathing stops again. If there are no head or neck injuries, turn the victim on one side or in the recovery position (see page 342).

TIPS FOR GIVING MOUTH-TO-MOUTH RESUSCITATION

◆If the chest does not rise, adjust the position of the head, as the airway may not be open properly. Make sure you are holding the nostrils shut and your mouth is forming a tight seal around the victim's mouth.

◆If, after you have adjusted the head, the chest still doesn't rise, try treating the victim as for choking (see page 349).

Give mouth-to-nose-and-mouth. *If you are resuscitating a baby or young child, it is often easier to put your mouth around both the mouth and nose.*

Checking for heartbeat

◆**For an adult.** Check the pulse in the arteries in the neck (the carotid arteries)—these are the easiest arteries to find.

◆**For a child.** Place your hand over the child's heart; the neck is too short for you to be able to find the arteries easily.

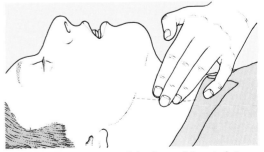

Finding the pulse. *Find the front of the windpipe and slide your fingers across into the groove between the windpipe and the large muscle in the neck.*

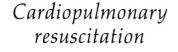
Cardiopulmonary resuscitation

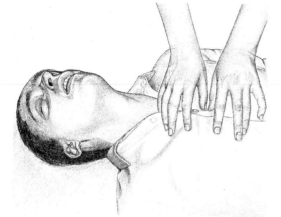

1 With the victim on a firm surface, kneel alongside him level with the chest and in line with the heart. Find the lower part of the breastbone: Feel for the "V" of the ribs at right above the bottom of the breastbone. Place your thumbs in the "V".

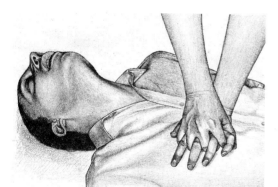

2 Keeping your fingers open and off the ribs, place the heel of one hand over the lower part of the breastbone. Cover this hand with the heel of the other one and lock your fingers together.

3 Keep your arms straight and move forward until they are vertical. Press down on the lower half of the breastbone about $1\frac{1}{2}$ to 2 inches. Move backward to release pressure. Pump 15 times at the rate of 80 to 100 per minute, with two breaths of mouth-to-mouth resuscitation given after every 15 pushes.

4 Continue on with 15 pushes, then two 1-second breaths, and repeat the heart check after a minute. Check the heartbeat after every 12 cycles of pushes and breaths.

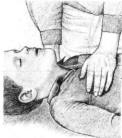

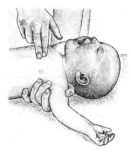

For children. *Perform cardiopulmonary resuscitation (CPR) with light pressure, using only one hand, to a depth of $\frac{1}{2}$ to 1 inch at a rate of 100 times per minute.*

For babies. *Use just two fingers, pressing at a rate of 100 times per minute to a depth of $\frac{1}{2}$ to 1 inch.*

The recovery position

◆ When an unconscious person is breathing and the heart is beating, check for head or neck injury. If there is a head or neck injury or you are unsure, leave the person on his back. If the head or neck seems unhurt, turn the victim on one side or put him into what is called the recovery position, which is described below. This ensures an open airway; keeps the tongue from falling into the back of the throat; keeps the head and neck extended; and allows any vomit, fluids, or other debris to drain freely.

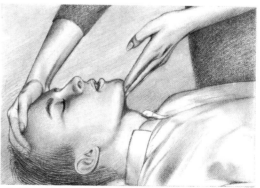

1 Kneel alongside the victim, level with the chest. Turn the head toward you, tilting it back, to open the airway.

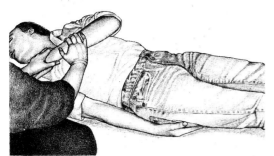

2 Place the victim's arm nearest to you by his side, and slide the hand, palm up, under the buttock. Cross the leg farthest from you over the near leg at the ankle, then lay the other arm across his chest, pointing toward the shoulder.

3 With one hand protecting and supporting the victim's head, use the other to grasp the clothing near the hip farthest from you and quickly pull the victim toward you until he is against your knees.

4 Readjust the head so the airway is open. Bend the victim's uppermost arm so that it supports the upper body, and bend the uppermost leg at the knee so the thigh comes forward to support the lower body.

5 Pull the other arm from under the victim and leave it lying parallel to the body to keep the victim from rolling onto his back.

WOUNDS AND BLEEDING

◆ If the injury is a small cut or scrape, clean and dress it to prevent infection.

▼▼ EMERGENCY: If the wound is serious,
◆ ◆ control bleeding immediately and call an ambulance, or take the victim to the hospital, whichever is easier and quicker.

Foreign body in a wound

◆ Apply direct pressure above and below the object to compress the blood vessels supplying blood to the area.
◆ Lay the victim down and, if possible, raise and support the injured part, then apply a

EMERGENCY ACTION FOR SEVERE BLEEDING

1 *Act quickly to stop any bleeding. Place a pad or dressing over the wound, and apply direct pressure against it.*

2 *Raise the injured part above the victim's heart; this will slow down the flow of blood to the injury. Help the victim lie down, keeping the injured part raised. Support the injured part, if necessary.*

3 *Place a sterile dressing over the wound, large enough to extend beyond the edges. Secure it with a bandage tied firmly enough to maintain pressure but not so tight as to cut off circulation (see page 355).*

4 *If blood begins to show through the first dressing, put another one on top of the first one and bandage all dressings snugly. Don't remove the original dressing; you'll disturb any clot that is forming.*

◆Pinch the lower part of the nostrils for about 15 minutes. The victim should breathe through the mouth.

◆Release the nostrils slowly and avoid touching or blowing the nose. If the bleeding has not stopped after 20 minutes, seek medical attention.

Displaced tooth

1 Have the victim sit down and lean her head to the injured side. Put a small pad of gauze against the gum wound or on (not *into*) the empty tooth socket so that it projects above the remaining teeth. (If you put the pad into the tooth socket, you could worsen the injury.) Get the victim to bite down on the pad for 10 to 20 minutes.

2 If the bleeding continues, gently remove the pad and replace it with another clean one. Maintain the pressure on the new pad for another 10 minutes.

3 If the bleeding persists, call a physician or take the victim to the hospital.

SAVING THE TOOTH

If a person has knocked out a tooth, keep the tooth; it may be possible for it to be replaced.

▼▼ Don't wash a broken tooth; put it in
◆ ◆ a clean plastic bag or get the victim to hold it in his mouth. Take the victim (with the tooth) to the dentist or hospital as soon as possible. Washing the tooth reduces the likelihood of being able to replace it, because it can destroy the bacteria in it.

UNCONSCIOUSNESS

This is a dangerous condition because the body's normal reflexes, which allow you to breathe while asleep, for example, stop working properly.

◆If a person has been unconscious, even for a short time, take her to a physician or to the hospital; there may be an underlying injury or condition that needs treatment.

▼▼ Don't give an unconscious person any-
◆ ◆ thing by mouth; it could cause choking.

EMERGENCY ACTION FOR UNCONSCIOUSNESS

1 *Shake the person by the shoulders or pinch an earlobe, and ask a question such as "Are you alright?" Give the person 10 seconds to respond.* **For a baby.** *Tap the sole of a foot—she should respond immediately if conscious.*

2 *If there is no response, tilt the head back to open the airway then check breathing (see page 340). If victim is breathing but is making gurgling sounds, try clearing the airway.*

3 *If victim is breathing normally and there are no head or neck injuries, move her on one side or into the recovery position (see page 342). If there are head or neck injuries, keep her on her back. Watch the victim while you are waiting for medical help and note any changes in condition.*

4 *If she is not breathing, begin mouth-to-mouth resuscitation and cardiopulmonany resuscitation (see pages 340–342), as necessary.*

5 *Examine the body for any signs of injury, or if you don't know the victim, for any bracelet or cards indicating the victim has a condition that can result in unconsciousness. Once normal breathing has resumed, or if you see fluid coming from an ear, move her into recovery position.*

▼▼ Don't leave an unconscious victim un-
♦ ♦ attended; his condition could worsen
suddenly.

Fainting

Fainting is a temporary spell of unconsciousness, and recovery is usually quick and
complete.

1 Anyone who feels faint should sit down
and lean forward with head down between the knees, and take deep breaths.

♦ If the person collapses and is unconscious,
turn her onto her back and raise the legs
above chest level to get the blood flowing
back to the heart. If she doesn't recover, treat
as described for unconsciousness.

2 Loosen tight clothes at the neck, chest,
and waist. Provide plenty of fresh air.
When she has come to, raise her into a sitting
position, and let her sit quietly for a while.

BONE, JOINT, AND MUSCLE INJURIES

These include broken bones or fractures,
sprained or torn ligaments (ligaments are the
bands of tissue that hold joints together), and
strained muscles. In some cases, it's difficult
to differentiate between a broken bone and a
sprain or a dislocated joint, as they all can be
extremely painful. If in doubt, treat the
injury as a break.

Broken bones

♦ Treat breathing difficulties, severe bleeding, or unconsciousness before treating a
broken bone because these conditions can
be life-threatening.

▼▼ If you have to move a victim (because his
♦ ♦ life is in danger, for example), temporarily immobilize the broken limb first;
broken bone ends can be sharp and can cause
serious internal injury.

♦ Note any symptoms, but don't move any
part unnecessarily; you could make the
injury worse.

♦ Compare injured with uninjured limbs to
help you locate the injury. The victim may
have heard and/or felt the bone snap. If not,
other clues are:

◇ Movement of the part is difficult or impossible, and attempts to move increase the
pain at or near the injury

◇ Tenderness when pressure is applied

◇ Swelling, and later, bruising

◇ The limb looks deformed—shortened,
rotated, or sticking out at an unnatural
angle; this will be particularly noticeable if
the top of the thighbone or both bones in the
lower leg are broken

◇ The victim is in shock. This is more
common if the thigh or pelvis is broken,
because both injuries are often accompanied
by severe blood loss (see page 345).

♦ Anyone with a suspected fracture should
be taken to the hospital. Do not try to fix a
broken bone yourself. If the injured person
cannot walk, summon an ambulance; otherwise take him to the hospital yourself, if
possible.

▼▼ If a spinal injury is suspected, do not
♦ ♦ move the person at all unless his life is in
immediate danger or if he is choking.

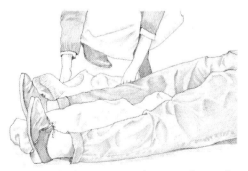

1 If the ambulance is on the way, keep the
injured part supported by placing rolled-
up blankets or coats, or a folded newspaper
along either side of it. Make the victim as
comfortable as possible.

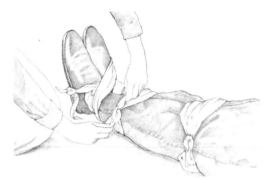

◆ Splinting is usually necessary, especially if the injured person needs to be moved or if there is a delay before help arrives.

2 Secure the injured limb to a sound part of the body with a sling or wide bandages. If an injured arm can be bent comfortably across the chest, splint it first and then apply a sling.

3 Raise the injured part after immobilizing it to slow down blood flow to the area, and minimize swelling and discomfort.

Sprains

A sprain is caused when one or more of the ligaments and tissues around a joint is wrenched and torn.

◆ Suspect a sprain if, after a fall:

◇ The victim complains of pain and tenderness around the joint, which are made worse by movement

◇ You notice swelling, or later, bruising

◆ If in doubt, treat as a fracture; it can be difficult to differentiate between a bad sprain and a fracture.

1 Raise the injured limb and support it in a comfortable position. Apply a cold compress to reduce swelling and pain (a bag of frozen peas wrapped in a thin towel is ideal because it molds to the shape of the limb).

2 Support the joint with cotton secured with a bandage. Don't apply a tight bandage because the joint will probably swell quickly. Take the victim to the hospital or to a physician.

Supporting a sprained ankle. *If the victim has a tight shoe or boot on, don't remove it since it is supporting the injury. Tie a bandage in a figure eight around the ankle and over the shoe and seek medical help.*

Dislocated joints

These occur when the ligaments that hold a joint together are torn, displacing the bones so that they are no longer in contact. Sometimes it is hard to tell the difference between a dislocated joint and a broken bone because they are both extremely painful. If in doubt, treat as a fracture.

◆ Suspect dislocation if you notice deformity at a joint and any signs of a sprain.

◆ Support the part in the position the victim finds most comfortable and, if possible, immobilize it with a splint or a sling. Get the victim to the hospital.

▼▼ Don't attempt to reposition dislocated
◆◆ bones or you may do more damage.

Strained or "pulled" muscles

◆ Muscle fibers can be torn or stretched as a result of suddenly pulling them too far. Strains are most common in athletes; warming up before activity can reduce the risk of strains.

Supporting the injury. Rest the injured part on a cushion in a raised position and apply an ice pack or cold compress to reduce pain and swelling. Seek medical help.

COOLING FOR PAIN RELIEF

Cooling an injury slows down the blood flow to it, minimizing swelling and easing pain. This works particularly well for sprains, strained muscles, dislocated joints, bruises, small cuts, and scrapes.

◆ Hold the injury under cold running water for up to half an hour to cool it. Don't do this for too long with a baby or young child, though, because he could become chilled.

◆ If the site of the injury makes it difficult to put the injury under cold water, make a cold compress or ice pack, or wrap a package of frozen peas in a thin towel and use that. Leave the compress on for up to half an hour, taking it off every few minutes to prevent frostbite.

Making an ice pack. *Put some crushed ice or ice cubes in a plastic bag. Pour some salt into the bag to lower the melting temperature of the ice (above left). Exclude any air from the bag, seal it, and wrap it in a thin towel. Crush ice cubes by hitting the bag with a rolling pin (above right) so the compress will mold to the shape of the injured area; then place it on the injury as required.*

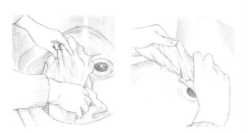

Making a cold compress. *Soak a large roll of cotton or a small towel in cold water, preferably iced water (above left). Wring it out so that it is damp (above right) and place it on the injury; replace it when it starts to feel warm, or drip more iced water onto it.*

CHOKING

Young children are particularly at risk of choking because of their tendency to put things into their mouths.

◆ Suspect choking and act quickly if you notice that a person:

◇ Is trying to cough, gripping his throat, and is unable to speak or breathe

◇ Looks blue around the face and lips and has prominent veins in the neck and face.

▼▼ EMERGENCY: If the person becomes
◆ ◆ unconscious, treat as described on page 346 and get medical help.

EMERGENCY ACTION FOR CHOKING

1 *If the person is coughing, encourage him to keep coughing hard; this may be enough to clear the airway.*

2 *If he is not coughing, help him to bend over until the head is lower than the lungs. Slap him sharply with the heel of your hand between the shoulder blades. Repeat if needed.*

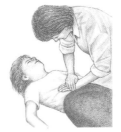

For a child. *Place the heel of one hand slightly above the navel. Place the other hand on top and press down with a quick, upward thrust.*

For a baby. *Pick him up and lay him head down, with the head lower than the chest, and whack between the shoulder blades.*

3 *Once the obstruction is dislodged, hook it out with your finger, being very careful not to push it back down the throat.*

The Heimlich maneuver for choking. *To perform the abdominal thrust, clasp the victim from behind and place your fist between the navel and sternum. Grasp your fist with your other hand and give four quick thrusts by squeezing and pulling inward and upward into the abdomen. This usually forces the object out.*

OTHER INJURIES

Most minor injuries can be treated easily at home. If you are ever in any doubt call your physician or take the person to the nearest emergency room.

Burns and scalds

◆ If the victim is an infant or sick elderly person, always get medical help.

EMERGENCY ACTION FOR SEVERE BURNS

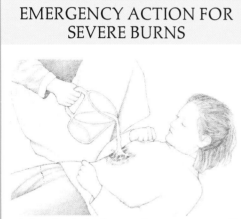

1 *Lay the victim down and get someone to call an ambulance while you cool the injury by carefully pouring cold water over it. Remove any constricting clothing or jewelry as long as it is not sticking to the injury; otherwise, do not remove.*

2 *Cover the injury with a dressing or clean non-fluffy material (a pillowcase is ideal) to minimize infection.*

3 *Treat as described for shock (see page 345); there can be severe fluid loss.*

BURNS TO THE MOUTH AND THROAT

1 *Give frequent sips of cold water to cool the throat (the tissues in the throat swell very quickly). Remove constricting clothing or jewelry from around the neck and chest if it is not sticking. Call an ambulance.*

2 *If the victim loses consciousness, place victim in the recovery position (see page 342). Check breathing and heartbeat and start mouth-to-mouth and cardiopulmonary resuscitation as necessary (see pages 340–342).*

◆ Cool a burn to minimize the damage. Use cold water if possible, but if there isn't any clean water available, use any cold liquid, such as milk or beer.

▼▼ Don't put butter, oil, grease, or oint-
◆ ◆ ments onto a burn; the residual heat can heat up the cream and make the injury worse.

▼▼ Don't break blisters, remove loose skin
◆ ◆ or anything that is sticking to a burn, or otherwise interfere with the injured area; burns are easily infected.

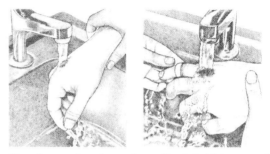

Treating a minor burn. *Immediately hold the injured area under cold running water or immerse it in cold water for at least 10 minutes (above left). Gently remove any constricting clothing or jewelry from the injured area (above right). Do this before it starts to swell. Cover the burn with a clean or sterile dressing of nonfluffy material that is larger than the wound.*

Electric shock

▼▼ Don't touch the victim until you are
◆ ◆ sure you are in no danger yourself. Either turn off the main power supply at the fuse box or circuit breaker, or push the victim clear (see below). If the victim is unconscious, follow steps for emergency action for unconsciousness (see page 346).

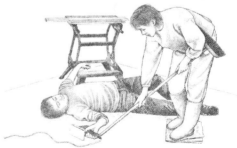

Breaking electrical contact. *If you are some distance from the power switch, wear rubber boots or stand on a wad of newspaper and push the victim away from the electrical source with a nonconductive object such as a wooden broomstick.*

Head injuries

Scalp wounds often look worse than they are because the skin is stretched so tightly across the head that even a minor injury can bleed profusely.

◆ If a scalp wound is bleeding, press a clean pad or handkerchief on it for about 10 minutes until the bleeding stops. If it is a small wound, wash the area with soap and water and place a clean bandage over it to keep pressure on the wound. If it is jagged or long, the wound will require stitches.

◆ A head injury resulting in unconsciousness, dizziness, or vomiting should always be treated as serious. If there is any blood or a straw-colored discharge from the nose or ear after a blow to the head, get medical help immediately; it could be a skull fracture.

◆ When a person has suffered a blow to the head and sometime later begins vomiting, becomes vague and can't remember anything, or loses consciousness, this is evidence of a concussion—medical attention should be sought immediately.

For an unconscious victim. *If a person is unconscious after a head injury, place a victim in the recovery position (see page 342) and call an ambulance. If you see any fluid coming from the ear, put a pad of material against the ear to absorb it, and position the victim so she is lying on that ear. This is to allow fluid to drain and prevent a buildup of pressure.*

Poisoning

◆ Suspect poisoning if you find a person collapsed with an empty or open container nearby that you think contained a poisonous substance or with some poisonous berries or leaves in his hand or nearby.

EMERGENCY ACTION FOR POISONING

CONSCIOUS VICTIM

1 *If the victim is conscious, quickly ask him to tell you, or point to, what he has taken because he could lose consciousness at any moment. Call a poison control center immediately (post the number by the phone), or call a hospital emergency room.*

2 *If the victim's lips or mouth show signs of burning, cool them by dabbing milk or water onto them. If the victim has swallowed a corrosive poison, don't try to induce vomiting; anything that burns going to the stomach will burn again on its way up.*

3 *Syrup of ipecac may help with a noncorrosive poison. Do not, however, induce vomiting with syrup of ipecac unless directed to do so by a physician.*

UNCONSCIOUS VICTIM

1 *If the victim is unconscious, call an ambulance immediately or get someone to drive you and the victim to the hospital, while you administer first aid.*

2 *Place the victim in the recovery position (see page 342). If breathing or heartbeat stops, begin mouth-to-mouth and cardiopulmonary resuscitation as necessary (see pages 340–342). If you suspect there is poison around the victim's mouth, try to wash it off, or use mouth-to-nose resuscitation so you don't burn your lips.*

◆ Act quickly if you notice any of the following symptoms and signs:

◇ Burns around lips and mouth, intense stomach pains; these may indicate that the victim has swallowed a corrosive substance, such as bleach, or toilet bowl or oven cleaner

◇ Convulsions

◇ Vomiting and, later on, diarrhea.

▼▼ EMERGENCY: Call your local poison
◆ ◆ control center, or the nearest emergency room and tell them what you think the victim has swallowed.

◆ Get the victim to the hospital as soon as possible, taking samples of vomit and any pill bottles or boxes, plants, etc., found near him or that he is known to have eaten.

Sunburn

◆Get the victim into the shade and soothe the skin with calamine lotion or tepid water. Advise the victim not to expose the skin to direct sun for at least 48 hours.

◆If there is extensive blistering, get medical help at once; don't break the blisters.

▼▼EMERGENCY: If the person has a fever ◆ ◆ and hot dry skin, she may be suffering from the early stages of heatstroke (see below); call a physician immediately.

Heat exhaustion

Caused by loss of salt and water from the body through profuse sweating, heat exhaustion can be aggravated by extra fluid loss as a result of a stomach upset.

◆Suspect heat exhaustion, if during hot weather, a person starts to feel tired and

EMERGENCY ACTION FOR HEATSTROKE

If, in very hot weather, a person has a high fever and hot *dry* skin, he may have heatstroke, which requires immediate treatment by a physician.

1 Get the victim into the shade, remove the clothes, and wrap him in a cold wet sheet or towel, or sponge the body with tepid water. Call a physician immediately.

2 Once the skin has cooled down, replace the wet towel with a dry one and stay with the victim. If he loses consciousness, treat as necessary (see page 346).

weak, and dizzy or faint, or if he is nauseated and has muscle cramps. The skin will be pale and clammy, and the pulse may be rapid.

◆Lay the victim down in a cool place with his feet raised about 12 inches above the ground. Sponge the body with lukewarm water to cool the skin down quickly. Give plenty of fluids; if there are cramps, diarrhea, and vomiting, give salt water, about $\frac{1}{4}$ teaspoon to a glass.

Hypothermia

If the body gets very cold, the body's systems slow down, and less blood is supplied to the limbs and skin in order to keep the vital organs, such as the heart, supplied with blood. Elderly people and babies are particularly susceptible to hypothermia because their body temperature control is not very efficient.

◆Suspect hypothermia and act quickly if a person is shivering, his skin feels very cold and looks pale, and if he becomes irrational, and has very slow breathing and pulse rates. In severe hypothermia, he may become unconscious.

◇**In a baby.** The skin will feel cold, but he may look very pink and healthy; he probably will be unusually drowsy and limp.

1 Wrap the victim in a sleeping bag, comforter, or quilt, covering everything except the face. You can lie under the comforter or in the sleeping bag, too, so your body heat helps to warm him; or, put a well-wrapped hot-water bottle against the body (not the limbs). Call a physician.

◇If the victim is unconscious, lay him in the recovery position (see page 342).

2 Put a conscious adult in a warm bath. When his skin feels warm, put him in a warm bed, and give hot, sweet drinks.

3 If breathing or heartbeat stops, begin mouth-to-mouth or cardiopulmonary resuscitation (see pages 340–342) as necessary.

▼▼ Don't rub or massage limbs or warm·
♦ ♦ them with a hot-water bottle because it will increase the blood flow to them and away from the center of the body. Don't give alcohol—it dilates the blood vessels, encouraging blood to flow throughout the body and not remain in the center of the body where it is needed most.

Removing a bee stinger. *Remove a stinger that is still in the skin by flicking it off with a fingernail or scraping it out with a knife blade. Do not use tweezers because you might squeeze the sac, which will release more poison into the skin.*

Bites and stings

Stings from insects such as bees, wasps, and hornets are not normally dangerous, although they are both painful and alarming. Spiders in some countries are poisonous; if in doubt, treat as for snake bites (see right).

▼▼ EMERGENCY: Get the victim to the
♦ ♦ hospital as soon as possible if:

◇He is known to be allergic to stings. (The effect of stings is cumulative, and there can be a severe reaction.)

◇He is stung in the mouth or throat, because the tissues swell quickly and can block the airway and prevent breathing.

◇He has several stings (if, for example, he has disturbed a nest).

♦If the stinger is still in the skin, try to scrape it off (see above right).

♦Soothe a wasp sting with a cold compress of diluted white vinegar and a bee sting with a baking-soda-and-water paste. Ice packs and calamine lotion also help to soothe bites and stings.

♦For a jellyfish sting, lay the victim down and flood the area of the sting and any attached tentacles with vinegar to inactivate them, then scrape the tentacle fragments off, cover with a sterile dressing, and get medical help as soon as possible.

For a stinger in the throat. *Wrap a cold pack around the victim's neck, and give him an ice cube to suck to keep the swelling down. Get him to the hospital quickly.*

Animal bites

For anything more serious than a minor bite or scratch, or if there is any possibility of rabies, seek medical treatment. If possible, the animal that inflicted the bite should be held and checked for rabies.

Snakebites

♦Lay the victim down so that the site of the bite is lower than the heart, and advise him not to move. Apply a pad or sterile dressing, immobilize the limb, and get the victim to a hospital. Don't apply a tourniquet or suck out the poison.

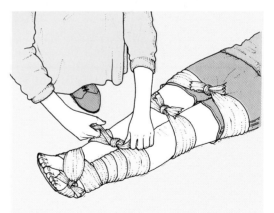

Treating a snakebite. *Keep the victim as still as possible. Bandage the affected area, then immobilize it. If the bite is on the victim's arm, put it in a sling, then tie a bandage around the body and affected arm; if the bite is on the leg, tie both legs together at the ankles, knees, and thighs.*

Splinters

1 Sterilize a pair of tweezers by holding them over a flame; don't wipe the soot off or you'll have to sterilize them again.

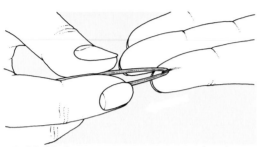

2 Hold the tweezers as near to the skin as possible, and grasp the splinter. Gently pull it out in the opposite direction to which it entered the skin.
◆ If glass is embedded in the skin or the splinter is too deep to get at with tweezers, don't try to remove it; seek medical help.
◆ Cleanse the area with soap and water and apply antiseptic cream. An adhesive bandage is not necessary.

Foreign body in the nose

◆ Have the person hold a finger against the unaffected nostril and blow out through the affected one. If this doesn't work, shine a light into the nostril and remove the object with tweezers if it is near the entrance to the nose; if not, get medical help.

Foreign body in the ear

Children are particularly prone to this type of injury.
◆ Tilt the head so that the affected area is facing downward; this may help the object drop out. If it doesn't, take the victim to a physician.
▼▼ *Don't* try to dislodge any object yourself
♦♦ even if you can see it clearly. You may perforate the eardrum.
◆ If the victim can hear an insect buzzing in his ear, try "floating" it out with tepid water (see above right) or take him to a physician as soon as possible.

Removing an insect from an ear. *Tilt the person's head so that the affected ear is facing upward and gently flood the ear with tepid water. It must not be too hot or too cold; you could damage the eardrum.*

Foreign body in the eye

▼▼ *Don't* let the victim rub the eye; the
♦♦ object could become embedded.
◆ Sit the person down facing a bright light. Separate the eyelids, then ask him to look left, right, up, and down so you can look at the whole eye. If you can see the object, remove it as shown below. If it is under the upper lid, pull the upper lid downward and outward over the lower lid and ask the person to blink; the lashes may lift it. If it is on the eye under the upper lid, expose the area by pulling the lid back over a matchstick, then use the moistened corner of a handkerchief to get the object out.
◆ **If the object is embedded or on the iris (colored part of the eye).** Tell the person to keep the eye closed and do not try to remove the object. Cover the eye with a pad or clean handkerchief, taped in position; tell him to keep both eyes still (cover up the other eye if necessary). Take the victim to the hospital immediately.

Removing dust from an eye. *Remove it with the dampened corner of a clean cloth, handkerchief, or cotton swab.*

BANDAGING TECHNIQUES

◆ When you have finished securing a bandage or sling, check the limb to make sure the blood is circulating. Press one of the nearby exposed fingernails or toenails until it turns white, then release the pressure. If the nail turns pink again immediately, blood is circulating through the area; if not, remove the bandage and start again.

SLING

◆ Make an improvised sling by folding the bottom of the victim's jacket up over the arm and pinning it to the top of the jacket.

◆ Use a triangular bandage or a piece of material about 1 square yard folded in half diagonally to make a sling.

1 *Place the arm across the victim's chest, with the hand slightly higher than the elbow and tell him to support it.*

2 *Fold the long edge of the bandage to make a hem, and slide it through the gap between the victim's elbow and body, leaving the long edge parallel to the other arm; take the top corner around the victim's neck to the front.*

3 *Carry the lower end of the bandage up over the arm and tie a square knot in the hollow below his shoulder.*

4 *Fold back the corner of the bandage at the elbow, then bring the point forward and pin it to the front.*

STRAIGHT BANDAGE

Use to secure a dressing to a leg or arm or to support strained muscles.

1 *Unroll the bandage slightly and, holding it with the rolled part on top, place the end of the bandage on the limb and make a straight turn.*

2 *Work up the limb, making spiral turns so that each layer covers two-thirds of the previous one. Finish off with a straight turn and fasten with a safety pin.*

ANKLE/FOOT BANDAGE

1 *Holding the bandage with the roll on top and working from the inner side of the leg outward, make one straight turn.*

2 *Take the bandage across the top of the foot to the little toe, around under the foot, and up at the base of the big toe. Make two complete turns around the foot.*

3 *Take the bandage across the top of the foot to the ankle. Continue figure-eight turns around the foot and ankle until the foot is covered, overlapping each turn.*

4 *Finish off with two turns at the ankle, and secure the bandage.*

ACTION FOR EMERGENCIES

Iᴺ ᴀɴʏ emergency, speed is of paramount importance: Seconds can mean the difference between life or death, minor and serious injury, or minor and major damage to property.

Make sure you are safe; the calmer you are, the more you can help and comfort others. Deal with the incident as quickly as you can. If possible, get everyone to safety while someone else calls for help.

INJURIES

Following are summaries of immediate actions to take in cases where someone is injured in the home. (For more detailed advice, see pages 339-355.)

Serious bleeding

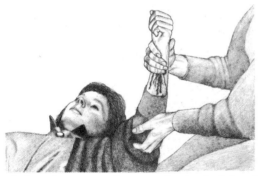

1 Lay the person down, and *raise the injured area* higher than the chest.

2 Apply *direct pressure* to the wound through a clean pad or dressing.
3 Send someone to call for an ambulance.

Unconsciousness

1 Tilt the person's head back to *open the airway* (see page 340) and *check the breathing* (see page 340).

2 If victim is breathing, move to the *recovery position* (see page 342).

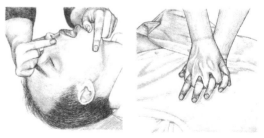

3 If breathing stops, begin *mouth-to-mouth* and *cardiopulmonary resuscitation* as necessary (see pages 340–342).
4 Phone for an ambulance if someone has not already done so for you.

Choking

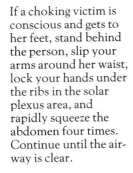

If a choking victim is conscious and gets to her feet, stand behind the person, slip your arms around her waist, lock your hands under the ribs in the solar plexus area, and rapidly squeeze the abdomen four times. Continue until the airway is clear.

If the victim is sitting, go behind the person's chair and lean her forward. Encircle the victim's body with your arms. Locking your hands under the ribs, squeeze the abdomen.

If the choking victim is unconscious, place her on her back, jaw jutting upward to provide an airway. Kneel to one side of the victim. Compress the lower part of the person's chest four times.

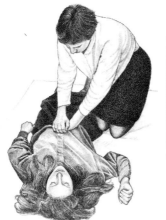

Immediately turn the victim's head to one side and clear the mouth of secretions, then repeat the maneuver.

GAS LEAK

▼▼ Don't try to repair a gas leak yourself;
◆◆ you could cause an explosion.

Small gas leak

1 Search for the leak by checking all knobs on a gas stove (*above left*), the gas taps, and pipes (*above right*), and make sure that pilot lights have not gone out.
◆Put out any open flames and cigarettes before searching for the leak.
▼▼ If in the dark, use a flashlight and *not* a
◆◆ match or candle to search for the leak. Don't turn on an electric light—the spark could ignite the gas.

2 If the smell lingers and you can't find the source, telephone your gas company.

Serious gas leak

1 If there is a very strong smell of gas, open all doors and windows, and put out all open flames.
▼▼ Don't turn electric switches either on or
◆◆ off—you could cause an explosion.

2 Call gas company immediately. Turn off the gas at the main shutoff valve.

FIRE

◆ Get everyone out of a building before treating any injuries.

Major fire

1 Get everyone out of the building. Don't stop to gather up possessions.

2 Call the fire department from a neighbor's home or a telephone booth.

IF TRAPPED ON AN UPPER FLOOR

1 Go into a room, close the door, and stuff the gap at the bottom with clothing, bedding, or rugs to stop smoke from entering *(above left)*. Open a window and shout for help *(above right)*.

2 If the room fills with smoke, lean out of the window or lie down on the floor to get below the level of the smoke.

3 If possible, tie a wet rag around your mouth and nose to keep some of the smoke fumes out. Make a rope of sheets, towels, belts, etc., to use only as a last resort.

Small fire

1 Get out of the room, and close the door so that drafts cannot fan the flames. (A fire can take half an hour to burn through a solid door.)

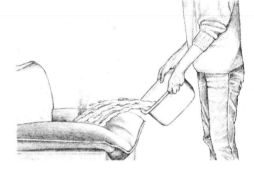

◆ If upholstery is burned by a cigarette falling on it and is just beginning to smolder, pour water over it.

◆ If the fire is smoldering seriously or is already burning, get out of the room and the house; the foam used in some upholstered furniture gives off lethal fumes.

2 Report the fire to your local emergency number (911 in some communities).

Clothes on fire

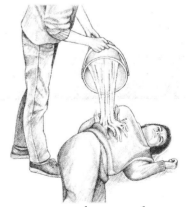

Get the person on the ground to stop the flames from rising up toward the face; douse the flames with water; or wrap her with a blanket or coat to smother the flames—the heavier the material the better.

▼▼ Don't roll the victim on the ground
♦♦ because the hot clothes could burn her, or the flames could spread to other areas of the body.

▼▼ Make sure you do not grab a plastic
♦♦ material to smother the flames; it will melt and could cause severe burns.

Grease fire

1 Turn off the heat under the pan or turn off the main power supply.

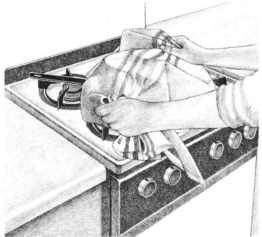

2 Smother the flames with a lid, a large plate, a baking pan, or a damp (not wet) dish towel.

♦ Don't move the pan or pour water over it; you'll fan the flames.

♦ **Oven fire.** Turn off the heat and let the fire burn itself out. Don't open the oven door; air will feed the fire.

Electrical fire

1 Turn off the main power supply at the circuit breaker or fuse box.

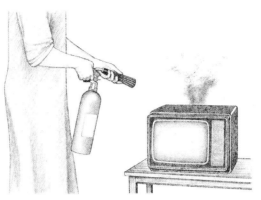

2 Extinguish the fire with an all-purpose fire extinguisher or one that is designed for use on electrical fires.

♦ If you don't have a suitable fire extinguisher, smother a burning appliance with a heavy rug or blanket; the heavier the better.

▼▼ Don't use water unless you know that
♦♦ the main power supply is turned off.

3 If you can't control the fire quickly, shut the door to the affected room and get everyone out of the house; call the fire department from a neighbor's home.

▼▼ Never use water to put out a fire in a
♦♦ television, stereo, or computer even if it is turned off, because there may be residual current in the machine and you could get an electric shock.

FLOOD

◆Act quickly to stop the flow of water and minimize the structural damage.

Burst pipe

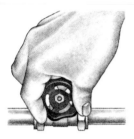

1 Stop the source of the water. Turn off water at the main shutoff valve if necessary.

Mopping up water. *Use towels, kitchen paper towels, or other absorbent material that will soak up the water. Press down hard with your hands to force the water up into the towels.*

2 If water is coming down through a light fixture, remove the relevant fuse from the main fuse box or trip the appropriate circuit breaker. Don't replace the fuse or reset the breaker until the area is completely dry.

3 If there is a bulge in the ceiling, pierce it with a screwdriver to minimize damage to the ceiling.

4 Do emergency repairs if you can (see pages 230–231), and call the plumber.

5 Mop up the water with towels as quickly as you can, and, if it is safe, put a fan in the room to speed up the drying time. (Use a long extension cord from another part of the house if necessary.) Lift up all floor coverings to let air circulate around them; they'll dry faster.

Floods from outside

1 Turn off the electricity, gas, and water to prevent a fire.

2 Put plastic garbage bags full of soil or rolled-up blankets on the outside of all the exterior doors. If the water keeps rising, put more bags along the sills of the ground floor windows to keep as much water out of the house as possible.

3 If you have time, put valuables on an upper floor and lift the carpets, or at least any rugs, and move them to a safer place.

4 If the water continues to rise, take any food you have in the house to an upper floor and wait for the emergency services, or if advised to, evacuate the building before access routes are cut off.

◆Act quickly to limit the flooding and prevent further damage that could be caused by fire due to electrical or gas sources being interfered with.

Appendix

GLOSSARY OF COOKING TERMS

Age: 1. To tenderize meat by allowing it to hang for a specified length of time in carefully controlled conditions.
2. To store cheese until it is mature and flavorful.
3. To store wine to improve flavor.

À la grecque: Vegetables cooked in olive oil with coriander seeds and other seasonings; served cold.

À la mode: Desserts à la mode are served with ice cream; meats cooked à la mode are braised with vegetables and served with gravy.

Al dente: Describes spaghetti or other pasta that is cooked only till it offers a slight resistance to the bite.

Amandine: Dishes made or garnished with almonds.

Aspic: Jellied meat, fish, or poultry stock or vegetable liquid often used for molding meat, fish, poultry, or vegetables.

Au gratin: Usually a pre-cooked dish topped with a sauce and bread crumbs or grated cheese, then browned in the oven or under the broiler.

Baste: To moisten foods during cooking with pan drippings or a special sauce in order to add flavor and prevent drying.

Batter: A mixture of fairly thin consistency, made of flour, liquid, and other ingredients.

Béarnaise sauce: Sauce made with egg yolks, butter, vinegar, and a spice mixture.

Beat: To make a mixture smooth by briskly whipping or stirring it with a spoon, wire whisk, rotary beater, or electric mixer.

Béchamel sauce: Basic white sauce made with flour, milk, and fat.

Bias-slice: To cut foods, usually vegetables, into elongated slices by holding a knife at a 45-degree angle to the cutting surface.

Bind: To add egg or liquid to a mixture to hold it together.

Blanch: To partially cook fruits, vegetables, or nuts in boiling water or steam to prepare for canning or freezing.

Bouillabaisse: A hearty stew made with several kinds of fish and shellfish.

Bouquet garni: Bunch of herbs, normally wrapped in cheesecloth and added to casseroles and stocks. Remove before serving.

Braise: To cook food slowly in a small amount of liquid in a tightly covered pan on the range top or in the oven.

Brine: Saltwater solution used to preserve fish, meat, or vegetables.

Broil: To cook food a measured distance from an overhead dry heat source. A broiler can be used to brown or toast foods or melt cheese.

Brush: To use a pastry brush to spread food lightly with a liquid such as salad oil, melted fat, milk, heavy cream, or beaten egg.

Butterfly: To split foods such as shrimp or steak through the middle without completely separating the halves, then spreading the halves to resemble a butterfly.

Candy: To cook in sugar or syrup when applied to vegetables. For fruit or fruit peel, to cook in heavy syrup till translucent.

Caramel: 1. Concentrated sugar syrup boiled until thick and brown.
2. A rich, chewy candy.

Caramelize: To stir sugar in skillet over low heat until it melts and develops a characteristic flavor and golden-brown color.

Carbonnade: Beef stew made with beer.

Cassoulet: French stew made with white beans, pork, ham, sausages, and duck or goose.

Clarify: Take the impurities out of fats, stocks, and consommés by melting them slowly, letting them cool down, and skimming.

Coat: To evenly cover food with crumbs, flour, or a batter.

Compote: Fruit cooked in sugar syrup, and seasoned with spices (e.g., cinnamon and cloves).

Condiment: 1. Sauces and relishes to add to food at the table, such as catsup or prepared mustard.
2. Seasoning, often pungent, used to bring out the flavor of foods.

Consommé: Clear meat broth (bouillon).

Court bouillon: Liquid used for poaching fish, made from water and wine or vinegar, with herbs and vegetables.

Cream: To beat butter or margarine (sometimes with sugar, until it is of a light consistency and nearly white.

Crisp-tender: Describes vegetables cooked until they're just tender and still somewhat crisp.

Croquette: Chopped or minced food, usually shaped as a ball or cone, coated with egg and crumbs, then deep-fried.

Cut in: To combine shortening with dry ingredients using a pastry blender or two knives.

Dash: An ingredient measure that equals about half of $\frac{1}{8}$ teaspoon.

Deglaze: Add wine, brandy, or stock to the roasting pan and scrape browned, solidified cooking juices off the bottom to make stock or gravy.

Degorge: Soak foods in water to remove excess liquid or strong or bitter flavors, or to improve color. Some are sprinkled with salt while soaking.

Devil: Season with spicy ingredients such as mustard, cayenne and Worcestershire sauce.

Dissolve: To stir a dry substance in a liquid, such as sugar in coffee or gelatin in water, till no solids remain. Heating the liquid is sometimes necessary.

Dollop: To place a scoop or spoonful of a semiliquid food, such as whipped cream or sour cream, on top of another food.

Dot: To scatter bits, as of butter or margarine, over surface of food.

Draw: To remove entrails from and clean poultry or game. Drawn fish are whole fish that have been cleaned but not boned.

Dredge: Sprinkle foods lightly with flour, icing sugar, or other fine powder.

Dress: 1. Mix salad with a dressing. 2. Pluck, clean, and trim (game and poultry).

En croûte: Cooked in a pastry shell.

Fillet: To cut lean meat or fish into pieces without bones.

Fines herbes: A mixture of herbs used for seasoning that traditionally includes parsley, chervil, chives, and tarragon.

Flake: To break food gently into small pieces.

Flame: To ignite warmed brandy or other alcohol poured over food. Also known as flambé.

Fold: To gently mix ingredients, using a folding motion. With a spatula, cut down through the mixture; cut across the bottom of the bowl, then up and over, close to the surface. Turn the bowl frequently.

Freeze: To reduce the temperature of foods so the liquid content solidifies.

Fry, deep: Immerse food, usually coated in batter or bread crumbs, in very hot, deep fat.

Fry, shallow: Cook food in a little fat in a shallow pan.

Frying, stir: Chinese method of cooking quickly, stirring constantly, in a little fat in a wok or frying pan.

Garnish: To add visual appeal to finished food by decorating it with small pieces of food, herbs, or edible flowers.

Glaze: To brush a mixture on a food to give it a glossy appearance or a hard finish.

Gnocchi: Italian dish of potato or semolina shaped into small rounds or squares.

Goulash: Hungarian meat stew with paprika.

Grind: To use a food grinder or food processor to cut food such as meat or fruit into fine pieces.

Gumbo: A thick, Cajun stew made with a roux, sausage or meat, poultry, shellfish, vegetables, and sometimes filé powder.

Infuse: Extract flavor by steeping food in hot liquid.

Julienne: To cut vegetables, fruit, or meat into matchlike strips.

Kabob: Cubes of meat, poultry, or fish and vegetables threaded on a skewer and grilled.

Knead: To work dough with the heel of your hand in a pressing and folding motion.

Macerate: Steep in sugar or liqueurs.

Marinate: Soak food in spicy or herby liquid to make it more tender and tasty, often used for grilled or barbecued food.

Melt: To heat a solid food, such as butter, margarine, or sugar, till it is liquid.

Mince: To chop food into very small pieces.

Mirepoix: Diced vegetables, usually carrots, onion, and celery, used as a basis for a braised dish.

Mix: To stir, usually with a spoon, till ingredients are thoroughly combined.

Mocha: Coffee-flavored or coffee combined with chocolate.

Mull: To slowly heat beverages, such as red wine or cider, with spices and sugar.

Paella: Spanish rice dish with fish or shellfish, meat, and saffron.

Panbroil: To cook meats in a skillet without added fat, removing any fat as it accumulates.

Panfry: To cook meats, poultry, or fish in a small amount of hot fat.

Parboil: To boil until partially cooked, usually before completing cooking by another method.

Partially set: Describes a gelatin mixture chilled until its consistency resembles unbeaten egg whites.

Pasteurize: To destroy, by heating, certain undesirable bacteria in juices and dairy foods.

Peel: To remove the outer layer or skin from a fruit or vegetable.

Petits fours: Small, rich, decoratively iced sweet cakes.

Pickle: To preserve or flavor meat, fish, vegetables, etc., in a brine or a solution made of vinegar, spices, and other seasonings.

Pilaf: Seasoned rice, often with meat or poultry added.

Pit: To remove the seed from a piece of fruit.

Poach: To cook gently by immersing food in simmering liquid such as a court bouillon.

Pot roast: 1. A large piece of meat, usually beef, that is cooked by braising. 2. To cook meat or poultry in a covered pot with liquid.

Preheat: To heat an oven to the recommended temperature before cooking in it.

Pressure cook: Cook quickly in pressurized saucepan at very high temperatures.

Prosciutto: Italian-style cured and spiced ham, served paper thin.

Provençale: Food cooked with tomatoes and garlic.

Puree: To chop food into a liquid or heavy paste, usually in a blender, food processor, or food mill.

Quiche: Baked pastry shell with savory filling, generally made with egg.

Ragout: French stew of meat and vegetables.

Ragu: Italian meat stew or sauce.

Ratatouille: A well seasoned vegetable stew from France. Traditional ingredients include eggplant, zucchini, green pepper, tomatoes, garlic, and olive oil.

Reduce: To rapidly boil liquids such as pan juices or sauces so that some of the liquid evaporates, thickening the mixture.

Render: To melt animal fat slowly to a liquid and then strain.

Risotto: Creamy Italian rice dish, traditionally made with an absorbent rice.

Roast: To cook meats, uncovered, in the oven.

Roux: Butter and flour cooked together as a basis for sauces.

Sauerkraut: German pickled white cabbage.

Sauté: To cook or brown food in a small amount of hot fat.

Scald: Heat milk or cream to just below boiling point when bubbles form in pan.

Score: To cut narrow grooves or slits partway through the outer surface of a food.

Shortening: Produced from bleached, refined, hydrogenated vegetable oil or animal fat; used as an ingredient in pastry or baked goods, and for frying.

Shuck: To remove the shells or husks from foods such as oysters, clams, or corn.

Sift: To put one or more dry ingredients through a sifter or sieve to incorporate air and break up any lumps.

Simmer: To heat liquids over low heat till bubbles form slowly and burst below the surface.

Skim: To remove melted fat or other substances from the surface of a liquid.

Souse: To pickle with vinegar or brine; most commonly used for oily fish such as herring.

Steam: To cook food in steam in perforated container, set above boiling water, to preserve nutrients.

Stew: To cook food in liquid for a long time till the food is tender, usually in a covered pot.

Stir: To mix ingredients with a spoon in a circular or figure-eight motion till combined.

Stroganoff: A main dish made with meat, sour cream, seasonings, and mushrooms. It is frequently served over noodles.

Tapas: Spanish snack served with drinks before a meal.

Terrine: 1. Oblong pottery dish used for cooking pâté. 2. A meat, fish or game mixture similar to pâté, which is baked in a terrine dish and served cold.

Timbale: 1. Cup-shaped earthenware or metal mold used for savory preparations. 2. A custard or creamed meat mixture baked in a small round mold.

Toast points: Toast slices, cut in halves or quarters diagonally.

Tofu: Made from pressed soybean curd, with the consistency of soft cheese.

Toss: To mix ingredients lightly by lifting and dropping them with a spoon or a fork and spoon.

Truss: To secure poultry with string or skewers to hold its shape while cooking.

Vol-au-vent: Puff pastry shell, filled with diced meat, vegetables, or fish in a sauce.

Whey: Watery liquid that separates out from milk or cream when making cheese.

Whip: To beat food lightly and rapidly using a wire whisk, rotary beater, or electric mixer to incorporate air into the mixture and increase its volume.

Wok: Traditional Chinese convex-bottomed pan for stir-frying. (Flat-bottomed ones also are available.)

Zest: Thin shavings of orange or lemon peel used as flavoring.

CALORIE TALLY

A-B

ALFALFA SPROUTS, fresh; 1 cup 10
APPLE, fresh; 1 medium 80
APPLESAUCE, canned
    sweetened; ½ cup 98
    unsweetened; ½ cup 53
APRICOTS
    canned, in syrup; ½ cup 108
    fresh; 3 medium 50
ASPARAGUS
    cooked, drained; 4 spears 15
AVOCADO, peeled; ½ avocado 170
BACON
    Canadian-style, cooked; 2 slices 85
    crisp strips, medium thickness;
        3 slices 110
BANANA; 1 medium 105
BEANS
    baked, with tomato sauce and pork,
        canned; ½ cup 155
    garbanzo, cooked, drained; ½ cup 135
    green snap, cooked, drained; ½ cup 23
    navy, dry, cooked, drained; ½ cup 113
    red kidney, canned; ½ cup 115
BEEF, corned, canned; 3 ounces 185
BEEF CUTS, cooked
    flank steak, lean only; 3 ounces 207
    ground beef, lean; 3 ounces 234
    ground beef, regular; 3 ounces 260
    pot roast, chuck, lean only;
        3 ounces 196
    rib roast, lean only; 3 ounces 204
    round steak, lean only; 3 ounces 165
    sirloin steak, lean only; 3 ounces 177
BEEF LIVER, braised; 3 ounces 137
BEETS, cooked, diced; ½ cup 28
BEVERAGES
    beer; 12 ounces 150
    cola; 12 ounces 160
    dessert wine; 3½ ounces 140
    ginger ale; 12 ounces 125
    gin, rum, vodka (80 proof);
        1½ ounces 95
    table wine, white; 3½ ounces 80
BLUEBERRIES
    fresh; ½ cup 40
    frozen, sweetened; ½ cup 93

BREADS
    bagel; 1 (3½-inch diameter) 200
    bun, frankfurter or hamburger; 1 119
    English muffin, plain; 1 140
    French; 1 slice (1 inch thick) 100
    pita; 1 (6½-inch diameter) 165
    raisin; 1 slice 65
    white; 1 slice 65
    whole wheat; 1 slice 70
BROCCOLI
    cooked, drained; 1 medium stalk 50
    frozen chopped, cooked, drained;
        ½ cup 25
BRUSSELS SPROUTS
    cooked, drained; ½ cup 30
BUTTER; 1 tablespoon 100

C

CABBAGE
    common varieties, raw, shredded;
        1 cup 15
    red, raw, shredded; 1 cup 20
CAKES, baked from mixes
    angel, no icing; $\frac{1}{12}$ cake 125
    devil's food or yellow, 2 layers,
        9-inch diameter, chocolate frosting;
        $\frac{1}{16}$ cake 235
CANDIES
    caramel; 1 ounce 115
    gumdrops; 1 ounce 100
    hard; 1 ounce 110
    milk-chocolate bar; 1 ounce 145
CANTALOUPE; ½ of a 5-inch-diameter
    melon 95
CARROTS
    cooked, drained, sliced; ½ cup 35
    raw; 1 large 30
CATSUP; 1 tablespoon 15
CAULIFLOWER
    cooked, drained; ½ cup 15
    raw, whole flowerets; 1 cup 25
CELERY, raw, chopped; ½ cup 10
CEREALS, ready to eat
    bran flakes; about ¾ cup 90
    cornflakes; about 1¼ cups 110
    granola; about ⅓ cup 125
    wheat flakes; about 1 cup 100

CHEESES
American, process; 1 ounce 105
blue; 1 ounce 100
Camembert; 1 ounce.......................... 86
Cheddar; 1 ounce 115
cottage, cream-style, large curd;
  1 cup 235
cottage, low fat (2% fat); 1 cup........... 205
cream cheese; 1 ounce 100
cream cheese, reduced calorie;
  1 ounce.. 60
Monterey Jack; 1 ounce 106
mozzarella, part skim milk; 1 ounce.... 72
Neufchâtel; 1 ounce 74
Parmesan, grated; 1 tablespoon 25
ricotta, part skim milk; 1 cup 340
Swiss, natural; 1 ounce....................... 105

CHERRIES
canned, in syrup, sweet; $\frac{1}{2}$ cup 107
canned, water pack, tart, pitted;
  $\frac{1}{2}$ cup 45
fresh, sweet, whole; 10 cherries 50

CHICKEN
breast, skinned, roasted; $\frac{1}{2}$ breast 142
canned, with broth; 5 ounces 234
dark meat, skinned, roasted; 1 cup 286
light meat, skinned, roasted; 1 cup...... 242

CHOCOLATE
bitter; 1 ounce 145
semisweet; 1 ounce 143
sweet plain; 1 ounce........................... 150
syrup, fudge-type; 2 tablespoons 125
syrup, thin-type; 2 tablespoons 85
CLAMS, canned; 3 ounces 85
COCONUT, sweetened, shredded;
  $\frac{1}{4}$ cup 118

COOKIES
chocolate chip; 1 ($2\frac{1}{4}$-inch diameter).... 45
cream sandwich, chocolate; 1 49
fig bar; 1 53
sugar; 1 ($2\frac{1}{2}$-inch diameter).................... 59
vanilla wafer; 3 ($1\frac{3}{4}$-inch diameter)....... 56

CORN
canned, cream-style; $\frac{1}{2}$ cup................... 93
canned, vacuum pack, whole kernel;
  $\frac{1}{2}$ cup... 83
sweet, cooked; 1 ear (5 × $1\frac{3}{4}$ inches) 85
CORNSTARCH; 1 tablespoon............. 29
CORN SYRUP; 1 tablespoon 59
CRABMEAT, canned; $\frac{1}{2}$ cup.................. 68

CRACKERS
cheese; 1 (1-inch square)..................... 5
graham; 2 ($2\frac{1}{2}$-inch square) 60
saltine; 2 (2-inch square)..................... 25

CREAM
half-and-half; 1 tablespoon................. 20
whipping; 1 tablespoon....................... 50
CUCUMBER; 6 large slices 5

D-G

DATES, fresh or dried, pitted; 10.......... 230
DOUGHNUTS
cake, plain; 1 ($3\frac{1}{4}$ × 1 inch)................... 210
yeast; 1 ($3\frac{3}{4}$ × $1\frac{1}{4}$ inches)................. 235
EGG
fried; 1 large 95
poached, or hard or soft cooked;
  1 large.. 80
scrambled, plain; made with
  1 large egg 110
white; 1 large 15
yolk; 1 large..................................... 65
EGGNOG; 1 cup 340
EGGPLANT, cooked, diced; $\frac{1}{2}$ cup 13
FISH
haddock, breaded, fried; 3 ounces 175
halibut, broiled; 3 ounces................... 140
herring, pickled; 3 ounces 190
salmon, broiled or baked; 3 ounces 140
salmon, canned, pink; 3 ounces 120
sardines, canned, in oil, drained;
  3 ounces 175
tuna, canned, in oil, drained;
  3 ounces 165
tuna, canned, in water, drained;
  3 ounces 135
FLOUR
all-purpose; 1 cup 455
whole wheat; 1 cup 400
FRANKFURTER, cooked; 1................ 145
GRAPEFRUIT
fresh; $\frac{1}{2}$ medium................................ 40
juice, canned, sweetened; 1 cup 115
juice, fresh; 1 cup.............................. 95
GRAPES
green, seedless; 10............................. 35

H-O

HAM, fully cooked, lean only;
  2.4 ounces 105
HONEYDEW MELON; $\frac{1}{10}$ of a
  $6\frac{1}{2}$-inch-diameter melon...................... 45

ICE CREAM, vanilla
    ice milk; 1 cup (about 4% fat) 185
    regular; 1 cup (about 11% fat) 270
    soft serve; 1 cup 223
JAM; 1 tablespoon 55
JELLY; 1 tablespoon 50
KALE, cooked, drained; ½ cup 20
KIWIFRUIT; 1 45
KOHLRABI, cooked, drained, diced;
    ½ cup 25
LAMB, cooked
    loin chop, lean only; 2.3 ounces 140
    roast leg, lean only; 2.6 ounces 140
LEMONADE, frozen concentrate,
    sweetened, reconstituted; 1 cup 106
LETTUCE
    Boston; ¼ of a medium head 5
    iceberg; ¼ of a medium compact head .. 20
LIMEADE, frozen concentrate,
    sweetened, reconstituted; 1 cup 100
LOBSTER, cooked; ½ cup 69
LUNCHEON MEATS
    bologna; 1 slice (1 ounce) 90
    salami, cooked; 1 slice (1 ounce) 73
MAPLE SYRUP; 1 tablespoon 50
MARGARINE, soft or regular;
    1 tablespoon 100
MARSHMALLOWS; 1 ounce 90
MAYONNAISE; 1 tablespoon 100
MILK
    buttermilk; 1 cup 100
    chocolate drink (2% fat); 1 cup 180
    condensed, sweetened, undiluted;
      1 cup 980
    dried nonfat, instant; 1 cup 245
    evaporated, skim, undiluted; 1 cup 200
    evaporated, whole, undiluted; 1 cup ... 340
    low fat (2% fat); 1 cup 120
    skim; 1 cup 85
    whole; 1 cup 150
MOLASSES, light; 2 tablespoons 85
MUFFINS
    blueberry; 1 135
    bran; 1 125
    corn; 1 145
MUSHROOMS
    canned, drained; ⅓ cup 12
    raw, sliced; 1 cup 20

NUTS
    almonds; 1 ounce 165
    cashews, roasted in oil; 1 ounce 165
    peanuts, roasted in oil, shelled;
      1 ounce 165
    pecans; 1 ounce 190
    walnuts; 1 ounce 170
OIL; 1 tablespoon 125
OLIVES
    green; 4 medium 15
    ripe; 3 small 15
ONIONS
    green, without tops; 6 small 10
    mature, raw, chopped; ½ cup 28
ORANGES
    fresh; 1 medium 60
    juice, canned, unsweetened;
      1 cup 105
    juice, fresh; 1 cup 110
    juice, frozen concentrate,
      reconstituted; 1 cup 110
OYSTERS
    raw; ½ cup (6 to 10 medium) 80

P-S

PANCAKE; 1 (4-inch diameter) 60
PEACHES
    canned, in juice; ½ cup 55
    canned, in syrup; ½ cup...................... 95
    fresh; 1 medium 35
PEANUT BUTTER; 1 tablespoon 95
PEA PODS, cooked, drained; ½ cup 33
PEARS
    canned, in juice; 2 halves 63
    canned, in syrup; ½ cup...................... 95
    fresh; 1 medium 100
PEAS, green, cooked; ½ cup 63
PEPPERONI; 1 slice (⅛ inch thick) 27
PEPPERS, green, sweet, chopped;
    ¾ cup 20
PICKLES
    dill; 1 medium 5
    sweet; 1 small 20
PIES; ⅛ of a 9-inch pie
    apple 303
    blueberry 286
    cherry 308
    lemon meringue 268
    pumpkin 240

PINEAPPLE
    canned, in juice; ½ cup 75
    fresh, diced; ½ cup 38
    juice, canned, unsweetened: 1 cup 140

PLUMS
    canned, in juice; ½ cup 73
    fresh; 1 (2-inch diameter).................... 3

POPCORN
    plain, air-popped; 1 cup 30
    plain, popped in oil; 1 cup 55

PORK, cooked
    chop, loin center cut, lean only;
        2½ ounces................................... 165
    sausage, links; 3 ounces 150

POTATO CHIPS; 10 medium.............. 105

POTATOES
    baked; 1 (about 8 ounces).................... 220
    boiled; 1 (about 5 ounces) 120
    mashed with milk; ½ cup..................... 80
    sweet, baked; 1 medium 115

PRUNE JUICE, canned; 1 cup............. 180

PRUNES, dried, uncooked, pitted;
    5 large 115

PUDDINGS, cooked
    chocolate; ½ cup 150
    vanilla; ½ cup 145

PUMPKIN, canned; 1 cup 85

RAISINS; 1 cup (not packed) 435

RASPBERRIES
    fresh; ½ cup....................................... 30
    frozen, sweetened; ½ cup..................... 128

RHUBARB
    cooked, sweetened; ½ cup 140
    raw, diced; 1 cup.............................. 26

RICE
    brown, cooked; ½ cup........................ 115
    white, cooked; ½ cup 113
    white, quick cooking, cooked;
      ½ cup... 93

ROLLS
    cloverleaf; 1 (2½-inch diameter).......... 85
    hard; 1 (3¾-inch diameter).................... 155
    sweet; 1 medium................................ 220

SALAD DRESSINGS
    blue cheese; 1 tablespoon 75
    French; 1 tablespoon 85
    Italian; 1 tablespoon 80
    mayonnaise; 1 tablespoon 100
    mayonnaise-type; 1 tablespoon 60
    Thousand Island; 1 tablespoon........... 60

SAUERKRAUT, canned; ½ cup 23

SHERBET, orange; ½ cup...................... 135

SHORTENING; 1 tablespoon.............. 115

SHRIMP, canned; 3 ounces................. 100

SOUPS, condensed, canned
    (diluted with water unless
    specified otherwise)
    beef bouillon, broth, consommé;
      1 cup 15
    chicken noodle; 1 cup 75
    cream of chicken,
      diluted with milk; 1 cup.................. 190
    cream of mushroom,
      diluted with milk; 1 cup.................. 205
    tomato; 1 cup 85
    tomato, diluted with milk; 1 cup 160

SOUR CREAM, dairy; ½ cup.............. 248

SPINACH
    canned, drained; ½ cup 25
    frozen, cooked, drained; ½ cup............ 28
    raw, torn; 1 cup 10

SQUASH
    summer, cooked, drained, sliced;
      ½ cup... 18
    winter, baked, cubed; ½ cup 40

STRAWBERRIES
    fresh, whole; ½ cup........................... 23
    frozen, sweetened, sliced; ½ cup 123

SUGARS
    brown, packed; ½ cup 410
    granulated; 1 tablespoon 45
    powdered; ½ cup 193

T-Z

TOMATOES
    canned; ½ cup................................... 25
    fresh; 1 medium................................ 25
    juice, canned; 1 cup 40
    paste, canned; 1 cup......................... 220
    sauce; 1 cup 75

TURKEY
    roasted, light and dark; 1 cup 240

TURNIPS, cooked, diced; ½ cup 15

VEAL, cooked, cutlet; 3 ounces............ 185

WAFFLE; 1 section
    (4½ × 4½ × ⅝ inch)............................ 140

WATERMELON; 1 wedge
    (8 × 4 inches)................................... 155

YOGURT
    low fat, fruit flavored;
      8 ounces 230
    low fat, plain; 8 ounces...................... 145

COOKING TIMES

ROASTING MEAT

To roast: Place meat, fat side up, on a rack in a shallow roasting pan. (Rib roasts do not need a rack.) For ham, if desired, score the top in a diamond pattern. Insert a meat thermometer. Do not add water or liquid and do not cover. Roast in a 325° oven, unless chart or recipe says otherwise, for the time given or till the thermometer registers the specified temperature.

CUT	WEIGHT (POUNDS)	DONENESS	ROASTING TIME (HOURS)
Beef Boneless rolled rump roast	4–6	150°–170°	1½–3
Boneless sirloin roast	4–6	140° rare 160° medium 170° well-done	2¼–2¾ 2¾–3¼ 3¼–3¾
Eye round roast	2–3	140° rare 160° medium 170° well-done	1¼–1¾ 1¾–2¼ 2¼–2¾
Rib eye roast (roast at 350°)	4–6	140° rare 160° medium 170° well-done	1¼–2 1¼–2¼ 1½–2½
Rib roast	4–6	140° rare 160° medium 170° well-done	1¾–3 2¼–3¾ 2¾–4¼
Tenderloin roast Half Whole (roast at 425°)	2–3 4–6	140° rare 140° rare	¾–1 1¼–1½
Tip roast	3–5 6–8	140°–170° 140°–170°	1¾–3¼ 3–4½
Top round roast	4–6	140°–170°	1½–3
Veal Boneless rolled breast roast	2½–3½	170° well-done	1¾–2¼
Boneless rolled shoulder roast	3–5	170° well-done	2¾–3¼
Loin roast	3–5	170° well-done	2–2½

CUT	WEIGHT (POUNDS)	DONENESS	ROASTING TIME (HOURS)
Veal (cont) Rib roast	3–5	170° well-done	$1\frac{3}{4}$–$2\frac{3}{4}$
Lamb Boneless leg roast	4–7	160° medium	2–4
Boneless rolled shoulder roast	2–3	160° medium	$1\frac{1}{2}$–$3\frac{1}{4}$
Rib crown roast	3–4	140° rare 160° medium 170° well-done	1–$1\frac{1}{4}$ $1\frac{1}{4}$–$1\frac{3}{4}$ $1\frac{1}{2}$–2
Whole leg roast	5–7	140° rare 160° medium 170° well	$1\frac{3}{4}$–3 2–3 $2\frac{1}{2}$–$4\frac{1}{2}$
Pork Boneless top loin roast Single loin Double loin, tied	2–4 3–5	170° well-done 170° well-done	1–$2\frac{1}{4}$ $1\frac{3}{4}$–$3\frac{1}{4}$
Loin back ribs, spareribs, country-style ribs (roast at 350°)	2–4	Well-done	$1\frac{1}{2}$–2
Loin blade or sirloin roast	3–4	170° well-done	2–3
Loin center rib roast (backbone loosened)	3–5	170° well-done	$1\frac{1}{2}$–3
Rib crown roast	4–6	170° well-done	$1\frac{3}{4}$–3
Tenderloin	$\frac{3}{4}$–1	170° well-done	$\frac{1}{2}$–1
Ham (fully cooked) Boneless half	4–6	140°	$1\frac{1}{4}$–$2\frac{1}{2}$
Boneless portion	3–4	140°	$1\frac{1}{2}$–$2\frac{1}{4}$
Smoked picnic	5–8	140°	2–4

ROASTING POULTRY

TYPE OF BIRD	WEIGHT	OVEN	ROASTING TIME
Capon	5–7 pounds	325°	$1\frac{3}{4}$–$2\frac{1}{2}$ hours
Chicken, broiler-fryer, whole	$2\frac{1}{2}$–3 pounds	375°	$1\frac{1}{4}$–$1\frac{1}{2}$ hours
	$3\frac{1}{2}$–4 pounds	375°	$1\frac{1}{4}$–$1\frac{3}{4}$ hours
	$4\frac{1}{2}$–5 pounds	375°	$1\frac{1}{2}$–2 hours
Chicken, roasting, whole	5–6 pounds	325°	$1\frac{3}{4}$–$2\frac{1}{2}$ hours
Cornish game hen	1–$1\frac{1}{2}$ pounds	375°	$1\frac{1}{4}$–$1\frac{1}{2}$ hours
Duckling, domestic	3–5 pounds	375°	$1\frac{3}{4}$–$2\frac{1}{4}$ hours
Goose, domestic	7–8 pounds	350°	2–$2\frac{1}{2}$ hours
	8–10 pounds	350°	$2\frac{1}{2}$–3 hours
	10–12 pounds	350°	3–$3\frac{1}{2}$ hours
Pheasant	2–3 pounds	350°	$1\frac{1}{2}$–$1\frac{3}{4}$ hours
Quail	4–6 ounces each	375°	30–50 minutes

TYPE OF BIRD	WEIGHT	OVEN	ROASTING TIME
Squab	12–14 ounces each	375°	45–60 minutes
Turkey, boneless whole	2½–3½ pounds	325°	2–2½ hours
	4–6 pounds	325°	2½–3½ hours
Turkey, unstuffed*	6–8 pounds	325°	3–3½ hours
	8–12 pounds	325°	3–4 hours
	12–16 pounds	325°	4–5 hours
	16–20 pounds	325°	4½–5 hours
	20–24 pounds	325°	5–6 hours
Turkey breast, whole	4–6 pounds	325°	1½–2¼ hours
	6–8 pounds	325°	2¼–3¼ hours
Turkey drumstick	1–1½ pounds	325°	1¼–1¾ hours
Turkey thigh	1½–1¾ pounds	325°	1½–1¾ hours

Note: Birds vary in size, shape, and tenderness; use these times as a general guide.
* Stuffed birds generally require 30 to 45 minutes more roasting time than unstuffed birds.

CONVERSION TABLES

It is rarely possible to make an exact comparison between the different measuring systems. All of the following figures have been rounded up slightly to make it easier to read equivalents quickly. If you need a more precise conversion for any reason, calculate the conversion using the formula that is given below each table.

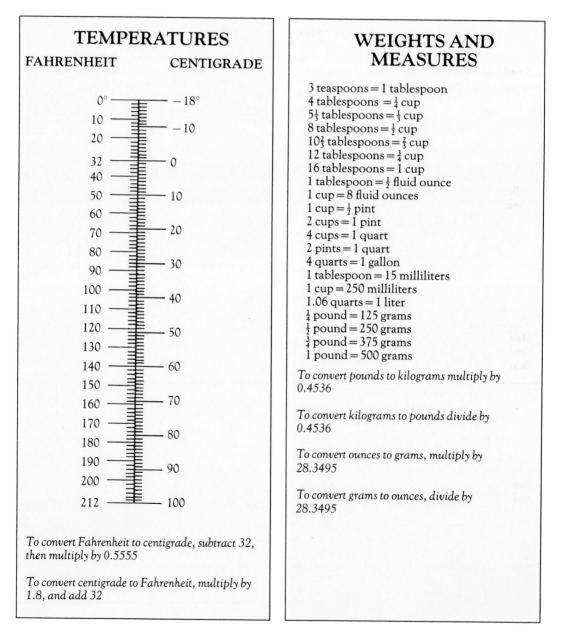

TEMPERATURES

FAHRENHEIT		CENTIGRADE
0°		−18°
10		−10
20		
32		0
40		
50		10
60		
70		20
80		
90		30
100		
110		40
120		50
130		
140		60
150		
160		70
170		
180		80
190		90
200		
212		100

To convert Fahrenheit to centigrade, subtract 32, then multiply by 0.5555

To convert centigrade to Fahrenheit, multiply by 1.8, and add 32

WEIGHTS AND MEASURES

3 teaspoons = 1 tablespoon
4 tablespoons = $\frac{1}{4}$ cup
$5\frac{1}{3}$ tablespoons = $\frac{1}{3}$ cup
8 tablespoons = $\frac{1}{2}$ cup
$10\frac{2}{3}$ tablespoons = $\frac{2}{3}$ cup
12 tablespoons = $\frac{3}{4}$ cup
16 tablespoons = 1 cup
1 tablespoon = $\frac{1}{2}$ fluid ounce
1 cup = 8 fluid ounces
1 cup = $\frac{1}{2}$ pint
2 cups = 1 pint
4 cups = 1 quart
2 pints = 1 quart
4 quarts = 1 gallon
1 tablespoon = 15 milliliters
1 cup = 250 milliliters
1.06 quarts = 1 liter
$\frac{1}{4}$ pound = 125 grams
$\frac{1}{2}$ pound = 250 grams
$\frac{3}{4}$ pound = 375 grams
1 pound = 500 grams

To convert pounds to kilograms multiply by 0.4536

To convert kilograms to pounds divide by 0.4536

To convert ounces to grams, multiply by 28.3495

To convert grams to ounces, divide by 28.3495

The Basic Food Groups

	Foods in Group	Number of Daily Servings	Serving Size	Major Nutrients
Vegetables and Fruits	All vegetables and fruits (fresh, canned, frozen, or dried) and their juices.	4 servings. (For vitamin C use citrus fruits, melons, berries, tomatoes, or dark green vegetables daily. For vitamin A use dark green or deep yellow vegetables.)	$\frac{1}{2}$ cup or a typical portion such as 1 medium orange, $\frac{1}{2}$ of a medium grapefruit, 1 medium potato, or 1 wedge of lettuce.	Carbohydrates, fiber, and vitamins A and C. Dark green vegetables are good sources of riboflavin, folacin, iron, and magnesium. Some greens contain calcium.
Breads and Cereals	All foods based on whole grains or enriched flour or meal. Includes breads, biscuits, muffins, waffles, pancakes, pasta, rice, and cereals.	4 servings. (For fiber, include some whole-grain bread or cereal every day.)	1 slice bread; 1 biscuit or muffin; 1 pancake or waffle; $\frac{1}{2}$ to $\frac{3}{4}$ cup cooked pasta, rice, bulgur, or cereal; or 1 ounce ready-to-eat cereal.	Carbohydrates, protein, thiamine, riboflavin, niacin, B vitamins, and iron. Whole-grain products provide magnesium, fiber, and folacin.
Milk and Cheese	All types of milk, yogurt, cheese, ice milk, ice cream, and foods prepared with milk (milk shakes, puddings, and creamed soups).	Children under 9, 2 to 3 servings. Children 9 to 12, 3 servings. Teens, 4 servings. Adults, 2 servings. Pregnant women, 3 servings. Nursing mothers, 4 servings.	1 cup milk or yogurt, 2 cups cottage cheese, $1\frac{1}{2}$ ounces cheese, 2 ounces process cheese food or spread. $\frac{1}{4}$ cup Parmesan cheese, or $1\frac{1}{2}$ cups ice cream.	Protein, calcium, riboflavin, and vitamins A, B_1, and B_{12}. When fortified, these products also provide vitamin D.
Meats, Fish Poultry, and Beans	Beef, veal, lamb, pork, poultry, fish, shellfish, variety meats, dry beans or peas, soybeans, lentils, eggs, peanuts and other nuts, peanut butter, and seeds.	2 servings.	2 to 3 ounces lean cooked meat, poultry, or fish; 1 to $1\frac{1}{2}$ cups cooked dry beans, peas, or lentils; 2 eggs; $\frac{1}{2}$ to 1 cup nuts or seeds; or $\frac{1}{4}$ cup peanut butter.	Protein, phosphorus, and vitamin B_6. Foods of animal origin provide vitamin B_{12}. Meats, dry beans, and dry peas provide iron. Liver and egg yolks provide vitamin A.
Fats, Sweets, and Alcohol	All fats and oils; mayonnaise and salad dressings; all concentrated sweets; highly sugared beverages; alcoholic beverages; unenriched, refined flour products.	No serving number is recommended. In moderation, these foods can be used to round out meals, as long as requirements from the other categories are satisfied.	No specific serving size is recommended.	These foods provide very few nutrients in proportion to the number of calories they contain. Vegetable oils provide vitamin E and essential fatty acids.

FAMILY HEALTH RECORDS

Name	
Date of birth	
Blood type	

IMMUNIZATIONS	Date
DPT (Diphtheria, pertussis/ whooping cough, tetanus) plus polio drops	1 2 3
Measles	
Diphtheria, tetanus plus polio drops preschool booster	
Rubella (German measles)	
Tetanus boosters	
Polio boosters	
Other immunizations	

IMPORTANT ILLNESSES (and treatments)	Date

ALLERGIES

OTHER INFORMATION

Name	
Date of birth	
Blood type	

IMMUNIZATIONS	Date
DPT (Diphtheria, pertussis/ whooping cough, tetanus) plus polio drops	1 2 3
Measles	
Diphtheria, tetanus plus polio drops preschool booster	
Rubella (German measles)	
Tetanus boosters	
Polio boosters	
Other immunizations	

IMPORTANT ILLNESSES (and treatments)	Date

ALLERGIES

OTHER INFORMATION

Name

_____

Date of birth

_____

Blood type

IMMUNIZATIONS	Date
DPT (Diphtheria, pertussis/ whooping cough, tetanus) plus polio drops	1 2 3
Measles	
Diphtheria, tetanus plus polio drops preschool booster	
Rubella (German measles)	
Tetanus boosters	
Polio boosters	
Other immunizations	

IMPORTANT ILLNESSES (and treatments)	Date

ALLERGIES	

OTHER INFORMATION

Name

_____

Date of birth

_____

Blood type

IMMUNIZATIONS	Date
DPT (Diphtheria, pertussis/ whooping cough, tetanus) plus polio drops	1 2 3
Measles	
Diphtheria, tetanus plus polio drops preschool booster	
Rubella (German measles)	
Tetanus boosters	
Polio boosters	
Other immunizations	

IMPORTANT ILLNESSES (and treatments)	Date

ALLERGIES

OTHER INFORMATION

BIRTH RECORD

NAME

| Date of birth | Time of birth |

| Born at | Duration of pregnancy |

MOTHER'S HEALTH DURING PREGNANCY

Illness

Medication

Problems

DELIVERY

Type

Monitoring

Drugs

Problems

Special care

Consultant

Hospital

Length of stay

BABY

| Height | Weight |

| Blood type | Head circumference |

Type of feeding:

| Breast | Bottle |

DEVELOPMENT RECORD

ACTIVITY	AGE
Smiles	
Holds head up for a few seconds	
Sleeps through night	
Rolls over	
Sits unsupported	
Crawls/shuffles	
Stands alone	
Walks	
Skips	
First tooth	
Starts solids	
Feeds self	
Looks for hidden toy	
First words	
Points to parts of the body	
Makes simple statements	
Pedals tricycle	
First visit to the dentist	
Gains bladder control	
Gains bowel control	
Can fasten buttons	
Fastens shoes	
Draws a circle	
Starts play group/nursery school	
Prints first name	

BIRTH RECORD

NAME
_____

Date of   Time of
birth   birth

Born at   Duration of
                 pregnancy

MOTHER'S HEALTH DURING PREGNANCY

Illness

Medication

Problems

DELIVERY

Type

Monitoring

Drugs

Problems

Special care

Consultant

Hospital

Length of stay

BABY

Height   Weight

Blood type   Head
                 circumference

Type of feeding:

Breast   Bottle

DEVELOPMENT RECORD

ACTIVITY	AGE
Smiles	
Holds head up for a few seconds	
Sleeps through night	
Rolls over	
Sits unsupported	
Crawls/shuffles	
Stands alone	
Walks	
Skips	
First tooth	
Starts solids	
Feeds self	
Looks for hidden toy	
First words	
Points to parts of the body	
Makes simple statements	
Pedals tricycle	
First visit to the dentist	
Gains bladder control	
Gains bowel control	
Can fasten buttons	
Fastens shoes	
Draws a circle	
Starts play group/nursery school	
Prints first name	

USEFUL ADDRESSES

GENERAL

Call for Action
575 Lexington Ave.
New York, New York 10022
212/537-0585
Refers callers on a confidential basis to places where they can get help with any type of consumer problem. The not-for-profit service is supported by broadcast organizations.

Center for Science in the Public Interest
1501 Sixteenth St. NW
Washington, DC 20036
202/332-9110
Provides information on food advertising, nutrition, diet and food safety; protects the public from scientific and health hazards.

Consumer Information Catalog
Pueblo, Colorado 81009
(written inquiries only)
Will send out a catalog containing about 200 federal consumer publications from which to choose.

Consumers Union of United States, Inc.
256 Washington St.
Mount Vernon, New York 10553
914/667-9400
Provides information and advice on goods, services, health, and personal finance; initiates and cooperates with individual and group efforts to maintain and enhance the quality of life for consumers; publishes Consumer Reports.

Council of the Better Business Bureau
1515 Wilson Blvd.
Suite 300
Arlington, Virginia 22209
703/276-0100
Network of local organizations that provides consumer education programs and materials, handles inquiries, mediates complaints, provides general information on companies, and maintains records of consumer satisfaction or dissatisfaction with individual companies.

Federal Deposit Insurance Corporation
Consumer Affairs
550 Seventeenth St. NW
Washington, DC 20429
800/424-5488 (9 a.m.–4 p.m. Eastern Standard Time)
Answers savings and loan and bank-related insurance questions and handles complaints about consumer protection and civil rights matters.

Office of Thrift Supervision
1700 G St. NW
Washington, DC 20552
800/842-6929
Handles complaints regarding savings and loan associations and distributes pamphlets about mortgage rates.

AUTOMOTIVE

American Automobile Association
1000 AAA Dr.
Heathrow, Florida 32746-5063
407/444-7000
Federation of local automobile clubs.

National Automobile Dealers Association
8400 Westpark Dr.
McLean, Virginia 22101
703/821-7144
Operates consumer-action panels throughout the country to resolve complaints against new car dealers.

BUILDING AND HOME IMPROVEMENT

Associated Landscape Contractors of America
405 N. Washington St.
Suite 104
Falls Church, Virginia 22046
703/241-4004
Answers technical questions; supplies information about a variety of subjects including how to use indoor foliage for clean air and where to purchase supplies for indoor/outdoor landscaping; puts you in touch with local chapters.

Home Owners Warranty Program
1110 N. Glebe Rd.
Arlington, Virginia 22201
800/CALL-HOW
Approved new home builders offer a full 10 years of warranty/insurance on all eligible homes they build. The program provides third-party dispute resolution for new homes built by HOW-member home builders.

Insulation Contractors Association of America
15819 Crabbs Branch Way
Rockville, Maryland 20855
301/590-0030
Will help you find a professional insulation contractor.

Mineral Insulation Manufacturers Association
1420 King St.
Alexandria, Virginia 22314
703/684–0084
Responds to specific questions about insulation requirements and levels of R-values and gives pointers on how to insulate your home.

National Appropriate Technology Assistance Service
P.O. Box 2525
Butte, Montana 59702
800/428–2525 or
800/428–1718 (in Montana)
Provides technical and business help to implement renewable-energy and energy-conservation projects using hot-water systems, energy-efficient building techniques, waste recycling, and renewable-energy forms.

National Association of Home Builders
Department of Consumer Affairs
Fifteenth and M Streets NW
Washington, DC 20005
202/822–0409
Answers questions about new homes and remodeling and makes referrals to local consumer protection agencies for handling complaints.

National Association of Plumbing, Heating and Cooling Contractors
180 S. Washington St.
Falls Church, Virginia 22041
703/237–8100
Will recommend members in local areas; also publishes brochures about such topics as choosing a contractor and winterizing a plumbing system.

National Association of the Remodeling Industry
1901 N. Moore St.
Suite 808
Arlington, Virginia 22209
703/276–7600
Publishes a consumer brochure and refers requests for information to association chapters, who, in turn, may furnish local listings for assistance.

National Kitchen and Bath Association
124 Main St.
Hackettstown,
New Jersey 07840
201/852–0033
Supplies basic consumer information about remodeling kitchens and bathrooms and helps consumers find someone to work with at the local level.

National Roofing Contractors Association
1 O'Hare Centre
Suite 8030
6250 River Rd.
Rosemont, Illinois 60018
800/USA–ROOF
Provides list of member contractors in local areas and publishes booklet that answers key questions roof buyers ask.

United States League of Savings Associations
111 E. Wacker Dr.
Chicago, Illinois 60601
Publishes "Energy Conservation and You," a free booklet listing items to ask about when considering home buying.

CHILD CARE

Child Care Action Campaign
330 Seventh Ave.
Eighteenth Floor
New York, New York 10001
212/239–0138
Supplies information about child-care-related issues and makes referrals for child care.

Child Welfare League
440 First St. NW
Suite 310
Washington, DC 20001
202/638–2952
Publishes child welfare materials, including an adoption directory.

National Association for the Education of Young Children
1834 Connecticut Ave. NW
Washington, DC 20009
(written inquiries only)
Provides resources about children from birth through age 8, including a brochure about choosing a good early childhood program.

National Association for Gifted Children
4175 Lovell Rd.
Suite 140
Circle Pines,
Minnesota 55014
612/784–3475
Disseminates information to school personnel, parents, and public officials related to the nature and education of the gifted; encourages and assists the development of state and local organizations that support gifted education.

National Center for Missing and Exploited Children
2101 Wilson Blvd.
Suite 550
Arlington, Virginia 22201
800/843–LOST
Assists communities in developing programs that protect children and pursues leads that will help in the recovery of a missing or exploited child.

National Child Safety Council
P.O. Box 1368
Jackson, Michigan 49204
517/764–6070
Makes referrals to direct or indirect service providers for a child at risk for a variety of reasons, from abuse to potential suicide.

Parents Without Partners
8807 Colesville Rd.
Silver Spring, Maryland
20910
301/588–9354
Support groups for single parents that provide advocacy and a variety of educational, family, and social activities for single parents and their children.

CLEANING AND LAUNDERING

Carpet and Rug Institute
P.O. Box 2048
Dalton, Georgia 30722
404/278-3176
Answers questions about purchasing carpets and rugs.

Cotton, Inc.
1370 Sixth Ave.
New York, New York 10019
212/586–1070
Provides consumer brochures and answers inquiries.

Wool Bureau Technical Center
225 Crossways Park Dr.
Woodbury, New York
11797
516/364–0890
Information on caring for wool, including wool carpets; list of suppliers of woolen upholstery, carpets, and wool fabrics.

COLLECTIBLES

American Gem Society
5901 W. Third St.
Los Angeles, California
90036
213/936–4367
Answers questions about jewelry, gems, jewelry care, and precious metals and gem investments; provides information on gem laboratories, member jewelers, and certified gemologists; and gives appraisals.

Bureau of Engraving and Printing
Treasury Department
14th and C Streets SW
Washington, DC 20228
202/447-0193
Answers questions about the history, design, or engraving of currency.

Telepraisal
P.O. Box 20686
New York, New York 10009
800/645–6002 or
212/614–9090 (in New York)
For a fee, an art expert gives computerized information regarding the value and marketability of a specific piece of art; also provides information on buying and authenticating.

U.S. Postal Service
Stamps Division
475 L'Enfant Plaza SW
Washington, DC 20260
202/245–4951
Besides giving pointers on stamp collecting, the division will provide information on the subject, design, history, and availability of various stamps.

ENVIRONMENTAL GROUPS

American Academy of Allergy & Immunology
611 E. Wells St.
Milwaukee, Wisconsin
53202
800/822-2762
Provides information on asthma and allergies.

Asbestos List
Laboratory Accreditation
ADMIN A527
National Institute of Standards and Technology
Gaithersburg, Maryland
20899
301/975–4016
Provides free listings of EPA-certified asbestos-detection agencies.

Environmental Assistance Division
Office of Toxic Substances
401 M St. SW
Washington, DC 20460
202/554–1404
Provides information on regulations to the chemical industry, labor and trade organizations, environmental groups, and the public.

Environmental Defense Fund
1616 P St. NW
Suite 150
Washington, DC 20036
202/387–3500
A public interest law firm seeking to tighten pollution control standards and ban harmful substances from the environment.

Friends of the Earth
218 D St. SE
Washington, DC 20003
202/544–2600
Organization that works at local, national, and international levels to protect the planet; preserve biological, cultural, and ethnic diversity; and to empower citizens to have a voice in decisions affecting their environment and their lives.

Greenpeace USA
1436 U St. NW
Washington, DC 20009
202/462–1177
International organization committed to preventing the destruction of wildlife and the environment.

Natural Resources Defense Council
40 W. Twentieth St.
New York, New York 10011
212/727–4400
Protects air, water, and food supplies through litigation and research.

FOOD AND DRINK

American Dairy Association
6300 N. River Rd.
Rosemont, Illinois 60018
708/696–1880
Helps answer questions about recipes and the use and care of dairy products.

American Egg Board
1460 Renaissance Dr.
Park Ridge, Illinois 60068
708/296–7043
Answers questions on a variety of topics from recipes to nutrition.

American Health Foundation
1 Dana Rd.
Valhalla, New York 10595
914/592–2600
Offers information on healthy nutrition.

American Institute Of Wine & Food
1550 Bryant St.
San Francisco, California 94103
800/274–AIWF
Advances the appreciation and understanding of wine and food and promotes quality.

American Meat Institute
Attention: Communications
P.O. Box 3556
Washington, DC 20007
703/841–2400
Provides information on safe food handling, meat inspection, nutrition, and fat.

Barbecue Industry Association
Myers CommuniCounsel
11 Penn Plaza
Suite 1000
New York, New York 10001
212/279–3580
Publishes brochures on barbecueing tips and recipes and answers consumer questions.

Canned Food Information Council
500 N. Michigan Ave.
Suite 200
Chicago, Illinois 60611
312/836–7279
Provides recipe tips and nutrition information and publishes cookbooks with recipes using canned food.

Distilled Spirits Council of the United States, Inc.
1250 I St. NW
Suite 900
Washington, DC 20005
202/628–3544
Provides brochures on responsible drinking and facts relating to alcohol; also provides "Know Your Limits" pocket-size cards.

Meat and Poultry Hotline
U.S. Department of Agriculture
Room 1165, South Bldg.
Washington, DC 20250
800/535-4555 or
202/472-4485 (in Washington, DC)
Answers food safety questions about wholesomeness, preparation, storage, and labeling of meat and poultry products.

National Food Processors Association
1401 New York Ave. NW
Washington, DC 20005
202/639–5994
Works with the Food and Drug Administration and other government agencies to assure the safety and quality of the food supply; addresses consumer concerns.

National Frozen Food Association
P.O. Box 398
Hershey, Pennsylvania 12033
717/534–1601
Offers information on frozen food.

Nutrition Action
1755 S St. NW
Washington, DC 20009
202/332–9110
Provides information about food contents and hazards, the food industry, and government regulation of food.

Office of Governmental and Public Affairs
U.S. Department of Agriculture
Washington, DC 20250
202/447–6311
Provides information on all USDA programs, including publications available free or for a minimal charge.

Public Voice for Food and Health Policy
1001 Connecticut Ave. NW
Suite 522
Washington, DC 20036
202/659–5930
Provides information on government and industry food policies and how consumers can work to improve these policies.

Safe Drinking Water Hotline
Environmental Protection Agency
800/426-4791
Interprets and clarifies drinking water regulations; explains EPA policies and guidelines; provides updates on the status of regulations and policies; and provides information on the availability of technical publications and public education materials.

United Fresh Fruit and Vegetable Association
727 N. Washington St.
Alexandria, Virginia 22314
703/836-3410
Provides information on the nutritional value, seasonal availability, and care and preservation of fruits and vegetables.

FURNISHINGS/ HOUSEHOLD PRODUCTS

American Council for an Energy-Efficient Economy
1001 Connecticut Ave. NW
Suite 535
Washington, DC 20036
202/429-8873
Provides information about the energy efficiency of household appliances.

American Furniture Manufacturers Association
918 Sixteenth St. NW
Suite 402
Washington, DC 20006
202/466-7362
Forwards consumer complaints to member firms.

Association of Home Appliances Manufacturers
20 N. Wacker Dr.
Chicago, Illinois 60606
312/236-3223
Citizen advisers investigate complaints about sellers of refrigerators, stoves, freezers, washers, dishwashers, dryers, air conditioners, garbage disposals, microwave ovens, humidifiers, dehumidifiers, compactors, and water heaters.

Direct Marketing Association
P.O. Box 3861
New York, NY 10163-3861
(written complaints only)
Mail Order Action Line handles consumer complaints on behalf of its members who market goods and services directly to consumers using direct mail, catalogs, telemarketing, magazine, newspaper and broadcast advertising. Individuals are removed from mail and telephone lists upon request. Consumer publications availble.

Major Appliance Consumer Action Panel
20 N. Wacker Dr.
Chicago, Illinois 60606
312/984-5858 or
800/621-0477 (outside Illinois)
Provides third-party dispute resolution for the major appliance industry.

HEALTH

American Association of Retired Persons
1909 K St. NW
Washington, DC 20049
202/872-4700
Provides information on a variety of nationwide services and resources for people older than 50.

American Holistic Medical Association
2002 Eastlake Ave. E
Seattle, Washington 98102
206/322-6842
Provides referrals to holistic physicians in a particular area and provides brochures on holistic health care.

American Medical Association
535 N. Dearborn
Chicago, Illinois 60610
312/645-5000
Handles complaints and answers questions regarding public policy.

American Red Cross National Headquarters
Seventeenth and D Streets NW
Washington, DC 20006
202/737-8300
Provides disaster relief at home and abroad; acts as a means of emergency communication between American families and the armed forces; collects and distributes voluntarily donated blood and blood products. For information on health and safety classes, contact local chapters.

American Speech-Language-Hearing Association
10801 Rockville Pike
Rockville, Maryland 20852
800/638-TALK or
301/897-8682 (in Maryland, Alaska, and Hawaii)
Provides information about speech, language, and hearing problems and makes referrals to qualified speech-language pathologists and audiologists.

Blue Cross and Blue Shield Associations
655 Fifteenth St. NW
Suite 350
Washington, DC 20005
202/626-4780
Consumer affairs office helps resolve complaints not solved by a state or local BC/BS office regarding hospital payments.

Health Research Group
Department 241
2000 P St. NW
Suite 708
Washington, DC 20036
202/872-0320
Organization concerned with improving the quality of medical care, removing harmful chemicals from food, and eliminating dangerous drugs from the market.

National Association of Retail Druggists
205 Daingerfield Rd.
Alexandria, Virginia 22314
703/683-8200
Organization of independent pharmacy owners provides information on prescription drugs, poison control, mail-order drug frauds, veterinary drugs, drug labeling and package inserts, and effective storage measures.

National Council of Senior Citizens
925 Fifteenth St. NW
Washington, DC 20005
202/347–8800
Addresses problems of the elderly, such as housing and national health insurance.

National Council on the Aging
600 Maryland Ave. SW
West Wing 100
Washington, DC 20024
800/424–9046
Serves as a national resource for family care givers and professionals who work with older adults.

National Family Planning and Reproductive Health Association
122 C St. NW
Suite 380
Washington, DC
20001–2109
202/628–3535
Makes referrals to family planning clinics and provides comprehensive, confidential information about family planning.

National Hospice Organization
1901 N. Moore St.
Suite 901
Arlington, Virginia 22209
800/658–8898
Provides general information about hospice care, a medically directed, patient-controlled program for care of terminally ill people and their families; also provides assistance throughout the United States in locating a hospice program.

Planned Parenthood Federation of America
810 Seventh Ave.
New York, New York 10019
212/603–4727
Provides advice on contraception, sterility, pregnancy, unwanted pregnancy, and abortion.

HEATING AND COOLING

Air Conditioning Contractors of America
1513 Sixteenth St. NW
Washington, DC 20036
202/483–9370
Provides consumer information about what to look for in a good heating and air conditioning contractor, as well as what consumers should know about chlorofluorocarbons (air conditioning refrigerant) and the ozone layer. Some local chapters provide contractor referrals.

Air Conditioning and Refrigeration Institute
1501 Wilson Blvd.
Suite 600
Arlington, Virginia 22209
703/524–8800
Provides consumer information pamphlets on central air conditioners, heat pumps, central-system air filters and humidifiers. Refers complaints to the Better Business Bureau.

American Gas Association
1515 Wilson Blvd.
Arlington, Virginia 22209
703/841–8501
Certifies gas equipment to national safety standards and provides AGA Blue Star seal of approval; also publishes consumer and safety information booklets.

Conservation and Renewable Energy Inquiry And Referral Service
P.O. Box 8900
Silver Spring,
Maryland 20907
800/523–2929 or
800/233–3971 (in Alaska and Hawaii)
Answers inquiries about the spectrum of renewable energy technologies—solar, wind, hydroelectric, photovoltaic, geothermal, and bioconversion.

Office of Consumer and Public Liaison
CP-34 Room 8G-070
U.S. Department of Energy
1000 Independence Ave. SW
Washington, DC 20585
202/586-5373
Handles complaints and comments directed at the agency and provides information on a wide range of energy-related topics.

HOME SAFETY

National Fire Protection Association
Public Affairs Department—BH
1 Batterymarch Park
P.O. Box 9109
Quincy, Massachusetts
02269–9101
(written inquiries only)
Public education department provides information on fire and its prevention.

U.S. Consumer Product Safety Commission
Washington, DC 20207
800/638–2772
Invites consumers to report unsafe consumer products used in and around the home. Does not include food, drugs, cosmetics, cars, baby car seats, or dissatisfaction with a store, product, or service. Product Safety Hotline takes calls about hazardous products or product-related injuries as well as inquiries about product recalls.

PAINTING AND DECORATING

American Institute of Architects
1735 New York Ave. NW
Washington, DC 20006
202/626–7492
Provides information on how to work with an architect and makes referrals to chapters nationwide for lists of local architects.
202/626–7475
Provides books, brochures, and other publications related to architecture and design.

American Society Of Interior Designers
1430 Broadway
New York, New York 10018
212/944–9220
Distributes information on how to choose a designer and how to become a designer.

Wallcovering Information Bureau
355 Lexington Ave.
New York, New York 10017
212/661–4261
Offers tips on design and application, and does research to find the manufacturer of a specific wallpaper.

PETS

American Animal Hospital Association
P.O. Box 150899
Denver, Colorado
80215–0899
303/279–2500
Refers consumers to association members throughout the country and provides brochures on a variety of topics regarding small companion animals, primarily dogs and cats.

American Humane Association
9725 E. Hampden
Denver, Colorado 80231
303/695–0811
National federation works to protect animals and children from abuse, neglect, and exploitation. Publishes a variety of educational materials.

American Veterinary Medical Association
930 N. Meacham Rd.
Schaumburg, Illinois 60196
800/248–2862
Provides brochures about pet health care.

Delta Society
P.O. Box 1080
Renton, Washington 98057
206/226–7357
Distributes information on the ways in which animals can help people with disabilities and on animals as companions.

Hearing Dog Resource Center
Delta Society
P.O. Box 1080
Renton, Washington 98057
800/869–6898 (Voice–TDD)
Provides information on dogs trained to assist the hearing impaired.

MISCELLANEOUS

American Movers Conference
1117 N. 19th St.
Suite 806
Arlington, Virginia 22209
703/524–5440
Consumer assistance office handles complaints against local, intrastate, and interstate movers of household goods.

American Society of Travel Agents
Consumer Affairs
Department
1101 King St.
Alexandria, Virginia 22314
703/739–2782
Informally mediates travel-related disputes and maintains information clearing house on travel firms.

National Coalition Against The Misuse of Pesticides
530 Seventh St. SE
Washington, DC 20003
202/543–5450
Provides information regarding chemicals used in the home and yard and suggests alternative products.

Index

Q

R

U

V